Practical VSAM
for Today's Programmers

James G. Janossy
DePaul University

Richard E. Guzik
Chicago Datacenter

WILEY

John Wiley & Sons

New York • Chichester • Brisbane • Toronto • Singapore

Library of Congress Cataloging in Publication Data:

Janossy, James G. (James Gustav), 1947–
    Practical VSAM for today's programmers.

Bibliography: p.
    1. Virtual computer systems. 2. Virtual storage
(Computer science) I. Guzik, Richard E. II. Title.
QA76.9.V5J36   1987   004.5'4   87-23139
ISBN 0-471-85107-8

Printed in the United States of America

10 9 8 7 6 5 4 3 2 1

esse quam videri

PREFACE

This book is purposely focused to be of immediate practical relevance to programmers and analysts in IBM mainframe installations, and to students of business data processing. You will find here early and in-depth emphasis on those elements of VSAM with which most business data processing programmers deal on a daily basis. Lesser used elements of the VSAM environment are purposely accorded later treatment, as appendix items.

We—the authors—design, program, and manage online systems supported by VSAM data sets. We wrote this book to help people we work with and train to use VSAM in a practical manner. While VSAM is well established as a software product, its complexity causes many journeymen to struggle with it. We set out to demystify the subject and to confront the challenge of securing widespread efficient, productive, and rapid acclimation to it. And we think you will find that our approach succeeds, because whether you are a programmer, trainer, or student, we all walk in the same shoes.

Virtual Storage Access Method—VSAM—is IBM's contemporary mechanism for the support of indexed files on its System/370-based computers. It is widely regarded as a complex subject for several reasons: it provides myriad options that affect data set performance; it is associated with the large general purpose utility program "IDCAMS," which has its own programming language; and it is taught in few courses. IBM manuals dealing with VSAM present all facets of the subject with the same emphasis; little differentiation exists in the manuals between aspects of VSAM that are relevant to a business data processing programmer and those aspects that are little used. *Practical VSAM*, on the other hand, homes in on the VSAM key sequenced data set knowledge and techniques needed to operate productively in the business data processing environment.

Why be limited to manual means to perform complex tasks such as VSAM data set design and management? It is high time to harness the horsepower of computing machinery and apply it to the work of VSAM key sequenced data set design and monitoring. We have done precisely this for you. We've included here tools in documented source code form—computational CLISTs, programs that read LISTCATs and automatically extract and analyze them, and prime or alternate key value distribution analysis routines. You can also obtain these tools on diskette ready to upload to a mainframe via a suitably equipped PC, for the cost of reproduction and mailing as described in Appendix A. Knowledge of VSAM and its efficient usage is critical for applications programming professionals; so are automated tools for dealing with it rapidly and consistently.

While it is crucial to provide VSAM file development and implementation guidance, it is also essential to monitor production VSAM key sequenced data sets on an ongoing basis. For this reason, we have addressed the subject of managing VSAM data sets in the production environment. Included here are in-depth illustrations of the means to provide true management capability for the scores of VSAM key sequenced data sets that populate the disk drives of a business data processing installation. Automated routines for these processes are also included on the nominal-cost distribution diskette described in Appendix A.

WITH THANKS

We drew upon the knowledge and skills of associates in developing this book and would like to thank them for their assistance. Pat Heafey, a skilled applications development and technical support supervisor, provided valuable insights and a practical perspective gained in her considerable VSAM experience. Tom Vari, an applications and database resource, lent his talents in a variety of ways.

We would like to thank Dr. Helmut Epp, chairman of the Department of Computer Science and Information Systems at DePaul University, Chicago, and Steve Samuels, director of the DePaul Computer Career Program, who suggested enhancements vital for academic text usage. A special thanks is due to Dawne Tortorella, director of Academic Computing Services at DePaul. Dawne prepared many of the illustrations for this book using an Apple Macintosh and laser printer, aiding not only with technical expertise but with artistic talent.

James G. Janossy
Richard E. Guzik

Chicago, Illinois
January 1988

____ CONTENTS ____

PART 1   EVERYDAY VSAM

PART 2   ADVANCED VSAM

PART 3   MANAGING VSAM

APPENDIXES

══ PART 1 ══

EVERYDAY VSAM

=== 1 ===

Introduction to VSAM

"Virtual Storage Access Method" is above all else a marketing term. VSAM is IBM's current technology for the support of indexed files, which are disk-stored files of records directly accessible by a key. It replaced ISAM—Indexed Sequential Access Method— IBM's initial means of implementing indexed files. As a sidelight VSAM also offers support for a form of sequential data set and a form of relative record data set, both of which are only lightly used.[1]

Online systems do not deal readily with simple sequential files. ISAM data sets, a mainstay for online systems throughout the early 1970s, received lagging support on IBM 3380 disk units, the current large mainframe disk device. To cap off ISAM entirely, IBM's teleprocessing monitor, CICS—Customer Information and Control System—dropped support for ISAM with its release 1.7. If your work on a mainframe involves online programming, you will come in contact with either VSAM data sets or a database.

WHY IS THERE VSAM AT ALL?

Newcomers to IBM mainframes as well as the initiated are often struck by the apparent complexity of the environment as opposed to micro- and mini-computers. On a Digital Equipment Corporation VAX system, for example, nothing comparable to VSAM and the IDCAMS utility exist for the purpose of creating a file of records that can be accessed by symbolic key. With a capable microcomputer COBOL, BASIC, Pascal, or C compiler, no special setup is needed to load records to an indexed file. Why then is there a need for something special and complex, outside of a programming language, to create and manipulate certain data sets on IBM mainframes?

Longevity of System/360 and 370 Operating Systems

One reason that VSAM exists is the longevity of the system software for the IBM 360/370 family—including mainframe DOS, OS/MVS, and VM. DOS and OS/MVS were developed in the early 1960s with the IBM 360/370 architecture; VM evolved as a laboratory and system support environment later in that decade. As time and progress have marched on, new capabilities have been required to meet the needs of devices and applications unknown in earlier days. Since the original operating systems did not provide great support for random access file operations, other subsystems of software were developed and evolved to support disk storage. An early such item for indexed files was ISAM. The current product for this purpose is VSAM.

3

Input/output subsystems exist by separate names under the umbrella of the IBM operating systems. BSAM, for Basic Sequential Access Method, QSAM, for Queued Sequential Access Method, BPAM, Basic Partitioned Access Method, BDAM, Basic Direct Access Method, TCAM, Telecommunications Access Method, and VTAM, Virtual Telecommunications Access Method are some of these subsystems. While it may seem that VSAM stands out as an item that requires the separate attention of a programmer, it is programmers new to IBM mainframes who are usually prone to the perception. After working in the environment for a time it becomes apparent that nearly all of IBM's I/O subsystems are regarded as creatures of their own, apart from mainframe operating systems.

Variety of IBM Operating Systems

Another reason that VSAM exists as a distinct subject area is that IBM mainframes are general-purpose data processing computers, of varying capacity. This means that they and the system software that controls them must be "tailorable" to a variety of different local requirements and situations. Customization has traditionally extended beyond the configuration of hardware, extending into the realm of support software as well.

It has been IBM's philosophy that no one operating system environment best serves all its customer base. IBM offers three mainframe business data processing operating systems. Mainframe DOS is offered for machines of lesser size; it demands fewer machine resources for operating system overhead, at the expense of additional programmer and operator attention to data set labeling, job handling, and housekeeping chores. MVS is offered to large machine environments and provides a wealth of support services but demands a larger mainframe and a greater share of machine horsepower for its own purposes. VM, Virtual Machine, is a timesharing operating system. It offers prime support for interactive work as a "super" operating system capable of running other operating systems under it, while being less inclined toward the running of large volumes of batch jobs.

Given that three mainframe operating systems exist, it made sense to IBM that the indexed file access method product be independent of any of them. VSAM and its utility IDCAMS is separately identified under the rubric of Access Method Services and is not buried within DOS, MVS, or VM.

Complexity of Mainframe Applications

A third basis for the VSAM and its complexity is the variety, nature, and large size of the application systems to which IBM mainframes are commonly dedicated. Small programs dealing with tiny files on a mini or micro can readily operate with a simple indexed file arrangement. The efficient operation of large production applications demands support more specific to individual file characteristics—the ability to best accommodate specific record sizes, concurrent access, data placement, internal arrangement, record addition/deletion activity, and so forth.

VSAM is more complex than other indexed file software for the same reason that a fine 35-millimeter camera is more complex than a snapshot camera. You have no settings on a snapshot camera for the different circumstances of lighting, distance, focus, and exposure that must be accommodated while creating a portrait- or publication-quality illustration. But a camera that provides these settings makes taking any picture more complicated than just pointing and clicking the button.

Support for Non-indexed Files

A final basis for apparent VSAM complexity is that it was developed with capabilities to support non-indexed as well as indexed files. VSAM supports Entry Sequenced Data Sets

(ESDS) and Relative Record Data Sets (RRDS), linear "data-in-virtual storage" data sets, and IDCAMS performs functions for sequential, partitioned, and generation data group data sets.

Editorially speaking, an unfortunate muddying of the waters results from the inclusion within VSAM and IDCAMS of so many functions. In the traditional arrangement of IBM's I/O support subsystems, the role of VSAM is really that of an indexed file support mechanism. Its ability to support a form of sequential file and a form of relative record file and the broadening of IDCAMS support to non-VSAM data sets lumps a tremendous amount of functionality into one product. This contributes to the difficulty sometimes associated with learning VSAM and IDCAMS, and certainly bogs down the documentation associated with it.

This book concentrates on key sequenced data sets. If, however, you wish to explore the creation and use of entry sequenced data sets, relative record data sets, or linear data sets Appendix D will guide you. It provides a concise discussion of the limited features, usage, IDCAMS control statements, and MVS JCL to work with them. A companion book in this series, *Practical MVS JCL For Today's Programmers* (James Janossy, John Wiley and Sons, Inc., 1987), ISBN 0-471-83648-6, provides extensive coverage of non-VSAM use of IDCAMS.

INDEXED FILES FOR BUSINESS DATA PROCESSING

Symbolic Keys

Production business data processing demands the capability to store and retrieve information by symbolic key. A symbolic key is a unique identifier that carries no information within it as to the physical storage location of the data it identifies. Social security number, customer account numbers, stock numbers, serial numbers, part numbers, and other such identifiers that "name" something are examples of symbolic keys.

Symbolic keys exhibit the characteristic that they may already have been in use prior to the advent of automation. For this reason alone—although it is not usually the only reason—storing records cannot involve the enforced use of some identifier such as "record number." A primitive random access organization offers the ability to store data on the condition that someone keep track of where on the disk device the record was stored. If such crude access were all that computers could supply, the development of application systems would be severely constrained. It is not possible to force-fit the real world into an arrangement where identifiers already in use are changed to accommodate disk storage requirements.

VSAM Replaces ISAM

Indexed files provide the means to store and retrieve information by symbolic key. Every commercial business data processing computer provides some form of indexed file support. IBM originally provided ISAM, the Indexed Sequential Access Method, for this purpose. ISAM was rendered obsolete by the introduction of VSAM in 1973, but its use lingered on due to the entrenched knowledge concerning it as well as the greater complexity of VSAM. ISAM files were created simply by using JCL, not with a utility program with its own control statement language such as IDCAMS.

ISAM was plagued by three quirks that made it inconsistent with the 1974 standards for COBOL: it provided no DELETE verb, it provided no FILE STATUS value, and it required coding of a "nominal key" in COBOL program working storage in addition to a record key field in the file description. ISAM also posed serious inefficiencies and limitations. VSAM eliminated all of these problems in indexed file support. Throughout the latter part of the 1970s and the decade of the 1980s, installations have converted ISAM-based systems to VSAM. Installations still running ISAM applications will be forced to convert them to VSAM in order to move ahead with new versions of CICS.

VSAM is unlike any other access method software that preceded it on IBM mainframes, and in the long run it may supplant the others.

VSAM: Data Tree Storage

VSAM indexed files are called "key sequenced data sets." This is a descriptive but unnecessarily verbose term; nearly all other implementors of indexed file support call such files indexed files. In this book we use the abbreviation "KSDS," for key sequenced data set, and the term "indexed file" synonymously.

Indexed files under VSAM are associated with data tree storage. One need not understand theories of data trees in order to use VSAM, but some explanation helps because many VSAM terms make more sense with such a background. A data tree can be viewed as an ordinary, woody tree; it is a skeleton to which leaves are attached. A data tree assigns a physical location to its "leaves" based on some characteristic of them. In the case of VSAM key sequenced data sets, the leaves on the tree are records. The factor that dictates where a given record is placed is the primary record key.

Data trees arrange and maintain their contents in an orderly manner. When a new leaf—a record—is to be hung on a tree, it is done so based on a series of tests between its primary key and those of the leaves already on the tree. The tests, conducted by VSAM software, determine on which branch of the tree to hang the new record. The same tests repeated by VSAM for retrieval of the record allow it to be found again later very quickly by its primary key.

New leaves burst forth in spring on a winter-barren tree. The leaves usually appear uniformly over the tree. But what if more leaves were to be added to the tree in late spring, and every branch was already full? The tree would have to grow more branches to accommodate the new leaves. If VSAM were "managing" the tree, we could arrange to not load the branches heavily in early spring but would instead keep some proportion of every branch empty for the addition of new leaves, and even some proportion of the trunk free for the addition of new limbs. This is called "free space," and its size and placement is only one of scores of characteristics that can be specified when a new VSAM KSDS is created. VSAM deals with record insertions automatically using free space, but figuring out how much and what type of free space to allow is the data set designer or programmer's job.

Botany is replete with thousands of specialized terms. VSAM has its jargon too, partly to be uniquely descriptive and partly, it might appear, to impose a rite of passage on the uninitiated. To whisper bits of the secret: VSAM calls the basic KSDS data tree a "base cluster." As Figure 1.1 illustrates, VSAM calls major limbs, attached to the main trunk, "control areas." It calls the branches of the tree, attached to major limbs, "control intervals." If you shinny up the main trunk and trace out the limbs, branches, and leaves in a sequential order, you are accessing the "sequence set." Room intentionally left empty within branches for more leaves is called "control interval free space." The places on the major limbs, intentionally left empty for the addition of branches, are called "control area free space."

IDCAMS, THE ACCESS METHOD SERVICES UTILITY

It's easiest to think of VSAM as a "black box," a self-contained entity under the wing of the MVS, DOS/VSE, and VM operating systems. VSAM is associated with "Access

FIGURE 1.1 Conceptual organization of a VSAM key sequenced data set

Method Services," an umbrella term that covers all VSAM system software. VSAM data sets are a creation of one large utility program, "IDCAMS," usually pronounced—when it is pronounced at all—as "eye dee khams," much like "hi dee ho!" The origin of this non-word is mundane. "IDC" is a meaningless three-letter prefix assigned by IBM to the VSAM product for use in its error message reporting, and "AMS" is the abbreviation for Access Method Services.

IDCAMS is a large and powerful utility. It is impossible to create VSAM data sets without IDCAMS; JCL alone is insufficient. But IDCAMS also performs non-VSAM data set services, in connection with catalog management, data set copying, and generation data group base creation and examination. It can even perform yeoman duty as a hex dump utility for non-VSAM sequential files.[2]

IDCAMS is a program. It is executed by JCL, and it is driven by control statements that enter it at the MVS DDname //SYSIN or following the // EXEC statement under DOS/VSE. The syntax of IDCAMS control statements forms a complete file definition and manipulation language all its own. Creating, loading, reorganizing, and maintaining VSAM files means using IDCAMS control statements. Crawling out of the application programmer's COBOL or PL/I syntax foxhole to learn VSAM means learning IDCAMS. It need not be a pitched battle, but it is usually more strenuous than a tranquil nature walk because IDCAMS and the considerations involved in creating efficient VSAM key sequenced data sets are not trivial.

Simple data tree structures are often the subject of computer science classes, and they can be demonstrated in languages such as BASIC and Pascal. IBM's VSAM, on the other hand, is a complete and general-purpose support product that was developed to offer external control over scores of parameters that govern the structure and operation of a given key sequenced data set. These controlling parameters are centralized and stored in the system catalog. IDCAMS control statements make or change entries in the catalog definition for a given VSAM data set.

When a new key sequenced data set is defined, using the DEFINE command of the IDCAMS control statement language, over 60 parameters may be specified, associated with the "base cluster," the "data component," and the "index component," the three elements of a KSDS. The knowledge needed to arrive at effective parameter choices for a specific KSDS and communicating these choices to IDCAMS via its control statement syntax are the major focus of this book.

KEY SEQUENCED DATA SET (KSDS) COMPONENTS

The base cluster, the data, and the index are the three components of a VSAM key sequenced data set. Each of these components carries a name analogous to the data set name of a simple sequential file. As with simple data sets, if a name for a data set is omitted in JCL, a default name is created by the operating system, composed of cryptic fields such as the Julian date, system time, job name, and some literals. But default names are usually avoided for VSAM data set components because explicit names, formed according to an installation naming convention, are a great aid in keeping track of the myriad parts or components of a VSAM data set.

Three names, following whatever conventions and data set naming pattern an installation enforces, exist for a key sequenced data set. The base cluster names the tree trunk, the data component names just the leaves, or records, and the index component names an overall map of the limbs, branches, and leaves of the tree.

Comparison to a tree is a convenient starting point, but the analogy quickly becomes strained. The base cluster is really a place in the catalog where the KSDS definition is stored, not the identifier of data or index records. Since it is the base cluster name, however, that is cited in JCL in referring to a VSAM data set, it is particularly easy to become confused on this point.

Similarly, while the index carries one name, it has at least two physical parts: various higher levels of roadmaps to roadmaps, and a lowest level that when read sequentially points to each control interval in a sequential manner. The lowest level is called the index "sequence set"; when a KSDS is accessed for sequential processing, it is the sequence set that is read to guide data accesses. The sequence set may even be housed with the data portion of the data set to speed sequential processing of it. The higher levels of the index are collectively called the index set. Together with the sequence set they provide for keyed access to any record in the data set.

PHYSICAL STRUCTURE OF A KEY SEQUENCED DATA SET

Figure 1.2 is a traditional representation of VSAM key sequenced data set. Here we see how a KSDS might appear internally after updating activity has caused records to be inserted after initial data set loading.

The records within a CI are maintained in key sequence. But due to the splits necessary when free space is depleted in a CI it is the sequence set of the index that keeps track of the order in which CIs themselves must be accessed in order to obtain all records in key sequence. It is for this reason that an option allows the sequence set to be stored "imbedded" within the data component. For sequential processing, only the sequence set of the

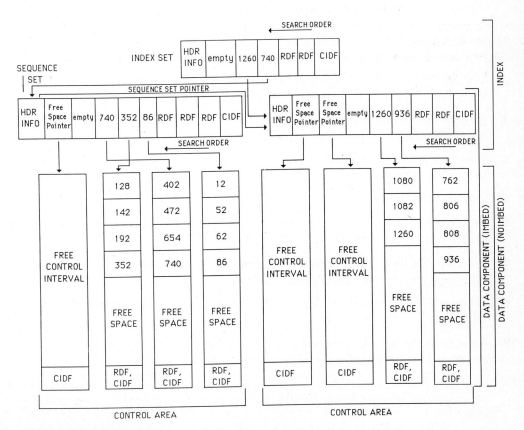

FIGURE 1.2 Internal organization of a key sequenced data set and its component parts

index and the sequence set pointers are involved; having it physically in the data component speeds access.

Also illustrated in Figure 1.2 is the manner in which the index set and the sequence set interrelate. The entries in the various levels of the index are small. A given index entry contains the highest key value in the item it indexes and the physical location in which that item starts. When a record is to be accessed by key, VSAM reads the highest level of the index that exists and tests each entry until a key value is noted that exceeds the key value sought. When it finds this entry, VSAM follows the pointer to the next lower level of index or the data component and conducts similar actions there.

You can follow the process VSAM performs when it handles symbolic key record access. Find a record with a specific key value in Figure 1.2; try, for example, seeking key value 192. Start with the higher level index and find that its first entry, 740, exceeds the key value sought. This points to the sequence set control interval starting with key entry 86 and ending with 740. Testing each of its entries from 86 leftward determines that the second one, 352, exceeds the key value sought. We finally settle on the CI housing as its highest key value 352, and after a few tests locate key 192 there. An identical process serves for record additions; the differences lie in the nature of the outcome and the need for a CI, or CA and CI, split if free space in the appropriate control interval has been depleted.

As we discuss some of the VSAM performance features you need to understand as a programmer, you will see how much of the attention required by good KSDS practices is aimed at minimizing the need for VSAM to do internal splitting to accommodate activity.

REVIEW QUESTIONS AND (*) EXERCISES

1. What are some reasons that a program in the contemporary IBM mainframe application environment will make use of VSAM key sequenced data sets?

2. VSAM often seems a complex indexed file support mechanism when compared to that of the DEC VAX and microcomputers. Cite some reasons why this is so.

3. Discuss the nature of symbolic key access and why it is essential for business data processing applications, as opposed to relative record access.

4. What are three reasons why VSAM was created to replace ISAM as a mechanism to support indexed file access?

5. Explain the term "free space" in connection with VSAM data tree storage.

6. Indicate the basis for the name "IDCAMS" and explain the connection of this large utility program to VSAM.

7. What are the three components of a VSAM key sequenced data set, what function does each serve, and what does each contain?

8. When a key sequenced data set is referenced in JCL, which of its components is cited?

*9. Refer to Figure 1.2 and describe step by step the actions taken by VSAM when the record with key 1082 is to be retrieved by symbolic key.

*10. Refer to Figure 1.2 and indicate the order in which the control intervals will be processed for sequential access and the role of the index sequence set in this process.

NOTES

1. Two forms of non-indexed data sets are supported by VSAM. The simplest of these is the entry sequenced data set or "ESDS." Entry sequenced data sets are very much like simple sequential data sets except that they are handled by VSAM and not by older access method software such as the Queued Sequential Access Method, QSAM. VSAM itself makes use of ESDS's on occasion for sort work files when it builds an alternate index. ESDS's are normally not used by applications systems, because they provide no advantage over simple sequential files, VSCO-BOL cannot deal with them in advanced ways, and they lack the ability to be handled as generation data group data sets.

    Relative record data sets, "RRDS," are very much like relative files of the old Basic Direct Access Method, BDAM. As described in Appendix D, RRDS files are analogous to the simple "store-it-by-slot-number" files supported by Microsoft BASIC on microcomputers. Random access via physical location "record number" is nearly always insufficient for contemporary business data processing. Relative record data sets are essentially irrelevant to applications programming.

    If VSAM supported only key sequenced data sets, its use would be exactly the same as it is for nearly all personnel employing it. However, if VSAM supported only ESDS and RRDS data sets, fewer than one person in a hundred would be using it. While it is unlikely that as an applications programmer you will ever have any significant contact with either ESDS or RRDS data sets, Appendix D provides coverage of these types of VSAM data sets.

2. This book concerns itself with VSAM and the IDCAMS functions that support it. For information on the non-VSAM services provided by IDCAMS for generation data group data sets (GDGs), the hexadecimal dumping of various formats of records, and data set and member cataloging, uncataloging, renaming and deletion, see Chapters 13 and 17 of *Practical MVS JCL For Today's Programmers* (James Janossy, John Wiley and Sons, Inc., 1987) ISBN 0-471-83648-6.

=== 2 ===

Designing the Key Sequenced Data Set

Creating a VSAM key sequenced data set involves the use of IDCAMS, the Access Method Services utility. IDCAMS provides what amounts to a complete language of control statements, only a few elements of which are used to define the base cluster, data component, and index component of the KSDS. An item of housekeeping—the elimination of a data set that might already exist with the intended KSDS name—and the actual copying of data from sequential form to the KSDS can also be accomplished with IDCAMS control statements.

A GOOD PATTERN EXAMPLE

Where do you start in using VSAM for key sequenced data set support? A good life-like example is a tremendous help. Let's jump right in with one here, which we will carry through this book.

Figure 2.1 depicts the format of records that will comprise a new key sequenced data set. The records are a fixed 250 bytes in length; each has a unique key eight bytes in length in positions 36 through 43.[1] Figure 2.2 is a listing of MVS JCL and IDCAMS control statements that can be used to allocate and load the KSDS, while Figure 2.3 provides DOS/VSE JCL and IDCAMS control statements to accomplish this task. Comments are provided in the code identifying the several IDCAMS tasks performed:

- eliminating any existing data set of the same name, if such exists, with a housekeeping DELETE
- resetting a possible nonzero completion posted by the DELETE if no existing data set exists to be eliminated
- KSDS definition and loading, accomplished with the DEFINE and REPRO commands
- a LISTCAT to produce a formatted report of the KSDS attributes and statistics concerning its contents.

These statements and test data to load the data set are listed in Appendix F and are available on diskette. You can readily experiment with key sequenced data set definition and loading by uploading these items to your mainframe. If you do this, however, change CYLINDERS to TRACKS to minimize undue use of disk space resources. After illustrating the manual development of RECORDSIZE, CONTROLINTERVALSIZE, CYLINDERS, and

12

	Old ID no. X(9) (not a key)	Customer name		Account number X(8)	Street direction X(1)	Street name X(15)	House number X(5)	Apartment number X(5)	Rest of record... (180 bytes)
		Last X(18)	First X(9)						
Real	1 9	10 27	28 36	37 44	45	46 60	61 65	66 70	71 250
Offset	0 8	9 26	27 35	36 43	44	45 59	60 64	65 69	70 249

Prime key 8 bytes

FIGURE 2.1   Format of records to be loaded to a VSAM key sequenced data set

FREESPACE parameters, we explore automated aids for their determination, also provided in Appendix F and on diskette.

Choices exist for the placement of various parameters in the CLUSTER, DATA, or INDEX component coding. We reserve discussion of those non-quantitative issues for Chapter 3; they rest simply on an understanding of what each option controls and the basis for overriding IDCAMS defaults.

KEY SEQUENCED DATA SET DESIGN FACTORS

A properly designed VSAM data set performs efficiently and delivers rapid response when accessed online. Effective design of a VSAM KSDS follows a step-by-step process. The initial step is the development of a concise understanding of the key sequenced data set in terms of several characteristics:

1. *Length of the data record,* which for fixed-length records is the actual record length and for variable-length records is the average and maximum record length
2. *The primary access manner,* online or batch
3. *Distribution characteristics* of the record key values
4. *The number of records to be added or deleted* between data set reorganizations
5. *The type of disk device* to be used
6. *The number of records to be loaded initially*
7. *The maximum number of records to be housed*
8. *The primary mode of record access:* random, sequential, or start/browse skip sequential
9. *Length, nature, and location of the primary key*
10. *The quantity, length, nature and physical location of alternate keys* and the necessity of concurrently updating any alternate index during online and batch processing
11. *Data set reorganization strategy,* including the length of time between the data set "unload" and "reload," which has an especially important bearing on data set characteristics if the data set is large or if it supports an online system.

```
//FSBT686A   JOB AK00TEST,'DP2-JANOSSY',CLASS=T,MSGCLASS=X,
//  MSGLEVEL=(1,1),NOTIFY=BT05686
//*
//*    THIS JCL = BT05686.SOURCE.CNTL(F22)
//*
//************************************************************
//*                                                          *
//*    DEFINE AND LOAD/RELOAD VSAM DATA SET                  *
//*                                                          *
//************************************************************
//STEPA      EXEC  PGM=IDCAMS
//SYSPRINT   DD    SYSOUT=*
//SYSUDUMP   DD    SYSOUT=A
//MASTIN     DD    DSN=AK00.C98.CUSTBKUP(0),
//  UNIT=(TAPE,,DEFER),
//  DISP=(OLD,KEEP)
//SYSIN      DD  *
                                        /* HOUSEKEEPING DELETES */
    DELETE       AK00.C98.CUSTMAST -
                 CLUSTER

  SET LASTCC=0                          /* SOME ABOVE MAY NOT BE  */
  SET MAXCC=0                           /* FOUND; GET RID OF RC=8 */

  /* - - - - - - - - CREATE THE BASE CLUSTER AND PRIMARY INDEX- - */

    DEFINE -
      CLUSTER    (   NAME(AK00.C98.CUSTMAST) -
                     VOLUMES(FSDC14) -
                     RECORDSIZE(250 250) -
                     KEYS(8 36) -
                     CYLINDERS(2 1) -
                     SHAREOPTIONS(2 3) -
                     SPEED -
                     IMBED                          ) -
                     -
      DATA       (   NAME(AK00.C98.CUSTMAST.BASE.DATA) -
                     CONTROLINTERVALSIZE(4096) -
                     FREESPACE(18 1)                ) -
                     -
      INDEX      (   NAME(AK00.C98.CUSTMAST.BASE.INDEX) )

  /* - - - - - - - - IF CREATION SUCCESSFUL LOAD THE KSDS - - - - */

  IF LASTCC = 0 -
  THEN -
    REPRO        INFILE(MASTIN) -
                 OUTDATASET(AK00.C98.CUSTMAST)

  /* - - - - LIST CATALOG TO SEE INFO ON THE DATA SET - - - - - - */

    LISTCAT -
      ENTRIES    (  AK00.C98.CUSTMAST   ) -
                 ALL
/*
//
```

FIGURE 2.2 MVS JCL and IDCAMS control statements to allocate and load a key sequenced data set

```
              // JOB DEFINE VSAM SPACE
              // ASSGN SYS007,DISK,VOL=FSDC14,SHR
              // DLBL NUSPACE,,,VSAM
              // EXTENT SYS007,FSDC14,,,1500,600
              // EXEC IDCAMS,SIZE=AUTO
                  DEFINE -
                     SPACE     (    FILE(NUSPACE) -
                                    VOLUMES(FSDC14) -
                                    CYLINDERS(50) -                            ) -
                     CATALOG      (CUSTMAST.CATALOG/A187P332)
              /&


              // JOB DEFINE AND LOAD A SUBALLOCATED KSDS
              // ASSGN SYS007,DISK,VOL=FSDC14,SHR
              // ASSGN SYS004,TAPE,VOL=010932
              // TLBL SYS004,'AK00.C98.CUSTBKUP'
              // DLBL MASTOUT,'AK00.C98.CUSTMAST',,VSAM
              // EXTENT SYS007,FSDC14
              // EXEC IDCAMS,SIZE=AUTO
                                                  /* HOUSEKEEPING DELETES    */
                  DELETE      AK00.C98.CUSTMAST -
                              CLUSTER

                  SET LASTCC = 0                  /* SOME ABOVE MAY NOT BE  */
                  SET  MAXCC = 0                  /* FOUND; GET RID OF RC-8 */

              /* - - - - - - -  CREATE BASE CLUSTER AND PRIMARY INDEX  - - - */

                  DEFINE -
                     CLUSTER  (    NAME(AK00.C98.CUSTMAST) -
                                   FILE(MASTOUT) -
                                   VOLUMES(FSDC14) -
                                   RECORDSIZE (250 250 ) -
                                   KEYS(8 36) -
                                   CYLINDERS(2 1) -
                                   IMBED                               ) -
                                   -
                     DATA     (    NAME(AK00.C98.CUSTMAST.BASE.DATA) -
                                   CONTROLINTERVALSIZE(4096) -
                                   FREESPACE(18 1)                     ) -
                                   -
                     INDEX    (    NAME(AK00.C98.CUSTMAST.BASE.INDEX)   )

              /* - - - - - - -  IF CREATION SUCCESSFUL, LOAD THE KSDS  - - - */

                  IF LASTCC = 0 -
                  THEN -
                     REPRO    INFILE(SYS004 -
                                   ENVIRONMENT( RECORDFORMAT(FB) -
                                                BLOCKSIZE(5000) -
                                                RECORDSIZE(250) -
                                                PRIMEDATADEVICE(2400)   ) -
                              OUTFILE(MASTOUT)
              /&
```

FIGURE 2.3   DOS/VSE JCL and IDCAMS control statements to allocate and load a key sequenced data set

Physical Features of Records and Control Interval (CI) Size

The control interval or "CI" is usually the physical unit of transfer between the disk device and memory, and is analogous to a block of data. Three data set characteristics are important in determining the control interval size for both the data component and the index component. These are the length of the record, the primary mode of processing, and the type of disk device the data set will occupy.

The CI size of the data component and the index component need not be the same. These can both be left to VSAM to choose or can be specified at data set definition. Because the data component CI size has a major impact on data set performance, it is necessary to specify it explicitly in order to gain efficient operation; VSAM does an adequate job of choosing the index component CI size.

Valid CI sizes for the data component exist in multiples of 512 bytes up to 8,192 bytes, and in multiples of 2,048 bytes beyond 8,192 bytes, up to 32,768 bytes. The index component is constrained to a CI size no greater than 4,096 bytes.

The CI size of the data component affects the distribution of free space within the data set. Larger data CI sizes generally allow more records per CI, and a more even distribution of free space. But maximum CI size is limited by other factors, related to online performance, which tend to force selection of 4,096 as a control interval size.

Data Component CI Size for an Online KSDS

A value of 4,096 bytes should be considered the maximum CI size for the data component for a data set accessed randomly online. Small data CI sizes are beneficial to CICS performance for random processing, where only one record from a CI is usually required at a time. The primary advantage of a small CI size lies in the reduction of CICS buffer space requirements and the minimization of the quantity of data transferred with each I/O.

Data Component CI Size for a Batch-processed KSDS

Sequential or batch skip sequential—START, READ/NEXT—processing benefits by using a data component CI size as large as provides good utilization of disk space. With larger data CI sizes, more data is transferred with each I/O request, reducing the total number of I/Os needed. Since contiguous records are being accessed, a single I/O can satisfy a series of sequential or skip sequential requests and minimize I/O activity.

The data component CI size has major bearing on buffer space requirements. Batch programs are far less constrained for buffer space than online programs, and their efficiency is enhanced with larger buffers. The operation of systems with limited real memory, however, will be degraded by virtual storage paging if too large a data component CI size is used, so it is unwise to attempt to gain efficiency by simply using a large CI size for a batch-processed data set without calculation of its impact.

CHOOSING THE DATA COMPONENT CONTROL INTERVAL SIZE

Very nearly all VSAM key sequenced data sets are accessed both randomly online and via batch processes such as IDCAMS REPRO backups during hours of non-teleprocessing access. It is the usual practice to optimize KSDS data component CI size for online processing, and to enhance sequential processing of the same VSAM data set by adding data buffers or buffer space via JCL executing the batch jobs.[2] This means that for all practical purposes the choice of data component CI size is limited to 4,096, 3,584, 3,072, 2,560, 2,048, 1,536, 1,024, or 512 bytes.

A straightforward method exists for the determination of an efficient CI size for a given VSAM KSDS. This process demands computation based on certain formulas as illustrated here. Skip ahead to the end of this chapter if you are in a hurry, however, because we have provided for your use interactive tools that automate these design computations.

1. Using the fixed or average record length, compute the number of records that will fit in CIs of 4,096; 3,584; 3,072; 2,560; 2,048; 1,536; 1,024; and 512 bytes, applying the appropriate formula:

$$\text{number of fixed-length records per CI} = \frac{(\text{CI size} - 10)}{\text{record length}}$$

or

$$\text{number of variable-length records per CI} = \frac{(\text{CI size} - 4)}{(\text{average record length} + 3)}$$

IDCAMS deals only in whole numbers and it rounds down when possible. The 10, 4, and 3 shown here are constants and represent bytes within the CI that are used by VSAM to house overhead information within each CI.[3] If only one record fits per CI, then the formula for fixed length records is slightly different:

$$\text{one fixed-length record per CI} = \frac{(\text{CI size} - 7)}{\text{record length}}$$

2. For each of the practical CI sizes, use the table in Figure 2.4 to find how many CIs will fit in one control area of one cylinder size on the disk device to be used to house the data set.[4]

| Control interval size | Number of Control Intervals per Control Area | | | | | |
| | 3330 | | 3350 | | 3380 | |
	IMBED	NOIMBED	IMBED	NOIMBED	IMBED	NOIMBED
4,096	54	57	116	120	140	150
3,584	51	54	111	115	92	98
3,072	66	69	145	150	144	155
2,560	72	75	156	162	128	138
2,048	108	114	232	240	252	270
1,536	120	126	261	270	214	230
1,024	198	209	435	450	434	465
512	360	380	783	810	644	690

FIGURE 2.4 Number of control intervals per one-cylinder sized control area, various disk devices and control interval sizes (subset of Appendix E, Figure E.2 for example purposes)

3. Multiply the number of records per CI for the disk by the number of CIs of that size accommodated in one control area, for each of the practical CI sizes. The CI size storing the largest number of records per control area is most efficient and desirable.

Some record lengths will leave unusable a large amount of space in the control interval. These formulas indicate how to calculate the amount of the CI that is unusable once the CI size has been chosen:

Bytes of CI unusable, fixed-length records:
   (CI size − 10) − (records per CI * record length)

or

Bytes of CI unusable, variable-length records:
   (CI size − 4) − (records per CI * (avg record length + 3))

If only one record fits per CI, the formula for unusable space for fixed length records is slightly different:

Bytes of CI unusable, one fixed-length record in CI:
(CI size − 7) − (records per CI * record length)

or

Bytes of CI unusable, one variable-length record in CI:
(CI size − 4) − (records per CI * (avg record length + 3))

Should the chosen CI size exhibit a large amount of unusable space, consider making the record length itself longer by apportioning the unused bytes equally among the records in the CI to make the extra space accessible to programs.

Burdened by the arithmetic involved? At the end of this chapter we present the computational aids of Appendix F, which entirely automate the process of control interval size selection.

CHOOSING THE INDEX COMPONENT CONTROL INTERVAL SIZE

The index component of a key sequenced data set contains the pointers maintained by VSAM to manage the data set structure. The "index" discussed here is the primary index. It is an integral part of the KSDS and is fundamentally different in nature from any alternate index that might optionally be created for the KSDS. The primary index consists of two main parts as illustrated in Figure 1.2:

- the "sequence set," which is the lowest level of the KSDS tree structure map. This may optionally be imbedded within the control areas of the data component itself to speed sequential access;
- the higher levels of the index, identified as the "index set," stored in separate control intervals that need not be of the same size as the data component control intervals.

For the higher levels of the index component of the KSDS, valid CI sizes are 512, 1,024; 2,048; and 4,906 bytes.[5] Smaller index component CI sizes are often the most efficient because of the compact nature of the pointer information.

IDCAMS itself usually chooses the most efficient CI size for the KSDS index component. IDCAMS's internal algorithm for determining the index CI size takes into consideration the number of data component CIs per CA and the length of the record key. CI size is therefore usually omitted from the IDCAMS specifications for the index component.

If the keys of the data component consist mostly of alphabetic characters, the index component CI size chosen by IDCAMS can be too small to be efficient. The IDCAMS default index CI size algorithm assumes that these keys can be compressed; only numeric keys can easily be compressed. An indication that IDCAMS has chosen an index component CI size that is too small is the occurrence of control interval splits in the index component, measured by a LISTCAT report as discussed in Chapter 8. The index CI size should always be kept small but at a value great enough to minimize index component control interval splits.

One way to empirically derive an effective CI size for the index is to load one control area's worth of data with a FREESPACE specification of (0 0). List the catalog entry for the data set with the LISTCAT option of IDCAMS. If the index component CI size is appropriate, there should be only one record in the index—the index itself will not have undergone any internal CI split. If more than one record exists in the index with this controlled trial loading, the index component CI size is too small. Use IDCAMS to delete the data set, increase the index component CI size to the next higher increment, and do the data set definition, load, and LISTCAT again. Repeat this process until there is only one record in the index component for a full control area's worth of data and use the index CI size that produces this result.

CONTROL AREA (CA) SIZE

Whereas a control interval, or "CI," is similar to a block of data in an ordinary sequential data set, no handy analogy exists for a control area. Control areas, or "CAs," are a creature of VSAM's structure. They are the greater of the two increments of space that may be split and "cloned" by VSAM to cope with the insertion of records as a normal function. CIs exist within CAs. When a CI split is needed to cope with a record insertion but it cannot be handled due to lack of free space within the CA, the CA itself is split and cloned by VSAM, creating another new CA out of unused space or a secondary allocation. The occurrence of a CI split or CA split requires VSAM to update the index, since the tree structure of the data set is changed by these events. Excessive CA splits pose serious inefficiencies in creation and for sequential access.

The minimum number of CIs in a CA is two. The minimum CA is one track of disk space and the maximum is one cylinder rendered in increments of whole tracks. *The CA size cannot be dictated directly but results from the means used to specify the space allocation.*

Control area size is determined by IDCAMS when the data set is defined. The space allocation options of CYLINDERS, TRACKS, and RECORDS have a direct bearing on CA size. One of these must be specified to indicate the unit of measure for the primary and secondary space allocation. If CYLINDERS is specified, the data set will be allocated in terms of cylinders. If TRACKS or RECORDS is specified, the data set will be allocated in terms of tracks. RECORDS causes IDCAMS to compute the number of tracks required for the data set and to use tracks as the unit of allocation.

Always allocate a VSAM file that consumes more than one cylinder in terms of CYL-INDERS, because the performance of a VSAM KSDS is improved when its control area is one *cylinder in size.* RECORD or TRACK allocation for a data set can result in a CA size of less than one cylinder. The rules by which the CA size is chosen by IDCAMS are:

- if the unit of allocation coded is CYLINDERS the CA size will be one cylinder
- if the unit of allocation coded is TRACKS, IDCAMS chooses the smaller of the primary allocation and the secondary allocation values, and uses it as the CA size. If this number amounts to more than one cylinder, IDCAMS chooses one cylinder as the CA size
- if the unit of allocation coded is RECORDS, IDCAMS chooses the smaller of the primary and secondary allocation values, converts the number of records into tracks for the given disk device, and determines the CA as if the unit of allocation was coded as TRACKS.

When the IMBED option is specified and the CA size is one cylinder, the sequence set, or lowest level of the index component, is maintained on the first track of the cylinder. When the IMBED option is specified and the CA size is less than one cylinder, the CA size will be made one track larger to accommodate the sequence set.

Some examples illustrate how IDCAMS handles control area allocation:

1. A space allocation of CYLINDERS (10 2) will make the control area size one cylinder. When CYLINDERS is coded as the unit of allocation, the CA size becomes one cylinder regardless of the numbers used for the primary and secondary allocations.

2. A space allocation of TRACKS (10 5) will make the control area size five tracks. When TRACKS is coded as the unit of allocation, the CA size becomes the smaller of the primary allocation and the secondary allocation.

3. A space allocation of TRACKS(100 50) will make the control area one cylinder. When the total of the primary and secondary track values are both greater than one cylinder, IDCAMS will make the CA one cylinder.

4. A space allocation of RECORDS(50000 500) will cause IDCAMS to determine the number of tracks required to hold 500 records, and allocate the CA size as this value, up to one cylinder in size. Assuming in this example a record length of 100 for fixed-length records, a CI size of 4,096 and 3380 disk, IDCAMS will make the control area two tracks. This is because 40 such fixed-length records will fit in a CI of 4,096, and 10 CIs of 4,096 bytes will fit on a track of a 3380 disk device. This will house 400 records per track. Dividing 500 records by 400 records per track indicates that two whole tracks are needed to house a CA. This will be an inefficient data set. Coding CYLINDERS with the equivalent amount of space would be much better.

Most of the benefits in performance arising from a CA size of one cylinder are realized in a reduction of I/O when records are retrieved.

The use of RECORDS allocation for a large production VSAM data set is a common VSAM efficiency error. Most production VSAM data sets will house more than a cylinder of data. It is especially important to understand the effect of CA size on the performance of large data sets and to define the data set in terms of CYLINDERS after determining the quantity of cylinders needed to house it. Allocating such a data set using the RECORDS option may appear to be similar to specifying ordinary sequential data set disk space by blocks, a practice that is encouraged. Using RECORDS specification with a small secondary space specification can, however, result in inefficient CA size usage by IDCAMS. The computational aids for designing VSAM data sets, provided in this book in Appendix F, automatically develop the values needed to employ CYLINDER allocation.

FREE SPACE

Background

Parts of control intervals and control areas can be reserved to accommodate record insertions and, in the case of variable length records, record expansion. The locations within the data set and the amount of area reserved is controlled by the FREESPACE specification of the DEFINE command. Free space specifications can be changed with the ALTER command after initial data set loading to change the amount of free space reserved during subsequent CI and CA split actions.

Free space is a particularly confusing issue because it is allocated as a *percent* of CIs and CAs. For example, the FREESPACE specification of:

```
FREESPACE (10 15)
```

means that 10% of each CI and 15% of the number of CIs per CA are to be reserved for free space. But control interval free space exists in terms of *bytes* at the end of each CI, while control area CA free space exists in terms of free CIs at the end of each CA. *The issue of developing the free space values warrants considerably more attention and care than does the specification of a secondary disk allocation amount for a simple sequential data set.*

If developed incorrectly, free space choices can have a negative impact on data set performance. An overallocation of free space will consume more disk space than required and waste I/O resources for sequential processing. But insufficient free space can cause an unwarranted number of CI splits and CA splits.

Free space is required only if records will be added to the data set after the initial load. If no records will be added after the initial load, free space can and should be specified as FREESPACE (0 0). For example, when data is loaded to a key sequenced VSAM data set solely for "lookup" or inquiry purposes, absolutely no need exists for free space.

Control Interval Free Space

```
FREESPACE ( CI-free-space-% CA-free-space-%)
```

CI free space is requested in terms of a percentage of the number of bytes in the CI. It is important to determine whether the percentage specified for CI free space will yield adequate space for records to be inserted and not simply create space in unusable quantities in each CI.

This formula chooses a CI free space percentage that will result in free space for one record in the CI:

$$\text{CI free space \% for one free record per CI} = \frac{\text{record length}}{\text{CI size}} \quad \text{round down}$$

CI free space should be specified in multiples of this value. If a value less than this is used for CI free space, the space reserved will not be large enough to hold one record; this will result in dead space in each CI and cause an excessive amount of CI splits. Because all decimal positions are dropped for this calculation, the resultant percentage may not guarantee that space for one free record will be reserved. Therefore this value should be tested by multiplying it and the CI size to verify that the resultant number of free bytes can in fact accommodate a record. If it cannot, the CI free space percentage should be adjusted upward. Double check the choice of value for CI free space since it is usually impossible to find a percentage that reserves exactly the amount of space for one record.

The three formulas following are used in sequence to calculate the total number of free record spaces that will be available in the KSDS following its initial loading. These formulas are for fixed-length records; the results are always to be rounded down:

$$\begin{aligned} \text{number of fixed-length records per CI} &= \frac{(\text{CI size} - 10)}{\text{record length}} \\[2ex] \text{number of records per CI after loading} &= \frac{\text{CI size} - 10 - (\text{CI size} * \text{CI free space \%})}{\text{record length}} \\[2ex] \text{number of record spaces in free space} &= \text{number of fixed-length records per CI} - \text{number of records per CI after loading} \end{aligned}$$

The "CI free space %" should be a multiple of the percentage that represents one free record per CI, computed with the formula presented earlier. The final figure should be checked to see if a downward adjustment still provides room for an integral number of records. CI free space governs the capacity of the CI to absorb randomly added records before VSAM will split the CI in two. Absorption of records without CI splits is desirable but dependent not only on availability of the free space but also on the key values of the records added.

For variable-length records, the formulas for free space will be less precise because the average record length is used:

$$\begin{aligned} \text{number of variable-length records per CI} &= \frac{(\text{CI size} - 4)}{(\text{average record length} + 3)} \\[2ex] \text{number of records per CI after loading} &= \frac{\text{CI size} - 4 - (\text{CI size} * \text{CI free space \%})}{\text{record length} + 3} \\[2ex] \text{number of record spaces in free space} &= \text{number of fixed-length records per CI} - \text{number of records per CI after loading} \end{aligned}$$

Once again, the "CI free space %" should be a multiple of the percentage that represents one free record per CI.

Control Area Free Space

```
FREESPACE ( CI-free-space-% CA-free-space-% )
```

The second portion of the FREESPACE specification deals with control area free space. While it is stated as a percentage, CA free space exists in terms of the number of free control intervals allowed per control area.

A formula similar to that for computing CI free space exists for developing the percentage of free CIs per CA. In order to consider it, we must first examine the means that IDCAMS uses to interpret the FREESPACE specification:

$$\text{number of free CIs per CA} = (\text{CIs per CA} \times \text{CA free space \%}) \quad\quad \textit{round down}$$

The number of CIs per CA is obtained from the disk space capacity chart in Appendix E; it is necessary to know the type of disk device on which the data set will reside and whether or not the IMBED option is to apply. When IDCAMS acts on the FREESPACE specification, it makes use of the algorithm discussed earlier in this chapter for the determination of CA size.

When calculating CI free space, we determined the percentage of a CI occupied by one record. The same general procedure can be used to determine the percentage of a CA occupied by one CI:

$$\text{CA free space \% for one free CI per CA} = \frac{1}{\#\ \text{CIs per CA}}$$

The computed percentage should be checked by using it to calculate the actual number of free CIs it produces, because of the imprecision inherent in rounding downward to integers. If a calculated percentage produces insufficient free space to house a CI, add a value of 1 to the calculated percentage and recheck it.

Effects of Free Space

How does the specification of FREESPACE affect the amount of space that will be used to store records on the initial load of the data set? Figure 2.5 provides some graphic illustrations.

For a specification of FREESPACE (40 20), 40% of each CI loaded initially will remain free and 60% of each CI used will contain data; 20% of all the CIs will be free. Only 80% of the CIs will be occupied with data. Simple multiplication of 60% and 80% indicates that 48% of the total space allocation is available to house data records at loading. The top part of Figure 2.5 illustrates this.

For FREESPACE (10 30), .9 × .7, or 63%, of the space allocation can be used at loading. A graphic depiction of this free space amount is shown in the middle part of Figure 2.5.

For FREESPACE (18 1) the "1" secures one free CI per CA, and the proportion of the CA that this represents depends on the number of CIs accommodated in a CA. In this example, with 10 CIs in a control area, FREESPACE (18 1) results in .82 × .9 = 73.8% of the space in each CA being available at initial loading. The lower part of Figure 2.5 shows how this can be visualized.

Determining Free Space Requirements

CA free space is used only when record additions or expansions cause a CI split within the CA—the CA free space is where the newly created CI resulting from a split is housed. If insert activity will be distributed evenly over the data set, emphasis should be given to

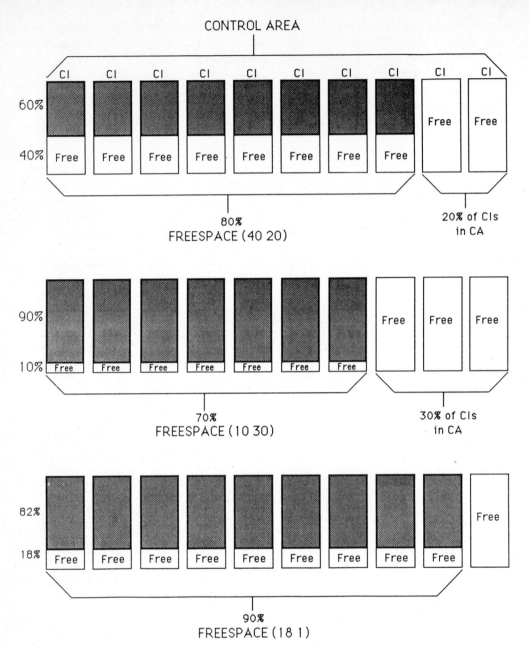

FIGURE 2.5 Free space in records after loading for various FREESPACE specification values

CI free space more than CA free space, in order to accommodate the insertions within a CI without forcing a CI split.

An easy way to pepper a data set with a minimum amount of free space to accommodate a few record additions over its entire expanse is to specify a small but nonzero value for CA free space. Free space specified as FREESPACE (0 1) secures no free space in any CI but a minimum of one free CI per CA. A CI will be split as soon as a record is added anywhere in the CA.

The opposite of requesting no free space is to request complete free space with FREE-SPACE (100 100). This seems meaningless, but results in one record being stored in the first CI in each CA at initial loading. This "preformats" the data set.

If a KSDS is to be used for data entry purposes, where large quantities of new records are to enter the data set online, records will probably enter it in random order. Preformatting the data set with dummy records carrying keys spaced evenly throughout the key range will make a significant difference in performance, since it establishes a "skeleton" for the data set ahead of time, within which the newly entered records will be placed. This avoids the rampant CI and CA splits that would occur if the data set were defined, loaded with one record only to initialize it, and records added at random. The dummy records which would exist in the first CI of each CA must be stripped out by program logic during sequential batch processing.

When the distribution of insert activity over the key values of the data set is unpredictable, little emphasis needs to be placed on control interval free space, and stress should be on control area free space. Unevenly distributed record insertions will inevitably force CI splits, making it necessary for VSAM to use a free CI within the CA for the newly "cloned" CI.

Various strategies can be used to accommodate the situation when insert activity is distributed in an extremely uneven manner. One not very appealing alternative is to specify little or no CI and CA free space but to allow secondary disk extent allocations for the data set. This will cause CI and CA splits to develop exactly where the space is needed, but can become troublesome since secondary extents are inefficient and can potentially cause other problems. If this is done, make the secondary allocations at least half as large as the primary, or even the same size as the primary, in order to avoid massive fragmentation.

Altering Free Space After Loading

An alternative for accommodating large numbers of record insertions concentrated in a small range of key values is to load the data set with a small amount of both CI and CA free space and then alter the FREESPACE values to larger quantities after the file load. FREESPACE values are stored within the KSDS definition (its "entry") in the catalog. They can be modified at any point in the life of a data set through use of the ALTER subcommand as illustrated in Appendix C. The altered values will be honored for all subsequent CI and CA splits, providing greater free space in newly created CIs and CAs resulting from record insertions. This technique is perhaps the single most effective design and processing strategy but is often overlooked. Let's discuss it.

Tailored Free Space Loading

A refined variant of free space tailoring involves interplay between system design and the loading and use of a key sequenced data set. An example illustrates how free space can be employed effectively when taken into consideration early in system development.

Let's suppose that a key sequenced data set is being designed to accommodate records supporting a system, and that the high-order byte of the primary key has been developed to facilitate efficient KSDS operation. Let's say three different types of records will be housed in the data set. One type of record will be added periodically in a batch load, and will never be added online or between these points. Another type of record will be added online, in relatively small quantities. A third type of record will be added online in large quantities. All three types are now housed in the data set, and we are structuring the IDCAMS control statements for an effective load.

It makes sense in this case to make the first type of record carry a high order byte of "A" or at least a value that sorts ahead of the other two. No free space is required in the area in which these records are stored; the area will be static. Bulk loading of additional records of this type will occur in a batch backup/merge/reload job, and no such records will be added at random.

The second type of record—light random insertion in ascending key order—demands that some free space be used. A small proportion of free control intervals within these areas will be effective. Control area free space can be minimal or not provided at all. These types of records can carry a high-order byte that sorts after the "A" above, and before the high-order byte of the key of the third type of record.

The third type of record in the data set, added in large quantity at random, will be best accommodated by allowance of control interval free space for a few records in each CI, and some free CIs in each CA as control area free space. Let's say we give this type of record a high-order primary key value of "C."

To recap:

Record key	Nature of record
Annnnnnn	Bulk batch load, not added at random
Bnnnnnnn	Small quantity of at-random adds
Cnnnnnnn	Large quantity of random adds

An effective way to structure the loading of the key sequenced data set would be to define it with FREESPACE (0 0) and to REPRO from key value A0000000 through A9999999 to the data set, using REPRO as shown in Figure 4.7 of Chapter 4. This will load all of the records of the first type with no free space in their storage area.

The free space attribute can then be altered, using the IDCAMS ALTER command, to a value such as FREESPACE (nn 1). Here nn is the computed value particular to the record size, which gives enough empty space room for one or two new records in each control interval. The minimal one free CI per CA is specified. After this ALTER, another REPRO is executed, this time specifying key values from B0000000 through B9999999.

Finally, an ALTER command is executed, changing free space to FREESPACE (yy zz), where yy is a computed value particular to the record size which gives empty room for several new records in each control interval, and zz is a computed value that allows two or more free CIs in each CA. A REPRO is then executed to read the load data set and process key values from C0000000 through Z9999999. The final free space attribute remains in effect for all subsequent online activity.

These IDCAMS actions can be performed in separate job steps, or within one step using several commands. The net effect is to create a KSDS in which the amount of distributed free space is tailored to the type of record insertion activity anticipated. This type of system design/KSDS design interplay is particularly effective and can produce highly space-efficient and responsive online data sets. KSDS reorganization is, of course, still performed on a periodic basis, using the same loading strategy.

Note that these actions involve the REPRO key value FROM and TO specifications, not the DEFINE command KEYRANGES specification, which assigns ranges of key values to different disk volumes.

Automated Key Spread Analysis

Appendix F contains the source code for a COBOL program named VANALYZE that can be used to analyze the spread of keys in a data file to be loaded to a key sequenced data set. The input record description of this program can be modified to describe the primary and alternate key fields of the specific record format for a given case.

When compiled, linkage edited, and run on the load file, VANALYZE sorts the data as needed to break it into equal-sized categories of records and reports on the number of records in each key range. Alternate keys are covered in the analysis as well as primary keys. The use of VANALYZE eliminates the imprecision of guesswork often present in the analysis leading to composition of IDCAMS control statements for new key sequenced data sets.

STEP-BY-STEP CALCULATIONS

The best way to become familiar with VSAM key sequenced data set development is to examine and analyze an actual case. We use the following assumptions for the non-trivial example introduced at the beginning of this chapter. Note that the percentage of record additions and their key distribution characteristics are, practically speaking, usually educated guesses:

- record length of 250 bytes
- 100,000 records to load initially
- 15% record additions between reorganizations evenly distributed across key values
- 3380 disk device
- online processing with batch backup and access.

Control Interval Size

The first step is to choose a control interval size for the data component of the data set. Because the data set if to be accessed online, its CI size should not exceed 4,096, and the IMBED option should be specified. All possible CI sizes up to and including this value should be examined to determine the one most efficient for the type of disk on which the data set will reside.

Let's evaluate the performance of each of the valid control interval sizes, keeping in mind that fewer tracks per control area will be available for data because the IMBED option will be used:

1. 4,096 bytes:
   $(4096 - 10) / 250 = 16$ records per CI
   $(4096 - 10) - (250 \times 16) = 86$ unusable bytes
   140 CIs per CA
   $(140 \times 16) = 2,240$ records per CA

2. 3,584 bytes:
   $(3584 - 10) / 250 = 14$ records per CI
   $(3584 - 10) - (250 \times 14) = 74$ unusable bytes
   92 CIs per CA
   $(92 \times 14) = 1,288$ records per CA

3. 3,072 bytes:
   $(3072 - 10) / 250 = 12$ records per CI
   $(3072 - 10) - (250 \times 12) = 62$ unusable bytes
   144 CIs per CA
   $(144 \times 12) = 1,728$ records per CA

4. 2,560 bytes:
   $(2560 - 10) / 250 = 10$ records per CI

$(1560 - 10) - (250 \times 10) = 50$ unusable bytes
128 CIs per CA
$(128 \times 10) = 1{,}280$ records per CA

5. 2,048 bytes:
    $(2048 - 10) / 250 = 8$ records per CI
    $(2048 - 10) - (250 \times 8) = 38$ unusable bytes
    252 CIs per CA
    $(252 \times 8) = 2{,}016$ records per CA

6. 1,536 bytes:
    $(1536 - 10) / 250 = 6$ records per CI
    $(1536 - 10) - (250 \times 6) = 26$ unusable bytes
    214 CIs per CA
    $(214 \times 6) = 1{,}284$ records per CA

7. 1,024 bytes:
    $(1024 - 10) / 250 = 4$ records per CI
    $(1024 - 10) - (250 \times 4) = 14$ unusable bytes
    434 CIs per CA
    $(434 \times 4) = 1{,}736$ records per CA

8. 512 bytes:
    $(512 - 10) / 502 = 2$ records per CI
    $(512 - 10) - (250 \times 2) = 2$ unusable bytes
    644 CIs per CA
    $(644 \times 2) = 1{,}288$ records per CA

Based on these calculations, 4,096 bytes is the most efficient data CI size because it stores the most records in a control area of one cylinder on the type of disk device to be used. The next step is to determine the appropriate percentage of CI free space to allow for 15% record additions spread evenly across the file:

$250 / 4{,}096 = 0.06135$ $= 0.06$	6% is approximately the portion of a CI occupied by one record
$.15/.6 = 2.5$	15% free CI space holds 2.5 records
$.06 \times 3 = 0.18$	The multiplier of 3 is used since 15% divided by 6% is more than 2 and not as great as 3. A control interval free space specification of 18% might allow 3 records to be added per CI.
$4{,}096 \times .18 = 737.0$	18% free space is 737 bytes, but three records of 250 bytes demand at least 750 bytes.

Why don't we have room for three records in CI free space? The last calculation above ignores the imprecision of rounding down from a decimal percentage to an integer as well as the overhead bytes in the control interval used by VSAM itself. Let's see how much space in addition to the 737 bytes obtained by a CI free space of 18% really exists in the 4,096-byte control interval unusable for the storage of data. We must take into account these bytes:

unusable CI bytes $= (4096 - 10) - (16 \times 250) = 86$

$(4096 \times .18) + 86$
$\qquad 737 + 86 = 823$

A total of 823 bytes of free space exist here with a CI free space value of 18 percent. This readily accommodates three whole records and leaves 73 bytes in the CI totally inaccessible:

823/250 = 3 plus a remainder of 73 unused bytes

If this check still did not yield enough space for three records, we would have to add 1 to the calculated CI free space percent and repeat the calculation.

The next step is to insure that 18% CI free space still allows enough room for 13 records during the initial load:

$$((4096 - 10) - (4096 \times .18)) / 250$$
$$4086 - 778 / 250$$
$$3308 / 250 = 13.2$$

Determining a workable CI free space value is a "fitting in" process that requires checking both ends of the fit—the free space record holding end and the non-free space end. This is an inevitable consequence of the IDCAMS syntax, which uses integer percentage specifications instead of a direct specification expressed in bytes.

The original calculations indicate that 16 records will fit per CI. After specifying 18% for CI free space, there is still room for 13 records to be loaded during the initial load. We can safely code:

FREESPACE (*18* CA-free-space-%)

Control Area Free Space

The last step is to determine the appropriate percentage of CA free space. Since the record additions will be spread evenly over the entire data set and ample CI free space will be specified, a minimum amount of CA free space is required. Let's set aside one free CI per CA; any nonzero value for CA free space will provide this. The exact amount needed can be calculated:

1 / 140 = .007 = 0%

The numerator of 1 represents one CI and the denominator represents 140 CIs per CA. Since 0% will not reserve free space, 1 will be used to guarantee that at least one CI will be reserved per CA for free space. We therefore code FREESPACE as:

FREESPACE (18 *1*)

under the data component of the DEFINE command.

Determining Disk Space Requirements

To determine the amount of disk space that a VSAM KSDS will require, it is necessary first to calculate the net number of CIs that each control area will allow to be used for initial loading. Let's continue to use the example developed in the foregoing paragraphs, with one free CI in each CA. Hence 140 − 1 = 139 CIs in each CA will be available for data loading.

Next, we must find out how many records can be loaded to each CI. According to our calculations, a CI free space value of 18% will reserve free space for three records. Thus the CI capacity of 16, minus 3, produces a net loading value of 13 records per CI.

Multiplying 13 records per CI times 139 CIs per CA gives us a figure of 1,807 records. This means that upon initial loading we will need one CA—one cylinder of disk space—for every 1,807 records to be loaded to the new KSDS. Since there are 100,000 records to be loaded, 100,000 divided by 1,807 yields the figure of 55.3, or 56 cylinders. The actual capacity of this space will be slightly greater than 100,000 records due to rounding up to the cylinder; the capacity will be 56 times 1,807, or 101,192 records. One extra cylinder should be allocated to accommodate the index, making the primary space allocation 57 cylinders.

Prudence dictates that since the data set is being designed to accommodate record insertions, some proportion of secondary space allocation must be specified, especially if the inserts are to occur online. A value of 5, roughly 10% that of the primary space allocation, is suitable. We can specify the disk space allocation using the CYLINDERS option, as:

```
CYLINDERS (57 5)
```

Should the data set actually grow into secondary space, as detected on a LISTCAT in monitoring data set performance, it would be advisable to examine the data set for possible purging of inactive records, to modify the primary space allocation to a greater value, copy the data set to tape using REPRO, delete and redefine the data set, and then reload the data to it.

AUTOMATING KSDS DESIGN: TSO CLISTS *VSAMCISZ* AND *VSAMSPAC*

After stepping through the lengthy arithmetic computations involved in assessing control interval size and free space, it may have occurred to you that these are excellent candidates for automation. After all, we're in the business of computerizing things, aren't we? Why not provide a tool that prompts for entry of the essential characteristics of a new KSDS, and does the many computations for us, returning the results? In fact, we have done this and provide such a tool with this book.

An easier way than manual computations exists to determine the optimal values for CI size, free space, and space allocation. Appendix F provides source code for VSAMCISZ and VSAMSPAC, two TSO CLISTs.[6]

VASMCISZ is a computational CLIST that prompts for record size, use or non-use of the IMBED option, and the type of disk device to house a KSDS, and returns the computations illustrated in Figure 2.6. The CLIST itself suggests the most efficient control interval size for these input values, for both online and strictly batch-processed data sets. The best CI sizes for both the batch and online environments are highlighted.

VSAMSPAC is a computational CLIST that handles fixed-length record calculations on 3330, 3350, and 3380 disk devices. VSAMCISZ calculates the number of records that will fit in each valid CI size for a specified record length, disk device, and IMBED option. VSAMSPAC prompts for the following information using the screen illustrated in Figure 2.7:

control interval size of the data component
record length
number of records for CI free space
number of CIs for CA free space
use of the IMBED or NOIMBED option
type of disk device

```
        PRACTICAL VSAM - JOHN WILEY AND SONS, 1988 - ISBN 0-471-85107-8
        BEST CI SIZE FOR FIXED LENGTH RECORD KSDS WITH CA SIZE ONE CYLINDER
               BY BT05677 AT 18:57:53 ON 01/19/88
  ENTER RECSIZE ==> 250
  WILL YOU USE THE IMBED OPTION - Y OR N ==> Y
  ENTER DEVICE TYPE - 3330, 3350 OR 3380 ==> 3380
  CISIZE    REC/CI    REC/TRK    REC/CA    CISIZE    REC/CI    REC/TRK    REC/CA
     512       2         92       1288      1,024       4         124       1736
   1,536       6         91       1284      2,048       8         144       2016
   2,560      10         91       1280      3,072      12         123       1728
   3,584      14         92       1288      4,096      16         160       2240
  BEST ONLINE  CI = 4096 WITH 2240 RECORDS PER CA
   4,608      18         91       1278      5,120      20         122       1720
   5,632      22         91       1276      6,144      24         144       2016
   6,656      26         91       1274      7,168      28         124       1736
   7,680      30         90       1260      8,192      32         160       2240
  10,240      40        142       2000     12,288      49         161       2254
  14,336      57        146       2052     16,384      65         162       2275
  18,432      73        146       2044     20,480      81         162       2268
  22,528      90        141       1980     24,576      98         161       2254
  26,624     106        143       2014     28,672     114         162       2280
  30,720     122        139       1952     32,768     131         159       2227
  BEST BATCH   CI = 28672 WITH 2280 RECORDS PER CA
  ***
```

FIGURE 2.6 Screen produced by VSAMCISZ computational TSO CLIST for control interval size determination

```
        PRACTICAL VSAM - JOHN WILEY AND SONS, 1988 - ISBN 0-471-85107-8
        SPACE CALC FOR FIXED LENGTH RECORD KSDS WITH CA SIZE ONE CYLINDER

        ANSWER ALL PROMPTS WITH NUMERIC ENTRIES EXCEPT IMBED/DSN

  ENTER CISIZE ==> 4096
  ENTER RECSIZE ==> 250
  16 RECORDS WILL FIT PER CI

  WHAT IS THE MINIMUM # RECORDS PER CI YOU WANT FOR CIFREESPACE?
  ENTER A NUMBER LESS THAN 16 ==> 3
  WILL YOU USE THE IMBED OPTION - Y OR N ==> Y
  ENTER DEVICE TYPE - 3330, 3350 OR 3380 ==> 3380
  MAX RECORDS PER CI = 16
     WITH 3 RECORDS FOR CIFREESPACE
     PLUS 13 RECORDS PER CI AT INITIAL LOAD
  MAX CIS PER CA = 140

  ENTER MINIMUM # OF CIS PER CA YOU WANT FOR CAFREESPACE ==> 1
  ENTER THE NUMBER OF RECORDS YOU WANT TO LOAD ==> 100000

  ENTER DATA SET NAME ==> AK00.C98.CUSTMAST
```

FIGURE 2.7 Screen prompting of VSAMSPAC computational TSO CLIST for free space and disk space calculation

number of records for the initial load
data set name

VSAMSPAC can be used after VSAMCISZ to compute space allocation quantities, producing a concise summary suggesting specifications that can be coded to define the data set. Figure 2.8 illustrates the screen returned by VSAMSPAC, including fully developed IDCAMS parameter coding, if these choices are input:

control interval size of 4,096
record length of 250
3 records for control interval free space
IMBED option
3380 disk
1 control interval for control area free space
100,000 records for the initial load
data set name of AK00.C98.CUSTMAST

VSAMCISZ and VSAMSPAC save a significant amount of time in performing VSAM key sequenced data set calculations and can be used across programming groups to standardize VSAM data set design practices or to analyze the effectiveness of present parameter choices. The use of these aids can be required in an installation, documented by the screen printing of their results, for every new VSAM data set developed. This is a simple and painless way to secure significant VSAM performance improvement on a consistent basis as well as speed KSDS design.

TSO CLIST source code for VSAMCISZ and VSAMSPAC is available in printed form in Appendix F and is also available on diskette for uploading to a mainframe. See Appen-

```
     PRACTICAL VSAM - JOHN WILEY AND SONS, 1988 - ISBN 0-471-85107-8
     SPACE CALC FOR FIXED LENGTH RECORD KSDS WITH CA SIZE ONE CYLINDER
        BY BT05677 AT 18:57:53 ON 01/19/88
        FOR DATA SET AK00.C98.CUSTMAST

     SEQ PROCESSING BUFFERS: // AMP=('AMORG,BUFNI=1,BUFND=21')
     CLUSTER OPTIONS ARE CYLINDERS ( 57 5 )
                         IMBED
                         RECORDSIZE ( 250 , 250 )
                         VOLUMES (        )         <== FOR 3380 UNIT
     DATA    OPTIONS ARE FREESPACE ( 18 , 1 )
                         CISIZE ( 4096 )
     ************** FILE STATISTICS ******************
     86 BYTES OF THE CI ARE UNUSABLE
     MAX RECORDS PER CI = 16
     MAX CIS PER CA = 140
     MAX RECORDS PER CA = 2240
     MAX RECS FOR THE FILE = 125440
     ************** STATISTICS AT INITIAL LOAD *******
     RECORDS PER CI = 13  - FREE RECORDS PER CI = 3
     CIS PER CA     = 139   - FREE CIS PER CA     = 1
     RECORDS PER CA = 1807
     MAX RECORDS WITH NO SPLITS = 101192
     ***
```

FIGURE 2.8   Space allocation, IDCAMS control statements, and optimal sequential access buffer parameters computed and returned by VSAMSPAC TSO CLIST

dix A for information on how to obtain a copy of the distribution diskette at nominal cost. These aids are original to this book. It is time to put shoes on the cobbler's children.

REVIEW QUESTIONS AND (*) EXERCISES

1. Why is the key sequenced data set control interval roughly analogous to a block of data?

2. Must the size of the control interval of the KSDS data component and the control interval size of the KSDS index component be the same? Please discuss the basis for your answer.

3. What is the maximum practical control interval size for a key sequenced data set accessed online, and why?

4. Discuss the most effective control area size for a KSDS and what specifications are necessary in defining a KSDS to achieve it.

*5. A file contains 8,000 fixed-length records, each 335 bytes in length. Determine the best data component control interval size for a key sequenced data set to house these records, which will be accessed online.

*6. For the KSDS discussed in exercise 5, what is the amount of unusable space in each control interval for the optimal control interval size?

*7. Describe the steps used to determine the optimal index component control interval size for a new key sequenced data set to be accessed online and apply these steps to arrive at the optimal index component CI size for the data set in exercise 5.

*8. Test data to load the key sequenced data set defined and created in Figure 2.2 exists in Appendix F and is available on diskette for upload to your mainframe. Appendix F also provides the control statements for a run of IEBGENER to expand this test data from 80-byte card-image format to the 250-byte records needed for the load. Copy or upload the JCL and IDCAMS control statements of Figure 2.2, customize it for your installation, and run the define and load. Examine the output from IDCAMS and circle the messages it generates in response to the control statements. Note: Change the space allocation from CYLINDERS(1 1) to TRACKS(2 1) before running this job to preclude wasting a large amount of disk space.

*9. After performing exercise 8, use IDCAMS control statements as illustrated in Figure 4.14 in Chapter 4 to print and see the contents of the key sequenced data set. Explain why the records are in the order you find them. (Omit COUNT/SKIP).

*10. After performing exercises 8 and 9, manipulate the records in the test data to be loaded to the KSDS, putting them out of ascending sequence of primary key. Rerun the define and load job, noting how IDCAMS responds. Indicate why you have received these results.

NOTES

1. The key of the records housed in a VSAM key sequenced data set need not be located in the first field in the record. Neither does the first byte of the record serve as a "delete indicator" as was the case with IBM's ISAM. The example used here makes apparent these facts.

   The record illustrated in Figure 2.1 appears to have only a primary key and the JCL of Figure 2.2 defines only a basic KSDS with no alternate indexes. In Chapter 5 we modify the JCL and

IDCAMS control statements of Figure 2.2, expanding the processing tasks to define and create two alternate indexes for the data set. Two fields already contained in the record layout of Figure 2.1 are intended to serve as alternate keys, but are not so defined here in order to focus the present discussion. Chapter 5 builds on this example, and Chapter 9 illustrates production-oriented refinements.

2. Chapter 6 illustrates the JCL to increase the number of buffers for batch processing of VSAM key sequenced data sets and provides guidance on buffer quantity determination.

3. The nature of the VSAM overhead information in each control interval is not germane to KSDS use, but it is not mysterious either. At the end of every CI is a four-byte field called the "control interval description field," or CIDF. This contains information about free space.

   Immediately preceding the CIDF at the end of the CI are one or more three-byte "record description fields," RIDF. VSAM uses two RIDFs to fully describe the length and position of any group of records that are the same length. Therefore, if a data set contains only records of the same fixed length, only two RIDFs are needed. The two three-byte RIDFs plus the single four-byte CIDF field make up the 10 bytes of VSAM overhead.

   A KSDS can contain records of different lengths. No explicit indicator exists marking a KSDS as "variable-length record format" as there is with JCL for a sequential data set containing variable-length records. Instead, different RECORDSIZE values for average and maximum record length denote a variable-length record KSDS. VSAM still uses two RIDF fields to describe groups of records of the same length in a CI in such a data set, but records of different lengths following one another each receive one RIDF.

   If only one record fits within a CI, only one RIDF field is required. This is the basis for the seven bytes of VSAM overhead in the CI in such a case.

   CIDF and RIDF fields are internal to VSAM and are neither accessible nor of use to application programs. They need to be taken into account only because of the space they consume, which has an effect on CI size and space calculation formulas.

4. The table associated with control interval size determination shows values for both the IMBED and NOIMBED options. But the issue of NOIMBED versus IMBED is not a factor in judging the relative merit of one CI size as opposed to another for a given KSDS.

5. An index control interval size of 512 bytes is permitted on 3330 and 3350 disk units but not on the 3380. For the 3380, 1,024 bytes is the smallest CI size possible; if 512 is coded, VSAM ignores it and uses 4,096 as the index CI size.

6. VSAMCISZ and VSAMSPAC were developed as CLISTs by Richard E. Guzik. Available on the same distribution diskette as these CLISTs is the source code for a CLIST named VSAMBUFS, discussed in Chapter 6, and for several COBOL programs and the JCL to execute them. These programs can be used to evaluate sequential data set key ranges and monitor the performance of all VSAM data sets in an installation on a regular basis as discussed in Chapters 3 and 8, and Appendix F.

3

Defining the Key Sequenced Data Set

The IDCAMS utility is driven by a control statement language. Some elements of this language are used to define VSAM data sets and manipulate them; other elements of the language invoke IDCAMS functions to perform services similar to those of more primitive copy and print utilities. In this chapter we focus on the elements of the IDCAMS control statement language that provide the means to define a key sequence data set.

KEY SEQUENCED DATA SET ATTRIBUTES

The attributes of a key sequenced data set are controlling parameters; these are stored in the system catalog and control VSAM software when the data set is accessed. Definition options are provided in the IDCAMS control statement language to set the attributes of a KSDS; the number of attribute definition options is almost overwhelming. Adding to the apparent complexity of VSAM data sets is the fact that many of the options can be specified either at the base cluster, the data component, the index, and in optional alternate indexes.

Figure 3.2 in this chapter presents the entire array of control statement KSDS definition options. That listing is purposely arranged in pseudo-syntax format in order to aid you in recognizing how the options are actually coded. But there is a reason the complete listing is buried in the middle of this chapter: the complete listing is actually a reference item and not a practical working tool of KSDS development. Such a listing obscures the optimal choice of options and definition points—cluster, data component, or index component. Figure 3.2 is like a raw technical manual.

Figure 3.1 is, on the other hand, a practical rendition of KSDS definition options arranged in the manner that best serves most purposes. This was prepared from the complete listing but shows a given item only at the definition point where it is most desirable to code it and drops all but the important specifications. Figure 3.1 shows the default specifications underlined. If you compare Figure 2.2 with Figure 3.1 you will see that the real IDCAMS coding statements stem directly from this abridged listing. The actual code simplifies matters further by omitting mention of the options for which the default is suitable.[1]

In this chapter we discuss the general nature of the IDCAMS KSDS definition mechanism and all of the options that may be coded. In keeping with our focus on practicality, the options first described are those non-default items shown in Figure 3.1. The lesser-used options are discussed in alphabetical order following 3.2. The point: if you are like

```
            DEFINE -
              CLUSTER    (    NAME ( data-set-name ) -
                              VOLUMES ( volser  volser  volser  volser ) -
                              RECORDSIZE ( average   maximum ) -
                              KEYS ( length   offset ) -
                              CYLINDERS( primary   secondary ) -
                              SHAREOPTIONS ( crossregion   crosssystem ) -
                              SPEED -
                              NODESTAGEWAIT -
                              NOERASE -
                              NOIMBED -
                              INDEXED -
                              UNORDERED -
                              NORECATALOG -
                              NOREPLICATE -
                              NOREUSE -
                              NONSPANNED -
                              STAGE -
                              UNIQUE -
                              NOWRITECHECK                                )  -
                              -
              DATA       (    NAME ( data-set-name.DATA ) -
                              CONTROLINTERVALSIZE( size ) -
                              FREESPACE( CI-percent   CA-percent )         )  -
                              -
              INDEX      (    NAME ( data-set-name.INDEX )                 )
```

FIGURE 3.1 Practical key sequenced data set definition options with optimal placement of important attributes in cluster, data, and index components (italics show defaults for ICF environment that need not be coded)

most busy professionals, you will appreciate the ability to hit the ground running with Figure 3.1.

DEFINE CLUSTER

Background

All VSAM data sets are defined as "clusters." The base cluster name is the umbrella that encompasses the data and index component, any alternate index components, and any paths that connect alternate indexes to the base cluster.[2] Since each component also has its own unique name, each can be processed independently of the others, but such processing is unusual.

Each data set component can reside on a different disk device or device type and each can be given its own attributes when defined. Attributes specified at the cluster level are applied to all the components as the default unless the component also has that attribute defined; specification in the component takes precedence over the attribute coded for the cluster.[3]

Several parameters are always required when defining a key sequenced data set. These include CLUSTER, NAME, VOLUMES, and CYLINDERS, TRACKS, or RECORDS. If MODEL is specified, the VOLUMES and space allocation are not required since these are copied from a model data set, in the same way that DCB specifications can be copied for non-VSAM data sets by naming a model data set.

The DEFINE CLUSTER option is divided into four sections; each section is self-contained with all of its attributes coded within an overall set of parentheses. The four sections are CLUSTER, DATA, INDEX, and CATALOG. The CATALOG section identifies the unique catalog in which reference to the data set will be recorded. CATALOG can be omitted when the default catalog is used to house the KSDS definition, the most common instance.

NAME (data-set-name)
Default: none   **Abbreviation: none**

The data set name specified is the name that will be entered by the system in the catalog. This is called the "entryname" in VSAM parlance. This name identifies the cluster, data component, and index component as an umbrella for access purposes, and is required. NAME can, however, also be coded for the index component and data component definitions, and its use in those places is strongly recommended to explicitly identify the components rather than allowing VSAM to assign unique but essentially meaningless names to them. When naming the two components, you should use the cluster name plus ".DATA" for the data component and ".INDEX" for the index component, because these names must be different from the cluster name. This is a convention only; VSAM imposes no requirement to do this, but it is a great help in organizing the many elements of a KSDS. The cluster name does *not* appear in the volume table of contents (VTOC) for a UNIQUE data set; the data component and index component names do.

The rules for NAME formation are identical to those for ordinary data set names. The name can be from 1 to 44 alphanumeric characters, national characters such as @, #, or $, or two special characters, hyphen and 12-0 overpunch (hexadecimal C0).[4] A name can be segmented into levels by periods that count as name characters. A maximum of eight characters can exist in any name level, and the first character of each level must be either alphabetic or national. The most leftward level of the name is called the high-level qualifier or high-level index, a term associated with cataloging functions and having nothing to do with a primary or alternate index.

KEYS (length offset)
Default: (64 0)   **Abbreviation: none**

KEYS defines the length of the key and its offset from the beginning of the record relative to the first byte. Offset is a number that is one less than the ordinal position of the byte in the record; the first byte of a record has an offset of zero. The key can be from 1 to 255 bytes in length. The offset can be from zero to one less than the length of the shortest record in the data set.

RECORDSIZE (average maximum)
Default: (4089 4089)   **Abbreviation: RECSZ**

RECORDSIZE specifies the average record length and the maximum record length. In the case of fixed-length records, both numbers are the same.

For nearly all purposes, data sets are created with records shorter than block size or control interval size. These are called "nonspanned" records because they do not span across what is traditionally considered an I/O action. For nonspanned records, the minimum record size is one byte and the maximum is the CI size minus seven. The default RECORDSIZE shown above is for nonspanned records.

Spanned records are logical records of such a length that they spread across control intervals. The maximum record size for a spanned record is the CI size minus 10, times the number of CIs per CA:

$$\text{Maximum record size for a spanned record} = (\text{CI} - 10) \times (\text{number of CIs per CA})$$

The default RECORDSIZE for spanned records is 4,089 bytes average record size; 32,600 bytes is the maximum record size.[5]

SPEED | RECOVERY
Default: RECOVERY   **Abbreviation: RCVY**

The choice of SPEED or RECOVERY is meaningful only during the initial loading of the data set. RECOVERY causes VSAM to preformat each control area with an end-of-file marker as the data set is loaded, and allows resumption of data set loading at a point just prior to abend. To use it you must arrange the data being loaded to resume the load at this point. This is worthwhile only for very large data sets; in most cases the cure for a load that failed due to interruption is to eliminate the partially created data set and to repeat the load.

SPEED will significantly reduce the I/O required to load a data set because it avoids the task of preformatting each control area, something that VSAM must do to allow the recovery capability. After a data set is loaded, VSAM always processes it in the RECOVERY mode.

SHAREOPTIONS (cross-region cross-system)
Default: (1 3)   **Abbreviation: SHR**

The first of the two values deals with cross-partition or cross-region sharing, the sharing of the data set between batch or online programs executing concurrently on the same machine. The second value deals with applicability of the sharing specification to programs executing on different machines, that is, different central processing units or "CPUs."

The cross-region SHAREOPTIONS specification sets the level of read and write integrity for the data set. The default values are assumed during the initial loading of the file. After the initial load the specified values are used.

The values of (1 3) indicate that the data set can be shared by any number of users for read processing or the data set can be accessed by only one user for write processing, but not both. This specification insures both read and write integrity for the data set.

The values of (2 3) indicate that the data set can be accessed by any number of users for read processing *and* can at the same time be accessed by one user for write processing. These values insure only write integrity for the data set, but this is usually sufficient for most applications and (2 3) are the SHAREOPTIONS recommended.

A SHAREOPTIONS value of (3 3) indicates that the data set can be shared by any number of users with any or all doing concurrent updating of the data set. These values provide no file integrity and are not recommended for any purpose.

The values of (4 3) allow the data set to be fully shared with no system-provided integrity checking as with (3 3), but the VSAM buffers are refreshed for each request.

A specification of 4 as the cross-system specification, as in (2 4), indicates that sharing of the data set between programs executing on different machines is desired, with the integrity provisions of the first specification. Integrity specified with a cross-region value of 1 or 2 cannot, however, automatically be insured for data sets shared between machines when COBOL programs are involved. To insure data set integrity between machines with SHAREOPTIONS values of (x 4) programs attempting access must issue either the ENQ/DEQ supervisor call or the RESERVE/RELEASE supervisor call. This cannot be done with COBOL. Even with this option in effect all write attempts by either program that result in the need for a CI split will receive a "NO SPACE AVAILABLE" file status value from VSAM.

An enhancement to the operating environment called "single image software" provides cross-system integrity. This is available only when the Integrated Catalog Facility of VSAM is installed; when in use, all programs accessing the data set must do so with the JCL disposition parameter of DISP = SHR.

VOLUMES
Default: none   **Abbreviation: VOL**

VOLUMES specifies the volume serial numbers of disk media on which the data set will reside. VOLUMES is also used in conjunction with KEYRANGES to identify the storage volume for each of several specified key ranges. If SUBALLOCATION is specified, a VSAM data space must exist on the single volume coded at VOLUMES. If UNIQUE and KEYRANGES are specified, a VSAM space will be created on each of potentially several volumes coded at VOLUMES. When the Integrated Catalog Facility is installed, SUBALLOCATION is eliminated as an option and all allocations are treated as UNIQUE.

VSAM catalogs have special interpretations for an attribute named VOLUME, which is not pluralized and is not the same as the VOLUMES attribute of DEFINE.

Important Defaults

Certain of the many key sequenced data set definition specifications are more relevant to everyday concerns than others. The 12 attributes described in the following section are important enough to warrant attention. The default of each, however, is usually the most appropriate, and for this reason none of these is shown in the actual IDCAMS example of Figure 2.2. They are shown on Figure 3.1 underlined, denoting that each is the default for an attribute that has two or more possible states. In Figure 3.2, on the other hand, these attributes are shown interspersed among the many others in alphabetical sequence with the other possible states of the attributes.

Your most concise guide to key sequenced data set definition is the actual coding of Figure 2.2. Figure 3.1 and this discussion are a good second step to practical KSDS background. The full listing of Figure 3.2, later in this chapter, is provided primarily for reference purposes.

DESTAGEWAIT | NODESTAGEWAIT
Default: NODESTAGEWAIT   **Abbreviation: NDSTGW**

DESTAGEWAIT is in effect only when the KSDS cluster is stored on a mass storage device, a unit employing automatically mounted tape spool cartridges.[6] Such a device appears to be a disk, but data is actually retrieved in bulk from a tape spool and staged to disk when access is requested. DESTAGEWAIT is recommended for clusters that are stored on mass storage devices because this attribute triggers notification to a program that closed a VSAM data set of the success or failure of destaging. DESTAGEWAIT allows the program itself to check the success or failure of data set destaging activities, making it possible to catch a destaging error earlier than would otherwise be the case.

ERASE | NOERASE
Default: NOERASE   **Abbreviation: NERAS**

ERASE is meaningful only when a data set is deleted. If ERASE is specified, the entire data component is overwritten with binary zeros by VSAM when the data set is deleted. If NOERASE is specified, just the VTOC entry for a UNIQUE data set is removed. ERASE

```
                                                                        Abbreviation


        DEFINE -                                                        DEF
           CLUSTER  (    NAME ( data-set-name ) -                       CL
                         VOLUMES( volser  volser  volser  volser ) -    VOL
                         RECORDSIZE( average    maximum ) -             RECSZ
                         KEYS( length    offset ) -                     —
                         SHAREOPTIONS( crossregion    crosssystem ) -   SHR
                         SPEED or RECOVERY -                            RCVY
                         ATTEMPTS( number ) -                           ATT
                         AUTHORIZATION( entrypoint    string ) -        AUTH
                         BUFFERSPACE( size ) -                          BUFSP
                         CODE( code ) -                                 —
                         CONTROLINTERVALSIZE( size ) -                  CISZ
                         CONTROLPW( password ) -                        CTLPW
                one of (   CYLINDERS( primary    secondary ) -          CYL
                these  (   RECORDS( primary    secondary ) -            REC
                three  (   TRACKS( primary    secondary ) -             TRK
                         DESTAGEWAIT or NODESTAGEWAIT -         DSTGW   NDSTGW
                         ERASE or NOERASE -                     ERAS    NERAS
                         EXCEPTIONEXIT( entrypoint ) -                  EEXT
                         FILE( DDname ) -                               —
                         FREESPACE( CI-percent    CA-percent ) -        FSPC
                         IMBED or NOIMBED -                     IMBD    NIMBD
  use   KSDS (           INDEXED -                                      IXD
  only  ESDS (           NONINDEXED -                                   NIXD
  one!  RRDS (           NUMBERED -                                     NUMD
        DIV  (           LINEAR -
                         KEYRANGES( ( lowkey    highkey ) -             KRNG
  up to      (                    ( lowkey    highkey ) -
  123        (                    ( lowkey    highkey ) -
  ranges     (                    ( lowkey    highkey ) ) -
                         MASTERPW( password ) -                         MRPW
                         MODEL( data-set-name/password   catname/password ) -  —
                         ORDERED or UNORDERED -                ORD     UNORD
                         OWNER( up-to-eight-characters ) -
                         READPW( password ) -                           RDPW
                         RECATALOG or NORECATALOG -            RCTLG   NRCTLG
                         REPLICATE or NOREPLICATE -            REPL    NREPL
                         REUSE or NOREUSE -                    RUS     NRUS
                         SPANNED or NONSPANNED -               SPND    NSPND
                         STAGE or BIND or CYLINDERFAULT -              CYLF
                         TO( Julian date ) or FOR( days ) -
                         UNIQUE or SUBALLOCATION -              UNQ    SUBAL
                         UPDATEPW( password ) -                         UPDPW
                         WRITECHECK or NOWRITECHECK            ) -  WCK NWCK
                         -

           DATA    (    NAME ( data-set-name.data ) -                   —
                         ATTEMPTS( number ) -                           ATT
                         AUTHORIZATION( entrypoint    string ) -        AUTH
                         BUFFERSPACE( size ) -                          BUFSP
                         CODE( code ) -                                 —
                         CONTROLINTERVALSIZE( size ) -                  CISZ
                         CONTROLPW( password ) -                        CTLPW
                one of (   CYLINDERS( primary    secondary ) -          CYL
                these  (   RECORDS( primary    secondary ) -            REC
                three  (   TRACKS( primary    secondary ) -             TRK
                         DESTAGEWAIT or NODESTAGEWAIT -         DSTGW   NDSTGW
                         ERASE or NOERASE -                     ERAS    NERAS
                         EXCEPTIONEXIT( entrypoint ) -                  EEXT
                         FILE( DDname ) -                               —
                         FREESPACE( CI-percent    CA-percent ) -        FSPC
                         KEYRANGES( ( lowkey    highkey ) -             KRNG
  up to          (                 ( lowkey    highkey ) -
```

FIGURE 3.2 Complete key sequenced data set definition options showing all attribute specifications (defaults for ICF environment in italics)

```
    123         {                    ( lowkey   highkey ) -
    ranges      {                    ( lowkey   highkey ) ) -
                        KEYS( length    offset ) -                          —
                        MASTERPW( password ) -                             MRPW
                        MODEL( data-set-name/password  catname/password ) -   —
                        ORDERED or UNORDERED -                        ORD  UNORD
                        OWNER( up-to-eight-characters ) -                   —
                        READPW( password ) -                               RDPW
                        RECORDSIZE( average    maximum ) -                 RECSZ
                        SPEED or RECOVERY -                                RCVY
                        REUSE or NOREUSE -                           RUS  NRUS
                        SHAREOPTIONS( crossregion   crosssystem ) -        SHR
                        SPANNED or NONSPANNED -                     SPND  NSPND
                        STAGE or BIND or CYLINDERFAULT -                   CYLF
                        UNIQUE or SUBALLOCATION -                    UNQ  SUBAL
                        UPDATEPW( password ) -                             UPDPW
                        VOLUMES( volser  volser  volser  volser ) -        VOL
                        WRITECHECK or NOWRITECHECK            ) -   WCK  NWCK
                        -
    INDEX      (    NAME ( data-set-name.index ) -                         IX
                    ATTEMPTS( number ) -                                  ATT
                    AUTHORIZATION( entrypoint   string ) -               AUTH
                    CODE( code ) -                                        —
                    CONTROLINTERVALSIZE( size ) -                        CISZ
                    CONTROLPW( password ) -                              CTLPW
    one of   {      CYLINDERS( primary   secondary ) -                   CYL
    these    {      RECORDS( primary   secondary ) -                    REC
    three    {      TRACKS( primary   secondary ) -                     TRK
                    DESTAGEWAIT or NODESTAGEWAIT -            DSTGW  NDSTGW
                    EXCEPTIONEXIT( entrypoint ) -                       EEXT
                    FILE( DDname ) -                                     —
                    IMBED or NOIMBED -                        IMBD  NIMBD
                    MASTERPW( password ) -                             MRPW
                    MODEL( data.set.name/password  catname/password ) -   —
                    ORDERED or UNORDERED -                     ORD  UNORD
                    OWNER( up-to-eight-characters ) -                   —
                    READPW( password ) -                               RDPW
                    REPLICATE or NOREPLICATE -                 REPL  NREPL
                    REUSE or NOREUSE -                         RUS  NRUS
                    SHAREOPTIONS( crossregion   crosssystem ) -        SHR
                    STAGE or BIND or CYLINDERFAULT -                   CYLF
                    UNIQUE or SUBALLOCATION -                  UNQ  SUBAL
                    UPDATEPW( password ) -                             UPDPW
                    VOLUMES( volser  volser  volser  volser ) -        VOL
                    WRITECHECK or NOWRITECHECK            ) -   WCK  NWCK
                    -
    CATALOG( catname/password )                                        CAT
```

FIGURE 3.2   (*Continued*)

should be specified if the data set contains confidential data to insure that the data is completely destroyed when the data set is deleted.

In most instances the default, NOERASE, is suitable since it eliminates performance of a time-consuming data obliteration process. Specifying ERASE also causes the formatting of control intervals during initial data set loading, as with the RECOVERY option. This additional action renders unnecessarily inefficient the operation of a KSDS. Chapter 11 elaborates on an optional feature called "erase on scratch " that also implements deleted data set obliteration through a security system.

NOIMBED | IMBED
Default: NOIMBED   Abbreviation: NIMBD

IMBED will reserve the first track of the data component for the lowest level of the index component. It will copy this, called the sequence set, around the track as many times as it fits. IMBED can be specified only for the data component. IMBED is recommended for online files and should only be used if the CA size of the data component is a cylinder. Use of IMBED will reduce the seek time for randomly accessed data sets and will also improve performance when the data set is accessed sequentially. REPLICATE, dealing with the index component, is easily confused with IMBED, but performs a different function.

INDEXED | NOINDEXED | NUMBERED
Default: INDEXED   Abbreviation: IXD

INDEXED specifies that the data set will be key sequenced. NOINDEXED indicates that the data set is of entry sequenced (ESDS) organization, and NUMBERED indicates a relative record data set (RRDS). INDEXED is the default and is nearly always appropriate since VSAM is used primarily for KSDS data sets. LINEAR allocates a special type of data set under the "Data-in-Virtual" enhancement announced for the ICF catalog environment in 1987. Appendix D discusses the non-indexed VSAM data set organizations.

ORDERED | UNORDERED
Default: UNORDERED   Abbreviation: UNORD

Specification of ORDERED will cause the volume serial numbers specified in VOLUMES to be used in the sequence coded to satisfy the space allocation. UNORDERED indicates that the sequence of volume serial numbers code at VOLUMES need not be honored for data set allocation. UNORDERED is the default. Your specific disk volume intentions for very large data sets dictates the choice between the ORDERED and UNORDERED.

RECATALOG | NORECATALOG
Default: NORECATALOG   Abbreviation: NRCTLG

RECATALOG is applicable only in an Integrated Catalog Facility environment and specifies whether the cluster component catalog entries are to be created or already exist and are to be recreated. If a cluster has been deleted, its recreation is considered a first-time creation. NORECATALOG, the default, indicates that the ICF catalog entries are being created for the first time.

RECATALOG will recreate the catalog entries only if valid VSAM Volume Data Set (VVDS) entries are found on the primary VVDS volume. Both the NAME and VOLUMES parameters must be specified as they were when the cluster was originally defined. If ATTEMPTS, AUTHORIZATION, CATALOG, CODE, CONTROLPW, FOR, MASTERPW, MODEL, OWNER, READPW, TO, or UPDATEPW were specified when the data set was originally defined, they should be specified again if RECATALOG is performed.

REPLICATE | NOREPLICATE
Default: NOREPLICATE   Abbreviation: NREPL

REPLICATE causes VSAM to write each index record on a separate track and copy it around the track as many times as it will fit. NOREPLICATE will leave the index in the form in which it develops, consisting of two or more logical levels within a physical control interval size chosen by VSAM. For time-critical applications, REPLICATE will have a beneficial effect on record seek time. However, for most applications, the amount of space required to replicate the index, especially on 3380 disk devices, is not worth the small benefit gained.

The default, NOREPLICATE, is recommended for most applications. REPLICATE should be used only in conjunction with IMBED, since the use of either implies a strong concern for ultimate online responsiveness at the expense of disk space.

REUSE | NOREUSE
Default: NOREUSE
Abbreviation: NRUS

REUSE allows a data set to be regarded as empty when it is opened for output. The first record written to a data set will thus be written at the beginning of the data set. REUSE is employed when it is desirable to use a VSAM data set for more than one purpose within a program. REUSE makes sense in such cases since the file may be opened more than once, but prior use should not affect subsequent use.

When REUSE is specified, KEYRANGES cannot be specified, and alternate indexes cannot be built for the data set. The default, NOREUSE, is recommended for nearly all data sets except for work files, such as the ESDS sort work files used by VSAM itself in connection with the BLDINDEX command. If UNIQUE is specified in a non-Integrated Catalog Facility (ICF) environment, REUSE cannot be specified. ALTER cannot be employed to change the REUSE/NOREUSE status of a data set.

SPANNED | NONSPANNED
Default: NONSPANNED
Abbreviation: NSPND

SPANNED indicates that the logical record length can exceed the size of a control interval. Use of SPANNED is recommended only when a small percentage of the records in a data set vastly exceeds the average record length; for other purposes ordinary variable-length records are more suitable. The maximum record length that can be specified with SPANNED is the CI size minus 10, times the number of CIs per CA as discussed in connection with the RECORDSIZE specification.

STAGE | BIND | CYLINDERFAULT
Default: STAGE
Abbreviation: none

These attributes are meaningful only for a mass storage device such as the IBM 3850, an obsolete device. The default of STAGE stages data from a mass storage device to disk when the cluster is opened. BIND stages the data at open time and holds it until the data set is closed. CYLINDERFAULT stages data as the processing program needs it.

UNIQUE | SUBALLOCATION
Default: SUBALLOCATION
Abbreviation: SUBAL

In an Integrated Catalog Facility (ICF) environment, all data sets are allocated UNIQUE and the UNIQUE and SUBALLOCATE specifications are ignored. In a non-ICF environment the choice remains, but UNIQUE, abbreviated UNQ, is recommended.

UNIQUE indicates that the data set will be allocated in a VSAM space of its own and will receive an entry in the disk volume table of contents, the VTOC, for the disk. SUB-ALLOCATION, the default, indicates that the data set will be allocated within a pre-defined VSAM space on the disk and the data set will not receive its own VTOC entry. A data space is created for each key range when KEYRANGES is specified, and VSAM must own all of the volumes except the first specified in the VOLUMES attribute.

WRITECHECK | NOWRITECHECK
Default: NOWRITECHECK   **Abbreviation: NWCK**

The default of NOWRITECHECK should always be used unless the data set resides on the obsolete 2314 disk device. WRITECHECK causes performance degradation because it forces the system to reread each record after it is written. This is not necessary for data set integrity verification on contemporary disk drives, because these drives themselves constantly monitor integrity, log performance, and warn of uncorrectable I/O errors.

DEFINE DATA

Background

When the definitions described above are coded at the base cluster definition, relatively few attributes must be coded for the data component. However, the specification of those noted here is far from arbitrary. NAME, CONTROLINTERVALSIZE, space allocation values, and FREESPACE are cited here rather than at the base cluster in order to avoid imposing these on the index component.

NAME (data-set-name)
Default: meaningless system-created name   **Abbreviation: none**

When naming the data component, you should use the cluster name plus ".DATA" in order to visually associate the two items. For example, if the cluster name is AK00.-C98.CUSTMAST, the data component name can be formed as AK00.C98.CUST-MAST.DATA. When one or more alternate indexes will also be established, however, it is advisable to extend the convention a bit further. An alternate index is actually a KSDS in its own right and will have its own cluster, data, and index components. In such a case, illustrated in Chapter 5, the overall naming convention includes the application of suffixes such as BASE for parts of the primary data set—the base cluster—and meaningful names for any alternate index. This suggested naming convention could be followed:

primary cluster	AK00.C98.CUSTMAST
primary data component	AK00.C98.CUSTMAST.BASE.DATA
primary index component	AK00.C98.CUSTMAST.BASE.INDEX
address alt index cluster	AK00.C98.CUSTMAST.ADDRAIX
address alt index data component	AK00.C98.CUSTMAST.ADDRAIX.DATA
address alt index index component	AK00.C98.CUSTMAST.ADDRAIX.INDEX
address alt index path	AK00.C98.CUSTMAST.ADDRAIX.PATH

The rules for NAME formation are identical to those for ordinary data set names. The name can be from 1 to 44 alphanumeric characters, national characters such as @, #, or $, or two special characters, hyphen and 12-0 overpunch (hexadecimal C0).[4] A name can be segmented into levels by periods that count as name characters. A maximum of eight characters can exist in any name level and the first character of each level must be either alphabetic or national.

CONTROLINTERVALSIZE
Default: determined by VSAM   **Abbreviation: CISZ**

The CONTROLINTERVALSIZE (CI size) is the basic unit of data transfer between disk and memory. The CI size should not be specified for the cluster but only for the data component. This will force VSAM to choose a CI size for the index component which it usually does very well. Chapter 2 provides an extensive discussion of the calculations leading to the choice of an appropriate control interval size.

CYLINDERS (primary secondary) |	Abbreviation: **CYL**
TRACKS (primary secondary) |	**TRK**
RECORDS (primary secondary)	**REC**
Default: none	

The CYLINDER, TRACKS, and RECORDS define the unit of space allocation for the data set. One of the space allocation parameters must be specified unless the MODEL specification is coded, naming a model data set from which attributes are copied. Use of CYLINDER is recommended to insure that the control area size becomes one cylinder. Use of RECORDS as the space allocation parameter should be avoided for any but insignificant test data sets because it can result in generation of an inefficient control area size.

The primary space allocation should be large enough to accommodate the number of records to be loaded initially, taking into account the amount of distributed free space in the data set.

If records will never be expanded or added to the data set, the secondary allocation can be omitted. The secondary allocation is used by the system to dynamically allocate additional space when the primary allocation becomes insufficient. When secondary allocation is specified, the data set can expand to a maximum of 123 extents, unlike the case with ordinary sequential data sets, which are limited to 16 extents on a volume. Allowing a KSDS to expand to more than three extents, however, is not recommended.

If UNIQUE is specified and more than one volume is coded for the data component, the data set can grow to a maximum of 16 extents on each volume. If a data component is divided into KEYRANGES on more than one volume, the primary allocation is used to allocate space for each key range. The initial allocation of the cluster must be satisfied in five extents or the DEFINE option will terminate abnormally. If UNIQUE is specified and the space allocation is not a multiple of a cylinder, VSAM will round the allocation up to a multiple of a cylinder. VSAM catalogs have special interpretations for these attributes. See Chapter 2 and the computational CLISTs of Appendix F for additional information on computing the cylinder space allocation for key sequenced data sets.

FREESPACE (CI-percent CA-percent)	
Default: FREESPACE (0 0)	Abbreviation: **FSPC**

FREESPACE reserves free space in each control interval and in each control area to accommodate record additions and record expansion. FREESPACE should be specified only for the data component. A complete discussion on the method for computing free space specifications can be found in Chapter 2.

DEFINE INDEX

Background

It is usually desirable to specify a unique name for the index component only in order to avoid inheriting a name for it constructed by IDCAMS. The name should be constructed according to a convention such as that suggested in the foregoing discussion of the data component name.

CONTROLINTERVALSIZE should not be specified explicitly for the index component. VSAM will determine for itself a suitable CI size for the index component, and this value is usually the best possible. No space allocation is specified for the index, and VSAM allocates an appropriate quantity on its own. The index does not usually consume more than a negligible amount of space.

NAME (data-set-name)
Default: meaningless system-created name   **Abbreviation: none**

When naming the index component, you should use the cluster name plus ".INDEX" in order to visually associate these items. For example, if the cluster name is AK00.-C98.CUSTMAST, then the data component name can be formed as AK00.C98.CUST-MAST.INDEX. When one or more alternate indexes will also be established, it is advisable to extend the convention further:

primary cluster	`AK00.C98.CUSTMAST`
primary index component	`AK00.C98.CUSTMAST.BASE.INDEX`
address alt index cluster	`AK00.C98.CUSTMAST.ADDRAIX`
address alt index index component	`AK00.C98.CUSTMAST.ADDRAIX.INDEX`

The rules for NAME formation are identical to those for ordinary data set names. See the discussion concerning the naming of the data component for a full recitation of these rules and the suggested naming convention.

LITTLE-USED KSDS DEFINITION OPTIONS

Many of the IDCAMS KSDS definition options listed in Figure 3.2—the reason this "complete" recitation of options is so lengthy—find little use in the contemporary applications programming environment. For this reason, these are listed here only in alphabetical order, without discrete grouping as to base cluster, data component, or index component applicability.

ATTEMPTS (number)
Default: ATTEMPTS (2)   **Abbreviation: ATT**

The ATTEMPTS parameter defines the number of times an operator can attempt to enter a correct password for the data set in response to a prompt by VSAM. Allowable values are 0 to 7. A value of zero indicates that no prompts are given and passwords are not permitted to be entered via the system console. As discussed further in Chapter 11, it is usually unwise to provide passwords to console operators for VSAM data sets unless there are no other means of securing the data set.

If the VSAM data set is accessed via TSO the verification of the TSO logon password is considered one attempt to obtain the password of the VSAM data set.

AUTHORIZATION (entrypoint string)
Default: none   **Abbreviation: AUTH**

AUTHORIZATION identifies a program entry point that will be invoked when a VSAM protected data set is accessed and the user provides a correct password other than the cluster's master password. A string of data can also be passed to the user security verification routine when the authorization program is called. This attribute will be invoked only when the data set master password is not null. VSAM data set security and the AUTHORIZATION attribute is discussed fully in Chapter 11. Use of AUTHORIZATION requires the local creation of a program that will be given control under the circumstances described.

BUFFERSPACE
Default: one index CI and two data CIs   **Abbreviation: BUFSP**

BUFFERSPACE carries the number of bytes reserved in memory for I/O buffers used in processing the data set. The default KSDS buffer space, that required to hold one index CI and two data CIs, is usually not adequate for efficient performance, but the value should not be specified directly. Instead, the BUFND and BUFNI specifications of the JCL AMP parameter can be used to indicate directly the number of buffers desired for data and index components. VSAM calculates and assigns BUFFERSPACE appropriate for the number of data and index buffers specified. Manual computation and underspecification of buffer space poses a danger of forcing VSAM to decrease the CA size for the data component.

The optimal number of buffers is discussed in Chapter 6. For purely random processing, performance is enhanced by allocating three index buffers and two data buffers. For sequential processing, including dumps and restores, performance can be enhanced by allocating one buffer for the index component and a minimum of four buffers for the data component. The maximum number of buffers that should be allocated for the data component can be determined with the use of a simple formula, discussed in Chapter 6, or via the VSAMBUFS CLIST provided in Appendix F. This number may range as high as 21 or more.

CODE (code)
Default: none   **Abbreviation: none**

CODE is a one- to eight-byte alphanumeric or special character code that is used as a prompt for the system operator when an attempt is made to access a password-protected entry without a password. CODE is in effect only when the master password of the cluster or component is not null. If a CODE is not specified, then the data set name is used as a prompt. The use of CODE is a viable security option when no systemwide security system, such as ACF2 or RACF, is in place, as discussed in Chapter 11. If passwords are used, CODE should be specified in order to avoid having VSAM divulge the data set name each time a password is required, the display of which might pique the curiosity of the uninformed.

CONTROLPW (password)
Default: next lower level password   **Abbreviation: CTLPW**

Specification of CONTROLPW allows control interval access to the base cluster and, when specified for an alternate index, it allows control interval access for the alternate index. When specified for a path, it allows the same access as the UPDATPW. CONTROLPW and UPDATPW and data set security are discussed in Chapter 11. The password is from one to eight characters in length.

EXCEPTIONEXIT (entrypoint)
Default: none   **Abbreviation: EEXT**

The entrypoint specified in EXCEPTIONEXIT is the name of a program or entry point of a program that will receive control when an I/O processing error occurs. This exit is taken prior to the SYNAD exit specifiable in job control language. Since VSAM provides an extensive error-detection mechanism through the FILE STATUS field in COBOL, it is not recommended that the EXCEPTIONEXIT be used. The entrypoint character string must be from one to eight alphanumeric or national characters, and may include the hyphen and/or the 12-0 overpunch.[4]

FILE (DDname)
Default: none   Abbreviation: none

FILE names the DD statement identifying the disks and volumes on which space is to be allocated for the cluster. The volumes specified at VOLUMES must agree with the volumes specified on the DD statement named by FILE. FILE is of limited use since it duplicates the information at VOLUMES. The DD statement named by FILE must be in the form:

```
//DDname DD UNIT=(SYSDA,3),
//   VOL=SER=(volser1,volser2,volser3)
```

VSAM catalogs have special interpretations for FILE. If FILE is specified and refers to more than one volume of the same device type, the DD statement cannot be concatenated.

KEYRANGES (low-key high-key)
Default: none   Abbreviation: KRNG

The use of KEYRANGES causes specific segments of the data set to be stored on different extents. Up to 123 ranges can be specified, but they cannot overlap. Keys can be up to 64 bytes in length and can be specified in either character or hexadecimal as either full or partial keys. Gaps can exist in the ranges but records with keys within the ranges not specified cannot be added to the data set. KEYRANGES can be used to eliminate records with specific key ranges from a data set or to spread designated portions of the file over several extents. Unless these two needs exist, KEYRANGES should not be used.

VOLUMES is used in conjunction with KEYRANGES. The number of volume serial numbers specified should equal the number of key ranges. If fewer key ranges are specified than volume serial numbers, all remaining key ranges will reside on the last volume. If UNIQUE is specified, each key range must be mapped to a different volume.

If key ranges are used to store groups of records on separate volumes, a danger exists that the data set may lose synchronization if a failure occurs and only one or some of the volumes are restored. Reliance on data record backups rather than full disk volume backups is highly preferable. VSAM catalogs have special interpretations for KEYRANGES.

MASTERPW (password)
Default: next lower level password   Abbreviation: MRPW

When MASTERPW, for master password, is specified for the cluster or a path, all operations for the cluster are permitted. When specified for an alternate index, MASTERPW allows all operations for the alternate index. The password can be from one to eight characters in length and is discussed further in Chapter 11.

MODEL (data-set-name/password catname/password)
Default: none   Abbreviation: none

MODEL names a cluster, data or index name that will be used as a model for the cluster or component being defined. All attributes of the model will be used to define the new data set, unless attributes are specifically overridden in the new definition. MODEL may be useful in defining test or temporary data sets, but it is recommended that a MODEL not be used since the entire DEFINE parameter provides explicit documentation on each data set. It is difficult to cross-reference and locate all clusters that refer to the MODEL. If for some reason the attributes of the MODEL are changed, a potential problem exists in identifying the impact on other data sets.

OWNER (up-to-eight characters)
Default: TSO id if allocated by TSO   Abbreviation: none

OWNER is a one- to eight-character identifier that may be used to indicate the application or actual owner of the cluster. OWNER has no special use except to serve as documentation and as an audit trail. It can, for example, be used to identify the person who initially defined the cluster.

READPW (password)
Default: none   Abbreviation: RDPW

READPW allows reads against cluster data when specified for the cluster or path. When specified for an alternate index, it allows reads for the alternate index data records. The password can be from one to eight characters in length and is discussed in Chapter 11.

TO (Julian-date) |
FOR (number-of-days)
Default: none   Abbreviation: none

TO and FOR specify the retention period for the cluster being defined. TO specifies the Julian date on which the cluster can be deleted. FOR indicates a range of 0 thru 1830 days which must elapse before the cluster can be deleted. If PURGE is specified in the IDCAMS DELETE command, these attributes are overridden. The use of TO or FOR is not recommended unless there are no other means of preventing unauthorized deletion of a cluster. If a number between 1831 and 9999 is used in FOR, January 1, 1999, becomes the expiration date.

UPDATEPW
Default: next lower level password   Abbreviation: UPDPW

The UPDATEPW allows reads and writes against cluster records when specified for the cluster or path. When specified for an alternate index, it allows reads and writes of the alternate index data records. The password can be from one to eight characters in length and is discussed in Chapter 11.

REVIEW QUESTIONS AND (*) EXERCISES

1. What are data set attributes, and where are they stored?

2. Must each of the three components of a key sequenced data set reside on the same physical disk device? Please explain the basis for your answer.

3. Definition attributes defined at the cluster level apply to what data set components?

4. What are the four sections of the IDCAMS DEFINE command?

5. Explain why the SPEED specification makes the loading of a data set proceed faster.

6. What attributes should be specified only in the DATA portion of the DEFINE command for a key sequenced data set, and why?

7. When defining a key sequenced data set, under what conditions is the default BUFFERSPACE optimum?

8. Based on recommendations presented in this chapter, cite three attributes for a key sequenced data set for which the default should ordinarily *not* be taken.

*9. A key sequenced data set base cluster designed to store an inventory master file has been named BT54.C03.PARTINVT. The data set as well as an alternate index for the file using a federal commodity code field are to be defined. Establish a suitable naming convention for all the KSDS and alternate index components that will exist, and list suitable names for each of the seven components that will exist.

*10. Code the minimum IDCAMS statements to define a key sequenced data set. Highlight all of the default values assumed.

NOTES

1. The following default attributes are assumed and not coded in the real IDCAMS control statements of Figure 2.2:

    BUFFERSPACE
    NODESTAGEWAIT   (for mass storage devices)
    NOERASE
    INDEXED
    UNORDERED
    NORECATALOG
    NOREPLICATE
    NOREUSE
    NONSPANNED
    STAGE   (for mass storage devices)
    UNIQUE   (for an ICF environment)
    SUBALLOCATION   (for a non-ICF environment)
    NOWRITECHECK

    If you wish to code these attributes, they should all be coded under the CLUSTER section.

2. An occasion when the base cluster name is not the name specified for access to a key sequenced data set occurs when a batch program accesses a KSDS with an alternate key. In that instance the PATH name related to the alternate index is specified in a JCL DD statement, but the base cluster name is still specified as well. See Chapter 5 for illustration of alternate key JCL coding.

A path can also be defined directly for a base cluster. This type of path can be used as an alternate name for the base cluster with access capabilities different from that attributed to the base cluster name.

3. The only exceptions to the rule that attributes coded in the base cluster provide the default for the data and index components are protection attributes such as passwords. The protection attributes, coded in the base cluster, are not carried over to the individual components. Components must specify their own passwords if passwords are to be required for access.

4. The 12-0 overpunch refers to the punching of a card column, moving the card backward a column, and punching a second symbol in the same column. This amounted to creating a "plus zero" or +0 signed value. In current usage hexadecimal C0 prints as the left brace "{" symbol. It has no special significance for data set naming and is a relic of the punched-card ancestry of IBM mainframes.

5. When the default maximum record size of 32,600 bytes is taken, the secondary allocation, if specified, should be at least as large as the maximum record size plus VSAM control information so that at least one maximum-size record can be stored in each extent to which the data set expands.

6. The IBM 3850 Mass Storage Unit is now obsolete and no direct replacement for it exists. While tape cartridges are mentioned in connection with the DEFINE DESTAGEWAIT| NODESTAGEWAIT option, this does not refer to manually mounted 3840 tape cartridges.

4

IDCAMS as a Multipurpose VSAM Utility

IDCAMS is a utility program used to establish and maintain VSAM data sets. It can also manipulate non-VSAM data sets. IDCAMS is executed via job control language.

The operation of IDCAMS is controlled with statements given to it at the MVS DDname SYSIN or after the DOS EXEC statement. Unlike the case with controlling input to older utilities, IDCAMS provides myriad syntax options and accepts freeform coding constrained only by the rule that statements must be housed within the first 72 positions of card-image 80-byte records. The IDCAMS commands and their keyword options can be specified in their full-length format or with abbreviations. Full-length renditions of the commands and keywords are used in this book for clarity. The sheer number of commands and keywords has forced their abbreviations to be cryptic, consonant-laden groups of letters that, out of context, make little sense.

FUNCTIONAL AND MODAL COMMANDS

The commands available through IDCAMS are divided into two categories: functional commands that direct IDCAMS to perform actual work, and "modal" commands that allow the conditional execution of the functional commands. Functional commands may be executed via IBM's Time Sharing Option, TSO, but not modal commands. IDCAMS functions are used to:

- copy VSAM and non-VSAM data sets
- print VSAM and non-VSAM data sets
- recover data sets not closed properly
- define and build alternate indexes
- list catalog entries and their attributes
- delete, define, and alter data set attributes
- move and return data sets from one system to another.

It would be possible to consolidate information about all of the IDCAMS functional commands in one chapter or reference, but this is not conducive to acclimation to the VSAM environment. In fact, such an approach exists in the IBM manuals and is a major reason that it is difficult to learn VSAM from manuals. A better approach is to treat the functional commands functionally—no pun intended—and to consider them in the light of what they do, in a sequence that matches common use.

In this book, we have already introduced and illustrated the IDCAMS DELETE, DE-FINE, and REPRO commands, which are used to create and load VSAM data sets. In this chapter, we round out illustration of IDCAMS commands used most often to manipulate VSAM data sets, analyze their contents, and insure that continued access is possible. These include REPRO, PRINT, and VERIFY.

Certain IDCAMS functional commands exist to support alternate indexes. We will discuss these commands, including DEFINE ALTERNATEINDEX, BLDINDEX, and DEFINE PATH in Chapter 5, which focuses on alternate indexes. In a similar way, a comprehensive discussion is dedicated to LISTCAT and its many options in Chapter 8, although you have already seen a usage of it in the KSDS creation and load example of Figure 2.2.

The remaining IDCAMS commands, such as ALTER, DELETE, EXPORT, and IMPORT are lesser used. When employed, these tend to be used in specialized situations. For these reasons, we have housed discussion of them in Appendix C.

The IDCAMS modal commands are few in number and serve to set condition codes and conditionally control the execution of functional commands. Modal commands present elements of a programming language, but in actual fact their practical utility is limited to simple condition code manipulation and functional command execution.

MVS JCL AND IDCAMS

The JCL required for IDCAMS depends on the function it is directed to perform and the environment in which it is operated. Many examples here are for the MVS environment. Figure 4.1 shows all possible DD statements associated with it.

JOB and JOBCAT Statements

The JOB statement identifies and describes the job to the system. While the one illustrated here is typical, each installation has its own defaults and requirements for the JOB statement.[1]

```
//FSBT677A  JOB AK00TEST,'DP4-GUZIK',CLASS=E,MSGCLASS=X,
//  MSGLEVEL=(1,1),NOTIFY=BT05677
//JOBCAT    DD  DSN=AK00.MASTER.CAT,      'NOT USUALLY REQUIRED
//  DISP=SHR
//*
//*    THIS JCL = BT05677.SOURCE.CNTL(V41)
//*
//************************************************************
//*                                                         *
//*    GENERAL IDCAMS EXECUTION JCL                         *
//*                                                         *
//************************************************************
//STEPA      DD  PGM=IDCAMS
//STEPCAT    DD  DSN=AK00.C98.CAT,        'NOT USUALLY REQUIRED
//  DISP=SHR
//SYSPRINT   DD  SYSOUT=*
//SYSUDUMP   DD  SYSOUT=A
//ddname     DD  VOL=SER=DISK01,          'NOT USUALLY USED
//  DISP=SHR
//ddnamein   DD  DSN=     data set to copy from
//ddnamout   DD  DSN=     data set to copy to
//SYSIN      DD  *
                      IDCAMS control statements
/*
//
```

FIGURE 4.1   MVS JCL to execute IDCAMS

//JOBCAT is an optional statement. It identifies a user catalog or catalogs that will be used for all steps within the job. //JOBCAT is not used when data sets are defined in the master catalog. Unless directed by your installation to use //JOBCAT it is most likely not necessary in your JCL and you should not code it.

EXEC and STEPCAT

//STEPA identifies the EXEC statement that invokes IDCAMS. //STEPA is just one of any of the possible names for the step. The step name can be formed of any eight letters or numbers, but must start with a letter. For some IDCAMS functions you may need to code REGION on the EXEC statement to obtain sufficient memory for a task.[1]

//STEPCAT is an optional statement. This statement identifies a user catalog or catalogs that will be used for the step. Use //STEPCAT only if your installation specifically directs it, in which case you may be advised of the catalog to specify. //STEPCAT is not required if your local default catalog is appropriate for your work.

DDnames Associated with IDCAMS

//SYSPRINT is a required statement; it identifies SYSOUT or the device that will receive IDCAMS messages and print. As defined in Figure 4.1, SYSOUT, the system spool, will receive print output. You may on occasion wish to direct the IDCAMS output messages to a data set for later printing or, as illustrated in Chapter 8, as input to a program for automated analysis. IDCAMS //SYSPRINT output is unusual in that it consists of blocked variable-length records rather than the fixed-length 121-byte records of IBM compilers and older utilities. IDCAMS //SYSPRINT characteristics are:

- record format of VBA, which cannot be changed or overridden
- blocksize of 629; five records per block are present, plus four bytes to identify the size of the block
- record length of 125; the first four characters are the length of the record. The actual print data length is 121 bytes, the first byte conveying carriage control.

//AMSDUMP is an optional statement. It identifies the output device that will receive a dump if IDCAMS abends. If this statement is missing and IDCAMS abends, an abbreviated dump is produced at //SYSUDUMP. Your installation standards may govern the use of this DD statement. The dump produced at //SYSUDUMP is adequate for applications programming purposes.

//DDname is an optional statement. It is required when the FILE attribute is coded as part of a cluster definition defined by the SYSIN DD statement. The use of this optional DD statement is not recommended unless it is necessary to identify a VSAM volume.

//DDnamein is an optional statement. It can be used to identify a data set to be read as input. The data set can also be identified as part of the IDCAMS command statements. It is recommended that the input data set be named in the //DDnamein DD statement rather than as part of the command statements when possible. This generalizes the IDCAMS control statements; data set name can easily be changed or overridden in JCL. It may then be possible to use the IDCAMS control statements in many steps of JCL.

//DDnameout is an optional statement. It can be used to identify a data set to be written to by the IDCAMS commands. It is recommended that the output data set be named in the //DDnameout DD statement rather than as part of the IDCAMS commands, for the same reasons noted in the foregoing discussion of //DDnamein.

Control Statement Input

//SYSIN is a required statement. It identifies the control card input to IDCAMS. Most examples show the IDCAMS control statements as instream card-image input. Since cataloged procedures cannot accept instream data, a given set of IDCAMS control statements is customarily housed within a member of a partitioned data set when job stream testing is finished and the job stream is to be placed into production.

DD Statements Pointing to VSAM Data Sets

If a VSAM data set is defined by a DD statement, it can take several forms, depending on the presence or absence of unit and volume parameters. DISP=OLD or DISP=SHR can be coded. The minimum JCL for an existing VSAM data set specifies the base cluster name and the disposition:

```
//DDNAME DD DSN=AKOO.C98.CUSTMAST,
// DISP=SHR
```

If you wish to allocate extra buffers when loading or unloading a VSAM data set, the AMP parameter is also coded:

```
//DDNAME DD DSN=AKOO.C98.CUSTMAST,
// DISP=SHR,
// AMP=('BUFNI=1,BUFND=21')
```

If the data set is being created, and the JCL is to specify the volume on which the data set is to reside, the AMP parameter is required even if buffers are not being specified. This is because MVS does not check the system catalog when UNIT and VOL parameters are coded; without such a check, MVS will not know that the data set is of Access Method ORGanization. The AMORG specification of the AMP parameter indicates this organization explicitly:

```
//DDNAME DD DSN=AKOO.C98.CUSTMAST,
// DISP=SHR,
// UNIT=3380,
// VOL=SER=FSDC03,
// AMP='AMORG'
```

Dynamic Data Set Allocation

A VSAM data set can be allocated dynamically instead of explicitly being defined through a DD statement. A dynamically allocated VSAM file must exist and be cataloged either in the master catalog or a user catalog identified by a JOBCAT or STEPCAT. When IDCAMS dynamically allocates a VSAM data set, it is allocated with a disposition of OLD. Dynamic allocation refers to use of the INDATASET and OUTDATASET keyword specifications that carry actual data set names, as opposed to the INFILE and OUTFILE specifications that point to //DDNAME JCL statements.

DOS JCL AND IDCAMS

VSAM is almost entirely operating system independent. But the MVS operating system allows omission of certain IDCAMS control statement parameters, producing some differences in coding between environments. Major examples in this book depict the IDCAMS control statement coding for processes in both the MVS and DOS environments. This brief description of DOS JCL is intended to parallel the DOS examples.

Unlike the syntax MVS JCL, in which no space is allowed between the initial two slashes and the start of a statement, DOS JCL *requires* that a space be present in the third position of each card image. The beginning of a DOS job stream is denoted by the JOB statement, and statements identifying disk and tape resource utilization appear *before* the EXEC statement that invokes a program using them, as depicted in Figure 4.2.

```
// JOB to execute IDCAMS under DOS/VSE
// ASSGN SYS006,DISK,VOL=volid,SHR
// DLBL filename,'data set name'
// EXTENT SYS006,volid,,,1500,600
// EXEC IDCAMS,SIZE=AUTO
                    IDCAMS control statements
/&
```

FIGURE 4.2   DOS/VSE JCL to execute IDCAMS

Each EXEC statement constitutes a job step. Instream or "immediate" card image data contained in a job stream is placed after the EXEC statement for a step, and its end is denoted by a statement carrying the symbols /*. A statement carrying the symbols /& denotes the end of a job stream.

DLBL and EXTENT Statements

The most common DOS JCL statements dealing with VSAM data sets are DLBL and EXTENT, specifying information about a data set housed on disk:

```
// DLBL filename,['file-id'][,scratch date],VSAM[,BUFSP=q][,CAT=name]
// EXTENT symbolic unit name,volid,[type],[sequence number],
        [relative track start],[track amount]
```

The DLBL statement carries a name of the form SYSnnn which is called the "filename" and corresponds to an MVS DDname; filename is sometimes referred to a "dname." In an application program this is the name coded at the right side of a SELECT/ASSIGN statement.

When the program being executed is IDCAMS, filename is specified in control statements with the FILE or INFILE specification, as dictated by the function being performed. Under MVS, FILE can be omitted causing dynamic allocation of the volume, but under DOS, when the FILE parameter, as opposed to INFILE, is appropriate, it is always required if the actions underway create or update a data set.

File-id on the DLBL statement corresponds to data set name (DSN) in MVS terminology, the actual name of a physical data set.

One or more EXTENT statements follow a DLBL statement immediately. *The presence of the EXTENT statements after the DLBL statement is the only means of associating them to the DLBL.* While of the same appearance as a filename, SYSnnn carried on EXTENT statements is a symbolic unit name and it does not have to be the same as the DLBL filename, although many examples do portray filename and symbolic unit name as the same value for convenience. The assignment of devices, by hardware address, to symbolic unit names is made at the time the operating system is generated, but these can be changed or supplemented for the duration of a job stream by the ASSGN statement.

The location at which a data set is to be placed on a disk is specified by relative track, numbered from 0 for the first track on the first usable cylinder of a disk. The amount of space is indicated by the number of tracks. Since different disk units provide differing numbers of cylinders and track capacities, the specification of space is device dependent.

In the foregoing discussion, items depicted in brackets are optional. The letter q represents a number of bytes of memory that, if greater, will supercede a value specified in the VSAM catalog or a program. "Name" cites a catalog name that owns the data set, and overrides the default, which is the master catalog or the current user or job catalog.

EXTENT is required for all VSAM data sets. The "short form" of the statement, with only symbolic unit name and volid, is sufficient for access to an existing VSAM data set. The definition of VSAM spaces, UNIQUE data sets, and master and user catalogs requires start and track amount information. Start and track amount information is not required for the definition of a suballocated data set.

When a VSAM data set that spans multiple volumes is accessed, the EXTENT statement for the data set must specify all volumes on which the data set resides. The only exceptions to this are data sets defined with the KEYRANGE specification and when access is to be limited to a specific volume of a multiple volume data set.

When alternate indexes are built using the EXTERNALSORT specification, BLDINDEX normally defines the two ESDS sort work files in the same VSAM space as the data set, using the default filenames IDCUT1 and IDCUT2. Two sets of DLBL and EXTENT statements are required, one set for each work file. The IDCUT1 and IDCUT2 default filenames must be used unless the IDCAMS WORKFILES parameter has been coded to specify other filenames. The EXTENT statements carry only volume information, not disk track location and amount of tracks.

TLBL Statement

TLBL is analogous to DLBL but identifies a tape data set:

```
// TLBL filename,['file-id'][,optional file specifications]
```

Filename corresponds to a name coded at the right side of a SELECT/ ASSIGN statement in a program or specified with FILE or INFILE in IDCAMS control statements.

File-id on TLBL is, as with the DLBL statement, the name of a data set, corresponding to DSN in MVS terminology.

Optional file specifications, the usage of which is often specific to local installations, is not usually necessary unless a tape file is being created, multiple data sets exist on the same tape, or a generation data group data set is being accessed.

ASSGN Statement

Some symbolic unit names may by default be associated to specific devices in an installation, making it unnecessary to code ASSGN statements in a DOS job stream. Symbolic unit name assignments to devices can be established or modified for a job stream using the ASSGN statement:

```
// ASSGN SYSnnn,DISK,VOL=volid,SHR
```

In its most primitive form the ASSGN statement establishes a correspondence between a symbolic unit name and device by the device hardware address. The generic assignment format of ASSGN, illustrated here, is more powerful and flexible and allows device specification by device type. With generic assignment, carrying volid, disks in ready status are scanned by DOS until the unit with the disk pack carrying the stated volid is found; the unit so located is then assigned the symbolic unit name. The SHR parameter allows the device to be assigned to other jobs and is normally specified.

When tape operations are involved with IDCAMS, specific symbolic unit names are required:

```
SYS004 for input tapes
SYS005 for output tapes
```

ASSGN can reiterate the VSAM default for these symbolic units:

```
// ASSGN,SYS005,TAPE,VOL=010932
```

In contrast, any symbolic unit names can be chosen for disk data sets, even though SYS006 is the VSAM default for input disk data sets and SYS007 the default for output disk data sets.

EXEC Statement

The execution of a step is initiated with an EXEC statement, coded *after* the DLBL and other specifications:

```
// EXEC IDCAMS,SIZE=mK
```

where m is the number of kilobytes of memory to be used by the program. The AUTO specification is recommended, making it unnecessary to specify an exact amount of memory.

Card Image Input

Card image input, or instream data, is handled under DOS with the special system logical unit SYSIPT. The card image data is placed after the EXEC statement and after the IDCAMS control statements. If, for example, card input is to be copied to a data set using IDCAMS, coding such as this can be used:

```
// EXEC IDCAMS,SIZE=AUTO
      REPRO   INFILE(SYSIPT) -
              OUTFILE(dname)
instream data such as cards or card-images are placed here
instream data such as cards or card-images are placed here
instream data such as cards or card-images are placed here
instream data such as cards or card-images are placed here
/*
/&
```

As under MVS, /* denotes the end of instream data; the resource statements for the next step then appear. If the step happens to be the last in a job stream, /& suffices to end the data as well as the job stream.

Suballocation Under DOS

Suballocation of VSAM data sets in VSAM space, using the SUBALLOCATION parameter, is more prevalent in the DOS environment than under MVS. A VSAM space is defined in a single operation after which other separate jobs can define VSAM data sets to be housed within it. Secondary space allocation is not used in defining VSAM space under DOS/VS. If it is specified it is simply recorded in the VSAM catalog to create compatibility with MVS.

Suballocation is convenient under DOS/VS since this relieves the need to code the quantity of tracks and location in the DOS JCL. Only one set of DLBL and EXTENT statements are required, and the VSAM data set name in the DLBL statement is optional. The statements can be of short form with EXTENT specifying only the volume on which a VSAM data space exists.

For UNIQUE data sets, the DOS JCL must specify the starting track by relative track number and the amount of tracks in the DLBL EXTENT statement when the key sequenced data set is defined. Two pairs of full form DLBL and EXTENT statements are required: one pair deals with the data component, and a separate one is associated with the index component.

The ENVIRONMENT Parameter

Under DOS, IDCAMS requires complete specifications for any non-VSAM data set to be processed, using the ENVIRONMENT parameter. ENVIRONMENT allows specification of many more items under DOS than under MVS, where its sole purpose is to allow dummy records to be copied from an ISAM data set. The items of information required by DOS to be stated with the ENVIRONMENT parameter of INFILE are record format, block size, record size, and physical device type, as illustrated in Figures 2.3 and 4.3.

REPRO

The REPRO command is used to copy all or part of a data set. It can process ordinary sequential data sets and ISAM data sets as well as VSAM data sets, at least for some functions. The only required specification for REPRO is INFILE or INDATASET and OUTFILE or OUTDATASET. This command is usually used to create a backup copy of a data set or to reload a data set from a backup copy. The output of the REPRO command can be directed via JCL to a data set or to SYSOUT. Figure 4.3 illustrates the specification options of the REPRO command. The selection options for REPRO are similar to those of the PRINT command.

INFILE | INDATASET

INFILE or INDATASET indicate the data set that will be copied to the data set specified by OUTFILE or OUTDATASET. This command can be used to copy VSAM and non-VSAM data sets.

INFILE specifies the name of the DD statement that identifies the data set to be copied. A base cluster can be copied in the sequence of the alternate index key by specifying the path name. If the data set to be copied is large, INFILE should be used instead of INDATASET so that additional buffers can be specified, improving performance. REPRO reads data sets sequentially and, as illustrated in Chapter 6, additional buffers can speed sequential input and output operations.

INDATASET directly identifies the name of the data set to be copied. Since no DD statement is specified for the data set, IDCAMS will allocate it dynamically at run time. As with the INFILE a base cluster can be printed in the sequence of the alternate index by specifying the PATH name. The data set to be copied will be dynamically allocated,

```
Required *
Choice needed >
Recommended +     Command        Option                              Abbreviation


        *          REPRO   -
        > +                       INFILE(ddname)|                         IFILE
        >                           INDATASET(entryname/password          IDS

MVS: limited usage                ENVIRONMENT(DUMMY)                  ENV DUM

DOS: describes nature             ENVIRONMENT(                        ENV
     of a non-VSAM file              BLOCKSIZE(bytes)                 BLKSZ
                                     HINDEXDEVICE                     HDEV
                                     NOLABEL|STDLABEL                 NLBL  SLBL
                                     NOREWIND|                        NREW
                                         REWIND|                           REW
                                         UNLOAD                            UNLD
                                     PRIMEDATADEVICE                  PDEV
                                     RECORDFORMAT(                    RECFM
                                         FIXUNB|                           F
                                         FIXBLK|                           FB
                                         VARUNB|                           V
                                         VARBLK|                           VB
                                         SPNUNB|                           S
                                         SPNBLK|                           SB
                                            UNDEF )                        U
                                     RECORDSIZE(bytes)               RECSZ

        > +                       OUTFILE(ddname/password)|               OFILE
        >                           OUTDATASET(entryname/password)        ODS
                                  FROMKEY(key)|                           FKEY
                                     FROMADDRESS(address)|                FADDR
                                     FROMNUMBER(number)|                  FNUM
                                     SKIP(quantity)
                                  REPLACE|NOREPLACE                  REP NREP
                                  REUSE|NOREUSE                      RUS NRUS
                                  TOKEY(key)|
                                     TOADDRESS(address)|                  TADDR
                                     TONUMBER(number)|                    TNUM
                                     COUNT(quantity)
```

Note: The | symbol represents a logical "or" meaning that only one of the items can be specified. Underlined print indicates the IDCAMS default. The usage of passwords is optional.

FIGURE 4.3   REPRO command options, abbreviations, and recommended usage

meaning that it is not sought by the operating system at the time the JCL is scheduled for execution, but is sought only when IDCAMS itself initiates access to it.

ENVIRONMENT

Under MVS, ENVIRONMENT is used only when the input data set is of Indexed Sequential Access Method organization, ISAM. ISAM is obsolete, but an installation converting from it to VSAM may have a need to copy ISAM-stored data.

ENVIRONMENT with the DUMMY parameter indicates that logically deleted records within an indexed sequential data set will be copied. If ENVIRONMENT with DUMMY is not specified, logically deleted records in the ISAM file will not be copied. Logically deleted records, also called dummy records, are identified in ISAM data sets with high values (hexadecimal "FF") in the first byte of the record.

ENVIRONMENT is used in more ways under DOS/VSE, as illustrated in Figure 4.3. The DOS implementation of VSAM provides for indication of record and device characteristics using the ENVIRONMENT specification.

OUTFILE | OUTDATASET

OUTFILE specifies the name of the DD statement that identifies the data set to receive the copied information. It functions in a manner similar to INFILE in that it requires a matching DD statement in the JCL executing IDCAMS.

OUTDATASET identifies directly the name of the target data set. When OUTDATASET is specified, the target data set is allocated dynamically at run time. An ISAM data set cannot be specified for either OUTFILE or OUTDATASET; IDCAMS cannot be used to load an ISAM data set.

FROMKEY | FROMADDRESS | FROMNUMBER, COUNT and SKIP

These attributes indicate the starting location within the data set from which the copy operation will begin or, in the case of COUNT, how many records to copy. If none of these attributes are coded, the copy operation will begin with the first record in the data set. Corresponding destination options named TOKEY, TOADDRESS, and TONUMBER exist and can be used with the like "from" specification.

FROMKEY The value coded is the full or partial key value of the first record to be copied. If the key value specified cannot be found in the data set, the record with the next higher key will be the first one copied. The key value specified can be from 1 to 255 characters but cannot exceed the actual key length defined for the data set. The records will be copied in sequential order. FROMKEY can only be specified for a KSDS, alternate index, or an indexed sequential (ISAM) data set. TOADDRESS cannot be coded when the FROMKEY attribute is coded.

FROMADDRESS The value coded is the relative byte address (RBA) of the first record to be copied and must be a value representing the start of a logical record. The value can be specified as an eight-byte decimal, hexadecimal (X'n'), or binary (B'n') quantity. If FROMADDRESS is coded for a KSDS, alternate index, or either of their components, the records copied will be in physical sequence rather than in logical key sequence. Only VSAM KSDS or ESDS data sets or their components can be specified when using FROMADDRESS. Entry name cannot represent a path name or a data set with spanned records if FROMADDRESS is coded and the spanned records are within the group to be copied.

FROMNUMBER The value coded is the relative record number of the first record to be copied. FROMNUMBER applies only to relative record data sets. The value specified can be an eight-byte decimal, hexadecimal (X'n'), or binary (B'n') number.

COUNT The value coded is the number of records to be copied. The value can be specified as an eight-byte decimal, hexadecimal (X'n'), or binary (B'n') number. COUNT and SKIP are the only specifications possible for a sequential data set, but these can be quite handy as a means of creating a test file from a large sequential data set. The results of the copy operation will be unpredictable if the entry name specified is a path.

SKIP The value coded is the number of records to be skipped before the copy operation begins. The value specified can be an eight-byte decimal, hexadecimal (X'n'), or binary (B'n') number. Do not specify SKIP when the item being copied is a path.

REPLACE | NOREPLACE

REPLACE and NOREPLACE indicate whether or not the records from the source data set will replace records with like keys on the target data set. For KSDS and RRDS data sets, the REPLACE attributes causes records with like keys or relative record numbers to replace records in the target data set. The NOREPLACE attribute causes a "duplicate record" condition and warning message to be generated when records with like keys or relative record numbers exist on both the source and target data sets. When a duplicate record is encountered with NOREPLACE, the target record is not replaced.

REPLACE can be used to merge data sets with different key values. Merging data sets with like keys will merge the data sets by replacing records with like keys and adding records with unlike keys. The use of IDCAMS REPRO to merge data sets complements the merge capability of the sort/merge utility. Unlike IDCAMS REPRO, the sort/merge requires only that records be sorted in like sequence on the merge field, but has no regard for duplicate merge keys or actual symbolic record keys.

REUSE | NOREUSE

REUSE as a REPRO specification is possible only if a data set was originally defined with REUSE as one of its attributes. When so defined, the data in the data set can be eliminated with a COBOL program opening the data set for OUTPUT. It will appear as if the data set had been empty; it will contain only the records output by the program.

REPRO ordinarily operates to supplement the records in a VSAM data set, or in other words to merge the records being written with those already in the data set. It will do this even if the data set is defined with REUSE. By coding REUSE, REPRO simulates the operation that would occur with a COBOL program using an open for OUTPUT. The REPROed records will be the only ones in the data set after the operation; any records originally there will no longer exist.

If the target data set was originally defined with the NOREUSE attribute, then it must be empty when the REUSE attribute is specified with the REPRO command. Otherwise, the REPRO command will terminate. It thus makes no sense to code REUSE on a REPRO if the target data set was not already defined with REUSE.

TOKEY | TOADDRESS | TONUMBER

These attributes indicate the ending location within the data set or the last record to be copied. If none of these attributes are coded, the copy operation will end with the last record in the data set. If any of these attributes are coded, their corresponding attributes should be specified for the starting location for the copy operation: FROMKEY and TOKEY, FROMADDRESS, and TOADDRESS, FROMNUMBER and TONUMBER.

TOKEY The value coded is the full or partial key value of the last record to be copied. If the key value specified cannot be found in the data set, the last record that matches the

TOKEY value will be the last record copied. The key value specified can be from 1 to 255 characters and cannot exceed the actual key length defined for the data set. TOKEY can only be specified for a KSDS, alternate index, or an ISAM data set.

TOADDRESS   The value coded for this attribute is the relative byte address (RBA) of the last record to be copied. The value specified can be an eight-byte decimal, hexadecimal (X'n'), or binary (B'n') number. If this attribute is coded for a KSDS, alternate index, or either of their components, the records copied will be in physical sequence rather than in key sequence. The entry name specified cannot represent a path name or a data set with spanned records if TOADDRESS is coded and the spanned records are within the group to be printed.

TONUMBER   The value coded for this attribute is the relative record number of the last record to be copied. The value specified can be an eight-byte decimal, hexadecimal (X'n'), or binary (B'n') number.

Examples

Assume that you wish to make a backup copy of the entire AK00.C98.CUSTMAST data set. The backup file will be on tape and have a data set name of AK00.C98.CUSTTAPE. The required JCL and IDCAMS commands to perform the REPRO operation are shown in Figure 4.4.

INFILE was used so that the default one index buffer and two data buffers could be overridden for better performance. The REPLACE/NOREPLACE and REUSE/NOREUSE attributes have not been used because they are meaningless for non-VSAM target data sets.

Figure 4.5 illustrates how the IDCAMS REPRO can be used to select records and build a test sequential data set from a large sequential data set. The SKIP specification skips over a quantity of records, while COUNT limits the number of records copied to the output data set.

```
//FSBT686A  JOB AK00TEST,'DP2-JANOSSY',CLASS=T,MSGCLASS=X,
//  MSGLEVEL=(1,1),NOTIFY=BT05686
//*
//*    THIS JCL = BT05686.SOURCE.CNTL(JCL44)
//*
//***********************************************************
//*                                                         *
//*    REPRO A VSAM KSDS TO TAPE                             *
//*                                                         *
//***********************************************************
//STEPA     EXEC  PGM=IDCAMS
//SYSPRINT  DD    SYSOUT=*
//FLUTE     DD    DSN=AK00.C98.CUSTMAST,
//  DISP=SHR,
//  AMP=('BUFNI=1,BUFND=21')
//CELLO     DD    DSN=AK00.C98.CUSTTAPE,
//  DISP=(NEW,CATLG,DELETE),
//  UNIT=(TAPE,,DEFER),
//  DCB=(RECFM=FB,LRECL=250,BLKSIZE=32750),
//  LABEL=RETPD=30
//SYSUDUMP  DD    SYSOUT=A
//SYSIN     DD    *
     REPRO        INFILE(FLUTE) -
                  OUTFILE(CELLO)
/*
//
```

FIGURE 4.4   Backing up a KSDS to tape using REPRO

```
//FSBT686A  JOB AK00TEST,'DP2-JANOSSY',CLASS=T,MSGCLASS=X,
//  MSGLEVEL=(1,1),NOTIFY=BT05686
//*
//*     THIS JCL = BT05686.SOURCE.CNTL(JCL45)
//*
//*****************************************************************
//*                                                               *
//*     CREATE A TEST SEQUENTIAL DATA SET                         *
//*                                                               *
//*****************************************************************
//STEPA     EXEC  PGM=IDCAMS
//SYSPRINT  DD    SYSOUT=*
//DD1       DD    DSN=AK00.C72.UPDTRANS,
//  DISP=(OLD,KEEP),
//  UNIT=(TAPE,,DEFER)
//DD2       DD    DSN=AK00.C72.TESTTRAN,
//  DISP=(NEW,CATLG,DELETE),
//  UNIT=SYSDA,
//  DCB=(RECFM=FB,LRECL=250,BLKSIZE=6000),
//  SPACE=(6000,(20,5),RLSE)
//SYSUDUMP  DD    SYSOUT=A
//SYSIN     DD    *
     REPRO -
               INFILE(DD1) -
               OUTFILE(DD2) -
               SKIP(1000) -
               COUNT(450)
/*
//
```

FIGURE 4.5 Creating a test sequential data set with REPRO

Figure 4.6 illustrates the loading of an already-defined key sequenced data set directly from an ISAM data set. This is a "straight" REPRO, and the entire input data set is copied to the output data set.

In Figure 4.7 we see the repeated use of REPRO with the FROMKEY and TOKEY specifications to perform a three-stage load of a key sequenced data set. Ranges of key values from the input file are loaded to the KSDS separately. Unrelated to REPRO, the IDCAMS


```
//FSBT677A  JOB AK00TEST,'DP4-GUZIK',CLASS=T,MSGCLASS=X,
//  MSGLEVEL=(1,1),NOTIFY=BT05677
//*
//*     THIS JCL = BT05677.SOURCE.CNTL(JCL46)
//*
//*****************************************************************
//*                                                               *
//*     REPRO AN ISAM DATA SET TO A KSDS                          *
//*                                                               *
//*****************************************************************
//STEPA     EXEC  PGM=IDCAMS
//SYSPRINT  DD    SYSOUT=*
//DD1       DD    DSN=AK00.C98.ISAMMAST,
//  DISP=(OLD,KEEP),
//  DCB=DSORG=IS
//DD2       DD    DSN=AK00.C98.CUSTMAST,
//  DISP=SHR,
//  AMP=('AMORG,BUFNI=1,BUFND=21')
//SYSUDUMP  DD    SYSOUT=A
//SYSIN     DD    *
     REPRO     INFILE(DD1) -
               OUTFILE(DD2)
/*
//
```

FIGURE 4.6 Copying an ISAM data set to a KSDS using REPRO

```
//FSBT686A   JOB AK00TEST,'DP2-JANOSSY',CLASS=T,MSGCLASS=X,
//  MSGLEVEL=(1,1),NOTIFY=BT05686
//*
//*     THIS JCL = BT05686.SOURCE.CNTL(JCL47)
//*
//*********************************************************
//*                                                        *
//*    IDCAMS REPRO TO LOAD AN ALREADY DEFINED KSDS        *
//*    IN THREE STAGES ALTERING FREESPACE FOR              *
//*    DIFFERENT KEY RANGES                                *
//*                                                        *
//*********************************************************
//STEPA      DD   PGM=IDCAMS
//SYSPRINT   DD   SYSOUT=*
//MASTIN     DD   DSN=AK00.C75.INSPBKUP,
//  UNIT=(TAPE,,DEFER),
//  DISP=(OLD,KEEP)
//MASTOUT    DD   DSN=AK00.C75.INSPMAST,
//  DISP=SHR,
//  AMP=('BUFNI=1,BUFND=21')
//SYSUDUMP   DD   SYSOUT=A
//SYSIN      DD   *
                                    /*  THE DATA SET WAS       */
                                    /*  ORIGINALLY DEFINED     */
                                    /*  WITH NO FREE SPACE;    */
                                    /*  COPY IN FIRST RANGE    */
           REPRO      INFILE(MASTIN) -
                      OUTFILE(MASTOUT) -
                      FROMKEY(AAAAAAAAAAA) -
                      TOKEY(A9999999999)
                                    /*  CHANGE TO A SMALL      */
                                    /*  AMOUNT OF FREE SPACE   */
                                    /*  AND LOAD MORE RECORDS  */
                                    /*  IN NEXT KEY RANGE      */
           ALTER      AK00.C75.INSPMAST -
                      FREESPACE(6 1)

           REPRO      INFILE(MASTIN) -
                      OUTFILE(MASTOUT) -
                      FROMKEY(BAAAAAAAAAA) -
                      TOKEY(B9999999999)
                                    /*  CHANGE TO A LARGE      */
                                    /*  AMOUNT OF FREE SPACE   */
                                    /*  AND LOAD MORE RECORDS  */
                                    /*  NOW AND LATER ONLINE   */
           ALTER      AK00.C75.INSPMAST -
                      FREESPACE(24 1)

           REPRO      INFILE(MASTIN) -
                      OUTFILE(MASTOUT) -
                      FROMKEY(CAAAAAAAAAA) -
                      TOKEY(99999999999)
       /*
       //
```

FIGURE 4.7   REPRO with key range specifications for a three-stage KSDS load in which free space is altered between parts of the load

ALTER command is invoked between parts of the load to change the free space specification in effect, in order to tailor free space to the requirements of different key ranges for a specific application.

PRINT

The PRINT command is used to print a data set on paper or to a specified data set. The entire data set or a specified portion of it can be printed. The data set can be printed in hEX, in character, or in both formats. PRINT can be used to print both VSAM and non-VSAM data sets. The only required attribute for the PRINT command is either the INFILE attribute or the INDATASET attribute.

Figure 4.8 illustrates the specification options of the PRINT command. The selection options for PRINT are similar to those of REPRO.

INFILE | INDATASET

INFILE or INDATASET identifies the data set to be printed at //SYSPRINT or output to the data set specified by OUTFILE. INFILE specifies a DD statement that identifies the data set or component to be printed. The base cluster can be printed in the sequence of the alternate index key by specifying the path name, as illustrated in Figure 4.9(a) under MVS and in Figure 4.9(b) for DOS/VSE. If the actual name of an alternate index is specified, the alternate index records themselves are printed, as illustrated in Figure 4.9(c). Both of these examples refer to alternate indexes for data set AK00.C98.CUSTMAST, the definition and loading of which is discussed in Chapter 5.

```
Required *
Choice needed >
Recommended +    Command         Option                          Abbreviation


     *              PRINT   -
     > +                        INFILE(ddname)|                       IFILE
     >                            INDATASET(entryname)                IDS

DOS: describes nature           ENVIRONMENT(                    ENV
     of a non-VSAM file            BLOCKSIZE(bytes)             BLKSZ
                                   HINDEXDEVICE                 HDEV
                                   NOLABEL|STDLABEL             NLBL   SLBL
                                   NOREWIND|                    NREW
                                       REWIND|                         REW
                                       UNLOAD                          UNLD
                                   PRIMEDATADEVICE              PDEV
                                   RECORDFORMAT(                RECFM
                                       FIXUNB|                         F
                                       FIXBLK|                         FB
                                       VARUNB|                         V
                                       VARBLK|                         VB
                                       SPNUNB|                         S
                                       SPNBLK|                         SB
                                       UNDEF )                         U
                                   RECORDSIZE(bytes)            RECSZ

                                OUTFILE(ddname)                       OFILE
     >                          CHARACTER|                            CHAR
     > +                          DUMP|
     >                            HEX
                                FROMKEY(key)|                         FKEY
                                    FROMADDRESS(address)|             FADDR
                                    FROMNUMBER(number)                FNUM
                                SKIP(count)
     >                          TOKEY(key)|
     >                              TOADDRESS(address)|               TADDR
     >                              TONUMBER(number)|                 TNUM
     > +                            COUNT(count)
```

Note: The | symbol represents a logical "or" meaning that only one of the items can be specified. Underlined print indicates the IDCAMS default. The usage of passwords is optional.

FIGURE 4.8 PRINT command options, abbreviations, and recommended usage

```
//FSBT686A  JOB AK00TEST,'DP2-JANOSSY',CLASS=E,MSGCLASS=X,
//  MSGLEVEL=(1,1),NOTIFY=BT05686
//*
//*    THIS JCL = BT05686.SOURCE.CNTL(JCL49A)
//*
//***********************************************************
//*                                                         *
//*    PRINT A KSDS IN ALTERNATE KEY SEQUENCE               *
//*                                                         *
//***********************************************************
//STEPA       DD   PGM=IDCAMS
//SYSPRINT    DD   SYSOUT=A
//DD1         DD   DSN=AK00.C98.CUSTMAST.NAMEAIX.PATH,
//  DISP=SHR
//SYSUDUMP    DD   SYSOUT=A
//SYSIN       DD   *
     PRINT        INFILE(DD1)
/*
//
```

FIGURE 4.9a   Printing a KSDS in alternate key sequence by specifying the alternate index path name (MVS JCL)

```
// JOB PRINT KSDS IN ALT INDEX SEQUENCE
// ASSGN SYS006,DISK,VOL=FSDC14,SHR
// DLBL ALTPATH,'AK00.C98.CUSTMAST.NAMEAIX.PATH',,VSAM
// EXTENT SYS006,FSDC14
// EXEC IDCAMS,SIZE=AUTO
     PRINT        INFILE(ALTPATH)
/&
```

FIGURE 4.9b   Printing a KSDS in alternate key sequence by specifying the alternate index path name (DOS/VSE JCL)

```
//FSBT686A   JOB AK00TEST,'DP2-JANOSSY',CLASS=E,MSGCLASS=X,
//  MSGLEVEL=(1,1),NOTIFY=BT05686
//*
//*    THIS JCL = BT05686.SOURCE.CNTL(JCL49C)
//*
//***********************************************************
//*                                                         *
//*    PRINT ALTERNATE INDEX RECORDS THEMSELVES             *
//*                                                         *
//***********************************************************
//STEPA       DD   PGM=IDCAMS
//SYSPRINT    DD   SYSOUT=A
//DD1         DD   DSN=AK00.C98.CUSTMAST.NAMEAIX,    'AIX BASE CLUSTER
//  DISP=SHR
//SYSUDUMP    DD   SYSOUT=A
//SYSIN       DD   *
     PRINT        INFILE(DD1)
/*
//
```

FIGURE 4.9c   Printing KSDS alternate index records by specifying the alternate index base cluster name

INDATASET identifies directly the name of the data set or component to be printed. As with INFILE, a base cluster can be printed in the sequence of the alternate index by specifying the path name. INDATASET causes dynamic allocation of the data set with the implied disposition of OLD.

OUTFILE

OUTFILE is an optional specification that identifies a DD statement which carries the name of a data set to receive the print output. If OUTFILE is coded, a DD statement other than //SYSPRINT can be specified.

The default DCB parameters for the records written to the OUTFILE data set follow the same rules as the //SYSPRINT DD statement. They are written as if an MVS JCL DCB had been coded in this manner:

```
DCB = (RECFM = VBA, LRECL = 125, BLKSIZE = 629)
```

The record format and record length cannot be changed. The printlines are written to the OUTFILE data set as variable-length blocked records of 121-byte length. Outputting print-lines to OUTFILE is normally of little utility.

CHARACTER | DUMP | HEX

CHARACTER, DUMP, and HEX indicate the format for the output of the PRINT command. CHARACTER lists the data set in character format as illustrated in Figure 4.10. Individual bytes that do not have a character representation are printed as a period.

DUMP, the default, produces a listing of the data set in both hexadecimal and character format. As illustrated in Figure 4.11, this is similar to an abend memory dump with hexadecimal representation on the left and the character representation on the right. DUMP is the most useful specification for programming purposes when PRINT is used for data set content analysis.

HEX produces a listing in hexadecimal only as illustrated in Figure 4.12. Pure HEX listings are generally very difficult to interpret and serve little purpose.

For DUMP and HEX, the key of each record is printed in hexadecimal. With CHARACTER the key of each record is printed in character format. In all cases the key fields are printed on a separate line, and the full content of the record, including the key field, is then presented.

FROMKEY | FROMADDRESS | FROMNUMBER, COUNT and SKIP

These specifications indicate the starting location within the data set from which the PRINT operation will begin. If none of these are coded, print will begin with the first record in the KSDS according to key sequence.

FROMKEY The value coded is the full or partial key value of the first record to be printed. If the key value specified cannot be found in the data set, the record with the next higher key will be the first record printed. The key value specified can be from 1 to 255 characters but cannot exceed the actual key length defined for the data set. The records will be printed in key sequence. FROMKEY can be specified only for a KSDS, alternate index, or an indexed sequential (ISAM) data set. TOADDRESS cannot be coded when the FROMKEY attribute is coded.

FROMADDRESS The value coded is the relative byte address (RBA) of the first record to be printed and must be a value representing the start of a logical record. The value can

```
KEY OF RECORD - 08716293
414943675FORESTER           ALVIN      08716293SDORCHESTER ST   09710      AA


KEY OF RECORD - 22168028
312872548WASIK              CHARLES    22168028NKILDARE AVE      02009      BB


KEY OF RECORD - 24307091
886376533KUREK              BESSIE     24307091WFULLERTON AVE    058004-B   CC


KEY OF RECORD - 25656631
934064961HAMPSTER           HERBERT    25656631SHALLDALE AV      08711      DD


KEY OF RECORD - 28441269
206931482HAMPSTER           HENRIETTA28441269SHALLDALE AV        08711      EE


KEY OF RECORD - 28799201
968312814HAMPSTER           HARVEY     28799201SHALLDALE AV      08711      FF


KEY OF RECORD - 32613729
650038142KALKINS            JANET      32613729NSHERIDAN RD      03016      GG


KEY OF RECORD - 32817132
624925399HAMPSTER           HELEN      32817132SHALLDALE AV      08711      HH


KEY OF RECORD - 33841546
364787800ANCONA             MINNIE     33841546SKOLINA PL        0431017    II


KEY OF RECORD - 37667140
030606384EASTON             JESSIE     37667140WPRYOR RD         02059      JJ
```

FIGURE 4.10 CHARACTER print sample of IDCAMS PRINT

be specified as an eight-byte decimal, hexadecimal (X′n′), or binary (B′n′) quantity. If FROMADDRESS is coded for a KSDS, alternate index, or either of their components, the records printed will be in physical sequence rather than in key sequence. Only VSAM KSDS or ESDS data sets or their components can be specified when using FROM-ADDRESS. The entry name specified cannot represent a path name or a data set with spanned records if FROMADDRESS is coded and the spanned records are within the group to be printed.

FROMNUMBER The value coded is the relative record number of the first record to be printed. FROMNUMBER applies only to relative record data sets. The value specified can be an eight-byte decimal, hexadecimal (X′n′), or binary (B′n′) number.

COUNT The value coded is the number of records to be printed. The value can be specified as an eight-byte decimal, hexadecimal (X′n′), or binary (B′n′) number. COUNT and SKIP are the only specifications possible for a sequential data set, but these can be quite handy as a means of dumping a sampling of a data set.

```
KEY OF RECORD - FOF8F7F1F6F2F9F3
000000  F4F1F4F9 F4F3F6F7 F5C6D6D9 C5E2E3C5   D9404040 40404040 404040C1 D3E5C9D5   *414943675FORESTER       ALVIN*
000020  40404040 FOF8F7F1 F6F2F9F3 E2C4D6D9   C3C8C5E2 E3C5D940 E2E34040 FOF9F7F1   *      08716293DORCHESTER ST  0971*
000040  F0404040 4040C1C1 40404040 40404040   40404040 40404040 40404040 40404040   *O    AA                      *
000060  40404040 40404040 40404040 40404040   40404040 40404040 40404040 40404040   *                            *
000080  40404040 40404040 40404040 40404040   40404040 40404040 40404040 40404040   *                            *
0000A0  40404040 40404040 40404040 40404040   40404040 40404040 40404040 40404040   *                            *
0000C0  40404040 40404040 40404040 40404040   40404040 40404040 40404040 40404040   *                            *
0000E0  40404040 40404040 40404040 40404040   40404040 40404040 4040               *                            *

KEY OF RECORD - F2F2F1F6F8FOF2F8
000000  F3F1F2F8 F7F2F5F4 F8E6C1E2 C9D24040   40404040 40404040 404040C3 C8C1D9D3   *312872548WASIK          CHARL*
000020  C5E24040 F2F2F1F6 F8FOF2F8 D5D2C9D3   C4C1D9C5 40C1E5C5 40404040 FOF2FOFO   *ES  22168028NKILDARE AVE  0200*
000040  F9404040 4040C2C2 40404040 40404040   40404040 40404040 40404040 40404040   *9    BB                      *
000060  40404040 40404040 40404040 40404040   40404040 40404040 40404040 40404040   *                            *
000080  40404040 40404040 40404040 40404040   40404040 40404040 40404040 40404040   *                            *
0000A0  40404040 40404040 40404040 40404040   40404040 40404040 40404040 40404040   *                            *
0000C0  40404040 40404040 40404040 40404040   40404040 40404040 40404040 40404040   *                            *
0000E0  40404040 40404040 40404040 40404040   40404040 40404040 4040               *                            *

KEY OF RECORD - F2F4F3FOF7FOF9F1
000000  F8F8F6F3 F7F6F5F3 F3D2E4D9 C5D24040   40404040 40404040 404040C2 C5E2E2C9   *886376533KUREK          BESSI*
000020  C5404040 F2F4F3FO F7FOF9F1 E6C6E4D3   D3C5D9E3 D6D540C1 E5C54040 FOF5F8FO   *E   24307091WFULLERTON AVE  0580*
000040  FOF460C2 4040C3C3 40404040 40404040   40404040 40404040 40404040 40404040   *04-B CC                      *
000060  40404040 40404040 40404040 40404040   40404040 40404040 40404040 40404040   *                            *
000080  40404040 40404040 40404040 40404040   40404040 40404040 40404040 40404040   *                            *
0000A0  40404040 40404040 40404040 40404040   40404040 40404040 40404040 40404040   *                            *
0000C0  40404040 40404040 40404040 40404040   40404040 40404040 40404040 40404040   *                            *
0000E0  40404040 40404040 40404040 40404040   40404040 40404040 4040               *                            *

KEY OF RECORD - F2F5F6F5F6F6F3F1
000000  F9F3F4FO F6F4F9F6 F1C8C1D4 D7E2E3C5   D9404040 40404040 404040C8 C5D9C2C5   *93406961HAMPSTER        HERBE*
000020  D9E34040 F2F5F6F5 F6F6F3F1 E2C8C1D3   D3C4C1D3 C540C1E5 40404040 FOF8F7F1   *RT  25656631SHALLDALE AV  0871*
000040  F1404040 4040C4C4 40404040 40404040   40404040 40404040 40404040 40404040   *1    DD                      *
000060  40404040 40404040 40404040 40404040   40404040 40404040 40404040 40404040   *                            *
000080  40404040 40404040 40404040 40404040   40404040 40404040 40404040 40404040   *                            *
0000A0  40404040 40404040 40404040 40404040   40404040 40404040 40404040 40404040   *                            *
0000C0  40404040 40404040 40404040 40404040   40404040 40404040 40404040 40404040   *                            *
0000E0  40404040 40404040 40404040 40404040   40404040 40404040 4040               *                            *

KEY OF RECORD - F2F8F4F4F1F2F6F9
000000  F2FOF6F9 F3F1F4F8 F2C8C1D4 D7E2E3C5   D9404040 40404040 404040C8 C5D5D9C9   *206931482HAMPSTER       HENRI*
000020  C5E3E3C1 F2F8F4F4 F1F2F6F9 E2C8C1D3   D3C4C1D3 C540C1E5 40404040 FOF8F7F1   *ETTA28441269SHALLDALE AV  0871*
000040  F1404040 4040C5C5 40404040 40404040   40404040 40404040 40404040 40404040   *1    EE                      *
000060  40404040 40404040 40404040 40404040   40404040 40404040 40404040 40404040   *                            *
000080  40404040 40404040 40404040 40404040   40404040 40404040 40404040 40404040   *                            *
0000A0  40404040 40404040 40404040 40404040   40404040 40404040 40404040 40404040   *                            *
0000C0  40404040 40404040 40404040 40404040   40404040 40404040 40404040 40404040   *                            *
```

FIGURE 4.11 DUMP print sample of IDCAMS PRINT

```
KEY OF RECORD - FOF8F7F1F6F2F9F3
F4F1F4F9F4F3F6F7F5C6D6D9C5E2E3C5D94040404040404040404040C1D3E5C9D540404040FOF8F7F1F6F2F9F3E2C4D6D9C3C8C5E2E3C5D940E2E34040
FOF9F7F1F0404040404040C1C140404040404040404040404040404040404040404040404040404040404040404040404040404040404040404040
4040404040404040404040404040404040404040404040404040404040404040404040404040404040404040404040404040404040404040404040
4040404040404040404040404040404040404040404040404040404040404040404040404040404040404040404040404040404040404040404040
404040404040404040404040

KEY OF RECORD - F2F2F1F6F8FOF2F8
F3F1F2F8F7F2F5F4F8E6C1E2C9D2404040404040404040404040404040C3C8C1D9D3C5E24040F2F2F1F6F8FOF2F8D5D2C9D3C4C1D9C540C1E5C540404040
FOF2FOFOF9404040404040C2C240404040404040404040404040404040404040404040404040404040404040404040404040404040404040404040
4040404040404040404040404040404040404040404040404040404040404040404040404040404040404040404040404040404040404040404040
4040404040404040404040404040404040404040404040404040404040404040404040404040404040404040404040404040404040404040404040
40404040404040404040

KEY OF RECORD - F2F4F3FOF7FOF9F1
F8F8F6F3F7F6F5F3F3D2E4D9C5D2404040404040404040404040404040C2C5E2E2C9C5404040F2F4F3FOF7FOF9F1E6C6E4D3D3C5D9E3D6D540C1E5C540
FOF5F8FOFOF460C24040C3C340404040404040404040404040404040404040404040404040404040404040404040404040404040404040404040404040
4040404040404040404040404040404040404040404040404040404040404040404040404040404040404040404040404040404040404040404040
4040404040404040404040404040404040404040404040404040404040404040404040404040404040404040404040404040404040404040404040
404040404040404040404040

KEY OF RECORD - F2F5F6F5F6F6F3F1
F9F3F4F0F6F4F9F6F1C8C1D4D7E2E3C5D94040404040404040404040C8C5D9C2C5D9E34040F2F5F6F5F6F6F3F1E2C8C1D3D3C4C1D3C540C1E540404040
FOF8F7F1F1404040404040C4C4404040404040404040404040404040404040404040404040404040404040404040404040404040404040404040404040
4040404040404040404040404040404040404040404040404040404040404040404040404040404040404040404040404040404040404040404040
4040404040404040404040404040404040404040404040404040404040404040404040404040404040404040404040404040404040404040404040
404040404040404040404040

KEY OF RECORD - F2F8F4F4F1F2F6F9
F2FOF6F9F3F1F4F8F2C8C1D4D7E2E3C5D94040404040404040404040C8C5D5D9C9C5E3E3C1F2F8F4F4F1F2F6F9E2C8C1D3D3C4C1D3C540C1E540404040
FOF8F7F1F1404040404040C5C5404040404040404040404040404040404040404040404040404040404040404040404040404040404040404040404040
4040404040404040404040404040404040404040404040404040404040404040404040404040404040404040404040404040404040404040404040
4040404040404040404040404040404040404040404040404040404040404040404040404040404040404040404040404040404040404040404040
40404040404040404040

KEY OF RECORD - F2F8F7F9F9F2FOF1
F9F6F8F3F1F2F8F1F1F4C8C1D4D7E2E3C5D94040404040404040404040C8C1D9E5C5E840404040F2F8F7F9F9F2FOF1E2C8C1D3D3C4C1D3C540C1E540404040
FOF8F7F1F1404040404040C6C640404040404040404040404040404040404040404040404040404040404040404040404040404040404040404040404040
4040404040404040404040404040404040404040404040404040404040404040404040404040404040404040404040404040404040404040404040
4040404040404040404040404040404040404040404040404040404040404040404040404040404040404040404040404040404040404040404040
404040404040404040404040

KEY OF RECORD - F3F2F6F1F3F7F2F9
F6F5FOFOF3F8F1F4F2D2C1D3D2C9D5E2404040404040404040404040D1C1D5C5E34040404040F3F2F6F1F3F7F2F9D5E2C8C5D9C9C4C1D5404D9C44040404040
FOF3FOF1F6404040404040C7C7404040404040404040404040404040404040404040404040404040404040404040404040404040404040404040404040
4040404040404040404040404040404040404040404040404040404040404040404040404040404040404040404040404040404040404040404040
4040404040404040404040404040404040404040404040404040404040404040404040404040404040404040404040404040404040404040404040
404040404040404040
```

FIGURE 4.12 HEX print sample of IDCAMS PRINT

SKIP The value coded is the number of records to be skipped before printing begins. The value specified can be an eight-byte decimal, hexadecimal (X'n'), or binary (B'n') number.

TOKEY | TOADDRESS | TONUMBER

These specifications indicate the ending location within the data set or the last record to be printed. If none of these are coded, the PRINT operation will terminate with the last record in the data set. If any of these are coded, their counterparts should be specified for the starting print location: FROMKEY and TOKEY, FROMADDRESS and TOADDRESS, FROMNUMBER and TONUMBER.

TOKEY The value coded is the full or partial key value of the last record to be printed. If the key value specified cannot be found in the data set, the last record that matches the TOKEY value will be the last record printed. The key value specified can be from 1 to 255 characters and cannot exceed the actual key length defined for the data set. TOKEY can only be specified for a KSDS, alternate index, or an ISAM data set.

TOADDRESS The value coded is the relative byte address (RBA) of the last record to be printed. The value specified can be an eight-byte decimal, hexadecimal (X'n'), or binary (B'n') number. If coded for a KSDS, alternate index, or either of their components, the records printed will be in physical sequence rather than in key sequence. The entry name specified cannot represent a path name or a data set with spanned records if TOADDRESS is coded and the spanned records are within the group to be printed.

TONUMBER The value coded is the relative record number of the last record to be printed. The value specified can be an eight-byte decimal, hexadecimal (X'n'), or binary (B'n') number.

Examples

Suppose we want to print records in character and hexadecimal from a key sequenced data set named AK00.C98.CUSTMAST, starting the record carrying a primary key that

```
//FSBT677A  JOB AK00TEST,'DP4-GUZIK',CLASS=E,MSGCLASS=X,
//  MSGLEVEL=(1,1),NOTIFY=BT05677
//*
//*     THIS JCL = BT05677.SOURCE.CNTL(JCL413)
//*
//***********************************************************
//*                                                         *
//*     IDCAMS PRINT WITH FROMKEY AND TOKEY                 *
//*                                                         *
//***********************************************************
//STEPA      DD  PGM=IDCAMS
//SYSPRINT   DD  SYSOUT=*
//DD1        DD  DSN=AK00.C98.CUSTMAST,
//  DISP=SHR,
//  AMP=('AMORG,BUFNI=1,BUFND=21')
//SYSUDUMP   DD  SYSOUT=A
//SYSIN      DD  *
     PRINT -
                INFILE(DD1) -
                FROMKEY(32753) -
                TOKEY(34000)
/*
//
```

FIGURE 4.13 FROMKEY/TOKEY use of IDCAMS PRINT

begins with "32753." The required JCL and IDCAMS command to perform this PRINT operation is illustrated in Figure 4.13. INFILE was used so that a DD statement could exist to carry an AMP parameter overriding the default quantity of buffers, providing more buffers for efficient sequential processing. Since none of the print format specifications were coded, the file will be printed in dump format, both character and hexadecimal.

In another case, we wish to list in character a sampling of a sequential data set so that an idea can be gained of its contents. Figure 4.14 illustrates JCL and IDCAMS coding that will skip 3,000 records, then start printing records until 150 have been listed.

```
//FSBT686A  JOB AK00TEST,'DP2-JANOSSY',CLASS=T,MSGCLASS=X,
//  MSGLEVEL=(1,1),NOTIFY=BT05686
//*
//*     THIS JCL = BT05686.SOURCE.CNTL(JCL414)
//*
//************************************************************
//*                                                         *
//*      IDCAMS PRINT DUMP PART OF DATA SET                 *
//*                                                         *
//************************************************************
//STEPA       DD   PGM=IDCAMS
//SYSPRINT    DD   SYSOUT=*
//DD1         DD   DSN=AK00.C72.UPDTRANS,
//  DISP=(OLD,KEEP),
//  UNIT=(TAPE,,DEFER)
//SYSUDUMP    DD   SYSOUT=A
//SYSIN       DD   *
       PRINT -
                   INFILE(DD1) -
                   SKIP(3000) -
                   COUNT(150)
   /*
   //
```

FIGURE 4.14 Dumping part of a data set for analysis using IDCAMS PRINT and the SKIP and COUNT options

VERIFY

Background

The VERIFY command is used to reset a VSAM data set's end-of-data indicator in the catalog. When a VSAM data set is closed improperly by an application abend or system failure, its end-of-data information is not updated by VSAM. This may leave the data component and index out of agreement. If not corrected, VSAM will detect this condition, post a return code to indicate that data set integrity is suspect, and terminate at the next attempt to open the data set. VERIFY corrects the condition if it exists, and is a common precautionary action in the VSAM catalog environment prior to access to a VSAM data set. The general syntax of the VERIFY command is illustrated in Figure 4.15.

In the Integrated Catalog Facility (ICF) environment, which offers enhancements over the VSAM catalog environment, explicit VERIFY actions are not necessary prior to data set access. With ICF, VSAM itself attempts to cure an inconsistency in data set end indication and catalog information by invoking an implicit VERIFY if necessary. Since VERIFY involves I/O actions, it is preferable not to invoke it directly when the installation uses ICF, but to instead allow the implicit VERIFY to handle a problem situation when one arises.

```
Required *
Choice needed >
Recommended +    Command        Option                      Abbreviation


      *          VERIFY -
      > +                   FILE(ddname/password)|              VFY
      >                        DATASET(entryname/password)      DS
```

Note: The | symbol represents a logical "or" meaning that only one of the
items can be specified. Underlined print indicates the IDCAMS default. The
usage of passwords is optional.

FIGURE 4.15   VERIFY command options, abbreviations, and recommended usage

In a shared disk environment where multiple central processors may access a VSAM data set concurrently, a potential integrity problem can arise which will corrupt the data set. Regardless of the SHAREOPTIONS and DISP parameter, if a VSAM data set is accessed concurrently from two different machines, neither machine may be aware of the actions of the other. If both update the same data set at the same time, the index and the data component can lose synchronization.

IBM provides software that can resolve the problem of data set integrity with multiple processors, presenting a "single image" to the VSAM data set of all machine involvement with it. This software is optional, however, and not all installations running multiple machines have it. With multiple processors but without single image software, VERIFY should be run on each VSAM data set prior to processing it even if the Integrated Catalog Facility is in use.

FILE | DATASET and Examples

FILE or DATASET defines the data set to be processed. FILE specifies a DD statement that carries the data set name. DATASET identifies directly the name of the data set. Figure 4.16(a) illustrates processing of a data set using the FILE specification under MVS, and Figure 4.16(b) illustrates the same process under DOS/VSE, while Figure 4.16(c) shows the same data set processed using DATASET coding.

```
//FSBT677A  JOB AKOOTEST,'DP4-GUZIK',CLASS=E,MSGCLASS=X,
//  MSGLEVEL=(1,1),NOTIFY=BT05677
//*
//*    THIS JCL = BT05677.SOURCE.CNTL(JCL416A)
//*
//*********************************************************
//*                                                      *
//*    IDCAMS VERIFY USING THE FILE SPECIFICATION         *
//*                                                      *
//*********************************************************
//STEPA      DD  PGM=IDCAMS
//SYSPRINT   DD  SYSOUT=*
//DD1        DD  DSN=AKOO.C98.CUSTMAST,
//  DISP=SHR
//SYSUDUMP   DD  SYSOUT=A
//SYSIN      DD  *
     VERIFY -
              FILE(DD1)
 /*
 //
```

FIGURE 4.16a   Verifying a data set using the FILE specification (MVS JCL)

```
// JOB VERIFY A KSDS
// ASSGN SYS006,DISK,VOL=FSDC14,SHR
// DLBL DD1,'AK00.C98.CUSTMAST',,VSAM
// EXTENT SYS006,FSDC14
// EXEC IDCAMS,SIZE=AUTO
   VERIFY -
                FILE(DD1)
  /&
```

FIGURE 4.16b   Verifying a data set using the FILE specification (DOS/VSE)

```
//FSBT677A  JOB AK00TEST,'DP4-GUZIK',CLASS=E,MSGCLASS=X,
//  MSGLEVEL=(1,1),NOTIFY=BT05677
//*
//*     THIS JCL = BT05677.SOURCE.CNTL(JCL416C)
//*
//*************************************************************
//*                                                          *
//*     IDCAMS VERIFY USING THE DATASET SPECIFICATION         *
//*                                                          *
//*************************************************************
//STEPA        DD  PGM=IDCAMS
//SYSPRINT     DD  SYSOUT=*
//SYSUDUMP     DD  SYSOUT=A
//SYSIN        DD  *
    VERIFY -
                DATASET(AK00.C98.CUSTMAST)
  /*
  //
```

FIGURE 4.16c   Verifying a data set using the DATASET specification

MODAL COMMANDS

Every IDCAMS functional command sets a condition code value when it executes. By convention, a condition code of zero is posted when execution of a command was successful; values of 4, 8, and upward, in increments of 4, indicate successively more serious problems in the execution of a command.

The condition code for a command just executed is housed in a value called LASTCC. IDCAMS also retains the highest condition code value posted in execution as a value called MAXCC. All condition code setting and testing are internal to the job step executing IDCAMS. Condition codes set by other steps within the job stream cannot be set or tested by the MODAL commands.

Modal commands provide the means to control the execution of IDCAMS functional commands, depending on the condition code set by each functional command. Three sets of modal commands are of primary concern. These are: IF-THEN-ELSE, DO-END, and SET. A list of valid MODAL commands and their options is provided in Figure 4.17.

LASTCC and MAXCC

LASTCC and MAXCC can assume values of 0, 4, 8, 12, and 16. The meaning of these values is:

0   The command executed successfully. Some informational messages may have been written to //SYSPRINT.

```
IF    LASTCC comparand number
      THEN command
      ELSE command
```

```
IF    LASTCC comparand number
      THEN DO
                functional-command-set
           END
      ELSE DO
                functional-command-set
           END
```

```
SET   LASTCC = number
```

```
IF    MAXCC comparand number
      THEN command
      ELSE command
```

```
IF    MAXCC comparand number
      THEN DO
                functional-command-set
           END
      ELSE DO
                functional-command-set
           END
```

```
SET   MAXCC = number
```

FIGURE 4.17   Modal command options

4   Some problem was encountered during the execution of the command, but subsequent commands could still be processed. A warning message will be issued. An example of this type of condition is the failure of the LISTCAT command to locate the entry it was directed to list.

8   The command was completed, but major specific directives of the command were bypassed. An error message will be issued. An example of this type of condition is the failure of the DELETE or ALTER command to locate the entry to be acted on; it occurs when an entry to be deleted could not be found.

12   The command could not be executed due to a logical error such as inconsistent syntax, invalid values specified, mutually exclusive specifications, or missing specifications. An error message will be issued.

16   A fatal error occurred and the remainder of functional commands were bypassed, terminating the execution of the IDCAMS step. An error message will be issued. Examples of this type of condition are a missing //SYSPRINT DD statement, an unrecoverable system error, or an invalid IF-THEN-ELSE sequence.

SET

The SET command can set LASTCC or MAXCC to one of their valid values. The setting of MAXCC does not affect the value of LASTCC. The setting of LASTCC affects the value of MAXCC only when the value being assigned to LASTCC is greater than the current setting of MAXCC.

The SET command is most often used to reset the condition codes set by functional commands. This is done when functional commands that are not critical to the command sequence within the IDCAMS step post non-zero condition codes. For example, it is recommended for safety that a DELETE should be processed for a data set prior to a DEFINE for it. If the entry does not exist and therefore the DELETE is not successful, LASTCC is set to 8.

The execution of IDCAMS can be forced to terminate by setting either LASTCC or MAXCC to 16. Such an action is a drastic one and is done only under the control of the IF modal command if a condition can be detected that should cause complete termination of processing. It is rare to find this type of action necessary.

DO-END

The DO-END commands delineate a group of commands that are to be treated as a single unit. The hyphen continuation character should not be used within a DO-END command sequence. Commands following the DO command must start on a new line and the END command must be on a line by itself. If more than one command is to be executed after an IF, THEN or ELSE statement, the functional commands to be executed must be grouped by the DO-END commands.

IF-THEN-ELSE

The IF-THEN-ELSE command tests either LASTCC or MAXCC for a specific or inclusive value; depending on the result of the test, it can execute a set of commands. The set of commands can be null—without any commands at all—or a single command, or a group of commands.

Figure 4.18 illustrates the use of IF-THEN-ELSE coding, where we wish to define a key sequenced data set named AK00.C98.CUSTMAST. If the data set definition is successful, we want to load the file from AK00.C98.CUSTTAPE and list the first ten records. If the definition is not successful, we want to list the catalog information for AK00.C98.-CUSTMAST. The condition code of the DELETE command is tested and reset to zero if the data set cannot be found, and the cluster is loaded only if the cluster definition is successful.

It is possible to encounter errors with IF-THEN-ELSE in IDCAMS because of its manner of processing. If the IF-THEN-ELSE statement is not followed by either a continuation character or a command on the same line, a null or no command situation is assumed. This does not cause an IDCAMS failure, but results in the unconditional execution of the commands that visually appear to be under the control of the IF-THEN-ELSE. Figure 4.19 illustrates the end of the control statements of Figure 4.18 with this error present. The lack of a continuation after THEN causes the THEN actions to be null. REPRO and PRINT will always be processed in this case.

The comparands that can be used to test the value of either LASTCC or MAXCC include the following:

Equal	=	or EQ
Not equal	¬=	or NE
Greater than	>	or GT
Less than	<	or LT
Less than or equal	<=	or LE
Greater than or equal	>=	or GE

```
//FSBT677A  JOB AK00TEST,'DP4-GUZIK',CLASS=T,MSGCLASS=X,
//  MSGLEVEL=(1,1),NOTIFY=BT05677
//*
//*    THIS JCL = BT05677.SOURCE.CNTL(JCL418)
//*
//***********************************************************
//*                                                         *
//*    IDCAMS DELETE, DEFINE, LOAD WITH MODAL               *
//*    COMMANDS TO CONTROL PROCESSING                       *
//*                                                         *
//***********************************************************
//STEPA       DD  PGM=IDCAMS
//SYSPRINT    DD  SYSOUT=*
//MASTIN      DD  DSN=AK00.C98.CUSTTAPE,
//  UNIT=(TAPE,,DEFER),
//  DISP=(OLD,KEEP)
//SYSUDUMP    DD  SYSOUT=A
//SYSIN       DD  *
      DELETE        AK00.C98.CUSTMAST -
                    CLUSTER

   IF LASTCC = 8 -
      THEN DO
              SET LASTCC = 0
              SET MAXCC = 0
          END

      DEFINE -
         CLUSTER   (   NAME(AK00.C98.CUSTMAST) -
                       VOLUMES(FSDC14) -
                       RECORDSIZE(250 250) -
                       KEYS(8 36) -
                       CYLINDERS(52 5) -
                       SHAREOPTIONS(2 3) -
                       IMBED -
                       SPEED                            ) -
                   -
         DATA      (   NAME(AK00.C98.CUSTMAST.BASE.DATA) -
                       CONTROLINTERVALSIZE(4096) -
                       FREESPACE(18 1)                  ) -
                   -
         INDEX     (   NAME(AK00.C98.CUSTMAST.BASE.INDEX)  )

   IF LASTCC = 0 -
      THEN DO
              REPRO         INFILE(MASTIN) -
                            OUTDATASET(AK00.C98.CUSTMAST)
              PRINT         INDATASET(AK00.C98.CUSTMAST) -
                            SKIP(500)
                            COUNT(100)
          END
      ELSE -
              LISTCAT       ENTRY(AK00.C98.CUSTMAST) -
                            ALL
/*
//
```

FIGURE 4.18 Controlling IDCAMS operation using modal commands

Coded as:

```
IF LASTCC = 0 -
    THEN
        REPRO           INFILE(BACKUP) -
                        OUTDATASET(AK00.C98.CUSTMAST)
        PRINT           INDATASET(AK00.C98.CUSTMAST) -
                        SKIP(500) -
                        COUNT(100)
```

is interpreted as:

```
IF LASTCC = 0 -
    THEN

REPRO           INFILE(BACKUP) -
                OUTDATASET(AK00.C98.CUSTMAST)
PRINT           INDATASET(AK00.C98.CUSTMAST) -
                SKIP(500) -
                COUNT(100)
```

> Lack of continuation hyphen after
> THEN makes it a null statement...
> the REPRO and PRINT always execute

FIGURE 4.19 Modal command error resulting from missing hyphen continuation after THEN

Values between 0 and 16 can be tested. Numbers specified greater than 16 are reduced to 16.

The command or commands specified after the THEN statement are executed if the IF comparison was true. The command or commands following the ELSE statement are executed if the IF comparison was false. Up to ten IF-THEN-ELSE commands can be nested. IDCAMS pairs the innermost THEN and ELSE statements. Continuation characters are required for the IF-THEN-ELSE command.

REVIEW QUESTIONS AND (*) EXERCISES

1. What are the two categories of IDCAMS commands, and what general services do the commands of each category perform?

2. Four of the many IDCAMS commands allow the definition, copying, and printing of a VSAM data set and the resetting of the data set end of file indicator. Cite these four IDCAMS commands.

3. Certain IDCAMS exist to support the use of alternate indexes. Tell what these three commands are.

4. Four IDCAMS commands are used much less than the others, to change data set parameters, eliminate data sets, and to transfer or move data sets. Tell what these four commands are.

5. Explain what the term "dynamic allocation" means in connection with the INDATASET and OUTDATASET keyword specifications and how these specifications contrast in operation with INFILE and OUTFILE.

6. When can the REUSE specification be used in a REPRO command and what is the effect of it?

*7. Code a REPRO that will read a sequential data set named BT45.C90. UPDTRANS and create a test data set consisting of 600 records starting with record number 5500. The test data set will be named AK45.C90.UPDTRANS.TESTDAT3.

*8. Code the IDCAMS control statements to print, in dump format, the first 500 records of sequential data set BT45.C90.TRANLOG7.

*9. Code a minimal REPRO command and job control language to copy records in the key range DTR130 to PPP999 from key sequenced data set BT45.C90.SRMASTER to a sequential file named BT45.C90.SRMASTER.SUBSET29.

*10. Code an IDCAMS step and the MVS or DOS/VSE job control language to verify data set BT45.C90.RECSUSP; explain in plain language what the verify action will accomplish and the hazard of not doing this.

NOTES

1. The MVS JOB statement provides over a dozen parameters affecting job stream labeling, processing priority, and memory allocation with the REGION parameter. The EXEC statement invoking a program within a step may also carry some of these parameters, including REGION. When REGION is coded at either point, it conveys the amount of memory to be allowed in kilobytes. This value should be specified in even increments of 2K, such as REGION = 2048K. An insufficient memory allocation results in a job failure with system completion code of 80A or 804. For more information on the specifications of the MVS JCL JOB and EXEC statements, see Appendix A of *Practical MVS JCL For Today's Programmers* (James Janossy, John Wiley and Sons, Inc., 1987) ISBN 0-471-83648-6.

——— PART 2 ———

ADVANCED VSAM

$$===== 5 =====$$

Alternate Indexes for Key Sequenced Data Sets

A powerful but often intimidating feature of key sequenced data sets lies in the area of alternate indexes. Simply speaking, an alternate key allows retrieval of a record, or positioning of a file for sequential access, via a field other than the primary key. Practically speaking, the design, definition, building, and use of alternate keys can be a complicated process. The steps in this process are straightforward, but you must understand them and the pitfalls that exist in several areas.

In this chapter we cover alternate index concepts and design, the IDCAMS control statements to define alternate keys, and some of the job control language to execute ID-CAMS in connection with alternate indexes. Many of the COBOL programming examples in Chapter 7 are oriented to accessing a KSDS via an alternate key.

A GOOD PATTERN EXAMPLE FOR ALTERNATE INDEXES

Chapter 2 began by illustrating the primary key area and other fields of a typical record housed in a key sequenced data set. Figure 2.1 is a graphic illustration of this record, identifying the primary record key as an eight-byte field named account number.

Figure 5.1 illustrates the enhancement of the customer data record with the specification of two alternate keys. No magic exists concerning the use of two alternate keys; we could have instead defined only one or the other. We have chosen to present both a unique alternate key as well as a nonunique alternate key in order to provide a complete example. The customer data record was originally developed with this purpose in mind, but the mention of alternate key fields was omitted in earlier chapters in order not to unduly burden the initial discussion.

Figure 5.2 provides the complete listing of MVS job control language and IDCAMS control statements necessary to define the AK00.C98.CUSTMAST key sequenced data set, load it, and define and build the two alternate indexes. You will recognize that this has been built from Figure 2.2; this code represents the addition of some JCL and some ID-CAMS control statements. In this chapter we'll discuss how the extra JCL and IDCAMS statements are composed.

You can copy to your mainframe the coding of Figure 5.2, or obtain it on the distribution diskette for this book as described in Appendix A, upload it, and customize it. If you then run it loading the test data provided at the end of Appendix F, you will note from the LISTCAT at the bottom that three separate KSDS entities will exist, not just the orig-

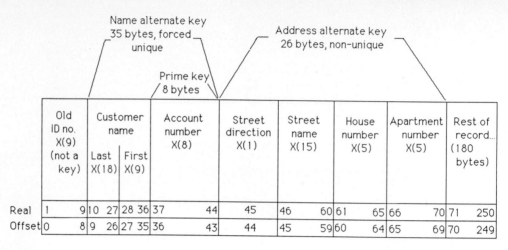

Old ID no. X(9) (not a key)	Customer name		Account number X(8)	Street direction X(1)	Street name X(15)	House number X(5)	Apartment number X(5)	Rest of record... (180 bytes)
	Last X(18)	First X(9)						
Real 1 9	10 27	28 36	37 44	45	46 60	61 65	66 70	71 250
Offset 0 8	9 26	27 35	36 43	44	45 59	60 64	65 69	70 249

FIGURE 5.1 Format of records to be loaded to a key sequenced data set with two alternate indexes

```
//FSBT686A  JOB AK00TEST,'DP2-JANOSSY',CLASS=T,MSGCLASS=X,
// MSGLEVEL=(1,1),NOTIFY=BT05686
//*
//*     THIS JCL = BT05686.SOURCE.CNTL(JCL52)
//*
//****************************************************************
//*                                                             *
//*     DEFINE AND LOAD/RELOAD VSAM DATA SET                     *
//*     WITH TWO ALTERNATE INDEXES                               *
//*                                                             *
//****************************************************************
//STEPA     EXEC  PGM=IDCAMS
//SYSPRINT   DD   SYSOUT=*
//SYSUDUMP   DD   SYSOUT=A
//MASTIN     DD   DSN=AK00.C98.CUSTBKUP(0),
//  UNIT=(TAPE,,DEFER),
//  DISP=(OLD,KEEP)
//WORKSRT1   DD   DSN=AK00.C98.IDCUT1,
//  UNIT=SYSDA,                          'AIX IDCAMS WORKFILE;
//  DISP=OLD,                            'VSAM REQUIRES DISP=OLD
//  AMP='AMORG',                         'EVEN THOUGH DOES NOT
//  VOL=SER=FSDC03                       'EXIST PRIOR TO USE!
//WORKSRT2   DD   DSN=AK00.C98.IDCUT2,
//  UNIT=SYSDA,                          'AIX IDCAMS WORKFILE;
//  DISP=OLD,                            'VSAM REQUIRES DISP=OLD
//  AMP='AMORG',                         'EVEN THOUGH DOES NOT
//  VOL=SER=FSDC03                       'EXIST PRIOR TO USE!
//SYSIN      DD   *
                                         /* HOUSEKEEPING DELETES */
       DELETE      AK00.C98.CUSTMAST -
                   CLUSTER

       DELETE      AK00.C98.IDCUT1 -
                   CLUSTER

       DELETE      AK00.C98.IDCUT2 -
                   CLUSTER

     SET LASTCC=0                        /* SOME ABOVE MAY NOT BE */
     SET MAXCC=0                         /* FOUND; GET RID OF RC=8 */

  /* - - - - - - - - - CREATE THE BASE CLUSTER AND PRIMARY INDEX- - */
```

FIGURE 5.2 MVS JCL and IDCAMS control statements to allocate and load a key sequenced data set with nonunique and unique alternate indexes

```
     DEFINE -
        CLUSTER    (   NAME(AK00.C98.CUSTMAST) -
                       VOLUMES(FSDC14) -
                       RECORDSIZE(250 250) -
                       KEYS(8 36) -
                       CYLINDERS(2 1) -
                       SHAREOPTIONS(2 3) -
                       SPEED
                       IMBED                          ) -
                       -
        DATA       (   NAME(AK00.C98.CUSTMAST.BASE.DATA) -
                       CONTROLINTERVALSIZE(4096) -
                       FREESPACE(18 1)                ) -
                       -
        INDEX      (   NAME(AK00.C98.CUSTMAST.BASE.INDEX) )

/* - - - - - - - - IF CREATION SUCCESSFUL LOAD THE KSDS - - - - */

IF LASTCC = 0 -
THEN -
     REPRO        INFILE(MASTIN) -
                  OUTDATASET(AK00.C98.CUSTMAST)

/* FIRST AIX - - - CREATE THE NONUNIQUE ADDRESS ALTERNATE INDEX */

     DEFINE -
        AIX        (   NAME(AK00.C98.CUSTMAST.ADDRAIX) -
                       RELATE(AK00.C98.CUSTMAST) -
                       VOLUMES(FSDC14) -          /* RECORDSIZE (AVG  MAX) */
                       RECORDSIZE(47 79) -        /* MAX 6 OCCURRENCES SO  */
                       KEYS(26 44) -              /* 5 + AIX + (N x PRIME) */
                       NONUNIQUEKEY -             /* GIVES 5+26+(2x8)=47   */
                       CYLINDERS(2 1) -           /* AND    5+26+(6x8)=79  */
                       SHAREOPTIONS(2 3) -
                       UNIQUE -
                       UPGRADE -
                       SPEED
                       IMBED                          ) -
                       -
        DATA       (   NAME(AK00.C98.CUSTMAST.ADDRAIX.DATA) -
                       CONTROLINTERVALSIZE(4096) -
                       FREESPACE(15 15)               ) -
                       -
        INDEX      (   NAME(AK00.C98.CUSTMAST.ADDRAIX.INDEX) )

     BLDINDEX     INDATASET(AK00.C98.CUSTMAST) -
                  OUTDATASET(AK00.C98.CUSTMAST.ADDRAIX) -
                  WORKFILES(WORKSRT1 WORKSRT2)

     DEFINE -
        PATH       (   NAME(AK00.C98.CUSTMAST.ADDRAIX.PATH) -
                       PATHENTRY(AK00.C98.CUSTMAST.ADDRAIX)  )

/* SECOND AIX - - -CREATE THE FORCED UNIQUE NAME ALTERNATE INDEX */

     DEFINE -
        AIX        (   NAME(AK00.C98.CUSTMAST.NAMEAIX) -
                       RELATE(AK00.C98.CUSTMAST) -
                       VOLUMES(FSDC14) -
                       RECORDSIZE(48 48) -        /* 5 + AIX + PRIME */
                       KEYS(35 9) -               /* GIVES 5+35+8=48 */
                       UNIQUEKEY -
                       CYLINDERS(2 1) -
                       SHAREOPTIONS(2 3) -
                       UNIQUE -
                       UPGRADE -
                       SPEED
```

FIGURE 5.2   (Continued)

```
                          IMBED                                    ) -
                            -
            DATA      (    NAME(AK00.C98.CUSTMAST.NAMEAIX.DATA)  -
                          CONTROLINTERVALSIZE(4096) -
                          FREESPACE(15 15)                         ) -
                            -
            INDEX     (    NAME(AK00.C98.CUSTMAST.NAMEAIX.INDEX) )

         BLDINDEX     INDATASET(AK00.C98.CUSTMAST) -
                      OUTDATASET(AK00.C98.CUSTMAST.NAMEAIX) -
                      WORKFILES(WORKSRT1 WORKSRT2)

          DEFINE -
            PATH      (    NAME(AK00.C98.CUSTMAST.NAMEAIX.PATH) -
                          PATHENTRY(AK00.C98.CUSTMAST.NAMEAIX)   )

      /* - - - - LIST CATALOG TO SEE INFO ON THE DATA SET AND INDEXES */

          LISTCAT -
            ENTRIES   (    AK00.C98.CUSTMAST -
                          AK00.C98.CUSTMAST.ADDRAIX -
                          AK00.C98.CUSTMAST.NAMEAIX      ) -
                      ALL
   /*
   //
```

FIGURE 5.2   (Continued)

inal KSDS base cluster. Each alternate index is in itself a KSDS, complete with its own "umbrella-named" cluster called an "AIX," a data component, and an index component. And in addition, "paths" have been created associating each alternate index with the original base cluster.

For comparison purposes, Figure 5.3 presents the DOS/VSE JCL and IDCAMS control statements necessary to define a KSDS, load it, and build alternate indexes.

```
// JOB DEFINE AND LOAD A SUBALLOCATED KSDS
// ASSGN SYS004,TAPE,VOL=010932
// ASSGN SYS007,DISK,VOL=FSDC14,SHR
// TLBL SYS004,'AK00.C98.CUSTBKUP'
// DLBL MASTOUT,'AK00.C98.CUSTMAST',,VSAM
// EXTENT SYS007,FSDC14
// DLBL ADDALT,'AK00.C98.CUSTMAST.ADDRAIX',,VSAM
// EXTENT SYS007,FSDC14
// DLBL NAMALT,'AK00.C98.CUSTMAST.NAMEAIX',,VSAM
// EXTENT SYS007,FSDC14
// DLBL ADDPATH,'AK00.C98.CUSTMAST.ADDRAIX.PATH',,VSAM
// EXTENT SYS007,FSDC14
// DLBL NAMPATH,'AK00.C98.CUSTMAST.NAMEAIX.PATH',,VSAM
// EXTENT SYS007,FSDC14
// DLBL WRKSRT1,,,VSAM
// EXTENT SYS007,FSDC14
// DLBL WRKSRT2,,,VSAM
// EXTENT SYS007,FSDC14
// EXEC IDCAMS,SIZE=AUTO
                                   /* HOUSEKEEPING DELETES    */
     DELETE      AK00.C98.CUSTMAST -
                 CLUSTER

     SET LASTCC = 0                /* SOME ABOVE MAY NOT BE */
```

FIGURE 5.3   DOS/VSE JCL and IDCAMS control statements to allocate and load a key sequenced data set with nonunique and unique alternate indexes

```
      SET  MAXCC = 0                          /* FOUND; GET RID OF RC-8 */

   /* - - - - - - - CREATE BASE CLUSTER AND PRIMARY INDEX  - - - */

      DEFINE -
         CLUSTER   (   NAME(AK00.C98.CUSTMAST) -
                       FILE(MASTOUT) -
                       VOLUMES(FSDC14) -
                       RECORDSIZE (250 250 ) -
                       KEYS(8 36) -
                       CYLINDERS(2 1) -
                       IMBED                                    ) -
                   -
         DATA      (   NAME(AK00.C98.CUSTMAST.BASE.DATA) -
                       CONTROLINTERVALSIZE(4096) -
                       FREESPACE(18 1)                      ) -
                   -
         INDEX     (   NAME(AK00.C98.CUSTMAST.BASE.INDEX)   )


   /* - - - - - - - IF CREATION SUCCESSFUL, LOAD THE KSDS  - - - */

      IF LASTCC = 0 -
      THEN -
         REPRO     INFILE(SYS004 -
                       ENVIRONMENT( RECORDFORMAT(FB) -
                                    BLOCKSIZE(5000) -
                                    RECORDSIZE(250) -
                                    PRIMEDATADEVICE(2400)   ) -
                   OUTFILE(MASTOUT)

   /* - - - - - - - CREATE NONUNIQUE ADDRESS ALT INDEX - - - - - */

      DEFINE -
         AIX       (   NAME(AK00.C98.CUSTMAST.ADDRAIX) -
                       FILE(ADDALT) -
                       RELATE(AK00.C98.CUSTMAST) -
                       VOLUMES(FSDC14) -         /* RECORDSIZE (AVG  MAX) */
                       RECORDSIZE(47 79) -       /* MAX 6 OCCURRENCES SO  */
                       KEYS(26 44) -             /* 5 + AIX + (N x PRIME) */
                       NONUNIQUEKEY -            /* GIVES 5+26+(2x8)=47   */
                       CYLINDERS(2 1) -          /* AND   5+26+(6x8)=79   */
                       UNIQUE -
                       UPGRADE -
                       IMBED                                    ) -
                   -
         DATA      (   NAME(AK00.C98.CUSTMAST.ADDRAIX.DATA)  -
                       CONTROLINTERVALSIZE(4096) -
                       FREESPACE(15 15)                     ) -
                   -
         INDEX     (   NAME(AK00.C98.CUSTMAST.ADDRAIX.INDEX) )

      BLDINDEX   INFILE(MASTOUT) -
                 OUTFILE(ADDALT) -
                 WORKFILES(WRKSRT1 WRKSRT2)


      DEFINE -
         PATH      (   NAME(AK00.C98.CUSTMAST.ADDRAIX.PATH) -
                       FILE(ADDPATH) -
                       PATHENTRY(AK00.C98.CUSTMAST.ADDRAIX)   )

   /* SECOND AIX - - -CREATE THE FORCED UNIQUE NAME ALTERNATE INDEX */

      DEFINE -
         AIX       (   NAME(AK00.C98.CUSTMAST.NAMEAIX) -
                       FILE(NAMALT) -
                       RELATE(AK00.C98.CUSTMAST) -
```

FIGURE 5.3 (Continued)

```
                    VOLUMES(FSDC14) -
                    RECORDSIZE(48 48) -        /* 5 + AIX + PRIME */
                    KEYS(35 9) -               /* GIVES 5+35+8=48 */
                    UNIQUEKEY -
                    CYLINDERS(2 1) -
                    UNIQUE -
                    UPGRADE -
                    IMBED                                       ) -
                    -
        DATA      ( NAME(AK00.C98.CUSTMAST.NAMEAIX.DATA) -
                    CONTROLINTERVALSIZE(4096) -
                    FREESPACE(15 15)                           ) -
                    -
        INDEX     ( NAME(AK00.C98.CUSTMAST.NAMEAIX.INDEX) )

  BLDINDEX        INFILE(MASTOUT) -
                  OUTFILE(NAMALT) -
                  WORKFILES(WRKSRT1 WRKSRT2)

  DEFINE -
    PATH        ( NAME(AK00.C98.CUSTMAST.NAMEAIX.PATH) -
                  FILE(NAMPATH) -
                  PATHENTRY(AK00.C98.CUSTMAST.NAMEAIX)  )

/* - - - - LIST CATALOG TO SEE INFO ON THE DATA SET AND INDEXES */

  LISTCAT -
    CATALOG(CUSTCAT) -
    ENTRIES   ( AK00.C98.CUSTMAST -
                AK00.C98.CUSTMAST.ADDRAIX -
                AK00.C98.CUSTMAST.NAMEAIX    ) -
            ALL
```

FIGURE 5.3   *(Continued)*

WHAT IS AN ALTERNATE INDEX?

VSAM replaces ISAM, IBM's first mechanism for the support of indexed files. In the 1970s IBM introduced key sequenced data sets coupling them with terminology familiar to personnel who knew ISAM. "Index" is one of these terms, but its use creates an element of potential confusion.

Nature of the Primary Index

VSAM refers to the part of the key sequenced data set that is used to access records by the primary key as the index, but the primary index is not at all like the separate index of a book. The primary index of a KSDS—to be specific, the lowest level of it, called the "sequenced set"—is inherent in the KSDS tree structure. The leaves of a tree, separate from its trunk, limbs, and branches, form nothing more than a pile. The records of a KSDS similarly have no utility without the structure by which they are stored and retrieved. They cannot even be read sequentially without the involvement of the index.

The situation regarding VSAM key sequenced data sets becomes semantically convoluted when alternate indexes are considered. Alternate indexes provide a means to directly access records via keys others than the primary key. For example, account number may be a primary key. Customer name might be an alternate key; customer address could be another. Every key sequenced data set must have a primary key and index, but alternate keys are entirely optional. They are defined and created only when a need exists to access records in a key sequenced data set by a key other than the primary key, and they exist mainly for online "browse" access.

The primary index of a KSDS and its alternate indexes, if any exist, are categorically different. *An alternate index is a complete KSDS in itself.* An alternate index has its own

KSDS base cluster, data component, and index component, comprised of an index set and a sequence set. All of these components carry their own names. The primary keys of the alternate index records are the alternate keys of the "real" KSDS. The data content of these records are the primary keys of the "real" KSDS records, serving as pointers to their access.

A Simple Alternate Key Example

Figure 5.4(a) graphically depicts the keys and part of the content of records in a small key sequenced data set. In this data set, the primary key of each record is a four-position

```
PRIMARY KEY        <---------- data content ---------->
                                      ALTERNATE KEY
Part number        Description        Product a part of

   2837            Polished blade     Letter opener
   2842            3' starter rope    Power mower
   2844            Drill chuck        Electric drill
   2845            Serrated wheel     Can opener           5.4(a)
   2847            Plastic handle     Electric drill
   2850            Wire cord          Electric drill
   2852            Circular bowl      Food processor
   2855            Rubber wheels      Power mower
```

```
   Letter opener        2837
   Power mower          2842
   Electric drill       2844
   Can opener           2845            5.4(b)
   Electric drill       2847
   Electric drill       2850
   Food processor       2852
   Power mower          2855
```

```
   Can opener           2845
   Electric drill       2844
   Electric drill       2847
   Electric drill       2850            5.4(c)
   Food processor       2852
   Letter opener        2837
   Power mower          2842
   Power mower          2855
```

```
PRIMARY KEY        <-- data content -->

Product a Part of    Part number

Can opener           2845
Electric drill       2844 2847 2850          5.4(d)
Food processor       2852
Letter opener        2837
Power mower          2842 2855
```

FIGURE 5.4 Development of a simple *nonunique* key alternate index; (a) the data records in a key sequenced data set, (b) first stage of alternate index formation, (c) sorted raw alternate index records, and (d) final alternate index records constructed with variable number of primary key pointers

part number; each part documented in the data set has a unique symbolic key. The data content of the records includes a description of the part, and a field that carries the name of the product in which the part is used. This example purposely omits excess detail.

The key sequenced data set of Figure 5.4(a) can exist quite well by itself without any alternate keys at all. But let's develop an alternate index for it. Let's define the "product a part of" field as an alternate key, and build what amounts to a set of cross-reference records to the KSDS. We want to be able to look up a product and find all of the parts that are used in it. Let's say we did this on common manila cards, making a separate card for each original record. On the card for a record we write the "product a part of" field, and then the part number, as shown in Figure 5.4(b).

After preparing one alternate index card for each original record, we sort the cards into ascending sequence on the product field as shown in Figure 5.4(c). Then, for compactness, we condense the records of Figure 5.4(c) in a "control break" fashion, listing one line for each product name, followed by all of the part numbers for the separate index cards of Figure 5.4(c).

An Alternate Index Is Really a KSDS

To facilitate access to the alternate index developed for the example in Figure 5.4(d), let's load these records to a key sequenced data set. Since we want to be able to access product names at random, we make the product name field the primary key of this second KSDS.

The resultant alternate index data set appears in Figure 5.4(d). The "primary key" of each alternate index record is the field in the original KSDS that we defined as the alternate key, namely, "product a part of." The data content of each alternate index record is formed by the key or keys of the original KSDS records. There is no other data content to the alternate index records; they serve only as a means of getting to the records in the original KSDS.

The alternate index in Figure 5.4(d) is very much like a real key sequenced data set alternate index. In fact, the only thing missing from the alternate index records illustrated is a five-byte field at the beginning of each record in which VSAM stores housekeeping information. Had we illustrated this field, invisible to application programs, the alternate index records illustrated would have been *exact* renditions of KSDS alternate index records.

Figure 5.5 lists the contents of a small test data set that can be used in conjunction with the JCL and IDCAMS control statement coding of Figure 5.2 to create and experiment with a key sequenced data set with two alternate indexes. As described in Appendix F, these 80-byte records provide the key areas for the 250-byte records illustrated in the record layout at the start of this chapter. Appendix F explains how to use a small IEBGENER run to expand these records to the full 250-byte length depicted in the examples throughout this book. This data is available on diskette for uploading to a mainframe as described in Appendix A.

When the test data of Figure 5.5 is loaded to a key sequenced data set and address and name alternate indexes are created for the KSDS, it is possible to view the actual content of an alternate index. Figure 5.6 shows the MVS JCL and IDCAMS control statements necessary to print the contents of the alternate index; Figure 5.7 illustrates the same process under DOS/VSE.

Figure 5.8 illustrates the actual content of the address alternate index records built using the customer test data. The "key of record" cited by the IDCAMS PRINT function is, for the alternate index, the alternate key field of the original KSDS. Note that this is, as defined in the record layout, a 26-byte field spanning ordinal positions 45 through 70 in the original KSDS records. It is made up of several contiguous fields in the record, such as street direction, street name, house number, and apartment number, which accounts for the appearance of the PRINT "key of record."

```
BROWSE - AK00.C98.CUSTTEST ------------------------ LINE 000000 COL   001 080
COMMAND ===>                                           SCROLL ===> PAGE
----+----1----+----2----+----3----+----4----+----5----+----6----+----7----+----8
******************************** TOP OF DATA *********************************
414943675FORESTER        ALVIN    08716293SDORCHESTER ST   09710      AA
312872548WASIK           CHARLES  22168028NKILDARE AVE     02009      BB
886376533KUREK           BESSIE   24307091WFULLERTON AVE   058004-B   CC
934064961HAMPSTER        HERBERT  25656631SHALLDALE AV     08711      DD
206931482HAMPSTER        HENRIETTA28441269SHALLDALE AV     08711      EE
968312814HAMPSTER        HARVEY   28799201SHALLDALE AV     08711      FF
650038142KALKINS         JANET    32613729NSHERIDAN RD     03016      GG
624925399HAMPSTER        HELEN    32817132SHALLDALE AV     08711      HH
364787800ANCONA          MINNIE   33841546SKOLINA PL       0431017    II
030606384EASTON          JESSIE   37667140WPRYOR RD        02059      JJ
008290945CHEROSO         JEROME   42705117NELSTON AVE      00418      KK
463586621DEKOVEN         FRANK    46712001SLARAMIE DR      04408      LL
726321341SMITH           JOHN     48077449W69TH            01349      MM
468384552SMITH           JOHN     63735122 KILBOURNE       00911      NN
385726351SMITH           JOHN     63817627E135TH ST        02415      OO
878952284FLAGG           ALLAN    64070301NKOSTNER AV      0562543    PP
679912244MADISON         MONROE   73724695WWRIGHTWOOD LANE04849       QQ
036505341BILECKI         PATRICIA 88389992SLEAVITT ST      0060916    RR
***************************** BOTTOM OF DATA *********************************
```

FIGURE 5.5   Test data for AK00.C98.CUSTMAST to illustrate its loading and the creation of two alternate indexes (see also Figure F.13 in Appendix F)

The second line of each item printed in Figure 5.8 is the actual alternate index record content. The five periods at the start of each record represent the five bytes of IDCAMS housekeeping or "header" information. The contents of these fields are not meaningful for character presentation. Next comes the actual key field of the alternate index record, a repetition of the "key of record." Finally, at the end of the alternate index record is the primary key of a record in the original KSDS, the pointer to the actual data record.

The eighth alternate index record listed in Figure 5.8 appears different from the others. It has four original KSDS primary keys listed at its end, not just one. In the major example of the customer data master file, the address alternate index is nonunique; it is similar in

```
//FSBT686A  JOB AK00TEST,'DP2-JANOSSY',CLASS=E,MSGCLASS=X,
// MSGLEVEL=(1,1),NOTIFY=BT05686
//*
//*      THIS JCL = BT05686.SOURCE.CNTL(JCL56)
//*
//*******************************************************************
//*                                                                *
//*      PRINT A DATA SET USING IDCAMS                             *
//*                                                                *
//*******************************************************************
//STEPA    EXEC  PGM=IDCAMS
//SYSPRINT DD    SYSOUT=*
//SYSIN    DD    *
   PRINT          INDATASET(AK00.C98.CUSTMAST.ADDRAIX) -
                  CHARACTER -
                  COUNT(100)
/*
//
```

FIGURE 5.6   MVS JCL and IDCAMS control statements to print the actual ADDRAIX alternate index records for AK00.C98.CUSTMAST

```
// JOB PRINT ALTERNATE INDEX RECORDS
// ASSGN SYS006,DISK,VOL=FSDC14,SHR
// DLBL ALTRECS,'AK00.C98.CUSTMAST.ADDRAIX',,VSAM
// EXTENT SYS006,FSDC14
// EXEC IDCAMS,SIZE=AUTO
      PRINT        INFILE(ALTRECS) -
                   CHARACTER -
                   COUNT(100)
/&
```

FIGURE 5.7   DOS/VSE JCL and IDCAMS control statements to print the actual ADDRAIX alternate index records for AK00.C98.CUSTMAST

```
KEY OF RECORD -  KILBOURNE         00911
.....KILBOURNE          00911      63735122

KEY OF RECORD - E135TH ST          02415
.....E135TH ST          02415      63817627

KEY OF RECORD - NELSTON AVE        00418
.....NELSTON AVE        00418      42705117

KEY OF RECORD - NKILDARE AVE       02009
.....NKILDARE AVE       02009      22168028

KEY OF RECORD - NKOSTNER AV        0562543
.....NKOSTNER AV        0562543    64070301

KEY OF RECORD - NSHERIDAN RD       03016
.....NSHERIDAN RD       03016      32613729

KEY OF RECORD - SDORCHESTER ST     09710
.....SDORCHESTER ST     09710      08716293

KEY OF RECORD - SHALLDALE AV       08711
.....SHALLDALE AV       08711      25656631 28441269 28799201 32817132

KEY OF RECORD - SKOLINA PL         0431017
.....SKOLINA PL         0431017    33841546

KEY OF RECORD - SLARAMIE DR        04408
.....SLARAMIE DR        04408      46712001

KEY OF RECORD - SLEAVITT ST        0060916
.....SLEAVITT ST        0060916    88389992

KEY OF RECORD - WFULLERTON AVE     058004-B
.....WFULLERTON AVE     058004-B   24307091

KEY OF RECORD - WPRYOR RD          02059
.....WPRYOR RD          02059      37667140

KEY OF RECORD - WWRIGHTWOOD LANE04849
.....WWRIGHTWOOD LANE04849         73724695

KEY OF RECORD - W69TH              01349
.....W69TH              01349      48077449

IDC0005I NUMBER OF RECORDS PROCESSED WAS 15

IDC0001I FUNCTION COMPLETED, HIGHEST CONDITION CODE WAS 0
```

FIGURE 5.8   Printed ADDRAIX alternate index records, showing five bytes of VSAM header, alternate key, and primary key or keys of records in the AK00.C98.CUSTMAST key sequenced data set

this way to the "product a part of" alternate index of Figure 5.4. The address of 8711 S. Halldale Avenue, found in the test data, occurs on four customer records. This means that when it appears as an alternate key, it is not unique to one original KSDS record, it is nonunique.

Accessing Records via Alternate Key

Let's return to Figure 5.4, in which an inventory of parts is housed in records in a key sequenced data set. In this simple example we could use the alternate index to list all of the parts contained in a given product. To do this, we access the alternate index by its primary key, product name. To list the parts that are found in an electric drill we obtain the second record of the alternate index. We then access the record in the original key sequenced data set with the key of 2844, then the record with key 2847, and then the record with key 2850.

Figure 5.9 illustrates how to access a key sequenced data set under sequential, random, and alternate key access. For sequential access, the original KSDS base cluster definition in the catalog is examined by VSAM and access proceeds to the data component via the original KSDS index sequence set. No other elements of the data set are involved. For

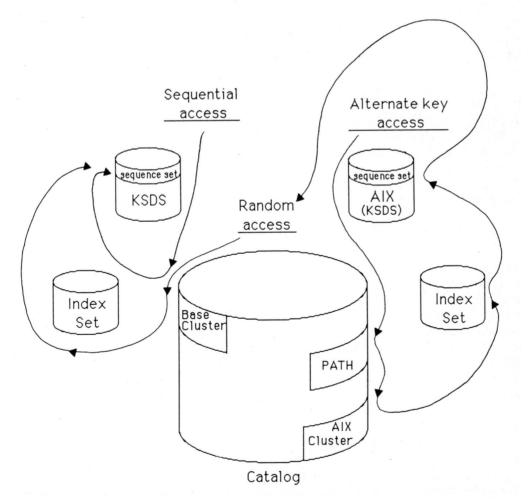

FIGURE 5.9 How processing differs depending on the sequential, random, or alternate index access to a key sequenced data set

random access to the original KSDS, VSAM first consults the original KSDS base cluster definition in the catalog, then the index set and the sequence set, and access proceeds to the data component.

For access via an alternate index, far different processing is involved. The item referenced for access is the alternate index path. For alternate index access, the path is the first item sought by VSAM in the system catalog; then the base cluster definition for the KSDS holding the alternate index records is examined. Following this the index set of the alternate index is accessed, and then the sequence set and data component of the alternate index. Obtaining the primary key of the record desired from the original KSDS, VSAM performs a random access to the original KSDS, consulting the original KSDS index set, then its sequence set, and finally its data component.

Figure 5.9 makes obvious some of the reasons that alternate key access to key sequenced data sets is accorded in a conservative manner in most application systems. Alternate key access involves significant I/O actions and resources. When batch access to an entire data set in a sequence other than primary key is desired, it is more efficient to sort the data set into the desired sequence rather than design and specify an alternate index for this purpose.

The Role of the Path

When we use the capabilities of VSAM to define and build the alternate index we gain a convenience: we do not have to manually juggle accesses to the alternate index and then the original base cluster. Once established, the alternate index is associated with the original base cluster by the establishment of a path carrying its own name. Stated most succinctly, a path for an alternate index is a linkage between a path name and an alternate index (AIX) cluster name. The path is established using the IDCAMS DEFINE command, specifying the path name and, as the "pathentry," the name of the alternate index.

When a key sequenced data set is to be accessed via an alternate index, the action is taken by citing the path name, the name by which the path is stored in the catalog. If, on the other hand, an alternate index is accessed by its own name, one obtains precisely this as we did in Figures 5.6 and 5.7. The records of the alternate index KSDS itself, not the records in the original base cluster indexed by the alternate index, are obtained.

Nonunique Alternate Keys

The alternate index records in the simple parts file example of Figure 5.4(d) can "point" to more than one original key sequenced data set record; this alternate key is said to be "nonunique." The terminology is somewhat backward; it is not the given alternate index key, as the primary key of the alternate index KSDS—in this case, product name—that is nonunique. Rather, nonunique means that the alternate key value is not unique to one original KSDS record. Reading the data set via one alternate index key in this example will not acquire just one record. When such an alternate key is identified in a COBOL program, it is cited with the phrase "WITH DUPLICATES" which is clearer language. Nonunique alternate index keys cause alternate index records to be of variable length because the potential exists for many record pointers to exist for a given alternate index key.

Nonunique alternate keys suffer from a certain awkwardness in performance. Suppose, for example, the alternate index illustrated in Figure 5.4(d) were defined and created, and the original data set and the alternate index made accessible to online processing. A record is added to the data set carrying key 2839, and it is a part for an electric drill. The record is written into the original KSDS and appears as in Figure 5.10(a). Assuming that

```
   PRIMARY KEY        <---------- Data content ----------->
                                   ALTERNATE KEY
      Part number     Description   Product a part of

         2837         Polished blade    Letter opener
         2839         Chuck key         Electric drill
         2842         3' starter rope   Power mower
         2844         Drill chuck       Electric drill
         2845         Serrated wheel    Can opener          5.10(a)
         2847         Plastic handle    Electric drill
         2850         Wire cord         Electric drill
         2852         Circular bowl     Food processor
         2855         Rubber wheels     Power mower
```

```
   PRIMARY KEY        <-- data content -->

      Part of         Part number

   Can opener         2845
   Electric drill     2844 2847 2850 2839           5.10(b)
   Food processor     2852
   Letter opener      2837
   Power mower        2842 2855
```

FIGURE 5.10 Updating of an alternate index containing nonunique alternate keys; multiple primary key pointers are not maintained in sequence by VSAM

the alternate index was defined with the UPGRADE option, the alternate index is updated automatically and now appears as in Figure 5.10(b).

When an alternate index is created, the keys of the original KSDS records pointed to by alternate index records are sorted in ascending sequence. When original KSDS records are accessed via an alternate index key, they are retrieved in this sequence, and a browse conducted in this manner appears quite natural.

When updates to the data set occur, however, the original KSDS keys stored as the data content of an alternate index record are not sorted or kept in ascending sequence. When the insertion of a record with key value 2839, a part of an electric drill, occurs as in Figure 5.10(a), the corresponding alternate index record acquires the additional pointer at the end of the existing pointers as in Figure 5.10(b). Access via the alternate key now produces a browse that gives record 2844, 2847, 2850, and then record 2839. This does not appear natural and will usually provoke concern that a problem exists. It appears that the sort order of the records being presented is flawed.

Nonunique alternate keys also pose an efficiency problem for online access where a browse is limited by the number of lines on a screen and forward screen paging is to be provided. Forward paging involves allowing the terminal user viewing records to indicate that the "next" screenful of records in the browse is to be presented. No efficient way exists to interrupt the reading of records from the original KSDS in the middle of a series of primary key pointers in an alternate index record and continue from this location later. To do this with nonunique alternate keys requires rereading and bypassing records in the alternate key pointer series until the key value last presented is reached. This repetitive I/O is wasteful and potentially degrading to online system performance.

Making Alternate Keys Unique

Unique alternate keys exist when every alternate value points to one and only one original key sequenced data set record. Given the nature of most alternate keys, such as "product a part of," customer name, and customer address, this is not ordinarily the case. But *it is always possible to force an alternate key field to be unique, and it is common to do this to gain the advantages of unique alternate keys.*

Figure 5.11(a) reproduces Figure 5.4(a) for convenience. The single field within any key sequenced data set record that we always know is unique to that record is its primary key. Suppose we append a copy of the primary key onto the tail end of the alternate key field, as in Figure 5.11(b). This is not done by or even known to the terminal operator entering the information for a new record; rather, it is accomplished entirely by program action with a simple field MOVE statement. The presence of this field within the defined alternate key field guarantees that no other original KSDS record will have entirely the same value for an alternate key.

When we now sort the raw alternate index records of Figure 5.11(b) into the order shown in Figure 5.11(c), the sort includes the longer alternate key field. When we build the alternate index, this produces it in the form shown in Figure 5.11(d). No alternate index record contains more than one original KSDS record pointer; all alternate index keys are unique.

Browse access to the data set via the alternate index proceeds much as in the case of a nonunique alternate index key, except that the browse is started on a *partial* alternate key as illustrated in Chapter 7. The browse continues until a full screen of records is presented, and then the full alternate key of the last record displayed is saved. To resume forward browsing, a read is done on the full alternate key field previously saved, and records presentation resumes immediately at this point.

An alternate key field can always be forced to be unique by appending a copy of the primary record key in the low order positions. While this may appear wasteful of space, the overhead of alternate indexes and their concurrent automatic updating in parallel with the original key sequenced data set usually limits the number of alternate indexes used. Two or perhaps three alternate indexes on a given data set is usually the maximum employed, and use of only one alternate index, or none, by far predominates.

At least one alternate index can always be forced to be unique with no extra record space overhead at all by judicious placement of the alternate key field physically ahead of the primary key field. It is for this reason that Figure 5.1 depicts the customer name field in positions 10 through 36, while the primary key field is located in positions 37 through 44. VSAM imposes no requirement that the primary key occur first in the record. Placing one alternate key field in front of it allows that alternate key field to include the primary key, forcing the alternate key to be entirely unique. An alternate key field can overlap or be entirely contained within another alternate key field or the primary key field.

Selection of Alternate Keys

The alternate keys developed for a given key sequenced data set must be designed with care since these have a great deal to do with data set efficiency and online responsiveness. Alternate keys should be chosen specifically for what they contribute to online functionality.

Common usage of alternate key fields is to make possible the initiation of an online browse of records, starting at some point such as a partial name or address. In designing an alternate key for this purpose, it is important to analyze the typical online access desired by the users of the data set. A name or address alternate key will be used to help locate information for a party or product when the exact primary key is not known. The access will be a limited "fishing expedition" undertaken to apply human judgment to the process of finding an identifiable item within a list presented on a screen. The fact that the list of items for which the front part of the defined alternate index duplicates may be

```
     PRIMARY KEY        <---------- data content ----------->
                                             ALTERNATE KEY
     Part number        Description        Product a part of

        2837            Polished blade     Letter opener
        2842            3' starter rope    Power mower
        2844            Drill chuck        Electric drill
        2845            Serrated wheel     Can opener          5.11(a)
        2847            Plastic handle     Electric drill
        2850            Wire cord          Electric drill
        2852            Circular bowl      Food processor
        2855            Rubber wheels      Power mower
```

```
     Letter opener  2837        2837
     Power mower    2842        2842
     Electric drill 2844        2844
     Can opener     2845        2845          5.11(b)
     Electric drill 2847        2847
     Electric drill 2850        2850
     Food processor 2852        2852
     Power mower    2855        2855
```

```
     Can opener     2845        2845
     Electric drill 2844        2844
     Electric drill 2847        2847
     Electric drill 2850        2850          5.11(c)
     Food processor 2852        2852
     Letter opener  2837        2837
     Power mower    2842        2842
     Power mower    2855        2855
```

```
     PRIMARY KEY            <-- data content -->

     Product a Part of       Part number

     Can opener     2845        2845
     Electric drill 2844        2844
     Electric drill 2847        2844
     Electric drill 2850        2844          5.11(d)
     Food processor 2852        2852
     Letter opener  2837        2837
     Power mower    2842        2842
     Power mower    2855        2842
```

FIGURE 5.11 Development of a simple *unique* key alternate index; (a) the data records in a key sequenced data set, (b) first stage of alternate index formation, (c) sorted raw alternate index records, and (d) final alternate index records constructed with one primary key pointer per alternate index record

longer than can be accommodated on one screen makes it necessary to provide for multiple screen paging, a process facilitated by entirely unique alternate keys.

If it is determined that a nonunique alternate index key is to be used, a program should be used to analyze the spread of alternate key values to determine the maximum duplication that exists. Such a program is provided in Appendix F. If alternate key duplication is found to occur to an excessive degree, the nature of the proposed alternate key should be modified. If this is not possible, such an alternate index should be defined with NOUP-GRADE, in order to omit it from the upgrade set kept updated online.

DEFINING AN ALTERNATE INDEX

An alternate index is a key sequenced data set in its own right. Most of the definition specifications for a KSDS apply to and have the same meaning for an alternate index. The INDEXED/NOINDEXED/NUMBERED attribute of a base cluster, however, does not apply to an alternate index, because it is always a KSDS data set; it is therefore always IN-DEXED.

DEFINE ALTERNATEINDEX

DEFINE ALTERNATEINDEX is a subcommand of the IDCAMS DEFINE command and is used to allocate an alternate index. Since it is a KSDS, an alternate index has three catalog entries: one for the alternate index base cluster, one for its data component, and one for its index component. As with an ordinary KSDS, each entity is assigned a unique name, either explicitly via the NAME specification or implicitly by VSAM itself.

The required parameters to define an alternate index are NAME, RELATE, VOLUMES, KEYS, and one of the space allocation attributes, CYLINDERS, RECORDS, or TRACKS. If MODEL is specified indicating an existing data set, the attributes of which are to serve as a pattern, VOLUMES is not required.

NAME

NAME specifies the name by which the alternate index KSDS is known to the system catalog. It is this name that can be used to access the alternate index as a KSDS independent of the base cluster to which it is related. The name chosen for an alternate index should include the name of the base cluster plus a standard identifier such as "AIX," in order to best organize JCL.

If more than one alternate index is defined for a KSDS, an extended naming convention should be employed. Such a convention is established in Figure 5.2, providing a clear and consistent format for the components of the alternate index KSDS.

RELATE

RELATE identifies the key sequenced data set indexed by the alternate index. Only a KSDS and an ESDS can have an alternate index, and only if the data set does not carry the REUSE attribute. If an alternate index were related to a reuseable KSDS, the alternate index would become useless at the point at which the KSDS was opened for output because this would render the KSDS empty. An alternate index itself, however, can be reusable.

VOLUMES

VOLUMES specifies the disk volume or volumes on which the KSDS containing the alternate index records will reside. While this can be the same as the disk volume housing the KSDS to which the alternate index is related, it need not be the same. It is often desirable to place an alternate index on a different disk volume to minimize disk arm contention. This can allow more rapid access to the original KSDS data records by eliminating a certain amount of disk arm motion.

RECORDSIZE

Alternate index record size is normally computed and specified, because the default average alternate index record size is 4,086 bytes; this is 4,096 minus 10 bytes of VSAM control fields consisting of one RIDF and two CIDFs. The default maximum record length is 32,600 bytes. Because of restrictions within VSAM, an alternate index with records larger than 32,600 bytes should not be made part of an upgrade set. Attempting to update KSDS with an alternate index with records larger than 32,600 bytes will result in failure and an error message from VSAM.

An alternate index record contains VSAM housekeeping header information, the alternate index key, and one or more original KSDS primary record keys. Header information includes data on the type of base cluster to which the alternate index is related, either an ESDS or KSDS, the number of base cluster keys carried in the alternate index record, and the length of the alternate key. The header information is created and maintained by VSAM and is always five bytes in length. The second portion of the alternate index record contains the alternate key. Its length is the length of the alternate key field within the original KSDS. The third portion of the record contains, in plain characters, all of the KSDS primary keys to which the alternate index record points. The length of this can be calculated by multiplying the length of the KSDS primary key by the maximum number of occurrences estimated for the most duplicated alternate key.

The RECORDSIZE specification of an alternate index is calculated in the following manner:

> Average alternate index record length =
> 5 + alternate key length + (A × primary key length)

> Maximum alternate index record length =
> 5 + alternate key length + (M × primary key length)

In connection with the address alternate index, AK00.C98.CUSTMAST.ADDRAIX, in the IDCAMS coding of Figure 5.2, these formulas are applied in this manner:

- It was estimated that on the average two original KSDS records would carry the same address, due to a spouse or at least one teenage child residing at the same address and being carried on the file. The value of "A" is thus 2 and the average alternate index record length is computed as:

        =   5 + alternate key length + (2 × primary key length)
        =   5 + 26 + (2 × 8)
        =   5 + 26 + 16
        =   47

- It was estimated that a maximum of six original KSDS records would carry the same address. The value of "M" is thus 6 and the maximum alternate index record length is computed as:

        =   5 + alternate key length + (6 × primary key length)
        =   5 + 26 + (6 × 8)
        =   5 + 26 + 48
        =   79

If a load file exists at the time the IDCAMS specifications are being developed, a key analysis program such as that provided in Appendix F is invaluable in making accurate estimates of alternate key frequency of occurrence. Allowing a large enough record length is of critical importance for a nonunique alternate index.

KEYS

The position of the alternate key in the original key sequenced data set record is defined in the KEYS specification. The length of the alternate key is stated first, then the offset of this field in the KSDS record. Thus in Figure 5.2, KEYS is coded as:

```
KEYS (26 44)
```

for the address alternate index. The address alternate key is 26 bytes in length, made up of the street direction, street name, house number, and apartment number. KEYS for the name alternate key is coded as

```
KEYS (35 9)
```

since this key is 35 bytes in length and includes the customer last name, customer first name, and, at the end, the primary key field to insure uniqueness.

Alternate key fields can overlap or be entirely contained within other alternate key fields or the primary key. There is no requirement that the primary key field for a record occur at the beginning of the record. Designing the record placing one of the alternate key fields physically ahead of the primary key is a clever technique that allows at least this alternate key field to be unique with no special concern at all.

The position and length of the alternate key must be within the original KSDS record and the fields that make up an alternate key must be contiguous. The length of an alternate key field cannot exceed that of the KSDS record. When the KSDS contains spanned records, alternate key fields must be contained within the first segment or control interval of each record.

UNIQUEKEY|NONUNIQUEKEY

UNIQUEKEY indicates that only one data record in the KSDS indexed can contain a given alternate key value. UNIQUEKEY is the default. If UNIQUEKEY is specified and the BLDINDEX command encounters more than one original KSDS record with the same alternate index key value, the building of the alternate index terminates.

NONUNIQUEKEY allows multiple original KSDS records to carry the same alternate index key. A maximum of 32,768 base cluster records can carry the same alternate key value, but serious drawbacks exist for such alternate key duplication. When NON-UNIQUEKEY is specified, the maximum record length for the alternate index record must be large enough to accommodate the keys of all of the original KSDS records to which it points.

SHAREOPTIONS

Share options control access to a data set by more than one program at a time. The values coded here should be the same as those coded for the original key sequenced data set.

UPGRADE/NOUPGRADE

These attributes indicate whether or not the alternate index will be kept updated as its base cluster is modified. An alternate index with UPGRADE becomes part of the "upgrade set" of the original key sequenced data set. Alternate indexes that are part of the upgrade set are normally updated when records in the KSDS are added, changed, and deleted.

UPGRADE becomes effective only after the alternate index is built with the BLDINDEX command. If the KSDS is open at the time the alternate index is built, UPGRADE goes into effect the next time it is opened.

NOUPGRADE coded on an alternate index excludes it from the upgrade set of the original KSDS. This means that the alternate index will not be updated along with the original KSDS; it will reflect new or modified alternate keys only when it is subsequently recreated in a separate batch operation. An alternate index not in the upgrade set of its KSDS can be brought up to currency by deleting it, redefining it, and recreating it with the BLDINDEX command.

UPGRADE is the default. But for each alternate index included in the KSDS upgrade set, at least two extra I/O operations can be incurred for each record addition, deletion, or alternate key modification in the base cluster. UPGRADE is recommended for alternate indexes that are required to be kept in synchronization with the original KSDS and do not have extremely large alternate index records. The more KSDS record keys contained in an alternate index record—that is, the greater degree of nonuniqueness—the larger the alternate index record.

Space Allocation

The space allocation for an alternate index must be considered just as in the case of any key sequenced data set, since it really is a KSDS in its own right. The same computational considerations discussed in Chapter 3 for KSDS space apply to alternate indexes, with additional complications. For data sets that are large, space for an alternate index should be allocated in cylinders for the same reasons of efficiency that exist for normal key sequenced data sets.

For alternate indexes defined as UNIQUEKEY, the alternate index record will contain only one KSDS primary key. This will make the alternate index record a fixed length, as is the NAMEAIX in Figure 5.2; RECORDSIZE is coded with the same value in both average and maximum record length fields. The formulas of Chapter 3 can be used manually to determine a suitable control interval size, or the VSAMCISZ and VSAMSPAC CLISTs can be employed. The number of records to be housed in the alternate index will equal the number of records in the KSDS to which the unique alternate key index is related.

For alternate indexes defined as NONUNIQUEKEY, the alternate index will contain a variable number of KSDS primary keys. In this case the average record length should be used either manually or with the VSAMCISZ and VSAMSPAC CLISTs to develop the space allocation. The number of records to be housed in the alternate index can be estimated less precisely because of the condensing of primary keys into alternate index records. The larger the degree of nonuniqueness in the alternate key, the greater will be this reduction in the number of alternate index records. Estimating a number of alternate records equal to the number of records in the KSDS errs on the side of conservatism, however, and this can be taken as a starting point. The space estimate can be reduced if monitoring of data set performance indicates a high degree of unused space in the alternate index.

The key analysis program discussed in Chapter 3 and provided in Appendix F is a valuable aid in understanding the nature of the records in the key sequenced data to which an alterate index is related. You can use this program, also available on diskette for uploading, to analyze the file being loaded to a KSDS and establish accurate figures for record size and space computations.

Miscellaneous Attributes

Recommendations for specification of the remaining alternate index attributes are identical to those discussed in in Chapter 3 for key sequenced data sets. CONTROLINTERVALSIZE should be chosen for the data component, but VSAM should be allowed to choose it for the alternate index's index component by omitting the specification there. NOERASE is recommended for non-confidential data sets. SPEED and IMBED should be specified to optimize loading and online performance.

BUILDING ALTERNATE INDEXES

Background

The BLDINDEX command is used to create an alternate index. The alternate index must already be defined, and the KSDS it indexes must have at least one record in it. BLDINDEX reads all the records in the KSDS, extracts the primary keys and the alternate keys and forms a record for each KSDS record. This is then sorted in sequence by the alternate key and within it, the primary key, just as in the foregoing index-card example. The final variable-length alternate index record is then created and output to the alternate index KSDS.

IDCAMS attempts to perform the sort process involved in creating an alternate index in memory. This is not usually possible and BLDINDEX can be provided with disk space and work files to perform an external sort. When directed to sort the records externally, IDCAMS uses two ESDS work files which it deletes after use. The default MVS DDnames or DOS Dnames for statements referencing these work files are IDCUT1 and IDCUT2. The origin of these unusual names leads to pronunciations that heighten the aura of mystery. "IDC" is the standard IDCAMS name and message prefix, while "UT" is a traditional IBM abbreviation for "OUT." *De asini umbra disceptare.*[1]

Sort work files can be identified at DDnames other than IDCUT1 and IDCUT 2. Coding WORKFILES(DDname1 and DDname2) and additional DD statements, as illustrated in Figure 5.2, allows this.

After IDCAMS completes the sort of the extracted information from the base cluster, it starts to build and load the alternate index records. As duplicate base cluster primary keys are encountered, they are all loaded in sequence into the same alternate index record if NONUNIQUEKEY was specified for the alternate index. If multiple primary keys occur and UNIQUEKEY was specified for the alternate index, the BLDINDEX command will terminate with an appropriate message.

BLDINDEX

The BLDINDEX command has two required parameters: INFILE or INDATASET, and OUTFILE or OUTDATASET. INFILE or INDATASET identifies the KSDS from which the alternate records are to be built. OUTFILE or OUTDATASET identifies the alternate index to be built.

INFILE|INDATASET

INFILE specifies the DD statement that identifies the KSDS for which the alternate index is to be built, or a path that points to this KSDS. The KSDS and the alternate index specified by OUTFILE or OUTDATASET must be related and defined in the same catalog.

INDATASET directly identifies the data set name of the KSDS or path. The KSDS specified will be dynamically allocated. It will be obtained for exclusive use as if DISP = OLD had been coded in MVS JCL.

OUTFILE|OUTDATASET

OUTFILE and OUTDATASET identify either the alternate index or a path that points to this. More than one alternate index can be built for a base cluster by identifying more than one alternate index within this specification. The alternate index must be related to and in the same catalog as the original KSDS. The alternate index also must either be empty or carry the REUSE attribute.

OUTFILE specifies a DD statement that identifies the alternate index. OUTDATASET identifies the data set name of the alternate index. The alternate index specified will be dynamically allocated, and no DD statement for it is coded.

EXTERNALSORT|INTERNALSORT

These specifications indicate whether the information extracted from the original KSDS is to be sorted internally in virtual storage or externally using two work files. INTERNAL-SORT indicates that the sort will be performed internally and is the default. EXTER-NALSORT indicates that the sort will be performed externally using two work files. EXTERNALSORT should be used when the size of the KSDS to be indexed is unpredictable or known to be larger than a few hundred records.

WORKFILES

WORKFILES is optional but identifies two DD statements that indicate the sort work files to be used in lieu of the DDnames IDCUT1 and IDCUT2. WORKFILES is applicable only when EXTERNALSORT is specified. The sort work files are deleted by IDCAMS itself when they are no longer needed for creating the index.

When coded at DD statements, the work files must carry a disposition of OLD even though they do not exist prior to the run. Unlike the case with ordinary sort utility sort work files, no SPACE parameter is coded in JCL for these IDCAMS work files. The JCL required for the sort work files can be found in Figure 5.2. If enough virtual storage is available the sort work data sets will not be used.

CATALOG

This attribute names the catalog in which the work files will be defined. If not specified, the work files will be defined in the master catalog.

ESTABLISHING THE PATH

Define Path

The definition of a path for access to a key sequenced data set through an alternate index establishes the necessary linkage to process the KSDS in this manner. The path is only a catalog entry. It is not a data set and therefore does not have a data component or an index component. The alternate index can be accessed independently of the path and more than one path involving the same alternate index and KSDS can be created. While this is rarely done, it affords a means of allowing different types of access privileges to the same KSDS, depending on the path name by which the KSDS is accessed.

Figure 5.12 lists the definition specifications for a path. The path has certain attributes identical to those associated with a KSDS or an alternate index, including many of the same VSAM protection attributes.

NAME

The NAME attribute defines the path entry name, the name of its entry in the catalog. This name must adhere to the same rules of formation that apply to data set names. The path name should include the name of the original key sequenced data set with the word "path" appended. If more than one path is defined for a KSDS, each should have an additional identifying qualification within a naming convention.

In our major example, AK00.C98.CUSTMAST is the name of a key sequenced data set. The naming convention we have used is applied to the KSDS components, alternate index and components, and paths created in the MVS JCL and IDCAMS coding of Figure 5.2 in this way:

```
Required *
Choice needed >
Recommended +    Command        Option                              Abbreviation      o


        *        DEFINE -
        *          PATH     (NAME( entryname ) -
        *                   PATHENTRY(name/password) -                    PENT
                            ATTEMPTS( number ) -                          ATT
                            AUTHORIZATION( entrypoint    string ) -       AUTH
                            CODE( code ) -
                            CONTROLPW( password ) -                       CTLPW
                            FILE( DDname ) -
                            MASTERPW( password ) -                        MRPW
                            MODEL( data-set-name/password  catname/password) -
                            OWNER( up-to-eight-characters ) -
                            READPW( password )                            RDPW
                            RECATALOG|NORECATALOG -             RCTLG    NRCTLG
                            TO( Julian date ) or FOR( days ) -
                            UPDATE|NOUPDATE -                    UPD      NUPD
                            UPDATEPW( password )  ) -                     UPDPW
                       CATALOG ( name / password )                       CAT
```

Note: The | symbol represents a logical "or" meaning that only one of the items can be specified. Underlined print indicates the IDCAMS default. The usage of passwords is optional.

FIGURE 5.12   DEFINE options and abbreviations for definition of PATH

```
*AK00.C98.CUSTMAST                  original KSDS name (cluster)
 AK00.C98.CUSTMAST.BASE.DATA        KSDS data component
 AK00.C98.CUSTMAST.BASE.INDEX       KSDS index component

*AK00.C98.CUSTMAST.ADDRAIX          alternate index name (cluster)
 AK00.C98.CUSTMAST.ADDRAIX.DATA     alternate index data component
 AK00.C98.CUSTMAST.ADDRAIX.INDEX    alternate index index component

*AK00.C98.CUSTMAST.ADDRAIX.PATH     alternate index access path

*AK00.C98.CUSTMAST.NAMEAIX          alternate index name (cluster)
 AK00.C98.CUSTMAST.NAMEAIX.DATA     alternate index data component
 AK00.C98.CUSTMAST.NAMEAIX.INDEX    alternate index index component

*AK00.C98.CUSTMAST.NAMEAIX.PATH     alternate index access path
```

The names marked with an asterisk (*) can be thought of as "umbrella" names in that reference to them automatically causes reference to the items immediately under them. That is, reference to AK00.C98.CUSTMAST causes VSAM to reference AK00.C98.-CUSTMAST.BASE.DATA and AK00.C98.CUSTMAST.BASE.INDEX. Reference to AK00.C98.CUSTMAST in JCL or a LISTCAT does not cause automatic reference to AK00.C98.CUSTMAST.ADDRAIX or the other alternate index or any paths.

PATHENTRY

PATHENTRY usually identifies the name of the alternate index itself. A path can, however, be defined without connection to an alternate index as a means of providing "screened" access to a key sequenced data set. This is done when access to a KSDS for a given purpose is to be tightly controlled or to disengage the upgrade set; the protection and update attributes coded in the path prevail over those defined for the KSDS. The second use of PATH is rare; paths are almost universally associated with the use of alternate indexes.

UPDATE|NOUPDATE and UPGRADE|NOUPGRADE Interplay

UPDATE and NOUPDATE affect the handling of the entire upgrade set of the key sequenced data set. This is often confusing because UPDATE or NOUPDATE is coded in a path, but the placement of an alternate index in the upgrade set is specified in the alternate index definitions themselves using the similar-sounding UPGRADE or NOUPGRADE specifications.

UPGRADE coded or assumed by default in an alternate index definition includes the alternate index in the active set of components that are automatically allocated, opened, and updated when the original key sequenced data set is updated. NOUPGRADE in an alternate index definition excludes membership of the alternate index in the upgrade set. When an alternate index carries NOUPGRADE, it is presumed that it will be periodically recreated to gain currency with the actual content of the KSDS it indexes.

UPDATE coded in the path of a given alternate index tells VSAM to abide by the membership of the upgrade set established by individual alternate index definitions, and to activate the entire upgrade set as usual. When a KSDS is accessed via a path carrying or defaulting to UPDATE, the upgrade set is handled in the manner in which it is intended to function. UPDATE is the default assumed if neither UPDATE or NOUPDATE is coded in a path definition.

NOUPDATE coded in the path by which a KSDS is accessed tells VSAM to ignore the membership of the KSDS upgrade set and not to allocate for access the members of it. Alternate indexes defined with UPGRADE are thus excluded from update in spite of their UPGRADE specification.

The primary use of NOUPDATE is in a path associated directly with a key sequenced data set, as in the case of path C in Figure 5.13. When coded in such a path, it is possible to gain access to the KSDS without involving the upgrade set.

Figure 5.13 is an illustration of a hypothetical KSDS with four alternate indexes and six paths. It does not illustrate a typical situation but does aid in portraying path concepts. This figure shows the relationship between an original KSDS, the alternate indexes included in its upgrade set via their own coding or UPGRADE, and the UPDATE attribute of paths. Paths D, E, F, and G are each associated with a different alternate index. Paths B and C are associated only with the KSDS itself, an uncommon but possible form of association.

When the KSDS base cluster labeled "A" is allocated and opened, the alternate indexes in the base cluster's upgrade set are also automatically allocated and opened. Their own UPGRADE specifications have caused their names to be cataloged in a listing that identifies the upgrade set. These are alternate indexes 1 and 2. This is the customary and normal manner of operation.

Path B is associated directly with the KSDS and is coded or defaults to the UPDATE attribute. When it is allocated and opened the alternate indexes in the KSDS upgrade set are also automatically allocated and opened. These are alternate indexes 1 and 2. This is a customary manner of operation.

Path C is associated directly with the KSDS and is coded with NOUPDATE. When it is allocated and opened, only the KSDS base cluster and its index and data components are allocated and opened. NOUPDATE applies only to the upgrade set; reads and writes to the KSDS base cluster are processed normally. We might use a path such as C if batch direct access updates were to occur to the KSDS immediately prior to its backup and full restoration, with consequent redefinition and recreation of all alternate indexes. Disengaging the upgrade set will eliminate considerable I/O that is not necessary in this case.

When a path is defined for an alternate index and the path carries or defaults to UPDATE, such as Path D or Path F, the upgrade set is processed normally and is opened and allocated. In addition, the path's alternate index entry name, such as alternate index 3 in this case, is allocated as well, even if it is not a member of the upgrade set. When path F is specified, it is as if alternate index 3 had been defined with UPGRADE.

When a path defined with the NOUPDATE attribute, such as path G, is referenced, the KSDS base cluster and only the path's alternate index are allocated.

If a path such as E is referenced, the path's NOUPDATE precludes the upgrade set from bing updated. The alternate index named in the path is allocated, however, and becomes active for KSDS access.

In actual practice the number of alternate indexes created for a KSDS are normally limited to one or two and path coding is as simple as that indicated in Figure 5.2. Path coding beyond this in complexity is not often warranted for operation or effective system maintenance.

A Path Directly to a KSDS (Read-Only Access)

It is possible to process a base cluster in read-only mode. This is accomplished by defining a path with the base cluster as its entry name. The path will carry NOUPDATE and the READPW attribute. NOUPDATE excludes the KSDS upgrade set from being updated.

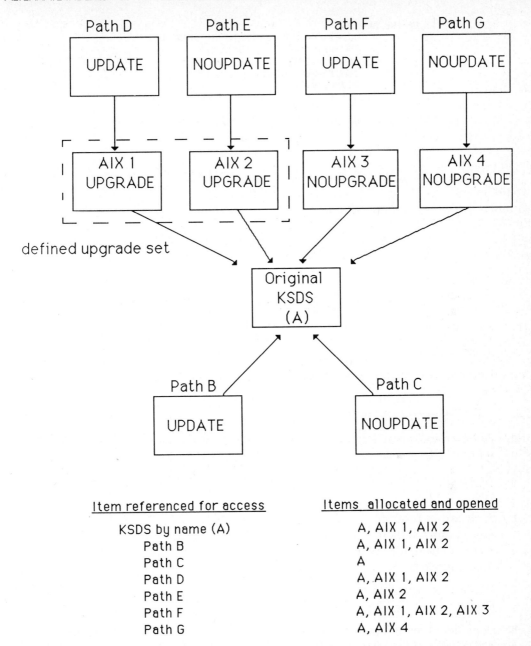

FIGURE 5.13 Entities involved in access for various UPDATE/NOUPDATE and UPGRADE/NOUP-GRADE specifications

READPW forces the console operator to supply the read password, not usually a workable security arrangement. The program will be able to obtain records from the data set but not write or rewrite to it or delete records from it.

Figure 5.14 illustrates the coding required to create a read-only path to a key sequenced data set named AK00.C98.CUSTMAST. A MASTERPW was also specified in this coding. If it had not been specified, the read password would also become the master password MASTERPW, control password CONTROLPW and the update password, UPDATEPW. This is an awkward consequence of the manner in which VSAM password security is implemented.

```
DEFINE PATH -
      (    NAME(AK00.C98.CUSTMAST.PATH.READONLY) -
           PATHENTRY(AK00.C98.CUSTMAST) -
           OWNER(RICHG) -
           MASTERPW(A629H327) -
           READPW(R781Z384)                              ) -
      CATALOG(CUSTMAST.CATALOG/CU332099)
```

FIGURE 5.14   Creating a read-only path for a key sequenced data set

By referencing the KSDS via path AK00.C98.CUSTMAST.PATH.READONLY a program would be authorized and allowed only to read the KSDS. The READPW would have to be supplied by the console operator at the time the program tried to open the data set. Since the ATTEMPTS attribute was not coded it would default to two; the system operator would have only two attempts to supply the correct password before the job failed. A more thorough discussion of VSAM password security is provided in Chapter 11.

REVIEW QUESTIONS AND (*)EXERCISES

1. Discuss the difference between the primary key of a key sequenced data set and an alternate key.

2. Describe how an alternate key is used to access a key sequenced data set.

3. How many alternate keys must be defined for a key sequenced data set? How many can be defined as an upper limit?

4. Alternate keys may be unique or nonunique. Discuss the difference between these types of alternate keys.

5. How can an alternate index key be made entirely unique without using any extra space in a record?

6. A record is inserted into a data set in a random mode. The field defined as the nonunique alternate key field contains a value already found in this field in other records in the file. Describe how this record insertion affects the applicable alternate index record.

7. When is it desirable to relate a PATH directly to a key sequenced data set base cluster?

8. Consider three alternate indexes named AIX1, AIX2, and AIX3 are related to a KSDS with paths named PATH1, PATH2, and PATH3. Indicate the UPDATE/UP-GRADE specifications that each alternate index and its corresponding PATH should have to satisfy the following conditions:

PATH accessed	AIX opened
PATH1	AIX1
PATH2	AIX2
PATH3	AIX1 and AIX3

*9. Code the RECORDSIZE specification for an alternate index when the following factors apply:

     original KSDS key length is 24 bytes
     alternate key is 11 bytes
     a maximum of 12 duplicates are allowed

*10. Enter the JCL and IDCAMS control statements from either Figure 5.2 or 5.3 or upload it from the diskette available to accompany this book as described in Appendix A. Customize the JCL for your installation and run it using the test data illustrated in Figure 5.5 and also available on diskette, expanding the records from 80 to 250 bytes as discussed in Appendix F. Examine the LISTCAT reports reproduced from this process, circle all of the data set component names that exist after the load, and explain in one sentence each what each of these components is.

NOTES

1. Those engaged in data processing are sometimes criticized for dwelling on detail. This Latin quotation, found in a novel named *Sybil*, by Benjamin Disraeli, literally means "to argue about the shadow of an ass." It can be taken idiomatically as "little things affect little minds."

6

VSAM Performance and Efficiency

It is easy to overlook the impact of KSDS attribute specifications and data set design characteristics, especially when VSAM is learned using test data sets where small data set size hides the realities of performance and efficiency. But the efficiency of online applications built using CICS and VSAM data sets and the batch processing of these same data sets is of overwhelming importance. Good performance can make or break the practicality of an entire application system, and the bulk of online system reponse time centers on input/output processes. *VSAM data set design is even more critical than CICS program logic efficiency in building practical online systems.* Proper consideration here can make an online system programmed in a fourth-generation language perform better than one programmed in raw CICS.

The performance of a VSAM data set is directly affected by its attributes as specified by the DEFINE command or as modified by the ALTER command. Critical attributes include IMBED, REPLICATE, CONTROLINTERVALSIZE, FREESPACE, VOLUMES, BUFFERSPACE, and CONTROLAREASIZE. Significant execution parameters include REGION, BUFNI, and BUFND. Important data set characteristics include the construction of the key, amount, type, and location of record maintenance, and the degree to which attributes and buffers are tailored to specific access requirements.

OVERVIEW OF FACTORS AFFECTING PERFORMANCE

Data Set Attributes

Use of the IMBED attribute will improve the performance of a data set accessed both randomly and sequentially. For time-critical applications that can afford the extra disk space, the REPLICATE attribute will reduce seek time of the index component, improving performance for random processing.

CONTROLINTERVALSIZE affects several areas of data set performance. For sequential or "browse" skip sequential processing, a very large CISIZE, such as 8,192 and up, will make more records available in a buffer than a smaller CISIZE by requiring fewer control interval accesses. Fewer index records are also required for larger CISIZEs. CONTROL-AREASIZE is determined by the space allocation attribute chosen. *A CONTROLAREA-SIZE of one cylinder guarantees that the data set will begin on a cylinder boundary, reducing I/O activity when it is accessed.* Larger CASIZEs also allow smaller index CI sizes.

The FREESPACE attribute leaves free space within control intervals and free CIs within control areas. A thorough understanding of insert and record expansion activity for the data set is required in order to determine where free space is required within the data set. Too much or too little free space or free space in the wrong area of a data set will waste disk space but, more seriously, will impede sequential and skip sequential processing.

VOLUMES can be used to physically separate the index and data component, eliminating physical disk arm contention between accesses to these components during random processing. The placement of the index component on a faster storage device will also improve performance during random processing.

BUFFERSPACE is one means of indicating the default amount of buffer space that will be allocated for the data set, but for reasons discussed in this chapter its specification should be avoided. The default that arises from its omission is insufficient for both batch random and batch sequential processing, but the appropriate place to specify the optimal quantity of buffers is in execution JCL using the AMP parameter or with CICS File Control Table (FCT) entries.

Execution Parameters

The BUFND and BUFNI options of the AMP parameter are used to allocate additional buffers for a data set at batch execution time. As illustrated in Figure 6.1 the greatest reduction in job execution time accrues from allocating the first additional buffers. The formulas for determining the maximum number of buffers that should be allocated for all types of processing follow in this chapter.

Additional buffers can be specified to obtain maximum performance with greater requirements for memory during execution. A guiding principle concerning buffers is that the use of memory resources is usually of less concern than processing performance.

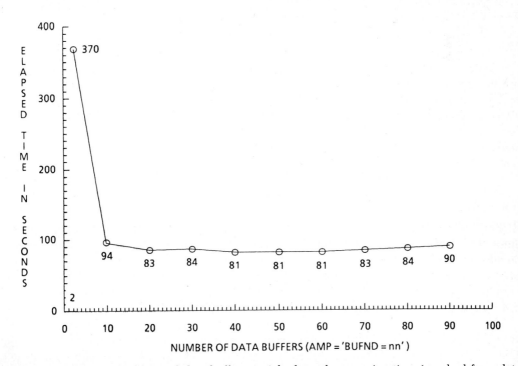

FIGURE 6.1   Effect of additional data buffers on job elapsed processing time (graphed from data provided in *VSAM Performance Study Foil Presentation*, IBM form GG22-9022).

Data Set Characteristics

The design of primary and alternate keys has a critical effect on data set performance. The most efficient keys are those that cause record additions to the data set to be spread throughout the data set. This allows control interval and control area free space to function effectively. Artificial keys such as those generated by a soundex phonetic routine are better suited to good performances than a purely alphabetic name key. Purely alphabetic keys, like last names, have certain ranges around which records will cluster—such as Smith and Jones—and other ranges that will contain relatively few records.

Keys that have a limited number of unique characters in their order (most leftward) position will cause record additions to cluster in certain locations of the data set. Keys that fall into this category include keys with a single leading alphabetic character or leading portion to which some meaning is ascribed. It is a poor design choice to form a primary key in this manner without considering how active certain of these key values will be.

Keys that start with dates or timestamps are particularly inefficient; all record additions will occur at the end of the data set since dates always advance. This makes both CA and CI free space entirely useless and will require appropriate space at the end of the data set or a secondary allocation to accommodate growth.

Keys developed with a traditional batch system approach, in which a key value is incremented upward by one for each record added, are poorly suited to online record addition. This type of key design concentrates record additions at the end of the dataset, rendering CI free space useless. To accommodate it efficiently where a particular application demands it, a technique such as preformatting of a data set with dummy records must be employed, as discussed later in this chapter.

BATCH-PROCESSING EFFICIENCY

Efficient batch access to a key sequenced data set requires some knowledge about the data set and the nature of the records being added in batch mode, but a main concern is the number of buffers allocated for the data set. The determination of an optimal number of buffers involves information about the entire data set obtainable on LISTCAT reports. This determination can be automated with a TSO CLIST. At the end of this chapter we present VSAMBUFS, a routine that not only performs the necessary computations, but also composes the actual AMP JCL parameters for various modes of data set access. Let's discuss here, however, the calculation bases for these values.

Buffer Space and the BUFFERSPACE Attribute

BUFFERSPACE, one of many data set DEFINE options, provides the means to specify the amount of space to be used for input/output buffers. *The BUFFERSPACE attribute should be omitted from DEFINE operations, however, because the number of buffers, and not the precise amount of space, is the important factor.* When the BUFFERSPACE specification is omitted, IDCAMS calculates the default buffer space so that it will accommodate one index component control interval and two data component control intervals.

The default buffer space of one index component CI and two data component CIs is always insufficient for sequential, skip sequential, random, and mixed mode processing. The number of buffers for batch processing should be set, via the AMP parameter of JCL on the DD statement for the VSAM data set, depending on the type of batch processing underway. BUFNI and BUFND subparameters of AMP control the number of buffers allocated for index and data component CIs. Similar entries in the File Control Table (FCT) for the data set govern buffer allocation for CICS access. BUFNI and BUFND override the buffer space amount arising from the data set definition and are the preferred method for specifying buffer requirements.[1]

Buffers and the AMP BUFND and BUFNI Subparameters

BUFND is the AMP subparameter used to request the number of buffers for the data component. BUFNI is the AMP subparameter that is used to request the number of buffers for the index component. The number of buffers is specified directly.

Formulas to calculate an optimal number of buffers involve strings, specified by the STRNO subparameter. Processing with COBOL in a batch environment allows for only one string, which means that only one access to a given VSAM data set is active at one time. Assembler, IMS, and CICS can use multiple strings. The process of setting the appropriate number of buffers for each type of access is called "buffer tuning."

BUFFER TUNING

Random Access Batch Processing

For purely random access batch processing, a simple rule of thumb dictates that two data buffers and at least three index buffers should be specified. For this mode of processing, additional data buffers will never be used by VSAM and will simply waste resources if specified.

Three index buffers will usually be sufficient to speed the search of the index component for the location of the data component CI in spite of CI and CA splits. Additional index buffers beyond three may allow the entire index to remain in memory, reducing to a minimum the number of I/Os required for each random access.

The following formulas should be used to determine the minimum and maximum number of buffers for random batch processing:

Minimum index buffers, random processing	=	STRNO + number of index levels − 1
Maximum index buffers, random processing	=	STRNO + number of index set records
Minimum and maximum data buffers, random processing	=	STRNO + 1

The value for STRNO will always be 1 for batch COBOL programs; for CICS programs this specification exists in control tables normally maintained by a systems programming group. The number of index levels can be found in the output of a LISTCAT command under the INDEX STATISTICS in the field called LEVELS. LISTCAT is discussed thoroughly in Chapter 8.

The number of index set records can be determined from four items of information found in the output of a LISTCAT command: INDEX REC-TOTAL, DATA CISIZE, DATA CI/CA, and DATA HI-USED-RBA. These formulas apply:

$$\frac{\text{number of sequence}}{\text{set records}} = \frac{\text{data HI-USED-RBA}}{(\text{data CI size} \times \text{data CI/CA})}$$

$$\frac{\text{number of index}}{\text{set records}} = \frac{\text{Total number of index records} -}{\text{number of sequence set records}}$$

Use these formulas and the following example as a guide in determining the number of index set records in key sequenced data sets:

Data component CISIZE   = 4,096
Data component CIs per CA   = 57
Data component HI-USED-RBA = 25,915,392
Number of sequence   = 25,915,392 / (4,096 * 57)
set records

                                = 25,915,392 / 233,472
                                = 111
Total index records   = 116
Number of index set   = 116 − 111
records

                                = 5

For this example, the minimum number of index buffers is STRNO + the number of index levels − 1, which is 1 + 3 − 1, or 3. The maximum number of index buffers is (STRNO + the number of index set records), which is 1 + 5, or 6. The optimal number of data buffers is (STRNO + 1), which is 1 + 1, or 2.

Figure 6.2 shows JCL for a job step executing a program using batch random access to a key sequenced data set. The DD statement AMP parameter is coded with the syntax necessary to use three index buffers and two data buffers.

Sequential Processing

For strictly sequential processing, one index buffer and a minimum of four data buffers should be specified. The single index buffer is sufficient for reading the index, and the

```
//STEPC     EXEC  PGM=FSBT2415,REGION=2048K
//STEPLIB    DD   DSN=SYS1.TESTLIB,
//  DISP=SHR
//BT2415E1   DD   DSN=AK00.C99.DRVTRANS,     'UPDATE TRANS
//  DISP=SHR
//BT2415E2   DD   DSN=AK00.C98.CUSTMAST,     'VSAM KSDS
//  AMP=('BUFNI=3,BUFND=2'),
//  DISP=(OLD,KEEP)
//BT2415E3   DD   SYSOUT=*                   'REPORT
//SYSOUT     DD   SYSOUT=*
//SYSUDUMP   DD   SYSOUT=A
```

FIGURE 6.2 Specifying buffers with the AMP parameter for improved batch random access processing

data buffers allow VSAM to read ahead and chain its I/O commands. The maximum number of buffers that should be specified depends on the number of CIs per track. The following formulas should be used to determine the minimum and maximum number of buffers for sequential processing:

$$
\begin{aligned}
&\text{Optimal number} \\
&\text{of index buffers,} &&= \text{STRNO} \\
&\text{sequential processing} \\
&\quad\text{Minimum data} \\
&\quad\text{buffers,} \\
&\quad\text{sequential} &&= 4 \\
&\quad\text{processing} \\
\\
&\text{Maximum data} \\
&\text{buffers,} &&= \frac{(2 \times \text{number of CIs per track})}{+ \text{STRNO}} \\
&\text{sequential} \\
&\text{processing}
\end{aligned}
$$

The number of CIs per CA is needed in order to use these formulas; it can be found in Appendix E. The number of tracks per CA where the CA is one cylinder can also be found in this appendix in the chart of physical device characteristics. The number of CIs per CA for the data component can be obtained from the output of the LISTCAT command. The determination of CIs per track is dependent on whether or not the IMBED attribute is specified. These simple formulas are used to compute it, for application in the foregoing computations:

$$
\begin{aligned}
&\text{Data CIs per} \\
&\text{track with} &&= \frac{\text{CIs per CA}}{\text{tracks per CA}} \\
&\text{NOIMBED} \\
&\text{Data CIs per} \\
&\text{track with} &&= \frac{\text{CIs per CA}}{\text{tracks per CA} - 1} \\
&\text{IMBED}
\end{aligned}
$$

A typical value for the maximum number of data buffers is 21, and results in the significant job elapsed time improvement shown in the graph of Figure 6.1. This graph deals with the use of a CI size of 4,096 on a 3380 disk device, where 10 CIs are accommodated on one track.

The foregoing formulas lead to determination of a buffer allocation that will allow one track of data to be read with one I/O operation, but the maximum number of data buffers can be adjusted upwards for larger machine environments to gain slightly more efficient I/O. In order to allow three tracks to be read with one I/O operation, the constant of "2" should be changed to "6":

$$
\begin{aligned}
&\text{Accessing three} \\
&\text{data tracks,} &&= \frac{(6 \times \text{number of CIs per track})}{+ \text{STRNO}} \\
&\text{sequential} \\
&\text{processing}
\end{aligned}
$$

Figure 6.3 shows a portion of the JCL for a job step executing a program accessing a key sequenced data set sequentially. The DD statement AMP parameter is coded to use one index buffer and 21 data buffers.

```
//STEPC      EXEC  PGM=FSBT2438,REGION=2048K
//STEPLIB    DD    DSN=SYS1.TESTLIB,
//  DISP=SHR
//BT2438E1   DD    DSN=AK00.C98.CUSTMAST,          'VSAM KSDS
//  AMP=('BUFNI=1,BUFND=21'),
//  DISP=SHR
//BT2438E2   DD    SYSOUT=*                        'REPORT
//SYSOUT     DD    SYSOUT=*
//SYSUDUMP   DD    SYSOUT=A
```

FIGURE 6.3   Specifying buffers with the AMP parameter for improved batch sequential access processing

Skip Sequential Processing

For skip sequential or mixed mode "START/browse" processing, at least three index buffers and four data buffers should be specified. The increased number of index buffers accommodates random processing to locate the desired group of keys; additional data buffers facilitate browse sequential processing.

Skip sequential processing is very much a hybrid of random and sequential processing. To compute the appropriate number of index buffers use the formula for random processing. To compute the appropriate number of data buffers use the formula for sequential processing.

Overallocation of Buffers

While providing adequate buffers is desirable, allocating too many buffers can be detrimental to performance. Buffers require memory. Using an excessive number of buffers can affect the entire computer system by causing extra virtual storage paging operations. In the graph of Figure 6.1, the slight rise in the job elapsed time in the vicinity of 70 to 90 buffers results from this fact.

Sequential Access Buffer Tuning Example

Let's assume the following conditions apply and perform buffer tuning calculations:

- control interval size of 4,096
- 3380 disk
- sequential processing

Using the chart in Appendix E we find that there are 150 CIs per CA for a CISIZE of 4,096 on a 3380 disk. For computational purposes, it's always easier to choose the number of CIs per CA with the NOIMBED option and to divide by the number of tracks per cylinder regardless of whether the IMBED or NOIMBED attribute is used. Appendix E indicates 15 tracks per cylinder on a 3380:

CIs per Track $= 150 / 15 = 10$

Maximum buffers
for sequential $= (2 * 10) + 1 = 21$
processing

and this AMP parameter will request the buffers:

```
// AMP = ('AMORG,BUFND=21,BUFNI=1'),
```

For processing a data set with these characteristics, between four and 21 data buffers should be allocated. The maximum value of 21 will allow two tracks of data to be read per I/O for maximum processing efficiency.

Memory for Buffers

The storage requirements for sequential processing of a key sequenced data set need not be calculated but are informative for example purposes. For a KSDS with index CI of 1,024 bytes and data CI of 8,192 bytes, the foregoing formulas indicate one index buffer and 21 data buffers. The memory requirement is thus:

$$\text{Required virtual storage} = \frac{\text{(number of index buffers} \times \text{index CI size)} +}{\text{(number of data buffers} \times \text{data CI size)}}$$

$= (1 \times 1,024) + (21 \times 8,192)$
$= 1,024 + 172,032$
$= 173,056$ or about 173K

A minor additional impact in buffer space requirements is imposed by the fact that buffers are allocated in 4K byte increments. The actual storage requirements imposed by the buffers specified will be rounded up to 176K. This is, of course, in addition to the memory required for the buffers dealing with I/O on other files and memory needed for the program itself.

Installations set a default amount of main storage to be obtained for each execution step or job stream. If this is insufficient, the REGION parameter must be used to obtain the amount required. The REGION parameter specifies the amount of memory to be reserved for the program and buffers for all data sets opened by the program. A practical approach is to begin testing a VSAM program specifying a large amount for the REGION parameter on the job step executing it, such as 2048K, and to reduce this in subsequent tests until the value proves insufficient.

AUTOMATING BUFFER TUNING: TSO CLIST *VSAMBUFS*

A computational TSO CLIST provides a convenient way to calculate the optimum number of key sequenced data set data and index buffers for random, sequential, and mixed mode processing. The source code for VSAMBUFS and the programs invoked by it are provided in Appendix F. Appendix A indicates how to obtain these on nominal-cost diskette for upload to a mainframe. The CLIST will function for all existing VSAM KSDS data sets with a CA size of one cylinder; the only input requirement is the data set name of the KSDS.

VSAMBUFS prompts for and passes the data set name to a COBOL program named VBUFCALC, which constructs a LISTCAT command and then invokes IDCAMS. The output from IDCAMS is written to a temporary data set opened by VBUFCALC. Several important items of information are extracted from the LISTCAT output, including the KSDS CISIZE, the number of CIs per CA, the status of the IMBED/NOIMBED attribute, HI-USED-RBA, the number of tracks per CA for the data component, and REC-TOTAL and LEVELS from the index component. The formulas described in this chapter are used by the program to determine the minimum and maximum batch buffer requirements for the three modes of processing.

Figure 6.4 shows VSAMBUF output for AK00.C98.CUSTMAST, the data set defined in Chapter 2. Not only does the CLIST calculate and tell the number of buffers for each component for each of the three processing modes, we built in a little fanciness. The CLIST composes the specific AMP subparameter coding for BUFND and BUFNI and writes this to the screen. A hardcopy taken with a screen print readily serves as a guide to composition or enhancement of JCL accessing this data set and for documentation.

If you input the name of an entry sequenced data set or a relative record data set to VSAMBUFS, the following message is displayed:

```
THE FOLLOWING IS NOT A KSDS
NONVSAM———AK00.C98.CNTLCARD : IN—CAT——VENDOR.UCAT1
   CLIST INVOKED BY RICHG at 08:43:24 on 01/31/88
```

If the data set name entered does not exist or is not cataloged, the following message is displayed:

```
THE FOLLOWING IS NOT A KSDS
IDC3012I ENTRY AK00.C98.CUSTMESS NOT FOUND.  IDC30091 ** VSAM
```

```
      PRACTICAL VSAM - JOHN WILEY AND SONS, 1988 - ISBN 0-471-85107-8
           OPTIMUM VSAM BATCH BUFFERS FOR AK00.C98.CUSTMAST

                              MIN  MAX
      RANDOM        INDEX     003  003
                    DATA      002  002
      SEQUENTIAL    INDEX     001  001
                    DATA      004  021
      MIXED MODE    INDEX     003  003
                    DATA      004  021

      AMP PARAMETER FOR RANDOM PROCESSING IS
           AMP=('BUFNI=003,BUFND=002')

      AMP PARAMETER FOR SEQUENTIAL PROCESSING IS
           AMP=('BUFNI=001,BUFND=009')

      AMP PARAMETER FOR MIXED PROCESSING IS
           AMP=('BUFNI=003,BUFND=009')

      CLIST INVOKED BY BT05686 AT 18:40:08 ON 01/03/88
```

FIGURE 6.4 Output of VSAMBUFS CLIST showing automatic computation of optimal AMP buffer parameters for random, sequential, and mixed processing modes (3350 disk)

```
CATALOG RETURN CODE IS 8
  CLIST INVOKED BY RICHG AT 08:44:57 ON 01/31/88
```

If an unexpected problem occurs, VSAMBUFS displays:

```
PREMATURE EOF ON EXTRACT FILE
  CLIST INVOKED BY RICHG AT 08:45:31 ON 01/31/88
```

VSAMBUFS assumes that the control area size of the KSDS is one cylinder. If the control area is not one cylinder in size, VSAMBUFS will slightly miscalculate the buffer requirements, but the error will not have a negative effect on the performance of the data set.

PLANNING FOR DATA SET ACTIVITY

Free space in a VSAM key sequenced data set supports record insertion or extension. When a record is added to a data set or a record in a variable length data set is lengthened, all records with key values higher than the one affected are shifted farther in the control interval within the limit of available free space. If enough free space exists to allow a record insertion, the manipulation of data ends at this point. If insufficient room exists within the control interval to allow the insertion of a record, one or another series of events is triggered, depending on the availability of free space in the control area.

Control Interval Split

A control interval split occurs when insufficient free space exists within a control interval to accommodate the insertion or lengthening of a record. When a control interval split occurs, some of the records in the control interval remain within it and some of the records are moved to a free control interval within the control area. The determination of which records remain within the control interval and which records are moved to a free control interval depends on where within the control interval the new record is to be inserted and whether the insertion was accomplished randomly or sequentially.

Random and skip-sequential record insertions and record expansions cause splits near the middle of the control interval. Sequential insertions cause splits at the point in the control interval where the specified percentage of free space is reached. Each control interval split causes significant I/O: the data set index is updated, the sequence set is read, the old control interval is read, the new control interval is written, the sequence set is updated and rewritten, and the old control interval is updated and rewritten.

Control Area Split

A control area split is triggered by a control interval split that cannot be undertaken due to the lack of a free control interval within the applicable control area. The control interval split is postponed until after the control area split is accomplished.

At least five I/O operations are necessary to accomplish a control area split. For this split a new control area is created at the end of the data set, each control interval in the new control area is formatted, a sequence set record is created for the new control area, the index set is updated, and one-half of the control intervals are moved, one at a time, to the new control area. These actions precede the control interval split, which is then processed. Control interval splits can now occur within both control areas without the need for additional control area splits until a control area again cannot accommodate a control interval split.

Figure 6.5(a) depicts a completely filled control area and one completely empty, containing "control area free space," or CAFS. Figure 6.5(b) shows how a control area split is processed when record additions are occurring in sequential mode. Figure 6.5(c) illustrates how the split is processed when the need for it arises in random access or skip sequential mode.

Each control area split causes the catalog to be updated, allocation processing to occur to create a new control area, and prompts extensive updating of the index component. Control area splits have a more significant effect on sequential access than on direct processing because records are no longer in physical sequence after a control area split. More

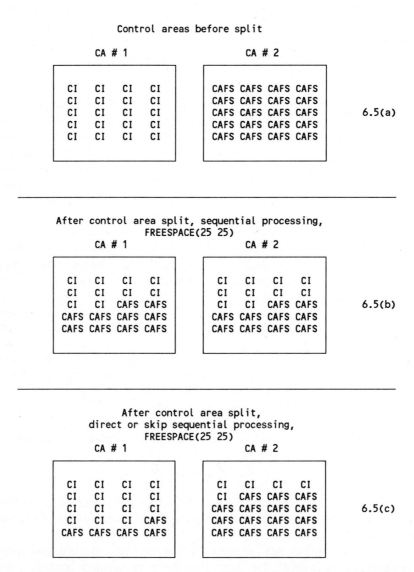

FIGURE 6.5 (a) Graphic depiction of a completely filled control area and a control area consisting completely of control area free space (CAFS); (b) the two control areas as they would appear after a control area split that occurred during sequential mode processing; (c) the two control areas as they would appear after a control area split that occurred during random or skip sequential mode processing

accesses to the index set occur and greater I/O activity is required to deliver the records in sequence when a large number of control area splits exist.

Direct (Key Access) Inserts

If room exists within the control interval, records added randomly will be added to the control interval using either space formerly occupied by a deleted record or existing free space. When no room exists within a control interval to accommodate a new record, a control interval split occurs or a single record is either added or moved to an empty control interval, as shown in Figure 6.6(a).

If the record being inserted in a keyed access belongs in the beginning of a filled control interval, the last record in the control interval is moved to a free control interval. If the record being added to a filled control interval belongs in the middle of the control interval, a split occurs with the higher half of the keys being moved to the new control interval. If the record belongs at the end of a filled control interval, it will be put into a new control interval by itself. Figure 6.6(b) illustrates these procedures when freespace has been specified and exists.

Sequential Inserts

If room exists within the control interval, records added sequentially will be inserted into the control interval using either space formerly occupied by deleted records or existing free space. When no room exists within a control interval to accommodate a new record, either a control interval split occurs or a single record is added or moved to an empty control interval, as illustrated in Figure 6.7(a).

The handling of a control interval split for sequential insert depends on certain factors. If the record being added belongs in the beginning of the control interval, it is added to a free control interval. If the record being added belongs in the middle of the control interval, a split occurs at the point of the insert, and all records with higher key value are move to a free control interval. If the record belongs at the end of the control interval, it alone will be put into a new control interval.

Free space is used within a control interval when records are inserted after the first record in the control interval and before the last record within the control interval. When records are added after the last record within a control interval, free space is honored, and the new record goes into a free control interval. Figure 6.7(b) shows the effect of sequential inserts when the data set has free space.

Mass Insertion

VSAM automatically uses a special mode for the insertion of records under certain conditions. The mass insertion technique reserves free space as defined for the data set and does not perform control interval or control area splits. Only one control interval split occurs if records are to be inserted between two existing records. After the control interval split, VSAM adds the records into free control intervals. Because there are no control interval splits, except the first, this technique improves loading time and dramatically reduces disk space usage.

Mass insertion with ACCESS MODE IS SEQUENTIAL differs from mass insertion with DYNAMIC mode. The conditions that initiate it in sequential mode are:

- the data set is opened for OUTPUT
- ACCESS MODE IS SEQUENTIAL is coded
- records to be inserted are sorted in ascending sequence

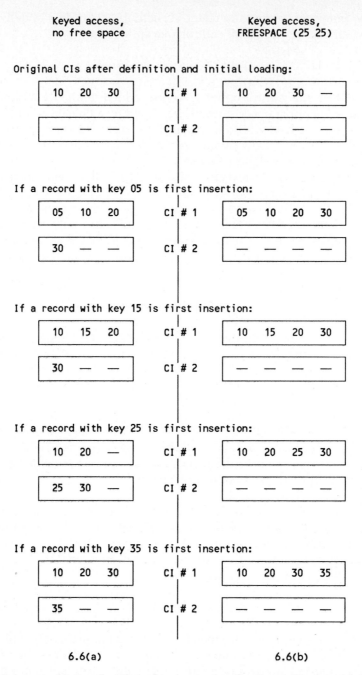

FIGURE 6.6 (a) A control interval with no free space specification as it appears initially and after each of four separate random access record inserts (each insert illustrated occurs into the CI as initially found, they are not accumulative); (b) a control interval with a free space specification as it appears initially and after each of four separate random access record inserts.

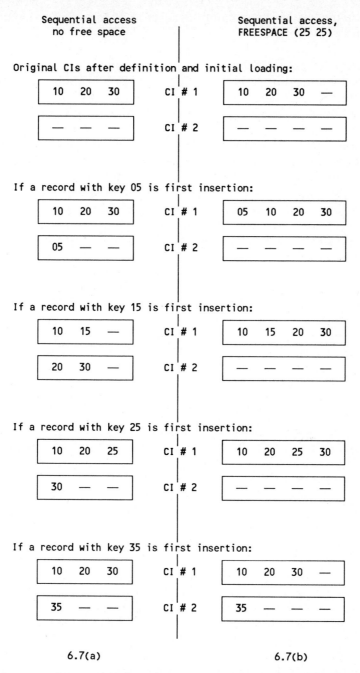

6.7(a)   6.7(b)

FIGURE 6.7 (a) A control interval with no free space specification as it appears initially and after each of four separate sequential access record inserts (each insert illustrated occurs into the CI as initially found, they are not accumulative); (b) a control interval with a free space specification as it appears initially and after each of four separate sequential access record inserts.

- records are being written to an empty data set or fit between two existing records, or are at the end of the data set

When ACCESS MODE IS DYNAMIC is specified and a series of write requests are issued for adjacent ascending records, COBOL invokes VSAM mass insertion mode, and it remains in effect until the sequential chain of records is broken. Depending on the keys to be added, a COBOL program can switch between the direct insert mode and the mass insertion mode.

The mass insertion technique reserves free space in control intervals and control areas on the assumption that more records will be added at random later, with key values between those being written to the data set. If the records being written early carry keys with no key values possible between them—such as with a numeric key incremented by one for each record—it is wise to alter data set FREESPACE to (0 0) before the mass insertion and then alter it again afterward to the appropriate amount. This way no free space is specified for the records that comprise a solid block; free space is not needed for such records unless they are of variable-length format and are subject to lengthening by updates.

SUMMARY OF VSAM EFFICIENCY GUIDELINES

It is wise to choose data elements for a data set primary key that tend to spread record insertion activity across the whole data set. Alternatively, accommodate concentrated or clumped random insertions with either preformatted control intervals or adequate free space and reorganizations.

Do not specify BUFFERSPACE when defining a key sequenced data set; let VSAM set assign the default.

Obtain additional buffers for batch processing with the JCL AMP BUFNI and the BUFND parameters, according to the formulas shown here, or by using TSO CLIST VSAMBUFS. Take care not to overallocate buffers, however, becauses this reaches the point of diminishing returns and may be counterproductive.

Obtain additional buffers for online processing with BUFNI and BUFND parameters in the File Control Table (FCT) for the data set, or use the Local Shared Resource facility, the default starting with CICS release 1.7, to allow CICS to allocate buffers from a pool. To optimize online response time, monitor the CICS "waiting on strings" count and add strings until no waiting on strings occurs, but allocate enough data buffers—one per string, plus one—to accommodate this.

Control interval splits and especially control area splits are costly in terms of extra I/O operations for access as well as initial handling. Arrange batch jobs to reorganize a data set with a frequency suited to its activity as indicated by condition monitoring described in Chapter 8 and the job streams described in Chapter 9.

Sort record addition transactions into ascending sequence to make batch programs use the direct insert technique. Even better, segregate processing so that bulk record additions are integrated with data set backup and reloading, making the record additions a logical merge of transactions with a tape-stored copy of the data set. The reloading of this to the VSAM data set will produce no free space impairment of CI/CA splits and will take only slightly more time than regular KSDS reorganization processing.

REVIEW QUESTIONS AND (*)EXERCISES

1. Explain the nature of FREESPACE specification coding and what the two values coded within it mean.

2. What JCL coding features are used to allocate additional buffers for the index and data components of a key sequenced data set?

3. The greatest impact in sequential processing speed is gained by changing from the default of two data component buffers to approximately how many such buffers?

4. Discuss what types of keys are efficient for key sequenced data set construction as well as what types of keys are particularly inefficient.

5. Discuss the role and recommended handling of the BUFFERSPACE and BUFSP specifications.

6. Explain how these attributes can affect the performance of a key sequenced data set:

   IMBED
   REPLICATE
   CONTROLINTERVALSIZE
   FREESPACE
   VOLUMES

7. For both sequential and random modes of processing, explain what happens when a control interval split is necessary and there are no empty control intervals left in the control area. Tell what effect this has on efficiency.

*8. Based on the following information, determine the optimum number of index and data buffers for a data set for each of the three processing modes: a) sequential b) random and c) mixed mode skip sequential.

   Disk = 3380
   Data control interval size = 2,048
   IMBED option
   Number of index set records = 2

*9. Based on the answers for Question 8, determine the memory requirements for each processing mode.

*10. Modify the key sequenced data set delete, define, and loading job stream you created for exercise item 8 of Chapter 2 so that it specifies the appropriate number of index and data buffers for the data set. Rerun the job stream, increasing the memory allocated to the IDCAMS step if necessary, and note the effect on processing time. Note: Unless you expand the number of test data records to a few thousand or more, the processing efficiency of the additional buffers may be masked by other factors.

NOTES

1. Use of the BUFSP subparameter is not recommended. The BUFNI and BUFND subparameters provide precisely the means to specify the quantity of buffers needed, and their use is much simpler and more reliable. BUFSP directly overrides the BUFFERSPACE amount defined for a data set. If specified, it can only be used to increase buffer space; if BUFSP specifies an amount less than that already defined, the BUFSP subparameter is ignored, as is true for the BUFNI and BUFND subparameters.

When BUFSP is specified, VSAM divides buffer space between the data and index components, depending on how the data set is being processed. When BUFSP, BUFNI, and BUFND are specified and BUFSP requests more space than both BUFNI and BUFND combined, VSAM honors the BUFNI and BUFND requests. Excess memory is given to index buffers if processing is random, or one more buffer for the index and the excess to the data component if the access is sequential.

═══ 7 ═══

COBOL Programming and VSAM

Programs written in COBOL predominate in the business data processing environment. VSAM data sets are accessed as readily by COBOL programs as are ordinary sequential or partitioned data sets. When a COBOL program accesses a VSAM data set, however, source code and job control language specifications meeting the requirements of VSAM must be used.

In this chapter, we illustrate the COBOL and JCL needed to access key sequenced data sets for normal sequential, START and READ/NEXT, alternate key access, and add/change/delete keyed access.[1] We present a modularization of input-output logic made desirable by some of VSAM's processing requirements and the use of FILE-STATUS necessitated by VSAM. We also consider the benefits provided by modern I/O logic module patterns and how an add/change/delete program can make use of them.

Complete data set and program examples are vital to understanding KSDS and COBOL usage. Throughout this chapter we will use a data set created with the IDCAMS control statements and JCL illustrated in Chapter 5. The data set, named AK00.C98.CUSTMAST, contains fixed-length 250-byte records representing customer information for an enterprise. Two alternate indexes are defined for the data set. In the programs and discussion that follow, this data set is assumed to have been loaded with the test data records illustrated in Figure 5.4 of Chapter 5.

SEQUENTIAL ACCESS TO A KEY SEQUENCED DATA SET

The simplest COBOL access to a key sequenced data set occurs when the KSDS is read from beginning to end in a sequential manner. This is the best place to start in considering the programming requirements of VSAM because it is a type of access that nearly every programmer has already experienced with ordinary data sets.

Program PSD183 illustrated in Figure 7.1 is a simple file-to-print routine that was designed to access an ordinary sequential data set. This program reads 80-byte card image records, each carrying the name of a different state, and lists the records on paper with page and column headings. A program such as PSD183 is as simple a program as one might find in a business data processing environment.[2]

Accessing a KSDS Sequentially

Program VSD183 depicted in Figure 7.2 has been built from PSD183 for the purpose of producing a simple listing of key sequenced data set AK00.C98.CUSTMAST. The MVS

```
000100 IDENTIFICATION DIVISION.
000200 PROGRAM-ID.     PSD183.
000300 AUTHOR.         J JANOSSY.
000400 INSTALLATION.   DEPAUL UNIVERSITY.
000500 DATE-WRITTEN.   FEB 1984.
000600 DATE-COMPILED.
000700*REMARKS.        FOR IBM COBOL-VS
000800*                VERSION 02    LAST CHANGE 03-15-84   ORIG 02-07-84
000900*                FILE-TO-PRINT PROGRAM.  READS A FILE OF RECORDS
001000*                AND PRODUCES A PRINTLINE FOR EACH RECORD.
001100*
001200 ENVIRONMENT DIVISION.
001300 CONFIGURATION SECTION.
001400 SOURCE-COMPUTER. IBM-4381.
001500 OBJECT-COMPUTER. IBM-4381.
001600 SPECIAL-NAMES.  C01 IS PAGE-EJECT.
001700 INPUT-OUTPUT SECTION.
001800 FILE-CONTROL.
001900     SELECT DATAFILE  ASSIGN TO UT-S-INDATA1.
002000     SELECT REPORT1   ASSIGN TO UT-S-OTREPT1.
002100*
002200 DATA DIVISION.
002300 FILE SECTION.
002400*
002500 FD  DATAFILE
002600     LABEL RECORDS ARE STANDARD
002700     BLOCK CONTAINS 0 RECORDS
002800     RECORD CONTAINS 80 CHARACTERS.
002900 01  DATAFILE-REC                    PIC X(80).
003000*
003100 FD  REPORT1
003200     LABEL RECORDS ARE OMITTED
003300     BLOCK CONTAINS 0 RECORDS
003400     RECORD CONTAINS 133 CHARACTERS.
003500 01  REPORT1-REC                     PIC X(133).
003600/
003700 WORKING-STORAGE SECTION.
003800 01  FILLER  PIC X(23)  VALUE   '*WORKING STORAGE START*'.
003900*
004000 01  WS-FLAGS.
004100     12 F1-EOF-FLAG                  PIC X(1)  VALUE 'M'.
004200        88 F1-EOF-DATAFILE-END                 VALUE 'E'.
004300*
004400 01  WS-COUNTERS.
004500     12 WS-DATAFILE-IN-COUNT         PIC S9(5) VALUE +0.
004600     12 WS-DATAFILE-OUT-COUNT        PIC S9(5) VALUE +0.
004700*
004800 01  DATAFILE-INPUT-AREA.
004900     12 DFI-STATE-NAME               PIC X(20).
005000     12 DFI-STATE-POP                PIC X(8).
005100     12 DFI-STATE-CAPITAL            PIC X(20).
005200     12 DFI-STATE-AREA               PIC X(8).
005300     12 DFI-STATE-ABBREV             PIC X(2).
005400     12 DFI-STATEHOOD-YR             PIC X(4).
005500     12 FILLER                       PIC X(18).
005600*
005700 01  REPORT1-COUNTERS.
005800     12 R1-LINE-LIMIT                PIC S9(2) VALUE +60.
005900     12 R1-NORMAL-LINE-SPACING       PIC S9(2) VALUE +2.
006000     12 R1-LINES-REMAINING           PIC S9(2) VALUE +0.
006100     12 R1-PAGE-COUNT                PIC S9(3) VALUE +0.
006200     12 R1-WANTED-LINE-SPACING       PIC S9(3) VALUE +0.
006300     12 R1-PRINT-SLOT                PIC X(133).
006400*
006500 01  R1-PAGE-HDR1.
006600     12 FILLER                       PIC X(1).
```

FIGURE 7.1 Program PSD183, a COBOL file-to-print program accessing an ordinary sequential data set

```
006700        12 FILLER                   PIC X(72)  VALUE ALL '*'.
006800        12 FILLER                   PIC X(60)  VALUE ALL ' '.
006900*
007000 01  R1-PAGE-HDR2.
007100        12 FILLER                   PIC X(1).
007200        12 FILLER                   PIC X(4)   VALUE '*   '.
007300        12 R1-PH2-PGM-TITLE         PIC X(18)  VALUE ALL 'X'.
007400        12 FILLER                   PIC X(14)  VALUE
007500            ' // PROGRAM '.
007600        12 R1-PH2-PGM-ID            PIC X(6)   VALUE ALL 'X'.
007700        12 FILLER                   PIC X(6)   VALUE '   *  '.
007800        12 R1-PH2-DATE              PIC X(8).
007900        12 FILLER                   PIC X(10)  VALUE '  *  PAGE '.
008000        12 R1-PH2-PAGE-NO           PIC ZZ9.
008100        12 FILLER                   PIC X(3)   VALUE '  *'.
008200        12 FILLER                   PIC X(60)  VALUE ALL ' '.
008300*
008400 01  R1-COL-HDR1.
008500        12 FILLER                   PIC X(1).
008600        12 FILLER   PIC X(22)  VALUE '      STATE NAME        '.
008700        12 FILLER   PIC X(22)  VALUE 'ABBREV    POP      AREA'.
008800        12 FILLER   PIC X(22)  VALUE '          CAPITAL      '.
008900        12 FILLER   PIC X(22)  VALUE '  YEAR                 '.
009000        12 FILLER   PIC X(22)  VALUE '                       '.
009100        12 FILLER   PIC X(22)  VALUE '                       '.
009200*
009300 01  R1-COL-HDR2.
009400        12 FILLER                   PIC X(1).
009500        12 FILLER   PIC X(22)  VALUE '<-----------------> '.
009600        12 FILLER   PIC X(22)  VALUE ' --   <------> <-----'.
009700        12 FILLER   PIC X(22)  VALUE '-> <----------------'.
009800        12 FILLER   PIC X(22)  VALUE '> <-->               '.
009900        12 FILLER   PIC X(22)  VALUE '                     '.
010000        12 FILLER   PIC X(22)  VALUE '                     '.
010100*
010200 01  R1-DETLINE.
010300        12 FILLER                   PIC X(1).
010400        12 R1-DL-NAME               PIC X(20).
010500        12 FILLER                   PIC X(4)   VALUE ALL ' '.
010600        12 R1-DL-ABBREV             PIC X(2).
010700        12 FILLER                   PIC X(3)   VALUE ALL ' '.
010800        12 R1-DL-POP                PIC X(8).
010900        12 FILLER                   PIC X(1)   VALUE ' '.
011000        12 R1-DL-AREA               PIC X(8).
011100        12 FILLER                   PIC X(1)   VALUE ' '.
011200        12 R1-DL-CAPITAL            PIC X(20).
011300        12 FILLER                   PIC X(1)   VALUE ' '.
011400        12 R1-DL-YR                 PIC X(4).
011500        12 FILLER                   PIC X(60)  VALUE ALL ' '.
011600*
011700 01  R1-ENDLINE.
011800        12 FILLER                   PIC X(1).
011900        12 FILLER   PIC X(22)  VALUE '*** END OF JOB        '.
012000        12 FILLER   PIC X(13)  VALUE 'RECORDS READ '.
012100        12 R1-EL-IN-COUNT           PIC ZZ,ZZ9.
012200        12 FILLER   PIC X(21)  VALUE '    RECORDS PRINTED '.
012300        12 R1-EL-OUT-COUNT          PIC ZZ,ZZ9.
012400        12 FILLER   PIC X(64)  VALUE ALL ' '.
012500/
012600 PROCEDURE DIVISION.
012700*
012800 0000-MAINLINE.
012900        PERFORM 1000-BOJ.
013000        PERFORM 2000-PROCESS UNTIL F1-EOF-FLAG EQUAL 'E'.
013100        PERFORM 3000-EOJ.
013200        STOP RUN.
013300*
```

FIGURE 7.1   (Continued)

```
013400 1000-BOJ.
013500     PERFORM 9000-INIT.
013600     OPEN  INPUT DATAFILE  OUTPUT REPORT1.
013700     PERFORM 2900-R1-NEWPAGE.
013800     PERFORM 2700-READ-DATAFILE.
013900*
014000 2000-PROCESS.
014100     PERFORM 2050-FILL-DETLINE.
014200     MOVE R1-NORMAL-LINE-SPACING TO R1-WANTED-LINE-SPACING.
014300     PERFORM 2100-WRITE-R1-OUTPUT.
014400     ADD +1 TO WS-DATAFILE-OUT-COUNT.
014500     PERFORM 2700-READ-DATAFILE.
014600*
014700 2050-FILL-DETLINE.
014800     MOVE DFI-STATE-NAME      TO R1-DL-NAME.
014900     MOVE DFI-STATE-ABBREV    TO R1-DL-ABBREV.
015000     MOVE DFI-STATEHOOD-YR    TO R1-DL-YR.
015100     MOVE DFI-STATE-POP       TO R1-DL-POP.
015200     MOVE DFI-STATE-AREA      TO R1-DL-AREA.
015300     MOVE DFI-STATE-CAPITAL   TO R1-DL-CAPITAL.
015400     MOVE R1-DETLINE TO R1-PRINT-SLOT.
015500*
015600 2100-WRITE-R1-OUTPUT.
015700     IF R1-LINES-REMAINING IS LESS THAN R1-WANTED-LINE-SPACING
015800         PERFORM 2900-R1-NEWPAGE.
015900     WRITE REPORT1-REC FROM R1-PRINT-SLOT
016000         AFTER ADVANCING R1-WANTED-LINE-SPACING LINES.
016100     COMPUTE R1-LINES-REMAINING =
016200         (R1-LINES-REMAINING - R1-WANTED-LINE-SPACING).
016300*
016400 2700-READ-DATAFILE.
016500     READ DATAFILE INTO DATAFILE-INPUT-AREA
016600         AT END
016700             MOVE 'E' TO F1-EOF-FLAG.
016800     IF F1-EOF-FLAG NOT EQUAL 'E'
016900         ADD +1 TO WS-DATAFILE-IN-COUNT.
017000*
017100 2900-R1-NEWPAGE.
017200     ADD +1 TO R1-PAGE-COUNT.
017300     MOVE R1-PAGE-COUNT TO R1-PH2-PAGE-NO.
017400     WRITE REPORT1-REC FROM R1-PAGE-HDR1
017500         AFTER ADVANCING PAGE-EJECT.
017600     WRITE REPORT1-REC FROM R1-PAGE-HDR2 AFTER ADVANCING 1 LINES.
017700     WRITE REPORT1-REC FROM R1-PAGE-HDR1 AFTER ADVANCING 1 LINES.
017800     WRITE REPORT1-REC FROM R1-COL-HDR1  AFTER ADVANCING 4 LINES.
017900     WRITE REPORT1-REC FROM R1-COL-HDR2  AFTER ADVANCING 1 LINES.
018000     MOVE SPACES TO REPORT1-REC.
018100     WRITE REPORT1-REC AFTER ADVANCING 2 LINES.
018200     COMPUTE R1-LINES-REMAINING = (R1-LINE-LIMIT - 10).
018300     MOVE R1-NORMAL-LINE-SPACING TO R1-WANTED-LINE-SPACING.
018400*
018500 3000-EOJ.
018600     MOVE WS-DATAFILE-IN-COUNT TO R1-EL-IN-COUNT.
018700     MOVE WS-DATAFILE-OUT-COUNT TO R1-EL-OUT-COUNT.
018800     MOVE R1-ENDLINE TO R1-PRINT-SLOT.
018900     MOVE +3 TO R1-WANTED-LINE-SPACING.
019000     PERFORM 2100-WRITE-R1-OUTPUT.
019100     CLOSE  DATAFILE  REPORT1.
019200*
019300 9000-INIT.
019400     MOVE 'STATE DATA LISTING' TO R1-PH2-PGM-TITLE.
019500     MOVE 'PSD183' TO R1-PH2-PGM-ID.
019600     MOVE CURRENT-DATE TO R1-PH2-DATE.
```

FIGURE 7.1   (Continued)

```
000100 IDENTIFICATION DIVISION.
000200 PROGRAM-ID.    VSD183.
000300 AUTHOR.        J JANOSSY.
000400 INSTALLATION. DEPAUL UNIVERSITY.
000500 DATE-WRITTEN. MAY 1987.
000600 DATE-COMPILED.
000700*REMARKS.       FOR IBM VSCOBOL
000800*               VERSION 01    LAST CHANGE 05-07-87    ORIG 05-07-87
000900*               FILE-TO-PRINT PROGRAM. READS A VSAM DATA SET
001000*               AND PRODUCES A PRINTLINE FOR EACH RECORD.
001100*
001200 ENVIRONMENT DIVISION.
001300 CONFIGURATION SECTION.
001400 SOURCE-COMPUTER.  IBM-4381.
001500 OBJECT-COMPUTER.  IBM-4381.
001600 SPECIAL-NAMES.  C01 IS PAGE-EJECT.
001700 INPUT-OUTPUT SECTION.
001800 FILE-CONTROL.
001900     SELECT VSAMFILE  ASSIGN TO       VSAMCSM
002000          ORGANIZATION IS INDEXED
002100          ACCESS MODE IS SEQUENTIAL
002200          RECORD KEY IS FD-ACCOUNT-NO-KEY
002300          FILE STATUS IS VSAM1-FS.
002400     SELECT REPORT1   ASSIGN TO UT-S-VSD183U1.
002500*
002600 DATA DIVISION.
002700 FILE SECTION.
002800*
002900 FD  VSAMFILE
003000     LABEL RECORDS ARE STANDARD
003100     BLOCK CONTAINS 0 RECORDS
003200     RECORD CONTAINS 250 CHARACTERS.
003300 01  VSAMFILE-REC.
003400     12 FILLER                      PIC X(36).
003500     12 FD-ACCOUNT-NO-KEY           PIC X(8).
003600     12 FILLER                      PIC X(206).
003700*
003800 FD  REPORT1
003900     LABEL RECORDS ARE OMITTED
004000     BLOCK CONTAINS 0 RECORDS
004100     RECORD CONTAINS 133 CHARACTERS.
004200 01  REPORT1-REC                    PIC X(133).
004300/
004400 WORKING-STORAGE SECTION.
004500 01  FILLER PIC X(23)  VALUE  '*WORKING STORAGE START*'.
004600*
004700*VSAM1STD  LAST CHANGED 04-02-84  ORIGINAL 01-22-84  J JANOSSY
004800*********************************************************************
004900*      STANDARD VSAM FILE STATUS FIELD DEFINITION (1)            *
005000*********************************************************************
005100 01  VSAM1-FS.
005200     05 VSAM1-FS-LEFT-RIGHT.
005300        10 VSAM1-FS-LEFT       PIC X(1).
005400           88 VSAM1-ACTION-OK              VALUE '0'.
005500           88 VSAM1-SEQ-EOF               VALUE '1'.
005600        10 FILLER          PIC X(1).
005700     05 VSAM1-FS-FULL   REDEFINES
005800        VSAM1-FS-LEFT-RIGHT     PIC X(2).
005900           88 VSAM1-WRITE-OUT-SEQ         VALUE '21'.
006000           88 VSAM1-DUP-PRIME-ALT-KEY     VALUE '22'.
006100           88 VSAM1-REC-NOT-FOUND         VALUE '23'.
006200           88 VSAM1-OPEN-OK               VALUE '00'.
006300*
006400 01  WS-FLAGS.
006500     12 F1-EOF-FLAG                 PIC X(1)  VALUE 'M'.
```

FIGURE 7.2 Program VSD183, built from PSD183 to sequentially access and print the records from KSDS

```
006600          88 F1-EOF-VSAMFILE-END                   VALUE 'E'.
006700*
006800 01  WS-COUNTERS.
006900      12 WS-VSAMFILE-IN-COUNT         PIC S9(5) VALUE +0.
007000      12 WS-VSAMFILE-OUT-COUNT        PIC S9(5) VALUE +0.
007100*
007200 01  VSAMFILE-INPUT-AREA.
007300      12 VFI-OLD-ID-NO                PIC X(9).
007400      12 VFI-NAME-AIX.
007500         15 VFI-NAMEAIX-CUSTOMER.
007600            18 VFI-NAMEAIX-LASTNAME   PIC X(18).
007700            18 VFI-NAMEAIX-FIRSTNAME  PIC X(9).
007800      12 VFI-ACCOUNT-NO-KEY           PIC X(8).
007900      12 VFI-ADDRAIX.
008000         15 VFI-ADDRAIX-ST-DIREC      PIC X(1).
008100         15 VFI-ADDRAIX-ST-NAME       PIC X(15).
008200         15 VFI-ADDRAIX-HOUSE-NO      PIC X(5).
008300         15 VFI-ADDRAIX-APT-NO        PIC X(5).
008400      12 VFI-RECORD-DATA.
008500         15 VFI-TWO-LETTERS           PIC X(2).
008600         15 FILLER                    PIC X(178).
008700*
008800 01  REPORT1-COUNTERS.
008900      12 R1-LINE-LIMIT                PIC S9(2) VALUE +60.
009000      12 R1-NORMAL-LINE-SPACING       PIC S9(2) VALUE +2.
009100      12 R1-LINES-REMAINING           PIC S9(2) VALUE +0.
009200      12 R1-PAGE-COUNT                PIC S9(3) VALUE +0.
009300      12 R1-WANTED-LINE-SPACING       PIC S9(3) VALUE +0.
009400      12 R1-PRINT-SLOT                PIC X(133).
009500*
009600 01  R1-PAGE-HDR1.
009700      12 FILLER                       PIC X(1).
009800      12 FILLER                       PIC X(72) VALUE ALL '*'.
009900      12 FILLER                       PIC X(60) VALUE ALL ' '.
010000*
010100 01  R1-PAGE-HDR2.
010200      12 FILLER                       PIC X(1).
010300      12 FILLER                       PIC X(4)  VALUE '*  '.
010400      12 R1-PH2-PGM-TITLE             PIC X(18) VALUE ALL 'X'.
010500      12 FILLER                       PIC X(14) VALUE
010600           ' // PROGRAM '.
010700      12 R1-PH2-PGM-ID                PIC X(6)  VALUE ALL 'X'.
010800      12 FILLER                       PIC X(6)  VALUE '   *  '.
010900      12 R1-PH2-DATE                  PIC X(8).
011000      12 FILLER                       PIC X(10) VALUE ' * PAGE '.
011100      12 R1-PH2-PAGE-NO               PIC ZZ9.
011200      12 FILLER                       PIC X(3)  VALUE ' *'.
011300      12 FILLER                       PIC X(60) VALUE ALL ' '.
011400*
011500 01  R1-COL-HDR1.
011600      12 FILLER                       PIC X(1).
011700      12 FILLER  PIC X(22) VALUE 'ACCOUNT NO       LAST'.
011800      12 FILLER  PIC X(22) VALUE ' NAME      FIRST NAME '.
011900      12 FILLER  PIC X(22) VALUE '           ADDRESS    '.
012000      12 FILLER  PIC X(22) VALUE '   APT  DATA          '.
012100      12 FILLER  PIC X(22) VALUE '                      '.
012200      12 FILLER  PIC X(22) VALUE '                      '.
012300*
012400 01  R1-COL-HDR2.
012500      12 FILLER                       PIC X(1).
012600      12 FILLER  PIC X(22) VALUE ' <------>   <-------- '.
012700      12 FILLER  PIC X(22) VALUE '--------> <--------> '.
012800      12 FILLER  PIC X(22) VALUE '<---> - <------------ '.
012900      12 FILLER  PIC X(22) VALUE '> <--->  --           '.
013000      12 FILLER  PIC X(22) VALUE '                      '.
013100      12 FILLER  PIC X(22) VALUE '                      '.
013200*
```

FIGURE 7.2 (Continued)

```
013300 01  R1-DETLINE.
013400     12 FILLER                    PIC X(1).
013500     12 FILLER                    PIC X(1)    VALUE ' '.
013600     12 R1-DL-ACCOUNT-NO-KEY      PIC X(8).
013700     12 FILLER                    PIC X(4)    VALUE ALL ' '.
013800     12 R1-DL-NAMEAIX-LASTNAME    PIC X(18).
013900     12 FILLER                    PIC X(1)    VALUE ' '.
014000     12 R1-DL-NAMEAIX-FIRSTNAME   PIC X(9).
014100     12 FILLER                    PIC X(3)    VALUE ALL ' '.
014200     12 R1-DL-ADDRAIX-HOUSE-NO    PIC X(5).
014300     12 FILLER                    PIC X(1)    VALUE ' '.
014400     12 R1-DL-ADDRAIX-ST-DIREC    PIC X(1).
014500     12 FILLER                    PIC X(1)    VALUE ' '.
014600     12 R1-DL-ADDRAIX-ST-NAME     PIC X(15).
014700     12 FILLER                    PIC X(1)    VALUE ' '.
014800     12 R1-DL-ADDRAIX-APT-NO      PIC X(5).
014900     12 FILLER                    PIC X(2)    VALUE ALL ' '.
015000     12 R1-DL-TWO-LETTERS         PIC X(2).
015100     12 FILLER                    PIC X(55)   VALUE ALL ' '.
015200*
015300 01  R1-ENDLINE.
015400     12 FILLER                    PIC X(1).
015500     12 FILLER                    PIC X(17)   VALUE
015600        '*** END OF JOB   '.
015700     12 R1-EL-IN-COUNT            PIC Z,ZZZ,ZZ9.
015800     12 FILLER                    PIC X(16)   VALUE
015900        ' RECORDS READ   '.
016000     12 R1-EL-OUT-COUNT           PIC Z,ZZZ,ZZ9.
016100     12 FILLER                    PIC X(16)   VALUE
016200        ' RECORDS PRINTED'.
016300     12 FILLER                    PIC X(65)   VALUE ALL ' '.
016400*
016500 01  R1-VSAM-PROBLEM-LINE.
016600     12 FILLER                    PIC X(1).
016700     12 FILLER                    PIC X(35)   VALUE
016800        '>>> RUN ABORTED -- FILE STATUS WAS '.
016900     12 R1-VPL-FILE-STATUS        PIC X(2).
017000     12 FILLER                    PIC X(4)    VALUE ' -- '.
017100     12 R1-VPL-MSG                PIC X(30).
017200     12 FILLER                    PIC X(61)   VALUE ALL ' '.
017300/
017400 PROCEDURE DIVISION.
017500*
017600 0000-MAINLINE.
017700     PERFORM 1000-BOJ.
017800     PERFORM 2000-PROCESS UNTIL F1-EOF-FLAG EQUAL 'E'.
017900     PERFORM 3000-EOJ.
018000     STOP RUN.
018100*
018200 1000-BOJ.
018300     PERFORM 9000-INIT.
018400     OPEN  OUTPUT REPORT1.
018500     PERFORM 9101-VSAM1-OPEN.
018600     PERFORM 2900-R1-NEWPAGE.
018700     PERFORM 2700-READ-VSAMFILE.
018800*
018900 2000-PROCESS.
019000     PERFORM 2050-FILL-DETLINE.
019100     MOVE R1-NORMAL-LINE-SPACING TO R1-WANTED-LINE-SPACING.
019200     PERFORM 2100-WRITE-R1-OUTPUT.
019300     ADD +1 TO WS-VSAMFILE-OUT-COUNT.
019400     PERFORM 2700-READ-VSAMFILE.
019500*
019600 2050-FILL-DETLINE.
019700     MOVE VFI-ACCOUNT-NO-KEY     TO R1-DL-ACCOUNT-NO-KEY.
019800     MOVE VFI-NAMEAIX-LASTNAME   TO R1-DL-NAMEAIX-LASTNAME.
019900     MOVE VFI-NAMEAIX-FIRSTNAME  TO R1-DL-NAMEAIX-FIRSTNAME.
```

FIGURE 7.2   (Continued)

```
020000      MOVE VFI-ADDRAIX-HOUSE-NO    TO R1-DL-ADDRAIX-HOUSE-NO.
020100      MOVE VFI-ADDRAIX-ST-DIREC    TO R1-DL-ADDRAIX-ST-DIREC.
020200      MOVE VFI-ADDRAIX-ST-NAME     TO R1-DL-ADDRAIX-ST-NAME.
020300      MOVE VFI-ADDRAIX-APT-NO      TO R1-DL-ADDRAIX-APT-NO.
020400      MOVE VFI-TWO-LETTERS         TO R1-DL-TWO-LETTERS.
020500      MOVE R1-DETLINE TO R1-PRINT-SLOT.
020600*
020700 2100-WRITE-R1-OUTPUT.
020800      IF R1-LINES-REMAINING IS LESS THAN R1-WANTED-LINE-SPACING
020900          PERFORM 2900-R1-NEWPAGE.
021000      WRITE REPORT1-REC FROM R1-PRINT-SLOT
021100          AFTER ADVANCING R1-WANTED-LINE-SPACING LINES.
021200      COMPUTE R1-LINES-REMAINING =
021300          (R1-LINES-REMAINING - R1-WANTED-LINE-SPACING).
021400*
021500 2700-READ-VSAMFILE.
021600      READ VSAMFILE INTO VSAMFILE-INPUT-AREA.
021700      IF VSAM1-ACTION-OK
021800        NEXT SENTENCE
021900       ELSE
022000      IF VSAM1-SEQ-EOF
022100        MOVE 'E' TO F1-EOF-FLAG
022200       ELSE
022300        MOVE VSAM1-FS TO R1-VPL-FILE-STATUS
022400        MOVE 'FAILED ON READ (VSAM1-FS)    ' TO R1-VPL-MSG
022500        MOVE R1-VSAM-PROBLEM-LINE TO R1-PRINT-SLOT
022600        PERFORM 9999-FORCED-ABORT.
022700      IF F1-EOF-FLAG NOT EQUAL 'E'
022800        ADD +1 TO WS-VSAMFILE-IN-COUNT.
022900*
023000 2900-R1-NEWPAGE.
023100      ADD +1 TO R1-PAGE-COUNT.
023200      MOVE R1-PAGE-COUNT TO R1-PH2-PAGE-NO.
023300      WRITE REPORT1-REC FROM R1-PAGE-HDR1
023400          AFTER ADVANCING PAGE-EJECT.
023500      WRITE REPORT1-REC FROM R1-PAGE-HDR2 AFTER ADVANCING 1 LINES.
023600      WRITE REPORT1-REC FROM R1-PAGE-HDR1 AFTER ADVANCING 1 LINES.
023700      WRITE REPORT1-REC FROM R1-COL-HDR1  AFTER ADVANCING 4 LINES.
023800      WRITE REPORT1-REC FROM R1-COL-HDR2  AFTER ADVANCING 1 LINES.
023900      MOVE SPACES TO REPORT1-REC.
024000      WRITE REPORT1-REC AFTER ADVANCING 2 LINES.
024100      COMPUTE R1-LINES-REMAINING = (R1-LINE-LIMIT - 10).
024200      MOVE R1-NORMAL-LINE-SPACING TO R1-WANTED-LINE-SPACING.
024300*
024400 3000-EOJ.
024500      MOVE WS-VSAMFILE-IN-COUNT TO R1-EL-IN-COUNT.
024600      MOVE WS-VSAMFILE-OUT-COUNT TO R1-EL-OUT-COUNT.
024700      MOVE R1-ENDLINE TO R1-PRINT-SLOT.
024800      MOVE +3 TO R1-WANTED-LINE-SPACING.
024900      PERFORM 2100-WRITE-R1-OUTPUT.
025000      CLOSE  VSAMFILE  REPORT1.
025100*
025200 9000-INIT.
025300      MOVE ' CUSTOMER LISTING ' TO R1-PH2-PGM-TITLE.
025400      MOVE 'VSD183' TO R1-PH2-PGM-ID.
025500      MOVE CURRENT-DATE TO R1-PH2-DATE.
025600*
025700 9101-VSAM1-OPEN.
025800      OPEN  INPUT VSAMFILE.
025900      IF VSAM1-OPEN-OK
026000        NEXT SENTENCE
026100       ELSE
026200        MOVE VSAM1-FS TO R1-VPL-FILE-STATUS
026300        MOVE 'FAILED ON OPENING (VSAM1-FS)  ' TO R1-VPL-MSG
026400        MOVE R1-VSAM-PROBLEM-LINE TO R1-PRINT-SLOT
026500        PERFORM 9999-FORCED-ABORT.
026600*
```

FIGURE 7.2   (Continued)

```
026700 9999-FORCED-ABORT.
026800     MOVE R1-NORMAL-LINE-SPACING TO R1-WANTED-LINE-SPACING.
026900     PERFORM 2100-WRITE-R1-OUTPUT.
027000     PERFORM 3000-EOJ.
027100     MOVE 3333 TO RETURN-CODE.
027200     STOP RUN.
```

FIGURE 7.2   (*Continued*)

job control language to execute VSD183 is shown in Figure 7.3, and output from the program is illustrated in Figure 7.4.

In order to adapt the simple file-to-print routine of PSD183 to report from the KSDS, the record length in the file description for the incoming data was changed to 250 bytes instead of 80, and print columns and column headings appropriate to the purpose were defined. But it was also necessary to make significant changes:

- the SELECT/ASSIGN statement was modified and enhanced to specify more information
- the VSAM data set key field was coded in the file description (FD) even though the record was fully defined in working storage
- a field was provided in working storage for the FILE-STATUS value by which VSAM communicates to a program
- a need to check the value of FILE-STATUS returned by VSAM at the OPEN of the data set and after each I/O action forced more logic to be provided for these program actions
- since VSAM will not abend at an I/O error as do other access methods, the program using the KSDS needs to consider how to attract attention when an abend or extraordinary error is encountered. VSD183 places a nonzero value in RETURN-CODE to do this; it could also trigger an abend if we so chose.

Let's consider each of these areas in detail; once they are understood, keyed access to a KSDS is stripped of excess complexity and becomes easier to consider.

SELECT/ASSIGN Coding

The SELECT/ASSIGN statement is an interface between the symbolic name a program uses for a file and the external, physical data set. A SELECT/ASSIGN statement referenc-

```
//FSBT686A  JOB AK00TEST,'DP2-JANOSSY',CLASS=E,MSGCLASS=X,
//  MSGLEVEL=(1,1),NOTIFY=BT05686
//*
//*     RUN PROGRAM VSD183
//*     THIS JCL = BT05686.SOURCE.CNTL(JCL73)
//*
//STEPA    EXEC  PGM=VSD183
//STEPLIB     DD  DSN=SYS1.TESTLIB,
//  DISP=SHR
//VSAMCSM     DD  DSN=AK00.C98.CUSTMAST,
//  DISP=SHR
//VSD183U1 DD  SYSOUT=*
//SYSOUT     DD  SYSOUT=*
//SYSUDUMP   DD  SYSOUT=*
//
```

FIGURE 7.3   MVS JCL to execute program VSD183

```
**********************************************************************
*     CUSTOMER LISTING    //   PROGRAM VSD183   *  05/09/87  *  PAGE    1   *
**********************************************************************
```

ACCOUNT NO	LAST NAME	FIRST NAME	ADDRESS	APT	DATA
<------>	<--------------->	<-------->	<---> - <------------->	<--->	--
08716293	FORESTER	ALVIN	09710 S DORCHESTER ST		AA
22168028	WASIK	CHARLES	02009 N KILDARE AVE		BB
24307091	KUREK	BESSIE	05800 W FULLERTON AVE	4-B	CC
25656631	HAMPSTER	HERBERT	08711 S HALLDALE AV		DD
28441269	HAMPSTER	HENRIETTA	08711 S HALLDALE AV		EE
28799201	HAMPSTER	HARVEY	08711 S HALLDALE AV		FF
32613729	KALKINS	JANET	03016 N SHERIDAN RD		GG
32817132	HAMPSTER	HELEN	08711 S HALLDALE AV		HH
33841546	ANCONA	MINNIE	04310 S KOLINA PL	17	II
37667140	EASTON	JESSIE	02059 W PRYOR RD		JJ
42705117	CHEROSO	JEROME	00418 N ELSTON AVE		KK
46712001	DEKOVEN	FRANK	04408 S LARAMIE DR		LL
48077449	SMITH	JOHN	01349 W 69TH		MM
63735122	SMITH	JOHN	00911 KILBOURNE		NN
63817627	SMITH	JOHN	02415 E 135TH ST		OO
64070301	FLAGG	ALLAN	05625 N KOSTNER AV	43	PP
73724695	MADISON	MONROE	04849 W WRIGHTWOOD LANE		QQ
88389992	BILECKI	PATRICIA	00609 S LEAVITT ST	16	RR

```
*** END OF JOB          18 RECORDS READ          18 RECORDS PRINTED
```

FIGURE 7.4 Output of program VSD183, sequential listing of records in a key sequenced data set

ing an ordinary sequential data set is nearly always coded as a subset of the complete specifications possible. Coding in a more extensive format is required when a KSDS is accessed:

```
SELECT VSAMFILE ASSIGN TO    VSAMCSM
   ORGANIZATION IS INDEXED
   ACCESS MODE IS SEQUENTIAL
   RECORD KEY IS FD-ACCOUNT-NO-KEY
   FILE STATUS IS VSAM1-FS
```

Linkage name (MVS)

Under MVS, the external linkage name for a data set is normally coded with prefixes such as "UT-S" when the data set is non-VSAM. The prefixes identify to MVS certain characteristics of the data set. When the data set is VSAM, such prefixes must *not* be coded. In the foregoing example only the linkage name is specified, which in this case is VSAMCSM. The linkage name becomes the DDname by which the data set will be referenced in JCL. To run this program we must have a DD statement in JCL such as:

```
//VSAMCSM DD DSN=AK00.C98.CUSTMAST,
// DISP=SHR
```

Of course, the actual linkage name could be any legitimate DDname of up to eight characters; installation naming conventions usually specify its form and content. The physical data set name is the KSDS base cluster, the umbrella name that encompasses all of the KSDS components.

Linkage name (DOS/VSE)

Under DOS/VSE the SELECT/ASSIGN is coded with a DLBL file-name of up to seven characters. This name is prefaced with SYSnnn:

```
SELECT VSAMFILE ASSIGN TO    SYS030-VSAMCSM
   ORGANIZATION IS INDEXED
   ACCESS MODE IS SEQUENTIAL
   RECORD KEY IS FD-ACCOUNT-NO-KEY
   FILE STATUS IS VSAM1-FS.
```

An installation may have local conventions establishing additional coding for the DLBL name prefix.

ORGANIZATION

The SELECT/ASSIGN organization of a data set defaults to SEQUENTIAL; for this reason the specification is usually omitted when an ordinary sequential data set is involved. For a key sequenced data set, it is necessary to specify INDEXED; a KSDS represents IBM's current implementation support for indexed files.[1]

ACCESS MODE and I/O Actions

Access mode specifies the type of processing that a program is to perform with a data set. As with organization, the default is sequential processing, as if ACCESS MODE IS SEQUENTIAL was coded; reading the data set obtains the first record in it, then the next, then the next, and so forth until all records have been read. This specification is usually omitted when an ordinary sequential data set is processed, but it should be specified with one of the three possible modes when the data set is a KSDS.

ACCESS MODE must be coded as one of three different specifications for a key sequenced data set:

```
ACCESS MODE IS SEQUENTIAL      Sequential access
ACCESS MODE IS RANDOM          Keyed access
ACCESS MODE IS DYNAMIC         Sequential and keyed access
```

The access mode coded in the SELECT/ASSIGN statement dictates which I/O verbs can be used within the program, as illustrated in Figure 7.5.

RECORD KEY

RECORD KEY within the SELECT/ASSIGN statement indicates the field within the KSDS record that has been defined as the primary key, sometimes also called the "prime" key. This field must be coded in its appropriate position in the file description for the data set.

```
SELECT vsamfile ASSIGN TO    DDname
    ORGANIZATION IS INDEXED
    ACCESS MODE IS ------------
    RECORD KEY IS fd-primary-key-field
    ALTERNATE RECORD KEY IS fd-alternate-key-field1
        WITH DUPLICATES
    ALTERNATE RECORD KEY IS fd-alternate-key-field2
    FILE STATUS IS vsam1-fs.
```

When ACCESS MODE is	and the OPEN verb is	these verbs can be used
SEQUENTIAL	OPEN INPUT vsamfile	READ READ/NEXT START
SEQUENTIAL	OPEN OUTPUT vsamfile	WRITE CLOSE
SEQUENTIAL	OPEN EXTEND vsamfile	WRITE CLOSE
SEQUENTIAL	OPEN I-O vsamfile	READ REWRITE DELETE CLOSE
RANDOM	OPEN I-O	READ WRITE REWRITE DELETE CLOSE
DYNAMIC	OPEN I-O	START READ READ/NEXT WRITE REWRITE DELETE CLOSE

FIGURE 7.5 Types of access possible to a key sequenced data set depending on the ACCESS MODE specified

A contemporary practice is to code a full record description in working storage rather than at the file description. When this is done, it is necessary to compose a special description at the FD, citing the appropriate amount of filler before the key field to position it correctly in the record, the key field, and filler for the remainder of the record length after it. Alternatively, the entire record description can be housed at the FD, but this relinquishes the ability to easily examine the data in the last record processed if the program abends.[3]

FILE STATUS

The SELECT/ASSIGN statement should cite the name of a two-byte alphanumeric field in working storage to be used as a "mailbox" by VSAM when OPEN, CLOSE, and I/O actions are executed. While the specification of FILE STATUS is actually optional, its use is essential in order to gain reliable operation and to be able to preserve data set integrity. FILE STATUS is called the "status key" in some IBM manuals; the terms are synonymous.

FILE STATUS can assume any of a dozen or more values, depending on the action undertaken. Zeroes (00) indicates a completely successful operation, as do certain other values for various actions. Some FILE STATUS values indicate the occurrence of situations that represent transaction errors with which a program should be able to deal. Other FILE STATUS values indicate situations that are not resolvable by program action. Appendix G presents all of the values and the course of action prescribed for each for the different I/O verbs. Note that some values carry different meanings for different I/O actions, and some values can be received only with one or a few of the verbs.

USING FILE STATUS

VSAM Data Set OPEN

In comparing programs PSD183 and VSD183, it is apparent that opening a key sequenced data set involves more actions than does opening a simple sequential data set. For a simple data set just coding the verb OPEN with an indication of the nature of access—INPUT or OUTPUT—and the symbolic name of the file is sufficient:

```
OPEN INPUT INDATA.
```

In the case of a key sequenced data set, the same coding forms only a part of the opening action. The open is arranged in VSD183 as a whole paragraph 9101-VSAM1-OPEN, it refers to the field cited as FILE STATUS, and it potentially directs the flow of program control to other paragraphs if the open has not been successful.

As Appendix G indicates more fully, nine FILE STATUS values can be returned by VSAM when the OPEN verb is executed:

00 Successful open
30 Permanent I/O error in data set
90 Unusable file, perhaps not yet loaded with any records
91 Password error
92 Logic error, file is already open
93 Data set or memory not available
95 Invalid or incomplete FD or JCL
96 No DD statement for the file in the JCL
97 File opened after an implicit VERIFY by VSAM

If an OPEN occurred successfully, the field cited in FILE STATUS will contain either 00 or 97.[4] If the OPEN was not successful, it is imperative that the program take action to abort operation because VSAM will not do this. Unlike older access methods, which would themselves abend if an OPEN could not be accomplished, VSAM will continue to operate even if the data set to be opened had a fatal I/O error (30), the wrong password had been supplied (91), a DD statement for the data set was missing (96), and so forth.

Without a successful OPEN, however, all other I/O actions directed to the data set will also fail.

KSDS Read

FILE STATUS checking is necessary after attempting to open a KSDS, but it is also possible after other I/O actions. In program VSD183, for example, file status should be checked after every sequential read to determine whether the read was successful. Let's look at this summary of READ values taken from Appendix G, which presents more information about these:

00	Successful read
10	End of file on non-keyed (sequential) READ
23	Record with specified key not found (keyed READ only)
30	Permanent I/O error in data set
90	Unusable file, perhaps not yet loaded with any records
92	Logic error, file may not be open
93	Data set or memory not available
95	Invalid or incomplete FD or JCL

FILE STATUS can reveal when end of file is reached, as well as the nature of several I/O errors. It can entirely supplant the "AT END" phase for sequential reading and the "INVALID KEY" phrase on indexed file actions. You can still code the older AT END for sequential access or INVALID KEY for indexed access, but it impossible to escape the need for FILE STATUS for OPEN actions. It is, therefore, customary to use FILE STATUS for all I/O actions instead of the older coding options.

Paragraph 2700 in program PSD183 is a short traditional rendition of a logic module that reads one record from a sequential data set every time it is performed. This paragraph in program VSD183 is expanded to several more lines of code, because it is necessary to identify, using the FILE STATUS value, one of three possible cases after a KSDS read. The read may have succeeded (00), it may have detected end of file (10), or it may have encountered a program-unresolvable error that warrants aborting the run with appropriate reporting.

It is possible to code "inline" tests of the FILE STATUS field after a READ and to specify branches to different points in a program, depending on whether a successful read, end of file, or abort condition was encountered. But it's best to recognize the fact that while the first two of these possibilities are acceptable to continued program operation, the third one is not. This makes modularization of I/O actions desirable to enhance reliability; all I/O actions involve the potential of that last case, and all such I/O failures should receive consistent handling through modularized logic.

Generalizing I/O Actions

Paragraph 2700 of program VSD183 illustrates in COBOL source code what is usually termed an "I/O module" in contemporary software engineering. This logic unit follows a standard pattern for a given VSAM I/O verb, in this case the READ verb. The paragraph is performed from whatever points in the program require the next record from the data set to be obtained; in VSD183 this occurs in beginning-of-job and in the processing loop.

The READ logic unit shown in VSD183 accomplishes these generic I/O module tasks:

- executes the verb

- determines which FILE STATUS condition applies and takes appropriate action for each case:

- I/O action was successful: return control
- I/O action was not successful but can be handled by the program: set a flag value to "tell" performing logic of the condition and return control
- I/O error not correctable by program was encountered; close files and abort the run with appropriate reporting of all of the key fields and the FILE STATUS value.

These tasks must be accomplished in the case of each of the KSDS verbs: for OPEN, READ, REWRITE, WRITE, DELETE, START, READ/NEXT, and CLOSE, yet the FILE STATUS values indicating an abort condition may differ for each. Given this fact, it makes sense to follow a generalized pattern in which each of the I/O verbs present in a program for a given KSDS is housed in a paragraph of its own. Each such I/O module invokes a standard pattern of reporting and program forced-abort for the uncorrectable errors particular to a given verb.

Program VSD183 illustrates a pattern in which uncorrectable errors detected by any I/O logic unit are reported by formation of a standard reporting line with a message and the FILE STATUS value. A single "forced-abort" logic unit, 9999-FORCED-ABORT, is performed by any I/O module to output the problem statement line and shut down the job with a nonzero RETURN-CODE or other reporting. The forced-abort paragraph could cause a visible operating system abend by calling an installation utility or the COBOL abend program ILBOABN0 (I-L-B-oh-A-B-N-zero) instead of executing STOP RUN.[5]

Figure 7.6 illustrates the output of VSD183 when an uncorrectable error is detected.

Generalizing FILE STATUS Checking

Appendix G summarizes all of the FILE STATUS values for the KSDS I/O verbs, but these can be distilled into a standard file status field definition with meaningful condition names. Figure 7.7 presents such a definition, used in program VSD183 as direct source code. The definition is suitable for placement in a copy library; a definition such as this is commonly made a copylib member in installations employing modern practices. A series of such copylib members, named VSAM1STD, VSAM2STD, VSAM3STD, and so forth, containing field names prefixed with the appropriate digits, provides the ability to have a different FILE STATUS field for each of perhaps several VSAM files being processed by a program.

The standardized FILE STATUS field definition is intended to provide the basis for clear source code development, not as a troubleshooting guide. Use of the 88 level names makes sense in code that tests the outcome of an I/O action. If, however, one of the program-uncorrectable situations has arisen, the printed FILE STATUS value can be found in a troubleshooting reference such as Appendix G. This provides detailed infor-

```
*********************************************************************
*    CUSTOMER LISTING    //   PROGRAM VSD183    *  05/09/87  *  PAGE   1  *
*********************************************************************


ACCOUNT NO          LAST NAME      FIRST NAME          ADDRESS          APT   DATA
<------>         <--------------->  <-------->    <--->  -  <-------------->  <--->   --


>>> RUN ABORTED -- FILE STATUS WAS 95 -- FAILED ON OPENING (VSAM1-FS)


*** END OF JOB          O RECORDS READ          O RECORDS PRINTED
```

FIGURE 7.6 Output of program VSD183 when an uncorrectable I/O error is detected

```
*VSAM1STD  LAST CHANGED 04-02-84  ORIGINAL 01-22-84  J JANOSSY
***************************************************************
*     STANDARD VSAM FILE STATUS FIELD DEFINITION            *
***************************************************************
 01  VSAM1-FS.
     05 VSAM1-FS-LEFT-RIGHT.
        10 VSAM1-FS-LEFT         PIC X(1).
           88 VSAM1-ACTION-OK                VALUE '0'.
           88 VSAM1-SEQ-EOF                   VALUE '1'.
        10 FILLER                PIC X(1).
     05 VSAM1-FS-FULL  REDEFINES
        VSAM1-FS-LEFT-RIGHT      PIC X(2).
           88 VSAM1-WRITE-OUT-SEQ            VALUE '21'.
           88 VSAM1-DUP-PRIME-ALT-KEY        VALUE '22'.
           88 VSAM1-REC-NOT-FOUND            VALUE '23'.
           88 VSAM1-OPEN-OK                  VALUE '00'.
 *
```

FIGURE 7.7   Standard FILE STATUS field definition suitable for placement in a copy library

mation on the meaning of the FILE STATUS value for the verb and actions to be taken to resolve the problem.

Standard Key Sequenced Data Set I/O Modules

When the FILE STATUS field and the meanings of the program-recoverable values are standardized as in Figure 7.7, it becomes possible to define standard I/O modules for KSDS access in generic form. These modules reduce the complexity of dealing with any of the KSDS I/O actions by relieving scattered units of processing logic of the need to check for all of the verb-specific uncorrectable FILE STATUS values.

Figure 7.8 illustrates the processing actions of a standard I/O logic module for each of the KSDS I/O actions. In cases where a "file-flag" is mentioned, the reference is to a work-

```
                                                          7.8(a)
OPEN I-O vsamfile.
IF VSAM1-ACTION-OK
   NEXT SENTENCE
ELSE
   reporting and forced abort actions.
```
___
```
                                                          7.8(b)
MOVE key-wanted TO FD-key-field.
PERFORM NNNN-READ.
IF fileflag = 'G'
   actions when record of desired key is obtained
ELSE
   actions when record of desired key not found.


NNNN-READ.
   READ vsamfile INTO working-storage-record-area.
   IF VSAM1-ACTION-OK
      MOVE 'G' TO fileflag
   ELSE
   IF VSAM1-REC-NOT-FOUND
      MOVE 'B' TO fileflag
```

FIGURE 7.8   Generic logic modules for each KSDS I/O verb: (a) OPEN, (b) READ, (c) REWRITE, (d) WRITE, (e) DELETE, (f) START on specific full key, (g) START on specific partial key, (h) START at or beyond partial key, (i) READ/NEXT after a START, and (j) CLOSE

```
        ELSE
            reporting and forced abort actions.
```

Note: <u>FD-key-field</u> can be the primary key field or an alternate key field. If it is an alternate key field the START statement must be coded

```
        START vsamfile KEY = FD-alt-key-field.
```

and will switch the "attention" of COBOL to the alternate index until a START involving the primary key or another alternate index.

7.8(c)

```
NNNN-REWRITE.
        REWRITE vsamfile-rec FROM working-storage-input-area.
        IF VSAM1-ACTION-OK
            NEXT SENTENCE
        ELSE
            reporting and forced abort actions.
```

Note: VSAM1-ACTION-OK tests the high order byte of the FILE STATUS value. If you test both bytes you may incorrectly think an error has occurred when you receive a FILE STATUS of 02. A value of 02 is returned when nonunique alternate keys are permitted, an alternate key value is changed to a duplicate and the record rewritten. The 02 does not indicate an error. See Appendix G for information on a FILE STATUS value of 22 on a REWRITE, which can be especially frustrating but is easy to resolve with that Appendix.

7.8(d)

```
        MOVE fields TO working storage record area.
        PERFORM NNNN-WRITE.
        IF fileflag = 'G'
            actions when record is written
        ELSE
            actions when record carries key of record on file.


NNNN-WRITE.
        WRITE vsamfile-rec FROM working-storage-record-area.
        IF VSAM1-ACTION-OK
            MOVE 'G' TO fileflag
        ELSE
        IF VSAM1-DUP-PRIME-ALT-KEY
            MOVE 'B' TO fileflag
        ELSE
            reporting and forced abort actions.
```

Note: VSAM1-ACTION-OK tests the high order byte of the FILE STATUS value. If you test both bytes you may incorrectly think an error has occurred when you receive a FILE STATUS of 02. A value of 02 is returned when nonunique alternate keys are permitted and a record is written with an alternate key that duplicates an alternate key already on file. The 02 does not indicate an error. See Appendix G for information on a FILE STATUS value of 22 on a WRITE, which can be especially frustrating but is easy to resolve with that Appendix.

7.8(e)

```
        MOVE key-to-delete TO FD-key-field.
        PERFORM NNNN-DELETE.
        IF fileflag = 'G'
            actions when record is deleted as desired
        ELSE
            actions when key to be deleted is not on file.
```

FIGURE 7.8   (Continued)

```
NNNN-DELETE.
    DELETE vsamfile.
    IF VSAM1-ACTION-OK
       MOVE 'G' TO fileflag
     ELSE
    IF VSAM1-REC-NOT-FOUND
       MOVE 'B' TO fileflag
     ELSE
       reporting and forced abort actions.
```

Note: A "raw" delete is rare. Usually the record is obtained first
with a keyed read as in (b) and written to a history file or printed
and then the DELETE issued. When that course of action is taken any
FILE STATUS received except VSAM1-ACTION-OK is regarded as indicative
of a program-uncorrectable error; VSAM1-REC-NOT-FOUND is not cited as
a second condition in the standard DELETE I/O logic module.

_____

                                                            7.8(f)

```
    MOVE key-to-start TO FD-key-field.
    PERFORM NNNN-START-FULL-SPECIFIC.
    IF fileflag = 'G'
       actions when start is possible
     ELSE
       actions when start is not possible.


NNNN-START-FULL-SPECIFIC.
    START vsamfile.
    IF VSAM1-ACTION-OK
       MOVE 'G' TO fileflag
     ELSE
    IF VSAM1-REC-NOT-FOUND
       MOVE 'B' TO fileflag
     ELSE
       reporting and forced abort actions.
```

Note: FD-key-field can be the primary key field or an alternate key
field. If it is an alternate key field the START statement must be
coded

```
    START vsamfile KEY = FD-alt-key-field.
```

and will switch the "attention" of COBOL tc the alternate index until a
START or READ involving the primary key or another alternate index.

_____

                                                            7.8(g)

```
    MOVE partial-key TO FD-part-key-field.
    PERFORM NNNN-START-PARTIAL-SPECIFIC.
    IF fileflag = 'G'
       actions when start is possible
     ELSE
       actions when start is not possible.


NNNN-START-PARTIAL-SPECIFIC.
    START vsamfile KEY = FD-part-key-field.
    IF VSAM1-ACTION-OK
       MOVE 'G' TO fileflag
     ELSE
    IF VSAM1-REC-NOT-FOUND
       MOVE 'B' TO fileflag
     ELSE
       reporting and forced abort actions.
```

FIGURE 7.8 (Continued)

Note: <u>FD-part-key-field</u> can be a leading part of the primary record key or a leading part of an alternate key. If it is the leading part of an alternate key the action switches the attention of COBOL to the alternate index until a START or READ involving the primary key or another alternate index.

7.8(h)

```
    MOVE partial-key TO FD-part-key-field.
    PERFORM NNNN-START-PARTIAL-AT-BEYOND.
    IF fileflag = 'G'
       actions when start is possible
    ELSE
       actions when start is not possible.


NNNN-START-PARTIAL-AT-BEYOND.
    START vsamfile KEY NOT LESS FD-part-key-field.
    IF VSAM1-ACTION-OK
      MOVE 'G' TO fileflag
    ELSE
    IF VSAM1-REC-NOT-FOUND
      MOVE 'B' TO fileflag
    ELSE
       reporting and forced abort actions.
```

Note: <u>FD-part-key-field</u> can be a leading part of the primary record key or a leading part of an alternate key. If it is the leading part of an alternate key the action switches the attention of COBOL to the alternate index until a START or READ involving the primary key or another alternate index.

7.8(i)

```
    PERFORM NNNN-READ-NEXT.


NNNN-READ-NEXT.
    READ vsamfile NEXT INTO working-storage-record-area.
    IF VSAM1-ACTION-OK
      MOVE 'M' TO eof-fileflag
    ELSE
    IF VSAM1-SEQ-EOF
      MOVE 'E' TO eof-fileflag
    ELSE
       reporting and forced abort actions.
```

Note: Since READ/NEXT is usually performed at the bottom of a processing loop in a "browse" action the value of the eof-fileflag is tested by the PERFORM...UNTIL driving the processing loop. This flag should be independent of a "fileflag" used to convey "G" or "B" values indicating the outcome of a keyed-READ, REWRITE, DELETE, or START.

7.8(j)

```
    CLOSE vsamfile.
    IF VSAM1-ACTION-OK
      NEXT SENTENCE
    ELSE
       reporting and forced abort actions.
```

FIGURE 7.8   *(Continued)*

ing storage field that will be made to carry either a value indicating a successful I/O or a value indicating that a record was not obtained. Program S802P165, illustrated later in this chapter, makes use of these generic I/O module patterns and provides a comprehensive picture of their use in a modern add/change/delete program. The modularized I/O logic also eases the handling of sequential "browse" access on the primary or alternate keys.

ALTERNATE KEY ACCESS TO KEY SEQUENCED DATA SETS

The foregoing discussion concerning sequential access to a key sequenced data set lays the groundwork for much more complex operations by establishing the essential "threshold" infrastructure of SELECT/ASSIGN, FILE STATUS, and I/O logic modularization. Let's now enhance the capability of program VSD183 by changing it into VSD383, a routine that still performs sequential access, but does so via one of the alternate indexes rather than by the primary KSDS index.

Alternate indexes are separate KSDS data sets arranged to provide pointers to primary record keys in the sequence of an alternate key field. Alternate keys are most often defined to provide a way to "home in" online on a record via imprecise information. Imagine, for example, a customer calling up to place an order and the resulting actions of an order clerk. The customer may not recall an account number, but can readily state his or her name. The clerk uses a "browse" screen, accessing a file such as AK00.C98.CUSTMAST via NAMEAIX, and queries the customer further for address or other data that distinguishes the customer from any others with the same or similar name. The end result is the identification of the appropriate customer account number and master file record.

Alternate indexes are rarely defined and created solely for the purpose of securing sequential access in an order other than primary key. Large-scale sequential reporting is more efficiently done by inputting the KSDS to a sort, sorting the records to the desired report order, and listing the records. However, some forms of batch update and processing involving alternate keys is typically present in the business data processing environment, and a demonstration of it is important. In addition to logic manipulations, both the MVS and DOS/VSE operating systems force some subtle job control language treatment for alternate key access.

Sequential Access via an Alternate Index

Alternate indexes need not be cited in a SELECT/ASSIGN statement unless they will be accessed in the program. In VSD183, the SELECT/ASSIGN statement for the VSAM data set being read did not mention either of the two alternate keys which exist for AK00.C98.CUSTMAST.

Program VSD383 is listed in Figure 7.9. This routine reads the customer master file and lists it via the name alternate index. The SELECT/ASSIGN cites the name alternate index, NAMEAIX, and the program accesses it. Figure 7.10 shows the MVS JCL to execute VSD383, and Figure 7.11 illustrates the output of it.

Code Differences Between Primary and Alternate Key Access

Several parts of program VSD183 have been affected by its transformation into program VSD383. These areas include the following:

• The ALTERNATE RECORD KEY specification has been added to the SELECT/ASSIGN statement, naming a field in the file description that describes the position of the alternate key field in the record.

```
000100 IDENTIFICATION DIVISION.
000200 PROGRAM-ID.      VSD383.
000300 AUTHOR.          J JANOSSY.
000400 INSTALLATION.    DEPAUL UNIVERSITY.
000500 DATE-WRITTEN.    MAY 1987.
000600 DATE-COMPILED.
000700*REMARKS.         FOR IBM VSCOBOL
000800*                 VERSION 01    LAST CHANGE 05-07-87   ORIG 05-07-87
000900*                 FILE-TO-PRINT PROGRAM. READS A VSAM DATA SET
001000*                 USING ONE OF TWO ALTERNATE KEYS (NAMEAIX).
001100*
001200 ENVIRONMENT DIVISION.
001300 CONFIGURATION SECTION.
001400 SOURCE-COMPUTER.  IBM-4381.
001500 OBJECT-COMPUTER.  IBM-4381.
001600 SPECIAL-NAMES.  C01 IS PAGE-EJECT.
001700 INPUT-OUTPUT SECTION.
001800 FILE-CONTROL.
001900     SELECT VSAMFILE  ASSIGN TO      VSAMCSM
002000         ORGANIZATION IS INDEXED
002100         ACCESS MODE IS SEQUENTIAL
002200         RECORD KEY IS FD-ACCOUNT-NO-KEY
002300         ALTERNATE RECORD KEY IS FD-NAME-AIX
002400         FILE STATUS IS VSAM1-FS.
002500     SELECT REPORT1   ASSIGN TO UT-S-VSD383U1.
002600*
002700 DATA DIVISION.
002800 FILE SECTION.
002900*
003000 FD  VSAMFILE
003100     LABEL RECORDS ARE STANDARD
003200     BLOCK CONTAINS 0 RECORDS
003300     RECORD CONTAINS 250 CHARACTERS.
003400 01  VSAMFILE-REC.
003500     12 FILLER                   PIC X(9).
003600     12 FD-NAME-AIX.
003700        15 FD-NAMEAIX-CUSTOMER.
003800           18 FD-NAMEAIX-LASTNAME    PIC X(18).
003900           18 FD-NAMEAIX-FIRSTNAME   PIC X(9).
004000        15 FD-ACCOUNT-NO-KEY     PIC X(8).
004100     12 FILLER                   PIC X(206).
004200*
004300 FD  REPORT1
004400     LABEL RECORDS ARE OMITTED
004500     BLOCK CONTAINS 0 RECORDS
004600     RECORD CONTAINS 133 CHARACTERS.
004700 01  REPORT1-REC                 PIC X(133).
004800/
004900 WORKING-STORAGE SECTION.
005000 01  FILLER PIC X(23)  VALUE  '*WORKING STORAGE START*'.
005100*
005200*VSAM1STD  LAST CHANGED 04-02-84  ORIGINAL 01-22-84  J JANOSSY
005300***********************************************************************
005400*   STANDARD VSAM FILE STATUS FIELD DEFINITION (1)            *
005500***********************************************************************
005600 01  VSAM1-FS.
005700     05 VSAM1-FS-LEFT-RIGHT.
005800        10 VSAM1-FS-LEFT         PIC X(1).
005900           88 VSAM1-ACTION-OK             VALUE '0'.
006000           88 VSAM1-SEQ-EOF              VALUE '1'.
006100        10 FILLER                PIC X(1).
006200     05 VSAM1-FS-FULL  REDEFINES
006300        VSAM1-FS-LEFT-RIGHT      PIC X(2).
006400           88 VSAM1-WRITE-OUT-SEQ        VALUE '21'.
006500           88 VSAM1-DUP-PRIME-ALT-KEY    VALUE '22'.
006600           88 VSAM1-REC-NOT-FOUND        VALUE '23'.
006700           88 VSAM1-OPEN-OK              VALUE '00'.
```

FIGURE 7.9 Source code for program VSD838, accessing a key sequenced data set sequentially via an alternate key

```
006800*
006900 01  WS-FLAGS.
007000     12 F1-EOF-FLAG                        PIC X(1)   VALUE 'M'.
007100        88 F1-EOF-VSAMFILE-END                        VALUE 'E'.
007200*
007300 01  WS-COUNTERS.
007400     12 WS-VSAMFILE-IN-COUNT               PIC S9(5) VALUE +0.
007500     12 WS-VSAMFILE-OUT-COUNT              PIC S9(5) VALUE +0.
007600*
007700 01  VSAMFILE-INPUT-AREA.
007800     12 VFI-OLD-ID-NO                      PIC X(9).
007900     12 VFI-NAME-AIX.
008000        15 VFI-NAMEAIX-CUSTOMER.
008100           18 VFI-NAMEAIX-LASTNAME         PIC X(18).
008200           18 VFI-NAMEAIX-FIRSTNAME        PIC X(9).
008300     12 VFI-ACCOUNT-NO-KEY                 PIC X(8).
008400     12 VFI-ADDRAIX.
008500        15 VFI-ADDRAIX-ST-DIREC            PIC X(1).
008600        15 VFI-ADDRAIX-ST-NAME             PIC X(15).
008700        15 VFI-ADDRAIX-HOUSE-NO            PIC X(5).
008800        15 VFI-ADDRAIX-APT-NO              PIC X(5).
008900     12 VFI-RECORD-DATA.
009000        15 VFI-TWO-LETTERS                 PIC X(2).
009100        15 FILLER                          PIC X(178).
009200*
009300 01  REPORT1-COUNTERS.
009400     12 R1-LINE-LIMIT                      PIC S9(2) VALUE +60.
009500     12 R1-NORMAL-LINE-SPACING             PIC S9(2) VALUE +2.
009600     12 R1-LINES-REMAINING                 PIC S9(2) VALUE +0.
009700     12 R1-PAGE-COUNT                      PIC S9(3) VALUE +0.
009800     12 R1-WANTED-LINE-SPACING             PIC S9(3) VALUE +0.
009900     12 R1-PRINT-SLOT                      PIC X(133).
010000*
010100 01  R1-PAGE-HDR1.
010200     12 FILLER                   PIC X(1).
010300     12 FILLER                   PIC X(72)  VALUE ALL '*'.
010400     12 FILLER                   PIC X(60)  VALUE ALL ' '.
010500*
010600 01  R1-PAGE-HDR2.
010700     12 FILLER                   PIC X(1).
010800     12 FILLER                   PIC X(4)   VALUE '*  '.
010900     12 R1-PH2-PGM-TITLE         PIC X(18)  VALUE ALL 'X'.
011000     12 FILLER                   PIC X(14)  VALUE
011100         ' // PROGRAM '.
011200     12 R1-PH2-PGM-ID            PIC X(6)   VALUE ALL 'X'.
011300     12 FILLER                   PIC X(6)   VALUE '  *  '.
011400     12 R1-PH2-DATE              PIC X(8).
011500     12 FILLER                   PIC X(10)  VALUE ' * PAGE '.
011600     12 R1-PH2-PAGE-NO           PIC ZZ9.
011700     12 FILLER                   PIC X(3)   VALUE ' *'.
011800     12 FILLER                   PIC X(60)  VALUE ALL ' '.
011900*
012000 01  R1-COL-HDR1.
012100     12 FILLER                   PIC X(1).
012200     12 FILLER  PIC X(22) VALUE 'ACCOUNT NO       LAST'.
012300     12 FILLER  PIC X(22) VALUE ' NAME       FIRST NAME '.
012400     12 FILLER  PIC X(22) VALUE '          ADDRESS       '.
012500     12 FILLER  PIC X(22) VALUE '    APT   DATA          '.
012600     12 FILLER  PIC X(22) VALUE '                        '.
012700     12 FILLER  PIC X(22) VALUE '                        '.
012800*
012900 01  R1-COL-HDR2.
013000     12 FILLER                   PIC X(1).
013100     12 FILLER  PIC X(22) VALUE ' <------>   <-------->'.
013200     12 FILLER  PIC X(22) VALUE '--------> <-------->  '.
013300     12 FILLER  PIC X(22) VALUE '<---> - <-------------->'.
013400     12 FILLER  PIC X(22) VALUE '> <--->  --            '.
```

FIGURE 7.9   (Continued)

```
013500         12 FILLER  PIC X(22)  VALUE '                        '.
013600         12 FILLER  PIC X(22)  VALUE '                        '.
013700*
013800 01  R1-DETLINE.
013900         12 FILLER                    PIC X(1).
014000         12 FILLER                    PIC X(1)   VALUE ' '.
014100         12 R1-DL-ACCOUNT-NO-KEY       PIC X(8).
014200         12 FILLER                    PIC X(4)   VALUE ALL ' '.
014300         12 R1-DL-NAMEAIX-LASTNAME      PIC X(18).
014400         12 FILLER                    PIC X(1)   VALUE ' '.
014500         12 R1-DL-NAMEAIX-FIRSTNAME     PIC X(9).
014600         12 FILLER                    PIC X(3)   VALUE ALL ' '.
014700         12 R1-DL-ADDRAIX-HOUSE-NO      PIC X(5).
014800         12 FILLER                    PIC X(1)   VALUE ' '.
014900         12 R1-DL-ADDRAIX-ST-DIREC      PIC X(1).
015000         12 FILLER                    PIC X(1)   VALUE ' '.
015100         12 R1-DL-ADDRAIX-ST-NAME       PIC X(15).
015200         12 FILLER                    PIC X(1)   VALUE ' '.
015300         12 R1-DL-ADDRAIX-APT-NO        PIC X(5).
015400         12 FILLER                    PIC X(2)   VALUE ALL ' '.
015500         12 R1-DL-TWO-LETTERS          PIC X(2).
015600         12 FILLER                    PIC X(55)  VALUE ALL ' '.
015700*
015800 01  R1-ENDLINE.
015900         12 FILLER                    PIC X(1).
016000         12 FILLER                    PIC X(17)  VALUE
016100           '*** END OF JOB   '.
016200         12 R1-EL-IN-COUNT            PIC Z,ZZZ,ZZ9.
016300         12 FILLER                    PIC X(16)  VALUE
016400           ' RECORDS READ   '.
016500         12 R1-EL-OUT-COUNT           PIC Z,ZZZ,ZZ9.
016600         12 FILLER                    PIC X(16)  VALUE
016700           ' RECORDS PRINTED'.
016800         12 FILLER                    PIC X(65)  VALUE ALL ' '.
016900*
017000 01  R1-VSAM-PROBLEM-LINE.
017100         12 FILLER                    PIC X(1).
017200         12 FILLER                    PIC X(35)  VALUE
017300           '>>> RUN ABORTED -- FILE STATUS WAS '.
017400         12 R1-VPL-FILE-STATUS         PIC X(2).
017500         12 FILLER                    PIC X(4)   VALUE ' -- '.
017600         12 R1-VPL-MSG                PIC X(30).
017700         12 FILLER                    PIC X(61)  VALUE ALL ' '.
017800/
017900 PROCEDURE DIVISION.
018000*
018100 0000-MAINLINE.
018200         PERFORM 1000-BOJ.
018300         PERFORM 2000-PROCESS UNTIL F1-EOF-FLAG EQUAL 'E'.
018400         PERFORM 3000-EOJ.
018500         STOP RUN.
018600*
018700 1000-BOJ.
018800         PERFORM 9000-INIT.
018900         OPEN  OUTPUT REPORT1.
019000         PERFORM 2900-R1-NEWPAGE.
019100         PERFORM 9101-VSAM1-OPEN.
019200         MOVE LOW-VALUES TO FD-NAME-AIX.
019300         PERFORM 2705-START-NAMEAIX.
019400         PERFORM 2710-READ-NEXT.
019500*
019600 2000-PROCESS.
019700         PERFORM 2050-FILL-DETLINE.
019800         MOVE R1-NORMAL-LINE-SPACING TO R1-WANTED-LINE-SPACING.
019900         PERFORM 2100-WRITE-R1-OUTPUT.
020000         ADD +1 TO WS-VSAMFILE-OUT-COUNT.
020100         PERFORM 2710-READ-NEXT.
```

FIGURE 7.9 (Continued)

```
020200*
020300 2050-FILL-DETLINE.
020400     MOVE VFI-ACCOUNT-NO-KEY        TO R1-DL-ACCOUNT-NO-KEY.
020500     MOVE VFI-NAMEAIX-LASTNAME      TO R1-DL-NAMEAIX-LASTNAME.
020600     MOVE VFI-NAMEAIX-FIRSTNAME     TO R1-DL-NAMEAIX-FIRSTNAME.
020700     MOVE VFI-ADDRAIX-HOUSE-NO      TO R1-DL-ADDRAIX-HOUSE-NO.
020800     MOVE VFI-ADDRAIX-ST-DIREC      TO R1-DL-ADDRAIX-ST-DIREC.
020900     MOVE VFI-ADDRAIX-ST-NAME       TO R1-DL-ADDRAIX-ST-NAME.
021000     MOVE VFI-ADDRAIX-APT-NO        TO R1-DL-ADDRAIX-APT-NO.
021100     MOVE VFI-TWO-LETTERS           TO R1-DL-TWO-LETTERS.
021200     MOVE R1-DETLINE TO R1-PRINT-SLOT.
021300*
021400 2100-WRITE-R1-OUTPUT.
021500     IF R1-LINES-REMAINING IS LESS THAN R1-WANTED-LINE-SPACING
021600         PERFORM 2900-R1-NEWPAGE.
021700     WRITE REPORT1-REC FROM R1-PRINT-SLOT
021800         AFTER ADVANCING R1-WANTED-LINE-SPACING LINES.
021900     COMPUTE R1-LINES-REMAINING =
022000         (R1-LINES-REMAINING - R1-WANTED-LINE-SPACING).
022100*
022200 2705-START-NAMEAIX.
022300     START VSAMFILE KEY NOT LESS FD-NAME-AIX.
022400     IF VSAM1-ACTION-OK
022500       NEXT SENTENCE
022600     ELSE
022700       MOVE R1-NORMAL-LINE-SPACING TO R1-WANTED-LINE-SPACING
022800       MOVE SPACES TO R1-VPL-FILE-STATUS
022900       MOVE 'NAMEAIX KEY AT FAILURE WAS    ' TO R1-VPL-MSG
023000       MOVE R1-VSAM-PROBLEM-LINE TO R1-PRINT-SLOT
023100       PERFORM 2100-WRITE-R1-OUTPUT
023200*
023300       MOVE FD-NAME-AIX                   TO R1-VPL-MSG
023400       MOVE R1-VSAM-PROBLEM-LINE TO R1-PRINT-SLOT
023500       PERFORM 2100-WRITE-R1-OUTPUT
023600*
023700       MOVE VSAM1-FS TO R1-VPL-FILE-STATUS
023800       MOVE 'START FAILED P2705 (VSAM1-FS) ' TO R1-VPL-MSG
023900       MOVE R1-VSAM-PROBLEM-LINE TO R1-PRINT-SLOT
024000       PERFORM 9999-FORCED-ABORT.
024100*
024200 2710-READ-NEXT.
024300     READ VSAMFILE NEXT INTO VSAMFILE-INPUT-AREA.
024400     IF VSAM1-ACTION-OK
024500       NEXT SENTENCE
024600     ELSE
024700     IF VSAM1-SEQ-EOF
024800       MOVE 'E' TO F1-EOF-FLAG
024900     ELSE
025000       MOVE VSAM1-FS TO R1-VPL-FILE-STATUS
025100       MOVE 'FAILED ON READ/NEXT (VSAM1-FS)' TO R1-VPL-MSG
025200       MOVE R1-VSAM-PROBLEM-LINE TO R1-PRINT-SLOT
025300       PERFORM 9999-FORCED-ABORT.
025400     IF F1-EOF-FLAG NOT EQUAL 'E'
025500       ADD +1 TO WS-VSAMFILE-IN-COUNT.
025600*
025700 2900-R1-NEWPAGE.
025800     ADD +1 TO R1-PAGE-COUNT.
025900     MOVE R1-PAGE-COUNT TO R1-PH2-PAGE-NO.
026000     WRITE REPORT1-REC FROM R1-PAGE-HDR1
026100         AFTER ADVANCING PAGE-EJECT.
026200     WRITE REPORT1-REC FROM R1-PAGE-HDR2 AFTER ADVANCING 1 LINES.
026300     WRITE REPORT1-REC FROM R1-PAGE-HDR1 AFTER ADVANCING 1 LINES.
026400     WRITE REPORT1-REC FROM R1-COL-HDR1  AFTER ADVANCING 4 LINES.
026500     WRITE REPORT1-REC FROM R1-COL-HDR2  AFTER ADVANCING 1 LINES.
026600     MOVE SPACES TO REPORT1-REC.
026700     WRITE REPORT1-REC AFTER ADVANCING 2 LINES.
026800     COMPUTE R1-LINES-REMAINING = (R1-LINE-LIMIT - 10).
```

FIGURE 7.9 (Continued)

```
026900        MOVE R1-NORMAL-LINE-SPACING TO R1-WANTED-LINE-SPACING.
027000*
027100 3000-EOJ.
027200        MOVE WS-VSAMFILE-IN-COUNT TO R1-EL-IN-COUNT.
027300        MOVE WS-VSAMFILE-OUT-COUNT TO R1-EL-OUT-COUNT.
027400        MOVE R1-ENDLINE TO R1-PRINT-SLOT.
027500        MOVE +3 TO R1-WANTED-LINE-SPACING.
027600        PERFORM 2100-WRITE-R1-OUTPUT.
027700        CLOSE  VSAMFILE  REPORT1.
027800*
027900 9000-INIT.
028000        MOVE 'CUSTOMERS BY NAME ' TO R1-PH2-PGM-TITLE.
028100        MOVE 'VSD383' TO R1-PH2-PGM-ID.
028200        MOVE CURRENT-DATE TO R1-PH2-DATE.
028300*
028400 9101-VSAM1-OPEN.
028500        OPEN  INPUT VSAMFILE.
028600        IF VSAM1-OPEN-OK
028700           NEXT SENTENCE
028800         ELSE
028900           MOVE VSAM1-FS TO R1-VPL-FILE-STATUS
029000           MOVE 'FAILED ON OPENING (VSAM1-FS)  ' TO R1-VPL-MSG
029100           MOVE R1-VSAM-PROBLEM-LINE TO R1-PRINT-SLOT
029200           PERFORM 9999-FORCED-ABORT.
029300*
029400 9999-FORCED-ABORT.
029500        MOVE R1-NORMAL-LINE-SPACING TO R1-WANTED-LINE-SPACING.
029600        PERFORM 2100-WRITE-R1-OUTPUT.
029700        PERFORM 3000-EOJ.
029800        MOVE 3333 TO RETURN-CODE.
029900        STOP RUN.
```

FIGURE 7.9   (*Continued*)

- The alternate key field has been defined in the file description. Note that since this alternate key was defined to encompass the primary key at its end—this automatically insures that this alternate key will always be unique—the coding for the alternate key field must include it. It was necessary for us to shift the primary key to a level that falls within the FD-NAME-AIX group name.[6]

- The movement of low-values to the alternate key field and the performance of a START action has been added to beginning-of-job actions.

```
//FSBT686A  JOB AK00TEST,'DP2-JANOSSY',CLASS=E,MSGCLASS=X,
//  MSGLEVEL=(1,1),NOTIFY=BT05686
//*
//*     RUN PROGRAM VSD383
//*     THIS JCL = BT05686.SOURCE.CNTL(JCL710)
//*
//STEPA     EXEC  PGM=VSD383
//STEPLIB   DD    DSN=SYS1.TESTLIB,
//  DISP=SHR
//VSAMCSM   DD    DSN=AK00.C98.CUSTMAST,
//  DISP=SHR
//VSAMCSM1  DD    DSN=AK00.C98.CUSTMAST.NAMEAIX.PATH,
//  DISP=SHR
//VSD383U1  DD    SYSOUT=*
//SYSOUT    DD    SYSOUT=*
//SYSUDUMP  DD    SYSOUT=*
//
```

FIGURE 7.10   MVS JCL to execute program VSD383

```
**************************************************************
*    CUSTOMERS BY NAME    //  PROGRAM VSD383  *  05/09/87  *  PAGE    1   *
**************************************************************
```

ACCOUNT NO	LAST NAME	FIRST NAME	ADDRESS	APT	DATA
<------>	<-------------->	<-------->	<---> - <------------->	<--->	--
33841546	ANCONA	MINNIE	04310 S KOLINA PL	17	II
88389992	BILECKI	PATRICIA	00609 S LEAVITT ST	16	RR
42705117	CHEROSO	JEROME	00418 N ELSTON AVE		KK
46712001	DEKOVEN	FRANK	04408 S LARAMIE DR		LL
37667140	EASTON	JESSIE	02059 W PRYOR RD		JJ
64070301	FLAGG	ALLAN	05625 N KOSTNER AV	43	PP
08716293	FORESTER	ALVIN	09710 S DORCHESTER ST		AA
28799201	HAMPSTER	HARVEY	08711 S HALLDALE AV		FF
32817132	HAMPSTER	HELEN	08711 S HALLDALE AV		HH
28441269	HAMPSTER	HENRIETTA	08711 S HALLDALE AV		EE
25656631	HAMPSTER	HERBERT	08711 S HALLDALE AV		DD
32613729	KALKINS	JANET	03016 N SHERIDAN RD		GG
24307091	KUREK	BESSIE	05800 W FULLERTON AVE	4-B	CC
73724695	MADISON	MONROE	04849 W WRIGHTWOOD LANE		QQ
48077449	SMITH	JOHN	01349 W 69TH		MM
63735122	SMITH	JOHN	00911 KILBOURNE		NN
63817627	SMITH	JOHN	02415 E 135TH ST		OO
22168028	WASIK	CHARLES	02009 N KILDARE AVE		BB

```
*** END OF JOB        18 RECORDS READ        18 RECORDS PRINTED
```

FIGURE 7.11   Output of program VSD383, records in master file listed in NAMEAIX order

- An I/O module has been created to house a START verb, located in paragraph 2705, to perform a number of tasks.
- The read verb in paragraph 2710 has been changed to READ/NEXT instead of READ. READ would have worked in VSD383, as it has for sequential access in VSD183. But when the access mode is coded as RANDOM or DYNAMIC, READ is used for keyed reads and READ/NEXT for sequential reads. As a matter of consistency this distinction should be made even when ACCESS MODE IS SEQUENTIAL is employed.

Functions of the START verb

The most significant difference between program VSD383 and its predecessor is that it makes use of the START verb for a dual purpose. START, when executed, performs two services for the program.

Current Record Pointer Position

START positions a value called the "current record pointer" to a specific record; it does not actually input a record. The current record pointer is used by VSAM to indicate the place in the data set from which the next READ/NEXT action will obtain a record. If a START fails, the current record pointer is left undefined, and subsequent sequential read attempts will fail. The purpose of START is directly implied by the word.

In beginning-of-job actions program VSD383 moves low-values to the NAMEAIX field, and then performs a START in which the condition is stated as NOT LESS THAN. This form of START succeeds except when the value of the key field exceeds any key value in the file, or alternate index in this case. In program VSD383, START positions the current record pointer to the first record according to the key value—alternate key value here— because no record will have a key composed of low-values. Figure 7.12 illustrates what happens in VSD383 if the NAMEAIX alternate is initialized 9999 instead of low values; this is higher than any key on the file, and a FILE STATUS of 23 results. This would not ordinarily be regarded as a cause for a forced abort, but program VSD383 was coded to serve a learning purpose, not a production one.

Changing the Key of Reference

START switches the attention of the program from the primary index to an alternate index if the alternate index key is named in the START verb. In this case START positions the current record pointer to an alternate index record, and subsequent accesses will occur via that index. READ/NEXT actions will obtain records as if they were stored in the order of the alternate index.

The second service performed by START is often obscured, but it is vital for programs such as VSD383. In technical terms the switching of attention is called changing the "key of reference." It is also possible to accomplish this change using the READ verb, but doing so requires that the specific alternate key value specified in the alternate key field is actually on the file. In practice, START is the method commonly used to change the key of reference.

MVS Job Control Language

The MVS job control language for alternate key access is, relatively speaking, unusual. The SELECT/ASSIGN statement carries as the "ASSIGN TO" name the DDname as always. The statement carries mention of at least the alternate index accessed by the program, or for AK00.C98.CUSTMAST, both alternate indexes if the program were to access

```
****************************************//*****************************************
*    CUSTOMERS BY NAME    //   PROGRAM VSD383    *   05/09/87  *  PAGE   1  *
****************************************//*****************************************


ACCOUNT NO          LAST NAME       FIRST NAME              ADDRESS           APT   DATA
<------>        <--------------->  <-------->      <--->  - <-------------->  <--->   --


>>> RUN ABORTED -- FILE STATUS WAS      -- NAMEAIX KEY AT FAILURE WAS

>>> RUN ABORTED -- FILE STATUS WAS      -- 9999

>>> RUN ABORTED -- FILE STATUS WAS 23 -- START FAILED P2705 (VSAM1-FS)


*** END OF JOB           0 RECORDS READ              0 RECORDS PRINTED
```

FIGURE 7.12 FILE STATUS value of 23 resulting from attempt to perform a START in program VSD383 at key "9999" which is greater than any key on file. (Program logic could and should intercept and resolve this error rather than treating it as grounds for a forced-abort.)

them both. But the JCL will have to cite at the DDname the base cluster of the VSAM data set, and *must also cite for each alternate index the name of the path by which it is accessed.*

COBOL SELECT/ASSIGN syntax provides the means only to specify a DDname for the base cluster. In order to provide a DDname for one or more alternate indexes, MVS does some behind-the-scenes work and generates additional DDnames using the DDname coded for the base cluster as a pattern. If this DDname is seven or fewer characters in length, MVS appends a "1" to it for the first alternate index cited, a "2" for the next alternate index stated, and so forth. If the base cluster DDname is eight characters in length, MVS overlays the last character with this generated digit.

In the case of program VSD383, the base cluster name is VSAMCSM, for "VSAM Customer Master." Since this is only seven characters in length, the DDname generated by MVS for the alternate index path is VSAMCSM1. This is the DDname shown in Figure 7.10, the MVS JCL used to run VSD383.

If a DDname is not coded in JCL for the alternate index path as required, the job fails. As Figure 7.13 indicates, the error message provided with the failure states that a DDname of the required form was missing. With the FILE STATUS checking performed by VSD383, the program itself produces a message if a DD statement for the alternate index is omitted. Figure 7.14 depicts the report produced in this case, presenting the FILE STATUS value of 96.

Some installations use a convention for DDnames that makes them eight positions in length and places a digit in the last position. Such a naming convention easily conflicts with the method used by MVS to generate alternate index path DDnames. For these cases DDnames composed of seven letters are clearer and offer less potential for confusion.[7]

```
          J E S 2   J O B   L O G  --  S Y S T E M   M 5 F S  --  N O D E   F S D C L A 0 1


     16.51.01 JOB  353  $HASP373 FSBT686A STARTED - INIT 15 - CLASS E - SYS M5FS
     16.51.01 JOB  353  SMF103I JOB FSBT686A  STEP 001 OF 003  STARTED  16:51
     16.51.01 JOB  353  IEF403I - FSBT686A - STARTED
     16.51.04 JOB  353  IEC130I VSAMCSM1 DD STATEMENT MISSING
     16.51.06 JOB  353  IEC999I IFG0200T,FSBT686A,STEPA                     ┌──────────────────┐
     16.51.39 JOB  353 *IEA911E COMPLETE DUMP ON SYS1.DUMP00      ├────────│  Error messages  │
                          FOR ASID (004C)                                  └──────────────────┘
                            ERROR ID = SEQ11216 CPU00 ASID004C TIME16.51.05.9
     16.51.39 JOB  353  IEC999I IFG0TCOA,IFG0TCOB,FSBT686A,STEPA    ,DEB ADDR = 8D1020
     16.51.39 JOB  353  IEF404I FSBT686A - ENDED
     16.51.39 JOB  353  $HASP373 FSBT686A ENDED
                    -
                    -
                    -
     IEF236I ALLOC. FOR FSBT686A STEPA
     IEF237I 92C  ALLOCATED TO STEPLIB
     IEF237I 711  ALLOCATED TO VSAMCSM
     IEF237I 716  ALLOCATED TO SYS00242
     IEF237I JES2 ALLOCATED TO VSD383U1
     IEF237I JES2 ALLOCATED TO SYSOUT
     IEF237I JES2 ALLOCATED TO SYSUDUMP
     IEC130I VSAMCSM1 DD STATEMENT MISSING       ├───────────┤ Error message │
     IEC999I IFG0200T,FSBT686A,STEPA                         └───────────────┘
     IEC999I IFG0TCOA,IFG0TCOB,FSBT686A,STEPA    ,DEB ADDR = 8D1020
     IEF142I FSBT686A STEPA - STEP WAS EXECUTED - COND CODE 3333
                    -
                    -
                    -
```

FIGURE 7.13   MVS error messages resulting from omission of DD statement for DDname generated for the alternate index from the base cluster name

```
*****************************************************************
*    CUSTOMERS BY NAME   //  PROGRAM VSD383   *  05/09/87  *  PAGE   1  *
*****************************************************************


ACCOUNT NO        LAST NAME        FIRST NAME         ADDRESS        APT  DATA
<------>       <--------------->  <-------->    <--->  -  <------------->  <--->   --


>>> RUN ABORTED -- FILE STATUS WAS 96 -- FAILED ON OPENING (VSAM1-FS)


*** END OF JOB            0 RECORDS READ            0 RECORDS PRINTED
```

FIGURE 7.14   Messages generated by program VSD383 when DD statement for generated DDname is omitted

DOS/VSE Job Control Language

DOS/VSE confronts the same situation as does MVS in connection with access to a KSDS via alternate keys. Each alternate key specified in the SELECT/ASSIGN statement needs to have a DLBL statement coded in the JCL executing the program.

Under DOS/VSE file-names on DLBL statements are limited to seven characters. The file-name generated from that used for the base cluster in the SELECT/ASSIGN statement is thus formed by adding the seventh character to a file-name of six characters or less, or overlaying the seventh position with the generated digit.

ALTERNATE KEYS: A REALISTIC EXAMPLE

Alternate key access to a key sequenced set purely for the purpose of listing records in a sequence other than ascending by primary key is not a commonly performed action, because external or internal sorting is a more efficient way to accomplish that. But access to a key sequenced data set by alternate key, driven by transactions that each cause a START and one or more READ/NEXT actions, is more common. The need for this type of processing arises when validation associated with an update requires cross-checking with other records on file, and in some cases where update transactions arrive coded with a partial key or a key other than the primary one.

Alternate Key Access Driven by Transactions

Let's take program VSD383 a step further, and modify it to respond to a transactions file containing transactions such as those depicted in Figure 7.15. We will access data set AK00.C98.CUSTMAST via the name alternate index NAMEAIX. But instead of starting the access at the record pointed to by the first record in the alternate index, we will start the access at the first alternate index record carrying the letter on the transaction present. We'll list all of the records from the master file that carry this first letter, then read the next transaction, START at that alternate index record, list those records, and so forth. So in fact access will not be on a complete alternate key, but rather on a partial one.

Figure 7.16 illustrates the output we wish to receive from our new version of the program. This output results from the transactions shown in Figure 7.15; the comments on each transaction simply note the anticipated result based on the test data to be used. The listing is now driven by the transactions; they initiate the sequential reading of the data set in alternate key sequence starting at different points.

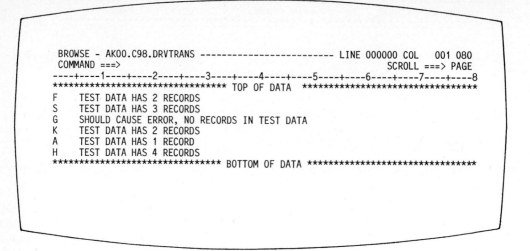

```
BROWSE - AK00.C98.DRVTRANS ------------------------ LINE 000000 COL   001 080
 COMMAND ===>                                               SCROLL ===> PAGE
 ----+----1----+----2----+----3----+----4----+----5----+----6----+----7----+----8
 ********************************* TOP OF DATA  *********************************
 F    TEST DATA HAS 2 RECORDS
 S    TEST DATA HAS 3 RECORDS
 G    SHOULD CAUSE ERROR, NO RECORDS IN TEST DATA
 K    TEST DATA HAS 2 RECORDS
 A    TEST DATA HAS 1 RECORD
 H    TEST DATA HAS 4 RECORDS
 ****************************** BOTTOM OF DATA *********************************
```

FIGURE 7.15 Driver transactions for alternate key START, READ/NEXT program VSD683, with comments based on test data

```
****************************************************************************
*    START/READ BY NAME   //   PROGRAM VSD683    *   C5/09/87  *   PAGE    1  *
****************************************************************************


ACCOUNT NO          LAST NAME      FIRST NAME           ADDRESS         APT  DATA
<------>        <--------------->  <-------->  <--->  - <-------------> <--->  --


 64070301     FLAGG              ALLAN        05625 N KOSTNER AV     43     PP

 08716293     FORESTER           ALVIN        09710 S DORCHESTER ST         AA


 48077449     SMITH              JOHN         01349 W 69TH                  MM

 63735122     SMITH              JOHN         00911   KILBOURNE            NN

 63817627     SMITH              JOHN         02415 E 135TH ST              OO


>>> START NOT POSSIBLE FOR DRIVER KEY "G" -- NO NAMES STARTING WITH THIS LETTER ON FILE
 32613729     KALKINS            JANET        03016 N SHERIDAN RD           GG

 24307091     KUREK              BESSIE       05800 W FULLERTON AVE  4-B    CC


 33841546     ANCONA             MINNIE       04310 S KOLINA PL      17     II


 28799201     HAMPSTER           HARVEY       08711 S HALLDALE AV           FF

 32817132     HAMPSTER           HELEN        08711 S HALLDALE AV           HH

 28441269     HAMPSTER           HENRIETTA    08711 S HALLDALE AV           EE

 25656631     HAMPSTER           HERBERT      08711 S HALLDALE AV           DD


*** END OF JOB        17 RECORDS READ        12 RECORDS PRINTED
```

FIGURE 7.16 Output of program VSD683 using test data and the driver transactions of Figure 7.15

Software-Engineered Logic for a Browse

Figure 7.17 is a software engineering profile diagram of the logic of VSD683. The program was actually designed using this blueprint. You will find it handiest to see the big picture of the program's logic using this diagram; in stepping up to the use of transactions to drive the START and READ/NEXT process, VSD683 becomes significantly more complicated than the simple file listings illustrated earlier. Each of the brackets shown on the profile represents a paragraph of source code, identified by the four-digit number shown.[8] Note that the location of some of the processing logic has changed from program VSD383 to VSD683.

The operation of VSD683 involves the prime reading of the transaction file to obtain the alternate first key value to be used in a START. This occurs in beginning of job paragraph 1000. The processing loop, paragraph 2000, moves this value to a defined portion of the alternate key field in the file description. Then a START is performed. If this start is successful, a browse is performed; note that the browse, paragraph 2200, is a repetition of the overall beginning/process/end pattern including iteration of the process within it. If the START was not successful, it means that no records exist on the file meeting the partial key condition; that is, the name field of no record matches the letter carried on the transaction. In this case an appropriate message is to be output on the report.

The iterative loop within the browse process itself, contained in paragraph 2200, is driven until one of two conditions is met. When the record obtained from the master file via the NAMEAIX alternate index carries a name field no longer meeting the starting-letter carried on the transaction, it is time to end the browse and return control to the main iterative process of paragraph 2000. It is possible, however, that the START occurred on the last group of records in the alternate index, as is the case with the fifth transaction, the letter "W." In this case the condition to end the loop within the browse must be end of file on the alternate index, which does not represent end of job.

COBOL Source Code and Syntax

Figure 7.18 lists the source code for program VSD683. The logic blueprint of figure 7.17 is implemented directly in this source code; the logic unit numbers on the profile are used within paragraph names.

These elements of the source code for VSD683 bear special attention:

- The nonunique ADDRAIX alternate key is cited in the SELECT/ASSIGN. This is not necessary since VSD683 continues to use only the NAMEAIX alternate key, but ADDRAIX is coded here to illustrate how two alternate indexes are coded and the MVS JCL necessary when this is done.
- The file description NAMEAIX alternate key definition has been modified to create FD-NAMEAIX-LASTNAME-BYTE1, the partial alternate key field on which the START will occur. This field name provides the name cited in the START verb at the top of paragraph 2000.
- Paragraph 2000 moves the transaction key value to FD-NAMEAIX-LASTNAME-BYTE1 and invokes the START I/O module, paragraph 2100. The START verb in paragraph 2100 is coded naming this field. The current record pointer will be positioned at the first record in the alternate index meeting this partial key condition, if such a record exists.
- The iterative loop within the browse process itself is driven, in paragraph 2200, with a PERFORM UNTIL statement satisfied by either a NOT EQUAL transaction key condition or the end of file flag for the master file reaching its ending condition value.

```
─0000
          ┌─1000
          │ Initialize (9000)
          │ Open non-VSAM files
   BOJ    │ Create report new page (2910)              ┌─9101
          │ Open VSAM file ─────────────────────────── │ Open file.
          │ Prime read driver file (2990)              │ If FILE-STATUS not OK
          └─                                           │   compose error message
                                                       │   do forced abort ───────
          ┌─2000


          │         Move driver file key to VSAM file FD


          │                   ┌─2100
          │                   │ START VSAM file
          │                   │ If START OK
          │                   │   move "G" to flag
          │                   │ else
          │          START    │ if record not found
          │                   │   move "B" to flag
          │                   │ else
          │                   │   compose and output messages (2900)
          │                   │   compose error message
          │                   │   do forced abort (9999)
 Perform  │                   └─
 until
PGM  end of
     driver
     file     If flag = "G"
          │     do browse ─────────────────────────────────────────────────
          │   else
          │     do no browse. ──────────────────────────────────────────────


          │                         ┌─2990
          │                         │ Read
          │          Read driver ── │   at end move "E" to file-flag.
          │          file           │ count
          │                         └─
          └─


          ┌─3000
          │ Form summary message printline
   EOJ    │ Write printline out (2900)
          └ Close files
─
```

FIGURE 7.17   Software engineering profile logic design for program

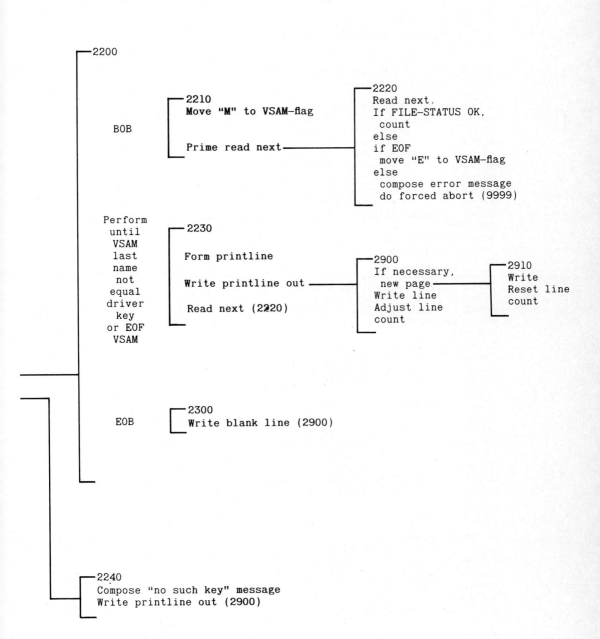

```
9999
Write message printline
Close files
Move 3333 to return-code
STOP RUN


2200

                    2210                        2220
                    Move "M" to VSAM-flag       Read next.
         BOB                                    If FILE-STATUS OK,
                                                 count
                    Prime read next             else
                                                if EOF
                                                 move "E" to VSAM-flag
                                                else
                                                 compose error message
                                                 do forced abort (9999)

    Perform
    until       2230
    VSAM
    last        Form printline               2900                      2910
    name                                     If necessary,             Write
    not         Write printline out           new page                 Reset line
    equal                                    Write line                count
    driver      Read next (2220)             Adjust line
    key                                      count
    or EOF
    VSAM


                    2300
         EOB        Write blank line (2900)




    2240
    Compose "no such key" message
    Write printline out (2900)
```

VSD683, each bracket representing a paragraph of source code

```
000100 IDENTIFICATION DIVISION.
000200 PROGRAM-ID.     VSD683.
000300 AUTHOR.         J JANOSSY.
000400 INSTALLATION.   DEPAUL UNIVERSITY.
000500 DATE-WRITTEN.   MAY 1987.
000600 DATE-COMPILED.
000700*REMARKS.        FOR IBM VSCOBOL
000800*                VERSION 01   LAST CHANGE 05-07-87   ORIG 05-07-87
000900*                FILE-TO-PRINT PROGRAM. READS A VSAM DATA SET
001000*                TO DEMONSTRATE START AND READ/NEXT PROCESSING.
001100*
001200 ENVIRONMENT DIVISION.
001300 CONFIGURATION SECTION.
001400 SOURCE-COMPUTER.  IBM-3081.
001500 OBJECT-COMPUTER.  IBM-3081.
001600 SPECIAL-NAMES.  C01 IS PAGE-EJECT.
001700 INPUT-OUTPUT SECTION.
001800 FILE-CONTROL.
001900     SELECT DRIVER      ASSIGN TO UT-S-BT1522E1.
002000     SELECT VSAMFILE    ASSIGN TO      B1522CSM
002100        ORGANIZATION IS INDEXED
002200        ACCESS MODE IS SEQUENTIAL
002300        RECORD KEY IS FD-ACCOUNT-NO-KEY
002400        ALTERNATE RECORD KEY IS FD-ADDR-AIX
002500           WITH DUPLICATES
002600        ALTERNATE RECORD KEY IS FD-NAME-AIX
002700        FILE STATUS IS VSAM1-FS.
002800     SELECT REPORT1    ASSIGN TO UT-S-BT1522U1.
002900*
003000 DATA DIVISION.
003100 FILE SECTION.
003200*
003300 FD   DRIVER
003400     LABEL RECORDS ARE STANDARD
003500     BLOCK CONTAINS 0 RECORDS
003600     RECORD CONTAINS 80 CHARACTERS.
003700 01   DRIVER-REC                  PIC X(80).
003800*
003900 FD   VSAMFILE
004000     LABEL RECORDS ARE STANDARD
004100     BLOCK CONTAINS 0 RECORDS
004200     RECORD CONTAINS 250 CHARACTERS.
004300 01   VSAMFILE-REC.
004400     12 FILLER                    PIC X(9).
004500     12 FD-NAME-AIX.
004600        15 FD-NAMEAIX-CUSTOMER.
004700           18 FD-NAMEAIX-LASTNAME.
004800              21 FD-NAMEAIX-LASTNAME-BYTE1 PIC X(1).
004900              21 FILLER           PIC X(17).
005000           18 FD-NAMEAIX-FIRSTNAME  PIC X(9).
005100        15 FD-ACCOUNT-NO-KEY      PIC X(8).
005200     12 FD-ADDR-AIX               PIC X(26).
005300     12 FILLER                    PIC X(180).
005400*
005500 FD   REPORT1
005600     LABEL RECORDS ARE OMITTED
005700     BLOCK CONTAINS 0 RECORDS
005800     RECORD CONTAINS 133 CHARACTERS.
005900 01   REPORT1-REC                 PIC X(133).
006000/
006100 WORKING-STORAGE SECTION.
006200 01  FILLER PIC X(23)  VALUE  '*WORKING STORAGE START*'.
006300*
006400*VSAM1STD  LAST CHANGED 04-02-84  ORIGINAL 01-22-84  J JANOSSY
006500****************************************************************
```

FIGURE 7.18 Source code for program VSD683, which performs START, READ/NEXT access to a key sequenced data set based on driver transactions

```
006600*    STANDARD VSAM FILE STATUS FIELD DEFINITION (1)              *
006700*****************************************************************
006800 01  VSAM1-FS.
006900     05 VSAM1-FS-LEFT-RIGHT.
007000         10 VSAM1-FS-LEFT         PIC X(1).
007100             88 VSAM1-ACTION-OK                  VALUE '0'.
007200             88 VSAM1-SEQ-EOF                    VALUE '1'.
007300         10 FILLER                PIC X(1).
007400     05 VSAM1-FS-FULL   REDEFINES
007500        VSAM1-FS-LEFT-RIGHT       PIC X(2).
007600             88 VSAM1-WRITE-OUT-SEQ             VALUE '21'.
007700             88 VSAM1-DUP-PRIME-ALT-KEY         VALUE '22'.
007800             88 VSAM1-REC-NOT-FOUND             VALUE '23'.
007900             88 VSAM1-OPEN-OK                   VALUE '00'.
008000*
008100 01  WS-FLAGS.
008200     12 F1-VSAM-EOF-FLAG          PIC X(1) VALUE 'M'.
008300         88 F1-VSAM-END                      VALUE 'E'.
008400     12 F2-VSAM-ACCESS-FLAG       PIC X(1).
008500         88 F2-VSAM-ACCESS-GOOD              VALUE 'G'.
008600         88 F2-VSAM-ACCESS-BAD               VALUE 'B'.
008700     12 F3-DRIVER-EOF-FLAG        PIC X(1) VALUE 'M'.
008800         88 F3-DRIVER-END                    VALUE 'E'.
008900*
009000 01  WS-COUNTERS.
009100     12 WS-DRIVER-IN-COUNT        PIC S9(5) VALUE +0.
009200     12 WS-VSAMFILE-IN-COUNT      PIC S9(5) VALUE +0.
009300     12 WS-VSAMFILE-OUT-COUNT     PIC S9(5) VALUE +0.
009400*
009500 01  DRIVER-FILE-INPUT-AREA.
009600     12 DRI-START-KEY             PIC X(1).
009700     12 FILLER                    PIC X(79).
009800*
009900 01  VSAMFILE-INPUT-AREA.
010000     12 VFI-OLD-ID-NO             PIC X(9).
010100     12 VFI-NAME-AIX.
010200         15 VFI-NAMEAIX-CUSTOMER.
010300             18 VFI-NAMEAIX-LASTNAME.
010400                 21 VFI-NAMEAIX-LASTNAME-BYTE1  PIC X(1).
010500                 21 FILLER                PIC X(17).
010600             18 VFI-NAMEAIX-FIRSTNAME     PIC X(9).
010700     12 VFI-ACCOUNT-NO-KEY        PIC X(8).
010800     12 VFI-ADDRAIX.
010900         15 VFI-ADDRAIX-ST-DIREC  PIC X(1).
011000         15 VFI-ADDRAIX-ST-NAME   PIC X(15).
011100         15 VFI-ADDRAIX-HOUSE-NO  PIC X(5).
011200         15 VFI-ADDRAIX-APT-NO    PIC X(5).
011300     12 VFI-RECORD-DATA.
011400         15 VFI-TWO-LETTERS       PIC X(2).
011500         15 FILLER                PIC X(178).
011600*
011700 01  REPORT1-COUNTERS.
011800     12 R1-LINE-LIMIT             PIC S9(2) VALUE +60.
011900     12 R1-NORMAL-LINE-SPACING    PIC S9(2) VALUE +2.
012000     12 R1-LINES-REMAINING        PIC S9(2) VALUE +0.
012100     12 R1-PAGE-COUNT             PIC S9(3) VALUE +0.
012200     12 R1-WANTED-LINE-SPACING    PIC S9(3) VALUE +0.
012300     12 R1-PRINT-SLOT             PIC X(133).
012400*
012500 01  R1-PAGE-HDR1.
012600     12 FILLER                    PIC X(1).
012700     12 FILLER                    PIC X(72) VALUE ALL '*'.
012800     12 FILLER                    PIC X(60) VALUE ALL ' '.
012900*
013000 01  R1-PAGE-HDR2.
013100     12 FILLER                    PIC X(1).
013200     12 FILLER                    PIC X(4) VALUE '*   '.
```

FIGURE 7.18   (Continued)

```
013300       12 R1-PH2-PGM-TITLE           PIC X(18)  VALUE ALL 'X'.
013400       12 FILLER                     PIC X(14)  VALUE
013500          ' // PROGRAM '.
013600       12 R1-PH2-PGM-ID              PIC X(6)   VALUE ALL 'X'.
013700       12 FILLER                     PIC X(6)   VALUE ' * '.
013800       12 R1-PH2-DATE                PIC X(8).
013900       12 FILLER                     PIC X(10)  VALUE ' * PAGE '.
014000       12 R1-PH2-PAGE-NO             PIC ZZ9.
014100       12 FILLER                     PIC X(3)   VALUE ' *'.
014200       12 FILLER                     PIC X(60)  VALUE ALL ' '.
014300*
014400 01  R1-COL-HDR1.
014500       12 FILLER                     PIC X(1).
014600       12 FILLER  PIC X(22)  VALUE 'ACCOUNT NO      LAST'.
014700       12 FILLER  PIC X(22)  VALUE ' NAME     FIRST NAME '.
014800       12 FILLER  PIC X(22)  VALUE '        ADDRESS      '.
014900       12 FILLER  PIC X(22)  VALUE '  APT  DATA          '.
015000       12 FILLER  PIC X(22)  VALUE '                     '.
015100       12 FILLER  PIC X(22)  VALUE '                     '.
015200*
015300 01  R1-COL-HDR2.
015400       12 FILLER                     PIC X(1).
015500       12 FILLER  PIC X(22)  VALUE ' <------>    <-------- '.
015600       12 FILLER  PIC X(22)  VALUE '--------> <-------->  '.
015700       12 FILLER  PIC X(22)  VALUE '<---> - <------------- '.
015800       12 FILLER  PIC X(22)  VALUE '> <---> --            '.
015900       12 FILLER  PIC X(22)  VALUE '                     '.
016000       12 FILLER  PIC X(22)  VALUE '                     '.
016100*
016200 01  R1-DETLINE.
016300       12 FILLER                     PIC X(1).
016400       12 FILLER                     PIC X(1)   VALUE ' '.
016500       12 R1-DL-ACCOUNT-NO-KEY       PIC X(8).
016600       12 FILLER                     PIC X(4)   VALUE ALL ' '.
016700       12 R1-DL-NAMEAIX-LASTNAME     PIC X(18).
016800       12 FILLER                     PIC X(1)   VALUE ' '.
016900       12 R1-DL-NAMEAIX-FIRSTNAME    PIC X(9).
017000       12 FILLER                     PIC X(3)   VALUE ALL ' '.
017100       12 R1-DL-ADDRAIX-HOUSE-NO     PIC X(5).
017200       12 FILLER                     PIC X(1)   VALUE ' '.
017300       12 R1-DL-ADDRAIX-ST-DIREC     PIC X(1).
017400       12 FILLER                     PIC X(1)   VALUE ' '.
017500       12 R1-DL-ADDRAIX-ST-NAME      PIC X(15).
017600       12 FILLER                     PIC X(1)   VALUE ' '.
017700       12 R1-DL-ADDRAIX-APT-NO       PIC X(5).
017800       12 FILLER                     PIC X(2)   VALUE ALL ' '.
017900       12 R1-DL-TWO-LETTERS          PIC X(2).
018000       12 FILLER                     PIC X(55)  VALUE ALL ' '.
018100*
018200 01  R1-ENDLINE.
018300       12 FILLER                     PIC X(1).
018400       12 FILLER                     PIC X(17)  VALUE
018500          '*** END OF JOB   '.
018600       12 R1-EL-IN-COUNT             PIC Z,ZZZ,ZZ9.
018700       12 FILLER                     PIC X(16)  VALUE
018800          ' RECORDS READ    '.
018900       12 R1-EL-OUT-COUNT            PIC Z,ZZZ,ZZ9.
019000       12 FILLER                     PIC X(16)  VALUE
019100          ' RECORDS PRINTED'.
019200       12 FILLER                     PIC X(65)  VALUE ALL ' '.
019300*
019400 01  R1-VSAM-PROBLEM-LINE.
019500       12 FILLER                     PIC X(1).
019600       12 FILLER                     PIC X(35)  VALUE
019700          '>>> RUN ABORTED -- FILE STATUS WAS '.
019800       12 R1-VPL-FILE-STATUS         PIC X(2).
019900       12 FILLER                     PIC X(4)   VALUE ' -- '.
```

FIGURE 7.18   (Continued)

```
020000      12 R1-VPL-MSG                PIC X(30).
020100      12 FILLER                    PIC X(61)  VALUE ALL ' '.
020200*
020300 01  R1-DRIVER-PROBLEM-LINE.
020400      12 FILLER                    PIC X(1).
020500      12 FILLER                    PIC X(39)  VALUE
020600      '>>> START NOT POSSIBLE FOR DRIVER KEY "'.
020700      12 R1-DPL-DRIVER-KEY         PIC X(1).
020800      12 FILLER                    PIC X(48)  VALUE
020900      '" -- NO NAMES STARTING WITH THIS LETTER ON FILE"'.
021000      12 FILLER                    PIC X(44)  VALUE ALL ' '.
021100/
021200 PROCEDURE DIVISION.
021300*
021400 0000-MAINLINE.
021500      PERFORM 1000-BOJ.
021600      PERFORM 2000-PROCESS UNTIL F3-DRIVER-EOF-FLAG EQUAL 'E'.
021700      PERFORM 3000-EOJ.
021800      STOP RUN.
021900*
022000 1000-BOJ.
022100      PERFORM 9000-INIT.
022200      OPEN  INPUT DRIVER  OUTPUT REPORT1.
022300      PERFORM 2910-R1-NEWPAGE.
022400      PERFORM 9101-VSAM1-OPEN.
022500      PERFORM 2990-READ-DRIVER.
022600*
022700 2000-PROCESS.
022800      MOVE DRI-START-KEY TO FD-NAMEAIX-LASTNAME-BYTE1.
022900      PERFORM 2100-START-NAMEAIX-PARTIAL.
023000      IF F2-VSAM-ACCESS-FLAG = 'G'
023100         PERFORM 2200-BROWSE
023200       ELSE
023300         PERFORM 2240-NO-BROWSE.
023400      PERFORM 2990-READ-DRIVER.
023500*
023600 2100-START-NAMEAIX-PARTIAL.
023700      START VSAMFILE KEY = FD-NAMEAIX-LASTNAME-BYTE1.
023800      IF VSAM1-ACTION-OK
023900         MOVE 'G' TO F2-VSAM-ACCESS-FLAG
024000       ELSE
024100        IF VSAM1-REC-NOT-FOUND
024200         MOVE 'B' TO F2-VSAM-ACCESS-FLAG
024300        ELSE
024400         MOVE R1-NORMAL-LINE-SPACING TO R1-WANTED-LINE-SPACING
024500         MOVE SPACES TO R1-VPL-FILE-STATUS
024600         MOVE 'NAMEAIX KEY AT FAILURE WAS      ' TO R1-VPL-MSG
024700         MOVE R1-VSAM-PROBLEM-LINE TO R1-PRINT-SLOT
024800         PERFORM 2900-WRITE-R1-OUTPUT
024900*
025000         MOVE FD-NAME-AIX                      TO R1-VPL-MSG
025100         MOVE R1-VSAM-PROBLEM-LINE TO R1-PRINT-SLOT
025200         PERFORM 2900-WRITE-R1-OUTPUT
025300*
025400         MOVE VSAM1-FS TO R1-VPL-FILE-STATUS
025500         MOVE 'START FAILED P2705 (VSAM1-FS) ' TO R1-VPL-MSG
025600         MOVE R1-VSAM-PROBLEM-LINE TO R1-PRINT-SLOT
025700         PERFORM 9999-FORCED-ABORT.
025800*
025900 2200-BROWSE.
026000      PERFORM 2210-BOJ-BROWSE.
026100      PERFORM 2230-PROCESS-BROWSE
026200         UNTIL FD-NAMEAIX-LASTNAME-BYTE1 NOT EQUAL DRI-START-KEY
026300            OR F3-DRIVER-EOF-FLAG = 'E'.
026400      PERFORM 2300-EOJ-BROWSE.
026500*
026600 2210-BOJ-BROWSE.
```

FIGURE 7.18 (Continued)

```
026700         MOVE 'M' TO F1-VSAM-EOF-FLAG.
026800         PERFORM 2220-READ-NEXT.
026900*
027000 2220-READ-NEXT.
027100         READ VSAMFILE NEXT INTO VSAMFILE-INPUT-AREA.
027200         IF VSAM1-ACTION-OK
027300           NEXT SENTENCE
027400         ELSE
027500         IF VSAM1-SEQ-EOF
027600           MOVE 'E' TO F1-VSAM-EOF-FLAG
027700          ELSE
027800           MOVE VSAM1-FS TO R1-VPL-FILE-STATUS
027900           MOVE 'FAILED ON READ/NEXT (VSAM1-FS)' TO R1-VPL-MSG
028000           MOVE R1-VSAM-PROBLEM-LINE TO R1-PRINT-SLOT
028100           PERFORM 9999-FORCED-ABORT.
028200         IF F1-VSAM-EOF-FLAG NOT EQUAL 'E'
028300           ADD +1 TO WS-VSAMFILE-IN-COUNT.
028400*
028500 2230-PROCESS-BROWSE.
028600         MOVE VFI-ACCOUNT-NO-KEY      TO R1-DL-ACCOUNT-NO-KEY.
028700         MOVE VFI-NAMEAIX-LASTNAME    TO R1-DL-NAMEAIX-LASTNAME.
028800         MOVE VFI-NAMEAIX-FIRSTNAME   TO R1-DL-NAMEAIX-FIRSTNAME.
028900         MOVE VFI-ADDRAIX-HOUSE-NO    TO R1-DL-ADDRAIX-HOUSE-NO.
029000         MOVE VFI-ADDRAIX-ST-DIREC    TO R1-DL-ADDRAIX-ST-DIREC.
029100         MOVE VFI-ADDRAIX-ST-NAME     TO R1-DL-ADDRAIX-ST-NAME.
029200         MOVE VFI-ADDRAIX-APT-NO      TO R1-DL-ADDRAIX-APT-NO.
029300         MOVE VFI-TWO-LETTERS         TO R1-DL-TWO-LETTERS.
029400         MOVE R1-DETLINE TO R1-PRINT-SLOT.
029500         MOVE R1-NORMAL-LINE-SPACING TO R1-WANTED-LINE-SPACING.
029600         PERFORM 2900-WRITE-R1-OUTPUT.
029700         ADD +1 TO WS-VSAMFILE-OUT-COUNT.
029800         PERFORM 2220-READ-NEXT.
029900*
030000 2240-NO-BROWSE.
030100         MOVE DRI-START-KEY TO R1-DPL-DRIVER-KEY.
030200         MOVE R1-DRIVER-PROBLEM-LINE TO R1-PRINT-SLOT.
030300         MOVE R1-NORMAL-LINE-SPACING TO R1-WANTED-LINE-SPACING.
030400         PERFORM 2900-WRITE-R1-OUTPUT.
030500*
030600 2300-EOJ-BROWSE.
030700         MOVE SPACES TO R1-PRINT-SLOT.
030800         MOVE R1-NORMAL-LINE-SPACING TO R1-WANTED-LINE-SPACING.
030900         PERFORM 2900-WRITE-R1-OUTPUT.
031000*
031100 2900-WRITE-R1-OUTPUT.
031200         IF R1-LINES-REMAINING IS LESS THAN R1-WANTED-LINE-SPACING
031300             PERFORM 2910-R1-NEWPAGE.
031400         WRITE REPORT1-REC FROM R1-PRINT-SLOT
031500             AFTER ADVANCING R1-WANTED-LINE-SPACING LINES.
031600         COMPUTE R1-LINES-REMAINING =
031700             (R1-LINES-REMAINING - R1-WANTED-LINE-SPACING).
031800*
031900 2910-R1-NEWPAGE.
032000         ADD +1 TO R1-PAGE-COUNT.
032100         MOVE R1-PAGE-COUNT TO R1-PH2-PAGE-NO.
032200         WRITE REPORT1-REC FROM R1-PAGE-HDR1
032300             AFTER ADVANCING PAGE-EJECT.
032400         WRITE REPORT1-REC FROM R1-PAGE-HDR2 AFTER ADVANCING 1 LINES.
032500         WRITE REPORT1-REC FROM R1-PAGE-HDR1 AFTER ADVANCING 1 LINES.
032600         WRITE REPORT1-REC FROM R1-COL-HDR1  AFTER ADVANCING 4 LINES.
032700         WRITE REPORT1-REC FROM R1-COL-HDR2  AFTER ADVANCING 1 LINES.
032800         MOVE SPACES TO REPORT1-REC.
032900         WRITE REPORT1-REC AFTER ADVANCING 2 LINES.
033000         COMPUTE R1-LINES-REMAINING = (R1-LINE-LIMIT - 10).
033100         MOVE R1-NORMAL-LINE-SPACING TO R1-WANTED-LINE-SPACING.
033200*
033300 2990-READ-DRIVER.
```

FIGURE 7.18   (Continued)

```
033400      READ DRIVER INTO DRIVER-FILE-INPUT-AREA
033500          AT END
033600              MOVE 'E' TO F3-DRIVER-EOF-FLAG.
033700      IF F3-DRIVER-EOF-FLAG NOT EQUAL 'M'
033800          ADD +1 TO WS-DRIVER-IN-COUNT.
033900*
034000 3000-EOJ.
034100      MOVE WS-VSAMFILE-IN-COUNT TO R1-EL-IN-COUNT.
034200      MOVE WS-VSAMFILE-OUT-COUNT TO R1-EL-OUT-COUNT.
034300      MOVE R1-ENDLINE TO R1-PRINT-SLOT.
034400      MOVE +3 TO R1-WANTED-LINE-SPACING.
034500      PERFORM 2900-WRITE-R1-OUTPUT.
034600      CLOSE  VSAMFILE  DRIVER  REPORT1.
034700*
034800 9000-INIT.
034900      MOVE 'START/READ BY NAME' TO R1-PH2-PGM-TITLE.
035000      MOVE 'VSD683' TO R1-PH2-PGM-ID.
035100      MOVE CURRENT-DATE TO R1-PH2-DATE.
035200*
035300 9101-VSAM1-OPEN.
035400      OPEN   INPUT VSAMFILE.
035500      IF VSAM1-OPEN-OK
035600        NEXT SENTENCE
035700      ELSE
035800        MOVE VSAM1-FS TO R1-VPL-FILE-STATUS
035900        MOVE 'FAILED ON OPENING (VSAM1-FS)  ' TO R1-VPL-MSG
036000        MOVE R1-VSAM-PROBLEM-LINE TO R1-PRINT-SLOT
036100        PERFORM 9999-FORCED-ABORT.
036200*
036300 9999-FORCED-ABORT.
036400      MOVE R1-NORMAL-LINE-SPACING TO R1-WANTED-LINE-SPACING.
036500      PERFORM 2900-WRITE-R1-OUTPUT.
036600      PERFORM 3000-EOJ.
036700      MOVE 3333 TO RETURN-CODE.
036800      STOP RUN.
```

FIGURE 7.18   (Continued)

- Paragraph 2990 now exists within the program to obtain the records from the transaction file, which is simply a sequential data set.

Program VSD683 conducts "inquire only" access to the master file. If it were using transaction data to update masterfile records, the record to be updated may be acquired with an alternate key read or browse, if appropriate. But the record should be reread with the primary key using the READ verb with KEY phrase, as described below, before attempting to perform the update and rewrite. Updates should always be done using the primary key.

Job Control Language for Two Alternate Indexes

VSD683 uses only the NAMEAIX alternate index, but its SELECT/ASSIGN cites both the ADDRAIX and NAMEAIX alternate indexes. The MVS JCL to execute VSD683, illustrated in Figure 7.19, must therefore contain DD statements for the base cluster, ADDRAIX path, and NAMEAIX path, in this sequence. Since ADDRAIX is named first in the SELECT/ASSIGN, the DDname generated by MVS for it will exist with a "1" appended or overlaid in the last position of the stated base cluster DDname. NAMEAIX will have a "2" appended or overlaid in the last position of the stated base cluster DDname.

The base cluster name coded in VSD683 is B1522CSM. Therefore the generated DDname for ADDRAIX is B1522CS1, and that for NAMEAIX is B1522CS2.

```
//FSBT686A   JOB AK00TEST,'DP2-JANOSSY',CLASS=W,MSGCLASS=X,
//  MSGLEVEL=(1,1),NOTIFY=BT05686
//*
//*     THIS JCL = BT05686.SOURCE.CNTL(JCL719)
//*
//***********************************************************
//*                                                         *
//*     EXECUTE PROGRAM VSD683 ACCESSING A KSDS             *
//*     WITH TWO ALTERNATE INDEXES                          *
//*                                                         *
//***********************************************************
//STEPA     EXEC  PGM=VSD683
//SYSOUT      DD  SYSOUT=*
//SYSUDUMP    DD  SYSOUT=A
//BT1522E1    DD  DSN=AK00.C99.DRVTRANS,
//  DISP=SHR
//B1522CSM    DD  DSN=AK00.C98.CUSTMAST,              'VSAM DATA SET
//  DISP=OLD
//B1522CS1    DD  DSN=AK00.C98.CUSTMAST.ADDRAIX.PATH, 'ADDR ALT INDEX
//  DISP=OLD
//B1522CS2    DD  DSN=AK00.C98.CUSTMAST.NAMEAIX.PATH, 'NAME ALT INDEX
//  DISP=OLD
//BT1522U1    DD  SYSOUT=*                            'REPORT
//
```

FIGURE 7.19   MVS JCL to execute program VSD683 (reprinted from *Practical MVS JCL for Today's Programmers*, James Janossy, John Wiley and Sons, Inc., 1987, ISBN 0-471-83648-6, by permission of the publisher)

MVS JCL Errors for Generated DDnames

If for some reason the generated DDnames and path specifications for alternate keys are incorrectly stated, the program attempting alternate key access will fail. The failure will occur at the attempt to open the key sequenced data set, and a FILE STATUS value of 95 will be posted, indicating invalid file information. The alternate key fields cited in the file description for the KSDS do not agree with those carried in the system catalog definition for the alternate keys.

Figure 7.20 illustrates the result of switching the alternate index path specifications in the JCL of Figure 7.19. Had one or both generated DD statements been omitted, the FILE STATUS value received would have been 96, indicating a missing DD statement.

```
*************************************************************************
*   START/READ BY NAME   //  PROGRAM VSD683   *  05/09/87  *  PAGE   1  *
*************************************************************************


ACCOUNT NO        LAST NAME       FIRST NAME          ADDRESS         APT  DATA
<------>       <-------------->  <-------->      <---> - <------------->  <--->   --


>>> RUN ABORTED -- FILE STATUS WAS 95 -- FAILED ON OPENING (VSAM1-FS)


*** END OF JOB            0 RECORDS READ          0 RECORDS PRINTED
```

FIGURE 7.20   Output of program VSD683 if alternate index path references in the DD statements for the two generated DDnames are switched, creating inconsistent SELECT/ASSIGN and JCL specifications

KEYED ACCESS TO KEY SEQUENCED DATA SETS

The "meat and potatoes" access ordinarily associated with key sequenced data sets deals with obtaining a record by its primary key, updating it by modifying one or more fields, and rewriting the record to the data set. These actions involve coding the SELECT/AS-SIGN statement in a program with access RANDOM or DYNAMIC, and opening the data set for I-O. The READ verb and the REWRITE verb are then used to obtain and replace the record in the data set. Records may be written to a key sequenced data set using the WRITE verb, and may be deleted with the DELETE verb.

A Major Update Program Example

Figure 7.21 is a graphic depiction showing how a major update program operates to perform add/change/delete keyed file maintenance. The update program is named S802P165 and accepts a data set containing transactions with the format shown in Figure 7.22, and applies them to the master file having records with the format shown in Figure 7.23, adding, changing, or deleting records. The program produces an update log report and a status report as well as a sequential history file to which deleted records are written. Figures 7.24(a) and 7.24(b) show samples of the output reports. The source code for program S802P165 is listed in full in Appendix B.

Using the Generic VSAM I/O Modules

Program S802P165 provides a complete example of the use of the generic I/O modules outlined in Figure 7.8. In addition, it carries further the use of standardized forced-abort provisions. It treats VSAM file open and close actions as a separate process controlled by

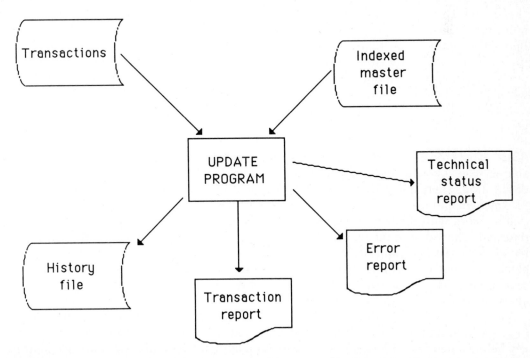

FIGURE 7.21 Graphic depiction of inputs and outputs of program S802P165, a major key sequenced data set keyed add/change/delete update

Account ID X(4)	Transaction Type X(1)	Transaction Subtype X(1)	Replacement Description X(25)	Filler X(21)
1 4	5	6	7 31	32 52

FIGURE 7.22   Format of transactions entering program S802P165

Account ID X(4)	Account Description X(25)	Active/Inactive Flag X(1)	Original Date X(6)	Last Change X(6)	Filler X(26)
1 4	5 29	30	31 36	37 42	43 68

FIGURE 7.23   Format of master file records accessed by program S802P165

flags and housed in a special processing paragraph. This pattern allows a program to "know" which of potentially several VSAM data sets are opened or closed, so that at any point the program can perform a clean forced-abort, closing only the data sets that are open. The status-reporting mechanism illustrated in S802P165 is also fully developed, directing automatically time-stamped program monitoring messages and tabled counts out to a separate status report. Figure 7.25 illustrates the status report output by S802P165 when a condition prompting a forced-abort is detected.[9]

Let's consider the processing actions applicable to each of the KSDS keyed access verbs. The use of most of these is illustrated in program S802P165.

READ   The processing actions required to access an individual record in a KSDS are simple. The key value of the record to be obtained is placed into the key field of the file description. Then, a READ on the file is executed. VSAM obtains the key value from the FD key field and uses it to seek a record in the KSDS.

If a record with the key in the FD key field is obtained, a FILE STATUS of 00 or 02 is returned. The value of 00 signifies that the read was successful and that the key of the record obtained is unique. A value of 02 means that the key by which the record was obtained is not unique and that the record obtained is not the last one to be obtained sequentially. The latter condition can arise only when the READ processing is on an alternate index with duplicates allowed.

The READ verb is illustrated in paragraph 3911 of program S802P165. Note that the logic performing this I/O module has already placed the key value wanted into the FD key field, named COA-KEY-ACCT. The READ paragraph moves the key value to a holding field in working storage from which it can be written to the status report in case a need arises to perform reporting for a forced-abort.

```
-------------------------------------------------------------------------
**   802 SYSTEM   **   COA TRANS LISTING      S802P165-R1   06/18/84   PAGE   2
-------------------------------------------------------------------------
```

ACCT ID <-->	T Y -	S T -	ACCOUNT NAME <---------------------->	RESULT	ERRORS
3395	A		MICROFICHE	ADDED	
3001	C	I		>>------>	F-01 ACCT ID NOT ON FILE
2121	C	R		>>------>	F-11 NEW NAME IS BLANK
2521	Y	R	ENTRANCE FEES	>>------>	F-06 TRANSACTION TYPE INVALID
2516	C	R	MISCELLANEOUS EXPENSES	>>------>	F-01 ACCT ID NOT ON FILE
3396	A		OPTICAL DISK ARCHIVAL	ADDED	
2511	C	R	AGENCY FEES	NAME CHANGED	
5204	D	D		DELETED	W-07 SUBTYPE SHOULD BE BLANK
3331	C	R		>>------>	F-11 NEW NAME IS BLANK
2723	A		RENTAL CARS	>>------>	F-02 ACCT ID ALREADY IN USE
2526	A	P	PROPS AND EXHIBITS	ADDED	W-07 SUBTYPE SHOULD BE BLANK
3392	C	X	REPRO AND BINDING	>>------>	F-08 SUBTYPE INVALID ON CHANGE
3336	A			>>------>	F-09 ACCT NAME BLANK FOR ADD
1215	A	B		>>------>	W-07 SUBTYPE SHOULD BE BLANK F-09 ACCT NAME BLANK FOR ADD F-02 ACCT ID ALREADY IN USE
5203		I		>>------>	F-06 TRANSACTION TYPE INVALID
2711	H	R		>>------>	F-06 TRANSACTION TYPE INVALID
2710	C	A		NOW ACTIVE	
2710	C	R	SHIPMENT OF GOODS	NAME CHANGED	

FIGURE 7.24a   Program S802P165 transaction listing report (portion)

```
-------------------------------------------------------------------------
**  802 SYSTEM  **     COA UPDATE LOG     S802P165-R2   06/18/84   PAGE   1
-------------------------------------------------------------------------


              ACCT                                    ORIGINAL   LAST CHANGE
              ID          ACCOUNT NAME       STATUS     DATE        DATE
              <-->   <------------------------>   -    <------>    <------>


      WAS:    3352   UTILITY LIGHT DUTY          A    07-02-83    11-14-83
  IS NOW:     3352   UTILITY LIGHT DUTY          I    07-02-83    06-18-84

      WAS:    3356   LICENSE AND REGISTRATION    A    07-02-83    11-14-83
  IS NOW:     3356   LICENSE AND REGISTRATION    I    07-02-83    06-18-84

      WAS:    3350   VEHICLES                    I    08-13-79    08-13-79
  IS NOW:     3350   VEHICLES                    A    08-13-79    06-18-84

      WAS:    ****   NEW ACCOUNT NOT PREVIOUSLY ON FILE
  IS NOW:     3371   MACHINE PRINTABLE PAPER     A    06-18-84    06-18-84

      WAS:    ****   NEW ACCOUNT NOT PREVIOUSLY ON FILE
  IS NOW:     3372   SPECIAL PRINT FORMS         A    06-18-84    06-18-84

      WAS:    ****   NEW ACCOUNT NOT PREVIOUSLY ON FILE
  IS NOW:     3373   STATIONERY SUPPLIES         A    06-18-84    06-18-84

      WAS:    3370   CONSUMMABLE SUPPLIES        A    08-13-79    08-13-79
  IS NOW:     3370   CONSUMMABLE SUPPLIES        I    08-13-79    06-18-84

      WAS:    2513   MEDIA DIRECT                I    03-17-80    07-15-83
  IS NOW:     2513   MEDIA DIRECT                A    03-17-80    06-18-84

      WAS:    1221   COMMISSION ADVANCES         A    01-15-81    01-15-81
  IS NOW:     1221   ADVANCE COMMISSIONS         A    01-15-81    06-18-84

      WAS:    3327   TELEGRAPH CHARGES           I    08-13-79    08-13-79
  IS NOW:     **** ACCOUNT DELETED AS REQUESTED

      WAS:    3394   MICROFILMING                A    05-01-80    05-01-80
  IS NOW:     3394   MICROFILMING                I    05-01-80    06-18-84

      WAS:    ****   NEW ACCOUNT NOT PREVIOUSLY ON FILE
  IS NOW:     3395   MICROFICHE                  A    06-18-84    06-18-84

      WAS:    ****   NEW ACCOUNT NOT PREVIOUSLY ON FILE
  IS NOW:     3396   OPTICAL DISK ARCHIVAL       A    06-18-84    06-18-84

      WAS:    2511   AGENCY                      A    03-17-80    07-15-83
  IS NOW:     2511   AGENCY FEES                 A    03-17-80    06-18-84

      WAS:    5204   MISCELLANEOUS               I    08-13-79    08-13-79
  IS NOW:     **** ACCOUNT DELETED AS REQUESTED
```

FIGURE 7.24b   Program S802P165 update log report (portion)

```
********************************************************************************
**   802 SYSTEM    **    ** STATUS REPORT **     S802P165-SR   06/18/84   PAGE   1
********************************************************************************


          TIME                      MESSAGE                    FILE STATUS
       <--------->    <--------------------------------------->     --


       09:03:22.47    PROGRAM STARTING

       09:03:22.47    STARTING TO OPEN I/O COA VSAM FILE

       09:03:22.88    FILE OPEN COMPLETED                             00

       09:03:22.88    OPEN OK

       09:03:24.20    END OF UPDATES


                      TRANSACTIONS READ ............      39

                      ADD TRANSACTIONS .............      10
                          SUCCESSFUL .................       6
                          INVALID DATA ...............       2
                          ACCT ID ALREADY IN USE .....       2

                      CHANGE TRANSACTIONS ..........      21

                          "CR" TRANSACTIONS ..........       8
                              SUCCESSFUL .............       3
                              INVALID DATA ...........       3
                              NO SUCH ACCT ID ........       2

                          "CI" TRANSACTIONS ..........       7
                              SUCCESSFUL .............       4
                              FOR INACTIVE ACCT .......       1
                              NO SUCH ACCT ID ........       2

                          "CA" TRANSACTIONS ..........       5
                              SUCCESSFUL .............       3
                              FOR ACTIVE ACCT .........       1
                              NO SUCH ACCT ID ........       1

                          BAD SUBTYPE CODE ...........       1

                      DELETE TRANSACTIONS ..........       4
                          SUCCESSFUL .................       2
                          ACCT NOT INACTIVE ..........       1
                          NO SUCH ACCT ID ............       1

                      INVALID TRAN TYPE CODE .......       4
                      RECORDS WRITTEN TO HISTORY ...       2
                      TOTAL ERRORS DETECTED ........      28

       09:03:24.20    CLOSING COA FILE

       09:03:24.59    COA FILE CLOSE CONCLUDED                        00
```

FIGURE 7.24c   Program S802P165 status report (complete)

```
         TIME                    MESSAGE                      FILE STATUS
      <--------->    <-------------------------------------->       --

      15:32:07.11    PROGRAM STARTING
      15:32:07.11    STARTING TO OPEN I/O COA VSAM FILE
      15:32:08.37    FILE OPEN COMPLETED                             00
      15:32:08.37    OPEN OK
      15:32:08.47    ABEND ON COA REWRITE                            23
      15:32:08.47    XRJV
                     TRANSACTIONS READ ............        64
      15:32:08.47    ABORTING ON I/O ERROR
      15:32:08.47    CLOSING COA FILE
      15:32:08.47    COA FILE CLOSE CONCLUDED
```

FIGURE 7.25 Status report produced by program S802P165 when a FILE STATUS condition arises that forces abort of execution

An optional KEY phrase may be stated on a READ:

```
READ vsamfile KEY IS FD-NAME-AIX.
```

If the alternate key of a record is placed into the alternate key field and this statement is executed, the READ obtains the first record in the data set with the alternate key stated. In addition, the attention of the program is switched to that alternate index for subsequent READ/NEXT actions; the key of reference becomes the key field stated. The key field stated can be qualified but not subscripted or indexed. When omitted, the key used by the READ is, by default, the primary key.

REWRITE   REWRITE replaces a record in the data set and can only be undertaken when a record was obtained via its primary key. It can be executed with ACCESS MODE IS SEQUENTIAL, but in such a case the last I/O statement executed against the data set prior to the REWRITE must have been a READ, and must have obtained the record being rewritten. In this case the primary key field of the record rewritten also must be the same as that obtained in the READ.

When ACCESS MODE IS RANDOM, or ACCESS MODE IS DYNAMIC, no requirement exists to have executed a READ immediately prior to the REWRITE, and the primary key of the record being rewritten need not be the same as that last read.

No restrictions exist concerning changes in alternate key fields between reading and rewriting a record. It is, however, possible that an alternate key defined to be unique is changed to a value that duplicates a key already on file. In such a case, an attempt to rewrite the record will result in a FILE STATUS value of 22, indicating a duplicate key. Because of the multiple keys involved, it is easy to assume that this value refers to the primary key, but it may instead refer to an alternate key. *Forced-abort reporting for a failure on a REWRITE should include presentation of all the key values, including alternate key fields as well as the primary key.*

REWRITE with ACCESS MODE IS RANDOM is illustrated in paragraph 3912 of program S802P165. The paragraph contains a statement that places the current date into the record being rewritten, for consistent "date stamping" of all updates.

WRITE   WRITE places records into the data set. If ACCESS MODE is SEQUENTIAL and the data set is open for OUTPUT or EXTEND, the records must be written in ascending key sequence. When opened for OUTPUT, the writing of records begins at the start of the data set; when opened for EXTEND, the records added are placed following any records already in the data set. For EXTEND the record keys to be written must be higher than any existing record in the data set. Execution of WRITE in this manner is uncommon because it simply loads the data set; REPRO is more often used for this purpose.

When a data set is being accessed with ACCESS MODE IS RANDOM or ACCESS MODE IS DYNAMIC, records may be written without being in ascending key sequence. The addition of large numbers of records in this manner by a batch program is inefficient. A better way to arrange batch processing is to logically merge the records to be added to a backup of the key sequenced data set, and to reload it with the file created from this process. This avoids the excessive control interval and control area splits that can be produced by a large volume of record inserts.

The addition of records to a key sequenced data set at random is illustrated in program S802P165 in paragraph 3913. As with REWRITE, forced-abort reporting for a failure on a WRITE should include presentation of all the key values, alternate key fields as well as the primary key. A FILE STATUS value of 22 can indicate that either the primary key or an alternate key defined to be unique is a duplicate of a key already on file. A FILE STATUS of 02 on a write means that an alternate key in the record is defined as nonunique and that it does in fact duplicate an alternate key already on file.

DELETE DELETE removes a record from the data set. To use it, the key of the record to be deleted is placed into the key field in the file description, and DELETE is executed as in paragraph 3914 of program S802P165. The syntax of the DELETE is ominous in that it makes it appear that the entire data set is being deleted, but in fact only the record with the key value contained in the key field of the file description is deleted. This record is physically deleted and the space it occupied becomes available immediately for use by another record.

When ACCESS MODE IS SEQUENTIAL, a record must first be read in order to be deleted. However, when ACCESS MODE IS RANDOM is coded in the SELECT/ASSIGN statement for the file, a record can be deleted simply by moving its key to the file description key field and executing a DELETE verb specifying the file name. A DELETE without prior READ is unusual, however, because it is nearly always desirable or necessary to report on or write the record being deleted to a history file.

More About Program S802P165

S802P165 is a fully functional key sequenced data set add/change/delete program that can be used as a pattern or learning device. It was originally published in *Commercial Software Engineering for Productive Program Design* (James Janossy, John Wiley and Sons, Inc., 1985) ISBN 0-471-81576-4, accompanied by a narrative specification and the complete software engineering profile diagram used to design it. The program uses comprehensive, production-oriented status reporting and illustrates how tabled counts and labeling, multiple-report generation, and contemporary VSAM I/O are arranged in a real-life program.

The source code for S802P165, test data files, and the job stream to execute it are available in machine readable form on diskette for upload to a mainframe, as described in Appendix A. If you are a student or trainer you may find the material on these diskettes an especially valuable way to gain experience with VSAM or to arrange training for others.

REVIEW QUESTIONS AND (*)EXERCISES

1. What changes are necessary in a COBOL program that was designed to access a simple sequential data set if it is to now access a VSAM key sequenced data set in sequential processing mode?

2. Explain what input/output actions are possible for each of the three processing modes, SEQUENTIAL, RANDOM, and DYNAMIC, when the key sequenced data set is open for I-0.

3. What is the purpose of the FILE-STATUS field, and in what two places is it cited besides the Procedure Division of a COBOL program?

4. What is the VSAM "status key"?

5. A program attempts to open a key sequenced data set. The action is performed, but the FILE STATUS value returned is 96. What is the likely cause of the problem and how can it be resolved?

*6. A record with the key value of "AZX27381034" is to be read from a key sequenced data set. The file description file name is ACCOUNT-FILE, and the key field in the program is named FD-ACCOUNT-ID. Using standard I/O module logic patterns, write the COBOL source code for the logic performing the read, using file status instead of INVALID KEY, taking into account the appropriate file status values for forced abort conditions as well as for program-resolvable conditions.

*7. An alternate key in a particular record format is composed of a field three bytes in length followed by a field eight bytes in length. The current record pointer is to be positioned to the first record carrying the value "DDY" in the three-byte field. Code the SELECT/ASSIGN statement for the program, the alternate key field in the file description, the START logic for this action, and the appropriate READ/NEXT.

*8. The SELECT/ASSIGN statement in a certain program accessing a key sequenced data set having two alternate keys appears like this:

```
SELECT ACCOUNT-FILE ASSIGN TO  B2319ACF
   ORGANIZATION IS INDEXED
   ACCESS MODE IS DYNAMIC
   RECORD KEY IS FD-ACCOUNT-ID
   ALTERNATE RECORD KEY IS FD-VOUCHER-NO
   ALTERNATE RECORD KEY IS FD-ORDER-NO
   FILE STATUS IS VSAM1-FS.
```

The program reads the data set, selecting certain records for printing, and produces two reports. Code the MVS or DOS/VSE JCL that executes the batch COBOL program involved.

*9. After performing exercise 8 of Chapter 2, creating a key sequenced data set housing AK00.C98.CUSTMAST records, write a simple file-to-print program to list the records from the data set. In accomplishing this, use the appropriate I/O modules discussed in this chapter.

*10. After completing exercise 9 above, modify the program you created so that it produces a second report, labeled a status report, and include on it messages relating to these actions and counts:

```
date and time of successful key sequenced data set open
count of records read
count of records written
date and time of successful key sequenced data set close
```

Include logic in the program to output a printline message and all key and alternate key field values if any I/O action receives a file status value indicating a program-unresolvable problem. After successfully running the program, test its failure message reporting by changing the length of the primary key field in the program to an incorrect value, recompiling, and running the program again. Indicate the file status value you receive and explain why this is produced.

NOTES

1. This chapter is concerned only with COBOL programming and key sequenced data sets, which are by far the most commonly employed VSAM data sets. See Appendix D for information about COBOL programming for entry sequenced data sets (ESDS) and relative record data sets (RRDS).

2. Program PSD183 is reproduced from pages 37–40 of *Commercial Software Engineering: For Productive Program Design*, (James G. Janossy, John Wiley and Sons, Inc., 1985) ISBN 0-471-81576-4. That book provides an extensive discussion of the software-engineered design of PSD183 as the first of several logical models for business data processing functions, and is recommended for guidance in contemporary COBOL program design and programming.

3. Receiving a record into a working storage input area is now common practice and makes analysis of abend dumps more rapid in the absence of a utility for this purpose. If, on the other hand, the record description is housed in the FD and no record area is used in working storage, the record in process will be presented within a memory dump in the I/O buffer area, not within the working storage of the program. That makes location of it difficult or impossible.

4. The FILE STATUS value of 97 indicating a successful open after an implied VERIFY is documented in early versions of VSCOBOL. Current releases of VSCOBOL, however, return a FILE STATUS value of 00 even when an implied VERIFY has been executed under the Integrated Catalog Facility (ICF).

5. For more information about the COBOL intentional dump utility, see the *IBM OS/VS COBOL Compiler and Library Programmer's Guide*, S28-6483. A sample forced-abort program that uses the utility, named ILBOABN0, is illustrated in Figure 14.5 in Chapter 14 of *Practical MVS JCL for Today's Programmers* (James Janossy, John Wiley and Sons, Inc., 1987) ISBN 0-471-83648-6.

6. The practice of placing an alternate key field physically adjacent to but ahead of the primary key and including the primary key within it is strongly recommended. It is a no-overhead means of insuring that the alternate key is entirely unique. Unique alternate keys provide significant benefits for alternate index management and the ability to provide efficient page scrolling in CICS programs. When more than one alternate key exists in a record, a copy of the primary key can be placed after each, at some expense in record space, to accomplish the same thing for each alternate key. Since the number of alternate keys is usually minimized and two is a common maximum, such a practice is not as demanding of record space as might first appear.

7. The authors wish to express their gratitude to Joe Massani, a co-worker who discovered what he thought was an element of extrasensory perception on the part of MVS in its error message concerning a missing DD statement for a generated DDname. Joe was testing a program accessing a key sequenced data set via an alternate index. The naming conventions in the installation dictated that the DDname for a VSAM data set can be composed in the form WC36IV01. In test, however, Joe coded the DDname as WC36IV00, and also omitted a DD statement for the alternate index path. He was amazed that MVS seemed to complain that he had not coded the DDname as WC36IV01 as he should have! MVS was, of course, complaining that no DDname for the alternate index path had been supplied, and was identifying it with a DDname generated from that indicated for the base cluster.

8. The profile diagram for transaction-driven START, READ/NEXT program VSD683 represents a generic software engineering logic pattern that is fully illustrated and discussed in Chapter 17, pages 321–330 and Appendix D, *Commercial Software Engineering: For Productive Program Design* (James Janossy, John Wiley and Sons, Inc., 1985) ISBN 0-471-81576-4.

9. Specifications, discussion, the complete software engineering profile logic design, and full illustrations of the program test inputs and output for S802P165 can be found in Chapter 17 of *Commercial Software Engineering: For Productive Program Design* (James Janossy, John Wiley and Sons, Inc., 1985) ISBN 0-471-81576-4. The source code, test data, job stream, and IDCAMS control statements to run and experiment with this program are available in machine readable form on diskette, suitable for upload to a mainframe. For more information on this, see Appendix A.

PART 3

MANAGING VSAM

===== 8 =====

LISTCAT and the Critical Measurements

The catalog stores all of the controlling parameters or attributes of a VSAM data set. It is itself a key sequenced data set. Its records are called "entries," and the prime keys of these records are base cluster, data set component, or path names. Entries for all base clusters, data components, index components, alternate indexes, and paths, and record count and activity information about them, are housed in the catalog. LISTCAT, or "LIST CATalog," provides the means to print these items for analysis and documentation.

LISTCAT is used by programming personnel for two purposes. It is handy to perform a LISTCAT of a data set when it is defined or loaded in order to retain a copy of the actual system-stored attributes. The IDCAMS control statements necessary to produce a LIST-CAT such as this for a specific data set have been illustrated at the end of data set definition and loading job streams such as Figure 2.2 on page 14. This coding is expanded in Figure 5.2 to include the alternate index clusters. The LISTCAT is simple to run and produces comprehensive print output.

The second use of LISTCAT involves data set performance monitoring. Concern for a VSAM data set cannot end once it has been placed into regular use in production; there remains the continuous task of monitoring data set condition and performance. The raw LISTCAT can be used for monitoring, but it is not at all handy when scores of data sets are involved. We present here some practical routines that make use of machine-readable LISTCAT output to produce summarized reports, with carryover from prior run cycles, facilitating real life VSAM data set monitoring.

EXECUTING LISTCAT

IDCAMS LISTCAT Control Statements

Figure 8.1 lists the JCL and IDCAMS control statements required to produce a LISTCAT. ENTRIES specifies the entries in the catalog for which we wish to obtain information. The names entered here are clusters or alternate index names. Because these are "umbrella" names, we obtain information on all of the components in a KSDS set or alternate index by specifying the cluster or alternate index name.

LISTCAT can be executed with various specification options. ALL as a display instruction coded in Figure 8.1 means just as it states—all information fields in the catalog for the named entries will be listed. ALL is the maximum display instruction; the minimum display instruction is NAME, or nothing at all—NAME is the default. Here is what LIST-

```
//FSBT677A  JOB AK00TEST,'DP4-GUZIK',CLASS=T,MSGCLASS=X,
//  MSGLEVEL=(1,1),NOTIFY=BT05677
//*
//*     THIS JCL = BT05677.SOURCE.CNTL(JCL81)
//*
//************************************************************
//*                                                          *
//*     LIST CATALOG INFORMATION FOR DATA SET                *
//*                                                          *
//************************************************************
//STEPA      EXEC  PGM=IDCAMS
//SYSPRINT   DD    SYSOUT=*
//SYSUDUMP   DD    SYSOUT=A
//SYSIN      DD    *
        LISTCAT -
          ENTRIES  (   AK00.C98.CUSTMAST -
                       AK00.C98.CUSTMAST.ADDRAIX -
                       AK00.C98.CUSTMAST.NAMEAIX    ) -
                   ALL
     /*
     //
```

FIGURE 8.1 JCL and IDCAMS control statements needed to produce a LISTCAT

CAT provides about data sets and other VSAM catalog entries for various display instructions, arranged in an accumulating hierarchy:

NAME Only the name and entry type, such as ALIAS, CLUSTER, DATA, INDEX, ALTERNATEINDEX, PATH, GENERATIONDATAGROUP, PAGESPACE, NONVSAM, SPACE, and USERCATALOG will be listed.

HISTORY Information fields will be limited to entry name, type, ownerid, creation date, and expiration date. HISTORY can be specified only for clusters, alternate indexes, paths, or their components.

VOLUME The volume serial numbers and device types are listed, in addition to the information provided by specifying HISTORY.

ALLOCATION Space allocation information and the information provided by HISTORY and VOLUME will be produced.

ALL All attribute and status fields in the catalog for the entry will be displayed, in addition to the information in the HISTORY, VOLUME, and ALLOCATION groups.

Figure 8.2 shows how a LISTCAT limited to HISTORY would be invoked. Limited information LISTCATs provide just a subset of catalog information and are not usually as helpful as presentation of all information.

LISTCAT Output

Figure 8.3 illustrates a portion of the output obtained when ALL is specified for a LISTCAT. Understanding what elements of the LISTCAT output are more important than others is, in itself, important.

LISTCAT arranges its output for a KSDS from the base cluster downward to the components of the data set. Listed under the base cluster are the "associations" of the object. The data and index components are associated with the base cluster, of course, and in this case we also see the entry names of two alternate indexes.

Each component of a data set receives its own group of information fields. The labels on the fields are nearly all self-explanatory, but the values provided for many represent

```
//FSBT677A  JOB AK00TEST,'DP4-GUZIK',CLASS=T,MSGCLASS=X,
//  MSGLEVEL=(1,1),NOTIFY=BT05677
//*
//*     THIS JCL = BT05677.SOURCE.CNTL(JCL82)
//*
//*************************************************************
//*                                                          *
//*      LIST CATALOG INFORMATION (HISTORY ONLY)             *
//*                                                          *
//*************************************************************
//STEPA     EXEC  PGM=IDCAMS
//SYSPRINT  DD    SYSOUT=*
//SYSUDUMP  DD    SYSOUT=A
//SYSIN     DD    *
       LISTCAT -
          ENTRIES  (   AK00.C98.CUSTMAST -
                       AK00.C98.CUSTMAST.ADDRAIX -
                       AK00.C98.CUSTMAST.NAMEAIX    ) -
                   HISTORY
    /*
    //
```

FIGURE 8.2   Producing a LISTCAT limited to HISTORY information

```
CLUSTER ------- AK00.C98.CUSTMAST
    IN-CAT --- CUSTMAST.CATALOG
    HISTORY
        OWNER-IDENT-------(NULL)       CREATION----------87.222
        RELEASE----------------2       EXPIRATION--------00.000
        PROTECTION-PSWD-----(NULL)     RACF---------------(NO)
    ASSOCIATIONS
        DATA-----AK00.C98.CUSTMAST.DATA
        INDEX----AK00.C98.CUSTMAST.INDEX
        AIX------AK00.C98.CUSTMAST.ADDRAIX
        AIX------AK00.C98.CUSTMAST.NAMEAIX

DATA ------- AK00.C98.CUSTMAST.DATA
    IN-CAT --- CUSTMAST.CATALOG
    HISTORY
        OWNER-IDENT-------(NULL)       CREATION----------87.222
        RELEASE----------------2       EXPIRATION--------00.000
        PROTECTION-PSWD-----(NULL)     RACF---------------(NO)
    ASSOCIATIONS
        CLUSTER--AK00.C98.CUSTMAST
    ATTRIBUTES
        KEYLEN----------------8        AVGLRECL------------250    BUFSPACE-----------8704     CISIZE-------------4096
        RKP------------------36        MAXLRECL------------250    EXCPEXIT----------(NULL)    CI/CA-----------------8
        SHROPTNS(2,3)     SPEED        UNIQUE          NOERASE    INDEXED     NOWRITECHK      NOIMBED     NOREPLICAT
        UNORDERED        NOREUSE       NONSPANNED
    STATISTICS
        REC-TOTAL------------18        SPLITS-CI-------------0     EXCPS-----------------5
        REC-DELETED-----------0        SPLITS-CA-------------0     EXTENTS---------------1
        REC-INSERTED----------0        FREESPACE-%CI--------18     SYSTEM-TIMESTAMP:
        REC-UPDATED-----------0        FREESPACE-%CA---------1        X'9D264A16F5694080'
        REC-RETRIEVED--------36        FREESPC-BYTES------28672
    ALLOCATION
        SPACE-TYPE--------TRACK        HI-ALLOC-RBA-------32768
        SPACE-PRI-------------2        HI-USED-RBA--------32768
        SPACE-SEC-------------2
    VOLUME
        VOLSER-----------DASD02        PHYREC-SIZE---------4096    HI-ALLOC-RBA-------32768     EXTENT-NUMBER----------1
        DEVTYPE------X'3050200B'       PHYRECS/TRK------------4    HI-USED-RBA--------32768     EXTENT-TYPE-------X'00'
        VOLFLAG-----------PRIME        TRACKS/CA-------------2
        EXTENTS:
        LOW-CCHH-----X'00F7001C'       LOW-RBA---------------0     TRACKS----------------2
        HIGH-CCHH----X'00F7001D'       HIGH-RBA-----------32767

INDEX ------ AK00.C98.CUSTMAST.INDEX
    IN-CAT --- CUSTMAST.CATALOG
    HISTORY
        OWNER-IDENT-------(NULL)       CREATION----------87.222
        RELEASE----------------2       EXPIRATION--------00.000
        PROTECTION-PSWD-----(NULL)     RACF---------------(NO)
    ASSOCIATIONS
        CLUSTER--AK00.C98.CUSTMAST
    ATTRIBUTES
        KEYLEN----------------8        AVGLRECL--------------0     BUFSPACE--------------0     CISIZE--------------512
        RKP------------------36        MAXLRECL------------505     EXCPEXIT----------(NULL)    CI/CA----------------27
        SHROPTNS(2,3)   RECOVERY       UNIQUE          NOERASE     NOWRITECHK      NOIMBED     NOREPLICAT    UNORDERED
        NOREUSE
    STATISTICS
        REC-TOTAL-------------1        SPLITS-CI-------------0     EXCPS-----------------5     INDEX:
        REC-DELETED-----------0        SPLITS-CA-------------0     EXTENTS---------------1     LEVELS----------------1
        REC-INSERTED----------0        FREESPACE-%CI---------0     SYSTEM-TIMESTAMP:           ENTRIES/SECT----------2
        REC-UPDATED-----------0        FREESPACE-%CA---------0        X'9D264A16F5694080'      SEQ-SET-RBA-----------0
        REC-RETRIEVED---------0        FREESPC-BYTES------13312                                HI-LEVEL-RBA----------0
    ALLOCATION
        SPACE-TYPE--------TRACK        HI-ALLOC-RBA-------13824
        SPACE-PRI-------------1        HI-USED-RBA----------512
        SPACE-SEC-------------1
    VOLUME
        VOLSER-----------DASD02        PHYREC-SIZE----------512    HI-ALLOC-RBA-------13824     EXTENT-NUMBER----------1
        DEVTYPE------X'3050200B'       PHYRECS/TRK-----------27    HI-USED-RBA----------512     EXTENT-TYPE-------X'00'
        VOLFLAG-----------PRIME        TRACKS/CA-------------1
        EXTENTS:
        LOW-CCHH-----X'01070002'       LOW-RBA---------------0     TRACKS----------------1
        HIGH-CCHH----X'01070002'       HIGH-RBA-----------13823
```

FIGURE 8.3   Comprehensive LISTCAT output produced when ALL is specified

arcane codings. Dates are universally printed in Julian format with year expressed in two digits, a decimal point, and then the ordinal day within the year in three digits. Values enclosed in apostrophes and prefaced by an X are rendered in hexadecimal as used internally by VSAM.

LISTCATS are usually helpful in these ways in developing an application or a program using a VSAM KSDS:

- Information in the attributes area of the DATA component documents choices made in defining the data set.
- Counts such as REC-TOTAL, REC-DELETED, REC-INSERTED, REC-UPDATED, and REC-RETRIEVED under STATISTICS reflect activity against the data set since it was created. These can be consulted to verify results of test runs.
- Information under STATISTICS about CI and CA splits, when examined after runs with test files approximating full-sized files, can confirm whether free space choices and index CI sizes are acceptable as described in Chapter 2.

The use of LISTCATS during program development generally does not involve the remainder of the fields displayed. At the end of this chapter we provide definitions of those fields and explain what they contain.

LISTCAT FOR CONVENIENT DATA SET MANAGEMENT

VSAM data sets are dynamic creations that demand informed attention on a day-by-day basis in terms of space allocation, use of disk extents, and record counts. From time to time some modification of controlling parameters such as free space and primary/secondary space specifications is usually required in order to maintain operating efficiency.

Various installations distribute the work of monitoring VSAM data sets in different ways. In some cases programmers who develop and install an application have the responsibility of "living with" a system and caring for the data sets supporting it. In other cases a technical support group or disk space management unit may be made responsible for data set performance monitoring. In other cases the tasks might default to one or the other technically inclined lead programmer assigned the duty along with normal programming tasks. In still other cases—too many cases—the task of monitoring VSAM data set performance is skirted and left to fall between the cracks of pressure-filled days; crises and teleprocessing system outages then occur.

While it is natural to regard the output of LISTCAT as a valuable tool, it is unwise to assume that it is sufficient in itself as a key sequenced data set management device. The comprehensive nature of LISTCAT output detracts from its convenience in this capacity. LISCAT is a good starting point for a very workable mechanism to monitor the scores or even hundreds of key sequenced data sets found in any moderate to large-scale mainframe installation. Such a mechanism need not be complex and simply relies on the use of IDCAMS printlines in machine-readable form.

Listing All Data Sets in a Catalog

If LISTCAT is invoked without naming an entry in the form:

```
LISTCAT -
 CATALOG ( SYS6.USERCAT )
```

output illustrated in Figure 8.4 is produced. This output consists of one printline for each

```
IDCAMS  SYSTEM SERVICES                          TIME: 19:44:37     08/03/87     PAGE  1
    LISTCAT CATALOG(CUSTMAST.CATALOG)                        00090000

                          LISTING FROM CATALOG -- CUSTMAST.CATALOG
CLUSTER ------- 0000000000000000000000000000000000000000000000
   DATA ------- CUSTMAST.CATALOG
   INDEX ------ CATINDEX.TB6244FO.VID84028.T96DO2D1
CLUSTER ------- AKOO.C98.CUSTMAST
   DATA ------- AKOO.C98.CUSTMAST.DATA
   INDEX ------ AKOO.C98.CUSTMAST.INDEX
AIX     ------- AKOO.C98.CUSTMAST.ADDRAIX
   DATA ------- AKOO.C98.CUSTMAST.ADDRAIX.DATA
   INDEX ------ AKOO.C98.CUSTMAST.ADDRAIX.INDEX
   PATH ------- AKOO.C98.CUSTMAST.ADDRAIX.PATH
AIX     ------- AKOO.C98.CUSTMAST.NAMEAIX
   DATA ------- AKOO.C98.CUSTMAST.NAMEAIX.DATA
   INDEX ------ AKOO.C98.CUSTMAST.NAMEAIX.INDEX
   PATH ------- AKOO.C98.CUSTMAST.NAMEAIX.PATH
CLUSTER ------- SYS1.VVDS.DASDO1
   DATA ------- SYS1.VVDS.DASDO1
VOLUME  ------- DASDO1
```

FIGURE 8.4   List of all data sets in catalog produced by LISTCAT with no ENTRIES specification

object in the catalog. LISTCAT output is normally sent to SYSOUT to be printed, but it can be directed from //SYSPRINT to a file. The nature of IDCAMS //SYSPRINT records is described by this MVS JCL:

$$DCB = (RECFM = VBA, LRECL = 125, BLKSIZE = 629)$$

Another way to obtain LISTCAT printlines in machine-readable form involves use of the optional OUTFILE specification as illustrated in Figure 8.5. This directs LISTCAT print-

```
//FSBT677A  JOB AKOOTEST,'DP4-GUZIK',CLASS=T,MSGCLASS=X,
// MSGLEVEL=(1,1),NOTIFY=BT05677
//*
//*     THIS JCL = BT05677.SOURCE.CNTL(JCL85)
//*
//*********************************************************
//*                                                       *
//*     LIST DATA SETS IN CATALOG, PRINTLINES TO A FILE   *
//*                                                       *
//*********************************************************
//STEPA      EXEC  PGM=IDCAMS
//SYSPRINT   DD    SYSOUT=*
//SYSUDUMP   DD    SYSOUT=A
//PRTFILE    DD    DSN=AKOO.C98.PRTFILE,
//  UNIT=SYSDA,
//  DISP=(NEW,CATLG,DELETE),
//  DCB=(RECFM=VBA,LRECL=125,BLKSIZE=629),
//  SPACE=(629,(100,20),RLSE)
//SYSIN      DD    *
        LISTCAT -
                  CATALOG (CUSTMAST.CATALOG) -
                  OUTFILE(PRTFILE)
   /*
   //
```

FIGURE 8.5   Invoking LISTCAT with the OUTFILE specification to capture printlines at the named DD statement

lines to a DD statement named in OUTFILE instead of to //SYSPRINT with the foregoing DCB characteristics.

Nothing prevents using an IDCAMS LISTCAT to list all of the entries in a catalog and then taking the output in machine-readable form. A program can then use this as input to form LISTCAT/ALL control statements as 80-byte card image records, one for each item to be monitored. These statements can then be fed to a second IDCAMS step to automatically generate full LISTCATs. This is exactly what we arrange in a group of tools for managing multiple VSAM data sets in the production environment, except that we go further and take the printlines from those second LISTCATs through an extraction program that picks off and prints only the critical monitoring fields for each data set. This lets the monitoring job stream, which we have called VMONITOR, consolidate critical KSDS measurements and automatically compare them from day to day. The net result is two highly condensed and pithy condition reports on all VSAM data sets.

The Critical Measurements

The critical measurements that must be monitored for VSAM data sets on a regular basis can be found, for the most part, in the statistics group of the LISTCAT command. When a VSAM data set is created, the bulk of these critical measurement fields are initialized with zero. These fields include all of the record count fields and the fields recording CI and CA splits.

Statistics group fields progressively accumulate data set activity since the point of data set definition. Examining the progression of these values on a regular basis provides the means to determine when the data set needs to be reorganized, reallocated, or altered to provide optimum batch and online performance. Looking at these statistics makes little sense unless you have the same statistics prior to each major outline or batch activity; only then is comparison possible.

The fields in the LISTCAT output that comprise the critical measurements include CISIZE, creation date, total records, CI splits, CA splits, number of records added, deleted, read, and updated, number of extents, percent of CI freespace, percent of CA freespace, and total number of bytes free. These statistics make no distinction between batch and online activity:

CISIZE is one of the most important attributes of a VSAM data set and determines the physical buffer requirements for programs that access it.

CREATION DATE monitoring is important for VSAM data sets carrying the NOREUSE attribute, since this data in combination with the specified disk space allocation and empty freespace determine whether reorganization is needed.

REC-TOTAL indicates the number of records that reside within the component. This field, as well as the other record count fields, are more important for the data component than they are for the index component. This count field will reflect data set progress towards the maximum number of records its space allocation will allow.

CI SPLITS reflect the expansion of records or the addition of new records and are to be expected as the data set grows. Records added at the end of the data set will not cause CI splits, so activity of that nature will not affect this count. A rapid increase in the number of CI splits indicates that the amount of free space is insufficient.

CA SPLITS are to be expected during the growth of a data set, but a peaking rate of CA splits is detrimental to performance. A larger number of I/O's is incurred when a CA is split and in subsequent sequential accesses. A rise in the rate of CA splits or a large number of CA splits should prompt reorganization of the data set and reexamination of the assumptions by which the free space specifications were determined. Free space may be insufficient or allocated improperly or more records are being added between reorganizations than originally estimated. The pattern or distribution of the record additions over the entire data set may have changed drastically or may have been ignored when free space requirements were determined.

REC-INSERTED   indicates the number of records that have been added to the component before the last record. Records added at the end of the data set are not reflected in this count. This value gives a fair indication of the day-to-day growth of the data set. A high number of record additions will cause CI splits, which can cause CA splits.

REC-DELETED   reveals the number of records that have been deleted from the component. This value subtracted from the REC-INSERTED field should, but will not always, equal the REC-TOTAL field. As with the number of record additions, the number of record deletions reflects day-to-day data set activity.

REC-RETRIEVED   indicates activity against the data set. Each record retrieved for update, deletion, or inquiry is counted here. A very high number of reads in an online environment may indicate a large volume of lengthy reporting-type inquiries by certain fourth-generation software, potentially having an adverse effect on other online functions. A high REC-RETRIEVED value may warrant the allocation of more strings or buffers for the data set for CICS access.

REC-UPDATED   counts all records modified or updated, but not those that were deleted. Each record that is processed in COBOL with the REWRITE verb is counted.

EXTENTS   indicates the number of physical disk extents occupied by the component. If secondary allocation was not specified when the data set was defined, this field will never change. If a secondary allocation was specified when the data set was defined, this becomes a very important field to monitor.

When a data set is allocated, the system will attempt to assign a contiguous amount of disk space for the primary allocation, in other words, to provide it in one extent. If a contigous amount of space is not available, the system will continue to allocate up to five extents. If the primary allocation cannot be satisfied in five extents, the DEFINE will fail.

The number five is significant because data set performance will noticeably degrade beyond this level of fragmentation. As more extents are acquired, it will take longer for the system to satisfy read and write requests. All the statistics for a data set with more than one extent should be examined. If records cannot be purged from it to reduce its size, it should be backed up, deleted, and then allocated enough space on disk so that it can be accommodated in one extent.

PERCENT OF CI FREESPACE AND CA FREESPACE   are specified when the data set is initially defined and can be altered afterward. The current values are shown.

FREESPC-BYTES   indicates the total number of bytes that are free in the empty control intervals only. If this is a large number and only slowly decreases in size, the initial specification of free space may have been too large. If this value decreases very rapidly, more activity against the data set may be occurring than anticipated. In any case, data sets that are static and have no record additions or expansions should have no free space.

PRACTICAL MONITORING OF PRODUCTION DATA SETS

Programs to Monitor All Data Sets

The source code for three COBOL programs that automate the listing of critical measurements is provided in this book as an aid to monitoring the VSAM data sets in your organization. We discuss the use of these programs here. As with other items in this book these programs are available in machine readable form at nominal cost as indicated in Appendix A.

If executed on a regular basis these programs can provide you with a concise means of monitoring scores or hundreds of VSAM data sets and rapidly seeing in highlighted form the ones that are in need of attention.

VMONITOR, a Monitoring Job Stream

Figure 8.6 illustrates the VMONITOR job stream, which runs the three monitoring programs. This job stream makes use of a generation data group data set to house summary data set statistics for comparison purposes from run to run. The job stream performs these steps:

//STEPA executes IDCAMS to obtain a list of entries in one or more catalogs. If the data sets you wish to monitor reside in different catalogs, several LISTCAT commands can be stacked, and the combined output of those commands will be processed.

//STEPB converts the variable-length records produced by the LISTCAT command to fixed-length records. This is done to simplify processing in the next program.

VCATSCAN

//STEPC of the VMONITOR job stream executes a COBOL program named VCATSCAN. This program accomplishes two tasks. It builds a card image carrying this type of LISTCAT command for each cluster and alternate index in the catalogs searched:

```
LISTCAT ENT(entryname) ALL
```

and it eliminates entries, such as test data sets, that you do not wish to monitor. You can tailor this program to be as selective as you wish by modifying the code within its main processing paragraph.

//STEPD executes IDCAMS to process all the LISTCAT statements produced by program VCATSCAN. This generates a large printline data set containing all of the catalog information for the VSAM data sets you wish to monitor.

//STEPE converts the variable-length records produced by the LISTCAT commands to fixed-length records to simplify subsequent processing.

VEXTRACT

//STEPF of the VMONITOR job stream executes program VEXTRACT, which extracts all of the critical measurements produced by the LISTCAT ALL commands and places them in the next generation of a generation data set. Also produced is a consolidated report that shows the attributes group of each monitored data set.

VREPORTR

//STEPG of the VMONITOR job stream executes a COBOL program named VREPORTR that reads the generation data group data set produced by program VEXTRACT, and the

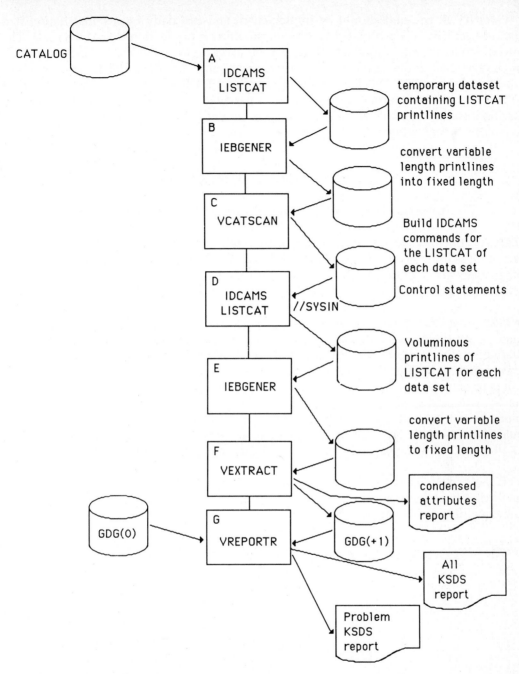

CATALOG

A
IDCAMS
LISTCAT

temporary dataset
containing LISTCAT
printlines

B
IEBGENER

convert variable
length printlines
into fixed length

C
VCATSCAN

Build IDCAMS
commands for
the LISTCAT of
each data set

D
IDCAMS
LISTCAT

//SYSIN

Control statements

Voluminous
printlines of
LISTCAT for each
data set

E
IEBGENER

convert variable
length printlines
to fixed length

F
VEXTRACT

condensed
attributes
report

G
VREPORTR

GDG(0)

GDG(+1)

All
KSDS
report

Problem
KSDS
report

FIGURE 8.6 Data set condition monitoring job stream invoking VCATSCAN, VEXTRACT, and VREPORTR programs

(− 1) generation, and creates the critical measurements summary report and a concise "data sets with problems" report. The problem report highlights data sets with multiple extents, a decline in record count, or CI or CA splits.

Figure F.9 of Appendix F shows a portion of the consolidated attributes report produced in //STEPF. Figure F.11 shows the type of information conveyed on the comparison report created by VREPORTR. Figure F.12 provides a part of a typical data set problem report.

VMONITOR can and should be implemented and run daily in any installation that does not yet have a consolidated facility for monitoring production VSAM data sets. The consolidated attributes report and the full monitoring report are useful for documentation and can be filed in the installation library for reference.[1] But the problem data set report produced by the VREPORTR program of the VMONITOR job stream is the single most critical output. Its examination should be an assigned responsibility within a data processing installation using VSAM, and the task should be regarded as critical to the mission of the organization.

LISTCAT OPTIONS OF LESSER UTILITY

Limiting LISTCAT to Certain Data Sets with Generic Names

LISTCAT provides several means of requesting information for groups of catalog entries. Two of these options—ENTRIES and LEVEL—deal with the selection of entries by name. Other specifiers, such as CREATION, EXPIRATION, FILES, and NOTUSABLE, limit LISTCAT output to catalog entries meeting specific requirements.

ENTRIES identifies the full or generic name of the catalog entries to be listed. If a cluster name is specified, all of its own components, such as data and index, will be listed; alternate index components will not be listed. To obtain LISTCAT output for alternate index components, the alternate index must itself be named in the LISTCAT command.

It is possible to specify a "generic" name using ENTRIES. Generic names are similar to the "*" wildcard specifier of VAX VMS and MS-DOS except that they are more crudely implemented. An asterisk can be used in place of a whole portion of a "qualifier" of a data set name and in this capacity stands in for all possible values of that qualifier. Figure 8.7 illustrates how the generic name feature is implemented by IDCAMS.

LEVEL is provided as a feature because the IDCAMS generic name does not actually have the flexibility of a true generic specifier. The generic asterisk stands in for only one entry name qualifier; for example, coding

```
LISTCAT -
  ENTRIES( AK00.* ) -
      ALL
```

Catalog ENTRYNAME	Does this LISTCAT specification obtain the data set?			
	ENT(AK00.*)	ENT(AK00.*.CUSTMAST)	LVL(AK00)	LVL(AK00.*.CUSTMAST)
AK00.C98.CUSTMAST	No	Yes	Yes	Yes
AK00.C98.CUSTMAST.ADDRAIX	No	No	Yes	Yes
AK00.C98.CUSTMAST.BASE.DATA	No	No	Yes	Yes
AK00.F17.PAYJOURN	No	No	Yes	No
AK00.SYSLOG	Yes	No	Yes	No

FIGURE 8.7   Effect of using generic names, entries, and the LEVEL specification

will not cause any data set such as AK00.C98.CUSTMAST to be included in the LISTCAT because this data set has three parts to its name. The asterisk can only stand in for one part of a name; only data sets named such as AK00.C01, AK00.C02, or AK00.C98 with no third name part would be selected. LEVEL works from the left side of the entry name and does allow selection of entries regardless of the number of name parts, or qualifiers, a name contains. Coding

```
LISTCAT -
  LEVEL ( AK00 ) -
        ALL
```

selects data sets such as those named in the form AK00.C98.CUSTMAST and even AK00.C98.CUSTMAST.ADDRAIX.DATA; the ALL causes maximum LISTCAT print display. A maximum of 1,456 entries can be listed when the LEVEL parameter is used. Figure 8.7 provides some examples of generic name and LEVEL use in combination.

ENTRY TYPES   that can be listed from a catalog are ALIAS, ALTERNATEINDEX, CLUSTER, DATA, GENERATIONDATAGROUP, INDEX, NONVSAM, PAGESPACE, PATH, SPACE, and USERCATALOG. The specification of one or more of these parameters indicates that only those types of entries will be listed.

EXPIRATION   indicates that items will be listed only if they will expire up to and including the specified number of days from the present. Valid values for days range from zero to 9999. Zero indicates that only those entries that have already expired will be listed, and 9999 indicates that all entries will be listed. Days can be expressed in decimal, hexadecimal, or binary. Most disk data sets do not carry expiration date. Reaching the expiration date, if one is used, does not mean automatic deletion of the data set, it simply allows unfettered deletion with the DELETE command. It is possible to delete an unexpired data set by using the PURGE specification.

CREATION   indicates that items will be listed only if they were created the specified number of days ago or earlier. Valid values for days range from zero through 9999. Zero indicates that all entries will be listed. Days can be expressed in decimal, hexadecimal, or binary.

FILE   specifies the name of the DD statement that identifies the volumes; entries listed in the VSAM Volume Data Set or VVDS on each volume specified will be selected for LISTCAT. FILE is applicable only to the Integrated Catalog Facility (ICF) environment.

NOTUSABLE   stipulates that only those data and index entries marked "unusable" by VSAM will be listed. An entry is marked unusable when a system failure occurs and results in damage to catalog information. This parameter applies only in the VSAM catalog environment, not the ICF environment.

CATALOG   specifies the name of the catalog that contains the entries to be listed. If the catalog is VSAM password-protected, the read level password or higher must also be specified. If entries are VSAM password-protected, the master password must be supplied in order to list their passwords. If the catalog is RACF-protected, read authority or higher is required; if entries are RACF protected, RACF alter authority to the catalog is required to list their passwords.

LISTCAT OUTPUT REFERENCE

LISTCAT output is segregated into 11 groups, seven of which are relevant to VSAM data sets. The nature of history, protection, associations, attributes, statistics, allocation, and volumes are explained in detail here.

History Group

The History Group identifies the entity's owner, VSAM release or version, creation date, expiration date, and for VSAM catalog environments, the catalog recovery volume, device type, and the control interval number in the catalog recovery area where the duplicate entry can be found. The expiration date indicates when the data set can be deleted without specifying PURGE. The creation data indicates when the data set was created or reorganized by unloading, deleting, defining, and reloading the data set.

The History Group can be listed for a cluster, alternate index, path, all data components, and all index components. To list only the history group for a VSAM catalog entry, use the following command:

```
LISTCAT -
  ENTRIES ( AK00.C98.CUSTMAST -
          ( AK00.C98.CUSTMAST.ADDRAIX -
          ( AK00.C98.CUSTMAST.NAMEAIX ) -
          HISTORY
```

Protection Group

The Protection Group indicates RACF protection and describes the VSAM password protection for the entity. RACF protection is indicated by either a YES or NO. The VSAM protection fields indicate NULL if they are not defined and SUPP for "suppressed" if they are defined but you do not have the authority to list them.

VSAM protection attributes displayed in this group include ATTEMPTS, CODE, CONTROLPW, MASTERPW, READPW, UPDATEPW, USAR, AND USVR. USVR is the name of the user security verification routine, while USAR represents the information specified in the AUTH attribute.

The Protection Group can be listed for a cluster, alternate index, path, all data components, and all index components. The Protection Group cannot be listed alone; it is listed only when the ALL subparameter of the LISTCAT command is specified.

Associations Group

The Associations Group lists the type and entry name of all objects associated with the entry. A cluster entry points to its data component, each path entry defined directly to the cluster, its index component, and each alternate index catalog entry. A cluster data component points to its cluster entry, as does the cluster index component.

An alternate index entry points to its associated data and index components, its base cluster entry, and the catalog entry for each of its paths. An alternate index data component points to its alternate index base cluster catalog entry. The index component of an alternate index points to the alternate index base cluster catalog entry.

A path associated directly with a KSDS base cluster points to its base cluster entry, the data component of its base cluster, and the index component of its base cluster. A path associated with an alternate index points to the alternate index entry, the alternate index data component, the alternate index's index component, the original KSDS base cluster, data component, and index component.

The Associations Group can be listed for a cluster, alternate index, path, all data components, and all index components. This group is listed when ALL is specified in a LIST-CAT; it cannot be listed alone.

Attributes Group

The Attributes Group lists most of the data set attributes in effect as well as some miscellaneous information. Attributes are set when the entity is defined and can be changed thereafter with the ALTER command as described in Appendix C. The VSAM attributes listed in this group are listed and explained in Figure 8.8.

The Attributes Group can be listed for an alternate index, path, all data components, and all index components. This group is listed when ALL is specified in a LISTCAT; it cannot be listed alone.

Statistics Group

The Statistics Group comprises the most important LISTCAT output. It contains numbers and percentages indicating the amount of activity that has taken place in the component

AVGLRECL	Average data record length
AXRKP	Offset of the alternate index key in base cluster records
BIND	The component is staged to disk storage from a mass storage device such as the IBM 3850 MSS
BUFSPACE	Minimum buffer space
CI/CA	Number of control intervals per control area control
CISIZE	Control interval size
CYLFAULT	The component is not staged to disk storage but parts are obtained as needed
ERASE	The data set and records are overwritten with binary zeroes when it is deleted
EXCPEXIT	The name of the entity's exception exit routine
IMBED	The index sequence set is stored with the data component
INH-UPDATE	Updates to the data component are inhibited (prevented)
INDEXED	Identifies a key sequenced data set (KSDS)
KEYLEN	Length of the base cluster key, the primary key
MAXLRECL	Maximum record length for the component
MAXRECS	The highest possible relative record number for an RRDS
NOERASE	The data set and records are not overwritten with binary zeroes when they are deleted
NOIMBED	The index sequence set is stored with the higher levels of the index component
NONINDEXED	Identifies an entry sequenced data set (ESDS)
NONSPANNED	Data records are not allowed to span a control interval
NONUNIQUEKEY	One alternate index key can point to many base cluster records
NOREPLICATE	Index records are not repeated around a full track to speed search time
NOREUSE	The data set can not be reused, that is, emptied by opening as OUTPUT
NOUPDATE	The base cluster's upgrade set is not opened when the path is opened for processing
NOTUSABLE	The entry is not usable, it may be flawed or corrupted as detected by VSAM
NOWRITECHK	Records written are not read back to check for write accuracy
NUMBERED	Identifies a relative record data set (RRDS)
ORDERED	The order of the volumes specified at definition is honored when space is allocated
RECOVERY	Each control area is preformatted with an end of file marker as the data set is loaded
RECORDS/CI	The number of slots in each control interval of an RRDS
RECVABLE	Each of the catalog volumes contain a catalog recovery area
REPLICATE	Index records are repeated around a full track to speed access
REUSE	The data set can be reused when it is opened as OUTPUT as if it was empty
RKP	Offset or displacement of the primary key relative to the start of the record as position 0
SHROPTNS	The types of sharing permitted for the data set as indicated in SHAREOPTIONS when defined
SPANNED	Data records can be longer than the control interval and can span control intervals
SPEED	Control areas are not preformatted when the data set is initially loaded
SUBALLOC	More than one VSAM data set can occupy the data space (ignored by Integrated Catalog Facility)
TEMP-EXP	This is an EXPORT copy of the data set, the original was not deleted by the EXPORT
UNIQUE	Only one VSAM data set can occupy the data space
UNIQUEKEY	Every alternate index key can identify only one base cluster record
UNORDERED	Volumes specified at data set definition may be allocated in any order by the system
UPDATE	The base cluster upgrade set is opened and updated when the path is opened for processing
UPGRADE	The base cluster alternate indexes are updated when it is updated
WRITECHECK	Records written are read back and checked for write accuracy

FIGURE 8.8   Meaning of the various LISTCAT Attribute Group indications

since the data set was created. The information in this group is updated when the data set is closed successfully. If a failure occurs during the data set close operation, the statistics may not be valid and cannot be corrected by the VERIFY command. The completeness of statistics can become questionable for VSAM files accessed by CICS if the online system abends.[2]

Figure 8.9 summarizes the information reported in the Statistics Group. Many fields are updated only when the data set is properly closed. The fields with the prefix *REC-* are not updated when the data set is processed in control interval mode, a technique available only with assembler language.

The Statistics Group can be listed for all data components and all index components. This group is listed when ALL is specified in a LISTCAT; it cannot be listed alone.

Allocation Group

The Allocation Group describes the physical disk storage space allocated to the component. The lower part of Figure 8.9 indicates the meaning of the fields in this group.

The Allocations Group can be listed for all data components and all index components. This group is listed when ALL is specified but can be listed alone by coding:

```
LISTCAT -
  ENTRIES ( AKOO.C98.CUSTMAST -
            ( AKOO.C98.CUSTMAST.ADDRAIX -
            ( AKOO.C98.CUSTMAST.NAMEAIX ) -
          ALLOCATION
```

STATISTICS GROUP:	
REC-TOTAL	Total number of records now in the component
REC-DELETED	Number of records deleted from component since its creation
REC-INSERTED	Number of records inserted since creation with key lower than the last logical record
REC-UPDATED	Number of records retrieved and rewritten since creation (does not include deletes)
REC-RETRIEVED	Number of records retrieved for either inquiry or update since creation
SPLITS-CI	Number of control area splits at present
SPLITS-CA	Number of control area splits at present
FREESPACE-%CI	Percentage of control interval left free for record expansion or insertion
FREESPACE-%CA	Percentage of control area left free for control interval splits or record insertion
FREESPC-BYTES	Actual number of bytes of free space in wholly unused control intervals only
EXCPS	Number of I/O operations performed by VSAM
EXTENTS	The number of physical disk extents occupied by the component
SYSTEM-TIMESTAMP	The encoded format of the date and time the component was last closed after update
(Index only)	
LEVELS	Number of levels in the index; a value of zero indicates the KSDS contains no records
ENTRIES/SECT	Number of entries in each section of an index record
SEQ-SET-RBA	The relative byte address of the first sequence set record
HI-LEVEL-RBA	The relative byte address of the highest level index record
ALLOCATION GROUP:	
SPACE-TYPE	Unit of space allocation, either CYLINDER or TRACK
SPACE-PRI	Number of units of primary space allocation in terms of SPACE-TYPE
SPACE-SEC	Number of units of secondary space allocation in terms of SPACE-TYPE
HI-ALLOC-RBA	Highest relative byte address plus 1 allocated for the component
HI-USED-RBA	Relative byte address plus 1 of the current end of file within the allocated space

FIGURE 8.9   Meaning of the various LISTCAT Statistics and Allocation Group indications

VOLUMES GROUP:	
VOLSER	Volume serial id of the media
DEVTYPE	Type of device to which the volume belongs:
	3010200E = 3380
	3040200A = 3340 (35M/70M)
	30502009 = 3330
	3050200B = 3350
	3050200D = 3330-1
	30582009 = 3330V
	30108003 = 9 track tape, 6250/1600 bpi
	30208003 = 9 track tape, 800/1600 bpi
	30808001 = 7 track tape
	32008003 = 9 track tape, 6250 bpi
	34008003 = 9 track tape, 1600 bpi
	78008080 = 3480 cartridge tape
VOLFLAG	Indicates whether the volume is a CANDIDATE, PRIME or OVERFLOW volume for a key range
PHYREC-SIZE	Physical record size for the component
PHYRECS/TRK	Number of physical records that can be written on a track on the volume
TRACKS/CA	The number of tracks per control area in the data component
LOW-KEY	For a KSDS with KEYRANGES, the lowest key value allowed on the volume
HIGH-KEY	For a KSDS with KEYRANGES, the highest key value allowed on the volume
HI-KEY-RBA	The relative byte address of the CI that contains the highest key value in the key range
HI-ALLOC-RBA	The highest relative byte address plus 1 available within in the space allocated
HI-USED-RBA	The highest used relative byte address that actually contains data
EXTENT-NUMBER	Number of extents allocated for the component on the volume
EXTENT-TYPE	Type of extent:
	00 = contiguous extents
	40 = extents are not preformatted
	80 = a sequence set occupies a track adjacent to a control area
Extents:	
LOW-CCHH	Physical device address of the beginning of the extent
HIGH-CCHH	Physical device address of the end of the extent
LOW-RBA	The relative byte address at the beginning of the extent
HIGH-RBA	The relative byte address at the end of the extent
TRACKS	Number of tracks in the extent

FIGURE 8.10   Meaning of the various LISTCAT Volume Group indications

Volumes Group

The Volumes Group identifies all the volumes occupied by the component and yet unoccupied candidate volumes for the component. Each extent or key range is described by a unique Volumes Group. The fields included in the group are explained by Figure 8.10. The Volumes Group can be listed only when ALL is specified in the LISTCAT command.

REVIEW QUESTIONS AND (*)EXERCISES

1. Explain the basis for the name of the LISTCAT function of IDCAMS and what it does.

2. What two purposes does LISTCAT serve for applications programmers?

3. Which of the LISTCAT display fields convey what are sometimes called the "critical measurements" for key sequenced data set performance and integrity management?

4. Examination of a LISTCAT for a key sequenced data set reveals that it is housed in nine extents. What would be a prudent course of action in regard to the data set?

5. Examination of the most recent of a series of LISTCATs for a key sequenced data set, taken at 4:30 p.m. each day, reveals that hundreds of control interval splits

exist. This is the case even though the data set is copied, eliminated, redefined, and reloaded nightly to reorganize it. What LISTCAT fields reveal the fact, what is a reasonable deduction concerning the data set, and what actions should be taken?

6. How may REC- . . . values in the LISTCAT Statistics Group be reset to zero?

*7. Code a LISTCAT to list the volume and history information for all cataloged entries starting with "BT34.C90." Note that some data set names have three qualifiers (one additional part after BT34.C90) and some have four (two additional parts after BT34.C90).

*8. Suppose a key sequenced data set base cluster is named BT34.C90.VEHREPAR. We wish to see a LISTCAT including allocation information. Code the necessary ID-CAMS commands to invoke the LISTCAT function to provide this.

*9. After performing exercise 8, code the IDCAMS commands to include allocation information for an alternate index named BT34.C90.VEHREPAR.VINAIX in the LISTCAT output.

*10. Modify the JCL and IDCAMS LISTCAT control statements in either Figure 2.2 or Figure 5.2 to reflect a FREESPACE specification of (1 1) for the data component of the key sequenced data set. Run the job stream to using the modified IDCAMS control statements to create and load a KSDS. Then change the FREESPACE specification to (0 0) and run the job stream again. Compare the two LISTCAT reports item by item, circle each difference in them, and explain why the difference is present.

NOTES

1. It is possible to create the generation data group base for the monitoring statistics with a number of generations greater than two and to retain historical data on disk. The monitoring job stream can then be modified to accept a parameter value for the earlier and current statistics set; VRE-PORTR can then produce a comparison report over a longer span of time. Another enhancement could be the application of a graphic display tool such as SPSS or SAS to the comparison statistics on a mainframe, or the downloading of earlier and current statistics in summary form to a microcomputer for charting.

2. LISTCAT statistics reflect the contents of the system catalog, updated only when a data set is successfully closed. A failure in an online program may not result in proper closure, leaving unposted many updates and record adds.

   Consider a data set with 10 records, opened by CICS. Let's say 1,000 records are added by CICS, then CICS abends and fails to close the VSAM data set properly. Since the CLOSE did not occur, catalog statistics are not updated. The data set contains 1,010 records, but the catalog indicates that only 10 records exist.

   Now suppose CICS is brought back up and 100 records are deleted, then CICS is shut down normally and closes the data set properly. The close for the data set causes VSAM to recalculate the total number of records in the data set by decrementing the total stored in the catalog by 100. This stores a negative number in the catalog statistics. Since LISTCAT prints the absolute value of the negative binary number, it will indicate that an extremely large number of records exist in the data set; the absolute value of a negative binary number is a large positive number.

   The statistics can be reset to zero only by deleting and then recreating the data set.

9

Backup and Reorganization Job Streams

Unloading a VSAM data set means making a copy of it using the REPRO utility option of IDCAMS, a process customarily called "taking a backup." Reloading or "restoring" the data set means copying the records to be housed in it from a tape or disk sequential data set into the VSAM data set.

The process of making a backup, deleting and redefining the VSAM data set, and restoring it from the backup is known as data set reorganization. This process is illustrated graphically in Figure 9.1. It eliminates any control interval and control area splits of the original VSAM data set because the new copy of the data set exists in pristine internal organization upon its creation and loading.

PURPOSE OF BACKUPS

Online System Integrity

Backup copies of disk-stored data sets are taken in the mainframe environment for the same reason that they are made in mini- and microcomputer environments: safety. Hard disks are reliable but rely on intricate mechanical devices that can fail. When a disk drive fails, the nature of the failure can be catastrophic and can lead to destruction of the information-carrying media. It is not as if a household audio disk player fails but once repaired can again play the same recordings; when a disk fails it usually destroys the medium, as if our record player physically gouged the audio or digital platter.

Timing plays a role in the taking of online VSAM data set backups. In most installations VSAM key sequenced data sets support online applications important to business and daily operations. Even if a disk device fails in circuitry that does not affect the subsequent readability of the magnetic media, it is often necessary to return an online application to operation faster than a disk device may be repaired. Beginning with the IBM 3350 and continuing with the IBM 3380s, disk media is no longer demountable from the disk spindle. To place an online application back in operation quickly an installation must be able to load data from independent media to a working disk device. Timely backups provide this capability.

While backups can be written with ordinary data set names, they are usually written to generation data group data sets in the MVS environment. This makes it possible to avoid changing JCL from one run to another and to restore a data set from its latest backup

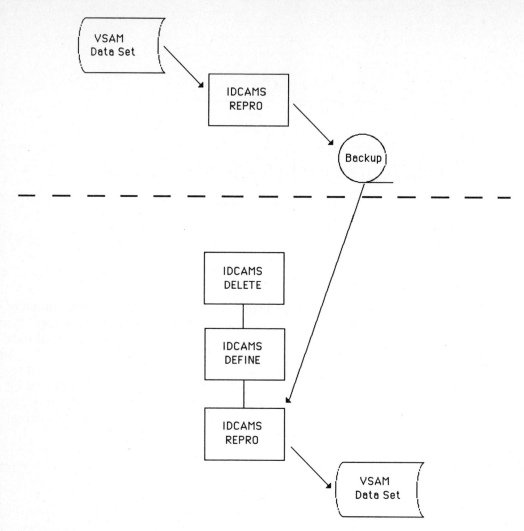

FIGURE 9.1   VSAM data set backup and reload processes for purpose of reorganization

by specifying the (0) generation, without having to modify a restoration job stream. The use of GDGs also makes it possible to insure that a given number of backup cycles, such as seven or more, is maintained to guarantee that a restoration is possible even if one or more backups is lost or destroyed. Different generation data group names are usually used for daily and weekly backups in order to have the ability to restore from any of several recent cycles, or from any of several weekly cycles further in the past.

REPRO Copies for Data Transfer to Other Applications

Both the REPRO and EXPORT commands of IDCAMS are associated with the copying of information from a VSAM data set to tape media. REPRO, however, creates records from the data component that can be read by any program or utility. EXPORT copies the VSAM data set environment and internal structure, producing the data sets on tape in a unique format that cannot be processed by other programs.

Backups are usually created with REPRO. The data set created by REPRO from a VSAM key sequenced data set consists of the data component records. REPRO can be used to create a copy of all or a portion of the records in a VSAM data set to provide these to another automated application on the same or another computer system.

When a REPRO backup is created, the records in the VSAM data set are automatically accessed via the sequence set of the index. Records that were not physically adjacent, due to CI or CA splits, are provided in their proper key sequence.

Sequential Update with Backup and Reload

A REPRO backup written to disk or tape is suitable as an input master file to a batch sequential update which creates a new updated master file. That master file can be used to reload the VSAM data set. Large-scale updates to a VSAM master file are customarily applied in this manner as shown in Figure 9.2 for efficiency reasons. Batch random access

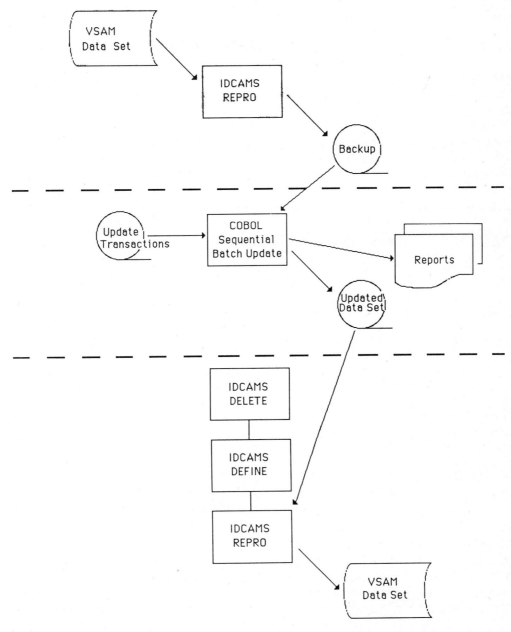

FIGURE 9.2   VSAM data set backup and reload processes including an intermediate batch sequential update

updates directly on a VSAM data set are normally avoided because these involve far greater disk I/O and are more time-consuming in execution than sequential processing.

A typical online application provides access to individual records for inquiry and update, and "browse" access on the primary or alternate keys for inquiry purposes. Batch sequential processing integrated with backup and reorganization often provides the best support for high volume updates that are inherently offline in nature.

For example, customer records and orders are usually accorded online treatment, but mailed-in payment posting is handled in a batch mode with a sequential update. If high-volume updates that expanded record lengths or added records to the key sequenced data set were handled in a random access mode, reorganization would likely be necessary immediately afterward anyway due to the control interval and control area splits generated by this processing.

DATA SET REORGANIZATION

Reorganizing a VSAM KSDS is a relatively simple task involving only IDCAMS. The JCL required to accomplish the reorganization is straightforward but should be organized in a way that avoids redundancy of JCL and IDCAMS control statements.

Figures 9.3 and 9.4 list two job streams that can be used to reorganize a key sequenced data set. Note that only the base cluster—specifically, its data component—is copied in a backup and then reloaded. The index for the base cluster is built from scratch as the reload proceeds, and any alternate indexes are built from scratch after the data component reload is finished. In truth the "re" in "reload" is purely semantic; the data set has existed in the past. To VSAM the reload is a data set delete, define, and load.

```
//FSBT677A  JOB AKOOTEST,'DP4-GUZIK',CLASS=T,MSGCLASS=X,
//  MSGLEVEL=(1,1),NOTIFY=BT05677
//*
//*     THIS JCL = BT05677.SOURCE.CNTL(JCL93)
//*
//************************************************************
//*                                                          *
//*     REPRO CUSTOMER MASTER FILE TO GENERATION             *
//*     DATA GROUP TAPE FOR BACKUP, USING EXTRA              *
//*     VSAM KSDS BUFFERS TO BOOST EFFICIENCY                *
//*                                                          *
//************************************************************
//STEPA     EXEC  PGM=IDCAMS,REGION=2048K
//SYSPRINT  DD   SYSOUT=*
//SYSUDUMP  DD   SYSOUT=A
//DD1       DD   DSN=AK00.C98.CUSTMAST,
//  AMP=('BUFNI=1,BUFND=21'),              'EXTRA BUFFERS
//  DISP=(OLD,KEEP)
//*
//* FOLLOWING GDG CREATION USES DUMMY MODEL DSCB INSTEAD OF A
//* SEPARATE MODEL DSCB FOR EVERY GDG IN THE INSTALLATION.
//* SEE CHAPTER 13, PRACTICAL MVS JCL (ISBN 0-471-83648-6)
//* IF YOU ARE NOT FAMILIAR WITH GENERATION DATA GROUPS OR
//* THIS CONVENIENCE AFFECTING THE DCB PARAMETER:
//*
//DD2       DD   DSN=AK00.C98.CUSTBKUP(+1),
//  UNIT=(TAPE,,DEFER),
//  DISP=(NEW,CATLG,DELETE),
//  DCB=(XX90.A00.DUMMYLBL,RECFM=FB,LRECL=250,BLKSIZE=32750),
//  LABEL=(1,SL,RETPD=90)
//SYSIN     DD   *
       VERIFY      FILE(DD1)
```

FIGURE 9.3   Key sequenced data set backup job stream with extra buffers for processing efficiency

```
               LISTCAT -
                  ENTRIES  (   AK00.C98.CUSTMAST -
                               AK00.C98.CUSTMAST.ADDRAIX -
                               AK00.C98.CUSTMAST.NAMEAIX     ) -
                          ALL

               REPRO        INFILE(DD1) -
                            OUTFILE(DD2)
          /*
          //
```

FIGURE 9.3   (*Continued*)

```
//FSBT686A  JOB AK00TEST,'DP2-JANOSSY',CLASS=T,MSGCLASS=X,
// MSGLEVEL=(1,1),NOTIFY=BT05686
//*
//*    THIS JCL = BT05686.SOURCE.CNTL(JCL94)
//*
//****************************************************************
//*                                                             *
//*    DEFINE AND LOAD/RELOAD VSAM DATA SET WITH                *
//*    TWO ALTERNATE INDEXES USING TWO STEPS AND                *
//*    THE AMP PARAMETER FOR EXTRA BUFFERS ON LOAD              *
//*                                                             *
//****************************************************************
//*
//****************************************************************
//*                                                             *
//*    STEPA -- DELETE AND DEFINE DATA SET                      *
//*                                                             *
//****************************************************************
//STEPA     EXEC  PGM=IDCAMS
//SYSPRINT   DD   SYSOUT=*
//SYSUDUMP   DD   SYSOUT=A
//SYSIN      DD   *
                                          /* HOUSEKEEPING DELETES  */
     DELETE     AK00.C98.CUSTMAST -
                CLUSTER

   SET LASTCC=0                           /* ABOVE MAY NOT BE      */
   SET MAXCC=0                            /* FOUND; ELIMINATE RC=8 */

   /* - - - - - - - - CREATE THE BASE CLUSTER AND PRIMARY INDEX- - */

     DEFINE -
       CLUSTER   (   NAME(AK00.C98.CUSTMAST) -
                     VOLUMES(FSDC14) -
                     RECORDSIZE(250 250) -
                     KEYS(8 36) -
                     CYLINDERS(2 1) -
                     SHAREOPTIONS(2 3) -
                     SPEED -
                     IMBED                           ) -
                     -
       DATA    (   NAME(AK00.C98.CUSTMAST.BASE.DATA) -
                   CONTROLINTERVALSIZE(4096) -
                   FREESPACE(18 1)                   ) -
                   -
       INDEX    (   NAME(AK00.C98.CUSTMAST.BASE.INDEX)  )
  /*
//****************************************************************
//*                                                             *
//*    STEPB -- USE REPRO WITH OUTFILE TO LOAD,                 *
//*             SPECIFYING EXTRA BUFFERS WITH AMP               *
//*                                                             *
//****************************************************************
```

FIGURE 9.4   Key sequenced data set restore job stream with extra buffers for processing efficiency

```
//STEPB     EXEC  PGM=IDCAMS,COND=(0,NE)
//SYSPRINT  DD    SYSOUT=*
//SYSUDUMP  DD    SYSOUT=A
//MASTIN    DD    DSN=AK00.C98.CUSTBKUP(0),
//  UNIT=(TAPE,,DEFER),
//  DISP=(OLD,KEEP)
//MASTOUT    DD   DSN=AK00.C98.CUSTMAST,
//  DISP=OLD,
//  AMP=('BUFNI=1,BUFND=21')              'EXTRA BUFFERS
//WORKSRT1   DD   DSN=AK00.C98.IDCUT1,
//  UNIT=SYSDA,                           'AIX IDCAMS WORKFILE;
//  DISP=OLD,                             'VSAM REQUIRES DISP=OLD
//  AMP='AMORG',                          'EVEN THOUGH DOES NOT
//  VOL=SER=FSDC03                        'EXIST PRIOR TO USE!
//WORKSRT2   DD   DSN=AK00.C98.IDCUT2,
//  UNIT=SYSDA,                           'AIX IDCAMS WORKFILE;
//  DISP=OLD,                             'VSAM REQUIRES DISP=OLD
//  AMP='AMORG',                          'EVEN THOUGH DOES NOT
//  VOL=SER=FSDC03                        'EXIST PRIOR TO USE!
//SYSIN      DD   *
                                          /* HOUSEKEEPING DELETES  */
     DELETE      AK00.C98.IDCUT1 -
                 PURGE

                 AK00.C98.IDCUT2 -
                 PURGE
     SET LASTCC=0                         /* ABOVE MAY NOT BE       */
     SET MAXCC=0                          /* FOUND; ELIMINATE RC=8 */

     /* - - - - - - - - - - - - - - - - - LOAD THE BASE CLUSTER */

     REPRO       INFILE(MASTIN) -
                 OUTFILE(MASTOUT)

     /* FIRST AIX - - - CREATE THE NONUNIQUE ADDRESS ALTERNATE INDEX */

     DEFINE -
       AIX       (  NAME(AK00.C98.CUSTMAST.ADDRAIX) -
                    RELATE(AK00.C98.CUSTMAST) -
                    VOLUMES(FSDC14) -         /* RECORDSIZE (AVG  MAX) */
                    RECORDSIZE(47 79) -       /* MAX 6 OCCURRENCES SO  */
                    KEYS(26 44) -             /* 5 + AIX + (N x PRIME) */
                    NONUNIQUEKEY -            /* GIVES 5+26+(2x8)=47   */
                    CYLINDERS(2 1) -          /* AND   5+26+(6x8)=79   */
                    SHAREOPTIONS(2 3) -
                    UNIQUE -
                    UPGRADE -
                    SPEED -
                    IMBED                          ) -
                    -
       DATA      (  NAME(AK00.C98.CUSTMAST.ADDRAIX.DATA)  -
                    CONTROLINTERVALSIZE(4096) -
                    FREESPACE(15 15)               ) -
                    -
       INDEX     (  NAME(AK00.C98.CUSTMAST.ADDRAIX.INDEX) )

     BLDINDEX    INDATASET(AK00.C98.CUSTMAST) -
                 OUTDATASET(AK00.C98.CUSTMAST.ADDRAIX) -
                 WORKFILES(WORKSRT1 WORKSRT2)

     DEFINE -
       PATH      (  NAME(AK00.C98.CUSTMAST.ADDRAIX.PATH) -
                    PATHENTRY(AK00.C98.CUSTMAST.ADDRAIX)  )

     /* SECOND AIX - - - - CREATE FORCED UNIQUE NAME ALTERNATE INDEX */

     DEFINE -
```

FIGURE 9.4 (Continued)

```
        AIX         (    NAME(AK00.C98.CUSTMAST.NAMEAIX) -
                         RELATE(AK00.C98.CUSTMAST) -
                         VOLUMES(FSDC14) -
                         RECORDSIZE(48 48) -        /* 5 + AIX + PRIME   */
                         KEYS(35 9) -               /* GIVES 5+35+8=48   */
                         UNIQUEKEY -
                         CYLINDERS(2 1) -
                         SHAREOPTIONS(2 3) -
                         UNIQUE -
                         UPGRADE -
                         SPEED -
                         IMBED                                    ) -
                         -
        DATA        (    NAME(AK00.C98.CUSTMAST.NAMEAIX.DATA)  -
                         CONTROLINTERVALSIZE(4096) -
                         FREESPACE(15 15)                         ) -
                         -
        INDEX       (    NAME(AK00.C98.CUSTMAST.NAMEAIX.INDEX) )

     BLDINDEX        INDATASET(AK00.C98.CUSTMAST) -
                     OUTDATASET(AK00.C98.CUSTMAST.NAMEAIX) -
                     WORKFILES(WORKSRT1 WORKSRT2)

     DEFINE -
        PATH        (    NAME(AK00.C98.CUSTMAST.NAMEAIX.PATH) -
                         PATHENTRY(AK00.C98.CUSTMAST.NAMEAIX)  )

  /* - - - - LIST CATALOG TO SEE INFO ON THE DATA SET AND INDEXES */

     LISTCAT -
        ENTRIES     (    AK00.C98.CUSTMAST -
                         AK00.C98.CUSTMAST.ADDRAIX -
                         AK00.C98.CUSTMAST.NAMEAIX    ) -
                    ALL
/*
//
```

FIGURE 9.4   *(Continued)*

Two job streams are created to perform the data set reorganization as a matter of economy. All master file data sets require a job to take backups; in the event of an abend or other disaster that would require a rerun, the master file must be restored. The two separate job streams perform these functions; a reorganization simply requires that the two job streams be run one after the other. If a batch sequential update is to be performed, a job stream for it is run after the backup but before the reload.

It is possible to omit deletion and redefinition of the VSAM data set in a reload operation if its cluster was originally defined with the REUSE attribute. Specifying REUSE, however, makes it impossible to build alternate indexes for a data set. As a practical matter this limits the applicability of REUSE.

MAXIMIZING REPRO EFFICIENCY USING EXTRA BUFFERS

The job streams illustrated in Figure 9.3 and 9.4 employ the AMP parameter BUFND and BUFNI on the DD statement for the key sequenced data set, providing appropriate buffers to speed processing. In a production environment the use of AMP for this purpose provides significant performance benefits. Specifying extra buffers for the backup of a KSDS is usually straightforward, but specifying them for the reload process is not.

In a job stream that combines key sequenced data set DELETE, DEFINE, and REPRO in one JCL step, efficiency is lost when the KSDS is allocated dynamically by naming it within an OUTDATASET specification. In this case there is no DD statement for the data set and no place to code the AMP parameter carrying extra buffers to speed the sequential access of REPRO. If OUTFILE is coded on the REPRO, however, referring to a DD statement, the job stream will fail if the data set to be deleted is not present. Flexibility is lost: the JCL cannot be used for an initial run and will fail if circumstances arise, such as a failed reload attempt, causing the data set to have been deleted prior to the run.

Figure 9.4 illustrates the means to both gain sequential processing efficiency for the reloading of the data set and to preserve flexibility. The DELETE and DEFINE actions are undertaken within one step of JCL and the reload within a subsequent step. The first step does not carry a DD statement for the data set, and its DELETE is permissive of not finding the data set. The DEFINE defines it fresh, using the control statements as they currently exist. The load step, which is barred from executing by the COND parameter if the DEFINE operation fails, makes use of OUTDATASET and a DD statement carrying the appropriate AMP subparameters BUFND and BUFNI for buffer allocation. See Chapter 6 for additional information on buffer tuning and an automated CLIST that will speed your composition of suitable AMP parameters for this purpose. COND is a JCL parameter; if you desire additional information on it, see Chapter 14 of *Practical MVS JCL for Today's Programmers* (James Janossy, John Wiley and Sons, Inc., 1987) ISBN 0-471-83648-6.

BACKUP, RESTORATION, REORGANIZATION CRITERIA

Backup

Each VSAM master file should be backed up after online updating ends for the business day *and* again after any subsequent batch random access or sequential updating is completed. If the data set is updated online, backing it up prior to other updating preserves the online modifications. Taking a second backup after batch updating for the night provides the capability to restore the data set rapidly if a disk fails during the next online processing cycle.

Backing up a data set immediately at the close of access to it online and again after any batch random access updates may appear redundant but is actually not. It appears so only when one carries over from batch days the idea that one day equals one update cycle. In fact, when a data set is updated online throughout the day, and directly in a batch random access mode after the close of online business, two daily update cycles are present. Taking a backup after each makes it possible to resume the next session of operation with the data set in the most expeditious manner. It is inexpensive insurance against an online system outage of any greater time duration than is absolutely necessary, especially when the AMP parameter is used to minimize REPRO processing time.

When Restoration Is Necessary

Two circumstances make it necessary to restore a VSAM key sequenced data set from a backup. The first of these deals with a failed online or batch update or a successful batch update that must be rerun due to incorrect transaction input. The second circumstance is the need to reorganize that data set to regain efficiency.

CICS provides an automatic mechanism called Dynamic Transaction Backout that restores a data set to its prior state when a transaction abends. This facility is not, however, universally employed. Dynamic Transaction Backout if employed with CICS in an installation will automatically return a VSAM data set being updated online to a usable condition if an individual online transaction terminates abnormally. Without DTB a failed online transaction may damage the VSAM data set and make it necessary to restore it from a backup and reapply online updates since the time of the backup, using the CICS journal. Reapplication of updates from the journal requires special programming to select the relevant items from the journal and apply them.

In a batch environment no automatic VSAM data set restoration facility exists. If a batch random access process writing to a VSAM data set ends abnormally, the data set will be left in a corrupted condition. The data set must be restored from a backup before use by the same or another program.

If a batch random access update acting directly on a VSAM master file completes successfully but it is discovered that the input transactions were not appropriate, it is of course necessary to restore the VSAM master file to its original condition in order to rerun the update. In this rare case a reload job stream can be executed using as input the last backup taken prior to the incorrect update.

When Reorganization Is Warranted

No automatic mechanism exists to flag the need for reorganization of a data set. Slow response time in an online environment can indicate a need to reorganize a data set. Longer than normal batch random access processing time can also indicate a need to reorganize. But slow response or processing time can also be caused by other situations such as temporary heavy loading of a machine, poor placement of data sets on specific disk units with high contention for access, or inefficient assignment of disk devices to system channels.

The only precise way to determine that a need exists to reorganize a data set is to monitor data set activity and condition using the IDCAMS LISTCAT utility function. Excessive CI or CA splits, multiple extents, or a large number of record additions or expansions dictate that a data set be reorganized. These statistics can be obtained directly from LISTCAT output or more conveniently from a job stream that monitors VSAM data sets, such as VMONITOR presented in Chapter 8.

It may appear that data set condition monitoring can be avoided by following a daily backup step with a restoration step. This simple approach may seem desirable but in many cases it is inefficient. In fact, it is always insufficient. Even if a reorganization is run after every backup, data set size must still be monitored to determine if the data set has expanded into multiple extents or if it is approaching its maximum file capacity.

Data Sets That Do Not Require Reorganization

Data sets with certain characteristics do not require reorganization. Data sets that are never modified after their initial load or which are defined with no free space do not require reorganization. Data sets that have minimal record insertion activity usually do not require reorganization. Reorganization can be avoided for data sets that are so seldom modified that their internal configuration is sufficient to absorb the activity, as indicated by a low level of CI and CA splits.

AUTOMATED MONITORING OF DATA SET CONDITION

The automated data set monitoring programs and job stream discussed in Chapter 8 take into account the foregoing criteria for differing levels of day-to-day attention that should be accorded to production VSAM data sets. Appendix F contains the source code for these items.

Source code for the automated monitoring tools presented in Appendix F is also available to you in machine-readable form, suitable for uploading to a mainframe. As described in Appendix A, these items are contained on a microcomputer diskette available by mail at nominal cost.

REORGANIZATION HINTS

It may be tempting to collapse the two steps in the job stream of Figure 9.4, but this should not be done. The main reason that the DELETE/DEFINE step is separated from the REPRO step is to gain the ability to specify appropriate buffers via the AMP parameter to maximize data set loading efficiency. Another aspect of this practice avoids a potential pitfall that may arise when it is necessary not only to reorganize a key sequenced data set but also to move it to a disk device other than the one on which it originally resides.

If the two steps were combined and the cluster allocated via a DD statement for the purpose of specifying buffers, and the VOLUME attribute is modified to reflect a different disk device, the job stream will abend on the REPRO command with the following IDCAMS error messages:

```
IDC3300I ERROR OPENING AK00.C98.CUSTMAST
IDC3351I ** VSAM OPEN RETURN CODE IS 184
```

and the REPRO command will terminate with a condition code of 12. This error message indicates that the data set that was located via the catalog and allocated for access by MVS at the DDname //MASTIN, then subsequently deleted by IDCAMS and defined on a different device, could not be found on the original device. A simple way to avoid this situation is to separate the DELETE/DEFINE and the reload operations. A temporary solution to the problem when it occurs with DELETE, DEFINE, and REPRO in one step is to rerun the job stream after it abends. The rerun will operate successfully the second time because at this point the data set will be allocated on the device to which it will be restored.

REVIEW QUESTIONS AND (*)EXERCISES

1. What is a more common term for the process of "unloading" a key sequenced data set?

2. What is the difference between data sets created by REPRO and EXPORT, and which is preferred for ordinary key sequenced backup purposes?

3. Discuss how bulk sequential update may be integrated with KSDS backup and reorganization processes on a cyclical basis and some of the advantages of this arrangement.

4. When a REPRO of a key sequenced data set is created, what components of the data set exist on the output media?

5. When should a key sequenced data set updated online be backed up?

6. When is restoration of a key sequenced data set from a backup necessary?

7. What actions can be taken to determine when a key sequenced data set should be reorganized?

8. Cite three types of key sequenced data sets that do not require reorganization.

*9. Extra buffers can be specified for sequential operations on a key sequenced data set to improve processing efficiency. Draw a diagram of a job stream that defines and loads a key sequenced data set named BT44.C90.TICKMAST, arranging functions to gain maximum flexibility. The job stream itself should delete the existing KSDS of this name but not require manual attention or change if that data set does not for some reason exist when the job stream is run.

*10.   A batch program is being executed at 2:15 a.m. to process random updates to a key sequenced data set. The program encounters a condition that causes it to abend with a system completion code of 0C7, and it terminates operation without closing any data sets normally. Write the recovery instructions that an operation group should have been given, describing actions that must be taken in order to avoid any delay in making the data set accessible to the teleprocessing network of the organization, which becomes active at 7:00 a.m. each day.

10

ISAM to VSAM Conversion
and the ISAM Interface

When VSAM was put forth as the replacement for the ISAM and BDAM access methods, most installations adopted VSAM for new applications. Older systems were, in many cases, not converted.

The conversion of ISAM data sets to VSAM data sets becomes a necessity as installations migrate to the more recent versions of COBOL and CICS software. VSCOBOL II, the latest IBM COBOL, does not directly support ISAM data sets; neither does CICS release 1.7. These current software releases provide access to memory above a machine size of 16 megabytes under IBM's "extended architecture" (XA) but make obsolete such things as ISAM, BDAM, and the COBOL Report Writer.

ISAM INTERFACE PROGRAM

The IIP as a Bridge from ISAM to VSAM

The ISAM Interface Program or IIP is support software that provides a means to run programs written with ISAM coding constructs against VSAM data sets that were converted from ISAM data sets. This interface enables completely debugged programs that process ISAM data sets to process key sequenced data sets instead. The IIP is the bridge away from ISAM towards VSAM. It allows an installation to eliminate ISAM data sets but to postpone the conversion of programs that still contain ISAM code, by intercepting communications between the program and VSAM as shown in Figure 10.1. The ISAM Interface Program deals with online CICS programs as well as batch programs.

Switching an ISAM application to VSAM is a straightforward process. An ISAM data set is first converted to a KSDS. The JCL identifying each converted ISAM data set is then modified—actually in most cases simplified—for VSAM. Finally, the ISAM processing program must be examined for coding practices that are not allowed by the interface and, if necessary, modified to conform to the coding structures acceptable to the interface.

How the IIP Is Invoked

The ISAM interface is invoked automatically when a program using ISAM coding syntax such as NOMINAL KEY is executed against a VSAM data set. When a program coded for ISAM issues an OPEN to what is now a key sequenced data set the IIP is given control to:

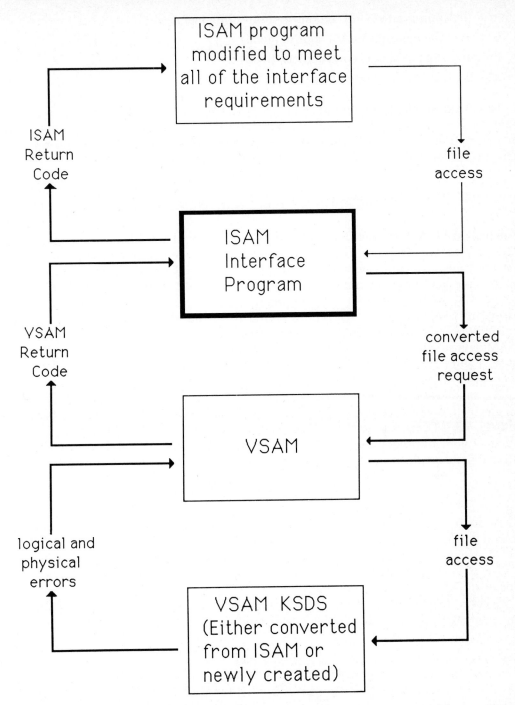

FIGURE 10.1 How the ISAM Interface Program intercepts communication to and from an ISAM-based program that accesses a VSAM key sequenced data set

- load the appropriate ISAM interface routines into memory
- construct the required VSAM control blocks
- initialize the ISAM data control block (DCB)
- take the DCB exit requested by the program.

The ISAM interface program intercepts each ISAM request, analyzes it, determines the equivalent KSDS request, and initiates the corresponding VSAM request. Return codes and exception codes from VSAM are translated to ISAM codes by the IIP and routed to the program or to the error-handling routine specified in the ISAM DCB.

CONVERTING AN ISAM DATA SET TO A KSDS

The physical ISAM data set can be converted to a key sequenced data set in several ways. The simplest way is to use IDCAMS to define the KSDS and then REPRO the ISAM data set to it from a backup tape. In lieu of loading the new KSDS with the REPRO command, an existing load program can be used, employing the IIP, after changing its JCL to that required by VSAM. If an existing load program is used, it should process the data set in ascending sequence to eliminate control interval splits during the load.

REPRO can be used to read an ISAM data set directly as input. When REPRO reads an ISAM data set, the JCL parameter DCB = DSORG = IS must be coded at the input DD statement. Figure 10.2 illustrates the JCL and IDCAMS control statements required to load a previously defined KSDS directly from an ISAM data set.

The specification of the ENVIRONMENT(DUMMY) subparameter as part of the INFILE parameter will allow records flagged for deletion in the ISAM data set also to be loaded into the VSAM data set. Such records carry high-values (hexadecimal FF) in the first byte. Figure 10.3 shows how the ENVIRONMENT(DUMMY) specification is coded. Omitting this subparameter causes records flagged for deletion to be dropped during the load.

An Example of ISAM to VSAM Conversion

In production JCL an ISAM data set is usually created in the same job stream that loads it. Converting the ISAM create/load to a VSAM DEFINE/REPRO is facilitated by using the ISAM specifications as a guide to free space determination. Figure 10.4 represents a typical set of job steps to create and load an ISAM data set. Let's create VSAM JCL to replace this in an ISAM to VSAM conversion.

//STEPA deletes any existing data set cataloged as AK00.C98.MASTER. //STEPB sorts the sequential data set, AK00.C98.SOURCE.FILE, into ascending sequence on the 25

```
//CNVTISAM    EXEC  IDCAMS
//SYSPRINT    DD    SYSOUT=*
//INPUT       DD    DSN=AK00.C98.ISAM.MASTER,
//  DISP=OLD,
//  DCB=DSORG=IS
//OUTPUT      DD    DSN=AK00.C98.VSAM.MASTER,
//  DISP=SHR
//SYSIN       DD    *
    REPRO -
          INFILE(INPUT) -
          OUTFILE(OUTPUT)
/*
```

FIGURE 10.2 IDCAMS control statements and JCL to REPRO an ISAM data set directly to an already defined KSDS

```
//CNVTISAM   EXEC  IDCAMS
//SYSPRINT    DD   SYSOUT=*
//INPUT       DD   DSN=AK00.C98.ISAM.MASTER,
//  DISP=OLD,
//  DCB=DSORG=IS
//OUTPUT      DD   DSN=AK00.C98.VSAM.MASTER,
//  DISP=SHR
//SYSIN       DD   *
    REPRO -
          INFILE(INPUT) -
          ENVIRONMENT(DUMMY) -
          OUTFILE(OUTPUT)
/*
```

FIGURE 10.3 Use of the ENVIRONMENT(DUMMY) specification on REPRO to cause KSDS loading of records carrying high-values in the first position

```
//FSBT677A  JOB AK00TEST,'DP4-GUZIK',CLASS=W,MSGCLASS=X,
//  MSGLEVEL=(1,1),NOTIFY=BT05677
//*
//*    THIS JCL = BT05677.SOURCE.CNTL(JCL104)
//*
//****************************************************************
//*                                                              *
//*    DELETE THE ISAM DATA SET                                  *
//*                                                              *
//****************************************************************
//STEPA       EXEC  PGM=IEFBR14
//DD1         DD  DSN=AK00.C98.ISAMMAST,
//  UNIT=SYSDA,
//  DISP=(MOD,DELETE),
//  SPACE=(TRK,0)
//****************************************************************
//*                                                              *
//*    SORT THE LOAD DATA, CREATE, AND LOAD THE ISAM DATA SET    *
//*    USING DYNAMIC SORT WORK SPACE ALLOCATION                  *
//*                                                              *
//****************************************************************
//STEPB       EXEC  PGM=SORT
//SYSOUT      DD  SYSOUT=A
//SORTIN      DD  DSN=AK00.C98.TESTDATA.FILE,DISP=OLD
//SORTOUT     DD  DSN=AK00.C98.ISAMMAST(INDEX),
//  UNIT=3380,
//  DISP=(NEW,CATLG,DELETE),
//  SPACE=(CYL,1),
//  DCB=(RECFM=FB,LRECL=250,BLKSIZE=2500,OPTCD=WIYLR,
//    RKP=1,KEYLEN=25,CYLOFL=3,DSORG=IS)
//            DD  DSN=AK00.C98.ISAMMAST(PRIME),
//  UNIT=3380,
//  SPACE=(CYL,55),
//  DISP=(NEW,KEEP,DELETE),
//  DCB=*.SORTOUT,
//  VOL=REF=*.SORTOUT
//            DD  DSN=AK00.C98.ISAMMAST(OVFLOW),
//  UNIT=3380,
//  SPACE=(CYL,1),
//  DISP=(NEW,KEEP,DELETE),
//  DCB=*.SORTOUT,
//  VOL=REF=*.SORTOUT
//SYSIN       DD  *
    SORT FIELDS=(2,25,CH,A),FILSZ=E85000,DYNALLOC=(SYSDA,4)
/*
//
```

FIGURE 10.4 Typical ISAM delete, sort, create, and load job stream

bytes starting in the second position, defines the ISAM data set, and loads it with the sorted records. Most of the information required to create IDCAMS control statements to define a corresponding VSAM data set is provided in the DCB parameters and space allocation for the ISAM data set. This information can be extracted from it:

* record length is 250 bytes
* the primary key starts in position 2 and is 25 bytes long
* the data set resides on a 3380 (which has 15 tracks per cylinder)
* The data set can hold 84,700 records in its prime area. Using the disk space capacity chart of Appendix E we find that 14 blocks will fit on a track for a keyed data set.[1] One track per cylinder is used for cylinder index and 3 tracks per cylinder are used for independent overflow, leaving 11 tracks per cylinder available for data. The number of records in the prime data area is determined by multiplying 10 records per block $\times$ 14 blocks per track $\times$ 11 tracks per cylinder $\times$ 55 cylinders = $10 \times 14 \times 11 \times 55$ producing a total of 84,700 records.
* Cylinder overflow of three tracks per cylinder represents approximately 21.4% of each cylinder. Since the cylinder index takes one track per cylinder, only 14 tracks per cylinder are available for data. The computation 3 / 14 indicates 21.4%.
* independent overflow represents 1.8% of the prime record area; 1 cylinder / 55 cylinders = 1.8.

Let's assume that the data set is accessed online and is reorganized weekly.

The attributes of a key sequenced data set to replace the ISAM data set can be determined using this information. The required MVS JCL and IDCAMS control statements are illustrated in Figure 10.5. SPEED and SHAREOPTIONS(2 3) are recommended for all VSAM data sets. KEYS(25 1) indicates that the key length is 25 bytes and starts with an offset of 1 from the first byte, in other words in position 2 of each record. RECORD-SIZE(250 250) specifies a fixed length record of 250 bytes: the average and maximum record length is the same. Since the data is accessed online, IMBED is recommended. The CLIST CISIZE indicates that the optimum value for the CISIZE of an online data set for a record length of 250 bytes on a 3380 is 4,096. This leaves only the space requirement for the data component and the free space requirement to be determined.

A simple formula can be used to convert cylinder overflow (CYLOFL) to CI free space. The three tracks of cylinder overflow specified as "CYLOFL = 3" represent 21.4% of a 3380 cylinder. For a CISIZE of 4,096 and a record length of 250, the number of records per CI are:

$$(4,096 - 10) / 250 = 16$$

21.4% of 16 is 3.4. Since the VSAM data set must accommodate at least as many records as did the ISAM data set, the value should be rounded up to 4. This value will be used with the CLIST VSAMSPAC when it prompts for the number of CIs to be reserved per CI for record additions. VSAMSPAC calculates a value of 24% for CI free space.

The independent overflow area of one cylinder can also be converted to CA free space. The one cylinder represents 1.8% of the prime area of the ISAM data set so 1.8% of each CA should be set aside for CA free space. The tables in Appendix E indicate that with a CISIZE of 4,096, 140 CIs will fit in a CA on a 3380 when the IMBED option is specified. 1.8% of 140 = 2.5; round up to 3. This value will be used with the CLIST VSAMSPAC when it prompts for the number of CIs per CA to reserve for CA free space. VSAMSPAC calculates a value of 3% for CA free space, which will reserve 4 CIs per CA for CA free space.

```
//FSBT686A  JOB AK00TEST,'DP2-JANOSSY',CLASS=W,MSGCLASS=X,
//  MSGLEVEL=(1,1),NOTIFY=BT05686
//*
//*     THIS JCL = BT05686.SOURCE.CNTL(JCL105)
//*
//*     SORT ISAM LOAD DATA, DEFINE KSDS, LOAD IT
//*
//************************************************************
//*                                                         *
//*     SORT DATA TO INSURE CORRECT ORDER TO LOAD           *
//*     USING DYNAMIC SORT WORK SPACE ALLOCATION            *
//*                                                         *
//************************************************************
//SORTINPT EXEC  PGM=SORT
//SYSOUT     DD  SYSOUT=A
//SORTIN     DD  DSN=AK00.C98.CUSTOMER,
//  DISP=(OLD,KEEP)
//SORTOUT    DD  DSN=&SORTDAT,
//  UNIT=SYSDA,
//  DISP=(NEW,PASS),
//  DCB=(RECFM=FB,LRECL=250,BLKSIZE=6000),
//  SPACE=(6000,(3600,700),RLSE)
//SYSIN      DD  *
    SORT  FIELDS=(2,25,CH,A),
          FILSZ=E85000,DYNALLOC=(SYSDA,4)
/*
//************************************************************
//*                                                         *
//*     DELETE, DEFINE, LOAD KSDS                           *
//*                                                         *
//************************************************************
//STEPB     EXEC  PGM=IDCAMS
//SYSPRINT   DD  SYSOUT=*
//SYSUDUMP   DD  SYSOUT=A
//MASTIN     DD  DSN=&&SORTDAT,
//  DISP=(OLD,DELETE)
//SYSIN      DD  *
                                    /* HOUSEKEEPING DELETES */
    DELETE      AK00.C98.CUSTMAST -
                CLUSTER

  SET LASTCC=0                      /* ABOVE MAY NOT BE      */
  SET MAXCC=0                       /* FOUND; GET RID OF RC=8 */

  /* - - - - - - - - CREATE THE BASE CLUSTER AND PRIMARY INDEX- - */

    DEFINE -
      CLUSTER  (   NAME(AK00.C98.CUSTMAST) -
                   VOLUMES(FSDC14) -
                   RECORDSIZE(250 250) -
                   KEYS(25 1) -
                   CYLINDERS(53 5) -
                   SHAREOPTIONS(2 3) -
                   SPEED -
                   IMBED                              ) -
                   -
      DATA     (   NAME(AK00.C98.CUSTMAST.BASE.DATA) -
                   CONTROLINTERVALSIZE(4096) -
                   FREESPACE(24 3)                    ) -
                   -
      INDEX    (   NAME(AK00.C98.CUSTMAST.BASE.INDEX)  )

  /* - - - - - - - - IF CREATION SUCCESSFUL LOAD THE KSDS - - - - */
```

FIGURE 10.5   JCL and IDCAMS control statements to sort, DELETE, DEFINE, and REPRO the data set converted to a VSAM key sequenced data set

```
         IF LASTCC = 0 -
         THEN -
            REPRO        INFILE(MASTIN) -
                         OUTDATASET(AK00.C98.CUSTMAST)

         /* - - - - LIST CATALOG TO SEE INFO ON THE DATA SET - - - - - - */

            LISTCAT -
                ENTRIES  (   AK00.C98.CUSTMAST   ) -
                         ALL
         /*
         //
```

FIGURE 10.5   (*Continued*)

The final specification to be determined is the disk space requirement. Using 84,700 for the number of records to be loaded initially, VSAMSPAC calculates 52 cylinders for the data component of the converted data set. A secondary allocation of 5 cylinders is specified to insure that the data set will not abruptly lose the ability to accommodate record additions during online updating. One extra cylinder is added to the primary space allocation to accommodate the index.

Converting ISAM JCL to VSAM MVS JCL

The typical DD statement for batch access to an ISAM data set:

```
//BT4510U1   DD DSN=AK00.C98.MASTER,
// DISP=OLD
```

can be replaced by a DD statement such as this when the data set has been converted to a KSDS:

```
//BT4510U1   DD DSN=AK00.C98.MASTER,
// DISP=SHR,
// AMP=('AMORG,OPTCD=IL,RECFM=FB',
// 'BUFNI=2,BUFND=4')
```

The disposition parameter of SHR does not present the potential for loss of data set integrity because share options of (2 3) defined for the data set in Figure 10.5 will allow only one task to update the data set at a time.

The AMP parameter in the new JCL performs several functions. AMORG indicates that data set is VSAM. OPTCD is communication to VSAM used only when the program being executed uses the ISAM interface. OPTCD determines whether or not records marked for deletion will be kept in the data set or physically deleted. Omitting OPTCD or coding OPTCD=L indicates that a record carrying hexadecimal FF in the first position will be rewritten to the data set. OPTCD=IL indicates that a record read by the program, marked with high-values in the first byte, and operated upon by a REWRITE verb will not be rewritten to the data set.

The AMP RECFM subparameter specifies the record format for which the processing program is coded. This is normally fixed-block FB. If no RECFM subparameter is specified in the program and this specification is omitted in the JCL, the data set is assumed to contain variable-length records.

The BUFND and BUFNI subparameters indicate the number of buffers to be allocated for the data component and the index component. For batch random processing, two index buffers and three data buffers should be specified. Sequential processing can be enhanced by specifying one index and a minimum of four data buffers. For skip sequential or mixed mode processing, two index and four data buffers can be used. The optimal number of buffers can be computed using the VSAMBUFS TSO CLIST or the formulas described in Chapter 6.

In the case of a variable-length record ISAM data set, a few of the ISAM JCL DCB parameters are treated differently. The KSDS record length is equal to the ISAM record length minus four bytes, and the KSDS key position is equal to the ISAM relative key position minus four bytes.

Program Restrictions

The final step to be taken in conversion to the use of the ISAM Interface Program is to examine the ISAM processing programs for coding practices that are not allowed by the interface. If any of these unacceptable coding practices are present the program must be modified to conform to coding structures acceptable to the interface program. The ISAM Interface Program imposes these restrictions:

- Programs that have two different select statements assigned to the same ISAM data set cannot have both of the data set references open at the same time. If this occurs, the IIP cannot insure the integrity of the data set. This is the most common coding pattern the IIP cannot handle.

- Program code that counts overflow records to determine when the ISAM data set requires reorganization will produce spurious results with VSAM data sets.

- VSAM data sets cannot be temporary data sets. A program coded on the assumption that the ISAM data sets it processes are temporary must be modified to regard them as permanent.

- A program must run successfully under ISAM using only standard ISAM interfaces. The IIP does not check for parameters that are invalid for ISAM.

- Code that creates dummy records with a maximum key in order to avoid overflow processing must be removed.

- Record definitions cannot be shorter than the actual record size.

- If the RECFM parameter (RECORDING MODE) is not specified in the program, it must be specified in the AMP parameter in the DD statement for the KSDS.

- The sequential processing of the data set with a key length defined smaller than the actual key length is not allowed.

- The OPEN TYPE=J macro, used in conjunction with the modification of a job file control block, is not allowed by VSAM. If use is made of OPEN TYPE=J it must be replaced by use of the OPEN macro.

- The ISAM Interface Program does not support the use of a job file control block extension (JFCBE) exit routine, a device-dependent JFCB feature.

- SETL I and SETL ID instructions must be removed or modified to some other form of the SETL instruction. The ISAM Interface Program cannot translate a request that depends on a specific device address or block.

- Since the ISAM Interface Program translates VSAM codes to appropriate ISAM codes, an associated SYNAD error routine must not invoke VSAM macros or check for VSAM return codes.

- CATALOG/DASDM macros must be replace by VSAM commands in the program.

The first eight restrictions can apply to COBOL programs and the last five restrictions apply only to assembler programs. The most difficult of the coding constructs to modify in a COBOL program is the first restriction since it can cause a major restructuring of program logic.

Modifying and Testing a Converted Program

One of the major requirements of the ISAM Interface Program is that the program must process successfully with ISAM. This can present a problem if the original ISAM data set is not retained for subsequent testing. Once a program has been modified to use the IIP the code peculiar to ISAM should not be changed. If changes are made to ISAM code, the program must be tested with a real ISAM data set prior to using it with the ISAM interface. This imposes a significant testing burden.

ISAM INTERFACE PROGRAM: PRO AND CON

Advantages of Using the ISAM Interface

Several advantages accrue to an installation in accepting the aid provided by the ISAM Interface Program and accelerating the migration to VSAM. VSAM uses less channel time than ISAM. For random operations the number of accesses required to obtain a record, from the highest level index entry down to the record, is always constant; record insertions have no effect on this. Under ISAM this processing path length varies and becomes longer as more records are inserted. The elapsed time and CPU time differences between using the interface IIP and native VSAM are negligible.

VSAM uses free space in a more efficient way than ISAM uses its overflow areas. A KSDS requires less reorganization than ISAM because of this.

Disadvantages of Using the ISAM Interface

While the ISAM Interface Program allows taking advantage of some VSAM benefits, the programs accessing VSAM data sets will run more slowly than they did under ISAM. It is well to know this ahead of time so that the effect on related job streams and schedules can be anticipated. OPEN and CLOSE in VSAM take significantly longer than OPEN and CLOSE in ISAM. Data set creation in VSAM takes longer than data set creation in ISAM, depending on the amount of free space specified, the number of buffers allocated, and the blocking factor.

VSAM requires more virtual storage than ISAM and generally uses more CPU time in sequential access operations. But direct access operations in VSAM usually require less CPU time than equivalent operations in ISAM. This is true for random batch and sorted batch operations. Using the ISAM interface program rather than native VSAM adds slightly to the CPU time required to execute the program.

FULL ISAM CONVERSION TO VSAM

On the surface it appears that using the ISAM Interface Program is a viable alternative to converting ISAM code and data sets to VSAM code and data sets. The data set conversion is a relatively simple task, as is the conversion of the JCL; for some programs little if any modification is necessary. The interface routines perform well and use only about 11K bytes of pageable memory. Why spend the extra time and effort to completely convert ISAM processing programs to VSAM processing programs?

The most compelling reason to fully convert programs to VSAM coding is to take full advantage of the extra capabilities of VSAM and of the new constructs that have been added to in the latest releases of COBOL and CICS.

VSAM Capabilities Not Available in ISAM

VSAM provides several capabilities that ISAM does not. Most of these additional capabilities provide the means to design and create more efficient and powerful programs with less code. The additional capabilities include concurrent request processing that allows a VSAM data set to perform both sequential and direct requests without closing and opening it, and with only one SELECT statement coded with ACCESS MODE IS DYNAMIC.

One or more alternate indexes can be built for a key sequenced data set, providing access to a single data set through different keys. Data for a single data set can be allocated on different volumes by ranges of key values. A secondary space allocation can be specified minimizing the chance that an online system will become inoperable due to exhaustion of its space allocation. In addition, automatic partial data set reorganization through control area splits occurs in a KSDS when there are no free control intervals to add or extend a record.

Finally, no abends occur in OPEN processing when using VSAM data sets. Instead, VSAM returns a file status code when it cannot open a data set. The value of this code pinpoints the problem without requiring printing and analysis of a memory dump.

VSCOBOL-II Capabilities

The VSCOBOL-II compiler, which can access VSAM data sets but not ISAM, provides significant benefits that become available under full conversion of programs from ISAM to VSAM. VSCOBOL-II provides several new language constructs lacking in its predecessors. The new constructs facilitate the implementation of better structured program logic.

An INITIALIZE verb is provided in VSCOBOL-II to assign either initial values or new values to data items. EVALUATE effectively replaces the GO TO DEPENDING ON verb with added functionality. Scope terminators such as ENDIF eliminate the use of periods to terminate conditional logic statements. AFTER with the PERFORM verb allows "test after perform" loops in addition to the already present "test before perform" loop. Expanded VSAM return codes in VSCOBOL-II assist in diagnosis of VSAM error conditions.

CICS 1.7 and Beyond

Release 1.7 adds many new performance and integrity features to the CICS telecommunications monitor. But, as with VSCOBOL-II, CICS 1.7 cannot access ISAM data sets. Some of the new features of CICS 1.7 include the ability to update a key sequenced data set directly through an alternate index, write spanned records when the logical record size is larger than the CI size, and the automatic performance of verification on a key sequenced data set.

Unlike the case with earlier CICS releases, empty data sets can be processed under CICS 1.7; it is no longer necessary to initialize a new KSDS with a dummy record to make it accessible. Dynamic calls can be made to VSCOBOL-II programs without CICS command dependencies.

CICS 1.7 does support the use of the ISAM Interface Program to allow ISAM-based programs to process VSAM data sets. But the application program cannot be written in VSCOBOL-II since VSCOBOL-II itself does not support ISAM.

COMPLETE CONVERSION EXAMPLE

A program that processes an ISAM data set and a version of the same program completely converted to VSAM processing can be found in Appendix B. All code altered or removed from the original program is identified, as is all new or modified code in the converted program. Note that the program illustrated uses a data set different from AK00.C98.-CUSTMAST, employed in earlier examples. This has no effect on the ISAM/VSAM coding and has been arranged in this book for variety.

ISAM to VSAM Conversion Guide

Completely converting a program to process a VSAM data set directly instead of using the IIP is straightforward. These conversion hints will help identify the code that must be converted and what the replacement code can be. These examples make use of the I/O code paragraphs or logical modules illustrated in Chapter 7 as comprehensive patterns for key sequenced data set access.

ISAM maintained three "quirks" in the form of a "nominal" key field, lack of a file status value, and lack of a delete verb. The coding to deal with these quirks must be removed or modified in the following ways:

SELECT Statement   NOMINAL KEY must be removed and FILE STATUS added, as in Figure 10.6.

FILE STATUS   FILE STATUS should be tested after each OPEN, START, READ, WRITE, REWRITE, DELETE, and CLOSE statement. Files should be closed and program operation aborted if FILE STATUS indicates a situation not recoverable through program logic statements.

RECORD KEY   VSAM obtains its key from RECORD KEY coded in the file description for the record rather than from a NOMINAL KEY coded in working storage. The value of the key of the record to be accessed must be moved to the RECORD KEY field prior to I/O operations. Figure 10.7 illustrates this change with representative field names.

```
ISAM code:

SELECT COA-FILE        ASSIGN TO DA-I-P165VC01
            ACCESS IS RANDOM
            RECORD KEY IS COA-KEY-ACCT-ID
            NOMINAL KEY IS WS-SAVE-ACCT-KEY.


_____


VSAM code:

SELECT COA-FILE        ASSIGN TO P165VC01
            ORGANIZATION IS INDEXED
            ACCESS IS RANDOM
            RECORD KEY IS COA-KEY-ACCT-ID
            FILE STATUS IS VSAM1-FS.
```

FIGURE 10.6   SELECT/ASSIGN statement in ISAM program and as modified in program converted to access a key sequenced data set

```
ISAM Code:

MOVE key-field  TO  WS-COA-NOMINAL-KEY.
```

```
VSAM Code:

MOVE key-field  TO  COA-KEY-ACCT-ID.
```

FIGURE 10.7   Record key of ISAM program changed from nominal key access to file description key field in converted program

LOGICAL DELETE (REWRITE WITH HIGH-VALUES)   VSAM provides a DELETE verb in keeping with the ANSI-74 standards for indexed file support in COBOL. ISAM, dating from before the drafting of those standards, implemented record deletion in a nonstandard manner by regarding as deleted any record carrying high-values (hexadecimal FF) in its first byte. Figure 10.8 illustrates the code change that can be made in an ISAM-based program when it is converted to VSAM.

Conversion Problems

Several problems can occur while converting an ISAM data set to a key sequenced data set for processing with the ISAM Interface Program. Most of these problems manifest themselves with an abend of the program. Potential problems and their causes include:

```
ISAM code:

MOVE key-value TO WS-nominal-key-field.
MOVE HIGH-VALUES TO COA-DELETE-BYTE.
REWRITE COA-RCORD FROM COA-INPUT-AREA
    INVALID KEY
        MOVE 'ABEND ON COA DELETE' TO SR-DL1-MSG
        PERFORM 3980-I-O-ABORT.
```

```
VSAM code:

(in WORKING-STORAGE)

*VSAM1STD  LAST CHANGED 04-02-84  ORIGINAL 01-22-84   J JANOSSY
****************************************************************
*      STANDARD VSAM FILE STATUS FIELD DEFINITION             *
****************************************************************
01  VSAM1-FS.
    05 VSAM1-FS-LEFT-RIGHT.
       10 VSAM1-FS-LEFT         PIC X(1).
          88 VSAM1-ACTION-OK              VALUE '0'.
          88 VSAM1-SEQ-EOF               VALUE '1'.
       10 FILLER               PIC X(1).
    05 VSAM1-FS-FULL   REDEFINES
       VSAM1-FS-LEFT-RIGHT      PIC X(2).
          88 VSAM1-WRITE-OUT-SEQ         VALUE '21'.
          88 VSAM1-DUP-PRIME-ALT-KEY     VALUE '22'.
```

FIGURE 10.8   ISAM delete-byte manipulation changed to COBOL DELETE verb in program converted from ISAM to VSAM

```
                      88 VSAM1-REC-NOT-FOUND            VALUE '23'.
                      88 VSAM1-OPEN-OK                  VALUE '00'.
              *
                         -
                         -
                         -

              (in the PROCEDURE DIVISION)
                         -
                         -
              MOVE key-value TO FD-key-field.
              DELETE COA-FILE.
              IF VSAM1-ACTION-OK
                 NEXT SENTENCE
              ELSE
                 MOVE 'ABEND ON COA DELETE' TO SR-DR1-MSG
                 PERFORM 3980-I-O-ABORT.
```

FIGURE 10.8   (*Continued*)

- An OC1 will occur on the first read of the KSDS converted from an ISAM file if you inadvertently reference the original ISAM data set with the AMP parameter coded on its DD statement instead of the VSAM data set.

- If an empty KSDS—one that has never had any records in it—is referenced through the ISAM Interface Program, a condition code of 12 will be posted with an IKF111I error message indicating an "unreachable block."

- A failure to code DSORG-IS on the DD statement used by IDCAMS to REPRO an ISAM data set to a KSDS will result in the following error messages and a condition code of 12:

```
IDC3300I ERROR OPENING isam-file-data-set-name
IDC3321I ** OPEN/CLOSE/EOV ABEND EXIT TAKEN
```

If this error is ignored the KSDS will be created empty and the first access to it will result in the error above.

- If the OPTCD=IL subparameter is omitted from the AMP parameter of a VSAM data set accessed via the ISAM Interface Program, the application program will function properly but the records flagged for deletion with hexadecimal FF in the first byte will be written to the KSDS.

REVIEW QUESTIONS AND (*)EXERCISES

1. Why does conversion of data sets and applications from ISAM-based support to VSAM support appear as a major work item for many IBM mainframe installations?

2. What is the ISAM Interface Program and what services does it perform?

3. How is the ISAM interface program invoked when it is needed?

4. A programmer copying an ISAM data set to a key sequenced data set erroneously omits the ENVIRONMENT(DUMMY) specification in the REPRO. What is the effect of this on the loading process and on the key sequenced data set?

5. Of what assistance, if any, is the job control language for an ISAM data set load when a key sequenced data set is to be designed to house the same data?

6. You are examining some existing MVS JCL and see OPTCD=IL in an AMP parameter at a DD statement. What three facts can you deduce from its presence?

7. A programmer is developing the job control language for an update routine originally written for ISAM but which is now being run against a key sequenced data
set. She codes the AMP parameter with OPTCD = L instead of OPTCD = IL. What is
the effect of this error on the data set?

8. A program originally written for ISAM is now being executed against a key sequenced data set. It has been run successfully for several months and a program
maintenance request has been received that, if fulfilled, affects some of the data set
access and record rewriting actions. Describe the steps in program testing imposed
by the use of the ISAM interface on the reinstallation of this program to production.

9. Describe the changes necessary in the SELECT statement, FILE STATUS, RECORD
KEY, and delete processing when a COBOL program originally written to access an
ISAM data set is converted to access a key sequenced data set.

10. A CYLOFL (cylinder overflow) value of 2 had been specified for an ISAM data set
residing on a 3350 disk unit. Compute an equivalent value of control interval free
space for a key sequenced data set.

NOTES

1. ISAM data sets made use of "hardware" keys on disk devices and for this reason the storage
capacity of the disk track, in terms of records, is less for ISAM than for ordinary data sets.
Figure E.3 in Appendix E lists track capacities for both non-keyed and keyed data sets. VSAM
does not make use of disk device hardware keys.

═══ 11 ═══

Security: VSAM Passwords, RACF, and ACF2

The type of security required for data sets depends on the nature and sensitivity of the data and installation standards. A centralized environment dictates one approach to security; a decentralized environment, in which programmer and user groups have wide technical latitude and autonomy requires a different approach. In either case security mechanisms must be well planned, audited, and administered to provide appropriate protection. This chapter describes the security mechanisms available for the protection of VSAM data sets.

CATEGORIES OF SECURITY MECHANISMS

Three categories of security mechanisms can be used either independently or in conjunction with one another. These include installation-developed security systems, operating system security facilities, such as OS and VSAM passwords, and external security systems, such as RACF and ACF2.

Installation-Developed Security

Installation-developed security systems are often created to provide security within the batch environment. They can protect data sets from access by unauthorized jobs and control the submission of job streams from remote work stations. A gross level of control is possible, allowing jobs not carrying appropriate names or other parametes on the JOB statement to be rejected. Access to specific VSAM and other data sets can be allowed only to jobs with names matching the application area involved.

In the MVS/JES2 environment, many reader-exit security arrangements make use of the job submission routine exit IEFUJV, at the input reader. While these arrangements work, they suffer from the major limitation that the exit logic must be modified, tested, and reinstalled in order to modify any aspect of the protection provided.

Application-Specific Security

Application-specific security systems are sometimes developed and implemented with online systems. Such systems can provide security by screen, transaction, terminal operator id, and application function such as read, update, add, and delete. Logic must be added to an application to provide this type of security, or else a whole subsystem must be developed to enforce it.

As with locally developed batch security mechanisms, "homemade" online application security involves several potential problems. Program code must be created, tested, and installed, and modified to meet the demands of a changing environment. Custom security mechanisms created for individual applications can present inconsistent end-user interfaces, a low threshold-to-breach (TTB), and varying levels of sophistication and capabilities.

Non-VSAM Operating System Security

Operating system security includes OS password protection, CICS security, and VSAM password security. These mechanisms are contained within the operating system, or CICS. Each provides limited security for certain environments; each mechanism varies as to the ease of accommodating changes in security requirements.

CICS provides a crude form of security in a 24-bit access authorization field accessible to systems programmers. It is possible to assign a small number of passwords and limit access to CICS transactions using sign-on passwords associated with these bit patterns. This provides a measure of security for VSAM data sets supporting an online application. Since the security is based on transaction, inquiry transactions must be segregated from update transactions in order to limit update access.

OS passwords provide data set security for individual data sets using a special system-resident data set named SYS1.PASSWORD, the entries in which are created and modified using the IEHPROGM utility.[1] This security feature stems from the earliest days of the System/360 architecture and is still employed for various operating system data sets.

OS passwords allow access to a data set only in the mode that the assigned password authorizes. A read-only password will only allow read access. An update password will allow read and write access. Only data sets for which passwords are explicitly established in the password data set are protected. The password data set itself must be explicitly protected or even it will not receive secure treatment.

Since VSAM provides a capability similar to OS passwords, OS passwords cannot be established for VSAM data sets. All VSAM data sets are automatically marked, however, as OS password-protected for both read and write operations by VSAM, as if all had been assigned OS password security.

VSAM PASSWORD SECURITY

VSAM provides a password protection scheme that can optionally be used to protect clusters, cluster components, alternate indexes, alternate index components, paths, and VSAM catalogs, if in effect VSAM passwords can be supplied at execution time for batch programs within the JCL or by the operator or by a programmer when the data set is accessed via TSO.

Levels of VSAM Password Security

Four levels of password protection can be established under VSAM:

MASTER PASSWORD   The master password allows complete access to read, write, update, and delete operations for the data set and its catalog entry. This authorization includes all IDCAMS operations and full access to cluster contents. If established, this password is required for altering and deleting the data set, and for creating an alternate index. The master password is the highest level password and bypasses any additional verification checking by the User Security Verification Routine, described in the following pages. The master password is assigned with the MASTERPW (MRPW) specification in DEFINE or ALTER actions.

CONTROL INTERVAL PASSWORD   The control interval password allows read, write and update operations against the data set as well as access at the control interval level. This level of password protection is usually not required since access at the control interval level is not supported by COBOL, but only in assembler language. The control interval password is assigned with the CONTROLPW (CTLPW) specification in DEFINE or ALTER actions.

UPDATE PASSWORD   The update password allows records to be read, added, updated, and deleted. If established, this password is required for defining, altering, and deleting data sets, including generation data groups and aliases. This password does not allow the altering of passwords or security information. The update password is assigned with the UPDATEPW (UPDPW) specification in DEFINE or ALTER actions.

READ PASSWORD   The read password, if established, allows only read access for the data set and its catalog entry, excluding password information. The master password is assigned with the READPW (RDPW) specification in DEFINE or ALTER actions.

Any one or combination of VSAM passwords can be specified for a data set; each higher level password allows all operations permitted by the lower levels. When multiple passwords are specified for a data set, the level of password specified at the time the data set is opened defines the level of access allowed for that access. If passwords are not specified for all of the four levels of protection, the highest level password established is automatically assigned to the higher levels, as illustrated in Figure 11.1. If the VSAM catalog is not password-protected and VSAM passwords established for it, security will be ignored and no data sets will be protected.

Passwords specified				Passwords assigned by VSAM			
READ	UPDATE	CI	MASTER	READ	UPDATE	CI	MASTER
			M				M
		C				C	C
		C	M			C	M
	U				U	U	U
	U		M		U		M
	U	C			U	C	C
	U	C	M		U	C	M
R				R	R	R	R
R			M	R	R		M
R		C		R		C	C
R		C	M	R		C	M
R	U			R	U	U	U
R	U		M	R	U		M
R	U	C		R	U	C	C
R	U	C	M	R	U	C	M

FIGURE 11.1   VSAM password relationships (read each line across)

```
        SELECT CUSTOMER-MASTER        ASSIGN TO BT4320E1
               ACCESS MODE IS SEQUENTIAL
               ORGANIZATION IS INDEXED
               RECORD KEY IS ...
               PASSWORD IS WS-PASSWORD-FIELD
               FILE STATUS IS ....


        WORKING-STORAGE SECTION.
        01  WS-PASSWORD-FIELD              PIC X(8) 'ABCD1234'.
```

FIGURE 11.2   COBOL PASSWORD clause within SELECT/ASSIGN and hardcoded password in working storage

Supplying the VSAM Password

If access to a VSAM password protected data set is attempted under TSO, TSO tests the TSO logon password prior to issuing a prompt for entry of the password. If the logon password matches the required password, access will be allowed and the prompt for the data set password will not be issued. Otherwise, this prompt will be generated:[2]

```
IEC113A ENTER PASSWORD FOR DATA SET data-set-name
```

In the batch environment the password must be made available to the PASSWORD clause within the SELECT/ASSIGN statement at execution time before the data set is opened. Figure 11.2 shows the format of a SELECT/ASSIGN clause that contains a PASSWORD clause for a VSAM key sequenced data set. The appropriate password must be present in the data element named PASSWORD-DATA-NAME prior to opening the data set. The COBOL program can be compiled and linked with the appropriate password or the password can be supplied at execution time via the PARM clause on the EXEC statement which invokes the program as shown in Figure 11.3. If an incorrect password or no password is supplied, execution of the program terminates.

```
        //STEPNAME   EXEC   PGM=FSBT4320,PARM='ABCD1234'


        SELECT CUSTOMER-MASTER        ASSIGN TO BT4320E1
               ACCESS MODE IS SEQUENTIAL
               ORGANIZATION IS INDEXED
               RECORD KEY IS ...
               PASSWORD IS WS-PASSWORD-INPUT
               FILE STATUS IS ....


        LINKAGE SECTION.
        01  USER-PARM.
            05 UP-LENGTH                   PIC S9(4)  COMP.
            05 UP-DATA                     PIC X(8).


        PROCEDURE DIVISION USING USER-PARM.
           MOVE UP-DATA TO WS-PASSWORD-INPUT.
           OPEN INPUT CUSTOMER-MASTER.
```

FIGURE 11.3   Using a PARM field to supply a VSAM password at execution time

Attributes Related to VSAM Password Security

Three attributes of a VSAM data set are related to VSAM password protection: AT-TEMPTS, AUTHORIZATION, and CODE:

ATTEMPTS specifies the maximum number of times that an operator can try to enter a password in response to a prompt. As discussed in Chapter 3 the ATTEMPTS value may range from 0 to 7. If 0 is defined no prompts are issued and passwords are not permitted to be entered at the system console, making the data set entirely inaccessible; ATTEMPTS should be 2 or greater.

AUTHORIZATION identifies a User Security Verification Routine (USVR) that will be invoked when a VSAM password protected data set is accessed.

The USVR, a locally written routine, is called only after the password specified is verified. If the master password for the data set is specified, the USVR is bypassed. The USVR must reside on SYS1.LINKLIB at the time its name is specified in the AUTHORIZATION attribute for a data set. Up to 255 bytes of information can be passed to the USVR as a subattribute of AUTHORIZATION called the user security authorization record, USAR. The same USVR can be used as the security verification routine for many data sets by using unique USARs for individual data sets.

The USVR is VSAM's way of allowing unique user-written security routines to exist for selective data sets in lieu of using the IEFUJV JES2 exit which is invoked for all jobs entering the system. The USVR must be reentrant if it will be used by more than one task in the system at a time.

CODE CODE is a one- to eight-byte alphanumeric or special character code that is used as a prompt for the system operator when an attempt is made to access a password-protected entry without a password. This attribute is in effect only when the master password of the cluster or component is not null. If a CODE is not specified, the data set name is used as a prompt; if passwords are used, CODE should be specified in order to avoid having VSAM divulge the data set name each time a password is required. Documentation for the system console operator must indicate the password to supply when the CODE prompt is issued.

VSAM Password Limitations

The following precautions must be observed when using VSAM data set protection:

- Accessing a key sequenced data set via its cluster name requires the proper level of password for the base cluster.
- Accessing a key sequenced data set data component or index component directly requires the appropriate data or index component password. If the cluster is password-protected, its master password can be specified instead of the data or index component password.
- If only the cluster is password-protected, individual components of a KSDS can be accessed without the specification of the cluster's passwords. Each catalog entry receives its own protection; all components have their own catalog entries. Because of this deficiency in the VSAM password protection scheme, it is wise to protect a cluster name and each of its components, paths, and alternate indexes and their paths if VSAM protection is desired.

- A KSDS with no assigned passwords may be accessed without the specification of any password even if its data and/or index components have passwords assigned. This allows totally unrestricted access to the VSAM data set but prevents the unauthorized access to the data and index as separate components. Whether this is a feature or a deficiency is subject to local interpretation.

EXTERNAL SECURITY SYSTEMS

Many security systems external to VSAM and the operating system are available to provide protection for data sets and other computer resources. Each such system maintains its own philosophy of security. The more advanced security systems have a means of phasing in the system from a "quiet mode," in which the system is installed and provides monitoring of access without denying it, to a "production mode," in which the system is installed and provides full protection. Two of the most common external security systems are Resource Access Control Facility (RACF) and Access Control Facility 2 (ACF2), marketed by Computer Associates, Inc.

Most external security systems work independently of VSAM's protection schemes, but RACF, an IBM product, is an exception. The main driving force behind external security systems is a set of data set access rules that defines the protection and access control for the systems resources. Specific data sets can be protected or a group of data sets with similar names can be protected. RACF and ACF2 provide read, write, and execute security, security for catalog functions such as uncatalog, rename and delete, and even control of access based on time-of-day, time zone, and verification from terminals and RJE stations.

IBM's RACF Product and VSAM Password Security

Under RACF only the data sets to which protection is explicitly applied, either by name or via a generic data set name "profile," will be protected. All other data sets on the system will remain unprotected. Protection indications are carried in the label of each data set.

RACF protection may be used in addition to or instead of VSAM's protection scheme. When a data set is protected by RACF and VSAM's protection scheme, and the data set's catalog is also protected by RACF, VSAM's protection scheme and the User Security Verification Routine (USVR) exits are bypassed. This leaves RACF as the sole system security mechanism in effect.

VSAM's protection scheme can be applied to a data set only if its catalog is RACF-protected or protected by VSAM passwords and the data set itself is not protected by RACF. Even though VSAM's protection schemes are bypassed when a data set is RACF-protected, the VSAM protection schemes can still provide protection for the data set when it is exported to a system that does not use RACF.

The catalog entry for a VSAM data set protected by RACF with a discrete profile is marked as RACF-protected as is its label, the entry for the data set in the volume table of contents (VTOC) on the disk on which it resides. Catalog entries for VSAM data sets protected by RACF with a generic profile are not so marked. It is the indication in the catalog that protects a data set when it is exported to another system that uses RACF. In an ICF environment the cluster's profile is used to protect the entire cluster and all of its components; profiles for individual components can exist but are not used.

RACF can verify the time of access and the source of the access. RACF levels of security named alter, control, update, and read correspond to the VSAM password levels of master, control, update, and read. Deleting a data set that carries RACF protection and is cataloged in a RACF-protected catalog requires alter authorization for the catalog and data set being deleted.

Protecting Key Sequenced Data Sets with RACF

Figure 11.4 lists the RACF commands to create a discrete profile for the cluster AK00.C98.CUSTMAST and to allow job FSBT4320 to read and update the cluster. The ADDSD command establishes a discrete profile for the cluster AK00.C98.CUSTMAST, allows no universal access and will cause all authorization failures to be recorded. The PERMIT command authorizes job FSBT4320 to read and update the cluster.

A computer user with the ADSP Automatic Data Set Protection RACF attribute can automatically have a discrete profile generated for all permanent disk data sets when he or she creates them. This attribute is RACF's way of protecting data sets by default for their creator.

Two forms of the ADDSD command are available to create a generic profile. The form to be used in a given case depends on the naming scheme employed for the group of data sets to be protected. Figure 11.5 shows the use of the two forms to establish a generic profile for all clusters and data sets with AK00.C98 as the first two levels of their name. Both RACF commands will establish a generic profile that will protect all data sets with AK00.C98 as its first two levels of data set naming qualification. But data sets protected by generic profiles are not marked as RACF-protected in the catalog or disk VTOC.

Two special characters are used by RACF in the creation of generic profiles. The percent sign (%) indicates that any single character except a period can occupy its position in the profile name. The asterisk (*) in a generic profile name indicates that any character in that position and all subsequent characters within the qualifier can occupy its position in the profile name.

Computer Associates' ACF2 Product and VSAM Security

ACF2 is a widely used security system marketed by Computer Associates, Inc. It was developed in the late 1970s by Barry Schrager, Scott Krueger, and Eberhard Klemens to meet the needs of complex batch and online MVS environments. ACF2 uses a philosophy quite the opposite of RACF. Under ACF2 all data sets on a system are automatically protected; permission must be granted by a data security officer to access any data set. ACF2 houses data set access rules apart from data set label and catalog entries.

ACF2 protection may be used in addition to or instead of VSAM's protection scheme. When a data set is protected by ACF2 and by VSAM's protection scheme, ACF2 authorization will be checked prior to the invocation of VSAM's protection scheme. Access will be allowed only when ACF2's data set access rules allow the access, an appropriate

```
ADDSD 'AK00.C98.CUSTMAST' UACC(NONE) AUDIT(FAILURES)
PERMIT 'AK00.C98.CUSTMAST' ID(FSBT4320) ACCESS(UPDATE)
```

FIGURE 11.4   RACF discrete profile and access authorization commands

```
ADDSD 'AK00.C98' UACC(NONE) AUDIT(FAILURES) GENERIC

      or

ADDSD 'AK00.C98.*' UACC(NONE) AUDIT(FAILURES)
```

FIGURE 11.5   RACF generic profile commands permitting data set access

VSAM password is supplied, and the User Security Verification Routine, if one exists for the data set, is satisfied.

VSAM's protection scheme is completely independent of ACF2. Its security scheme is checked only if ACF2 allows access to a data set. If ACF2 allows access and VSAM's security disallows access, the data set cannot be accessed. When a data set is exported to another system, the VSAM security scheme is also exported with the data set but the ACF2 data set access rules are not. Unlike RACF, which marks a data set with a discrete profile as RACF protected, ACF2 protection relies strictly on its own data set access rules.

The existence of VSAM catalogs or ICF catalogs have no direct impact on the protection of data sets under ACF2. A data set access rule for the cluster applies to all of the cluster components. ACF2 also allows for generic rules with its scheme of data set name specification similar to that of RACF.

ACF2 can verify the time of access and the source of the access. The levels of security for a data set are read, write, allocate, and execute. The security levels of read and write are obvious in their interpretation. Allocate refers to all catalog functions such as catalog, delete, and rename. Execute allows a load module to be executed from a load library but does not allow the load module to be copied or read.

Protecting Key Sequenced Data Sets with ACF2

Figure 11.6 illustrates an ACF2 rule set that will allow all users to read the cluster AK00.C98.CUSTMAST and allow only user FSBT6562 to read and write to the cluster. All disallowed accesses will be logged.

The high-level data set name qualifier or "index" AK00 is found in the $KEY parameter. All the rules for data sets with AK00 as the first qualifier will be found in this rule set. The second and subsequent levels of data set names are found in lines below the $KEY line. As with RACF, ACF2 stores and uses rules from the most specific or discrete to the most general or generic. Unlike RACF, ACF2 houses all rules for a high-level index, both discrete and generic, in one rule set.

ACF2 uses a set of rules to authorize access to data sets. Like RACF, ACF2 uses a set of special characters in its data set name authorizations. The asterisk(*) indicates that any single character, except a period, can occupy its position in the data set name. The hyphen indicates that any characters within the qualifier can occupy the data set name or that this qualifier and subsequent qualifiers can be empty.

Nothing appears in the catalog or disk VTOC to indicate that a data set is protected by ACF2 because all data sets are protected. The complete set of access rules authorizes individuals or groups of users or jobs to access data sets.

Erase-on-Scratch Facility Under RACF and ACF2

A data set can be physically erased from the disk device on which it resides by specifying the ERASE attribute for the IDCAMS DELETE command. NOERASE, the default, eliminates the entry from the VTOC but leaves the physical data on the device. In this form the data is still accessible albeit through highly unusual means.

An enhanced erase-on-scratch facility is available in MVS/XA environments. It is implemented through both RACF and ACF2. The extended capability enables the ERASE

```
$KEY(AK00)
C98.MASTER UID(FSBT6562) READ(A) WRITE(A)
C98.MASTER READ(A)
C98.MASTER
```

FIGURE 11.6   ACF2 cluster rules permitting data set access

option to be controlled through these external security systems. In order to use the extended capability of this feature, an installation that must employ the Integrated Catalog Facility (ICF).

Under RACF the SETROPTS command sets global parameters that determine if and how erase-on-scratch is implemented. The SETROPTS global command must be set to activate this feature across the entire system. The ERASE option of SETROPTS determines the manner in which the feature is implemented:

- ERASE with no suboptions activates erase-on-scratch
- the ALL suboption specifies that all data sets are always erased regardless of the erase indicator in the profile
- the SECLEVEL suboption specifies a security level at which all data sets at that security level or higher are always erased regardless of the erase indicator in the profile
- the NOSECLEVEL suboption specifies that RACF is not to use the security level in the data set profile to determine if the data set is to be erased.

NOERASE specifies that erase-on-scratch is not in effect. If NOERASE has been specified in SETROPTS an ERASE indicator in the data set RACF profile is disregarded.

RACF data set profiles can indicate whether or not the data set is to be erased when it is scratched. This is arranged using the ERASE/NOERASE option:

```
ADDSD 'data-set-name' ERASE
```

of either the ADDSD or the ALTDSD command.

ACF2 does not have a global option to turn erase-on-scratch on and off. Neither is there an indicator in ACF2 data set access rules to control this feature at the data set on generic data set group level. But ACF2 does have a global option that can control erase-on-scratch for all VSAM data sets by CPU and for all non-VSAM data sets by volume or generic volume by CPU. The Global System Option parameter controls this feature for ACF2.

```
SET CONTROL(GSO) SYSID(CPU1)
AUTOERAS VSAM NON-VSAM VOLS(DASD**,PUBL01)
```

SYSID identifies the CPU to which the AUTOERAS parameter will apply. AUTOERAS can activate or deactivate the automatic erasure of all VSAM data sets and all non-VSAM data sets when they are deleted on the specific CPU. A mask can be specified in the SYSID subparameter to indicate all CPUs in the network; disk volumes, either specific or generic, can be specified for non-VSAM data sets.

ACF2 cannot deactivate the erase-on-scratch, but it can activate it for all data sets whether or not the ERASE attribute is specified in the IDCAMS DELETE command.

REVIEW QUESTIONS AND (*)EXERCISES

1. What are the three main categories of security mechanisms found in IBM mainframe installations?

2. VSAM password security supersedes OS password security. Discuss the four levels of VSAM password and what type of data set access each allows.

3. When access to a VSAM data set protected with a VSAM password is attempted under TSO, how is the password sought by the system?

4. Cite three key sequenced data set definition attributes related to VSAM password security, and indicate the function or service provided by each one.

5. If the cluster name of a key sequenced data set is VSAM password-protected, is access to the data component also blocked? Discuss the basis for your answer.

6. Cite two well-known and widely used external security systems for the IBM mainframe environment, and discuss the general protection philosophy of each.

7. Explain briefly the nature and function of the erase-on-scratch facility of external security systems.

*8. Code the SELECT/ASSIGN statement for a program that accesses a key sequenced data set at DDname //BT3516E1 in a random access mode and is password-protected.

NOTES

1. For information on OS passwords and the IEHPROGM utility statement to establish and modify them, see Chapter 17, Item 21, in *Practical MVS JCL For Today's Programmers*, (John Wiley and Sons, Inc., 1987) ISBN 0-471-83648-6.

2. TSO automatically uses the TSO logon password for validation when access to a password-protected VSAM data set is made under TSO. This counts as an attempt to access the data set. If this password is not the same as the VSAM password, TSO will prompt for entry of the password. This means that the ATTEMPTS attribute of the data set must have a value of at least 2, or else access to the data set will fail.

Obtaining Source Code for *Practical VSAM* Tools, Programs, and Test Data on Diskette

Chapter 2 discusses the use of TSO CLISTs named VSAMCISZ and VSAMSPAC to automate the many calculations involved in designing efficient VSAM key sequenced data sets. Chapter 6 describes how VSAMBUFS, another CLIST, can rapidly compute optimal buffer allocations and compose AMP parameter coding to secure them. Chapter 8, in dealing with the day-to-day management of many KSDS's, provides output from automated routines that aid in these tasks.

Source code for all of the CLISTs and programs are printed in this book. They are also available in machine-readable form at nominal cost on MS-DOS 360K 5¼" microcomputer diskette, suitable for uploading to a mainframe. In addition, the diskette contains figures—JCL listings—from this book for instructional purposes and for use as patterns.

To obtain a copy of the *Practical VSAM* diskette shipped postpaid to destinations in North America, request diskette #287 and send $6 ($US) to:

Practical VSAM Distribution Diskettes
P.O. Box 46078
Chicago, Illinois 60646

For destinations other than North America, please add $2 ($US) for additional postage.

A second diskette is also available, containing among other things the source code, test data, and JCL for S802P165, the large VSAM keyed add/change/delete program discussed in Chapter 7. This diskette is associated with the book *Commercial Software Engineering: For Productive Program Design* (James Janossy, John Wiley and Sons, Inc., 1985) ISBN 0-471-81576-4. This diskette is also available from the source listed above as diskette #152 at a separate cost of $6 postpaid.

Using the ISAM Interface

The ISAM interface is a support routine built into VSAM. Invoked automatically when VSAM detects use of ISAM coding in the COBOL program, the interface allows a program originally coded for ISAM to access a key sequenced data set without extensive modification. The interface does this by translating codes and control functions between the program and VSAM, allowing the program to continue to "think" it is doing business with the obsolete Indexed Sequential Access Method. The use of the ISAM interface is covered in detail in Chapter 10. This appendix includes three sets of JCL and the source code for program S802P165, a major keyed add/change/delete program.

JCL IMPLICATIONS AND EXAMPLE

Figure B.1 lists the MVS job control language that was originally used to execute the program when it was coded to access an ISAM data set. //STEP01 uses IEFBR14 to delete the existing ISAM data set, and //STEP02 carries the JCL to create the ISAM master file at the DDname //MASTER. No utility program control statements are used in //STEP02 since the ISAM data set is allocated entirely with JCL. //STEP03 runs the update program, and //STEP04 takes a tape backup of the updated data set.

Figure B.2 is MVS JCL to execute program S802P165 against a VSAM key sequenced data set which is created in //STEP01. //STEP01 is now an execution of the IDCAMS utility. Control statements are shown to delete the existing KSDS, redefine it, and load it using the REPRO command. //STEP02 verifies the KSDS, and //STEP03 runs the update program. //STEP04 verifies the data set to insure that it was properly closed by the update, and //STEP05 creates a backup of it using the IDCAMS REPRO command. The AMP parameter is coded at //STEP01 and //STEP05 with extra data buffers to speed sequential access to the KSDS.

Figure B.3 lists MVS JCL for the update job stream after the program source code has been modified to eliminate the use of high-values in the first byte of the record to denote a deleted record. With this change, OPTCD = IL has been dropped from the JCL at //STEP03, although the AMP parameter is still coded in order to carry greater index and data buffer allocations than would exist by default.

```
//FSTB802A JOB AKOOTEST,'DP4-GUZIK',CLASS=T,MSGCLASS=X,
//  MSGLEVEL=(1,1),NOTIFY=BT05677
//*
//*      BATCH UPDATE OF ISAM FILE VMF0000.ISAM.ISMM1003
//*      BY PROGRAM S802P165 CODED FOR ISAM
//*      THIS JCL = BT05677.SOURCE.CNTL(JCLFB1)
//*
//**********************************************************************
//*                                                                    *
//*      DELETE OLD MASTER FILE                                        *
//*                                                                    *
//**********************************************************************
//STEP01    EXEC  PGM=IEFBR14
//DD1          DD  DSN=VMF0000.ISAM.ISMM1003,
//  UNIT=3350,
//  DISP=(MOD,DELETE),
//  SPACE=(TRK,0)
//**********************************************************************
//*                                                                    *
//*      ALLOCATE AND RELOAD MASTER FILE FROM BACKUP                   *
//*                                                                    *
//**********************************************************************
//STEP02    EXEC  PGM=S802P164,PARM='RELOAD'
//MASTER       DD  DSN=VMF0000.ISAM.ISMM1003,
//  UNIT=3350,
//  DISP=(NEW,CATLG,DELETE),
//  DCB=(RECFM=FB,LRECL=69,BLKSIZE=3036,
//     DSORG=IS,KEYLEN=4,RKP=1,OPTCD=IYLR,CYLOFL=1),
//  SPACE=(CYL,5)
//BACKUP       DD  DSN=VMF0000.ISAM.ISMM1003.BKUP(0),
//  DISP=OLD
//SYSPRINT     DD  SYSOUT=*
//SYSUDUMP     DD  SYSOUT=*
//**********************************************************************
//*                                                                    *
//*      RUN THE UPDATE PROGRAM                                        *
//*                                                                    *
//**********************************************************************
//STEP03    EXEC  PGM=S802P165
//STEPLIB      DD  DSN=S803.PRODLIB,DISP=SHR
//P165VC01     DD  DSN=VMF0000.ISAM.ISMM1003,        'ISAM FILE
//  DISP=OLD
//P165IN01     DD  DSN=VMF0000.C95.SORTTRAN,         'SORTED TRANSACTIONS
//  DISP=(OLD,KEEP)
//P165UT01     DD  DSN=VMF0000.C95.HISTFILE,         'HISTORY FILE
//  UNIT=SYSDA,
//  DISP=(NEW,PASS,DELETE),
//  DCB=(RECFM=FB,LRECL=69,BLKSIZE=6210),
//  SPACE=(6210,(1,1),RLSE)
//P165REP1     DD  SYSOUT=(S,,14RP),COPIES=1         'TRANS REPORT
//P165REP2     DD  SYSOUT=(S,,14RP),COPIES=1         'UPDATE REPORT
//P165STAT     DD  SYSOUT=(S,,14RP),COPIES=1         'STATUS REPORT
//SYSOUT       DD  SYSOUT=*
//SYSUDUMP     DD  SYSOUT=*
//**********************************************************************
//*                                                                    *
//*      BACK UP THE UPDATED ISAM FILE                                 *
//*                                                                    *
//**********************************************************************
//STEP04    EXEC  PGM=S802P164,PARM='BACKUP'
//MASTER       DD  DSN=VMF0000.ISAM.ISMM1003,
//  DISP=OLD
//*
//* FOLLOWING GDG CREATION USES DUMMY MODEL DSCB INSTEAD OF A
//* SEPARATE MODEL DSCB FOR EVERY GDG IN THE INSTALLATION.
//* SEE CHAPTER 13, PRACTICAL MVS JCL (ISBN 0-471-83648-6)
//* IF YOU ARE NOT FAMILIAR WITH GENERATION DATA GROUPS OR
```

FIGURE B.1   MVS JCL originally used to execute ISAM-based program S802P165

```
//* THIS CONVENIENCE AFFECTING THE DCB PARAMETER:
//*
//BACKUP       DD   DSN=VMF0000.ISAM.ISMM1003.BKUP(+1),
//  UNIT=(TAPE,,DEFER),
//  DISP=(NEW,CATLG,DELETE),
//  DCB=(XX90.A00.DUMMYLBL,RECFM=FB,LRECL=69,BLKSIZE=32706),
//  LABEL=RETPD=90
//SYSPRINT    DD   SYSOUT=*
//SYSUDUMP    DD   SYSOUT=*
//
```

FIGURE B.1   (Continued)

```
//FSBT802B JOB AK00TEST,'DP-GUZIK',CLASS=D,MSGCLASS=X,
//  MSGLEVEL=(1,1),NOTIFY=BT05677
//*
//*      BATCH UPDATE OF VSAM FILE AK00.C95.VMFMAST BY
//*      PROGRAM S802P165 CODED FOR ISAM, USING THE ISAM
//*      INTERFACE PROGRAM
//*
//*      THIS JCL = BT05677.SOURCE.CNTL(JCLFB2)
//*
//**********************************************************************
//*                                                                    *
//*      ALLOCATE VSAM FILE AND LOAD IT                                *
//*                                                                    *
//**********************************************************************
//STEP01     EXEC  PGM=IDCAMS
//SYSPRINT    DD   SYSOUT=*
//VSAM        DD   DSN=AK00.C95.VMFMAST,
//  DISP=SHR,
//  AMP=('AMORG,BUFNI=1,BUFND=21')
//MYSEQIN     DD DSN=AK00.C95.VMFMAST.BKUP(0),
//  DISP=OLD
//SYSIN       DD   *
     DELETE      AK00.C95.VMFMAST -
                    CLUSTER
     DEFINE -
       CLUSTER   (NAME(AK00.C95.VMFMAST) -
                    VOLUME(DASD01) -
                    RECORDSIZE(69 69) -
                    KEYS(4 1) -
                    CYLINDERS(2 1) -
                    IMBED -
                    SHAREOPTIONS(2 3) -
                    SPEED                                   ) -
       DATA      (NAME(AK00.C95.VMFMAST.DATA) -
                    FREESPACE(20 10) -
                    CONTROLINTERVALSIZE(4096)               ) -
       INDEX     (NAME(AK00.C95.VMFMAST.INDEX)    )
     IF LASTCC=0 -
     THEN -
       REPRO       INFILE(MYSEQIN) -
                   OUTFILE(VSAM)
//**********************************************************************
//*                                                                    *
//*      VERIFY VSAM FILE                                              *
//*                                                                    *
//**********************************************************************
//STEP02     EXEC  PGM=IDCAMS
//DD1         DD   DSN=AK00.C95.VMFMAST,
```

FIGURE B.2   MVS JCL to execute program S802P165 using the ISAM interface and key sequenced data set instead of an ISAM data set

```
//  DISP=SHR
//SYSPRINT   DD  SYSOUT=*
//SYSIN      DD  *
     VERIFY   FILE(DD1)
//**********************************************************************
//*                                                                    *
//*     RUN THE UPDATE PROGRAM USING THE ISAM INTERFACE                *
//*                                                                    *
//**********************************************************************
//STEP03   EXEC  PGM=S802P165
//STEPLIB   DD  DSN=S803.PRODLIB,DISP=SHR
//P165VC01  DD  DSN=AK00.C95.VMFMAST,         'VSAM FILE
//  DISP=SHR,                                 'CHANGED DISP
//  AMP=('AMORG,OPTCD=IL,BUFNI=2,BUFND=3')    'ADDED AMP
//P165IN01  DD  DSN=VMF0000.C95.SORTTRAN,     'TRANSACTIONS
//  DISP=(OLD,KEEP)
//P165UT01  DD  DSN=VMF0000.C95.HISTFILE,     'HISTORY FILE
//  UNIT=SYSDA,
//  DISP=(NEW,PASS,DELETE),
//  DCB=(RECFM=FB,LRECL=69,BLKSIZE=6210),
//  SPACE=(6210,(1,1),RLSE)
//P165REP1  DD  SYSOUT=(S,,14RP),COPIES=1     'TRANS REPORT
//P165REP2  DD  SYSOUT=(S,,14RP),COPIES=1     'UPDATE REPORT
//P165STAT  DD  SYSOUT=(S,,14RP),COPIES=1     'STATUS REPORT
//SYSOUT    DD  SYSOUT=*
//SYSUDUMP  DD  SYSOUT=*
//**********************************************************************
//*                                                                    *
//*     VERIFY VSAM FILE                                               *
//*                                                                    *
//**********************************************************************
//STEP04   EXEC  PGM=IDCAMS
//DD1       DD  DSN=AK00.C95.VMFMAST,
//  DISP=SHR
//SYSPRINT   DD  SYSOUT=*
//SYSIN      DD  *
     VERIFY   FILE(DD1)
//**********************************************************************
//*                                                                    *
//*     BACK UP THE UPDATED VSAM FILE                                  *
//*                                                                    *
//**********************************************************************
//STEP05   EXEC  PGM=IDCAMS
//MASTER    DD  DSN=AK00.C95.VMFMAST,
//  DISP=SHR,
//  AMP=('AMORG,BUFNI=1,BUFND=21')
//*
//* FOLLOWING GDG CREATION USES DUMMY MODEL DSCB INSTEAD OF A
//* SEPARATE MODEL DSCB FOR EVERY GDG IN THE INSTALLATION.
//* SEE CHAPTER 13, PRACTICAL MVS JCL (ISBN 0-471-83648-6)
//* IF YOU ARE NOT FAMILIAR WITH GENERATION DATA GROUPS OR
//* THIS CONVENIENCE AFFECTING THE DCB PARAMETER:
//*
//BACKUP    DD  DSN=AK00.C95.VMFMAST.BKUP(+1),
//  UNIT=(TAPE,,DEFER),
//  DISP=(NEW,CATLG,DELETE),
//  DCB=(XX90.A00.DUMMYLBL,RECFM=FB,LRECL=69,BLKSIZE=32706),
//  LABEL=RETPD=90
//SYSPRINT   DD  SYSOUT=*
//SYSIN      DD  *
     REPRO           INFILE(MASTER)  -
                     OUTFILE(BACKUP)
//
```

FIGURE B.2   (Continued)

```
//STEP03    EXEC  PGM=S802P165
//STEPLIB   DD    DSN=S803.PRODLIB,DISP=SHR
//P165VC01  DD    DSN=AK00.C95.VMFMAST,
//  DISP=SHR,
//  AMP=('AMORG,BUFNI=2,BUFND=3')                  'NO OPTCD=IL WHEN
//P165IN01  DD    DSN=VMF0000.C95.SORTTRAN,        'PROGRAM IS CHANGED
//  DISP=(OLD,KEEP)                                'TO USE VSAM VERBS
//P165UT01  DD    DSN=VMF0000.C95.HISTFILE,
//  UNIT=SYSDA,
//  DISP=(NEW,PASS,DELETE),
//  DCB=(RECFM=FB,LRECL=69,BLKSIZE=6210),
//  SPACE=(6210,(1,1),RLSE)
//P165REP1  DD    SYSOUT=(S,,14RP),COPIES=1
//P165REP2  DD    SYSOUT=(S,,14RP),COPIES=1
//P165STAT  DD    SYSOUT=(S,,14RP),COPIES=1
//SYSOUT    DD    SYSOUT=*
//SYSUDUMP  DD    SYSOUT=*
```

FIGURE B.3   MVS JCL to execute program S802P165 after modification to access a key sequenced data set directly, without the ISAM interface

COBOL ISAM PROGRAM AS MODIFIED TO ACCESS
A KEY SEQUENCED DATA SET

Figure B.4 provides the source code for program S802P165. The statements within it for ISAM access remain, but have been commented out. Statements added to access a key sequenced data set have been prefaced with comments in order to identify them. This major example provides the basis for comparison of ISAM and VSAM coding differences. The program is also referenced extensively from Chapter 7, which discusses COBOL programming for key sequenced data sets based on generic I/O module patterns that were employed in converting S802P165.

```
000100 IDENTIFICATION DIVISION.
000200 PROGRAM-ID.     S802P165.
000300 AUTHOR.         J JANOSSY.
000400 INSTALLATION.   DEPAUL UNIVERSITY.
000500 DATE-WRITTEN.   APRIL, 1984.
000600 DATE-COMPILED.
000700*REMARKS.        VER 02   LAST CHANGE 05-04-84   ORIG DATE 04-14-84
000800*
000900*               THIS PROGRAM UPDATES AN INDEXED FILE FROM
001000*               TRANSACTION-SUPPLIED DATA. THE PROGRAM PLACES
001100*               DELETED MASTER FILE RECORDS ONTO A HISTORY
001200*               FILE, AND PRODUCES THREE REPORTS:
001300*
001400*                    STATUS REPORT:  MESSAGES AND COUNTS
001500*
001600*                    REPORT1:        TRANSACTION LIST WITH
001700*                                    DISPOSITION INDICATION
001800*
001900*                    REPORT2:        BEFORE/AFTER IMAGES OF
002000*                                    MASTER FILE RECORDS
002100*                                    THAT WERE UPDATED
002200*
002300*   FORCED ABORTS
```

FIGURE B.4   Source code for COBOL program S802P165, a keyed add/change/delete update; statements originally coded to access an ISAM file are commented out and replaced by coding suited to KSDS access

```
002400*  RETURN CODES:
002500*                    2402  =  I/O ERROR ENCOUNTERED
002600*
002700********************ADDED FOR VSAM*********************
002800*                    2401  =  FILE OPEN FAILED
002900*                    2403  =  FILE CLOSE FAILED
003000******************************************************
003100 ENVIRONMENT DIVISION.
003200 CONFIGURATION SECTION.
003300 SOURCE-COMPUTER.  IBM-4381.
003400 OBJECT-COMPUTER.  IBM-4381.
003500 SPECIAL-NAMES.   C01 IS PAGE-EJECT.
003600*
003700 INPUT-OUTPUT SECTION.
003800 FILE-CONTROL.
003900********************OLD ISAM CODE********************
004000*     SELECT COA-FILE       ASSIGN TO DA-I-P165VC01
004100*          ACCESS IS RANDOM
004200*          RECORD KEY IS COA-KEY-ACCT-ID
004300*          NOMINAL KEY IS WS-SAVE-ACCT-KEY.
004400******************************************************
004500********************NEW VSAM CODE********************
004600     SELECT COA-FILE       ASSIGN TO P165VC01
004700          ORGANIZATION IS INDEXED
004800          ACCESS IS RANDOM
004900          RECORD KEY IS COA-KEY-ACCT-ID
005000          FILE STATUS IS VSAM1-FS.
005100******************************************************
005200     SELECT TRANS-FILE     ASSIGN TO UT-S-P165IN01.
005300     SELECT HIST-FILE      ASSIGN TO UT-S-P165UT01.
005400     SELECT REPORT1-FILE   ASSIGN TO UT-S-P165REP1.
005500     SELECT REPORT2-FILE   ASSIGN TO UT-S-P165REP2.
005600     SELECT STATREPT-FILE  ASSIGN TO UT-S-P165STAT.
005700*
005800 DATA DIVISION.
005900 FILE SECTION.
006000*
006100 FD  COA-FILE
006200     RECORD CONTAINS 69 CHARACTERS
006300*    BLOCK CONTAINS 0 RECORDS
006400     BLOCK CONTAINS 44 RECORDS
006500     LABEL RECORDS ARE STANDARD.
006600 01  COA-REC.
006700     12 FILLER                    PIC X(1).
006800     12 COA-KEY-ACCT-ID           PIC X(4).
006900     12 FILLER                    PIC X(64).
007000*
007100 FD  TRANS-FILE
007200     RECORD CONTAINS 52 CHARACTERS
007300     BLOCK CONTAINS 0 RECORDS
007400     LABEL RECORDS ARE STANDARD.
007500 01  TRANS-REC                    PIC X(52).
007600*
007700 FD  HIST-FILE
007800     RECORD CONTAINS 69 CHARACTERS
007900     BLOCK CONTAINS 0 RECORDS
008000     LABEL RECORDS ARE STANDARD.
008100 01  HIST-REC                     PIC X(69).
008200*
008300 FD  REPORT1-FILE
008400     RECORD CONTAINS 133 CHARACTERS
008500     BLOCK CONTAINS 0 RECORDS
008600     LABEL RECORDS ARE STANDARD.
008700 01  REPORT1-REC                  PIC X(133).
008800*
008900 FD  REPORT2-FILE
009000     RECORD CONTAINS 133 CHARACTERS
```

FIGURE B.4 (Continued)

```
009100      BLOCK CONTAINS 0 RECORDS
009200      LABEL RECORDS ARE STANDARD.
009300 01   REPORT2-REC                    PIC X(133).
009400*
009500 FD   STATREPT-FILE
009600      RECORD CONTAINS 133 CHARACTERS
009700      BLOCK CONTAINS 0 RECORDS
009800      LABEL RECORDS ARE STANDARD.
009900 01   STATREPT-REC                   PIC X(133).
010000/
010100 WORKING-STORAGE SECTION.
010200 01   FILLER  PIC X(21) VALUE 'WORKING STORAGE START'.
010300*
010400*******************ADDED FOR VSAM*******************
010500      COPY VSAM1STD.
       *VSAM1STD  LAST CHANGED 04-02-84  ORIGINAL 01-22-84  J JANOSSY
       ***********************************************************************
       *      STANDARD VSAM FILE STATUS FIELD DEFINITION (1)           *
       ***********************************************************************
         01   VSAM1-FS.
              05 VSAM1-FS-LEFT-RIGHT.
                 10 VSAM1-FS-LEFT        PIC X(1).
                    88 VSAM1-ACTION-OK              VALUE '0'.
                    88 VSAM1-SEQ-EOF                VALUE '1'.
                 10 FILLER               PIC X(1).
              05 VSAM1-FS-FULL  REDEFINES
                 VSAM1-FS-LEFT-RIGHT     PIC X(2).
                    88 VSAM1-WRITE-OUT-SEQ          VALUE '21'.
                    88 VSAM1-DUP-PRIME-ALT-KEY      VALUE '22'.
                    88 VSAM1-REC-NOT-FOUND          VALUE '23'.
                    88 VSAM1-OPEN-OK                VALUE '00'.
010600*********************************************************
010700 01   WS-COMMON-FLAGS.
010800      12 F1-TREOF-FLAG             PIC X(1)  VALUE 'M'.
010900         88 F1-TREOF-MORE-DATA               VALUE 'M'.
011000         88 F1-TREOF-END                     VALUE 'E'.
011100      12 F2-COA-FILE-FLAG          PIC X(1).
011200         88 F2-COA-ACCESS-GOOD               VALUE 'G'.
011300         88 F2-COA-ACCESS-BAD                VALUE 'B'.
011400      12 F3-TR-EDIT-FLAG           PIC X(1).
011500         88 F3-TR-EDITS-GOOD                 VALUE 'G'.
011600         88 F3-TR-EDITS-BAD                  VALUE 'B'.
011700      12 F4-NAME-EDIT-FLAG         PIC X(1).
011800         88 F4-NAME-EDITS-GOOD               VALUE 'G'.
011900         88 F4-NAME-EDITS-BAD                VALUE 'B'.
012000*
012100 01   WS-FILE-OPEN-CLOSE-FLAGS.
012200*      C = CLOSED     O = OPEN
012300*
012400      12 WS-COA-FILE-OC-FLAG       PIC X(1)  VALUE 'C'.
012500      12 WS-TRANS-FILE-OC-FLAG     PIC X(1)  VALUE 'C'.
012600      12 WS-HIST-FILE-OC-FLAG      PIC X(1)  VALUE 'C'.
012700      12 WS-REPORT1-FILE-OC-FLAG   PIC X(1)  VALUE 'C'.
012800      12 WS-REPORT2-FILE-OC-FLAG   PIC X(1)  VALUE 'C'.
012900      12 WS-STATREPT-FILE-OC-FLAG  PIC X(1)  VALUE 'C'.
013000/
013100 01   TRANS-REC-INPUT-AREA.
013200      12 TR-ACCT-ID                PIC X(4).
013300      12 TR-TYPE                    PIC X(1).
013400         88 TR-TYPE-ADD                      VALUE 'A'.
013500         88 TR-TYPE-CHANGE                   VALUE 'C'.
013600         88 TR-TYPE-DELETE                   VALUE 'D'.
013700*
013800*      SUBTYPES ARE VALID ONLY FOR TR-TYPE 'C':
013900*
```

FIGURE B.4   (Continued)

```
014000      12 TR-SUBTYPE                      PIC X(1).
014100          88 TR-SUBTYPE-REPLACE-NAME              VALUE 'R'.
014200          88 TR-SUBTYPE-INACTIVATE                VALUE 'I'.
014300          88 TR-SUBTYPE-ACTIVATE                  VALUE 'A'.
014400      12 TR-ACCT-NAME                    PIC X(25).
014500      12 FILLER                          PIC X(21).
014600*
014700 01  COA-INPUT-AREA.  COPY S802COA.
       *S802COA   LAST CHANGED 06-06-84  ORIGINAL 06-06-84  J JANOSSY
        ****************************************************************
        *     802 ACCOUNTING SYSTEM                                   *
        *     CHART OF ACCOUNTS RECORD DEFINITION                     *
        ****************************************************************
            12 COA-DELETE-BYTE                 PIC X(1).
            12 CHART-OF-ACCOUNTS-RECORD.
                15 COA-ACCT-ID                 PIC X(4).
                15 COA-ACCT-NAME               PIC X(25).
                15 COA-STATUS-FLAG             PIC X(1).
                    88 COA-STATUS-ACTIVE               VALUE 'A'.
                    88 COA-STATUS-INACTIVE             VALUE 'I'.
                15 COA-ORIGINAL-DATE.
                    18 COA-ORIGINAL-MO         PIC X(2).
                    18 COA-ORIGINAL-DA         PIC X(2).
                    18 COA-ORIGINAL-YR         PIC X(2).
                15 COA-LAST-CHANGE-DATE.
                    18 COA-LAST-CHANGE-MO      PIC X(2).
                    18 COA-LAST-CHANGE-DA      PIC X(2).
                    18 COA-LAST-CHANGE-YR      PIC X(2).
                15 FILLER                      PIC X(26).
014800*
014900*  PROGRAM INTERNAL WORK FIELDS
015000      COPY DTIMEWS.
       *DTIMEWS   LAST CHANGED 03-08-84  ORIGINAL 01-19-84  J JANOSSY
        ****************************************************************
        *     STANDARD WORKING STORAGE FOR DATE AND TIME             *
        *     USE WITH STANDARD CODE IN COPYLIB MEMBER 'DTIMECOD'    *
        ****************************************************************
            01 WS-CURRENT-DATE-WITH-SLASHES.
                12 WS-CDS-MO                    PIC X(2).
                12 FILLER                       PIC X(1).
                12 WS-CDS-DA                    PIC X(2).
                12 FILLER                       PIC X(1).
                12 WS-CDS-YR                    PIC X(2).
            *
            01 WS-CURRENT-GREG-DATE.
                12 WS-CURR-GREG-MO              PIC X(2).
                12 WS-CURR-GREG-DA              PIC X(2).
                12 WS-CURR-GREG-YR              PIC X(2).
            *
            01 WS-TIME-MASK.
                12 WS-HRS                       PIC X(2).
                12 WS-MIN                       PIC X(2).
                12 WS-SEC                       PIC X(2).
                12 WS-HUN                       PIC X(2).
015100*
015200*  FOLLOWING RETURN CODE ALWAYS MOVED TO RETURN CODE REGISTER
015300*  AT END OF RUN. REMAINS 0000 UNLESS CHANGED DURING RUN:
015400*
015500 01  WS-RET-CODE                         PIC 9(4)  VALUE 0000.
015600*
015700*
015800 01  WS-SAVE-ACCT-KEY                    PIC X(4).
015900/
016000*  COUNTERS ARE MAINTAINED BY REFERENCE TO INDIVIDUAL NAMES.
016100*  COUNTER LABELS AND MESSAGES ARE OUTPUT IN A PRINTING LOOP
016200*  IN EOJ. LABELS MATCH COUNTERS IN POSITION.
016300*
```

FIGURE B.4   (Continued)

```
016400 01  WS-COUNTER-VALUES.
016500     12 WS-TRANS-COUNT              PIC S9(5)  COMP-3  VALUE +0.
016600     12 WS-ADD-TRANS               PIC S9(5)  COMP-3  VALUE +0.
016700     12 WS-A-SUCCESSFUL            PIC S9(5)  COMP-3  VALUE +0.
016800     12 WS-A-BAD-DATA              PIC S9(5)  COMP-3  VALUE +0.
016900     12 WS-A-BAD-ACCT-ID           PIC S9(5)  COMP-3  VALUE +0.
017000*
017100     12 WS-CHANGE-TRANS            PIC S9(5)  COMP-3  VALUE +0.
017200     12 WS-CR-TRANS                PIC S9(5)  COMP-3  VALUE +0.
017300     12 WS-CR-SUCCESSFUL           PIC S9(5)  COMP-3  VALUE +0.
017400     12 WS-CR-INVALID-DATA         PIC S9(5)  COMP-3  VALUE +0.
017500     12 WS-CR-BAD-ACCT-ID          PIC S9(5)  COMP-3  VALUE +0.
017600*
017700     12 WS-CI-TRANS                PIC S9(5)  COMP-3  VALUE +0.
017800     12 WS-CI-SUCCESSFUL           PIC S9(5)  COMP-3  VALUE +0.
017900     12 WS-CI-FOR-INACTIVE-ACCT    PIC S9(5)  COMP-3  VALUE +0.
018000     12 WS-CI-BAD-ACCT-ID          PIC S9(5)  COMP-3  VALUE +0.
018100     12 WS-CA-TRANS                PIC S9(5)  COMP-3  VALUE +0.
018200*
018300     12 WS-CA-SUCCESSFUL           PIC S9(5)  COMP-3  VALUE +0.
018400     12 WS-CA-FOR-ACTIVE-ACCT      PIC S9(5)  COMP-3  VALUE +0.
018500     12 WS-CA-BAD-ACCT-ID          PIC S9(5)  COMP-3  VALUE +0.
018600     12 WS-C-BAD-SUBTYPE           PIC S9(5)  COMP-3  VALUE +0.
018700     12 WS-DELETE-TRANS            PIC S9(5)  COMP-3  VALUE +0.
018800*
018900     12 WS-D-SUCCESSFUL            PIC S9(5)  COMP-3  VALUE +0.
019000     12 WS-D-ACCT-NOT-INACTIVE     PIC S9(5)  COMP-3  VALUE +0.
019100     12 WS-D-BAD-ACCT-ID           PIC S9(5)  COMP-3  VALUE +0.
019200     12 WS-BAD-TRAN-TYPE           PIC S9(5)  COMP-3  VALUE +0.
019300     12 WS-RECS-TO-HIST            PIC S9(5)  COMP-3  VALUE +0.
019400*
019500     12 WS-TOTAL-ERRORS            PIC S9(5)  COMP-3  VALUE +0.
019600*
019700 01  WS-COUNTERS-BY-SUB  REDEFINES  WS-COUNTER-VALUES.
019800     12 WS-COUNTER-VALUE  OCCURS 26 TIMES  PIC S9(5) COMP-3.
019900/
020000 01  WS-COUNTER-LABELS.
020100     12 FILLER  PIC X(30) VALUE 'TRANSACTIONS READ .............'.
020200     12 FILLER  PIC X(30) VALUE 'ADD TRANSACTIONS .............'.
020300     12 FILLER  PIC X(30) VALUE '  SUCCESSFUL .................'.
020400     12 FILLER  PIC X(30) VALUE '  INVALID DATA ...............'.
020500     12 FILLER  PIC X(30) VALUE '  ACCT ID ALREADY IN USE .....'.
020600*
020700     12 FILLER  PIC X(30) VALUE 'CHANGE TRANSACTIONS ..........'.
020800     12 FILLER  PIC X(30) VALUE '  "CR" TRANSACTIONS ..........'.
020900     12 FILLER  PIC X(30) VALUE '    SUCCESSFUL ...............'.
021000     12 FILLER  PIC X(30) VALUE '    INVALID DATA .............'.
021100     12 FILLER  PIC X(30) VALUE '    NO SUCH ACCT ID ..........'.
021200*
021300     12 FILLER  PIC X(30) VALUE '. "CI" TRANSACTIONS ..........'.
021400     12 FILLER  PIC X(30) VALUE '    SUCCESSFUL ...............'.
021500     12 FILLER  PIC X(30) VALUE '    FOR INACTIVE ACCT ........'.
021600     12 FILLER  PIC X(30) VALUE '    NO SUCH ACCT ID ..........'.
021700     12 FILLER  PIC X(30) VALUE '  "CA" TRANSACTIONS ..........'.
021800*
021900     12 FILLER  PIC X(30) VALUE '    SUCCESSFUL ...............'.
022000     12 FILLER  PIC X(30) VALUE '    FOR ACTIVE ACCT ..........'.
022100     12 FILLER  PIC X(30) VALUE '    NO SUCH ACCT ID ..........'.
022200     12 FILLER  PIC X(30) VALUE '  BAD SUBTYPE CODE ...........'.
022300     12 FILLER  PIC X(30) VALUE 'DELETE TRANSACTIONS ..........'.
022400*
022500     12 FILLER  PIC X(30) VALUE '  SUCCESSFUL .................'.
022600     12 FILLER  PIC X(30) VALUE '  ACCT NOT INACTIVE ..........'.
022700     12 FILLER  PIC X(30) VALUE '  NO SUCH ACCT ID ............'.
022800     12 FILLER  PIC X(30) VALUE 'INVALID TRAN TYPE CODE .......'.
```

FIGURE B.4 (Continued)

```
022900        12 FILLER  PIC X(30) VALUE 'RECORDS WRITTEN TO HISTORY ...'.
023000        12 FILLER  PIC X(30) VALUE 'TOTAL ERRORS DETECTED ........'.
023100 01  WS-COUNTER-LABELS-BY-SUB  REDEFINES  WS-COUNTER-LABELS.
023200        12 WS-COUNTER-LABEL  OCCURS 26 TIMES  PIC X(30).
023300*
023400*  VALUES IN FOLLOWING 88 LEVEL INDICATE WHERE BLANK LINES ARE TO
023500*  PRINT IN FINAL SUMMARY COUNTS. NUMBERS SHOW LINES BEFORE WHICH
023600*  A BLANK LINE GETS GENERATED BY FINAL COUNT PRINT LOGIC
023700*
023800 01  WS-COUNTER-SUB                      PIC S9(4) COMP  VALUE +0.
023900        88 WS-COUNTER-SUB-SKIP-BEFORE
024000            VALUES +2  +6  +7  +11  +15  +19  +20  +24.
024100/
024200 01  WS-ERROR-MSG-SETUP.
024300        12 FILLER  PIC X(30) VALUE 'F-01 ACCT ID NOT ON FILE      '.
024400        12 FILLER  PIC X(30) VALUE 'F-02 ACCT ID ALREADY IN USE   '.
024500        12 FILLER  PIC X(30) VALUE 'W-03 ACCT ALREADY INACTIVE    '.
024600        12 FILLER  PIC X(30) VALUE 'W-04 ACCT ALREADY ACTIVE      '.
024700        12 FILLER  PIC X(30) VALUE 'F-05 CANNOT DELETE ACTIVE ACCT'.
024800        12 FILLER  PIC X(30) VALUE 'F-06 TRANSACTION TYPE INVALID '.
024900        12 FILLER  PIC X(30) VALUE 'W-07 SUBTYPE SHOULD BE BLANK  '.
025000        12 FILLER  PIC X(30) VALUE 'F-08 SUBTYPE INVALID ON CHANGE'.
025100        12 FILLER  PIC X(30) VALUE 'F-09 ACCT NAME BLANK FOR ADD  '.
025200        12 FILLER  PIC X(30) VALUE 'W-10 CHANGED NAME SAME AS OLD '.
025300        12 FILLER  PIC X(30) VALUE 'F-11 NEW NAME IS BLANK        '.
025400*
025500 01  WS-ERROR-MSG-TABLE  REDEFINES  WS-ERROR-MSG-SETUP.
025600        12 WS-ERROR-MSG  OCCURS 11 TIMES  PIC X(30).
025700*
025800 01  WS-ERRORS-FOR-A-TRAN.
025900        12 WS-ERROR-STACK  OCCURS 11 TIMES  PIC S9(3) COMP-3.
026000*
026100 01  WS-MSG-NO                     PIC S9(3)  COMP-3.
026200 01  WS-ERRORS-IN-TRAN-COUNT       PIC S9(3)  COMP-3.
026300 01  WS-SUB1                       PIC S9(4)  COMP  VALUE +0.
026400 01  WS-SUB2                       PIC S9(4)  COMP  VALUE +0.
026500/
026600 01  R1-HOUSEKEEPING.
026700        12 R1-LINE-LIMIT           PIC S9(3) COMP-3 VALUE +55.
026800        12 R1-NORMAL-LINE-SPACING  PIC S9(3) COMP-3 VALUE +2.
026900        12 R1-LINES-REMAINING      PIC S9(3) COMP-3 VALUE +0.
027000        12 R1-WANTED-LINE-SPACING  PIC S9(3) COMP-3 VALUE +0.
027100        12 R1-PAGE-COUNT           PIC S9(3) COMP-3 VALUE +0.
027200        12 R1-PRINT-SLOT           PIC X(133).
027300*
027400 01  R1-LINES.
027500        12 R1-PAGEHEADERS.  COPY S802STHD.
          *S802STHD  LAST CHANGED 03-07-84  ORIGINAL 01-19-84  J JANOSSY
          *****************************************************************
          *     802 ACCOUNTING SYSTEM                                    *
          *     STANDARD PAGE HEADER                                     *
          *****************************************************************
                  15 S802-PAGEHDR1.
                      18 FILLER  PIC X(1).
                      18 FILLER  PIC X(20) VALUE '--------------------'.
                      18 FILLER  PIC X(20) VALUE '--------------------'.
                      18 FILLER  PIC X(20) VALUE '--------------------'.
                      18 FILLER  PIC X(20) VALUE '--------------------'.
              *
                  15 S802-PAGEHDR2.
                      18 FILLER                  PIC X(1).
                      18 FILLER  PIC X(20) VALUE '**    802 SYSTEM    **'.
                      18 FILLER                  PIC X(3) VALUE ALL ' '.
                      18 PH2-REPORT-TITLE         PIC X(20).
                      18 FILLER                  PIC X(3) VALUE ALL ' '.
                      18 PH2-PGM-REPNO            PIC X(11).
                      18 FILLER                  PIC X(3) VALUE ALL ' '.
```

FIGURE B.4 (Continued)

```
                      18 PH2-DATE                   PIC X(8).
                      18 FILLER  PIC X(8) VALUE '  PAGE '.
                      18 PH2-PAGENO                 PIC ZZ9.
                      18 FILLER                     PIC X(1) VALUE ' '.
027600*
027700      12 R1-COLHEADERS.
027800          15 R1-COLHDR1.
027900              18 FILLER  PIC X(1).
028000              18 FILLER  PIC X(20) VALUE 'ACCT  T  S         '.
028100              18 FILLER  PIC X(20) VALUE '                   '.
028200              18 FILLER  PIC X(20) VALUE '                   '.
028300              18 FILLER  PIC X(20) VALUE '                   '.
028400*
028500          15 R1-COLHDR2.
028600              18 FILLER  PIC X(1).
028700              18 FILLER  PIC X(20) VALUE ' ID    Y  T      AC'.
028800              18 FILLER  PIC X(20) VALUE 'COUNT NAME         '.
028900              18 FILLER  PIC X(20) VALUE ' RESULT           E'.
029000              18 FILLER  PIC X(20) VALUE 'RRORS              '.
029100*
029200          15 R1-COLHDR3.
029300              18 FILLER  PIC X(1).
029400              18 FILLER  PIC X(20) VALUE '<-->  -  -  <-------'.
029500              18 FILLER  PIC X(20) VALUE '---------------->  '.
029600              18 FILLER  PIC X(20) VALUE '                   '.
029700              18 FILLER  PIC X(20) VALUE '                   '.
029800*
029900          15 R1-DETLINE1.
030000              18 FILLER                 PIC X(1).
030100              18 R1-DL1-ACCT-ID         PIC X(4).
030200              18 FILLER                 PIC X(2)  VALUE ALL ' '.
030300              18 R1-DL1-TRAN-TYPE       PIC X(1).
030400              18 FILLER                 PIC X(2)  VALUE ALL ' '.
030500              18 R1-DL1-TRAN-SUBTYPE    PIC X(1).
030600              18 FILLER                 PIC X(2)  VALUE ALL ' '.
030700              18 R1-DL1-ACCT-NAME       PIC X(25).
030800              18 FILLER                 PIC X(1)  VALUE ' '.
030900              18 R1-DL1-OVERALL-MSG     PIC X(12).
031000              18 R1-DL1-ERROR-TEXT      PIC X(30).
031100/
031200 01   R2-HOUSEKEEPING.
031300      12 R2-LINE-LIMIT             PIC S9(3) COMP-3 VALUE +55.
031400      12 R2-NORMAL-LINE-SPACING    PIC S9(3) COMP-3 VALUE +2.
031500      12 R2-LINES-REMAINING        PIC S9(3) COMP-3 VALUE +0.
031600      12 R2-WANTED-LINE-SPACING    PIC S9(3) COMP-3 VALUE +0.
031700      12 R2-PAGE-COUNT             PIC S9(3) COMP-3 VALUE +0.
031800      12 R2-PRINT-SLOT             PIC X(133).
031900*
032000 01   R2-LINES.
032100      12 R2-PAGEHEADERS.  COPY S802STHD.
      *S802STHD  LAST CHANGED 03-07-84  ORIGINAL 01-19-84  J JANOSSY
      ****************************************************************
      *     802 ACCOUNTING SYSTEM                                   *
      *     STANDARD PAGE HEADER                                    *
      ****************************************************************
              15 S802-PAGEHDR1.
                  18 FILLER  PIC X(1).
                  18 FILLER  PIC X(20) VALUE '--------------------'.
                  18 FILLER  PIC X(20) VALUE '--------------------'.
                  18 FILLER  PIC X(20) VALUE '--------------------'.
                  18 FILLER  PIC X(20) VALUE '--------------------'.
          *
              15 S802-PAGEHDR2.
                  18 FILLER                 PIC X(1).
                  18 FILLER  PIC X(20) VALUE '**    802 SYSTEM    **'.
```

FIGURE B.4   (Continued)

```
                    18 FILLER                  PIC X(3) VALUE ALL ' '.
                    18 PH2-REPORT-TITLE        PIC X(20).
                    18 FILLER                  PIC X(3) VALUE ALL ' '.
                    18 PH2-PGM-REPNO           PIC X(11).
                    18 FILLER                  PIC X(3) VALUE ALL ' '.
                    18 PH2-DATE                PIC X(8).
                    18 FILLER  PIC X(8) VALUE '  PAGE '.
                    18 PH2-PAGENO              PIC ZZ9.
                    18 FILLER                  PIC X(1) VALUE ' '.
032200*
032300     12 R2-COLHEADERS.
032400        15 R2-COLHDR1.
032500           18 FILLER  PIC X(1).
032600           18 FILLER  PIC X(20) VALUE '        ACCT        '.
032700           18 FILLER  PIC X(20) VALUE '                    '.
032800           18 FILLER  PIC X(20) VALUE '           ORIGINAL '.
032900           18 FILLER  PIC X(20) VALUE ' LAST CHANGE        '.
033000*
033100        15 R2-COLHDR2.
033200           18 FILLER  PIC X(1).
033300           18 FILLER  PIC X(20) VALUE '         ID         '.
033400           18 FILLER  PIC X(20) VALUE ' ACCOUNT NAME       '.
033500           18 FILLER  PIC X(20) VALUE ' STATUS      DATE   '.
033600           18 FILLER  PIC X(20) VALUE '    DATE            '.
033700*
033800        15 R2-COLHDR3.
033900           18 FILLER  PIC X(1).
034000           18 FILLER  PIC X(20) VALUE '          <-->  <---'.
034100           18 FILLER  PIC X(20) VALUE '--------------------'.
034200           18 FILLER  PIC X(20) VALUE '>   -       <------> '.
034300           18 FILLER  PIC X(20) VALUE '   <------>         '.
034400*
034500        15 R2-DETLINE1.
034600           18 FILLER                  PIC X(1).
034700           18 R2-DL1-WAS-IS-MSG       PIC X(7).
034800           18 FILLER                  PIC X(3) VALUE ALL ':  '.
034900           18 R2-DL1-ACCT-ID          PIC X(4).
035000           18 FILLER                  PIC X(2) VALUE ALL ' '.
035100           18 R2-DL1-ACCT-NAME        PIC X(25).
035200           18 FILLER                  PIC X(4) VALUE ALL ' '.
035300           18 R2-DL1-STATUS           PIC X(1).
035400           18 FILLER                  PIC X(5) VALUE ALL ' '.
035500           18 R2-DL1-ORIGINAL-DATE.
035600              21 R2-DL1-ORIG-MO        PIC X(2).
035700              21 FILLER                PIC X(1) VALUE '-'.
035800              21 R2-DL1-ORIG-DA        PIC X(2).
035900              21 FILLER                PIC X(1) VALUE '-'.
036000              21 R2-DL1-ORIG-YR        PIC X(2).
036100           18 FILLER                  PIC X(4) VALUE ALL ' '.
036200           18 R2-DL1-LAST-CHANGE-DATE.
036300              21 R2-DL1-LAST-CHG-MO    PIC X(2).
036400              21 FILLER                PIC X(1) VALUE '-'.
036500              21 R2-DL1-LAST-CHG-DA    PIC X(2).
036600              21 FILLER                PIC X(1) VALUE '-'.
036700              21 R2-DL1-LAST-CHG-YR    PIC X(2).
036800           18 FILLER                  PIC X(9) VALUE ALL ' '.
036900*
037000        15 R2-DETLINE2.
037100           18 FILLER  PIC X(1).
037200           18 FILLER  PIC X(20) VALUE '    WAS:  **** NEW A'.
037300           18 FILLER  PIC X(20) VALUE 'CCOUNT NOT PREVIOUSL'.
037400           18 FILLER  PIC X(20) VALUE 'Y ON FILE           '.
037500           18 FILLER  PIC X(20) VALUE '                    '.
037600*
037700        15 R2-DETLINE3.
037800           18 FILLER  PIC X(1).
037900           18 FILLER  PIC X(20) VALUE ' IS NOW:  **** ACCOU'.
```

FIGURE B.4   (Continued)

```
038000              18 FILLER  PIC X(20) VALUE 'NT DELETED AS REQUES'.
038100              18 FILLER  PIC X(20) VALUE 'TED                 '.
038200              18 FILLER  PIC X(20) VALUE '                    '.
038300*
038400 01  WS-WAS-MSG         PIC X(7) VALUE '    WAS'.
038500 01  WS-IS-MSG          PIC X(7) VALUE ' IS NOW'.
038600/
038700********************ADDED FOR VSAM********************
038800     COPY S802STA2.
      *S802STA1  LAST CHANGED 01-22-84  ORIGINAL 01-20-84   J JANOSSY
      ***********************************************************************
      *     802 ACCOUNTING SYSTEM                                       *
      *     STATUS REPORT CONTROL FIELDS, HEADINGS, DETAIL LINES        *
      ***********************************************************************
       01  SR-HOUSEKEEPING.
           12 SR-LINE-LIMIT              PIC S9(3) COMP-3 VALUE +56.
           12 SR-NORMAL-LINE-SPACING     PIC S9(3) COMP-3 VALUE +2.
           12 SR-LINES-REMAINING         PIC S9(3) COMP-3 VALUE +0.
           12 SR-WANTED-LINE-SPACING     PIC S9(3) COMP-3 VALUE +0.
           12 SR-PAGE-COUNT              PIC S9(3) COMP-3 VALUE +0.
           12 SR-PRINT-SLOT              PIC X(133).
      *
       01  SR-LINES.
           12 SR-PAGEHEADERS.
              15 S802-PAGEHDR1.
                 18 FILLER  PIC X(1).
                 18 FILLER  PIC X(20) VALUE '********************'.
                 18 FILLER  PIC X(20) VALUE '********************'.
                 18 FILLER  PIC X(20) VALUE '********************'.
                 18 FILLER  PIC X(20) VALUE '********************'.
      *
              15 S802-PAGEHDR2.
                 18 FILLER             PIC X(1).
                 18 FILLER  PIC X(20) VALUE '**    802 SYSTEM   **'.
                 18 FILLER             PIC X(3) VALUE ALL ' '.
                 18 PH2-REPORT-TITLE   PIC X(20).
                 18 FILLER             PIC X(3) VALUE ALL ' '.
                 18 PH2-PGM-REPNO      PIC X(11).
                 18 FILLER             PIC X(3) VALUE ALL ' '.
                 18 PH2-DATE           PIC X(8).
                 18 FILLER  PIC X(8) VALUE '   PAGE '.
                 18 PH2-PAGENO         PIC ZZ9.
                 18 FILLER             PIC X(1) VALUE ' '.
      *
           12 SR-COLHDR1.
              15 FILLER  PIC X(1).
              15 FILLER  PIC X(20) VALUE '     TIME           '.
              15 FILLER  PIC X(20) VALUE '           MESSAGE  '.
      ********************OLD ISAM CODE********************
      *       15 FILLER  PIC X(20) VALUE '                    '.
      *       15 FILLER  PIC X(20) VALUE '                    '.
      ***********************************************************
      ********************NEW VSAM CODE********************
              15 FILLER  PIC X(20) VALUE '                 FIL'.
              15 FILLER  PIC X(20) VALUE 'E STATUS            '.
      ***********************************************************
      *
           12 SR-COLHDR2.
              15 FILLER  PIC X(1).
              15 FILLER  PIC X(20) VALUE '<--------->   <-----'.
              15 FILLER  PIC X(20) VALUE '--------------------'.
              15 FILLER  PIC X(20) VALUE '------------->      '.
              15 FILLER  PIC X(20) VALUE '                    '.
      *
           12 SR-DETLINE1.
              15 FILLER  PIC X(1).
```

FIGURE B.4 (Continued)

```
         15 SR-DL1-TIME.
            18 SR-DL1-HRS              PIC X(2).
            18 FILLER  PIC X(1) VALUE ':'.
            18 SR-DL1-MIN              PIC X(2).
            18 FILLER  PIC X(1) VALUE ':'.
            18 SR-DL1-SEC              PIC X(2).
            18 FILLER  PIC X(1) VALUE '.'.
            18 SR-DL1-HUN              PIC X(2).
         15 FILLER  PIC X(3) VALUE ALL ' '.
         15 SR-DL1-MSG                 PIC X(40).
         15 FILLER  PIC X(8) VALUE ALL ' '.
*********************OLD ISAM CODE*********************
*        15 FILLER                     PIC X(2)  VALUE ALL ' '.
******************************************************
*********************NEW VSAM CODE*********************
         15 SR-DL1-FILESTAT            PIC X(2)  VALUE ALL ' '.
******************************************************
         15 FILLER  PIC X(16) VALUE ALL ' '.
*
      12 SR-ENDLINE.
         15 FILLER  PIC X(1).
         15 FILLER                     PIC X(14) VALUE ALL ' '.
         15 SR-ENDLINE-TEXT.
            18 SR-ENDLINE-MSG          PIC X(30).
            18 FILLER  PIC X(2).
            18 SR-DOLLAR-VALUE         PIC $Z,ZZZ,ZZZ.99-.
            18 SR-DECIMAL-VALUE  REDEFINES
               SR-DOLLAR-VALUE         PIC ZZ,ZZZ,ZZZ.99-.
            18 SR-COUNTER-VALUE  REDEFINES
               SR-DOLLAR-VALUE         PIC Z,ZZZ,ZZZ,ZZ9-.
         15 FILLER                     PIC X(20) VALUE ALL ' '.
*
038900****************************************************
039000/
039100 PROCEDURE DIVISION.
039200*
039300 0000-MAINLINE.
039400     PERFORM 1000-BOJ.
039500     PERFORM 3000-PROCESS
039600        UNTIL F1-TREOF-FLAG EQUAL 'E'.
039700     PERFORM 5000-EOJ.
039800     MOVE WS-RET-CODE TO RETURN-CODE.
039900     STOP RUN.
040000*
040100 1000-BOJ.
040200     PERFORM 9000-INITIALIZE.
040300     OPEN  INPUT TRANS-FILE
040400           OUTPUT STATREPT-FILE
040500                  REPORT1-FILE
040600                  REPORT2-FILE
040700                  HIST-FILE.
040800     MOVE 'O' TO WS-TRANS-FILE-OC-FLAG
040900                 WS-STATREPT-FILE-OC-FLAG
041000                 WS-REPORT1-FILE-OC-FLAG
041100                 WS-REPORT2-FILE-OC-FLAG
041200                 WS-HIST-FILE-OC-FLAG.
041300     PERFORM 4920-SR-NEWPAGE.
041400     MOVE 'PROGRAM STARTING' TO SR-DL1-MSG.
041500     PERFORM 4900-STAT-MSG.
041600     PERFORM 9101-ISAM1-OPEN.
041700     PERFORM 3820-R1-NEWPAGE.
041800     PERFORM 3399-R2-NEWPAGE.
041900     PERFORM 3901-READ-TRANS.
042000*
042100 3000-PROCESS.
042200     MOVE +0 TO WS-ERRORS-IN-TRAN-COUNT.
042300     MOVE '  >>------>  ' TO R1-DL1-OVERALL-MSG.
```

FIGURE B.4   (Continued)

```
042400      IF TR-TYPE EQUAL 'A'
042500          PERFORM 3100-ADD-PROCESS
042600       ELSE
042700      IF TR-TYPE EQUAL 'C'
042800          PERFORM 3300-CHANGE-PROCESS
042900       ELSE
043000      IF TR-TYPE EQUAL 'D'
043100          PERFORM 3600-DELETE-PROCESS
043200       ELSE
043300          PERFORM 3700-BAD-TR-TYPE.
043400      PERFORM 3800-WRITE-TRAN-REPORT.
043500      ADD WS-ERRORS-IN-TRAN-COUNT TO WS-TOTAL-ERRORS.
043600      PERFORM 3901-READ-TRANS.
043700/
043800***********************************************************************
043900*                                                                     *
044000*      ADD PROCESSING                                                  *
044100*                                                                     *
044200***********************************************************************
044300*
044400 3100-ADD-PROCESS.
044500      ADD +1 TO WS-ADD-TRANS.
044600      PERFORM 3110-ADD-EDITS.
044700      IF F3-TR-EDIT-FLAG EQUAL 'G'
044800          PERFORM 3120-FINISH-BUILD
044900          PERFORM 3125-WRITE-NEW-COA-REC
045000       ELSE
045100          PERFORM 3127-FINISH-BAD-DATA.
045200*
045300 3110-ADD-EDITS.
045400      MOVE 'G' TO F3-TR-EDIT-FLAG.
045500      PERFORM 3112-SUBTYPE-EDIT.
045600      PERFORM 3114-CONTENT-CHECK.
045700*
045800 3112-SUBTYPE-EDIT.
045900*
046000*   THIS IS A WARNING EDIT ONLY SO NO MOVE OF 'B' TO EDIT FLAG
046100*
046200      IF TR-SUBTYPE NOT EQUAL ' '
046300          MOVE +7 TO WS-MSG-NO
046400          PERFORM 4800-POST-ERROR-MSG.
046500*
046600 3114-CONTENT-CHECK.
046700      IF (TR-ACCT-NAME EQUAL SPACES)
046800         OR (TR-ACCT-NAME EQUAL LOW-VALUES)
046900          MOVE +9 TO WS-MSG-NO
047000          PERFORM 4800-POST-ERROR-MSG
047100          MOVE 'B' TO F3-TR-EDIT-FLAG
047200       ELSE
047300          MOVE TR-ACCT-NAME TO COA-ACCT-NAME.
047400*
047500 3120-FINISH-BUILD.
047600      MOVE TR-ACCT-ID            TO COA-ACCT-ID.
047700      MOVE 'A'                   TO COA-STATUS-FLAG.
047800      MOVE WS-CURRENT-GREG-DATE  TO COA-ORIGINAL-DATE
047900                                    COA-LAST-CHANGE-DATE.
048000      MOVE SPACE                 TO COA-DELETE-BYTE.
048100*
048200 3125-WRITE-NEW-COA-REC.
048300      PERFORM 3913-WRITE-COA.
048400      IF F2-COA-FILE-FLAG EQUAL 'G'
048500          PERFORM 3391-WRITE-UP-REP-BEFORE-A
048600          PERFORM 3394-WRITE-UP-REP-AFTER-A-C
048700          ADD +1 TO WS-A-SUCCESSFUL
048800          MOVE 'ADDED          ' TO R1-DL1-OVERALL-MSG
```

FIGURE B.4   (Continued)

```
048900        ELSE
049000           ADD +1 TO WS-A-BAD-ACCT-ID
049100           MOVE +2 TO WS-MSG-NO
049200           PERFORM 4800-POST-ERROR-MSG.
049300*
049400 3127-FINISH-BAD-DATA.
049500     ADD +1 TO WS-A-BAD-DATA.
049600     MOVE TR-ACCT-ID TO WS-SAVE-ACCT-KEY.
049700*******************ADDED FOR VSAM*********************
049800     MOVE TR-ACCT-ID TO COA-KEY-ACCT-ID.
049900****************************************************************
050000     PERFORM 3911-READ-COA.
050100     IF F2-COA-FILE-FLAG EQUAL 'G'
050200        MOVE +2 TO WS-MSG-NO
050300        PERFORM 4800-POST-ERROR-MSG.
050400/
050500*********************************************************************
050600*                                                                  *
050700*     CHANGE TRANS PROCESSING                                      *
050800*                                                                  *
050900*********************************************************************
051000*
051100 3300-CHANGE-PROCESS.
051200     ADD +1 TO WS-CHANGE-TRANS.
051300     IF TR-SUBTYPE = 'R'
051400        PERFORM 3310-CR-PROCESS
051500     ELSE
051600     IF TR-SUBTYPE = 'I'
051700        PERFORM 3400-CI-PROCESS
051800     ELSE
051900     IF TR-SUBTYPE = 'A'
052000        PERFORM 3500-CA-PROCESS
052100     ELSE
052200        MOVE +8 TO WS-MSG-NO
052300        PERFORM 4800-POST-ERROR-MSG
052400        ADD +1 TO WS-C-BAD-SUBTYPE.
052500/
052600*********************************************************************
052700*                                                                  *
052800*     CR --- CHANGE/REPLACE ACCT DESCRIPTION PROCESSING            *
052900*                                                                  *
053000*********************************************************************
053100*
053200 3310-CR-PROCESS.
053300     ADD +1 TO WS-CR-TRANS.
053400     MOVE 'G' TO F3-TR-EDIT-FLAG.
053500     PERFORM 3320-EDIT-CHANGED-NAME.
053600     IF F3-TR-EDIT-FLAG EQUAL 'G'
053700        PERFORM 3350-EDITS-GOOD
053800     ELSE
053900        PERFORM 3380-EDITS-BAD.
054000*
054100 3320-EDIT-CHANGED-NAME.
054200     IF (TR-ACCT-NAME EQUAL SPACES)
054300     OR (TR-ACCT-NAME EQUAL ALL LOW-VALUES)
054400        MOVE 'B' TO F3-TR-EDIT-FLAG
054500        MOVE +11 TO WS-MSG-NO
054600        PERFORM 4800-POST-ERROR-MSG.
054700*
054800 3324-COMPARE-NAMES.
054900     IF TR-ACCT-NAME EQUAL COA-ACCT-NAME
055000        MOVE 'B' TO F3-TR-EDIT-FLAG
055100        MOVE 'B' TO F4-NAME-EDIT-FLAG
055200        MOVE +10 TO WS-MSG-NO
055300        PERFORM 4800-POST-ERROR-MSG
055400        ADD +1 TO WS-CR-INVALID-DATA
055500     ELSE
```

FIGURE B.4   (Continued)

```
055600          MOVE 'G' TO F4-NAME-EDIT-FLAG.
055700*
055800 3350-EDITS-GOOD.
055900      MOVE TR-ACCT-ID TO WS-SAVE-ACCT-KEY.
056000********************ADDED FOR VSAM********************
056100      MOVE TR-ACCT-ID TO COA-KEY-ACCT-ID.
056200********************************************************
056300      PERFORM 3911-READ-COA.
056400      IF F2-COA-FILE-FLAG EQUAL 'G'
056500          PERFORM 3360-FINAL-EDIT-REWRITE
056600        ELSE
056700          ADD +1 TO WS-CR-BAD-ACCT-ID
056800          MOVE +1 TO WS-MSG-NO
056900          PERFORM 4800-POST-ERROR-MSG.
057000*
057100 3360-FINAL-EDIT-REWRITE.
057200      PERFORM 3324-COMPARE-NAMES.
057300      IF F4-NAME-EDIT-FLAG EQUAL 'G'
057400          PERFORM 3392-WRITE-UP-REP-BEFORE-C-D
057500          MOVE TR-ACCT-NAME TO COA-ACCT-NAME
057600          PERFORM 3912-REWRITE-COA
057700          PERFORM 3394-WRITE-UP-REP-AFTER-A-C
057800          ADD +1 TO WS-CR-SUCCESSFUL
057900          MOVE 'NAME CHANGED' TO R1-DL1-OVERALL-MSG.
058000*
058100 3380-EDITS-BAD.
058200      MOVE TR-ACCT-ID TO WS-SAVE-ACCT-KEY.
058300********************ADDED FOR VSAM********************
058400      MOVE TR-ACCT-ID TO COA-KEY-ACCT-ID.
058500********************************************************
058600      PERFORM 3911-READ-COA.
058700      IF F2-COA-FILE-FLAG EQUAL 'G'
058800          ADD +1 TO WS-CR-INVALID-DATA
058900        ELSE
059000          MOVE +1 TO WS-MSG-NO
059100          PERFORM 4800-POST-ERROR-MSG
059200          ADD +1 TO WS-CR-BAD-ACCT-ID.
059300/
059400*********************************************************************
059500*                                                                   *
059600*      UPDATE REPORT (R2) STANDARD OUTPUT ROUTINES                   *
059700*                                                                   *
059800*********************************************************************
059900*
060000 3391-WRITE-UP-REP-BEFORE-A.
060100      MOVE R2-NORMAL-LINE-SPACING TO R2-WANTED-LINE-SPACING.
060200      MOVE R2-DETLINE2 TO R2-PRINT-SLOT.
060300      PERFORM 3398-WRITE-R2-PRINT-SLOT.
060400*
060500 3392-WRITE-UP-REP-BEFORE-C-D.
060600      MOVE R2-NORMAL-LINE-SPACING TO R2-WANTED-LINE-SPACING.
060700      MOVE WS-WAS-MSG TO R2-DL1-WAS-IS-MSG.
060800      PERFORM 3395-FORM-AND-PRINT.
060900*
061000 3393-WRITE-UP-REP-AFTER-D.
061100      MOVE +1 TO R2-WANTED-LINE-SPACING.
061200      MOVE R2-DETLINE3 TO R2-PRINT-SLOT.
061300      PERFORM 3398-WRITE-R2-PRINT-SLOT.
061400*
061500 3394-WRITE-UP-REP-AFTER-A-C.
061600      MOVE +1 TO R2-WANTED-LINE-SPACING.
061700      MOVE WS-IS-MSG TO R2-DL1-WAS-IS-MSG.
061800      PERFORM 3395-FORM-AND-PRINT.
061900*
062000 3395-FORM-AND-PRINT.
```

FIGURE B.4 (*Continued*)

```
062100      MOVE COA-ACCT-ID              TO R2-DL1-ACCT-ID.
062200      MOVE COA-ACCT-NAME            TO R2-DL1-ACCT-NAME.
062300      MOVE COA-STATUS-FLAG          TO R2-DL1-STATUS.
062400      MOVE COA-ORIGINAL-MO          TO R2-DL1-ORIG-MO.
062500      MOVE COA-ORIGINAL-DA          TO R2-DL1-ORIG-DA.
062600      MOVE COA-ORIGINAL-YR          TO R2-DL1-ORIG-YR.
062700      MOVE COA-LAST-CHANGE-MO       TO R2-DL1-LAST-CHG-MO.
062800      MOVE COA-LAST-CHANGE-DA       TO R2-DL1-LAST-CHG-DA.
062900      MOVE COA-LAST-CHANGE-YR       TO R2-DL1-LAST-CHG-YR.
063000      MOVE R2-DETLINE1              TO R2-PRINT-SLOT.
063100      PERFORM 3398-WRITE-R2-PRINT-SLOT.
063200*
063300 3398-WRITE-R2-PRINT-SLOT.
063400      IF R2-LINES-REMAINING LESS R2-WANTED-LINE-SPACING
063500          PERFORM 3399-R2-NEWPAGE.
063600      WRITE REPORT2-REC
063700          FROM R2-PRINT-SLOT
063800          AFTER ADVANCING R2-WANTED-LINE-SPACING LINES.
063900      COMPUTE R2-LINES-REMAINING =
064000          R2-LINES-REMAINING - R2-WANTED-LINE-SPACING.
064100*
064200 3399-R2-NEWPAGE.
064300      ADD +1 TO R2-PAGE-COUNT.
064400      MOVE R2-PAGE-COUNT TO PH2-PAGENO OF R2-LINES.
064500      WRITE REPORT2-REC
064600          FROM S802-PAGEHDR1 OF R2-LINES
064700          AFTER ADVANCING PAGE-EJECT.
064800      WRITE REPORT2-REC
064900          FROM S802-PAGEHDR2 OF R2-LINES
065000          AFTER ADVANCING 1 LINES.
065100      WRITE REPORT2-REC
065200          FROM S802-PAGEHDR1 OF R2-LINES
065300          AFTER ADVANCING 1 LINES.
065400      MOVE SPACES TO REPORT2-REC.
065500      WRITE REPORT2-REC
065600          AFTER ADVANCING 3 LINES.
065700      WRITE REPORT2-REC
065800          FROM R2-COLHDR1
065900          AFTER ADVANCING 1 LINES.
066000      WRITE REPORT2-REC
066100          FROM R2-COLHDR2
066200          AFTER ADVANCING 1 LINES.
066300      WRITE REPORT2-REC
066400          FROM R2-COLHDR3
066500          AFTER ADVANCING 1 LINES.
066600      MOVE SPACES TO REPORT2-REC.
066700      WRITE REPORT2-REC
066800          AFTER ADVANCING 1 LINES.
066900      COMPUTE R2-LINES-REMAINING =
067000          R2-LINE-LIMIT - 9.
067100      MOVE R2-NORMAL-LINE-SPACING TO R2-WANTED-LINE-SPACING.
067200/
067300***************************************************************
067400*                                                             *
067500*      CI --- CHANGE/INACTIVATE PROCESSING                    *
067600*                                                             *
067700***************************************************************
067800*
067900 3400-CI-PROCESS.
068000      ADD +1 TO WS-CI-TRANS.
068100      MOVE TR-ACCT-ID TO WS-SAVE-ACCT-KEY.
068200******************ADDED FOR VSAM********************
068300      MOVE TR-ACCT-ID TO COA-KEY-ACCT-ID.
068400*************************************************
068500      PERFORM 3911-READ-COA.
068600      IF F2-COA-FILE-FLAG EQUAL 'G'
068700          PERFORM 3410-CI-REC-FOUND
```

FIGURE B.4 (Continued)

```
068800        ELSE
068900            MOVE +1 TO WS-MSG-NO
069000            PERFORM 4800-POST-ERROR-MSG
069100            ADD +1 TO WS-CI-BAD-ACCT-ID.
069200*
069300 3410-CI-REC-FOUND.
069400     IF COA-STATUS-FLAG EQUAL 'I'
069500         MOVE +3 TO WS-MSG-NO
069600         PERFORM 4800-POST-ERROR-MSG
069700         ADD +1 TO WS-CI-FOR-INACTIVE-ACCT
069800     ELSE
069900         PERFORM 3392-WRITE-UP-REP-BEFORE-C-D
070000         MOVE 'I' TO COA-STATUS-FLAG
070100         PERFORM 3912-REWRITE-COA
070200         PERFORM 3394-WRITE-UP-REP-AFTER-A-C
070300         ADD +1 TO WS-CI-SUCCESSFUL
070400         MOVE 'NOW INACTIVE' TO R1-DL1-OVERALL-MSG.
070500/
070600*****************************************************************
070700*                                                              *
070800*     CA --- CHANGE/ACTIVATE PROCESSING                        *
070900*                                                              *
071000*****************************************************************
071100*
071200 3500-CA-PROCESS.
071300     ADD +1 TO WS-CA-TRANS.
071400     MOVE TR-ACCT-ID TO WS-SAVE-ACCT-KEY.
071500*******************ADDED FOR VSAM********************
071600     MOVE TR-ACCT-ID TO COA-KEY-ACCT-ID.
071700*****************************************************
071800     PERFORM 3911-READ-COA.
071900     IF F2-COA-FILE-FLAG EQUAL 'G'
072000         PERFORM 3510-CA-REC-FOUND
072100     ELSE
072200         MOVE +1 TO WS-MSG-NO
072300         PERFORM 4800-POST-ERROR-MSG
072400         ADD +1 TO WS-CA-BAD-ACCT-ID.
072500*
072600 3510-CA-REC-FOUND.
072700     IF COA-STATUS-FLAG EQUAL 'A'
072800         MOVE +4 TO WS-MSG-NO
072900         PERFORM 4800-POST-ERROR-MSG
073000         ADD +1 TO WS-CA-FOR-ACTIVE-ACCT
073100     ELSE
073200         PERFORM 3392-WRITE-UP-REP-BEFORE-C-D
073300         MOVE 'A' TO COA-STATUS-FLAG
073400         PERFORM 3912-REWRITE-COA
073500         PERFORM 3394-WRITE-UP-REP-AFTER-A-C
073600         ADD +1 TO WS-CA-SUCCESSFUL
073700         MOVE 'NOW ACTIVE  ' TO R1-DL1-OVERALL-MSG.
073800/
073900*****************************************************************
074000*                                                              *
074100*     DELETE TRANSACTION PROCESSING                            *
074200*                                                              *
074300*****************************************************************
074400*
074500 3600-DELETE-PROCESS.
074600     ADD +1 TO WS-DELETE-TRANS.
074700     PERFORM 3612-SUBTYPE-EDIT.
074800     MOVE TR-ACCT-ID TO WS-SAVE-ACCT-KEY.
074900*******************ADDED FOR VSAM********************
075000     MOVE TR-ACCT-ID TO COA-KEY-ACCT-ID.
075100*****************************************************
075200     PERFORM 3911-READ-COA.
075300     IF F2-COA-FILE-FLAG EQUAL 'G'
```

FIGURE B.4   (*Continued*)

```
075400          PERFORM 3610-D-REC-FOUND
075500      ELSE
075600          MOVE +1 TO WS-MSG-NO
075700          PERFORM 4800-POST-ERROR-MSG
075800          ADD +1 TO WS-D-BAD-ACCT-ID.
075900*
076000 3610-D-REC-FOUND.
076100      IF COA-STATUS-FLAG EQUAL 'I'
076200          PERFORM 3620-ARCHIVE-AND-DELETE
076300      ELSE
076400          MOVE +5 TO WS-MSG-NO
076500          PERFORM 4800-POST-ERROR-MSG
076600          ADD +1 TO WS-D-ACCT-NOT-INACTIVE.
076700*
076800 3612-SUBTYPE-EDIT.
076900      IF TR-SUBTYPE NOT EQUAL ' '
077000          MOVE +7 TO WS-MSG-NO
077100          PERFORM 4800-POST-ERROR-MSG.
077200*
077300 3620-ARCHIVE-AND-DELETE.
077400      PERFORM 3392-WRITE-UP-REP-BEFORE-C-D.
077500      PERFORM 3903-WRITE-HIST.
077600      PERFORM 3914-DELETE-COA.
077700      PERFORM 3393-WRITE-UP-REP-AFTER-D.
077800      ADD +1 TO WS-D-SUCCESSFUL.
077900      MOVE 'DELETED      ' TO R1-DL1-OVERALL-MSG.
078000/
078100******************************************************************
078200*                                                                *
078300*      BAD TRAN TYPE AND TRAN REPORT PROCESSING                  *
078400*                                                                *
078500******************************************************************
078600*
078700 3700-BAD-TR-TYPE.
078800      ADD +1 TO WS-BAD-TRAN-TYPE.
078900      MOVE +6 TO WS-MSG-NO.
079000      PERFORM 4800-POST-ERROR-MSG.
079100      MOVE TR-ACCT-ID TO WS-SAVE-ACCT-KEY.
079200*******************ADDED FOR VSAM********************
079300      MOVE TR-ACCT-ID TO COA-KEY-ACCT-ID.
079400***************************************************
079500      PERFORM 3911-READ-COA.
079600      IF F2-COA-FILE-FLAG EQUAL 'B'
079700          MOVE +1 TO WS-MSG-NO
079800          PERFORM 4800-POST-ERROR-MSG.
079900*
080000 3800-WRITE-TRAN-REPORT.
080100      MOVE TR-ACCT-ID       TO R1-DL1-ACCT-ID.
080200      MOVE TR-TYPE          TO R1-DL1-TRAN-TYPE.
080300      MOVE TR-SUBTYPE       TO R1-DL1-TRAN-SUBTYPE.
080400      MOVE TR-ACCT-NAME     TO R1-DL1-ACCT-NAME.
080500      IF WS-ERRORS-IN-TRAN-COUNT GREATER +0
080600          MOVE WS-ERROR-STACK(1) TO WS-SUB2
080700          MOVE WS-ERROR-MSG(WS-SUB2) TO R1-DL1-ERROR-TEXT
080800      ELSE
080900          MOVE SPACES TO R1-DL1-ERROR-TEXT.
081000      MOVE R1-DETLINE1 TO R1-PRINT-SLOT.
081100      MOVE R1-NORMAL-LINE-SPACING TO R1-WANTED-LINE-SPACING.
081200      PERFORM 3810-WRITE-R1-PRINT-SLOT.
081300*
081400      IF WS-ERRORS-IN-TRAN-COUNT GREATER +1
081500          MOVE SPACES TO R1-DL1-ACCT-ID
081600                         R1-DL1-TRAN-TYPE
081700                         R1-DL1-TRAN-SUBTYPE
081800                         R1-DL1-ACCT-NAME
081900                         R1-DL1-OVERALL-MSG
082000          MOVE +1 TO R1-WANTED-LINE-SPACING
```

FIGURE B.4   (Continued)

```
082100          PERFORM 3830-WRITE-SECOND-PLUS-ERRORS
082200              VARYING WS-SUB1 FROM +2 BY +1
082300                  UNTIL WS-SUB1 GREATER WS-ERRORS-IN-TRAN-COUNT.
082400*
082500 3810-WRITE-R1-PRINT-SLOT.
082600     IF R1-LINES-REMAINING LESS R1-WANTED-LINE-SPACING
082700         PERFORM 3820-R1-NEWPAGE.
082800     WRITE REPORT1-REC
082900         FROM R1-PRINT-SLOT
083000         AFTER ADVANCING R1-WANTED-LINE-SPACING LINES.
083100     COMPUTE R1-LINES-REMAINING =
083200         R1-LINES-REMAINING - R1-WANTED-LINE-SPACING.
083300*
083400 3820-R1-NEWPAGE.
083500     ADD +1 TO R1-PAGE-COUNT.
083600     MOVE R1-PAGE-COUNT TO PH2-PAGENO OF R1-LINES.
083700     WRITE REPORT1-REC
083800         FROM S802-PAGEHDR1 OF R1-LINES
083900         AFTER ADVANCING PAGE-EJECT.
084000     WRITE REPORT1-REC
084100         FROM S802-PAGEHDR2 OF R1-LINES
084200         AFTER ADVANCING 1 LINES.
084300     WRITE REPORT1-REC
084400         FROM S802-PAGEHDR1 OF R1-LINES
084500         AFTER ADVANCING 1 LINES.
084600     MOVE SPACES TO REPORT1-REC.
084700     WRITE REPORT1-REC
084800         AFTER ADVANCING 3 LINES.
084900     WRITE REPORT1-REC
085000         FROM R1-COLHDR1
085100         AFTER ADVANCING 1 LINES.
085200     WRITE REPORT1-REC
085300         FROM R1-COLHDR2
085400         AFTER ADVANCING 1 LINES.
085500     WRITE REPORT1-REC
085600         FROM R1-COLHDR3
085700         AFTER ADVANCING 1 LINES.
085800     MOVE SPACES TO REPORT1-REC.
085900     WRITE REPORT1-REC
086000         AFTER ADVANCING 1 LINES.
086100     COMPUTE R1-LINES-REMAINING =
086200         R1-LINE-LIMIT - 9.
086300     MOVE R1-NORMAL-LINE-SPACING TO R1-WANTED-LINE-SPACING.
086400*
086500 3830-WRITE-SECOND-PLUS-ERRORS.
086600*
086700* EXTRACT SECOND AND HIGHER ERROR NUMBERS FOR TRAN FROM THE
086800* STACK, USING CONTENTS OF EACH STACK SLOT AS SUBSCRIPT TO
086900* THE TABLE OF ERROR MESSAGES
087000*
087100     MOVE WS-ERROR-STACK(WS-SUB1) TO WS-SUB2.
087200     MOVE WS-ERROR-MSG(WS-SUB2) TO R1-DL1-ERROR-TEXT.
087300     MOVE R1-DETLINE1 TO R1-PRINT-SLOT.
087400     PERFORM 3810-WRITE-R1-PRINT-SLOT.
087500/
087600*****************************************************************
087700*                                                               *
087800*     STANDARD INDEXED FILE LOGIC UNITS                         *
087900*                                                               *
088000*****************************************************************
088100*
088200 3901-READ-TRANS.
088300     READ TRANS-FILE INTO TRANS-REC-INPUT-AREA
088400         AT END
088500             MOVE 'E' TO F1-TREOF-FLAG.
088600     IF F1-TREOF-FLAG NOT EQUAL 'E'
```

FIGURE B.4 (Continued)

```
088700         ADD +1 TO WS-TRANS-COUNT.
088800*
088900 3903-WRITE-HIST.
089000     WRITE HIST-REC FROM COA-INPUT-AREA.
089100     ADD +1 TO WS-RECS-TO-HIST.
089200*
089300 3911-READ-COA.
089400*******************OLD ISAM CODE********************
089500*    MOVE 'G' TO F2-COA-FILE-FLAG
089600*    READ COA-FILE INTO COA-INPUT-AREA
089700*       INVALID KEY
089800*       MOVE 'B' TO F2-COA-FILE-FLAG.
089900***********************************************************
090000*******************NEW VSAM CODE********************
090100     READ COA-FILE INTO COA-INPUT-AREA.
090200     IF VSAM1-ACTION-OK
090300        MOVE 'G' TO F2-COA-FILE-FLAG
090400     ELSE
090500        IF VSAM1-REC-NOT-FOUND
090600           MOVE 'B' TO F2-COA-FILE-FLAG
090700        ELSE
090800           MOVE 'ABEND ON COA READ' TO SR-DL1-MSG
090900           PERFORM 3980-I-O-ABORT.
091000***********************************************************
091100*
091200 3912-REWRITE-COA.
091300     MOVE COA-KEY-ACCT-ID TO WS-SAVE-ACCT-KEY.
091400     MOVE WS-CURRENT-GREG-DATE TO COA-LAST-CHANGE-DATE.
091500*******************OLD ISAM CODE********************
091600*    REWRITE COA-REC FROM COA-INPUT-AREA
091700*       INVALID KEY
091800*       MOVE 'ABEND ON COA REWRITE' TO SR-DL1-MSG
091900*       PERFORM 3980-I-O-ABORT.
092000***********************************************************
092100*******************NEW VSAM CODE********************
092200     REWRITE COA-REC FROM COA-INPUT-AREA.
092300     IF VSAM1-ACTION-OK
092400        NEXT SENTENCE
092500     ELSE
092600        MOVE 'ABEND ON COA REWRITE' TO SR-DL1-MSG
092700        PERFORM 3980-I-O-ABORT.
092800***********************************************************
092900*
093000 3913-WRITE-COA.
093100     MOVE COA-ACCT-ID TO WS-SAVE-ACCT-KEY.
093200*******************OLD ISAM CODE********************
093300*    MOVE 'G' TO F2-COA-FILE-FLAG
093400*    WRITE COA-REC FROM COA-INPUT-AREA
093500*       INVALID KEY
093600*       MOVE 'B' TO F2-COA-FILE-FLAG.
093700***********************************************************
093800*******************NEW VSAM CODE********************
093900     WRITE COA-REC FROM COA-INPUT-AREA.
094000     IF VSAM1-ACTION-OK
094100        MOVE 'G' TO F2-COA-FILE-FLAG
094200     ELSE
094300        IF VSAM1-DUP-PRIME-ALT-KEY
094400           MOVE 'B' TO F2-COA-FILE-FLAG
094500        ELSE
094600           MOVE 'ABEND ON COA WRITE' TO SR-DL1-MSG
094700           PERFORM 3980-I-O-ABORT.
094800***********************************************************
094900*
095000 3914-DELETE-COA.
095100*
095200* RECORDS TO BE DELETED ARE READ FIRST TO COPY TO HISTORY SO
095300* A DELETE IMMEDIATELY SUBSEQUENT MUST FIND RECORD ON FILE OR
```

FIGURE B.4 (Continued)

```
095400*   A SERIOUS PROBLEM EXISTS!
095500*
095600      MOVE COA-KEY-ACCT-ID TO WS-SAVE-ACCT-KEY.
095700********************OLD ISAM CODE********************
095800*    MOVE HIGH-VALUES TO COA-DELETE-BYTE.
095900*    REWRITE COA-REC FROM COA-INPUT-AREA
096000*       INVALID KEY
096100*        MOVE 'ABEND ON COA DELETE' TO SR-DL1-MSG
096200*         PERFORM 3980-I-O-ABORT.
096300***********************************************************
096400********************NEW VSAM CODE********************
096500      DELETE COA-FILE.
096600      IF VSAM1-ACTION-OK
096700         NEXT SENTENCE
096800      ELSE
096900         MOVE 'ABEND ON COA DELETE' TO SR-DL1-MSG
097000         PERFORM 3980-I-O-ABORT.
097100***********************************************************
097200*
097300 3980-I-O-ABORT.
097400      PERFORM 4900-STAT-MSG.
097500      MOVE WS-SAVE-ACCT-KEY TO SR-DL1-MSG.
097600      PERFORM 4900-STAT-MSG.
097700*
097800      MOVE WS-COUNTER-LABEL(1) TO SR-ENDLINE-MSG.
097900      MOVE WS-COUNTER-VALUE(1) TO SR-COUNTER-VALUE.
098000      MOVE SR-ENDLINE TO SR-PRINT-SLOT.
098100      MOVE SR-NORMAL-LINE-SPACING TO SR-WANTED-LINE-SPACING.
098200      PERFORM 4910-WRITE-SR-PRINT-SLOT.
098300*
098400      MOVE 2402 TO WS-RET-CODE.
098500      MOVE 'ABORTING ON I/O ERROR' TO SR-DL1-MSG.
098600      PERFORM 9999-FORCED-ABORT.
098700/
098800 4800-POST-ERROR-MSG.
098900*
099000*  WS-MSG-NO IS MESSAGE NO DESIRED TO BE POSTED TO TRAN
099100*  WS-ERROR-STACK(1..11) IS LIST OF ERRORS FOR A GIVEN TRAN
099200*  WS-ERRORS-IN-TRAN-COUNT IS POINTER TO PUT ERROR-NO INTO
099300*     STACK FOR A TRAN AND COUNT OF ERRORS FOR THE TRAN
099400*
099500      ADD +1 TO WS-ERRORS-IN-TRAN-COUNT.
099600      MOVE WS-MSG-NO
099700         TO WS-ERROR-STACK(WS-ERRORS-IN-TRAN-COUNT).
099800*
099900 4900-STAT-MSG.
100000      ACCEPT WS-TIME-MASK FROM TIME.
100100      MOVE WS-HRS TO SR-DL1-HRS.
100200      MOVE WS-MIN TO SR-DL1-MIN.
100300      MOVE WS-SEC TO SR-DL1-SEC.
100400      MOVE WS-HUN TO SR-DL1-HUN.
100500      MOVE SR-DETLINE1 TO SR-PRINT-SLOT.
100600      MOVE SR-NORMAL-LINE-SPACING TO SR-WANTED-LINE-SPACING.
100700      PERFORM 4910-WRITE-SR-PRINT-SLOT.
100800      MOVE SPACES TO  SR-DL1-MSG.
100900********************ADDED FOR VSAM********************
101000      MOVE SPACES TO  SR-DL1-FILESTAT.
101100***********************************************************
101200*
101300 4910-WRITE-SR-PRINT-SLOT.
101400      IF SR-LINES-REMAINING LESS SR-WANTED-LINE-SPACING
101500         PERFORM 4920-SR-NEWPAGE.
101600      WRITE STATREPT-REC
101700         FROM SR-PRINT-SLOT
101800         AFTER ADVANCING SR-WANTED-LINE-SPACING LINES.
```

FIGURE B.4   (Continued)

```
101900       COMPUTE SR-LINES-REMAINING =
102000           SR-LINES-REMAINING - SR-WANTED-LINE-SPACING.
102100*
102200 4920-SR-NEWPAGE.
102300     ADD +1 TO SR-PAGE-COUNT.
102400     MOVE SR-PAGE-COUNT TO PH2-PAGENO OF SR-LINES.
102500     WRITE STATREPT-REC
102600         FROM S802-PAGEHDR1 OF SR-LINES
102700         AFTER ADVANCING PAGE-EJECT.
102800     WRITE STATREPT-REC
102900         FROM S802-PAGEHDR2 OF SR-LINES
103000         AFTER ADVANCING 1 LINES.
103100     WRITE STATREPT-REC
103200         FROM S802-PAGEHDR1 OF SR-LINES
103300         AFTER ADVANCING 1 LINES.
103400     MOVE SPACES TO STATREPT-REC.
103500     WRITE STATREPT-REC
103600         AFTER ADVANCING 3 LINES.
103700     WRITE STATREPT-REC
103800         FROM SR-COLHDR1
103900         AFTER ADVANCING 1 LINES.
104000     WRITE STATREPT-REC
104100         FROM SR-COLHDR2
104200         AFTER ADVANCING 1 LINES.
104300     MOVE SPACES TO STATREPT-REC.
104400     WRITE STATREPT-REC
104500         AFTER ADVANCING 1 LINES.
104600     COMPUTE SR-LINES-REMAINING =
104700         SR-LINE-LIMIT - 8.
104800     MOVE SR-NORMAL-LINE-SPACING TO SR-WANTED-LINE-SPACING.
104900*
105000 5000-EOJ.
105100     MOVE SR-NORMAL-LINE-SPACING TO SR-WANTED-LINE-SPACING.
105200     MOVE 'END OF UPDATES' TO SR-DL1-MSG.
105300     PERFORM 4900-STAT-MSG.
105400     MOVE SPACES TO SR-PRINT-SLOT.
105500     PERFORM 4910-WRITE-SR-PRINT-SLOT.
105600*  WRITE COUNTS TO USER REPORT R1 AS WELL AS TO STATUS REPORT
105700     PERFORM 3820-R1-NEWPAGE.
105800     MOVE +1 TO R1-WANTED-LINE-SPACING.
105900     MOVE +1 TO SR-WANTED-LINE-SPACING.
106000     PERFORM 5010-WRITE-COUNTS
106100         VARYING WS-COUNTER-SUB FROM +1 BY +1
106200             UNTIL WS-COUNTER-SUB GREATER +26.
106300     PERFORM 9900-CLOSE-ALL-FILES.
106400*
106500 5010-WRITE-COUNTS.
106600*  WRITE COUNTS TO USER REPORT R1 AS WELL AS TO STATUS REPORT
106700     IF WS-COUNTER-SUB-SKIP-BEFORE
106800         MOVE SPACES TO SR-PRINT-SLOT
106900         PERFORM 4910-WRITE-SR-PRINT-SLOT
107000         MOVE SPACES TO R1-PRINT-SLOT
107100         PERFORM 3810-WRITE-R1-PRINT-SLOT.
107200     MOVE WS-COUNTER-LABEL(WS-COUNTER-SUB) TO SR-ENDLINE-MSG.
107300     MOVE WS-COUNTER-VALUE(WS-COUNTER-SUB) TO SR-COUNTER-VALUE.
107400     MOVE SR-ENDLINE TO SR-PRINT-SLOT.
107500     PERFORM 4910-WRITE-SR-PRINT-SLOT.
107600     MOVE SR-ENDLINE TO R1-PRINT-SLOT.
107700     PERFORM 3810-WRITE-R1-PRINT-SLOT.
107800/
107900 9000-INITIALIZE.
108000     COPY DTIMECOD.
       *DTIMECOD  LAST CHANGED 03-08-84  ORIGINAL 01-19-84  J JANOSSY
       ****************************************************************
       *     STANDARD CODE TO INITIALIZE DATE AND TIME FIELDS        *
       *     USE WITH STANDARD CODE IN COPYLIB MEMBER 'DTIMEWS'      *
       ****************************************************************
```

FIGURE B.4 (Continued)

```
            MOVE CURRENT-DATE TO WS-CURRENT-DATE-WITH-SLASHES.
            MOVE WS-CDS-MO     TO WS-CURR-GREG-MO.
            MOVE WS-CDS-DA     TO WS-CURR-GREG-DA.
            MOVE WS-CDS-YR     TO WS-CURR-GREG-YR.
            ACCEPT WS-TIME-MASK FROM TIME.
108100      MOVE WS-CURRENT-DATE-WITH-SLASHES
108200        TO PH2-DATE OF R1-LINES
108300           PH2-DATE OF R2-LINES
108400           PH2-DATE OF SR-LINES.
108500*
108600      MOVE ' COA TRANS LISTING  '
108700        TO PH2-REPORT-TITLE OF R1-LINES.
108800      MOVE 'S802P165-R1'
108900        TO PH2-PGM-REPNO OF R1-LINES.
109000*
109100      MOVE '   COA UPDATE LOG   '
109200        TO PH2-REPORT-TITLE OF R2-LINES.
109300      MOVE 'S802P165-R2'
109400        TO PH2-PGM-REPNO OF R2-LINES.
109500*
109600      MOVE '** STATUS REPORT ** '
109700        TO PH2-REPORT-TITLE OF SR-LINES.
109800      MOVE 'S802P165-SR'
109900        TO PH2-PGM-REPNO OF SR-LINES.
110000*
110100 9101-ISAM1-OPEN.
110200      MOVE 'STARTING TO OPEN I/O COA ISAM FILE'
110300        TO SR-DL1-MSG.
110400      PERFORM 4900-STAT-MSG.
110500      OPEN I-O COA-FILE.
110600      MOVE 'FILE OPEN COMPLETED' TO SR-DL1-MSG.
110700*******************ADDED FOR VSAM*******************
110800      MOVE VSAM1-FS TO  SR-DL1-FILESTAT.
110900******************************************************
111000      PERFORM 4900-STAT-MSG.
111100*******************OLD ISAM CODE*********************
111200*     MOVE 'O' TO WS-COA-FILE-OC-FLAG
111300*     MOVE 'OPEN OK' TO SR-DL1-MSG
111400*     PERFORM 4900-STAT-MSG.
111500******************************************************
111600*******************NEW VSAM CODE********************
111700      IF VSAM1-OPEN-OK
111800         MOVE 'O' TO WS-COA-FILE-OC-FLAG
111900         MOVE 'OPEN OK' TO SR-DL1-MSG
112000         PERFORM 4900-STAT-MSG
112100      ELSE
112200         MOVE 2401 TO WS-RET-CODE
112300         MOVE 'OPEN FAILED' TO SR-DL1-MSG
112400         PERFORM 9999-FORCED-ABORT.
112500******************************************************
112600*
112700 9900-CLOSE-ALL-FILES.
112800      IF WS-COA-FILE-OC-FLAG EQUAL 'O'
112900         PERFORM 9911-CLOSE-ISAM1.
113000      IF WS-TRANS-FILE-OC-FLAG EQUAL 'O'
113100         CLOSE TRANS-FILE
113200         MOVE 'C' TO WS-TRANS-FILE-OC-FLAG.
113300      IF WS-HIST-FILE-OC-FLAG EQUAL 'O'
113400         CLOSE HIST-FILE
113500         MOVE 'C' TO WS-HIST-FILE-OC-FLAG.
113600      IF WS-REPORT1-FILE-OC-FLAG EQUAL 'O'
113700         CLOSE REPORT1-FILE
113800         MOVE 'C' TO WS-REPORT1-FILE-OC-FLAG.
113900      IF WS-REPORT2-FILE-OC-FLAG EQUAL 'O'
114000         CLOSE REPORT2-FILE
```

FIGURE B4   (Continued)

```
114100          MOVE 'C' TO WS-REPORT2-FILE-OC-FLAG.
114200     CLOSE STATREPT-FILE.
114300*
114400 9911-CLOSE-ISAM1.
114500     MOVE 'C' TO WS-COA-FILE-OC-FLAG.
114600     MOVE 'CLOSING COA FILE' TO SR-DL1-MSG.
114700     PERFORM 4900-STAT-MSG.
114800     CLOSE COA-FILE.
114900     MOVE 'COA FILE CLOSE CONCLUDED' TO SR-DL1-MSG.
115000*********************ADDED FOR VSAM********************
115100     MOVE VSAM1-FS TO  SR-DL1-FILESTAT.
115200********************************************************
115300     PERFORM 4900-STAT-MSG.
115400********************ADDED FOR VSAM********************
115500     IF VSAM1-ACTION-OK
115600        NEXT SENTENCE
115700     ELSE
115800        MOVE 2403 TO WS-RET-CODE
115900        MOVE 'CLOSE FAILED' TO SR-DL1-MSG
116000        PERFORM 9999-FORCED-ABORT.
116100********************************************************
116200*
116300 9999-FORCED-ABORT.
116400     PERFORM 4900-STAT-MSG.
116500     PERFORM 9900-CLOSE-ALL-FILES.
116600     MOVE WS-RET-CODE TO RETURN-CODE.
116700*  REPLACE STOP RUN WITH CALL TO DUMP IF DESIRED
116800     STOP RUN.
```

FIGURE B4   (Continued)

Reference Guide to IDCAMS ALTER, DELETE, EXPORT, and IMPORT

Certain IDCAMS functional commands such as DEFINE, REPRO, PRINT, VERIFY, and the alternate index commands receive major usage. In this book they are discussed in the chapter dedicated to the functions performed with them. Other IDCAMS functions are employed to a lesser extent and do not warrant prime attention. Information about these functions is provided here.

ALTER COMMAND

ALTER allows changes to be made in the controlling parameters for a data set stored in the catalog. It is used to change, add, or remove the attributes of a data set. ALTER options can play a role during the initial loading of a cluster when records in different key ranges will have different insertion or update characteristics. In such cases, the free space for the data set suitable for one key range can be defined, that key range loaded, the free space altered, another key range loaded, and so forth.

Example

Let's assume that a key sequenced data set exists with several disk volumes specified to house it, an owner attribute of CMILLER, FREESPACE defined as (25,5), no master password, and a retention period ending on April 22, 1992. We wish to modify its attributes in this way:

- remove FSDC05 as a candidate volume
- change the OWNER to RGUZIK
- change to FREESPACE to (10 10)
- add a MASTERPW of SRJ1043X
- remove the retention period and exception exit.

The MVS JCL and IDCAMS control statements required to accomplish these alterations is shown in Figure C.1.

Figure C.2 lists the options of the ALTER command. We discuss here only those options that are unique to ALTER or for which special limits or restrictions apply in the use of

```
//FSBT677A  JOB AKOOTEST,'DP4-GUZIK',CLASS=E,MSGCLASS=X,
//  MSGLEVEL=(1,1),NOTIFY=BT05677
//*
//*    THIS JCL = BT05677.SOURCE.CNTL(JCLC1)
//*
//************************************************************
//*                                                         *
//*    ALTER KSDS ATTRIBUTES                                *
//*                                                         *
//************************************************************
//STEPA     DD    PGM=IDCAMS
//SYSPRINT  DD    SYSOUT=A
//SYSUDUMP  DD    SYSOUT=A
//SYSIN     DD    *
     ALTER -
               AKOO.C98.CUSTMAST -
               REMOVEVOLUMES(FSDC05) -
               OWNER(RGUZIK) -
               FREESPACE(10 10) -
               MASTERPW(SRJ1043X) -
               NULLIFY(RETENTION  EXCEPTIONEXIT)
  /*
  //
```

FIGURE C.1   MVS JCL and the IDCAMS ALTER examples

```
Required *
Choice needed >
Recommended +   Command       Option                        Abbreviation


     *          ALTER      entryname/password
                           ADDVOLUMES(volser volser)           AVOL
                           ATTEMPTS(number)                    ATT
                           AUTHORIZATION(entrypoint string)    AUTH
                           BUFFERSPACE(size)                   BUFSP
                           BUFND(number)                       BFND
                           BUFNI(number)                       BFNI
                           CATALOG(catname/password)           CAT
                           CODE(code)
                           CONTROLPW(password)                 CTLPW
                           DESTAGEWAIT|NODESTAGEWAIT     DSTGW NDSTGW
                           EMPTY|NOEMPTY                 EMP   NEMP
                           ERASE|NOERASE                 ERAS  NERAS
                           EXCEPTIONEXIT(entrypoint)           EEXT
                           FILE(ddname)
                           FREESPACE(CI-percent  CA-percent)   FSPC
                           INHIBIT|UNINHIBIT             INH   UNINH
                           KEYS(length  offset)
                           MASTERPW(password)                  MRPW
                           NEWNAME(newname)                    NEWNM
                           NULLIFY(                            NULL
                             AUTHORIZATION(module|string)  AUTH MDLE STRG
                             CODE
                             CONTROLPW                         CTLPW
                             EXCEPTIONEXIT                     EEXT
                             MASTERPW                          MRPW
                             OWNER
                             READPW                            RDPW
                             RETENTION                         RETN
                             UPDATEPW      )                   UPDPW
```

FIGURE C.2   Complete list of ALTER options and abbreviations

```
OWNER(ownerid)
READPW(password)                                    RDPW
RECORDSIZE(average  maximum)                        RECSZ
REMOVEVOLUMES(volser  volser)                       RVOL
SCRATCH|NOSCRATCH                           SCR     NSCR
SHAREOPTIONS(crossregion  crosssystem)             SHR
STAGE|BIND|CYLINDERFAULT                            CYLF
STRNO(number)
TO(DATE)|FOR(days)
UNIQUEKEY|NONUNIQUEKEY                       UNQK    NUNQK
UPDATE|NOUPDATE                             UPD     NUPD
UPDATEPW(password)                                 UPDPW
UPGRADE|NOUPGRADE                           UPG     NUPG
WRITECHECK|NOWRITECHECK                     WCK     NWCK
```

Note: The | symbol represents a logical "or" meaning that only one of the
items can be specified. Underlined print indicates the IDCAMS default.
Passwords are needed only if they are defined for the entity for which
attributes are being altered.

FIGURE C.2   (*Continued*)

ALTER. The options not discussed carry the same potential for use as do their counter-parts in the DEFINE command discussed in Chapter 2.

ALTER Options Differing from DEFINE Options

ENTRYNAME   is the one required parameter of the ALTER option. It identifies the cluster, component, or other entity to be altered. The optional password is the master password for the catalog that contains the entry. This password can alternatively be provided in the CATALOG specification.

ADDVOLUMES   will add volume serial numbers to the list of candidate volumes on which the data set can be extended. Under the VSAM catalog environment, but not the Integrated Catalog Facility (ICF) environment, all of the volumes being added must be owned by the catalog that contains the entry being altered.

BUFFERSPACE   of a data component can be altered. The amount of BUFFERSPACE specified should not be less than the default buffer space of one index CI and two data CIs.

BUFND and BUFNI   Both BUFND for the quantity of data component buffers and BUFNI for the quantity of index component buffers can be modified with the ALTER command. However, it is recommended that these parameters assume default values in data set definition, and that they be set in the manner most appropriate to a given task via the AMP parameter of JCL. As discussed in Chapter 4, the quantity of data and index buffers has a significant impact on efficiency. No one setting is optimal for both random and sequential processing.

EMPTY | NOEMPTY and SCRATCH | NOSCRATCH   These attributes apply only to generation data group data sets (GDGs), which are non-VSAM entities. Generation data groups provide the means to reference sequential data sets and partitioned data sets by relative generation number. Ironically, VSAM data sets themselves may not be treated as generation data sets, a factor that seriously limits the utility of entry sequenced data sets (ESDS).

The creation, use, and deletion of generation data group data sets is covered in depth in Chapter 13 of *Practical MVS JCL For Today's Programmers* (1987, John Wiley and Sons, Inc.) ISBN 0-471-83684-6.

FILE   If NEWNAME is specified for a data component or index component which does not reside on the volume containing the catalog recovery area, that volume must be specified in the DD statement referenced by the FILE parameter.

FREESPACE   alters the free space specification of the data component. This makes it possible to change the way that free space is provided in previously empty control intervals when they are used for CI splits, and the way free space is provided when a new control area is created.

Figure 4.7 in Chapter 4 illustrates the alteration of the free space specification between the loading of portions of a key sequenced data set.

INHIBIT | UNINHIBIT   control read-only access to a data set. A read-only restriction can be set by using INHIBIT with the ALTER command; read-only access is also set by the EXPORT command. The read-only restriction is removed when UNINHIBIT is specified in a subsequent ALTER command. The INHIBIT attribute can be used to temporarily disallow updates to a data set but still make it available for inquiry processing.

KEYS   makes it possible to change the nature of a primary or alternate key. However, the instances when this is permitted are few. The nature, length, and position of record keys can be altered only when all of the following conditions are met:

- the entity being altered is a key sequenced data set, an alternate index, or a path
- the entity being altered is empty, containing no records in its data component
- the new length of the key does not exceed the RECORDSIZE of the entity being altered
- for spanned records, the new key fits in the first segment of the record, a length equal to CISIZE − 10
- the original entity definition either specified or took the default values for KEYS, which is a length of 64 and an offset of zero
- the new values for KEYS do not conflict with the original CISIZE specified.

It is highly unlikely that all of these requirements can be met. The possibility of altering the key specification of a KSDS is therefore so remote as to make it an item of trivia.

NEWNAME   defines a new name for the item at "entryname." The new name specified must follow the same rules as the NAME specified in the DEFINE option. If either the entryname or the new name is specified as a generic name, both names must be specified as generic names. A generic name is a data set or entity name with an asterisk in place of one of the levels within the name, such as AK00.*.CUSTMAST. A generic name represents a group of data sets, entities, or components. The asterisk is a place holder that represents from one to eight characters. Generic names can be used with ALTER to make mass changes to a group of items with similar names.

NULLIFY   removes attributes from an entity. Most of the attributes that can be removed by the NULLIFY attribute are related to security. If NULLIFY is specified, the attributes indicated are nullified before any are given new values. These attributes can be nullified:

- Either the AUTHORIZATION MODULE and STRING, or just the STRING
- CODE, CONTROLPW, EXCEPTIONEXIT, OWNER, READPW, and the UPDATEPW

- MASTERPW; if a new MASTERPW is not specified and other passwords exist, then the highest level password that does exist becomes the value for the higher level passwords

- RETENTION specified either by TO or FOR.

RECORDSIZE   of an alternate index or a base cluster can be altered directly or through its associated path. RECORDSIZE can be altered only when the following conditions are met:

- the entity to be altered is a cluster, data component, alternate index, or path
- the entity contains no records
- the original entity definition either specified the default values or took the default values for RECORDSIZE
- for alternate indexes that specified NONUNIQUEKEY the altered record length accommodates the increased record length resulting from multiple prime key entries
- for nonspanned records the altered maximum record length is at least seven bytes less than the control interval size.

It is unlikely that all of these requirements can be met. The possibility of altering the record size specification of a KSDS is therefore remote.

REMOVEVOLUMES   removes volumes as candidates for either data or index components after new volumes, if any, are added. The volume serial numbers specified in this parameter will be removed from the list of candidate volumes on which the data set can be extended.

SHAREOPTIONS   of data and index components of a base cluster and alternate index can be altered.

UNIQUEKEY | NONUNIQUEKEY   indicates that each alternate key value is unique across the entire data set. If NONUNIQUEKEY has been defined for the data set, UNIQUEKEY can be specified with ALTER only when the alternate index is defined but not yet built.

NONUNIQUEKEY indicates that multiple alternate keys can point to the same base cluster record. This can be specified with ALTER at any time. If UNIQUEKEY is altered to NONUNIQUEKEY, RECORDSIZE should also be altered to provide sufficient room in the alternate key record to house the multiple primary keys that can potentially be associated with a given alternate key.

UPDATE | NOUPDATE   indicates whether or not the base cluster's upgrade set, identified through a path, is to be allocated when a DD statement specifies the path name.

UPDATE indicates that both the base cluster and the associated alternate index are allocated when the corresponding path is carried on a DD statement.

NOUPDATE indicates that only the base cluster is allocated in this case. NOUPDATE spares the allocation of the alternate index even when it is part of the upgrade set, intended to be updated when alternate key values are changed or records added to the data set. NOUPDATE is useful only when a data set is being used for prime key inquiry purposes and it is known that no updates will occur.

More than one path can be defined for a given key sequenced data set and alternate index. UPDATE can be specified in one path, and NOUPDATE in another. By using the appropriate path to access the data set, the allocation or nonallocation of the alternate index can be tailored to a given task.

UPGRADE | NOUPGRADE   indicates whether or not an alternate index allocated through a path carrying UPDATE capability will be updated when alternate keys are changed in the base cluster or records are added to it.

When specified through the ALTER option, UPGRADE takes effect immediately if the alternate index is not open. If the alternate index is open, UPGRADE takes effect after the alternate index is closed and is no longer allocated to any job. NOUPGRADE will take effect immediately when specified with the ALTER option. This curtails alternate index updates without affecting the base cluster update process, by causing VSAM to omit the additional steps needed to update the alternate index.

Other Alterable Items

Other entity attributes can be altered with no restriction as to value except those that apply for original definition. These include ATTEMPTS, AUTHORIZATION, CODE, CONTROLPW, DESTAGEWAIT/NODESTAGEWAIT, ERASE/NOERASE, EXCEPTIONEXIT, MASTERPW, OWNER, READPW, SHAREOPTIONS, STAGE/BIND/CYLINDERFAULT, TO/FOR, UPDATEPW, and CATALOG. Consult the DEFINE options discussed in Chapter 2 for information on these options. ALTER coding for these is identical to DEFINE syntax.

DELETE COMMAND

The DELETE option is used to delete and uncatalog an entry, or a cluster and all of its components and related entities. DELETE is usually coded prior to the allocation and loading of a cluster. This will insure that the definition and subsequent loading of the data set will not be terminated due to the data set already existing. Figure C.3 is a list of options of the DELETE command. Figure C.4 illustrates common uses of the command to

```
Required *
Choice needed >
Recommended +    Command        Option                          Abbreviation


     *           DELETE     entryname/password                      DEL
                            ALIAS|
                               ALTERNATEINDEX|                      AIX
                               CLUSTER|                             CL
                               GENERATIONDATAGROUP|                 GDG
                               NONVSAM|                             NVSAM
                               PATH|
                               SPACE|                               SPC
                               TRUENAME|                            TNAME
                               USERCATALOG|                         UCAT
                               VVR
                            CATALOG(catname/password)         CAT
                            ERASE|NOERASE                     ERAS  NERAS
                            FILE(ddname)
                            FORCE|NOFORCE                     FRC   NFRC
                            PURGE|NOPURGE                     PRG   NPRG
                            RECOVERY|NORECOVERY               RCVRY NRCVRY
                            SCRATCH|NOSCRATCH                 SCR   NSCR
```

Note: The | symbol represents a logical "or" meaning that only one of the items can be specified. Underlined print indicates the IDCAMS default. Passwords are needed only if they are defined for the entity being deleted.

FIGURE C.3   Complete list of DELETE options, abbreviations, suggested choices

```
//FSBT686A  JOB AKOOTEST,'DP2-JANOSSY',CLASS=E,MSGCLASS=X,
// MSGLEVEL=(1,1),NOTIFY=BT05686
//*
//*     THIS JCL = BT05686.SOURCE.CNTL(JCLC4)
//*
//***********************************************************
//*                                                        *
//*     DELETE DATA SETS OR MEMBERS USING IDCAMS           *
//*                                                        *
//***********************************************************
//STEPA      EXEC  PGM=IDCAMS
//SYSPRINT   DD    SYSOUT=*
//SYSIN      DD    *
      DELETE  AKOO.C98.CUSTMAST -          /* DELETE A    */
              CLUSTER -                    /* CLUSTER     */
              PURGE                        /* EVEN IF     */
                                           /* UNEXPIRED   */

      DELETE  AKOO.C99.TESTDATA            /* DELETE A    */
                                           /* DATA SET    */

      DELETE  AKOO.C99.VEHMAST1 -          /* DELETE AN   */
              PURGE                        /* UNEXPIRED   */
                                           /* DATA SET    */

      DELETE  BT05686.SOURCE.COBOL(FSBT1522)  /* DELETE A    */
                                           /* PDS MEMBER  */
   /*
   //
```

FIGURE C.4   MVS JCL and IDCAMS DELETE examples

delete a VSAM cluster, delete an ordinary sequential data set, delete an unexpired sequential data set, and to delete a member of a partitioned data set.

ENTRYNAME   identifies the entry or cataloged item to be deleted. It can be a cluster, alternate index, individual component, path, non-VSAM data set, or generation data group entry. "Entryname" is the only required attribute of the DELETE command. Only if the base cluster or alternate index is missing or inaccessible, and you want to delete one of the components, the TRUENAME attribute is also required.

MASTERPW is required for VSAM data sets when deleting a password-protected entity. Either the UPDATEPW or higher password is required when deleting a password protected non-VSAM entity.

ALIAS   indicates that the entity to be deleted is an alias name for a cluster or other item. An alias is an alternate name by which the entity is also known, and is established with the DEFINE or ALTER command.

ALTERNATEINDEX   indicates that the alternate index entry and its data and index components are to be deleted. If a PATH is associated with the alternate index, it will be deleted also. If the alternate index is the only alternate index with the UPGRADE attribute associated with its cluster, the cluster's definition will be altered to carry NOUPGRADE if the alternate index is deleted.

CLUSTER   is an all-encompassing specification when DELETE is coded. CLUSTER indicates that the base cluster, its data and index components, all related alternate indexes with their data and index components, and all related path entities are to be deleted.

ERASE | NOERASE   ERASE indicates that the data component will be overwritten with binary zeroes when the KSDS is deleted. NOERASE omits this action. The specification in the DELETE command will override the ERASE/NOERASE specification established for the KSDS with its DEFINE. NOERASE is usually preferable since it eliminates a time-consuming write operation. Unless there exists some real security need to physically obliterate the information on the disk tracks assigned to the deleted data set, no need exists to use ERASE. The disk tracks will be overlaid with other information as soon as they are assigned to another data set by the operating system and written upon.

FILE   identifies the DD statement that contains the volume, VSAM data set, non-VSAM data set, or the partitioned data set to be deleted. FILE is an optional specification.

FORCE | NOFORCE   The FORCE specification allows a non-empty generation data group to be deleted along with all of its associated data sets. NOFORCE is the default; the DE-LETE command will fail if the generation data group to be deleted is not empty and still has data sets associated with it. NOFORCE should be used unless it is desirous to delete the catalog entry along with all of the associated generation data group data sets.[1]

GENERATIONDATAGROUP   indicates that the generation data group entry will be deleted if it is empty, that is, there are no data sets cataloged with the generation data group name. FORCE is required if there are data sets associated with the generation data group at the time of its deletion.[1]

NONVSAM   indicates that the item being deleted is not a VSAM data set. Any existing aliases for the item are also deleted. An individual member from a partitioned data set can be deleted by specifying the member name in parentheses immediately after the entryname. NONVSAM is an optional specification used for items that are not cataloged. The deletion of a cataloged item takes place even if this specification is not coded.[1]

PATH   A path can be deleted with the DELETE command. When a path is deleted its associated base cluster and alternate index remain unaffected.

PURGE | NOPURGE   PURGE will allow an entry to be deleted even if the retention date or period specified with either TO or FOR has not been reached. PURGE cannot be used with the TRUENAME attribute. The default attribute of NOPURGE will not allow the entry to be deleted if its retention period is unexpired. NOPURGE should normally be used.

RECOVERY | NORECOVERY   apply only to an ICF user catalog and do not apply to the type of VSAM data sets that have been discussed in this book.

SCRATCH | NOSCRATCH   The default of SCRATCH will both delete the data set and also remove its entry from the catalog. NOSCRATCH will simply remove the entry from the catalog. NOSCRATCH cannot be specified for alternate indexes. SCRATCH should be used at all times since it removes both the entry in the catalog and the data set.

SPACE   is related only to the VSAM catalog environment, and not the Integrated Catalog Facility (ICF) environment. SPACE allows the deletion of empty VSAM data spaces from a disk volume. A data space must be empty in order to be deleted, but the FORCE command can override this provision and delete a data space that contains VSAM data sets. Deletion of data spaces is not an action commonly undertaken by applications programmers, but is in the realm of systems programming or disk space management personnel.

TRUENAME is applicable to the Integrated Catalog Facility only. Records known as "true name records" exist as a part of the ICF catalog structure, which is in itself a KSDS. True name records relate the key of the ICF catalog "sphere record," which consists of hexadecimal zeros (low-values), to the user-defined name for the catalog, and to relate the catalog's index component to it.

TRUENAME allows an individual cluster or alternate index component to be deleted when its associated base cluster or alternate index is missing or inaccessible. TRUENAME should be used only after consultation with a systems programmer because the circumstances that usually lead to its use are complex and require careful diagnosis.

USERCATALOG is specified if the item to be deleted is a user catalog. The user catalog is deleted, as are its aliases if any exist, and the catalog connector entry in the master catalog. In order to be deleted, a catalog must contain nothing more than its own self-describing entries, unless FORCE is also specified. Deletion of usercatalogs is not an action commonly taken by application programmers.

VVR is applicable only to the Integrated Catalog Facility (ICF) environment, and allows deletion of the VSAM Volume Record related to the cluster or component name specified at the entryname parameter. The VVR is contained in the VSAM Volume Data Set (VVDS), a portion of the catalog structure that is housed on each individual disk. Deletion of VVRs is not an action commonly taken by application programmers.

EXPORT COMMAND

How EXPORT Differs from REPRO; Example

The EXPORT command is used to unload a VSAM data set for transportation to another system or to create a backup copy. The exported copy contains all data set components and all of the data set's attributes in an unusual format that cannot be processed except by IMPORT. EXPORT creates a portable version of the data set that can be loaded elsewhere with the IMPORT command. IMPORT automatically redefines the data set from the exported data and loads the data records into it, allocating the specified control interval and control area free space, and, in effect, reorganizing the data set. If a data set has alternate indexes they must be exported individually.

REPRO, on the other hand, copies only the data component records of a VSAM data set as simple sequential records. REPRO does not record any VSAM data set attributes. When used to restore a VSAM data set, REPRO requires that the existing data set be explicitly deleted and redefined. The data set created by REPRO is readable by any other program, and provides the basis for efficient batch processing of the data set. REPRO is more commonly used than EXPORT to create data set backups because of this last advantage.

Figure C.5 lists the valid specifications for the EXPORT command. Figure C.6 illustrates the exportation of a key sequenced data set and its two alternate indexes on tape.

ENTRYNAME identifies the base cluster or alternate index to be EXPORTed. The master password for the entry must be supplied if the entry has VSAM passwords. If any associated paths have VSAM passwords, the master password of the catalog containing the entries must be supplied.

OUTFILE | OUTDATASET OUTFILE indicates the DDname of the DD statement at which is named the data set to receive the exported data. Only BLKSIZE and DEN can be specified

```
Required *
Choice needed >
Recommended +    Command          Option                          Abbreviation


    *            EXPORT     entryname/password                    EXP
    >                       OUTFILE(ddname)|                      OFILE
    >                         OUTDATASET(entryname)               ODS
                            INFILE(ddname)                        IFILE
                            ERASE|NOERASE                         ERAS NERAS
                            INHIBITSOURCE|NOINHIBITSOURCE         INHS NINHS
    +                       INHIBITTARGET|                        INHT
                              NOINHIBITTARGET                          NINHT
                            PURGE|NOPURGE                         PRG NPRG
    +                       TEMPORARY|                            TEMP
                              PERMANENT                                PERM
```

Note: The | symbol represents a logical "or" meaning that only one of the
items can be specified. Underlined print indicates the IDCAMS default. The
usage of passwords is optional. INHIBITTARGET is recommended for use rather
than the default NOINHIBITTARGET, so that when imported the data set will be
protected from update until an ALTER is used to UNINHIBIT it. TEMPORARY is
recommended; if PERMANENT is left as the default the data set is deleted upon
completion of the export.

FIGURE C.5   Complete list of EXPORT options, abbreviations, suggested choices


```
//FSBT686A  JOB AK00TEST,'DP2-JANOSSY',CLASS=T,MSGCLASS=X,
//  MSGLEVEL=(1,1),NOTIFY=BT05686
//*
//*     THIS JCL = BT05686.SOURCE.CNTL(JCLC6)
//*
//**********************************************************
//*                                                        *
//*     EXPORT KEY SEQUENCED DATA SET AND ALT INDEXES       *
//*                                                        *
//*     ALTERNATE INDEXES ARE EXPORTED FIRST SO IN          *
//*     CASES WHERE THE DEFAULT OF "PERMANENT" IS           *
//*     ALLOWED TO REMAIN IN EFFECT THEY WILL BE            *
//*     AVAILABLE FOR EXPORT.  ("PERMANENT" EXPORT OF       *
//*     BASE CLUSTER DELETES ALTERNATE INDEXES WITH         *
//*     THE BASE, AND ALTERNATE INDEXES ARE LOST.)          *
//*     THIS JOB STREAM USES "TEMPORARY" SO THAT THE        *
//*     ORIGINAL DATA SETS ARE NOT DELETED BY EXPORT.       *
//*                                                        *
//**********************************************************
//STEPA     EXEC  PGM=IDCAMS
//SYSPRINT   DD   SYSOUT=*
//SYSUDUMP   DD   SYSOUT=A
//DD1        DD   DSN=AK00.C98.ADDREXPT,
//  UNIT=(TAPE,,DEFER),
//  DISP=(NEW,CATLG,DELETE),               'NO SERIAL NUMBER SO
//  VOL=(PRIVATE,RETAIN),                  'LET MVS CALL FOR A
//  DCB=BLKSIZE=32000,                     'SCRATCH TAPE; KEEP
//  LABEL=(1,SL,RETPD=90)                  'IT MOUNTED
//*
//DD2        DD   DSN=AK00.C98.NAMEEXPT,
//  UNIT=TAPE,
//  DISP=(NEW,CATLG,DELETE),
//  DCB=BLKSIZE=32000,                     'PUT AS SECOND FILE
//  VOL=(PRIVATE,RETAIN,REF=*.DD1),        'ON THE SAME SCRATCH
//  LABEL=(2,SL,RETPD=90)                  'TAPE; KEEP IT MOUNTED
//*
```

FIGURE C.6   MVS JCL and IDCAMS EXPORT example

```
//DD3          DD  DSN=AK00.C98.CUSTEXPT,
//  UNIT=TAPE,
//  DISP=(NEW,CATLG,DELETE),
//  DCB=BLKSIZE=32000,
//  VOL=REF=*.DD1,                         'PUT AS THIRD FILE
//  LABEL=(3,SL,RETPD=90)                  'ON SAME SCRATCH TAPE
//*
//SYSIN        DD  *
     EXPORT  AK00.C98.CUSTMAST.ADDRAIX -
             OUTFILE(DD1) -
             INHIBITTARGET -
             TEMPORARY

     EXPORT  AK00.C98.CUSTMAST.NAMEAIX -
             OUTFILE(DD2) -
             INHIBITTARGET -
             TEMPORARY

     EXPORT  AK00.C98.CUSTMAST -
             OUTFILE(DD3) -
             INHIBITTARGET -
             TEMPORARY
  /*
  //
```

FIGURE C.6   (Continued)

for the data set receiving the exported data, and the specification of these is optional. If BLKSIZE is not specified, EXPORT creates records of 2,048-byte length, into which the attributes, data, and index components of the data set are strung. BLKSIZE can be specified to increase this length to a value more efficient for processing. For an export of data to tape a maximum block size of 32,760 is possible and provides maximum processing speed.

OUTDATASET specifies the name of the data set that will receive the exported data. The system will attempt to dynamically allocate the data set. OUTFILE is recommended over OUTDATASET unless the data set receiving the exported data is located on disk and is already allocated.

ERASE | NOERASE   ERASE can be specified only with the PERMANENT attribute which indicates that the VSAM data set will automatically be deleted after the export. ERASE causes the data component of the base cluster or alternate index being exported to be obliterated with binary zeroes. If neither ERASE or NOERASE is specified, the choice specified at data set creation time or as last altered will be honored.

INFILE   identifies the DD statement carrying the name of the base cluster or alternate index to be exported. The name of the base cluster or alternate index is the same one coded as entryname.

The purpose of INFILE is to allow a means of stating the input data set on a DD statement to be able to specify other things for it via JCL. Use of INFILE is rare because it is preferable to have the system dynamically allocate the data set at the time the export occurs, which is what happens when INFILE is omitted.

INHIBITSOURCE | NOINHIBITSOURCE   EXPORT was originally viewed as very much an export: once exported, the disk-stored data set would either be deleted or at least left in a read-only condition. INHIBITSOURCE specifies this; it places a "lock" on the data set preventing further update. INHIBITSOURCE can be specified only when TEMPORARY is specified, because TEMPORARY omits deletion of the original data set.

These parameters govern the setting of the INHIBIT/NOINHIBIT attribute for the data set in the system catalog. This attribute can be modified with the ALTER command.

INHIBITTARGET | NOINHIBITTARGET   The "target" data set is the one created by the importation of exported data. INHIBITTARGET causes the target data set or alternate index to be accessible only for retrieval operations; NOINHIBITTARGET, the default, allows the imported data set to be updated. If EXPORT is used to transport a VSAM data set to another system, it is desirable to specify INHIBITTARGET to provide some initial protection for the data set. The ALTER command can be used after the importation to UNINHIBIT the data set at an appropriate time.

PURGE | NOPURGE   When a data set is exported and the default PERMANENT specification prevails, it will automatically be deleted upon completion of the export. The deletion can occur only if the data set expiration date, if it has one, has been reached. PURGE allows a data set to be deleted by PERMANENT even if the retention period specified for it at its creation by TO or FOR, or last changed by ALTER, has not been reached. PURGE can be specified only with PERMANENT. NOPURGE prevents deletion of unexpired data sets, and is the default.

TEMPORARY | PERMANENT   TEMPORARY indicates that the original data set is not to be deleted after the export operation. PERMANENT provides that the original data set is automatically deleted after the export operation. PERMANENT is in keeping with the original intention of the VSAM product designers to make EXPORT just that: the exportation of a data set and its removal from the "source" system. If the export copy is for backup purposes, TEMPORARY should be specified, so that the original data set remains after the operation.

IMPORT COMMAND

The IMPORT command is used to bring an EXPORTed data set back to its original system or to load it on another system. The attributes of the data set are taken from the portable copy and automatically placed into the catalog on the system executing the IMPORT. The data is taken from the portable copy and used to load the data set according to the free space attributes, resulting in a reorganization of the data on the new system. Figure C.7 lists the specifications valid for the IMPORT command.

INFILE | INDATASET   INFILE or INDATASET identifies the portable data set created by an EXPORT, containing the base cluster or alternate index to be imported.

INFILE specifies a DD statement citing the data set to be imported. If the portable copy resides on a non-labeled tape, the DCB parameters that were specified when the data set was exported must be specified when the data set is imported. INFILE must be used if the import operation is being executed on a system other than the one on which the export was made. In this case the exported data set will not be known to the receiving system's catalog, and the dynamic allocation of INDATASET would fail.

INDATASET cites the portable data set name for dynamic allocation. This attribute can be used only if the portable data set is cataloged on the system on which the import operation is being performed.

OUTFILE | OUTDATASET   If the data set was exported with the PERMANENT option, the original data set will have been deleted at the conclusion of the EXPORT. In this case

```
Required *
Choice needed >
Recommended +     Command        Option                              Abbreviation


     *            IMPORT -                                            IMP
     >                        INFILE(ddname)|                         IFILE
     >                         INDATASET(entryname)                   IDS
     >                        OUTFILE(ddname/password|                OFILE
     >                         OUTDATASET(entryname/password)         ODS
                              CATALOG(catname/password)               CAT
                              ERASE|NOERASE                    ERAS   NERAS
                              INTOEMPTY                               IEMPTY
                              OBJECTS( -                              OBJ
                                (entryname
                                  FILE(ddname)
                                  KEYRANGES((lowkey highkey)          KRNG
                                    (lowkey highkey) (lowkey highkey)
                                  NEWNAME(newname)                    NEWNM
                                  ORDERED|UNORDERED             ORD   UNORD
                                  VOLUMES(volser  volser  volser)     VOL
                                (entryname
                                  FILE(ddname)
                                  KEYRANGES((lowkey highkey)          KRNG
                                    (lowkey highkey) (lowkey highkey)
                                  NEWNAME(newname)                    NEWNM
                                  ORDERED|UNORDERED             ORD   UNORD
                                  VOLUMES(volser  volser  volser) )   VOL
                              PURGE|NOPURGE                     PRG   NPRG
                              SAVRAC|NOSAVRAC
```

Note: The | symbol represents a logical "or" meaning that only one of the
items can be specified. Underlined print indicates the IDCAMS default. The
usage of passwords is optional.

FIGURE C.7   Complete list of EXPORT options, abbreviations, suggested choices

OUTFILE should be used for the IMPORT operation, because it specifies a DD statement citing the name of the data set to receive the imported data.

The DD statement referenced by OUTFILE must specify the data set name of the data set being imported, the volume serial numbers to which the data set is being imported, the device type, AMP = 'AMORG' and DISP = OLD if the data set is being imported to a volume other than the original volume. The data set name on the DD statement must be the same as the name specified in the NEWNAME attribute, if it is coded.

If the components of the base cluster or the alternate index are being imported to different devices, a second DD statement must be concatenated to the first DD statement. The first DD statement will refer to the data component and carry volume serial numbers, device type, AMP = 'AMORG' and DISP = OLD. The second DD statement will refer to the index component and carry volume serial numbers, device type, AMP = 'AMORG' and DISP = OLD. The data set names specified on these concatenated DD statements specify the data and index component names.

OUTDATASET specifies the name of the data set that will receive the imported data set. The system will attempt to dynamically allocate the data set, a process that will fail unless the data set is already known to the system catalog. For all practical purposes this means that OUTDATASET can be specified only if the EXPORT was performed with a TEMPORARY specification and the original data set still exists, and the IMPORT is being done on the same computer system as the EXPORT. If NEWNAME is also specified, the data set name used at OUTDATASET must be the same as that specified at NEWNAME.

ERASE | NOERASE   The ERASE attribute indicates that the data component of the base cluster or alternate index being imported will be overwritten with binary zeroes before the data is loaded by the import. ERASE is possible only when the data set was exported with the TEMPORARY option; if exported with PERMANENT, it will have been deleted after the export and the ERASE/NOERASE specified on the EXPORT will have dictated handling. The option chosen for the import becomes the option in effect for the data set, overriding the ERASE/NOERASE choice carried by the exported data set.

INTOEMPTY   Data sets are usually imported into a system in which they do not exist, or into a system in which a data set of the same name exists and contains data. IMPORT causes the definition of a data set from the data set attributes stored in the portable data set created by EXPORT. INTOEMPTY allows the import operation to take place into a data set that has been defined but does not contain data. If a data set is defined but is empty, and INTOEMPTY is not specified, the IMPORT operation will fail as a matter of safety.

OBJECTS   "Entryname" and subsequent specifications of OBJECTS act similar to an AL-TER. These can be used to add or change selected attributes of the imported cluster, alternate index, or associated paths.

> **ENTRYNAME**   identifies the base cluster component, alternate index component, or path to be altered.

> **FILE**   refers to a DD statement citing the volumes on which the item resides. If this is not specified, the volumes will be dynamically allocated, which is recommended. FILE is required when the components were originally defined with the UNIQUE attribute and the data and index components reside on different device types.

> **KEYRANGES**   indicates that portions of the data set being imported will be loaded on different volumes even if the original data set did not have key ranges or had different key ranges. This subattribute acts in the same way as the KEYRANGES attribute when specified with the DEFINE command, but this subattribute can specify only 20 key ranges rather than the 123 key ranges of the DEFINE command.

> **NEWNAME**   alters the original entry name of the cluster that was exported, and any alternate indexes, their components, and associated paths. If the export was executed with TEMPORARY and the cluster or alternate index is given a new name, each of the components must also be assigned a new name.

> **ORDERED | UNORDERED**   indicates whether or not the volumes specified on VOLUMES in the original data set definition will be used in the order coded. This subattribute follows the same rules as if with the DEFINE command, including the default specification of UNORDERED. Whichever specification is used for a cluster or alternate index will apply to both the data and index component.

> **VOLUMES**   specifies the target volume or volumes on which the imported data set will reside. If specified for a cluster or alternate index, it applies to both the data and index component. The number of tracks or cylinders occupied by the original data set cannot be modified when the data set is imported. When IMPORTing a cluster or alternate index to a disk device of less capacity, the original device may fail for insufficient space. This potential problem can be avoided by defining an empty cluster or alternate index to be used as the object of the import command and specifying INTOEMPTY.

PURGE | NOPURGE   specifies whether or not the original cluster or alternate index will be deleted and replaced by the imported data set even if the date resulting from either TO or FOR for the original data set has not been reached. PURGE can be specified only when TEMPORARY was specified at the export of the data set and it is being imported back to the same system. NOPURGE is the default and will not allow the item to be deleted and the import to occur if the retention period has not expired.

SAVRAC | NOSAVRAC   SAVRAC applies to the RACF security system environment and indicates that existing security profiles will be used for the data set. NOSAVRAC applies in this environment and indicates that new security profiles are to be created. If the original data set was exported with TEMPORARY and is being imported back to the same system, SAVRAC should be specified.

CATALOG   names the catalog in which the imported data set will be cataloged. If not coded, the data set will be cataloged in the master catalog of the computer system. If the master catalog is password-protected this specification is required in order to indicate the password.

Examples

Figure C.8 illustrates the MVS JCL and IDCAMS control statements to import the key sequenced data set and alternate indexes exported with the job listed in Figure C. 6. The data sets will be imported to the same computer system, and the names and devices will be the same as existed at the time of the export.

Figure C.9 illustrates the handling of a different importation of the data sets exported in Figure C.6. Here we wish to import the key sequenced data set to another computer system, which has not previously existed. The portable data set is not known to the new system's catalog, and the JCL must therefore supply additional information about the tape conveying it. The portable copy created with the EXPORT command is named AK00.C98.CUSTEXPT and was exported with a BLKSIZE of 32000. The imported data set will reside on a disk carrying volume serial id FSDC57. The original data set name was AK00.C98.CUSTMAST, but we wish the imported data set to be known as

```
//FSBT686A  JOB AK00TEST,'DP2-JANOSSY',CLASS=T,MSGCLASS=X,
//  MSGLEVEL=(1,1),NOTIFY=BT05686
//*
//*     THIS JCL = BT05686.SOURCE.CNTL(JCLC8)
//*
//****************************************************************
//*                                                             *
//*     IMPORT A PREVIOUSLY EXPORTED KSDS AND INDEXES           *
//*                                                             *
//****************************************************************
//STEPA      EXEC  PGM=IDCAMS,REGION=2048K
//SYSPRINT   DD    SYSOUT=*
//SYSUDUMP   DD    SYSOUT=A
//DD1        DD    DSN=AK00.C98.ADDREXPT,
//  UNIT=(TAPE,,DEFER),
//  DISP=(OLD,KEEP),
//  VOL=(PRIVATE,RETAIN)
//DD2        DD    DSN=AK00.C98.NAMEEXPT,
//  UNIT=AFF=DD1,
//  DISP=(OLD,KEEP),
```

FIGURE C.8   MVS JCL and IDCAMS IMPORT example, importing an exported data set to the same computer system

```
//   VOL=(PRIVATE,RETAIN)
//DD3        DD  DSN=AK00.C98.CUSTEXPT,
//   UNIT=AFF=DD1,
//   DISP=(OLD,KEEP)
//SYSIN      DD  *
     IMPORT  -
             INFILE(DD1) -
             OUTDATASET(AK00.C98.CUSTMAST.ADDRAIX)

     IMPORT  -
             INFILE(DD2) -
             OUTDATASET(AK00.C98.CUSTMAST.NAMEAIX)

     IMPORT  -
             INFILE(DD3) -
             OUTDATASET(AK00.C98.CUSTMAST)
/*
//
```

FIGURE C.8   (Continued)

```
//FSBT686A  JOB AK00TEST,'DP2-JANOSSY',CLASS=T,MSGCLASS=X,
// MSGLEVEL=(1,1),NOTIFY=BT05686
//*
//*    THIS JCL = BT05686.SOURCE.CNTL(JCLC9)
//*
//****************************************************************
//*                                                              *
//*    IMPORT A KSDS AND INDEXES TO A NEW SYSTEM                  *
//*                                                              *
//*    DATA SET AND ALTERNATE INDEXES WERE EXPORTED              *
//*    BY ONE COMPUTER SYSTEM TO ANOTHER ON WHICH                *
//*    THE DATA SETS WERE NOT PREVIOUSLY ESTABLISHED             *
//*                                                              *
//****************************************************************
//STEPA     EXEC  PGM=IDCAMS,REGION=2048K
//SYSPRINT  DD  SYSOUT=*
//SYSUDUMP  DD  SYSOUT=A
//AMSDUMP   DD  SYSOUT=A
//DD1       DD  DSN=AK00.C98.ADDREXPT,
//  UNIT=(TAPE,,DEFER),
//  DISP=(OLD,KEEP),
//  DCB=BLKSIZE=32000,
//  VOL=(PRIVATE,RETAIN,SER=033146),
//  LABEL=(1,SL)
//DD2       DD  DSN=AK00.C98.NAMEEXPT,
//  UNIT=AFF=DD1,
//  DISP=(OLD,KEEP),
//  DCB=BLKSIZE=32000,
//  VOL=(PRIVATE,RETAIN,SER=033146),
//  LABEL=(2,SL)
//DD3       DD  DSN=AK00.C98.CUSTEXPT,
//  UNIT=AFF=DD1,
//  DISP=(OLD,KEEP),
//  DCB=BLKSIZE=32000,
//  VOL=SER=033146,
//  LABEL=(3,SL)
//SYSIN     DD  *
     DELETE    MA88.C90.CUSTMAST -
               CLUSTER -
               PURGE

  SET LASTCC=0
  SET MAXCC=0
```

FIGURE C.9   MVS JCL and IDCAMS IMPORT example, importing an exported data set to a different computer system

```
DEFINE -
  CLUSTER    (    NAME(MA88.C90.CUSTMAST) -
                  VOLUMES(FSDC57) -
                  RECORDSIZE(250 250) -
                  KEYS(8 36) -
                  CYLINDERS(1 1) -
                  SHAREOPTIONS(2 3) -
                  SPEED -
                  IMBED                                    ) -
                  -
  DATA       (    NAME(MA88.C90.CUSTMAST.BASE.DATA) -
                  CONTROLINTERVALSIZE(4096) -
                  FREESPACE(18 1)                          ) -
                  -
  INDEX      (    NAME(MA88.C90.CUSTMAST.BASE.INDEX)   ) -
  CATALOG    (    SYS3.MFG.PRODCAT/FJ38AA19              )

DEFINE -
  AIX        (    NAME(MA88.C90.CUSTMAST.ADDRAIX) -
                  RELATE(MA88.C90.CUSTMAST) -
                  VOLUMES(FSDC57) -          /* RECORDSIZE (AVG   MAX   */
                  RECORDSIZE(47 79) -        /* MAX 6 OCCURRENCES SO    */
                  KEYS(26 44) -              /* 5 + AIX + (N x PRIME)   */
                  NONUNIQUEKEY -             /* GIVES 5+26+(2x8)=47     */
                  SHAREOPTIONS(2 3) -        /* AND    5+26+(6x8)=79    */
                  UNIQUE -
                  UPGRADE -
                  SPEED                                    ) -
                  -
  DATA       (    NAME(MA88.C90.CUSTMAST.ADDRAIX.DATA)  -
                  CONTROLINTERVALSIZE(4096) -
                  CYLINDERS(1 1) -
                  FREESPACE(15 15)                         ) -
                  -
  INDEX      (    NAME(MA88.C90.CUSTMAST.ADDRAIX.INDEX) ) -
  CATALOG    (    SYS3.MFG.PRODCAT/FJ38AA19              )

DEFINE -
  AIX        (    NAME(MA88.C90.CUSTMAST.NAMEAIX) -
                  RELATE(MA88.C90.CUSTMAST) -
                  VOLUMES(FSDC57) -
                  RECORDSIZE(48 48) -        /* 5 + AIX + PRIME */
                  KEYS(35 9) -               /* GIVES 5+35+8=48 */
                  UNIQUEKEY -
                  SHAREOPTIONS(2 3) -
                  UNIQUE -
                  UPGRADE -
                  SPEED                                    ) -
                  -
  DATA       (    NAME(MA88.C90.CUSTMAST.NAMEAIX.DATA)  -
                  CONTROLINTERVALSIZE(4096) -
                  CYLINDERS(1 1) -
                  FREESPACE(15 15)                         ) -
                  -
  INDEX      (    NAME(MA88.C90.CUSTMAST.NAMEAIX.INDEX) ) -
  CATALOG    (    SYS3.MFG.PRODCAT/FJ38AA19              )

IMPORT   -
         INFILE(DD3) -
         OUTDATASET(MA88.C90.CUSTMAST) -
         INTOEMPTY -
         OBJECTS( -
           (AK00.C98.CUSTMAST) -
             NEWNAME(MA88.C90.CUSTMAST) -
             VOLUMES(FSDC57) -
```

FIGURE C.9   (Continued)

```
                          (AK00.C98.CUSTMAST.BASE.DATA) -
                            NEWNAME(MA88.C90.CUSTMAST.BASE.DATA) -
                            VOLUMES(FSDC57) -
                          (AK00.C98.CUSTMAST.BASE.INDEX) -
                            NEWNAME(MA88.C90.CUSTMAST.BASE.INDEX) -
                            VOLUMES(FSDC57)                           )
                        CATALOG(SYS3.MFG.PRODCAT/FJ38AA19)

        IMPORT   -
                 INFILE(DD1) -
                 OUTDATASET(MA88.C99.CUSTMAST.ADDRAIX) -
                 OBJECTS( -
                   (AK00.C98.CUSTMAST.ADDRAIX) -
                     NEWNAME(MA88.C90.CUSTMAST.ADDRAIX) -
                     VOLUMES(FSDC57) -
                   (AK00.C98.CUSTMAST.ADDRAIX.DATA) -
                     NEWNAME(MA88.C90.CUSTMAST.ADDRAIX.DATA) -
                     VOLUMES(FSDC57) -
                   (AK00.C98.CUSTMAST.ADDRAIX.INDEX) -
                     NEWNAME(MA88.C90.CUSTMAST.ADDRAIX.INDEX) -
                     VOLUMES(FSDC57)                        )
                 CATALOG(SYS3.MFG.PRODCAT/FJ38AA19)

        IMPORT   -
                 INFILE(DD2) -
                 OUTDATASET(MA88.C90.CUSTMAST.NAMEAIX) -
                 OBJECTS( -
                   (AK00.C98.CUSTMAST.NAMEAIX) -
                     NEWNAME(MA88.C90.CUSTMAST.NAMEAIX) -
                     VOLUMES(FSDC57) -
                   (AK00.C98.CUSTMAST.NAMEAIX.DATA) -
                     NEWNAME(MA88.C90.CUSTMAST.NAMEAIX.DATA) -
                     VOLUMES(FSDC57) -
                   (AK00.C98.CUSTMAST.NAMEAIX.INDEX) -
                     NEWNAME(MA88.C90.CUSTMAST.NAMEAIX.INDEX) -
                     VOLUMES(FSDC57)                        )
                 CATALOG(SYS3.MFG.PRODCAT/FJ38AA19)
    /*
    //
```

FIGURE C.9   (Continued)

MA88.C90.CUSTMAST, and its alternate index to use these identifiers in its naming convention. It and its alternate indexes will be cataloged in SYS3.MFG.PRODCAT.

For the new system importation, PURGE has been specified and a DELETE done on the data set name specified with NEWNAME to insure that the importation will not terminate due to a duplicate data set name in the catalog. An empty data set was defined prior to the import in order to have full control over the nature of the new data set, and the import specifies the INTOEMPTY attribute. This DEFINE actually subverts the "portable data set" feature of EXPORT/IMPORT. The data set could have as readily been transferred to the new system by using a REPRO copy of it and more familiar coding to load it and rebuild the alternate indexes after the definition as in Figure 5.2. Such coding would be required in any case on the new system to perform periodic reorganization of the data set.

NOTES

1. For information on the use of IDCAMS to create, display, and delete generation data group bases, see Chapter 13 of *Practical MVS JCL For Today's Programmers* (James Janossy, John Wiley and Sons, Inc., 1987) ISBN 0-471-83648-6. That book also provides examples of the coding for IDCAMS renaming and deletion of data sets or partitioned data set members using IDCAMS.

Entry Sequenced Data Sets (EDSD) and Relative Record Data Sets (RRDS)

Entry sequenced data sets are the VSAM equivalent of sequential files, and relative record data sets are very much like the relative disk files of the Basic Direct Access Method (BDAM) and many variants of the BASIC language. Neither of these types of VSAM data sets is very much used. This appendix contains essential information about them, examples of COBOL SELECT/ASSIGN statements for programs dealing with them, and IDCAMS control statements for their definition, loading, and backup.

ENTRY SEQUENCED DATA SETS (ESDS)

Background

Entry sequenced data sets are simple sequential files. They provide no benefits beyond ordinary sequential data sets for batch access, but do suffer from certain limitations. Unlike an ordinary sequential data set, an ESDS cannot be made a member of a generation data group, and it is not supported for access on tape, but only on disk. CICS deals with an ESDS in a more powerful manner than batch COBOL and in certain specialized instances, such as for logging files, an ESDS may prove useful in an online application.

IDCAMS Operations: Defining, Loading, Copying, and Printing

Figure D.1 illustrates the JCL and IDCAMS control statements necessary to define and load an entry sequenced data set. Once defined, the ESDS can receive records written by a CICS transaction or a batch COBOL program. Since the data set by definition cannot have a primary index, no requirement exists to sort the records being loaded on any particular key field. If there is no data to initially load to the data set, the REPRO operation in Figure D.1 can copy and load a single dummy record to insure appropriate initialization for online access.

The ESDS definition is similar to that for a key sequenced data set except that the word NONINDEXED is included in the base cluster definition. NONINDEXED is synonymous with ESDS; it is unfortunate that the designers of IDCAMS syntax felt compelled to create another word when perhaps "ESDS" itself would have sufficed in a plainer fashion. INDEXED, synonymous with a key sequenced data set, is a default; if NONINDEXED is not

```
//FSBT686A   JOB AK00TEST,'DP2-JANOSSY',CLASS=T,MSGCLASS=X,
//  MSGLEVEL=(1,1),NOTIFY=BT05686
//*
//*     THIS JCL = BT05686.SOURCE.CNTL(JCLD1)
//*
//************************************************************
//*                                                          *
//*     DEFINE AND LOAD ENTRY SEQUENCED DATA SET (ESDS)      *
//*                                                          *
//************************************************************
//STEPA      EXEC  PGM=IDCAMS
//SYSPRINT   DD    SYSOUT=*
//SYSUDUMP   DD    SYSOUT=A
//DD1        DD    DSN=AK00.C98.CFUPLOGB,
//  UNIT=(TAPE,,DEFER),
//  DISP=(OLD,KEEP)
//SYSIN      DD    *
       DELETE       AK00.C98.CFUPLOG -
                    CLUSTER

       SET LASTCC=0                           /* ABOVE MAY NOT BE      */
       SET MAXCC=0                            /* FOUND; ELIMINATE RC=8 */

       DEFINE -
         CLUSTER  (   NAME(AK00.C98.CFUPLOG) -
                      VOLUMES(FSDC14) -
                      RECORDSIZE(85 85) -
                      SHAREOPTIONS(2 3) -
                      CONTROLINTERVALSIZE(4096) -
                      CYLINDERS(1 1) -
                      NONINDEXED                        ) -
                      -
         DATA     (   NAME(AK00.C98.CFUPLOG.BASE.DATA)  )

       REPRO        INFILE(DD1) -
                    OUTDATASET(AK00.C98.CFUPLOG)

       LISTCAT -
         ENTRIES  (   AK00.C98.CFUPLOG                 ) -
                  ALL
   /*
   //
```

FIGURE D.1 MVS JCL and IDCAMS control statements to define and load an entry sequenced data set (ESDS)

coded, IDCAMS will assume that the data set being defined is a KSDS and will erroneously employ the other defaults for that organization, leading to confusing problems.

Since an ESDS cannot have a primary index, only the base cluster definition and a data component are specified. An ESDS cannot have imbedded free space; the FREESPACE specification is not present. No key field can be defined for an ESDS, so no KEYS specification is present. An ESDS can receive secondary space allocation.

RECORDSIZE is coded in a manner identical to that for a KSDS. The first figure within parentheses is the average record length and the second is the maximum record length. For fixed-length records the two values are the same.

SPANNED can optionally be coded to indicate that records can be larger than the control interval size. Spanned records can cross more than one CI boundary.

REUSE can be specified with the effect that each time the data set is opened, it is treated as if it were empty. It can be opened for output and records written to it; the records will overlay the existing records as if the data set had previously contained no records.

IDCAMS REPRO can be used to copy an ESDS to an ordinary sequential file for backup or provision to another application as illustrated in Figure D.2. IDCAMS PRINT can be used to print or dump an ESDS. The JCL and control statements for these operations are identical to those for a KSDS, as illustrated in Chapter 4.

Batch COBOL Operations

An ESDS can house fixed-length or variable-length records. In order to process variable-length records, the program must provide customary file description coding for variable-length record processing and contain the logic to know the format and record length of a given record. Multiple 01 descriptions in the FD and/or OCCURS DEPENDING ON clauses and fields within record descriptions are appropriate.

An ESDS can be accessed only in a sequential manner. The defaults for both the OR-GANIZATION and the ACCESS MODE clauses are SEQUENTIAL, so neither must be coded in a SELECT/ASSIGN statement. Unlike with a KSDS, for which no prefix is used on the DDname following the ASSIGN phrase, the letters AS- must precede the DDname in a COBOL program. Since the determination of successful file open, close, and I/O actions rests with the program, a two-byte alphanumeric working storage file status field should be designated and tested after each I/O action. This is a suitable SELECT/ASSIGNMENT statement for the example ESDS:

```
SELECT LOG-FILE ASSIGN TO AS-BT2817E1
                FILE STATUS IS WS-LOGFILE-FS.
```

A corresponding MVS JCL DD statement for this file could be:

```
//BT2817E1  DD DSN=AK00.C98.CFUPLOG,
// DISP=OLD
```

An existing ESDS can be opened for INPUT, I-O, or EXTEND. INPUT allows records to be read from the ESDS. I-O allows records to be read and rewritten with the REWRITE

```
//FSBT686A  JOB AK00TEST,'DP2-JANOSSY',CLASS=T,MSGCLASS=X,
//  MSGLEVEL=(1,1),NOTIFY=BT05686
//*
//*     THIS JCL = BT05686.SOURCE.CNTL(JCLD2)
//*
//*********************************************************
//*                                                       *
//*     BACK UP AN ENTRY SEQUENCED DATA SET WITH REPRO     *
//*                                                       *
//*********************************************************
//STEPA      EXEC  PGM=IDCAMS
//SYSPRINT   DD    SYSOUT=*
//SYSUDUMP   DD    SYSOUT=A
//DDOUT      DD    DSN=AK00.C98.CFUPLOGB,
//  UNIT=(TAPE,,DEFER),
//  DISP=(OLD,KEEP),
//  DCB=(RECFM=FB,LRECL=85,BLKSIZE=32725),
//  LABEL=(1,SL,RETPD=30)
//SYSIN      DD  *
     REPRO         INDATASET(AK00.C98.CFUPLOG) -
                   OUTFILE(DDOUT)
  /*
  //
```

FIGURE D.2   MVS JCL and IDCAMS control statements to back up an entry sequenced data set

verb so long as the record length is not changed. EXTEND provides the means to add records to the end of an existing ESDS. An ESDS can also be opened for OUTPUT, but it must not yet have any records in it for this type of operation. OPEN, READ, WRITE, and REWRITE and CLOSE are the only I/O verbs permitted. Appendix G includes all file status values that may be encountered for an ESDS.

Procedure division logic for dealing with an ESDS is identical to that for dealing with sequential reading of a KSDS except for the limitations noted. Records in an ESDS cannot be deleted so the DELETE verb cannot be employed. It is not possible to start reading records in an ESDS at any point except the beginning of the file; the START verb cannot be used.

Alternate Index on an Entry Sequenced Data Set

In an often confusing manner, it is possible to create from one to 253 alternate indexes for an entry sequenced data set. The alternate index is "alternate" not in the sense of a secondary index, but in the sense that an ESDS by nature does not have any internal structure for a primary index. Assembler language and CICS can make use of an alternate index on an ESDS, but batch COBOL cannot.

An alternate index for an ESDS is really a KSDS in its own right. Each record in the alternate index data set has as its key the field regarded as a key in the ESDS record it indexes. The "pointers" in the data portion of the alternate index records are not, as with an alternate index on a KSDS, symbolic keys. Rather, they are "relative byte addresses," or, in other words, the starting byte location of the record indexed. The relative byte address, or RBA, is a four-byte binary field and may be used to access a record in an ESDS. More commonly, records in an ESDS are read in sequence, one record after another, and the RBA is not known and is of no concern.

An alternate index for an ESDS is built using exactly the same IDCAMS control statements as are used to build an alternate index for a key sequenced data set, illustrated in Chapter 5. The only difference lies in the computation of the size for the alternate index records. For a unique alternate index on a KSDS, the record size is computed by summing five bytes for overhead, the length of the alternate key field, and the length of the KSDS primary key field. For an alternate index on an ESDS the formula is:

overhead + length of alternate key + RBA field

or

5 bytes + length of alternate key + 4

For an alternate index on an ESDS with nonunique keys, the record size computation must allow four bytes for the maximum number of duplications of the key. This introduces an additional factor into the formula:

5 bytes + length of alternate key + 4 × n

where n is the maximum number of duplicates for any key value. Figure D.3 illustrates JCL and IDCAMS control statements to define and build an alternate index on an ESDS. The field to be used as a key exists as the eight bytes starting in position 22 of each record.

```
//FSBT686A  JOB AK00TEST,'DP2-JANOSSY',CLASS=T,MSGCLASS=X,
//  MSGLEVEL=(1,1),NOTIFY=BT05686
//*
//*     THIS JCL = BT05686.SOURCE.CNTL(JCLD3)
//*
//************************************************************
//*                                                          *
//*     DEFINE AND BUILD A UNIQUE KEY ALTERNATE INDEX        *
//*     ON AN EXISTING ENTRY SEQUENCED DATA SET              *
//*                                                          *
//************************************************************
//STEPA     EXEC  PGM=IDCAMS
//SYSPRINT   DD   SYSOUT=*
//SYSUDUMP   DD   SYSOUT=A
//WORKSRT1   DD   DSN=AK00.C98.IDCUT1,
//  UNIT=SYSDA,                         'AIX IDCAMS WORKFILE;
//  DISP=OLD,                           'VSAM REQUIRES DISP=OLD
//  AMP='AMORG',                        'EVEN THOUGH DOES NOT
//  VOL=SER=FSDC03                      'EXIST PRIOR TO USE!
//WORKSRT2   DD   DSN=AK00.C98.IDCUT2,
//  UNIT=SYSDA,                         'AIX IDCAMS WORKFILE;
//  DISP=OLD,                           'VSAM REQUIRES DISP=OLD
//  AMP='AMORG',                        'EVEN THOUGH DOES NOT
//  VOL=SER=FSDC03                      'EXIST PRIOR TO USE!
//SYSIN      DD   *
                                        /* HOUSEKEEPING DELETES */
      DELETE       AK00.C98.CFUPLOG.SRNOAIX -
                   PURGE
                   AK00.C98.IDCUT1  -
                   PURGE
                   AK00.C98.IDCUT2  -
                   PURGE
    SET LASTCC=0                        /* SOME ABOVE MAY NOT BE */
    SET MAXCC=0                         /* FOUND; ELIMINATE RC=8 */
      DEFINE -
        AIX      (   NAME(AK00.C98.CFUPLOG.SRNOAIX) -
                     RELATE(AK00.C98.CFUPLOG) -
                     VOLUMES(FSDC14) -
                     RECORDSIZE(17 17) -     /* 5 + AIX + 4      */
                     KEYS(8 22) -            /* GIVES 5+8+4=17   */
                     UNIQUEKEY -             /* (8 BYTE AIX)     */
                     CYLINDERS(2 1) -
                     SHAREOPTIONS(2 3) -
                     UNIQUE -
                     UPGRADE -
                     SPEED -
                     IMBED                           ) -
                 -
        DATA     (   NAME(AK00.C98.CFUPLOG.SRNOAIX.DATA)  -
                     CONTROLINTERVALSIZE(4096) -
                     FREESPACE(15 15)                ) -
                 -
        INDEX    (   NAME(AK00.C98.CFUPLOG.SRNOAIX.INDEX) )

      BLDINDEX     INDATASET(AK00.C98.CFUPLOG) -
                   OUTDATASET(AK00.C98.CFUPLOG.SRNOAIX) -
                   WORKFILES(WORKSRT1 WORKSRT2)
      DEFINE -
        PATH     (   NAME(AK00.C98.CFUPLOG.SRNOAIX.PATH) -
                     PATHENTRY(AK00.C98.CFUPLOG.SRNOAIX)   )
      LISTCAT -
        ENTRIES  (   AK00.C98.CFUPLOG -
                     AK00.C98.CFUPLOG.SRNOAIX      ) -
                   ALL
/*
//
```

FIGURE D.3 MVS JCL and IDCAMS control statements to build an alternate index on an entry sequenced data set

RELATIVE RECORD DATA SETS (RRDS)

Background

Relative record data sets are arranged as fixed-length slots, end to end, similar to numbered pigeonholes in an old roll-top desk. They can house only fixed-length records. While the records are accessible at random, you must know the number of the record, relative to the first record which is numbered as zero, in order to read a specific record. As with the obsolete direct files of the Basic Direct Access Method (BDAM) this usually necessitates the use of a hashing algorithm to generate a record number from a true symbolic key contained within a record. Also as with direct files, this arrangement is simply too cumbersome and fraught with unreliability to be relevant to modern business data processing.

Why does VSAM provide the relative record data set organization at all? VSAM was introduced in 1973, quite a long time ago in terms of software and machine development. At that time VSAM was envisioned as a support mechanism to supplant a collection of access methods then in popular use. While the major focus of this process was ISAM, replaced by the KSDS, VSAM made provision to replace relative and direct files as well. The fact that the RRDS organization is unpopular reflects not on a shortcoming of VSAM but on the nature of contemporary keyed access requirements, which have surpassed reliance on relative file organizations in general. While relative files provide random access with the fewest possible machine I/O actions, this does not compensate for their lack of suitability for nearly all business data processing activities.

IDCAMS Operations: Defining, Loading, Copying and Printing

Figure D.4 illustrates the JCL and IDCAMS control statements necessary to define and load a relative record data set. The data set by definition cannot have an index, and no requirement exists to sort the records being loaded on any particular key field. If there is no data to initially load to the data set, the REPRO operation in Figure D.4 is omitted.

The definition is similar to that for an entry sequenced data set except that the word NUMBERED is specified instead of NONINDEXED. Here too it would have been plainer had IDCAMS syntax been designed to accept "RRDS" as opposed to "NUMBERED" because the latter word is really a synonym for RRDS.

The RRDS definition cannot make use of the KEYS specification. Only the base cluster and the data component are specified since no primary index will be present. Unlike the case with an ESDS, no alternate indexes can be built for an RRDS. Records can be logically deleted from an RRDS, freeing the record slot for use by another record, but free space cannot be defined. An RRDS can receive secondary space allocation.

A relative record data set can support only fixed-length records. The RECORDSIZE specification therefore must be coded with the average and maximum record length identical.

IDCAMS REPRO can be used to copy an RRDS to an ordinary sequential file for backup or provision to another application as illustrated in Figure D.5. IDCAMS PRINT can be used to print or dump an RRDS. The JCL and control statements for these operations are identical to that for a KSDS as illustrated in Chapter 4.

Batch COBOL Operations

Sequential and random access operations are possible with a relative record data set, but their scope is more limited than with a key sequenced data set. The I/O verbs OPEN, READ, REWRITE, WRITE, START, READ NEXT, DELETE, and CLOSE are available.

```
//FSBT686A  JOB AK00TEST,'DP2-JANOSSY',CLASS=T,MSGCLASS=X,
//  MSGLEVEL=(1,1),NOTIFY=BT05686
//*
//*     THIS JCL = BT05686.SOURCE.CNTL(JCLD4)
//*
//************************************************************
//*                                                          *
//*     DEFINE AND LOAD RELATIVE RECORD DATA SET (RRDS)      *
//*                                                          *
//************************************************************
//STEPA      EXEC  PGM=IDCAMS
//SYSPRINT   DD    SYSOUT=*
//SYSUDUMP   DD    SYSOUT=A
//DD1        DD    DSN=AK00.C98.XAMPLEBK,
//  UNIT=(TAPE,,DEFER),
//  DISP=(OLD,KEEP)
//SYSIN      DD    *
     DELETE      AK00.C98.XAMPLERR -
                 CLUSTER

     SET LASTCC=0                        /* ABOVE MAY NOT BE    */
     SET MAXCC=0                         /* FOUND; ELIMINATE RC=8 */

     DEFINE -
        CLUSTER   (   NAME(AK00.C98.XAMPLERR) -
                      VOLUMES(FSDC14) -
                      RECORDSIZE(92 92) -
                      SHAREOPTIONS(2 3) -
                      CONTROLINTERVALSIZE(4096) -
                      CYLINDERS(1 1) -
                      NUMBERED                         ) -
                      -
        DATA      (   NAME(AK00.C98.XAMPLERR.BASE.DATA)   )

     REPRO        INFILE(DD1) -
                  OUTDATASET(AK00.C98.XAMPLERR)

     LISTCAT -
        ENTRIES   (   AK00.C98.XAMPLERR          ) -
                  ALL
/*
//
```

FIGURE D.4 MVS JCL and IDCAMS control statements to define and load a relative record data set (RRDS)

```
//FSBT686A  JOB AK00TEST,'DP2-JANOSSY',CLASS=T,MSGCLASS=X,
//  MSGLEVEL=(1,1),NOTIFY=BT05686
//*
//*     THIS JCL = BT05686.SOURCE.CNTL(JCLD5)
//*
//************************************************************
//*                                                          *
//*     BACK UP A RELATIVE RECORD DATA SET WITH REPRO        *
//*                                                          *
//************************************************************
//STEPA      EXEC  PGM=IDCAMS
//SYSPRINT   DD    SYSOUT=*
//SYSUDUMP   DD    SYSOUT=A
//DDOUT      DD    DSN=AK00.C98.XAMPLEBK,
//  UNIT=(TAPE,,DEFER),
//  DISP=(NEW,CATLG,DELETE),
//  DCB=(RECFM=FB,LRECL=92,BLKSIZE=32752),
//  LABEL=(1,SL,RETPD=30)
//SYSIN      DD    *
     REPRO        INDATASET(AK00.C98.XAMPLERR) -
                  OUTFILE(DDOUT)
/*
//
```

FIGURE D.5 MVS JCL and IDCAMS control statements to back up a relative record data set

Which of these can be employed in a given program is dictated by the specifications made in the SELECT/ASSIGN statement of the program and the manner in which the data set is opened.

SELECT/ASSIGN   The SELECT/ASSIGN statement for a relative record data set is similar to that for a key sequenced data set in that no prefix is used on the DDname:

```
SELECT REF-FILE ASSIGN TO BT5413E1
                ORGANIZATION IS RELATIVE
                ACCESS MODE IS RANDOM
                RELATIVE KEY IS WS-RELKEY
                FILE STATUS IS WS-REFFILE-FS.
```

ORGANIZATION must be coded as RELATIVE. ACCESS MODE may be sequential, random, or dynamic; sequential is the default. RELATIVE KEY must be an unsigned integer field in working storage, not within the RRDS records. In order to access a particular record, its relative record number must be placed into the working storage field designated as the relative key before performing the read. Since the determination of successful file open, close, and I/O actions rests with the program, a two-byte working storage file status field should be designated and tested after each I/O action.

A corresponding MVS JCL DD statement for this file could be:

```
//BT5413E1  DD DSN=AK00.C98.XAMPLERR,
// DISP=OLD
```

OPEN   A relative record data set can be opened for INPUT, OUTPUT, or I-O, but not for EXTEND as with ESDS. Because records can be written into specific record slots, it is possible for some slots to be empty. OPEN for either INPUT or I-O positions the data set on the first record slot housing a record, skipping any empty slots at the beginning of the data set.

READ   The options and outcome of a read differ, depending on whether the SELECT/ ASSIGN statement indicates sequential or random/dynamic access. For SEQUENTIAL access, READ with AT END may be used, and each read will obtain the next record slot that contains a record—slots into which no records have been written are skipped by the read. The field specified as the relative key is updated by VSAM with each read and contains the relative record number of the record last read. It is thus possible to know after a read the relative record number of the record present.

For RANDOM or DYNAMIC access, READ is coded with the INVALID KEY phrase, or file status checking is performed in its stead. The number of the record to be read must be placed into the designated relative key field in working storage before the READ is attempted. If the record slot read with a given record number does not contain a record, a file status of 23 is returned meaning "no record with this relative key."

REWRITE   REWRITE allows return of a record to the data set. The record is written back to the same record slot. To use REWRITE, the data set must be opened for I/O. It is possible to use REWRITE even if the SELECT/ASSIGN statement carries ACCESS MODE IS SEQUENTIAL; in this case, the record rewritten is the last one read.

REWRITE without first reading a record is unusual but is permitted when the SELECT/ ASSIGN has been coded ACCESS MODE IS RANDOM or ACCESS MODE IS DYNAMIC. In this case the value placed in the designated relative key field in working storage determines the record slot that will receive the record being rewritten.

WRITE   WRITE can be executed only if the data set is opened for OUTPUT or I-O. The options available differ, however, depending on the combination of access mode and open specification.

When the SELECT/ASSIGN statement is coded ACCESS IS SEQUENTIAL and the data set is open for OUTPUT, records are written to the data set placing each in the next sequential record slot, starting with the first, slot zero. With ACCESS IS SEQUENTIAl the data set cannot be opened for I-O.

When the SELECT/ASSIGN statement is coded ACCESS IS RANDOM or ACCESS IS DYNAMIC, the data set can be opened for OUTPUT or for I-O. When opened for OUTPUT or I-O with this access mode, the relative record number identifying the slot to house a record must be placed into the relative key field before the write. The record is written into the designated slot if the slot is empty. If the slot is already occupied, INVALID KEY and a file status value of 22 is received, indicating that a record already exists in the designated record slot.

DELETE   DELETE can be executed in SEQUENTIAL access mode; the record read immediately prior to the delete is affected. For I-O and DYNAMIC access modes, the value in the relative key field dictates the record to be deleted.

DELETE causes a logical deletion only and the record slot remains after the action. Another record can be written into the slot in I-O or DYNAMIC access mode by placing the record slot number in the relative key field prior to the write.

START and READ/NEXT   It is possible to execute a START in either SEQUENTIAL or I-O access mode. The syntax of the START verb is identical to that for a key sequenced data set as illustrated in Chapter 7.

In a START using the KEY IS phrase, the data name in that phrase and the equal, greater than, or less than condition specified dictates where the file is positioned for the next READ or READ NEXT action. With a START verb lacking the optional KEY IS and data name phrase, it is implied that the start should occur as if the verb had been specified "KEY IS EQUAL" to the contents of the defined relative key field.

Starting a file establishes a positioning mechanism known as the "current record pointer," relevant only to READ or READ/NEXT actions. READ is used to input records when ACCESS MODE IS SEQUENTIAL has been specified in the SELECT/ASSIGN statement. When the access mode is RANDOM or I-O, READ/NEXT is used. The inputting action obtains the contents of the next record slot, according to the current record pointer, that contains a record. The access will then automatically move the current record pointer to the next record slot that contains a record.

An unsuccessful START evidenced by receipt of INVALID KEY or a file status value denoting I/O failure leaves the current record pointer undefined. It must be reestablished with a successful START or random READ prior to additional sequential read actions.

LINEAR DATA-IN-VIRTUAL DATA SETS

Announced in 1987, linear data sets allow access to virtual storage for the purpose of storing and directly manipulating large arrays. Assembler, FORTRAN, and PL/I, but not COBOL, can access linear data sets using special "Data-In-Virtual" assembler language macro instructions or language calls.

The records placed into a linear data set must be fixed length and are accessed based on location, not a symbolic key. Linear data sets are similar to Basic Direct Access Method (BDAM) or VSAM relative record (RRDS) data sets. For appropriate applications they can significantly speed processing since an entire file of data is read into what appears to be

```
//FSBT686A  JOB AK00TEST,'DP2-JANOSSY',CLASS=E,MSGCLASS=X,
// MSGLEVEL=(1,1),NOTIFY=BT05686
//*
//*    THIS JCL = BT05686.SOURCE.CNTL(JCLFD6)
//*
//************************************************************
//*                                                          *
//*    DEFINE A LINEAR (DATA IN VIRTUAL) DATA SET            *
//*    FOR ICF CATALOG ENVIRONMENT ONLY                      *
//*                                                          *
//************************************************************
//STEPA     EXEC  PGM=IDCAMS
//SYSPRINT  DD    SYSOUT=*
//SYSUDUMP  DD    SYSOUT=A
//SYSIN     DD    *
       DEFINE -
         CLUSTER   (  NAME(AK25.C00.DIVDATA) -
                      VOLUMES(FSDC42) -
                      CYLINDERS(20 20) -
                      SHAREOPTIONS(1 3) -
                      LINEAR                        )
```

FIGURE D.6   Allocating a linear data set ("Data-In-Virtual") with IDCAMS

contiguous memory. The access method houses this data in the same way that virtual memory is handled by the operating system, and I/O during program operation is minimized.

A linear data set is a VSAM data set and is allocated using IDCAMS. Once allocated, however, it is not accessed using ordinary VSAM commands and control statements, but via special Data-In-Virtual functions. Allocation of a linear data set can be done with JCL and IDCAMS control statements as illustrated in Figure D.6.

Linear data sets and their use are described in the following IBM publications:

GG66-0259	An Introduction to Data-In-Virtual
GC28-1154	MVS/Extended Architecture Supervisor and Macro Instructions
GC26-4135	MVS/XA Integrated Catalog: Access Method Services Reference
LY28-1655	MVS/XA SLL: Data-In-Virtual

Space Charts for 3330, 3350, and 3380 disks

The three charts provided here provide in one location the reference items needed to manually develop and refine record size, control interval, control area, and space allocation control statements for VSAM data sets. Figure E.1 provides an overall summary of disk device characteristics spanning the time period from the introduction of the System/360 to the present. Figure E.2 indicates the physical record size obtained, control intervals per control area, and the percentage control area utilization for each of the valid control intervals sizes for 3330, 3350, and 3380 disks. Figure E.3 is a table of raw block size and track capacities for these three widely used disk devices, for data sets with and without hardware keys.

Figure E.1 originally appeared in Appendix G of *Practical MVS JCL for Today's Programmers* (James Janossy, John Wiley and Sons, Inc., 1987) ISBN 0-471-83648-6, and is reproduced here with the permission of the publisher.

DISK DEVICE TYPES AND CHARACTERISTICS	2314	3330 Mod-1	3330 Mod-11	3350	3380	3380 Mod-E
Year available	1964	1972	1973	1977	1981	1985
Removable media?	yes	yes	yes	no	no	no
Capacity in megabytes	29.1	100	200	317.5	630.2	1,260.4
Number of tracks	4,000	7,676	15,352	16,650	13,275	26,550
Number of cylinders	200	404	808	555	885	1,770
Tracks per cylinder	20	19	19	30	15	15
Bytes per track	7,294	13,030	13,030	19,069	47,476	47,476
Bytes per cylinder	145,880	247,570	247,570	572,070	712,140	712,140
PDS directory blocks per track	17	28	28	36	46	46
VTOC DSCB records per track	25	39	39	47	53	53
Average head movement time, in milliseconds	75	30	30	25	16	16
Media rotation time, in milliseconds	25	16.7	16.7	16.7	16.7	16.7
Data transfer rate, megabytes per second	.312	.806	.806	1.1	3.0/6.0	3.0/6.0

FIGURE E.1   Disk device types and characteristics

KSDS Space Utilization Chart -- 3330 Disk Device

CI Size	Physical Rec Size	IMBED		NOIMBED	
		CIs per CA	CA Utilization	CIs per CA	CA Utilization
512	512	360	.83	380	.83
1,024	1,024	198	.92	209	.92
1,536	512	120	.83	126	.83
2,048	2,048	108	1.00	114	1.00
2,560	512	72	.83	75	.83
3,072	1,024	66	.92	69	.91
3,584	512	51	.83	54	.83
4,096	4,096	54	1.00	57	1.00
4,608	512	40	.83	42	.83
5,120	1,024	39	.90	41	.90
5,632	512	32	.81	43	.82
6,144	2,048	36	1.00	38	1.00
6,656	512	27	.81	29	.83
7,168	1,024	28	.91	29	.89
7,680	512	24	.83	25	.82
8,192	4,096	27	1.00	28	.98
10,240	2,048	21	.97	22	.96
12,288	4,096	18	1.00	19	1.00
14,336	2,048	15	.97	16	.98
16,384	4,096	13	.96	14	.98
18,432	2,048	12	1.00	12	.95
20,480	4,096	10	.93	11	.96
22,528	2,048	9	.92	10	.96
24,576	4,096	9	1.00	9	.95
26,624	2,048	8	.96	8	.91
28,672	4,096	7	.91	8	.98
30,720	2,048	7	.97	7	.92
32,768	4,096	6	.89	7	.98

FIGURE E.2   Reference table of control intervals per control area for each control interval size, and control area utilization percentages for IMBED/NOIMBED options

KSDS Space Utilization Chart -- 3350 Disk Device

CI Size	Physical Rec Size	IMBED CIs per CA	IMBED CA Utilization	NOIMBED CIs per CA	NOIMBED CA Utilization
512	512	783	.84	810	.84
1,024	1,024	435	.94	450	.94
1,536	512	261	.84	270	.84
2,048	2,048	232	1.00	240	1.00
2,560	512	156	.84	162	.84
3,072	1,024	145	.94	150	.94
3,584	512	111	.84	115	.84
4,096	4,096	116	1.00	120	1.00
4,608	512	87	.84	90	.84
5,120	1,024	87	.94	90	.94
5,632	512	71	.84	73	.84
6,144	2,048	77	1.00	80	1.00
6,656	512	60	.84	62	.84
7,168	1,024	62	.94	64	.93
7,680	512	52	.84	54	.84
8,192	4,096	58	1.00	60	1.00
10,240	2,048	46	.99	48	1.00
12,288	4,096	38	.98	40	1.00
14,336	2,048	33	1.00	34	.99
16,384	4,096	29	1.00	30	1.00
18,432	2,048	25	.97	26	.98
20,480	4,096	23	.99	24	1.00
22,528	2,048	21	1.00	21	.96
24,576	4,096	19	.98	20	1.00
26,624	2,048	17	.95	18	.98
28,672	4,096	16	.97	17	.99
30,720	2,048	15	.97	16	1.00
32,768	4,096	14	.97	15	1.00

FIGURE E.2   (Continued)

KSDS Space Utilization Chart -- 3380 Disk Device

CI Size	Physical Rec Size	IMBED		NOIMBED	
		CIs per CA	CA Utilization	CIs per CA	CA Utilization
512	512	644	.58	690	.58
1,024	1,024	434	.78	465	.78
1,536	512	214	.57	230	.58
2,048	2,048	252	.90	270	.90
2,560	512	128	.57	138	.58
3,072	1,024	144	.77	155	.78
3,584	512	92	.58	98	.57
4,096	4,096	140	1.00	150	1.00
4,608	512	71	.57	76	.57
5,120	1,024	86	.77	93	.78
5,632	512	58	.57	62	.57
6,144	2,048	84	.90	90	.90
6,656	512	49	.57	53	.57
7,168	1,024	62	.78	66	.77
7,680	512	42	.56	46	.58
8,192	4,096	70	1.00	75	1.00
10,240	2,048	50	.89	54	.90
12,288	4,096	46	.99	50	1.00
14,336	2,048	36	.90	38	.89
16,384	4,096	35	1.00	37	.99
18,432	2,048	28	.90	30	.90
20,480	4,096	28	1.00	30	1.00
22,528	2,048	22	.86	24	.88
24,576	4,096	23	.99	25	1.00
26,624	2,048	19	.88	20	.87
28,672	4,096	20	1.00	21	.98
30,720	2,048	16	.86	18	.90
32,768	4,096	17	.97	18	.96

FIGURE E.2 (Continued)

RAW TRACK CAPACITY FOR 3330, 3350, AND 3380 DISKS

Blocks per track	3330		3350		3380	
	Max block unkeyed	Max block keyed	Max block unkeyed	Max block keyed	Max block unkeyed	Max block keyed
1	13,030	12,974	19,069	18,987	47,476	47,240
2	6,447	6,391	9,442	9,360	23,476	23,240
3	4,253	4,197	6,233	6,151	15,476	15,240
4	3,156	3,100	4,628	4,546	11,476	11,240
5	2,498	2,442	3,665	3,583	9,076	8,840
6	2,059	2,003	3,024	2,942	7,476	7,240
7	1,745	1,689	2,565	2,483	6,356	6,120
8	1,510	1,454	2,221	2,139	5,492	5,256
9	1,327	1,271	1,954	1,872	4,820	4,584
10	1,181	1,125	1,740	1,658	4,276	4,040
11	1,061	1,005	1,565	1,483	3,860	3,624
12	962	906	1,419	1,337	3,476	3,240
13	877	821	1,296	1,214	3,188	2,952
14	805	749	1,190	1,108	2,932	2,696
15	742	686	1,098	1,016	2,676	2,440
16	687	631	1,018	936	2,484	2,248
17	639	583	947	865	2,324	2,088
18	596	540	884	802	2,164	1,928
19	557	501	828	746	2,004	1,768
20	523	467	777	695	1,876	1,640
21	491	435	731	649	1,780	1,544
22	463	407	690	608	1,684	1,448
23	437	381	652	570	1,588	1,352
24	413	357	617	535	1,492	1,256
25	391	335	585	503	1,396	1,160
26	371	315	555	473	1,332	1,096
27	352	296	528	446	1,268	1,032
28	335	279	502	420	1,204	968
29	318	262	478	396	1,140	904
30	303	247	456	374	1,076	840

Notes:

1. On this chart "keyed" refers to records that carry physical keys, not records that exist in a key sequenced data set. Physical keys are contained in additional space not part of the data content defined for the record, and are used by ISAM and other older system software. Block size information for keyed records is provided here only to aid in ISAM to VSAM conversion tasks, as discussed in Chapter 10. The "unkeyed" column should be used for any computations dealing with VSAM data sets.

2. A block can consist of one or more logical records.

3. Track size on a 3380 exceeds the MVS I/O block size limit of 32,760 bytes and single blocks of this size are not available through normal programming methods. Use 23,476 as the maximum attainable block size for 3380 disk devices, which will place two blocks on each track.

4. A maximum block size of 6,233 on a 3350 establishes the "compromise" target block size for a mixture of 3330, 3350, and 3380 devices. This target provides for housing two blocks on a 3330 track, three blocks on a 3350 track, and seven blocks on a 3380 track. The maximum efficiency of storage for a block of 6,233 bytes is 95.6% on a 3330, 98% on a 3350, and 91.9% on a 3380.

FIGURE E.3 Raw disk track capacity for 3330, 3350, and 3380 devices for data sets with and without hardware keys

Source Code for KSDS Design and Monitoring Tools

Chapters 2, 3, 6, and 8 have mentioned the use of computational TSO command lists (CLISTs), COBOL programs for LISTCAT output summarization, and a program to evaluate key range spreads to aid in key sequenced data set work. This appendix contains the source code for these tools. These items, as well as JCL to install them, are also available at nominal cost on diskette for upload to a mainframe, as described in Appendix A.

COMPUTATIONAL CLISTS

VSAMCISZ

VSAMCISZ, listed in Figure F.1, is a CLIST that calculates and lists the number of records that will fit in each valid CI size for a specific record length, disk device, and IMBED option. The most efficient CI size for both online and batch usage is highlighted. Two assumptions made by the CLIST are that the CA size will be one cylinder and that the record length is fixed or a reasonable average.

The TSO CLIST language does not provide a universal screen clear function. The only suggested modification that should be made to VSAMCISZ before you use it is to include a call to your installation's own CLIST screen clear function at the point marked by the comment:

```
/* CALL PROGRAM TO CLEAR THE SCREEN */
```

Clearing the screen prior to prompting for record length, device type, and IMBED option allows the prompts, responses, and CLIST output to fit on one 24-line TSO screen. A single hardcopy print is then easy to create for documentation purposes.

VSAMCISZ is invoked by name at the TSO READY mode function or on the TSO/ISPF command line by prefacing the name with "TSO":

```
COMMAND  = = = > TSO VSAMCISZ
```

If you prefer to execute it from your own TSO CLIST library rather than installing it into the installation default CLIST library, you can use it by entering:

```
/*                                                    */
/*  TSO CLIST  VSAMCISZ    BY RICH GUZIK    AUGUST, 1988   */
/*                                                    */
/*  FOR YOUR CONVENIENCE THIS ITEM IS AVAILABLE IN MACHINE   */
/*  READABLE FORM FOR UPLOADING TO AN IBM MAINFRAME.     */


/*                                                    */
PROC 0
CONTROL NOFLUSH NOMSG END(ENDO)
START:     SET &ANSWER EQ Y
/* CLIST TO LIST ALL VALID CISIZES AND MAX REC PER CA FOR A RECSIZE */
/* ------------------**** VSAMCISZ ***------------------------ */
       SET &IMBED    = IMBED  /* IMBED OR NOIMBED */
       SET &RECSIZE  = 0      /* RECORD LENGTH */
       SET &ANSWER   = Y      /* ANSWER TO ALL ?'S */
       SET &DASD     = 0      /* DEVICE TYPE */
       SET &TRACK    = 0      /* AVAILABLE DATA TRACKS PER CYL */
       SET &CIOVERHD = 10     /* CI CONTROL INFORMATION */
       SET &RECPERCA1 = 0     /* RECORDS PER CA COLUMN 1 */
       SET &RECPERCA2 = 0     /* RECORDS PER CA COLUMN 2 */
       SET &RECPERCI1 = 0     /* RECORDS PER CI COLUMN 1 */
       SET &RECPERCI2 = 0     /* RECORDS PER CI COLUMN 2 */
       SET &RECPERTRK1 = 0    /* RECORDS PER TRK COLUMN 1 */
       SET &RECPERTRK2 = 0    /* RECORDS PER TRK COLUMN 2 */
       SET &ONLINECI = 0      /* BEST RECORD PER CI ONLINE */
       SET &BESTOCI  = 0      /* BEST CISIZE FOR ONLINE */
       SET &BATCHCI  = 0      /* BEST RECORD PER CI BATCH */
       SET &BESTBCI  = 0      /* BEST CISIZE FOR BATCH */
       /* CALL CLEAR SCREEN PROGRAM HERE */
       WRITE    PRACTICAL VSAM - JOHN WILEY AND SONS, 1988 - ISBN 0-471--
85107-8
       WRITE    BEST CI SIZE FOR FIXED LENGTH RECORD KSDS WITH CA SIZE -
ONE CYLINDER
       WRITE         BY &SYSUID AT &SYSTIME ON &SYSDATE
ERECSIZE: SET &ANSWER EQ Y
       WRITENR ENTER RECSIZE ==>
       READ &RECSIZE
       IF &RECSIZE EQ 0 -
          THEN  GOTO BADRECSZ
       IF &RECSIZE GT 32761 -
          THEN  GOTO BADRECSZ
       IF &RECSIZE LT 12 -
          THEN  GOTO BADRECSZ
       ELSE     GOTO IFIMBED
BADRECSZ:   SET &ANSWER EQ Y
       WRITE RECSIZE ( &RECSIZE ) IS INVALID
       WRITENR DO YOU WANT TO TRY AGAIN - Y OR N ==>
       READ &ANSWER
       IF &ANSWER NE Y -
          THEN DO
                WRITE GOODBYE
                END
          ENDO
       ELSE  GOTO ERECSIZE
IFIMBED:    SET &ANSWER EQ Y
       WRITENR WILL YOU USE THE IMBED OPTION - Y OR N ==>
       READ &ANSWER
       IF &ANSWER NE Y -
          THEN SET &IMBED = NOIMBED
DISKTYPE:   SET &ANSWER EQ Y
/* PROMPT FOR TYPE OF DISK - 3330, 3350 OR 3380 */
       WRITENR ENTER DEVICE TYPE - 3330, 3350 OR 3380 ==>
       READ &DASD
       IF &DASD EQ 3330 -
          THEN  GOTO THIRTY
       IF &DASD EQ 3350 -
          THEN  GOTO FIFTY
       IF &DASD EQ 3380 -
          THEN  GOTO EIGHTY
       WRITE VALID RESPONSES ARE 3330, 3350 AND 3380
       WRITENR DO YOU WANT TO TRY AGAIN - Y OR N ==>
       READ &ANSWER
       IF &ANSWER EQ Y -
          THEN  GOTO DISKTYPE
       ELSE DO
                WRITE GOODBYE
                END
          ENDO
THIRTY:    SET &ANSWER EQ Y
/* PROCESS FOR 3330 DASD WITH NOIMBED */
       WRITE CISIZE   REC/CI   REC/TRK   REC/CA  -
CISIZE   REC/CI   REC/TRK   REC/CA
       IF &IMBED = IMBED -
          THEN GOTO ITHIRTY
       SET &C512 = 380
       SET &C1024 = 209
       SET &C1536 = 126
       SET &C2048 = 114
       SET &C2560 = 76
       SET &C3072 = 69
       SET &C3584 = 54
       SET &C4096 = 57
       SET &C4608 = 42
       SET &C5120 = 41
       SET &C5632 = 34
       SET &C6144 = 38
       SET &C6656 = 29
       SET &C7168 = 29
       SET &C7680 = 25
       SET &C8192 = 28
```

```
       SET &C10240 = 22
       SET &C12288 = 19
       SET &C14336 = 16
       SET &C16384 = 14
       SET &C18432 = 12
       SET &C20480 = 11
       SET &C22528 = 10
       SET &C24576 = 9
       SET &C26624 = 8
       SET &C28672 = 8
       SET &C30720 = 7
       SET &C32768 = 7
       SET &TRACK = 19
       GOTO C8512
ITHIRTY:   SET &ANSWER EQ Y
/* PROCESS FOR 3330 DASD WITH IMBED */
       SET &C512 = 360
       SET &C1024 = 198
       SET &C1536 = 120
       SET &C2048 = 108
       SET &C2560 = 72
       SET &C3072 = 66
       SET &C3584 = 51
       SET &C4096 = 54
       SET &C4608 = 40
       SET &C5120 = 39
       SET &C5632 = 32
       SET &C6144 = 36
       SET &C6656 = 27
       SET &C7168 = 28
       SET &C7680 = 24
       SET &C8192 = 27
       SET &C10240 = 21
       SET &C12288 = 18
       SET &C14336 = 15
       SET &C16384 = 13
       SET &C18432 = 12
       SET &C20480 = 10
       SET &C22528 = 9
       SET &C24576 = 9
       SET &C26624 = 8
       SET &C28672 = 7
       SET &C30720 = 7
       SET &C32768 = 6
       SET &TRACK = 18
       GOTO C8512
FIFTY:     SET &ANSWER EQ Y
/* PROCESS FOR 3350 DASD WITH NOIMBED */
       WRITE CISIZE   REC/CI   REC/TRK   REC/CA  -
CISIZE   REC/CI   REC/TRK   REC/CA
       IF &IMBED = IMBED -
          THEN GOTO IFIFTY
       SET &C512 = 810
       SET &C1024 = 450
       SET &C1536 = 270
       SET &C2048 = 240
       SET &C2560 = 162
       SET &C3072 = 150
       SET &C3584 = 115
       SET &C4096 = 120
       SET &C4608 = 90
       SET &C5120 = 90
       SET &C5632 = 73
       SET &C6144 = 80
       SET &C6656 = 62
       SET &C7168 = 64
       SET &C7680 = 54
       SET &C8192 = 60
       SET &C10240 = 48
       SET &C12288 = 40
       SET &C14336 = 34
       SET &C16384 = 30
       SET &C18432 = 26
       SET &C20480 = 24
       SET &C22528 = 21
       SET &C24576 = 20
       SET &C26624 = 18
       SET &C28672 = 17
       SET &C30720 = 15
       SET &C32768 = 15
       SET &TRACK = 30
       GOTO C8512
IFIFTY:    SET &ANSWER EQ Y
/* PROCESS FOR 3350 DASD WITH IMBED */
       SET &C512 = 783
       SET &C1024 = 435
       SET &C1536 = 261
       SET &C2048 = 232
       SET &C2560 = 156
       SET &C3072 = 145
       SET &C3584 = 111
       SET &C4096 = 116
       SET &C4608 = 87
       SET &C5120 = 87
       SET &C5632 = 71
       SET &C6144 = 77
       SET &C6656 = 60
       SET &C7168 = 62
       SET &C7680 = 52
       SET &C8192 = 58
       SET &C10240 = 46
```

FIGURE F.1   Source code for TSO CLIST VASMCISZ, which automates the calculation of KSDS control interval size (listed two columns per page)

```
        SET &C12288 = 38                                    SET &RECPERCI2 = ( ( 1024 - &CIOVERHD ) / ( &RECSIZE ) )
        SET &C14336 = 33                                    SET &RECPERCA2 = &RECPERCI2 * &C1024
        SET &C16384 = 29                                    SET &RECPERTRK2 = &RECPERCA2 / &TRACK
        SET &C18432 = 25                          WL1:    SET &ANSWER EQ Y
        SET &C20480 = 23                              WRITE      512       &RECPERCI1     &RECPERTRK1     &RECPERCA1  -
        SET &C22528 = 21                          1,024       &RECPERCI2     &RECPERTRK2     &RECPERCA2
        SET &C24576 = 19                              IF &RECPERCA1 GT &ONLINECI -
        SET &C26624 = 17                                 THEN  DO
        SET &C28672 = 16                                             SET &ONLINECI = &RECPERCA1
        SET &C30720 = 15                                             SET &BESTOCI EQ 512
        SET &C32768 = 14                                          ENDO
        SET &TRACK = 29                               IF &RECPERCA2 GT &ONLINECI -
        GOTO C8512                                       THEN  DO
EIGHTY:   SET &ANSWER EQ Y                                         SET &ONLINECI = &RECPERCA2
/* PROCESS FOR 3380 DASD WITH NOIMBED */                          SET &BESTOCI EQ 1024
        WRITE CISIZE   REC/CI   REC/TRK   REC/CA                 ENDO
CISIZE   REC/CI   REC/TRK   REC/CA           C81536:    SET &ANSWER EQ Y
        IF &IMBED = IMBED -                              SET &CIOVERHD = 10
             THEN GOTO IEIGHTY                           IF ( 1536  - &RECSIZE ) GT 6 AND ( 1536  - &RECSIZE ) LT 10 -
        SET &C512 = 690                                     THEN SET &CIOVERHD = 7
        SET &C1024 = 465                                 IF &RECSIZE GT ( 1536 - &CIOVERHD ) -
        SET &C1536 = 230                                    THEN  DO
        SET &C2048 = 270                                             SET &RECPERCA1 = 0
        SET &C2560 = 138                                             GOTO C82048
        SET &C3072 = 155                                          ENDO
        SET &C3584 = 98                               SET &RECPERCI1 = ( ( 1536 - &CIOVERHD ) / ( &RECSIZE ) )
        SET &C4096 = 150                              SET &RECPERCA1 = &RECPERCI1 * &C1536
        SET &C4608 = 76                               SET &RECPERTRK1 = &RECPERCA1 / &TRACK
        SET &C5120 = 93                           C82048:    SET &ANSWER EQ Y
        SET &C5632 = 62                               SET &CIOVERHD = 10
        SET &C6144 = 90                               IF ( 2048  - &RECSIZE ) GT 6 AND ( 2048  - &RECSIZE ) LT 10 -
        SET &C6656 = 53                                  THEN SET &CIOVERHD = 7
        SET &C7168 = 66                               IF &RECSIZE GT ( 2048 - &CIOVERHD ) -
        SET &C7680 = 46                                  THEN  DO
        SET &C8192 = 75                                          SET &RECPERCA2 = 0
        SET &C10240 = 54                                         GOTO WL2
        SET &C12288 = 50                                      ENDO
        SET &C14336 = 38                              SET &RECPERCI2 = ( ( 2048 - &CIOVERHD ) / ( &RECSIZE ) )
        SET &C16384 = 37                              SET &RECPERCA2 = &RECPERCI2 * &C2048
        SET &C18432 = 30                              SET &RECPERTRK2 = &RECPERCA2 / &TRACK
        SET &C20480 = 30                          WL2:    SET &ANSWER EQ Y
        SET &C22528 = 24                              WRITE 1,536       &RECPERCI1     &RECPERTRK1     &RECPERCA1  -
        SET &C24576 = 25                          2,048       &RECPERCI2     &RECPERTRK2     &RECPERCA2
        SET &C26624 = 20                              IF &RECPERCA1 GT &ONLINECI -
        SET &C28672 = 21                                 THEN  DO
        SET &C30720 = 18                                          SET &ONLINECI = &RECPERCA1
        SET &C32768 = 18                                          SET &BESTOCI EQ 1536
        SET &TRACK = 15                                        ENDO
        GOTO C8512                                   IF &RECPERCA2 GT &ONLINECI -
IEIGHTY:   SET &ANSWER EQ Y                              THEN  DO
/* PROCESS FOR 3380 DASD WITH IMBED */                          SET &ONLINECI = &RECPERCA2
        SET &C512 = 644                                          SET &BESTOCI EQ 2048
        SET &C1024 = 434                                       ENDO
        SET &C1536 = 214                         C82560:    SET &ANSWER EQ Y
        SET &C2048 = 252                              SET &CIOVERHD = 10
        SET &C2560 = 128                              IF ( 2560  - &RECSIZE ) GT 6 AND ( 2560  - &RECSIZE ) LT 10 -
        SET &C3072 = 144                                 THEN SET &CIOVERHD = 7
        SET &C3584 = 92                               IF &RECSIZE GT ( 2560 - &CIOVERHD ) -
        SET &C4096 = 140                                 THEN  DO
        SET &C4608 = 71                                          SET &RECPERCA1 = 0
        SET &C5120 = 86                                          GOTO C83072
        SET &C5632 = 58                                       ENDO
        SET &C6144 = 84                               SET &RECPERCI1 = ( ( 2560 - &CIOVERHD ) / ( &RECSIZE ) )
        SET &C6656 = 49                               SET &RECPERCA1 = &RECPERCI1 * &C2560
        SET &C7168 = 62                               SET &RECPERTRK1 = &RECPERCA1 / &TRACK
        SET &C7680 = 42                           C83072:    SET &ANSWER EQ Y
        SET &C8192 = 70                               SET &CIOVERHD = 10
        SET &C10240 = 50                              IF ( 3072  - &RECSIZE ) GT 6 AND ( 3072  - &RECSIZE ) LT 10 -
        SET &C12288 = 46                                 THEN SET &CIOVERHD = 7
        SET &C14336 = 36                              IF &RECSIZE GT ( 3072 - &CIOVERHD ) -
        SET &C16384 = 35                                 THEN  DO
        SET &C18432 = 28                                         SET &RECPERCA2 = 0
        SET &C20480 = 28                                         GOTO WL3
        SET &C22528 = 22                                      ENDO
        SET &C24576 = 23                              SET &RECPERCI2 = ( ( 3072 - &CIOVERHD ) / ( &RECSIZE ) )
        SET &C26624 = 19                              SET &RECPERCA2 = &RECPERCI2 * &C3072
        SET &C28672 = 20                              SET &RECPERTRK2 = &RECPERCA2 / &TRACK
        SET &C30720 = 16                          WL3:    SET &ANSWER EQ Y
        SET &C32768 = 17                              WRITE 2,560       &RECPERCI1     &RECPERTRK1     &RECPERCA1 -
        SET &TRACK = 14                           3,072       &RECPERCI2     &RECPERTRK2     &RECPERCA2
C8512:   SET &ANSWER EQ Y                                 IF &RECPERCA1 GT &ONLINECI -
        SET &CIOVERHD = 10                                  THEN  DO
        IF ( 512   - &RECSIZE ) GT 6 AND ( 512    - &RECSIZE ) LT 10 -          SET &ONLINECI = &RECPERCA1
             THEN SET &CIOVERHD = 7                                      SET &BESTOCI EQ 2560
        IF &RECSIZE GT ( 512 - &CIOVERHD ) -                          ENDO
             THEN  DO                                    IF &RECPERCA2 GT &ONLINECI -
                     SET &RECPERCA1 = 0                     THEN  DO
0164000               GOTO C81024                                   SET &ONLINECI = &RECPERCA2
                  ENDO                                               SET &BESTOCI EQ 3072
        SET &RECPERCI1 = ( ( 512 - &CIOVERHD ) / ( &RECSIZE ) )            ENDO
        SET &RECPERCA1 = &RECPERCI1 * &C512          C83584:    SET &ANSWER EQ Y
        SET &RECPERTRK1 = &RECPERCA1 / &TRACK            SET &CIOVERHD = 10
C81024:    SET &ANSWER EQ Y                               IF ( 3584  - &RECSIZE ) GT 6 AND ( 3584  - &RECSIZE ) LT 10 -
        SET &CIOVERHD = 10                                  THEN SET &CIOVERHD = 7
        IF ( 1024  - &RECSIZE ) GT 6 AND ( 1024  - &RECSIZE ) LT 10 -          IF &RECSIZE GT ( 3584 - &CIOVERHD ) -
             THEN SET &CIOVERHD = 7                               THEN  DO
        IF &RECSIZE GT ( 1024 - &CIOVERHD ) -                             SET &RECPERCA1 = 0
             THEN  DO                                                     GOTO C84096
                     SET &RECPERCA2 = 0                                ENDO
                     GOTO WL1                          SET &RECPERCI1 = ( ( 3584 - &CIOVERHD ) / ( &RECSIZE ) )
                  ENDO                                 SET &RECPERCA1 = &RECPERCI1 * &C3584
```

FIGURE F.1   (Continued)

```
        SET &RECPERTRK1 = &RECPERCA1 / &TRACK
C84096:   SET &ANSWER EQ Y
        SET &CIOVERHD = 10
        IF ( 4096 - &RECSIZE ) GT 6 AND ( 4096 - &RECSIZE ) LT 10 -
            THEN SET &CIOVERHD = 7
        IF &RECSIZE GT ( 4096 - &CIOVERHD ) -
            THEN DO
                    SET &RECPERCA2 = 0
                    GOTO WL4
            ENDO
        SET &RECPERCI2 = ( ( 4096 - &CIOVERHD ) / ( &RECSIZE ) )
        SET &RECPERCA2 = &RECPERCI2 * &C4096
        SET &RECPERTRK2 = &RECPERCA2 / &TRACK
WL4:     SET &ANSWER EQ Y
        WRITE 3,584      &RECPERCI1      &RECPERTRK1      &RECPERCA1
4,096        &RECPERCI2      &RECPERTRK2      &RECPERCA2
        IF &RECPERCA1 GT &ONLINECI -
            THEN DO
                    SET &ONLINECI = &RECPERCA1
                    SET &BESTOCI EQ 3584
            ENDO
        IF &RECPERCA2 GT &ONLINECI -
            THEN DO
                    SET &ONLINECI = &RECPERCA2
                    SET &BESTOCI EQ 4096
            ENDO
        WRITE BEST ONLINE CI = &BESTOCI WITH &ONLINECI RECORDS PER CA
        SET &BATCHCI = &ONLINECI
        SET BESTBCI = &BESTOCI
C84608:   SET &ANSWER EQ Y
        SET &CIOVERHD = 10
        IF ( 4608 - &RECSIZE ) GT 6 AND ( 4608 - &RECSIZE ) LT 10 -
            THEN SET &CIOVERHD = 7
        IF &RECSIZE GT ( 4608 - &CIOVERHD ) -
            THEN DO
                    SET &RECPERCA1 = 0
                    GOTO C85120
            ENDO
        SET &RECPERCI1 = ( ( 4608 - &CIOVERHD ) / ( &RECSIZE ) )
        SET &RECPERCA1 = &RECPERCI1 * &C4608
        SET &RECPERTRK1 = &RECPERCA1 / &TRACK
C85120:   SET &ANSWER EQ Y
        SET &CIOVERHD = 10
        IF ( 5120 - &RECSIZE ) GT 6 AND ( 5120 - &RECSIZE ) LT 10
            THEN SET &CIOVERHD = 7
        IF &RECSIZE GT ( 5120 - &CIOVERHD ) -
            THEN DO
                    SET &RECPERCA2 = 0
                    GOTO WL5
            ENDO
        SET &RECPERCI2 = ( ( 5120 - &CIOVERHD ) / ( &RECSIZE ) )
        SET &RECPERCA2 = &RECPERCI2 * &C5120
        SET &RECPERTRK2 = &RECPERCA2 / &TRACK
WL5:     SET &ANSWER EQ Y
        WRITE 4,608      &RECPERCI1      &RECPERTRK1      &RECPERCA1
5,120        &RECPERCI2      &RECPERTRK2      &RECPERCA2
        IF &RECPERCA1 GE &BATCHCI -
            THEN DO
                    SET &BATCHCI = &RECPERCA1
                    SET &BESTBCI EQ 4608
            ENDO
        IF &RECPERCA2 GE &BATCHCI -
            THEN DO
                    SET &BATCHCI = &RECPERCA2
                    SET &BESTBCI EQ 5120
            ENDO
C85632:   SET &ANSWER EQ Y
        SET &CIOVERHD = 10
        IF ( 5632 - &RECSIZE ) GT 6 AND ( 5632 - &RECSIZE ) LT 10 -
            THEN SET &CIOVERHD = 7
        IF &RECSIZE GT ( 5632 - &CIOVERHD ) -
            THEN DO
                    SET &RECPERCA1 = 0
                    GOTO C86144
            ENDO
        SET &RECPERCI1 = ( ( 5632 - &CIOVERHD ) / ( &RECSIZE ) )
        SET &RECPERCA1 = &RECPERCI1 * &C5632
        SET &RECPERTRK1 = &RECPERCA1 / &TRACK
C86144:   SET &ANSWER EQ Y
        SET &CIOVERHD = 10
        IF ( 6144 - &RECSIZE ) GT 6 AND ( 6144 - &RECSIZE ) LT 10 -
            THEN SET &CIOVERHD = 7
        IF &RECSIZE GT ( 6144 - &CIOVERHD ) -
            THEN DO
                    SET &RECPERCA2 = 0
                    GOTO WL6
            ENDO
        SET &RECPERCI2 = ( ( 6144 - &CIOVERHD ) / ( &RECSIZE ) )
        SET &RECPERCA2 = &RECPERCI2 * &C6144
        SET &RECPERTRK2 = &RECPERCA2 / &TRACK
WL6:     SET &ANSWER EQ Y
        WRITE 5,632      &RECPERCI1      &RECPERTRK1      &RECPERCA1
6,144        &RECPERCI2      &RECPERTRK2      &RECPERCA2
        IF &RECPERCA1 GE &BATCHCI -
            THEN DO
                    SET &BATCHCI = &RECPERCA1
                    SET &BESTBCI EQ 5632
            ENDO
        IF &RECPERCA2 GE &BATCHCI -
            THEN DO
                    SET &BATCHCI = &RECPERCA2
                    SET &BESTBCI EQ 6144
            ENDO

C86656:   SET &ANSWER EQ Y
        SET &CIOVERHD = 10
        IF ( 6656 - &RECSIZE ) GT 6 AND ( 6656 - &RECSIZE ) LT 10 -
            THEN SET &CIOVERHD = 7
        IF &RECSIZE GT ( 6656 - &CIOVERHD ) -
            THEN DO
                    SET &RECPERCA1 = 0
                    GOTO C87168
            ENDO
        SET &RECPERCI1 = ( ( 6656 - &CIOVERHD ) / ( &RECSIZE ) )
        SET &RECPERCA1 = &RECPERCI1 * &C6656
        SET &RECPERTRK1 = &RECPERCA1 / &TRACK
C87168:   SET &ANSWER EQ Y
        SET &CIOVERHD = 10
        IF ( 7168 - &RECSIZE ) GT 6 AND ( 7168 - &RECSIZE ) LT 10 -
            THEN SET &CIOVERHD = 7
        IF &RECSIZE GT ( 7168 - &CIOVERHD ) -
            THEN DO
                    SET &RECPERCA2 = 0
                    GOTO WL7
            ENDO
        SET &RECPERCI2 = ( ( 7168 - &CIOVERHD ) / ( &RECSIZE ) )
        SET &RECPERCA2 = &RECPERCI2 * &C7168
        SET &RECPERTRK2 = &RECPERCA2 / &TRACK
WL7:     SET &ANSWER EQ Y
        WRITE 6,656      &RECPERCI1      &RECPERTRK1      &RECPERCA1
7,168        &RECPERCI2      &RECPERTRK2      &RECPERCA2
        IF &RECPERCA1 GE &BATCHCI -
            THEN DO
                    SET &BATCHCI = &RECPERCA1
                    SET &BESTBCI EQ 6656
            ENDO
        IF &RECPERCA2 GE &BATCHCI -
            THEN DO
                    SET &BATCHCI = &RECPERCA2
                    SET &BESTBCI EQ 7168
            ENDO
C87680:   SET &ANSWER EQ Y
        SET &CIOVERHD = 10
        IF ( 7680 - &RECSIZE ) GT 6 AND ( 7680 - &RECSIZE ) LT 10 -
            THEN SET &CIOVERHD = 7
        IF &RECSIZE GT ( 7680 - &CIOVERHD ) -
            THEN DO
                    SET &RECPERCA1 = 0
                    GOTO C88192
            ENDO
        SET &RECPERCI1 = ( ( 7680 - &CIOVERHD ) / ( &RECSIZE ) )
        SET &RECPERCA1 = &RECPERCI1 * &C7680
        SET &RECPERTRK1 = &RECPERCA1 / &TRACK
C88192:   SET &ANSWER EQ Y
        SET &CIOVERHD = 10
        IF ( 8192 - &RECSIZE ) GT 6 AND ( 8192 - &RECSIZE ) LT 10 -
            THEN SET &CIOVERHD = 7
        IF &RECSIZE GT ( 8192 - &CIOVERHD ) -
            THEN DO
                    SET &RECPERCA2 = 0
                    GOTO WL8
            ENDO
        SET &RECPERCI2 = ( ( 8192 - &CIOVERHD ) / ( &RECSIZE ) )
        SET &RECPERCA2 = &RECPERCI2 * &C8192
        SET &RECPERTRK2 = &RECPERCA2 / &TRACK
WL8:     SET &ANSWER EQ Y
        WRITE 7,680      &RECPERCI1      &RECPERTRK1      &RECPERCA1
8,192        &RECPERCI2      &RECPERTRK2      &RECPERCA2
        IF &RECPERCA1 GE &BATCHCI -
            THEN DO
                    SET &BATCHCI = &RECPERCA1
                    SET &BESTBCI EQ 7680
            ENDO
        IF &RECPERCA2 GE &BATCHCI -
            THEN DO
                    SET &BATCHCI = &RECPERCA2
                    SET &BESTBCI EQ 8192
            ENDO
C810240:   SET &ANSWER EQ Y
        SET &CIOVERHD = 10
        IF ( 10240 - &RECSIZE ) GT 6 AND ( 10240 - &RECSIZE ) LT 10 -
            THEN SET &CIOVERHD = 7
        IF &RECSIZE GT ( 10240 - &CIOVERHD ) -
            THEN DO
                    SET &RECPERCA1 = 0
                    GOTO C812288
            ENDO
        SET &RECPERCI1 = ( ( 10240 - &CIOVERHD ) / ( &RECSIZE ) )
        SET &RECPERCA1 = &RECPERCI1 * &C10240
        SET &RECPERTRK1 = &RECPERCA1 / &TRACK
C812288:   SET &ANSWER EQ Y
        SET &CIOVERHD = 10
        IF ( 12288 - &RECSIZE ) GT 6 AND ( 12288 - &RECSIZE ) LT 10 -
            THEN SET &CIOVERHD = 7
        IF &RECSIZE GT ( 12288 - &CIOVERHD ) -
            THEN DO
                    SET &RECPERCA2 = 0
                    GOTO WL9
            ENDO
        SET &RECPERCI2 = ( ( 12288 - &CIOVERHD ) / ( &RECSIZE ) )
        SET &RECPERCA2 = &RECPERCI2 * &C12288
        SET &RECPERTRK2 = &RECPERCA2 / &TRACK
WL9:     SET &ANSWER EQ Y
        WRITE 10,240      &RECPERCI1      &RECPERTRK1      &RECPERCA1
12,288       &RECPERCI2      &RECPERTRK2      &RECPERCA2
        IF &RECPERCA1 GE &BATCHCI -
            THEN DO
```

FIGURE F.1   (Continued)

```
            SET &BATCHCI = &RECPERCA1
            SET &BESTBCI EQ 10240
        ENDO
    IF &RECPERCA2 GE &BATCHCI -
        THEN DO
            SET &BATCHCI = &RECPERCA2
            SET &BESTBCI EQ 12288
        ENDO
C814336:  SET &ANSWER EQ Y
    SET &CIOVERHD = 10
    IF ( 14336 - &RECSIZE ) GT 6 AND ( 14336 - &RECSIZE ) LT 10 -
    THEN SET &CIOVERHD = 7
    IF &RECSIZE GT ( 14336 - &CIOVERHD ) -
        THEN DO
            SET &RECPERCA1 = 0
            GOTO C816384
        ENDO
    SET &RECPERCI1 = ( ( 14336 - &CIOVERHD ) / ( &RECSIZE ) )
    SET &RECPERCA1 = &RECPERCI1 * &C14336
    SET &RECPERTRK1 = &RECPERCA1 / &TRACK
C816384:  SET &ANSWER EQ Y
    SET &CIOVERHD = 10
    IF ( 16384 - &RECSIZE ) GT 6 AND ( 16384 - &RECSIZE ) LT 10 -
    THEN SET &CIOVERHD = 7
    IF &RECSIZE GT ( 16384 - &CIOVERHD ) -
        THEN DO
            SET &RECPERCA2 = 0
            GOTO WL10
        ENDO
    SET &RECPERCI2 = ( ( 16384 - &CIOVERHD ) / ( &RECSIZE ) )
    SET &RECPERCA2 = &RECPERCI2 * &C16384
    SET &RECPERTRK2 = &RECPERCA2 / &TRACK
WL10:  SET &ANSWER EQ Y
    WRITE 14,336    &RECPERCI1    &RECPERTRK1    &RECPERCA1 -
16,384    &RECPERCI2    &RECPERTRK2    &RECPERCA2
    IF &RECPERCA1 GE &BATCHCI -
        THEN DO
            SET &BATCHCI = &RECPERCA1
            SET &BESTBCI EQ 14336
        ENDO
    IF &RECPERCA2 GE &BATCHCI -
        THEN DO
            SET &BATCHCI = &RECPERCA2
            SET &BESTBCI EQ 16384
        ENDO
C818432:  SET &ANSWER EQ Y
    SET &CIOVERHD = 10
    IF ( 18432 - &RECSIZE ) GT 6 AND ( 18432 - &RECSIZE ) LT 10 -
    THEN SET &CIOVERHD = 7
    IF &RECSIZE GT ( 18432 - &CIOVERHD ) -
        THEN DO
            SET &RECPERCA1 = 0
            GOTO C820480
        ENDO
    SET &RECPERCI1 = ( ( 18432 - &CIOVERHD ) / ( &RECSIZE ) )
    SET &RECPERCA1 = &RECPERCI1 * &C18432
    SET &RECPERTRK1 = &RECPERCA1 / &TRACK
C820480:  SET &ANSWER EQ Y
    SET &CIOVERHD = 10
    IF ( 20480 - &RECSIZE ) GT 6 AND ( 20480 - &RECSIZE ) LT 10 -
    THEN SET &CIOVERHD = 7
    IF &RECSIZE GT ( 20480 - &CIOVERHD ) -
        THEN DO
            SET &RECPERCA2 = 0
            GOTO WL11
        ENDO
    SET &RECPERCI2 = ( ( 20480 - &CIOVERHD ) / ( &RECSIZE ) )
    SET &RECPERCA2 = &RECPERCI2 * &C20480
    SET &RECPERTRK2 = &RECPERCA2 / &TRACK
WL11:  SET &ANSWER EQ Y
    WRITE 18,432    &RECPERCI1    &RECPERTRK1    &RECPERCA1 -
20,480    &RECPERCI2    &RECPERTRK2    &RECPERCA2
    IF &RECPERCA1 GE &BATCHCI -
        THEN DO
            SET &BATCHCI = &RECPERCA1
            SET &BESTBCI EQ 18432
        ENDO
    IF &RECPERCA2 GE &BATCHCI -
        THEN DO
            SET &BATCHCI = &RECPERCA2
            SET &BESTBCI EQ 20480
        ENDO
C822528:  SET &ANSWER EQ Y
    SET &CIOVERHD = 10
    IF ( 22528 - &RECSIZE ) GT 6 AND ( 22528 - &RECSIZE ) LT 10 -
    THEN SET &CIOVERHD = 7
    IF &RECSIZE GT ( 22528 - &CIOVERHD ) -
        THEN DO
            SET &RECPERCA1 = 0
            GOTO C824576
        ENDO
    SET &RECPERCI1 = ( ( 22528 - &CIOVERHD ) / ( &RECSIZE ) )
    SET &RECPERCA1 = &RECPERCI1 * &C22528
    SET &RECPERTRK1 = &RECPERCA1 / &TRACK
C824576:  SET &ANSWER EQ Y
    SET &CIOVERHD = 10
    IF ( 24576 - &RECSIZE ) GT 6 AND ( 24576 - &RECSIZE ) LT 10 -
    THEN SET &CIOVERHD = 7
    IF &RECSIZE GT ( 24576 - &CIOVERHD ) -
        THEN DO

            SET &RECPERCA2 = 0
            GOTO WL12
        ENDO
    SET &RECPERCI2 = ( ( 24576 - &CIOVERHD ) / ( &RECSIZE ) )
    SET &RECPERCA2 = &RECPERCI2 * &C24576
    SET &RECPERTRK2 = &RECPERCA2 / &TRACK
WL12:  SET &ANSWER EQ Y
    WRITE 22,528    &RECPERCI1    &RECPERTRK1    &RECPERCA1 -
24,576    &RECPERCI2    &RECPERTRK2    &RECPERCA2
    IF &RECPERCA1 GE &BATCHCI -
        THEN DO
            SET &BATCHCI = &RECPERCA1
            SET &BESTBCI EQ 22528
        ENDO
    IF &RECPERCA2 GE &BATCHCI -
        THEN DO
            SET &BATCHCI = &RECPERCA2
            SET &BESTBCI EQ 24576
        ENDO
C826624:  SET &ANSWER EQ Y
    SET &CIOVERHD = 10
    IF ( 26624 - &RECSIZE ) GT 6 AND ( 26624 - &RECSIZE ) LT 10 -
    THEN SET &CIOVERHD = 7
    IF &RECSIZE GT ( 26624 - &CIOVERHD ) -
        THEN DO
            SET &RECPERCA1 = 0
            GOTO C828672
        ENDO
    SET &RECPERCI1 = ( ( 26624 - &CIOVERHD ) / ( &RECSIZE ) )
    SET &RECPERCA1 = &RECPERCI1 * &C26624
    SET &RECPERTRK1 = &RECPERCA1 / &TRACK
C828672:  SET &ANSWER EQ Y
    SET &CIOVERHD = 10
    IF ( 28672 - &RECSIZE ) GT 6 AND ( 28672 - &RECSIZE ) LT 10 -
    THEN SET &CIOVERHD = 7
    IF &RECSIZE GT ( 28672 - &CIOVERHD ) -
        THEN DO
            SET &RECPERCA2 = 0
            GOTO WL13
        ENDO
    SET &RECPERCI2 = ( ( 28672 - &CIOVERHD ) / ( &RECSIZE ) )
    SET &RECPERCA2 = &RECPERCI2 * &C28672
    SET &RECPERTRK2 = &RECPERCA2 / &TRACK
WL13:  SET &ANSWER EQ Y
    WRITE 26,624    &RECPERCI1    &RECPERTRK1    &RECPERCA1 -
28,672    &RECPERCI2    &RECPERTRK2    &RECPERCA2
    IF &RECPERCA1 GE &BATCHCI -
        THEN DO
            SET &BATCHCI = &RECPERCA1
            SET &BESTBCI EQ 26624
        ENDO
    IF &RECPERCA2 GE &BATCHCI -
        THEN DO
            SET &BATCHCI = &RECPERCA2
            SET &BESTBCI EQ 28672
        ENDO
C830720:  SET &ANSWER EQ Y
    SET &CIOVERHD = 10
    IF ( 30720 - &RECSIZE ) GT 6 AND ( 30720 - &RECSIZE ) LT 10 -
    THEN SET &CIOVERHD = 7
    IF &RECSIZE GT ( 30720 - &CIOVERHD ) -
        THEN DO
            SET &RECPERCA1 = 0
            GOTO C832768
        ENDO
    SET &RECPERCI1 = ( ( 30720 - &CIOVERHD ) / ( &RECSIZE ) )
    SET &RECPERCA1 = &RECPERCI1 * &C30720
    SET &RECPERTRK1 = &RECPERCA1 / &TRACK
C832768:  SET &ANSWER EQ Y
    SET &CIOVERHD = 10
    IF ( 32768 - &RECSIZE ) GT 6 AND ( 32768 - &RECSIZE ) LT 10 -
    THEN SET &CIOVERHD = 7
    IF &RECSIZE GT ( 32768 - &CIOVERHD ) -
        THEN DO
            SET &RECPERCA2 = 0
            GOTO WL14
        ENDO
    SET &RECPERCI2 = ( ( 32768 - &CIOVERHD ) / ( &RECSIZE ) )
    SET &RECPERCA2 = &RECPERCI2 * &C32768
    SET &RECPERTRK2 = &RECPERCA2 / &TRACK
WL14:  SET &ANSWER EQ Y
    WRITE 30,720    &RECPERCI1    &RECPERTRK1    &RECPERCA1 -
32,768    &RECPERCI2    &RECPERTRK2    &RECPERCA2
    IF &RECPERCA1 GE &BATCHCI -
        THEN DO
            SET &BATCHCI = &RECPERCA1
            SET &BESTBCI EQ 30720
        ENDO
    IF &RECPERCA2 GE &BATCHCI -
        THEN DO
            SET &BATCHCI = &RECPERCA2
            SET &BESTBCI EQ 32768
        ENDO
    WRITE BEST BATCH  CI = &BESTBCI WITH &BATCHCI RECORDS PER CA
    END
```

FIGURE F.1 (Continued)

```
COMMAND  = = = >  TSO EXEC 'BT05686.SOURCE.CLIST(VSAMCISZ)'
```

or

```
COMMAND  = = = >  TSO EXEC SOURCE.CLIST(VSAMCISZ)
```

where you use your own local names for BT05686 and SOURCE, which are qualifiers on
the TSO data set name.

VSAMCISZ prompts for three items of information which it uses to determine the
optimal control interval size:

- length of records to be housed
- whether or not the IMBED option will be used
- type of disk device to house the data set.

The record length entered must be between 12 and 32761, and the device type can be
3330, 3350, or 3380. If an invalid record length or device type is specified, VSAMCISZ
provides a chance to start the computation over or to exit. The CLIST trusts you to enter
a numeric value for record length. A sample of the output from VSAMCISZ can be found
on page 31.

VSAMSPAC

VSAMSPAC, listed in Figure F.2, is a CLIST that calculates the required disk space and
free space attributes for a fixed-length VSAM KSDS or alternate index, and composes
IDCAMS control statements for the values. For variable-length records, the average record

```
/*                                                    */        SET &BUFND    = 0    /* DATA BUFFERS FOR SEQUENTIAL PROCESING */
/*  TSO CLIST  VSAMSPAC    BY RICH GUZIK   AUGUST, 1988 */        WRITE    PRACTICAL VSAM - JOHN WILEY AND SONS, 1988 - ISBN 0-471--
/*                                                    */     85107-8
/*  FOR YOUR CONVENIENCE THIS ITEM IS AVAILABLE IN MACHINE */    WRITE    SPACE CALC FOR FIXED LENGTH RECORD KSDS WITH CA SIZE ONE -
/*  READABLE FORM FOR UPLOADING TO AN IBM MAINFRAME.    */     CYLINDER
/*                                                    */        WRITE
/*                                                    */        WRITE    ANSWER ALL PROMPTS WITH NUMERIC ENTRIES EXCEPT IMBED/DSN
/*                                                    */        WRITE
PROC 0                                                          WRITENR ENTER CISIZE ==>
CONTROL NOFLUSH NOMSG END(ENDO)                                 READ &CISIZE
START:    SET &ANSWER EQ Y                                      IF &CISIZE LE 4096 -
/* CLIST TO CALCULATE SPACE FOR A FIXED KSDS VSAM FILE */          THEN GOTO ERECSIZE
/* ---------------****  VSAMSPAC  ****---------------- */       WRITENR  DID THE TP ADMINISTRATOR OK THIS CISIZE - Y OR N ==>
    /* CALL CLEAR SCREEN PROGRAM HERE */                        READ &ANSWER
    SET &TEMPCALC = 0    /* TEMPORARY CALCULATION FIELD */      IF &ANSWER NE Y -
    SET &CISIZE = 0      /* CISIZE */                              THEN DO
    SET &RECSIZE = 0     /* RECORD SIZE */                           WRITE GET THE TP ADMINISTRATOR'S APPROVAL AND TRY AGAIN
    SET &MAXRECS = 0     /* MAX # RECS FOR THE FILE */               WRITE GOODBYE
    SET &LOADRECS = 0    /* MAX RECS, INITIAL LOAD, EMPTY FREESPACE*/ END
    SET &CYLS = 0        /* # CYLS REQUIRED FOR FILE */            ENDO
    SET &SECONDARY = 0   /* 10% OF PRIMARY ALLOCATION (CYLS) */  ERECSIZE:    SET &ANSWER EQ Y
    SET &CIOVERHD = 0    /* CI CONTROL INFORMATION (7 OR 10) */  /* PROMPT FOR RECORD SIZE */
    SET &USABLECI  = 0   /* CISIZE - &CIOVERHD */                   WRITENR ENTER RECSIZE ==>
    SET &CIPERCA = 0     /* # MAX CIS PER CA */                     READ &RECSIZE
    SET &RECPERCA = 0    /* # RECS PER CA, INITIAL LOAD, EMPTY FREESPC*/ SET &CIOVERHD = 10
    SET &RECPERCI = 0    /* MAX REC PER CI */                       IF ( &CISIZE - &RECSIZE ) GT 6 AND ( &CISIZE - &RECSIZE ) LT 10 -
    SET &DASD = 0        /* DEVICE TYPE - 3330, 3350 OR 3380 */        THEN SET &CIOVERHD = 7
    SET &NUMRECS = 0     /* REQUESTED # RECS FOR INITIAL LOAD */     SET &USABLECI = &CISIZE - &CIOVERHD
    SET &ARECPERCI = 0   /* # RECS PER CI W/ EMPTY FREESPACE */      IF &RECSIZE LE &USABLECI -
    SET &MRECPERCA = 0   /* MAX # RECS PER CA (CYL) */                 THEN GOTO ECIFREE
    SET &CALCFREE = 0    /* CALCULATED # RECS IN CI FREESPACE */     WRITE RECSIZE ( &RECSIZE ) GT USABLECI ( &USABLECI )
    SET &CALCCAFREE = 0  /* CALCULATED # REC IN CA FREESPACE */     WRITENR DO YOU WANT TO TRY AGAIN - Y OR N ==>
    SET &CIAVAIL = 0     /* # RECS PER CI FOR FREESPACE */          READ &ANSWER
    SET &PERCENT = 0     /* % CI FREESPACE */                       IF &ANSWER NE Y -
    SET &CAPERCENT = 0   /* % CA FREESPACE */                          THEN DO
    SET &IMBEDANS = N    /* IS IMBED REQUESTED - Y OR N */                WRITE GOODBYE
    SET &ANSWER = Y      /* % ANSWER TO ALL OTHER ?S */                   END
    SET &CIFREECA = 0    /* REQUESTED # CIS PER CA FOR CAFREESPACE */   ENDO
    SET &UNUSABLE = 0    /* UNUSABLE PORTION OF CI IN BYTES */       ELSE GOTO ERECSIZE
    SET &CIFREERECS = 0  /* REQUESTED # RECS FOR CI FREESPACE */   ECIFREE:    SET &ANSWER EQ Y
    SET &FILENAME = ???  /* DATA SET NAME */                      /* PROMPT FOR CIFREESPACE */
    SET &TRKPERCA = 0    /* TRACKS PER CA */                         SET &RECPERCI = &USABLECI / &RECSIZE
    SET &CIPERTRK = 0    /* CIS PER TRACK */                         SET &UNUSABLE = &USABLECI - ( &RECPERCI * &RECSIZE )
```

FIGURE F.2 Source code for TSO CLIST VSAMSPAC, which automates the selection and composition of IDCAMS DEFINE parameters (listed two columns per page)

```
        WRITE &RECPERCI RECORDS WILL FIT PER CI                          SET &CIPERCA EQ 76
        WRITE WHAT IS THE MINIMUM # RECORDS PER CI YOU WANT FOR CIFREESPACE      GOTO ECAFREE
        WRITENR ENTER A NUMBER LESS THAN &RECPERCI ==>                    ENDO
        READ &CIFREERECS                                          IF &CISIZE EQ  3072 AND &IMBEDANS EQ Y -
        IF &CIFREERECS LT &RECPERCI -                                THEN DO
          THEN GOTO CALCFRCI                                             SET &CIPERCA EQ 66
        WRITE YOU REQUESTED &CIFREERECS AND &RECPERCI IS THE MAX         GOTO ECAFREE
        WRITENR DO YOU WANT TO TRY AGAIN - Y OR N ==>                    ENDO
        READ &ANSWER                                              IF &CISIZE EQ  3072 AND &IMBEDANS NE Y -
        IF &ANSWER EQ Y   -                                          THEN DO
          THEN GOTO ECIFREE                                              SET &CIPERCA EQ 69
        ELSE  DO                                                        GOTO ECAFREE
              WRITE GOODBYE                                             ENDO
              END                                                 IF &CISIZE EQ  3584 AND &IMBEDANS EQ Y -
            ENDO                                                      THEN DO
CALCFRCI:    SET &ANSWER EQ Y                                          SET &CIPERCA EQ 51
/* CALCULATE PRECENT OF CIFREE */                                     GOTO ECAFREE
        SET &PERCENT = ((&CIFREERECS * &RECSIZE) * 100) / &CISIZE       ENDO
LOOPONE:     SET &ANSWER EQ Y                                     IF &CISIZE EQ  3584 AND &IMBEDANS NE Y -
/* ADJUST PERCENT TO BE GE NUMBER OF FREE RECS REQUESTED */             THEN DO
        SET &TEMPCALC = (((&CISIZE * &PERCENT) + 99 ) / 100 + &UNUSABLE )    SET &CIPERCA EQ 54
        SET &CALCFREE = &TEMPCALC / &RECSIZE                            GOTO ECAFREE
        IF &CALCFREE GE &CIFREERECS -                                   ENDO
          THEN GOTO IMBED                                          IF &CISIZE EQ  4096 AND &IMBEDANS EQ Y -
        SET &PERCENT = &PERCENT + 1                                     THEN DO
        GOTO LOOPONE                                                   SET &CIPERCA EQ 54
IMBED:      SET &ANSWER EQ Y                                          GOTO ECAFREE
/* PROMPT FOR IMBED OPTION */                                         ENDO
        WRITENR WILL YOU USE THE IMBED OPTION - Y OR N ==>        IF &CISIZE EQ  4096 AND &IMBEDANS NE Y -
        READ &IMBEDANS                                               THEN DO
DISKTYPE:       SET &ANSWER EQ Y                                       SET &CIPERCA EQ 57
/* PROMPT FOR TYPE OF DISK - 3330, 3350 OR 3380 */                    GOTO ECAFREE
        WRITENR ENTER DEVICE TYPE - 3330, 3350 OR 3380 ==>             ENDO
        READ &DASD                                                IF &CISIZE EQ  4608 AND &IMBEDANS EQ Y -
        IF &DASD EQ 3330 -                                           THEN DO
          THEN GOTO THIRTY                                               SET &CIPERCA EQ 40
        IF &DASD EQ 3350 -                                              GOTO ECAFREE
          THEN GOTO FIFTY                                               ENDO
        IF &DASD EQ 3380 -                                        IF &CISIZE EQ  4608 AND &IMBEDANS NE Y -
          THEN GOTO EIGHTY                                            THEN DO
        WRITE VALID RESPONSES ARE 3330, 3350 AND 3380                 SET &CIPERCA EQ 42
        WRITENR DO YOU WANT TO TRY AGAIN - Y OR N ==>                 GOTO ECAFREE
        READ &ANSWER                                                   ENDO
        IF &ANSWER EQ Y   -                                       IF &CISIZE EQ  5120 AND &IMBEDANS EQ Y -
          THEN GOTO DISKTYPE                                          THEN DO
        ELSE  DO                                                        SET &CIPERCA EQ 39
              WRITE GOODBYE                                           GOTO ECAFREE
              END                                                     ENDO
            ENDO                                                  IF &CISIZE EQ  5120 AND &IMBEDANS NE Y -
THIRTY:     SET &ANSWER EQ Y                                          THEN DO
/* DETERMINE CIS PER CA FOR 3330 */                                   SET &CIPERCA EQ 41
        SET &TRKPERCA = 19                                             GOTO ECAFREE
        IF &IMBEDANS = Y -                                              ENDO
          THEN SET &TRKPERCA = &TRKPERCA - 1                     IF &CISIZE EQ  5632 AND &IMBEDANS EQ Y -
        IF &CISIZE EQ   512 AND &IMBEDANS EQ Y -                     THEN DO
          THEN DO                                                       SET &CIPERCA EQ 32
              SET &CIPERCA EQ 360                                      GOTO ECAFREE
              GOTO ECAFREE                                             ENDO
            ENDO                                                  IF &CISIZE EQ  5632 AND &IMBEDANS NE Y -
IF &CISIZE EQ   512 AND &IMBEDANS NE Y -                             THEN DO
  THEN DO                                                              SET &CIPERCA EQ 34
        SET &CIPERCA EQ 380                                           GOTO ECAFREE
        GOTO ECAFREE                                                   ENDO
        ENDO                                                     IF &CISIZE EQ  6144 AND &IMBEDANS EQ Y -
IF &CISIZE EQ  1024 AND &IMBEDANS EQ Y -                             THEN DO
  THEN DO                                                              SET &CIPERCA EQ 36
        SET &CIPERCA EQ 198                                           GOTO ECAFREE
        GOTO ECAFREE                                                   ENDO
        ENDO                                                     IF &CISIZE EQ  6144 AND &IMBEDANS NE Y -
IF &CISIZE EQ  1024 AND &IMBEDANS NE Y -                             THEN DO
  THEN DO                                                              SET &CIPERCA EQ 38
        SET &CIPERCA EQ 209                                           GOTO ECAFREE
        GOTO ECAFREE                                                   ENDO
        ENDO                                                     IF &CISIZE EQ  6656 AND &IMBEDANS EQ Y -
IF &CISIZE EQ  1536 AND &IMBEDANS EQ Y -                             THEN DO
  THEN DO                                                              SET &CIPERCA EQ 27
        SET &CIPERCA EQ 120                                           GOTO ECAFREE
        GOTO ECAFREE                                                   ENDO
        ENDO                                                     IF &CISIZE EQ  6656 AND &IMBEDANS NE Y -
IF &CISIZE EQ  1536 AND &IMBEDANS NE Y -                             THEN DO
  THEN DO                                                              SET &CIPERCA EQ 29
        SET &CIPERCA EQ 126                                           GOTO ECAFREE
        GOTO ECAFREE                                                   ENDO
        ENDO                                                     IF &CISIZE EQ  7168 AND &IMBEDANS EQ Y -
IF &CISIZE EQ  2048 AND &IMBEDANS EQ Y -                             THEN DO
  THEN DO                                                              SET &CIPERCA EQ 28
        SET &CIPERCA EQ 108                                           GOTO ECAFREE
        GOTO ECAFREE                                                   ENDO
        ENDO                                                     IF &CISIZE EQ  7168 AND &IMBEDANS NE Y -
IF &CISIZE EQ  2048 AND &IMBEDANS NE Y -                             THEN DO
  THEN DO                                                              SET &CIPERCA EQ 29
        SET &CIPERCA EQ 114                                           GOTO ECAFREE
        GOTO ECAFREE                                                   ENDO
        ENDO                                                     IF &CISIZE EQ  7680 AND &IMBEDANS EQ Y -
IF &CISIZE EQ  2560 AND &IMBEDANS EQ Y -                             THEN DO
  THEN DO                                                              SET &CIPERCA EQ 24
        SET &CIPERCA EQ 72                                            GOTO ECAFREE
        GOTO ECAFREE                                                   ENDO
        ENDO                                                     IF &CISIZE EQ  7680 AND &IMBEDANS NE Y -
IF &CISIZE EQ  2560 AND &IMBEDANS NE Y -                             THEN DO
  THEN DO                                                              SET &CIPERCA EQ 25
```

FIGURE F.2   (*Continued*)

```
              GOTO ECAFREE
              ENDO
   IF &CISIZE EQ  8192 AND &IMBEDANS EQ Y -
      THEN DO
              SET &CIPERCA EQ 27
              GOTO ECAFREE
              ENDO
   IF &CISIZE EQ  8192 AND &IMBEDANS NE Y -
      THEN DO
              SET &CIPERCA EQ 28
              GOTO ECAFREE
              ENDO
   IF &CISIZE EQ 10240 AND &IMBEDANS EQ Y -
      THEN DO
              SET &CIPERCA EQ 21
              GOTO ECAFREE
              ENDO
   IF &CISIZE EQ 10240 AND &IMBEDANS NE Y -
      THEN DO
              SET &CIPERCA EQ 22
              GOTO ECAFREE
              ENDO
   IF &CISIZE EQ 12288 AND &IMBEDANS EQ Y -
      THEN DO
              SET &CIPERCA EQ 18
              GOTO ECAFREE
              ENDO
   IF &CISIZE EQ 12288 AND &IMBEDANS NE Y -
      THEN DO
              SET &CIPERCA EQ 19
              GOTO ECAFREE
              ENDO
   IF &CISIZE EQ 14336 AND &IMBEDANS EQ Y -
      THEN DO
              SET &CIPERCA EQ 15
              GOTO ECAFREE
              ENDO
   IF &CISIZE EQ 14336 AND &IMBEDANS NE Y -
      THEN DO
              SET &CIPERCA EQ 16
              GOTO ECAFREE
              ENDO
   IF &CISIZE EQ 16384 AND &IMBEDANS EQ Y -
      THEN DO
              SET &CIPERCA EQ 13
              GOTO ECAFREE
              ENDO
   IF &CISIZE EQ 16384 AND &IMBEDANS NE Y -
      THEN DO
              SET &CIPERCA EQ 14
              GOTO ECAFREE
              ENDO
   IF &CISIZE EQ 18432 AND &IMBEDANS EQ Y -
      THEN DO
              SET &CIPERCA EQ 12
              GOTO ECAFREE
              ENDO
   IF &CISIZE EQ 18432 AND &IMBEDANS NE Y -
      THEN DO
              SET &CIPERCA EQ 12
              GOTO ECAFREE
              ENDO
   IF &CISIZE EQ 20480 AND &IMBEDANS EQ Y -
      THEN DO
              SET &CIPERCA EQ 10
              GOTO ECAFREE
              ENDO
   IF &CISIZE EQ 20480 AND &IMBEDANS NE Y -
      THEN DO
              SET &CIPERCA EQ 11
              GOTO ECAFREE
              ENDO
   IF &CISIZE EQ 22528 AND &IMBEDANS EQ Y -
      THEN DO
              SET &CIPERCA EQ 9
              GOTO ECAFREE
              ENDO
   IF &CISIZE EQ 22528 AND &IMBEDANS NE Y -
      THEN DO
              SET &CIPERCA EQ 10
              GOTO ECAFREE
              ENDO
   IF &CISIZE EQ 24576 AND &IMBEDANS EQ Y -
      THEN DO
              SET &CIPERCA EQ 9
              GOTO ECAFREE
              ENDO
   IF &CISIZE EQ 24576 AND &IMBEDANS NE Y -
      THEN DO
              SET &CIPERCA EQ 9
              GOTO ECAFREE
              ENDO
   IF &CISIZE EQ 26624 AND &IMBEDANS EQ Y -
      THEN DO
              SET &CIPERCA EQ 8
              GOTO ECAFREE
              ENDO
   IF &CISIZE EQ 26624 AND &IMBEDANS NE Y -
      THEN DO
              SET &CIPERCA EQ 8
              GOTO ECAFREE
              ENDO
   IF &CISIZE EQ 28672 AND &IMBEDANS EQ Y -

            THEN DO
              SET &CIPERCA EQ 7
              GOTO ECAFREE
              ENDO
   IF &CISIZE EQ 28672 AND &IMBEDANS NE Y -
      THEN DO
              SET &CIPERCA EQ 8
              GOTO ECAFREE
              ENDO
   IF &CISIZE EQ 30720 AND &IMBEDANS EQ Y -
      THEN DO
              SET &CIPERCA EQ 7
              GOTO ECAFREE
              ENDO
   IF &CISIZE EQ 30720 AND &IMBEDANS NE Y -
      THEN DO
              SET &CIPERCA EQ 7
              GOTO ECAFREE
              ENDO
   IF &CISIZE EQ 32768 AND &IMBEDANS EQ Y -
      THEN DO
              SET &CIPERCA EQ 6
              GOTO ECAFREE
              ENDO
   IF &CISIZE EQ 32768 AND &IMBEDANS NE Y -
      THEN DO
              SET &CIPERCA EQ 7
              GOTO ECAFREE
              ENDO
   WRITE YOU ENTERED AN INVALID CISIZE
   WRITENR DO YOU WANT TO TRY AGAIN - Y OR N ==>
   READ &ANSWER
   IF &ANSWER EQ Y   -
         THEN GOTO START
   ELSE  DO
              WRITE GOODBYE
              END
              ENDO
FIFTY:     SET &ANSWER EQ Y
/* DETERMINE CIS PER CA FOR 3350 */
      SET &TRKPERCA = 30
      IF &IMBEDANS = Y -
         THEN SET &TRKPERCA = &TRKPERCA - 1
      IF &CISIZE EQ    512 AND &IMBEDANS EQ Y -
         THEN DO
              SET &CIPERCA EQ 783
              GOTO ECAFREE
              ENDO
      IF &CISIZE EQ    512 AND &IMBEDANS NE Y -
         THEN DO
              SET &CIPERCA EQ 810
              GOTO ECAFREE
              ENDO
      IF &CISIZE EQ   1024 AND &IMBEDANS EQ Y -
         THEN DO
              SET &CIPERCA EQ 435
              GOTO ECAFREE
              ENDO
      IF &CISIZE EQ   1024 AND &IMBEDANS NE Y -
         THEN DO
              SET &CIPERCA EQ 450
              GOTO ECAFREE
              ENDO
      IF &CISIZE EQ   1536 AND &IMBEDANS EQ Y -
         THEN DO
              SET &CIPERCA EQ 261
              GOTO ECAFREE
              ENDO
      IF &CISIZE EQ   1536 AND &IMBEDANS NE Y -
         THEN DO
              SET &CIPERCA EQ 270
              GOTO ECAFREE
              ENDO
      IF &CISIZE EQ   2048 AND &IMBEDANS EQ Y -
         THEN DO
              SET &CIPERCA EQ 232
              GOTO ECAFREE
              ENDO
      IF &CISIZE EQ   2048 AND &IMBEDANS NE Y -
         THEN DO
              SET &CIPERCA EQ 240
              GOTO ECAFREE
              ENDO
      IF &CISIZE EQ   2560 AND &IMBEDANS EQ Y -
         THEN DO
              SET &CIPERCA EQ 156
              GOTO ECAFREE
              ENDO
      IF &CISIZE EQ   2560 AND &IMBEDANS NE Y -
         THEN DO
              SET &CIPERCA EQ 162
              GOTO ECAFREE
              ENDO
      IF &CISIZE EQ   3072 AND &IMBEDANS EQ Y -
         THEN DO
              SET &CIPERCA EQ 145
              GOTO ECAFREE
              ENDO
      IF &CISIZE EQ   3072 AND &IMBEDANS NE Y -
         THEN DO
              SET &CIPERCA EQ 150
              GOTO ECAFREE
              ENDO
```

FIGURE F.2   (Continued)

```
IF &CISIZE EQ  3584 AND &IMBEDANS EQ Y -
    THEN DO
        SET &CIPERCA EQ 111
        GOTO ECAFREE
    ENDO
IF &CISIZE EQ  3584 AND &IMBEDANS NE Y -
    THEN DO
        SET &CIPERCA EQ 115
        GOTO ECAFREE
    ENDO
IF &CISIZE EQ  4096 AND &IMBEDANS EQ Y -
    THEN DO
        SET &CIPERCA EQ 116
        GOTO ECAFREE
    ENDO
IF &CISIZE EQ  4096 AND &IMBEDANS NE Y -
    THEN DO
        SET &CIPERCA EQ 120
        GOTO ECAFREE
    ENDO
IF &CISIZE EQ  4608 AND &IMBEDANS EQ Y -
    THEN DO
        SET &CIPERCA EQ 87
        GOTO ECAFREE
    ENDO
IF &CISIZE EQ  4608 AND &IMBEDANS NE Y -
    THEN DO
        SET &CIPERCA EQ 90
        GOTO ECAFREE
    ENDO
IF &CISIZE EQ  5120 AND &IMBEDANS EQ Y -
    THEN DO
        SET &CIPERCA EQ 87
        GOTO ECAFREE
    ENDO
IF &CISIZE EQ  5120 AND &IMBEDANS NE Y -
    THEN DO
        SET &CIPERCA EQ 90
        GOTO ECAFREE
    ENDO
IF &CISIZE EQ  5632 AND &IMBEDANS EQ Y -
    THEN DO
        SET &CIPERCA EQ 71
        GOTO ECAFREE
    ENDO
IF &CISIZE EQ  5632 AND &IMBEDANS NE Y -
    THEN DO
        SET &CIPERCA EQ 73
        GOTO ECAFREE
    ENDO
IF &CISIZE EQ  6144 AND &IMBEDANS EQ Y -
    THEN DO
        SET &CIPERCA EQ 77
        GOTO ECAFREE
    ENDO
IF &CISIZE EQ  6144 AND &IMBEDANS NE Y -
    THEN DO
        SET &CIPERCA EQ 80
        GOTO ECAFREE
    ENDO
IF &CISIZE EQ  6656 AND &IMBEDANS EQ Y -
    THEN DO
        SET &CIPERCA EQ 60
        GOTO ECAFREE
    ENDO
IF &CISIZE EQ  6656 AND &IMBEDANS NE Y -
    THEN DO
        SET &CIPERCA EQ 62
        GOTO ECAFREE
    ENDO
IF &CISIZE EQ  7168 AND &IMBEDANS EQ Y -
    THEN DO
        SET &CIPERCA EQ 62
        GOTO ECAFREE
    ENDO
IF &CISIZE EQ  7168 AND &IMBEDANS NE Y -
    THEN DO
        SET &CIPERCA EQ 64
        GOTO ECAFREE
    ENDO
IF &CISIZE EQ  7680 AND &IMBEDANS EQ Y -
    THEN DO
        SET &CIPERCA EQ 52
        GOTO ECAFREE
    ENDO
IF &CISIZE EQ  7680 AND &IMBEDANS NE Y -
    THEN DO
        SET &CIPERCA EQ 54
        GOTO ECAFREE
    ENDO
IF &CISIZE EQ  8192 AND &IMBEDANS EQ Y -
    THEN DO
        SET &CIPERCA EQ 58
        GOTO ECAFREE
    ENDO
IF &CISIZE EQ  8192 AND &IMBEDANS NE Y -
    THEN DO
        SET &CIPERCA EQ 60
        GOTO ECAFREE
    ENDO
```

```
IF &CISIZE EQ 10240 AND &IMBEDANS EQ Y -
    THEN DO
        SET &CIPERCA EQ 46
        GOTO ECAFREE
    ENDO
IF &CISIZE EQ 10240 AND &IMBEDANS NE Y -
    THEN DO
        SET &CIPERCA EQ 48
        GOTO ECAFREE
    ENDO
IF &CISIZE EQ 12288 AND &IMBEDANS EQ Y -
    THEN DO
        SET &CIPERCA EQ 38
        GOTO ECAFREE
    ENDO
IF &CISIZE EQ 12288 AND &IMBEDANS NE Y -
    THEN DO
        SET &CIPERCA EQ 40
        GOTO ECAFREE
    ENDO
IF &CISIZE EQ 14336 AND &IMBEDANS EQ Y -
    THEN DO
        SET &CIPERCA EQ 33
        GOTO ECAFREE
    ENDO
IF &CISIZE EQ 14336 AND &IMBEDANS NE Y -
    THEN DO
        SET &CIPERCA EQ 34
        GOTO ECAFREE
    ENDO
IF &CISIZE EQ 16384 AND &IMBEDANS EQ Y -
    THEN DO
        SET &CIPERCA EQ 29
        GOTO ECAFREE
    ENDO
IF &CISIZE EQ 16384 AND &IMBEDANS NE Y -
    THEN DO
        SET &CIPERCA EQ 30
        GOTO ECAFREE
    ENDO
IF &CISIZE EQ 18432 AND &IMBEDANS EQ Y -
    THEN DO
        SET &CIPERCA EQ 25
        GOTO ECAFREE
    ENDO
IF &CISIZE EQ 18432 AND &IMBEDANS NE Y -
    THEN DO
        SET &CIPERCA EQ 26
        GOTO ECAFREE
    ENDO
IF &CISIZE EQ 20480 AND &IMBEDANS EQ Y -
    THEN DO
        SET &CIPERCA EQ 23
        GOTO ECAFREE
    ENDO
IF &CISIZE EQ 20480 AND &IMBEDANS NE Y -
    THEN DO
        SET &CIPERCA EQ 24
        GOTO ECAFREE
    ENDO
IF &CISIZE EQ 22528 AND &IMBEDANS EQ Y -
    THEN DO
        SET &CIPERCA EQ 21
        GOTO ECAFREE
    ENDO
IF &CISIZE EQ 22528 AND &IMBEDANS NE Y -
    THEN DO
        SET &CIPERCA EQ 21
        GOTO ECAFREE
    ENDO
IF &CISIZE EQ 24576 AND &IMBEDANS EQ Y -
    THEN DO
        SET &CIPERCA EQ 19
        GOTO ECAFREE
    ENDO
IF &CISIZE EQ 24576 AND &IMBEDANS NE Y -
    THEN DO
        SET &CIPERCA EQ 20
        GOTO ECAFREE
    ENDO
IF &CISIZE EQ 26624 AND &IMBEDANS EQ Y -
    THEN DO
        SET &CIPERCA EQ 17
        GOTO ECAFREE
    ENDO
IF &CISIZE EQ 26624 AND &IMBEDANS NE Y -
    THEN DO
        SET &CIPERCA EQ 18
        GOTO ECAFREE
    ENDO
IF &CISIZE EQ 28672 AND &IMBEDANS EQ Y -
    THEN DO
        SET &CIPERCA EQ 16
        GOTO ECAFREE
    ENDO
IF &CISIZE EQ 28672 AND &IMBEDANS NE Y -
    THEN DO
        SET &CIPERCA EQ 17
        GOTO ECAFREE
    ENDO
```

FIGURE F.2   (Continued)

```
IF &CISIZE EQ 30720 AND &IMBEDANS EQ Y -
   THEN DO
        SET &CIPERCA EQ 15
        GOTO ECAFREE
        ENDO
IF &CISIZE EQ 30720 AND &IMBEDANS NE Y -
   THEN DO
        SET &CIPERCA EQ 16
        GOTO ECAFREE
        ENDO
IF &CISIZE EQ 32768 AND &IMBEDANS EQ Y -
   THEN DO
        SET &CIPERCA EQ 14
        GOTO ECAFREE
        ENDO
IF &CISIZE EQ 32768 AND &IMBEDANS NE Y -
   THEN DO
        SET &CIPERCA EQ 15
        GOTO ECAFREE
        ENDO
WRITE YOU ENTERED AN INVALID CISIZE
WRITENR DO YOU WANT TO TRY AGAIN - Y OR N ==>
READ &ANSWER
IF &ANSWER EQ Y    -
   THEN GOTO START
ELSE  DO
        WRITE GOODBYE
        END
        ENDO
EIGHTY:      SET &ANSWER EQ Y
    SET &TRKPERCA = 15
    IF &IMBEDANS = Y -
       THEN SET &TRKPERCA = &TRKPERCA - 1
/* DETERMINE CIS PER CA FOR 3380 */
   IF &CISIZE EQ    512 AND &IMBEDANS EQ Y -
      THEN DO
           SET &CIPERCA EQ 644
           GOTO ECAFREE
           ENDO
   IF &CISIZE EQ    512 AND &IMBEDANS NE Y -
      THEN DO
           SET &CIPERCA EQ 690
           GOTO ECAFREE
           ENDO
   IF &CISIZE EQ   1024 AND &IMBEDANS EQ Y -
      THEN DO
           SET &CIPERCA EQ 434
           GOTO ECAFREE
           ENDO
   IF &CISIZE EQ   1024 AND &IMBEDANS NE Y -
      THEN DO
           SET &CIPERCA EQ 465
           GOTO ECAFREE
           ENDO
   IF &CISIZE EQ   1536 AND &IMBEDANS EQ Y -
      THEN DO
           SET &CIPERCA EQ 214
           GOTO ECAFREE
           ENDO
   IF &CISIZE EQ   1536 AND &IMBEDANS NE Y -
      THEN DO
           SET &CIPERCA EQ 230
           GOTO ECAFREE
           ENDO
   IF &CISIZE EQ   2048 AND &IMBEDANS EQ Y -
      THEN DO
           SET &CIPERCA EQ 252
           GOTO ECAFREE
           ENDO
   IF &CISIZE EQ   2048 AND &IMBEDANS NE Y -
      THEN DO
           SET &CIPERCA EQ 270
           GOTO ECAFREE
           ENDO
   IF &CISIZE EQ   2560 AND &IMBEDANS EQ Y -
      THEN DO
           SET &CIPERCA EQ 128
           GOTO ECAFREE
           ENDO
   IF &CISIZE EQ   2560 AND &IMBEDANS NE Y -
      THEN DO
           SET &CIPERCA EQ 138
           GOTO ECAFREE
           ENDO
   IF &CISIZE EQ   3072 AND &IMBEDANS EQ Y -
      THEN DO
           SET &CIPERCA EQ 144
           GOTO ECAFREE
           ENDO
   IF &CISIZE EQ   3072 AND &IMBEDANS NE Y -
      THEN DO
           SET &CIPERCA EQ 155
           GOTO ECAFREE
           ENDO
   IF &CISIZE EQ   3584 AND &IMBEDANS EQ Y -
      THEN DO
           SET &CIPERCA EQ 92
           GOTO ECAFREE
           ENDO
   IF &CISIZE EQ   3584 AND &IMBEDANS NE Y -
      THEN DO
           SET &CIPERCA EQ 98
           GOTO ECAFREE

           ENDO
IF &CISIZE EQ   4096 AND &IMBEDANS EQ Y -
   THEN DO
        SET &CIPERCA EQ 140
        GOTO ECAFREE
        ENDO
IF &CISIZE EQ   4096 AND &IMBEDANS NE Y -
   THEN DO
        SET &CIPERCA EQ 150
        GOTO ECAFREE
        ENDO
IF &CISIZE EQ   4608 AND &IMBEDANS EQ Y -
   THEN DO
        SET &CIPERCA EQ 71
        GOTO ECAFREE
        ENDO
IF &CISIZE EQ   4608 AND &IMBEDANS NE Y -
   THEN DO
        SET &CIPERCA EQ 76
        GOTO ECAFREE
        ENDO
IF &CISIZE EQ   5120 AND &IMBEDANS EQ Y -
   THEN DO
        SET &CIPERCA EQ 86
        GOTO ECAFREE
        ENDO
IF &CISIZE EQ   5120 AND &IMBEDANS NE Y -
   THEN DO
        SET &CIPERCA EQ 93
        GOTO ECAFREE
        ENDO
IF &CISIZE EQ   5632 AND &IMBEDANS EQ Y -
   THEN DO
        SET &CIPERCA EQ 58
        GOTO ECAFREE
        ENDO
IF &CISIZE EQ   5632 AND &IMBEDANS NE Y -
   THEN DO
        SET &CIPERCA EQ 62
        GOTO ECAFREE
        ENDO
IF &CISIZE EQ   6144 AND &IMBEDANS EQ Y -
   THEN DO
        SET &CIPERCA EQ 84
        GOTO ECAFREE
        ENDO
IF &CISIZE EQ   6144 AND &IMBEDANS NE Y -
   THEN DO
        SET &CIPERCA EQ 90
        GOTO ECAFREE
        ENDO
IF &CISIZE EQ   6656 AND &IMBEDANS EQ Y -
   THEN DO
        SET &CIPERCA EQ 49
        GOTO ECAFREE
        ENDO
IF &CISIZE EQ   6656 AND &IMBEDANS NE Y -
   THEN DO
        SET &CIPERCA EQ 53
        GOTO ECAFREE
        ENDO
IF &CISIZE EQ   7168 AND &IMBEDANS EQ Y -
   THEN DO
        SET &CIPERCA EQ 62
        GOTO ECAFREE
        ENDO
IF &CISIZE EQ   7168 AND &IMBEDANS NE Y -
   THEN DO
        SET &CIPERCA EQ 66
        GOTO ECAFREE
        ENDO
IF &CISIZE EQ   7680 AND &IMBEDANS EQ Y -
   THEN DO
        SET &CIPERCA EQ 42
        GOTO ECAFREE
        ENDO
IF &CISIZE EQ   7680 AND &IMBEDANS NE Y -
   THEN DO
        SET &CIPERCA EQ 46
        GOTO ECAFREE
        ENDO
IF &CISIZE EQ   8192 AND &IMBEDANS EQ Y -
   THEN DO
        SET &CIPERCA EQ 70
        GOTO ECAFREE
        ENDO
IF &CISIZE EQ   8192 AND &IMBEDANS NE Y -
   THEN DO
        SET &CIPERCA EQ 75
        GOTO ECAFREE
        ENDO
IF &CISIZE EQ  10240 AND &IMBEDANS EQ Y -
   THEN DO
        SET &CIPERCA EQ 50
        GOTO ECAFREE
        ENDO
IF &CISIZE EQ  10240 AND &IMBEDANS NE Y -
   THEN DO
        SET &CIPERCA EQ 54
        GOTO ECAFREE
        ENDO
IF &CISIZE EQ  12288 AND &IMBEDANS EQ Y -
   THEN DO
```

FIGURE F.2   (Continued)

```
        SET &CIPERCA EQ 46                              GOTO ECAFREE
        GOTO ECAFREE                                    ENDO
        ENDO                                    IF &CISIZE EQ 32768 AND &IMBEDANS NE Y -
IF &CISIZE EQ 12288 AND &IMBEDANS NE Y -            THEN DO
    THEN DO                                             SET &CIPERCA EQ 18
        SET &CIPERCA EQ 50                              GOTO ECAFREE
        GOTO ECAFREE                                    ENDO
        ENDO                                    WRITE YOU ENTERED AN INVALID CISIZE
IF &CISIZE EQ 14336 AND &IMBEDANS EQ Y -        WRITENR DO YOU WANT TO TRY AGAIN - Y OR N ==>
    THEN DO                                     READ &ANSWER
        SET &CIPERCA EQ 36                      IF &ANSWER EQ Y  -
        GOTO ECAFREE                                THEN GOTO START
        ENDO                                    ELSE  DO
IF &CISIZE EQ 14336 AND &IMBEDANS NE Y -                WRITE GOODBYE
    THEN DO                                             END
        SET &CIPERCA EQ 38                              ENDO
        GOTO ECAFREE                    ECAFREE:     SET &ANSWER EQ Y
        ENDO                            /* PROMPT FOR CAFREESPACE */
IF &CISIZE EQ 16384 AND &IMBEDANS EQ Y -            SET &ARECPERCI = &RECPERCI - &CALCFREE
    THEN DO                                     WRITE MAX RECORDS PER CI = &RECPERCI
        SET &CIPERCA EQ 35                      WRITE   WITH &CALCFREE RECORDS FOR CIFREESPACE
        GOTO ECAFREE                            WRITE    PLUS &ARECPERCI RECORDS AVAILABLE AT INITIAL LOAD
        ENDO                                    WRITE MAX CIS PER CA = &CIPERCA
IF &CISIZE EQ 16384 AND &IMBEDANS NE Y -        WRITENR ENTER MINIMUM # OF CIS PER CA YOU WANT FOR CAFREESPACE ==>
    THEN DO                                     READ &CIFREECA
        SET &CIPERCA EQ 37                      IF &CIFREECA LT &CIPERCA -
        GOTO ECAFREE                                THEN GOTO RECCA
        ENDO                                    WRITE YOU REQUESTED &CIFREECA AND &CIPERCA IS THE MAX
IF &CISIZE EQ 18432 AND &IMBEDANS EQ Y -        WRITENR DO YOU WANT TO TRY AGAIN - Y OR N ==>
    THEN DO                                     READ &ANSWER
        SET &CIPERCA EQ 28                      IF &ANSWER EQ Y   -
        GOTO ECAFREE                                THEN GOTO ECAFREE
        ENDO                                    ELSE  DO
IF &CISIZE EQ 18432 AND &IMBEDANS NE Y -                WRITE GOODBYE
    THEN DO                                             END
        SET &CIPERCA EQ 30                              ENDO
        GOTO ECAFREE                    RECCA:     SET &ANSWER EQ Y
        ENDO                            /* CALC CAFREESPACE */
IF &CISIZE EQ 20480 AND &IMBEDANS EQ Y -            SET &CAPERCENT = ( &CIFREECA * 100 ) / &CIPERCA
    THEN DO                             LOOPTWO:     SET &ANSWER EQ Y
        SET &CIPERCA EQ 28              /* ADJUST CAFREESPACE */
        GOTO ECAFREE                            SET &CALCCAFREE = ( &CIPERCA * &CAPERCENT ) / 100
        ENDO                                    IF &CALCCAFREE GE &CIFREECA -
IF &CISIZE EQ 20480 AND &IMBEDANS NE Y -                THEN GOTO CATOTAL
    THEN DO                                     SET &CAPERCENT = &CAPERCENT + 1
        SET &CIPERCA EQ 30                      GOTO LOOPTWO
        GOTO ECAFREE                    CATOTAL:     SET &ANSWER EQ Y
        ENDO                            /* CALC RECS PER CA AT INITIAL LOAD */
IF &CISIZE EQ 22528 AND &IMBEDANS EQ Y -            SET &CIAVAIL = &CIPERCA - &CALCCAFREE
    THEN DO                                     SET &RECPERCA = &CIAVAIL * &ARECPERCI
        SET &CIPERCA EQ 22              ERECS:     SET &ANSWER EQ Y
        GOTO ECAFREE                    /* PROMPT FOR NUMBER OF RECORDS */
        ENDO                                    WRITENR ENTER THE NUMBER OF RECORDS YOU WANT TO LOAD ==>
IF &CISIZE EQ 22528 AND &IMBEDANS NE Y -        READ &NUMRECS
    THEN DO                                     IF &NUMRECS GT 0 -
        SET &CIPERCA EQ 24                          THEN GOTO SETCYLS
        GOTO ECAFREE                            WRITE YOU ENTERED AN NUMBER LESS THAN 1
        ENDO                                    WRITENR DO YOU WANT TO TRY AGAIN - Y OR N ==>
IF &CISIZE EQ 24576 AND &IMBEDANS EQ Y -        READ &ANSWER
    THEN DO                                     IF &ANSWER EQ Y   -
        SET &CIPERCA EQ 23                          THEN GOTO ERECS
        GOTO ECAFREE                            ELSE  DO
        ENDO                                            WRITE GOODBYE
IF &CISIZE EQ 24576 AND &IMBEDANS NE Y -                END
    THEN DO                                             ENDO
        SET &CIPERCA EQ 25              SETCYLS:     SET &ANSWER EQ Y
        GOTO ECAFREE                    /* CALC NUMBER OF CYLINDERS NEEDED */
        ENDO                                    SET &CYLS = ((( &NUMRECS * 100 ) / &RECPERCA ) + 99 ) / 100
IF &CISIZE EQ 26624 AND &IMBEDANS EQ Y -            SET &MRECPERCA = &RECPERCI * &CIPERCA
    THEN DO                             LOOPTRE:     SET &ANSWER EQ Y
        SET &CIPERCA EQ 19              /* ADJUST REQUIRED CYLINDERS */
        GOTO ECAFREE                            SET &MAXRECS = &RECPERCI * &CIPERCA * &CYLS
        ENDO                                    SET &LOADRECS = &RECPERCA * &CYLS
IF &CISIZE EQ 26624 AND &IMBEDANS NE Y -        IF &LOADRECS LT &NUMRECS -
    THEN DO                                         THEN DO
        SET &CIPERCA EQ 20                              SET &CYLS = &CYLS + 1
        GOTO ECAFREE                                    GOTO LOOPTRE
        ENDO                                            ENDO
IF &CISIZE EQ 28672 AND &IMBEDANS EQ Y -        SET &SECONDARY = (&CYLS / 10)
    THEN DO                                     IF &SECONDARY < 1 -
        SET &CIPERCA EQ 20                          THEN SET &SECONDARY = 1
        GOTO ECAFREE                            SET &CYLS = &CYLS + 1         /* ADD 1 CYLINDER FOR THE INDEX */
        ENDO                                    WRITENR ENTER DATA SET NAME ==>
IF &CISIZE EQ 28672 AND &IMBEDANS NE Y -        READ &FILENAME
    THEN DO                                     SET &BUFND = (2 * (&CIPERCA / &TRKPERCA) + 1)
        SET &CIPERCA EQ 21                      IF &BUFND < 4 -
        GOTO ECAFREE                                THEN SET &BUFND = 4
        ENDO                                    /* CALL CLEAR SCREEN PROGRAM HERE */
IF &CISIZE EQ 30720 AND &IMBEDANS EQ Y -        WRITE     PRACTICAL VSAM - JOHN WILEY AND SONS, 1988 - ISBN 0-471--
    THEN DO                             85107-8
        SET &CIPERCA EQ 16                      WRITE    SPACE CALC FOR FIXED LENGTH RECORD KSDS WITH CA SIZE ONE -
        GOTO ECAFREE                    CYLINDER
        ENDO                                    WRITE           BY &SYSUID AT &SYSTIME ON &SYSDATE
IF &CISIZE EQ 30720 AND &IMBEDANS NE Y -        WRITE           FOR DATA SET &FILENAME
    THEN DO                                     WRITE
        SET &CIPERCA EQ 18                      WRITE SEQ PROCESSING BUFFERS: // AMP=('AMORG,BUFNI=1,BUFND=&BUFND')
        GOTO ECAFREE                            WRITE CLUSTER OPTIONS ARE CYLINDERS ( &CYLS &SECONDARY )
        ENDO                                    IF &IMBEDANS EQ Y -
IF &CISIZE EQ 32768 AND &IMBEDANS EQ Y -            THEN WRITE                    IMBED
    THEN DO                                     ELSE WRITE                    NOIMBED
        SET &CIPERCA EQ 17
```

FIGURE F.2   (Continued)

```
WRITE                    RECORDSIZE ( &RECSIZE , &RECSIZE )         WRITE MAX RECORDS PER CA = &MRECPERCA
WRITE                    VOLUMES(        )         <== FOR &DASD UNIT   WRITE MAX RECS FOR THE FILE = &MAXRECS
WRITE DATA     OPTIONS ARE FREESPACE ( &PERCENT , &CAPERCENT )      WRITE *************** STATISTICS AT INITIAL LOAD *******
WRITE                    CISIZE ( &CISIZE )                         WRITE RECORDS PER CI = &ARECPERCI  - FREE RECORDS PER CI = &CALCFREE
WRITE *************** FILE STATISTICS ******************            WRITE CIS PER CA      = &CIAVAIL    - FREE CIS PER CA   = &CALCCAFREE
WRITE &UNUSABLE BYTES OF THE CI ARE UNUSABLE                        WRITE RECORDS PER CA = &RECPERCA
WRITE MAX RECORDS PER CI = &RECPERCI                                WRITE MAX RECORDS WITH NO SPLITS = &LOADRECS
WRITE MAX CIS PER CA = &CIPERCA                                     END
```

FIGURE F.2   (Continued)

length can be used. As described in the foregoing discussion of VSAMCISZ, a local cus-tomization you will find helpful is to replace the comment concerning the clearing of the terminal screen with a call to your local CLIST screen clearing program.

VSAMSPAC is invoked by name at the TSO READY mode function or on the TSO/ISPF command line by prefacing the name with "TSO":

COMMAND = = > TSO VSAMSPAC

You can, if you prefer, house the CLIST in your own library and use it as described in the foregoing discussion of VSAMCISZ.

Since the determination of disk space and free space requirements are nontrivial, VSAMSPAC prompts for several items of information you must be prepared to supply:

- control interval size
- record size
- CI free space in records per CI
- whether or not the IMBED option is to be used
- disk device type
- number of empty CIs wanted per CA for free space
- number of records to be loaded to the data set
- name of the data set.

You will find it handy to have used VSAMCISZ to determine an optimal control interval size before using VSAMSPAC to complete your KSDS design tasks.

Two assumptions made by VSAMSPAC are that the control area size will be one cyl-inder and that the record length is fixed in length. The output of VSAMSPAC is compre-hensive and includes the actual IDCAMS FREESPACE, RECORDSIZE, and CISIZE control statements needed to define the data set. An example of the output is shown on page 32.

VSAMSPAC checks for valid record length and disk type, and that the requested num-ber of free space records per CI and free CIs per CA do not exceed the available space. The record length entered must be between 12 and 32,761 bytes and the entered device type must be 3330, 3350, or 3380. If an invalid response is entered, VSAMSPAC prompts for a chance to start over or exit. No numeric input checking is performed.

VSAMBUFS

VSAMBUFS, a combination of a TSO CLIST and a COBOL program that work together, is presented in Figure F.3(a) and F.3(b). VSAMBUFS is a routine that calculates the optimal number of data and index component buffers for a key sequenced data set, and composes the AMP parameter coding to specify them. VSAMBUFS requires only the entry of a key sequenced data set name at the CLIST prompt. It automatically obtains the necessary data

```
/*                                                              */
/*   TSO CLIST  VSAMBUFS    BY RICH GUZIK    AUGUST, 1987       */
/*                                                              */
/*   FOR YOUR CONVENIENCE THIS ITEM IS AVAILABLE IN MACHINE     */
/*   READABLE FORM FOR UPLOADING TO AN IBM MAINFRAME.           */
/*                                                              */
/*                                                              */
/*                                                              */
/*   NOTE: THIS CLIST CALLS A COBOL PROGRAM, IT CANNOT OPERATE  */
/*   WITHOUT IT.  SEE THE DISCUSSION IN APPENDIX F TO INSTALL IT.*/
/*                                                              */
PROC 1 KSDSNAME
CONTROL PROMPT NOFLUSH NOMSG NOLIST
/* CLIST TO CALCULATE VSAM BUFFER REQUIREMENTS */
/* ----------------**** VSAMBUFS ****---------------- */
     /* CALL CLEAR SCREEN PROGRAM HERE */
FREE FILE(SYSIN SYSPRINT SYSOUT) ATTR(SYSIN1 SYSPRNT2)
ATTR SYSIN1 BLKSIZE(80)
ATTR SYSPRNT2 RECFM(V) LRECL(125) BLKSIZE(6129)
ALLOC FILE(SYSIN) SPACE(1) TRACKS USING(SYSIN1)
ALLOC FILE(SYSPRINT) SPACE(5 1) TRACKS USING(SYSPRNT2)
ALLOC FILE(SYSOUT) DA(*)
CALL 'VSAM.LOADLIB(VBUFCALC)' '&KSDSNAME'
WRITE
WRITE          CLIST INVOKED BY &SYSUID AT &SYSTIME ON &SYSDATE
FREE FILE(SYSIN SYSPRINT SYSOUT) ATTR(SYSIN1 SYSPRNT2)
END
```

FIGURE F.3a   Source code for TSO CLIST VASMBUFS, which calls COBOL program VBUFCALC to compute optimal buffers and compose JCL AMP parameters to secure them

```
ID DIVISION.
PROGRAM-ID. VBUFCALC.
AUTHOR.  R. GUZIK.
DATE-WRITTEN.  MARCH 1987.
*    DETERMINE BUFFER REQUIREMENTS FOR A VSAM KSDS
*    FOR RANDOM, SEQUENTIAL AND MIXED MODE PROCESSING.
*
*    THIS SOURCE CODE IS AVAILABLE IN MACHINE READABLE FORM
*    FOR UPLOAD
*
*
ENVIRONMENT DIVISION.
INPUT-OUTPUT SECTION.
FILE-CONTROL.
     SELECT IDCAMS-INPUT    ASSIGN UT-S-SYSIN.
     SELECT EXTRACT-FILE    ASSIGN UT-S-SYSPRINT.
*
DATA DIVISION.
FILE SECTION.
*
FD  IDCAMS-INPUT               DATA RECORD ICDAMS-REC
    RECORDING F                LABEL RECORDS STANDARD
    BLOCK 0 RECORDS            RECORD  80 CHARACTERS.
01  IDCAMS-REC.
    05  IDCAMS-PREFIX          PIC X(11).
    05  IDCAMS-OUT-DSN         PIC X(69).
*
FD  EXTRACT-FILE
    RECORDING V                LABEL RECORDS STANDARD
    BLOCK 0 RECORDS            RECORD 24 TO 121 CHARACTERS.
01  LISTC-IN-TYPE.
```

FIGURE F.3b   Source code for COBOL program VBUFCALC, called by TSO CLIST VSAMBUFS

```
        03  FILLER       PIC X(01).
        03  LISTC-IN-TYPE-DATA.
            05  FILE-TYPE-IN   PIC X(03).
                88  RIGHT-TYPE-IN      VALUES 'CLU' 'AIX'.
            05  FILLER       PIC X(13).
            05  DSN-IN       PIC X(44).
            05  FILLER       PIC X(60).
    01  LISTC-IN-DATA.
        03  FRONT-1      PIC X(01).
        03  LISTC-IN-DATA120.
            05  FILLER     PIC X(1).
            05  FRONT-6      PIC X(06).
            05  LABEL-1-IN  PIC X(09).
                88  RIGHT-LABEL-1       VALUE 'KEYLEN---'.
                88  RIGHT-LABEL-2       VALUE 'RKP------'.
                88  RIGHT-LABEL-3       VALUE 'SHROPTNS('.
                88  RIGHT-LABEL-4       VALUE 'DEVTYPE--'.
                88  RIGHT-LABEL-5       VALUE 'VOLFLAG--'.
                88  RIGHT-LABEL-6       VALUE 'REC-TOTAL'.
                88  RIGHT-LABEL-7       VALUE 'REC-DELET'.
            05  FILLER       PIC X(03).
            05  DATA-1-IN   PIC X(12).
            05  FILLER       PIC X(05).
            05  LABEL-2-IN  PIC X(12).
            05  DATA-2-IN   PIC X(12).
            05  FILLER       PIC X(05).
            05  LABEL-3-IN  PIC X(12).
            05  DATA-3-IN   PIC X(12).
            05  FILLER       PIC X(05).
            05  LABEL-4-IN  PIC X(05).
                88  LABEL-4I    VALUE 'IMBED'.
                88  LABEL-4N    VALUE 'NOIMB'.
            05  FILLER       PIC X(07).
            05  DATA-4-IN   PIC X(12).
            05  FILLER       PIC X(02).
*
    WORKING-STORAGE SECTION.
    01  ALL-CONSTANT          PIC X(5)  VALUE ') ALL'.
    01  SPACE-CONSTANT        PIC X(5)  VALUE LOW-VALUE.
*
    01  LISTCAT-EXTRACTS.
        05  LC-CISIZE         PIC X(12).
        05  RD-CISIZE     REDEFINES LC-CISIZE      PIC 9(12).
        05  LC-CI-CA          PIC X(12).
        05  RD-CI-CA      REDEFINES  LC-CI-CA      PIC 9(12).
        05  LC-IMBED          PIC X(01).
        05  LC-HI-USED-RBA    PIC X(12).
        05  RD-HI-USED-RBA REDEFINES  LC-HI-USED-RBA PIC 9(12).
        05  LC-TRACKS-CA      PIC X(12).
        05  RD-TRACKS-CA  REDEFINES  LC-TRACKS-CA  PIC 9(12).
        05  LC-REC-TOTAL      PIC X(12).
        05  RD-REC-TOTAL  REDEFINES  LC-REC-TOTAL  PIC 9(12).
        05  LC-LEVELS         PIC X(12).
        05  RD-LEVELS     REDEFINES  LC-LEVELS     PIC 9(12).
*
    01  BUFFER-VALUES.
        05  RANDOM-INDEX-MIN      PIC 9(3)          VALUE 3.
        05  RANDOM-INDEX-MAX      PIC 9(3)          VALUE 0.
        05  RANDOM-DATA-MIN-MAX   PIC 9(3)          VALUE 2.
        05  SEQUEN-INDEX-MIN-MAX  PIC 9(3)          VALUE 1.
        05  SEQUEN-DATA-MIN       PIC 9(3)          VALUE 4.
        05  SEQUEN-DATA-MAX       PIC 9(3)          VALUE 0.
        05  SKPSEQ-INDEX-MIN      PIC 9(3)          VALUE 3.
        05  SKPSEQ-INDEX-MAX      PIC 9(3)          VALUE 0.
        05  SKPSEQ-DATA-MIN       PIC 9(3)          VALUE 4.
        05  TEMP-HOLD-AREA        PIC S9(3)         VALUE +0.
*
```

FIGURE F.3b (Continued)

```
01  ERROR-MSG.
    05  FILLER  PIC X(31)  VALUE
        'A DATA SET NAME WAS NOT ENTERED'.
*
LINKAGE SECTION.
01  INPUT-PARM.
    05  INPUT-LENGTH      PIC 9(4)   COMP.
    05  INPUT-DSN         PIC X(44).
/
PROCEDURE DIVISION USING INPUT-PARM.
CHECK-PARM.
    IF INPUT-LENGTH = 0
        DISPLAY ERROR-MSG
        GOBACK.
*
PROCESS-PARM.
    OPEN OUTPUT IDCAMS-INPUT.
    MOVE ' LISTC ENT(' TO IDCAMS-PREFIX.
    MOVE SPACES TO IDCAMS-OUT-DSN.
    STRING INPUT-DSN DELIMITED BY SPACE-CONSTANT
            ALL-CONSTANT DELIMITED BY SIZE
            INTO IDCAMS-OUT-DSN.
    WRITE IDCAMS-REC.
    CLOSE IDCAMS-INPUT.
    CALL 'IDCAMS'.
*
PROCESS-EXTRACT-FILE.
    OPEN INPUT EXTRACT-FILE.
*
READ-EXTRACT.
    READ EXTRACT-FILE  AT END  GO TO ABNORMAL-EOJ.
*
IS-IT-AIX-OR-CLUSTER.
    PERFORM READ-EXTRACT.
    PERFORM READ-EXTRACT.
    PERFORM READ-EXTRACT.
    IF RIGHT-TYPE-IN
        NEXT SENTENCE
    ELSE
        DISPLAY ' THE FOLLOWING IS NOT A KSDS'
        DISPLAY LISTC-IN-TYPE-DATA
        GO TO END-OF-JOB.
*
FIND-CISIZE.
    PERFORM READ-EXTRACT.
    IF RIGHT-LABEL-1
        MOVE DATA-4-IN TO LC-CISIZE
    ELSE
        GO TO FIND-CISIZE.
*
FIND-CI-PER-CA.
    PERFORM READ-EXTRACT.
    IF RIGHT-LABEL-2
        MOVE DATA-4-IN TO LC-CI-CA
    ELSE
        GO TO FIND-CI-PER-CA.
*
FIND-IMBED.
    PERFORM READ-EXTRACT.
    IF RIGHT-LABEL-3
        NEXT SENTENCE
    ELSE
        GO TO FIND-IMBED.
    IF LABEL-4N
        MOVE 'N' TO LC-IMBED
```

FIGURE F.3b   (Continued)

```
        ELSE
            MOVE 'Y' TO LC-IMBED.
*
    FIND-HI-USED-RBA.
        PERFORM READ-EXTRACT.
        IF RIGHT-LABEL-4
            MOVE DATA-3-IN TO LC-HI-USED-RBA
        ELSE
            GO TO FIND-HI-USED-RBA.
*
    FIND-TRACKS-PER-CA.
        PERFORM READ-EXTRACT.
        IF RIGHT-LABEL-5
            MOVE DATA-2-IN TO LC-TRACKS-CA
        ELSE
            GO TO FIND-TRACKS-PER-CA.
*
    FIND-INDEX-REC-TOTAL.
        PERFORM READ-EXTRACT.
        IF RIGHT-LABEL-6
            MOVE DATA-1-IN TO LC-REC-TOTAL
        ELSE
            GO TO FIND-INDEX-REC-TOTAL.
*
    FIND-INDEX-LEVELS.
        PERFORM READ-EXTRACT.
        IF RIGHT-LABEL-7
            MOVE DATA-4-IN TO LC-LEVELS
        ELSE
            GO TO FIND-INDEX-LEVELS.
*
    ADJUST-EXTRACT-FIELDS.
        INSPECT LC-CISIZE        REPLACING LEADING '-' BY '0'.
        INSPECT LC-CI-CA         REPLACING LEADING '-' BY '0'.
        INSPECT LC-HI-USED-RBA   REPLACING LEADING '-' BY '0'.
        INSPECT LC-TRACKS-CA     REPLACING LEADING '-' BY '0'.
        INSPECT LC-REC-TOTAL     REPLACING LEADING '-' BY '0'.
        INSPECT LC-LEVELS        REPLACING LEADING '-' BY '0'.
        IF RD-TRACKS-CA = 1
            GO TO PERFORM-CALCULATIONS.
*
******* ASSUME A CA SIZE OF 1 CYLINDER *******
*
        IF LC-IMBED = 'Y'
            SUBTRACT 1 FROM RD-TRACKS-CA.
*
    PERFORM-CALCULATIONS.
        IF RD-LEVELS GREATER RANDOM-INDEX-MIN
            MOVE RD-LEVELS TO RANDOM-INDEX-MIN.
        COMPUTE TEMP-HOLD-AREA =
        RD-REC-TOTAL - ((RD-HI-USED-RBA) / (RD-CISIZE * RD-CI-CA)).
        IF TEMP-HOLD-AREA LESS RANDOM-INDEX-MIN
            MOVE RANDOM-INDEX-MIN TO RANDOM-INDEX-MAX
        ELSE
            MOVE TEMP-HOLD-AREA TO RANDOM-INDEX-MAX.
        COMPUTE TEMP-HOLD-AREA = 2 * (RD-CI-CA / RD-TRACKS-CA) + 1.
            MOVE TEMP-HOLD-AREA TO SEQUEN-DATA-MAX.
        IF TEMP-HOLD-AREA LESS SEQUEN-DATA-MIN
            MOVE SEQUEN-DATA-MIN TO SEQUEN-DATA-MAX
        ELSE
            MOVE TEMP-HOLD-AREA TO SEQUEN-DATA-MAX.
        MOVE RANDOM-INDEX-MAX TO SKPSEQ-INDEX-MAX.
        MOVE SEQUEN-DATA-MAX  TO SKPSEQ-DATA-MAX.
*
    WRITE-DATA.
        DISPLAY 'PRACTICAL VSAM - JOHN WILEY AND SONS, 1988 - '
                'ISBN 0-471-85107-8'.
```

FIGURE F.3b   (Continued)

```
        DISPLAY '         OPTIMUM VSAM BATCH BUFFERS FOR ' INPUT-DSN.
        DISPLAY '                          MIN   MAX'.
        DISPLAY '          RANDOM      INDEX ' RANDOM-INDEX-MIN
           ' ' RANDOM-INDEX-MAX.
        DISPLAY '                       DATA ' RANDOM-DATA-MIN-MAX
           ' ' RANDOM-DATA-MIN-MAX.
        DISPLAY '          SEQUENTIAL  INDEX ' SEQUEN-INDEX-MIN-MAX
           ' ' SEQUEN-INDEX-MIN-MAX.
        DISPLAY '                       DATA ' SEQUEN-DATA-MIN
           ' ' SEQUEN-DATA-MAX.
        DISPLAY '          MIXED MODE  INDEX ' SKPSEQ-INDEX-MIN
           ' ' SKPSEQ-INDEX-MAX.
        DISPLAY '                       DATA ' SKPSEQ-DATA-MIN
           ' ' SKPSEQ-DATA-MAX.
        DISPLAY ' '.
        DISPLAY '         AMP PARAMETER FOR RANDOM PROCESSING IS'.
        DISPLAY '              AMP=(''BUFNI=' RANDOM-INDEX-MAX
           ',BUFND=' RANDOM-DATA-MIN-MAX ''')'.
        DISPLAY ' '.
        DISPLAY '         AMP PARAMETER FOR SEQUENTIAL PROCESSING IS'.
        DISPLAY '              AMP=(''BUFNI=' SEQUEN-INDEX-MIN-MAX
           ',BUFND=' SEQUEN-DATA-MAX ''')'.
        DISPLAY ' '.
        DISPLAY '         AMP PARAMETER FOR MIXED PROCESSING IS'.
        DISPLAY '              AMP=(''BUFNI=' SKPSEQ-INDEX-MAX
           ',BUFND=' SKPSEQ-DATA-MAX ''')'.
    *
     END-OF-JOB.
        CLOSE EXTRACT-FILE.
        GOBACK.
    *
     ABNORMAL-EOJ.
        DISPLAY ' PREMATURE EOF ON EXTRACT FILE'.
        GO TO END-OF-JOB.
    *    ******** LAST LINE OF VBUFCALC ********
```

FIGURE F.3b   (Continued)

```
//FSBT677A  JOB AK00PROD,'DP4-GUZIK',CLASS=W,MSGCLASS=X,
// MSGLEVEL=(1,1),NOTIFY=BT05677
//*
//*     CALCULATE BATCH BUFFERS FOR A KSDS IN A BATCH MODE
//*     THIS JCL = BT05677.SOURCE.CNTL(JCLFF3C)
//*
//*     NOTE:  THE VBUFCALC PROGRAM MAKES CREATIVE USE
//*     OF THE TEMPORARY DATA SETS NAMED AT //SYSIN AND
//*     //SYSPRINT AS A MEANS OF COMMUNICATING WITH
//*     IDCAMS WHEN IT CALLS IT.  THESE ARE REGARDED AS
//*     WORK FILES IN THIS JOB STREAM AND THEREFORE
//*     DO NOT CARRY ANY DISP PARAMETERS, IMPLYING A
//*     DISPOSITION OF (NEW,DELETE)
//*
//VSAMBUFS PROC  DASD='SYSDA',LOADMOD='VSAM.LOADLIB'
//CALCBUFS EXEC  PGM=VBUFCALC,PARM='&KSDSNAME'
//STEPLIB   DD   DSN=&LOADMOD,DISP=SHR
//SYSIN     DD   DSN=&IDCAMSIN,
//  UNIT=&DASD,
//  DCB=(RECFM=FB,LRECL=80,BLKSIZE=80),
//  SPACE=(TRK,1)
//SYSPRINT  DD   DSN=&IDCAMSUT,
//  UNIT=&DASD,
//  DCB=(RECFM=VB,LRECL=125,BLKSIZE=6129),
```

FIGURE F.3c   JCL to invoke program VBUFCALC in a batch mode rather than from a TSO CLIST

```
//   SPACE=(TRK,(5,1))
//SYSOUT      DD   SYSOUT=*
//SYSUDUMP    DD   SYSOUT=*
//   PEND
//*
//*       EXECUTE THE PROC INSTREAM
//*
//CALCIT    EXEC VSAMBUFS,KSDSNAME='key.sequenced.data.set.name'
//
```

FIGURE F.3c   (*Continued*)

set attribute information from the system catalog to perform its calculations. You can use VSAMBUFS to rapidly maximize the efficiency of job control language dealing with existing key sequenced data sets.

VSAMBUFS is a TSO CLIST that invokes a COBOL program named VBUFCALC; the COBOL program calls IDCAMS itself in a clever way. VBUFCALC calculates the minimum and maximum batch buffer requirements for any existing KSDS, base cluster, or alternate index. The minimum and maximum buffer requirements are determined for each of the three processing modes—random, sequential, and mixed mode. Appropriate error messages are returned if a data set specified to VSAMBUFS is not found. As with other CLISTs included in this book, this line within the source code:

```
/* CALL PROGRAM TO CLEAR THE SCREEN */
```

should be replaced by your local "clear the screen" CLIST function.

The input to VSAMBUFS, a KSDS data set name, can be entered along with the CLIST command in the TSO READY mode:

```
VSAMBUFS data-set-name
```

If just the CLIST name is entered, VSAMBUFS will prompt for the KSDS name. A sample of VSAMBUFS output appears on page 118 within Chapter 6, which discusses how to use VSAMBUFS to greatest advantage. Batch execution is shown in Figure F.3c.

VANALYZE

VANALYZE (V-analyze) is a straightforward batch COBOL program that aids in analyzing the range and distribution of keys on an existing file that must be loaded to a VSAM key sequenced data set. It can be used to quickly gain a picture of primary and alternate record key spread to lead to and support informed KSDS design choices, especially when an ISAM data set is to be converted to VSAM.

VANALYZE is listed in Figure F.4. The comments at the beginning of the source code indicate the simple changes necessary in the file description in order to use the program on a given data set. Figure F.5 provides typical JCL used to compile, load, and run the program, which reads the entire data set, builds counts, and performs internal sorts to produce five reports.

DATA SET PERFORMANCE MONITORING

Chapter 8 discusses the elements of a LISTCAT report on a data set that figure prominently in day-to-day monitoring of production VSAM data set performance. An auto-

```
        IDENTIFICATION DIVISION.
        PROGRAM-ID.    VANALYZE.
     *
     *    THIS SOURCE CODE IS AVAILABLE IN MACHINE READABLE FORM
     *    FOR UPLOAD
     *
     *
     *    THIS PROGRAM WILL PRODUCE FIVE REPORTS.
     *    VANALYZE1 - DUPLICATE PRIME KEYS
     *    VANALYZE2 - ALTERNATE KEYS WITH THE MOST POINTERS
     *    VANALYZE3 - PRIME KEY GROUPINGS
     *    VANALYZE4 - ALTERNATE KEY GROUPINGS
     *    VANALYZE5 - RECORD KEY COUNTS
     *
     *    THREE ITEMS MUST BE MODIFIED IN THIS PROGRAMM PRIOR TO
     *         ITS EXECUTION:
     *    1 - RECORD LENGTH OF THE INPUT RECORD FOR FILE 'FILE-IN'
     *    2 - ADJUST 'RECORD-IN-PRIME' TO REFLECT THE LENGTH OF
     *            THE INPUT DATA SET AND THE POSITION OF THE
     *            PRIMARY KEY
     *    3 - ADJUST 'RECORD-IN-ALT' TO REFLECT THE LENGTH OF
     *            THE INPUT DATA SET AND THE POSITION OF THE
     *            ALTERNATE KEY
     *        IF THERE IS NO ALTERNATE INDEX, THEN USE USE THE
     *            POSITION OF THE PRIMARY KEY FOR THE ALTERNATE
     *            KEY
     *
     *    IF MORE THAN TEN GROUPINGS ARE DESIRED FOR EITHER THE
     *        PRIMARY KEY OR THE ALTERNATE KEY, THEN REPLACE THE
     *        CONSTANTS FOR 'PRIME-GROUP' AND/OR 'ALT-GROUP' WITH
     *         VALUES LESS THAN 99
     *
     ENVIRONMENT DIVISION.
     CONFIGURATION SECTION.
     SOURCE-COMPUTER. IBM-370.
     OBJECT-COMPUTER. IBM-370.
     SPECIAL-NAMES. C01 IS T-O-P.
     *
     INPUT-OUTPUT SECTION.
     FILE-CONTROL.
         SELECT FILE-IN ASSIGN TO SEQFILIN
             FILE STATUS IS FILE-IN-STATUS.
         SELECT REPORT-FILE ASSIGN TO REPORTFL
             FILE STATUS IS REPORT-STATUS.
         SELECT WORK-FILE-1 ASSIGN TO TEMPFIL1
             FILE STATUS IS WORK-FILE-1-STATUS.
         SELECT WORK-FILE-2 ASSIGN TO TEMPFIL2
             FILE STATUS IS WORK-FILE-2-STATUS.
         SELECT SR1 ASSIGN TO SORTFIL1.
         SELECT SR2 ASSIGN TO SORTFIL2.
         SELECT SR3 ASSIGN TO SORTFIL3.
     *
     DATA DIVISION.
     FILE SECTION.
     *
     FD  FILE-IN
     ******************************************************************
     *    MODIFY THE AREA BELOW TO REFLECT INPUT FILE RECORD
     *    LENGTH AND POSITIONS OF KEY AND ALTERNATE KEYS:
     *
         RECORD CONTAINS 0234 CHARACTERS
         BLOCK CONTAINS 0 RECORDS
         LABEL RECORDS ARE STANDARD.
     01  RECORD-IN-PRIME.
```

FIGURE F.4   Source code for COBOL program VANALYZE, useful for analyzing the nature and spread of primary and alternate keys in a data set to be loaded to a KSDS

```
        05  FILLER                      PIC X(028).
        05  PRIME-KEY                   PIC X(009).
        05  FILLER                      PIC X(197).
    01  RECORD-IN-ALT.
        05  FILLER                      PIC X(011).
        05  ALT-KEY                     PIC X(004).
        05  FILLER                      PIC X(219).
   *
   ***********************************************************************
   *
   FD  WORK-FILE-1
       RECORD CONTAINS 250 CHARACTERS
       BLOCK CONTAINS 0 RECORDS
       LABEL RECORDS ARE STANDARD.
   01  WORK-RECORD-1.
        05  WR1-PRIME-KEY               PIC X(125).
        05  WR1-ALT-KEY                 PIC X(125).
   *
   FD  WORK-FILE-2
       RECORD CONTAINS 140 CHARACTERS
       LABEL RECORDS ARE STANDARD.
   01  WORK-RECORD-2.
        05  WR2-COUNT                   PIC 9(15).
        05  WR2-ALT-KEY                 PIC X(125).
   *
   SD  SR1
       RECORD CONTAINS 250 CHARACTERS.
   01  SR1-PRIME.
        05  SR1-PRIME-KEY               PIC X(125).
        05  SR1-ALT-KEY                 PIC X(125).
   *
   SD  SR2
       RECORD CONTAINS 250 CHARACTERS.
   01  SR2-ALT-PRIME.
        05  SR2-ALT-KEY                 PIC X(125).
        05  SR2-PRIME-KEY               PIC X(125).
   *
   SD  SR3
       RECORD CONTAINS 140 CHARACTERS.
   01  SR3-COUNT-ALT.
        05  SR3-COUNT                   PIC 9(15).
        05  SR3-ALT-KEY                 PIC X(125).
   *
   FD  REPORT-FILE
       RECORD CONTAINS 133 CHARACTERS
       BLOCK CONTAINS 0 RECORDS
       LABEL RECORDS ARE STANDARD.
   01  REPORT-RECORD                    PIC X(133).
   /
   WORKING-STORAGE SECTION.
   01  FILLER  PIC X(21)  VALUE 'WORKING STORAGE START'.
   *
   *   MODIFY CONSTANTS BELOW FOR MORE KEY GROUPINGS
   *
   01  RECORD-KEY-GROUPING-COUNTS.
        05  PRIME-GROUP                 PIC 9(02)    VALUE 10.
        05  ALT-GROUP                   PIC 9(02)    VALUE 10.
   *
   01  FILE-STATUS-FIELDS.
        05  ABEND-PLACE                 PIC S9(03)   COMP.
        05  FILE-IN-STATUS              PIC 9(02).
        05  REPORT-STATUS               PIC 9(02).
        05  WORK-FILE-1-STATUS          PIC 9(02).
        05  WORK-FILE-2-STATUS          PIC 9(02).
   *
   01  PRIME-BUCKETS.
        05  PRIME-KEY-COUNT             PIC 9(15).
```

FIGURE F.4   (Continued)

```
        05  DUP-PRIME-KEY-COUNT              PIC 9(15).
        05  UNIQUE-PRIME-KEY-COUNT           PIC 9(15).
        05  PRIME-INCREMENT                  PIC 9(15).
        05  ALT-KEY-COUNT                    PIC 9(15).
        05  DUP-ALT-KEY-COUNT                PIC 9(15).
        05  UNIQUE-ALT-KEY-COUNT             PIC 9(15).
        05  TEMP-ALT-GROUP-COUNT             PIC 9(15).
        05  ALT-GROUP-COUNT                  PIC 9(15).
        05  PRIME-GROUP-COUNT                PIC 9(15).
        05  TEMP-PRIME-GROUP-COUNT           PIC 9(15).
        05  TOP-50-CNT-ALT                   PIC 9(15).
        05  ALT-SORT-OUT-COUNT               PIC 9(15).
        05  LINE-COUNT                       PIC 99.
        05  SUB                              PIC 999.
        05  SUBA                             PIC 999.
    *
    01  KEY-AREAS.
        05  LOW-PRIME-KEY                    PIC X(125).
        05  HIGH-PRIME-KEY                   PIC X(125).
        05  LOW-ALT-KEY                      PIC X(125).
        05  HIGH-ALT-KEY                     PIC X(125).
    *
    01  SORT-PRIME-COUNT-TABLE.
        05  S-PRIME-GROUP OCCURS 201 TIMES.
            10  PRIME-GROUP-TAB-COUNT        PIC 9(15).
            10  PRIME-GROUP-TAB-LOW          PIC X(125).
            10  PRIME-GROUP-TAB-HIGH         PIC X(125).
    *
    01  SORT-ALT-COUNT-TABLE.
        05  S-ALT-GROUP OCCURS 201 TIMES.
            10  ALT-GROUP-TAB-COUNT          PIC 9(15).
            10  ALT-GROUP-TAB-LOW            PIC X(125).
            10  ALT-GROUP-TAB-HIGH           PIC X(125).
    *
    01  RPT-HD1.
        05  FILLER          PIC X(01)        VALUE SPACES.
        05  FILLER          PIC X(08)        VALUE SPACES.
        05  FILLER          PIC X(09)        VALUE 'VANALYZE-'.
        05  RPT-NUMBER      PIC X            VALUE '1'.
        05  FILLER          PIC X(30)        VALUE SPACES.
        05  FILLER          PIC X(31)
                VALUE 'VSAM DATA SET EVALUATION REPORT'.
        05  FILLER          PIC X(30)        VALUE SPACES.
        05  FILLER          PIC X(5)         VALUE 'PAGE '.
        05  PAGE-NO         PIC 9(5)         VALUE 0.
        05  FILLER          PIC X(13)        VALUE SPACES.
    *
    01  RPT-HD2.
        05  FILLER          PIC X(01)        VALUE SPACES.
        05  FILLER          PIC X(10)        VALUE SPACES.
        05  TODAYS-DATE     PIC X(8).
        05  FILLER          PIC X(30)        VALUE SPACES.
        05  RPT-DESC        PIC X(84)
                VALUE 'DUPLICATE PRIME KEYS'.
    *
    01  RPT-HD3.
        05  RPT-HD3-X1.
            10  FILLER          PIC X(01)        VALUE SPACES.
        05  RPT-HD3-X2.
            10  COL-HD          PIC X(50)
                    VALUE 'PRIMARY KEYS'.
            10  FILLER          PIC X(82)        VALUE SPACES.
    *
    01  DETAIL-LINE.
        05  FILLER          PIC X(01)        VALUE SPACES.
```

FIGURE F.4   (*Continued*)

```
     05  DETAIL-COUNT   PIC Z(14)9.
     05  FILLER         PIC X(17)       VALUE SPACES.
     05  DETAIL-KEY     PIC X(100).
*
 01  DETAIL-LINE2.
     05  FILLER           PIC X(01)       VALUE SPACES.
     05  DETAIL-LINE2-PART1.
         10  DETAIL-DESC    PIC X(25).
     05  DETAIL-LINE2-PART2.
         10  FILLER         PIC X(25)        VALUE SPACES.
         10  DETAIL-COUNT1  PIC Z(14)9.
         10  FILLER         PIC X(25)        VALUE SPACES.
         10  DETAIL-COUNT2  PIC Z(14)9.
         10  FILLER         PIC X(32)        VALUE SPACES.
     05  DETAIL-LINE2-PART3 REDEFINES DETAIL-LINE2-PART2.
         10  FILLER         PIC X(12).
         10  DETAIL-KEY1    PIC X(100).
*
 01  CONSTANT1.
     05  FILLER           PIC X(51)
     VALUE 'DESCRIPTION                                      PR'.
     05  FILLER           PIC X(51)
     VALUE 'IME KEY                              ALTERNATE KEY'.
*
 01  DATE-IN.
     05  DATE-IN-ALL    PIC 9(6).
     05  DATE-IN-ALL-X REDEFINES DATE-IN-ALL.
         10  YY-IN      PIC XX.
         10  MM-IN      PIC XX.
         10  DD-IN      PIC XX.
*
 01  DATE-OUT.
     05  MM-OUT         PIC XX.
     05  FILLER         PIC X           VALUE '/'.
     05  DD-OUT         PIC XX.
     05  FILLER         PIC X           VALUE '/'.
     05  YY-OUT         PIC XX.
*
 01  BLANKS             PIC X(133)      VALUE SPACES.
/
 PROCEDURE DIVISION.
*
 MAINLINE  SECTION.
     PERFORM HOUSEKEEPING.
*
*    SORT EXTRACT OF INPUT FILE IN PRIME KEY SEQUENCE
*
     SORT SR1 ON ASCENDING SR1-PRIME-KEY
         INPUT PROCEDURE SORT-PRIME-IN
         OUTPUT PROCEDURE SORT-PRIME-OUT.
     IF SORT-RETURN NOT EQUAL 0
         MOVE 01 TO ABEND-PLACE
         CALL 'ILBOABNO' USING ABEND-PLACE.
     PERFORM SET-PRIME-INCREMENT.
*
*    SORT WORK FILE IN ALTERNATE KEY SEQUENCE
*
     SORT SR2 ON ASCENDING SR2-ALT-PRIME
         INPUT PROCEDURE SORT-ALT-PRIME-IN
         OUTPUT PROCEDURE SORT-ALT-PRIME-OUT.
     IF SORT-RETURN NOT EQUAL 0
         MOVE 02 TO ABEND-PLACE
         CALL 'ILBOABNO' USING ABEND-PLACE.
     PERFORM SET-ALT-INCREMENT.
*
*    SORT WORK FILE BY ALTERNATE KEY WITHIN PRIMARY KEY POINTER
*    AND PRINT THE LAST THREE REPORTS
```

FIGURE F.4 (Continued)

```
*
        SORT SR3 ON DESCENDING SR3-COUNT-ALT
            USING WORK-FILE-2
            OUTPUT PROCEDURE SORT-CNT-ALT-OUT.
        IF SORT-RETURN NOT EQUAL 0
            MOVE 03 TO ABEND-PLACE
            CALL 'ILBOABNO' USING ABEND-PLACE.
        PERFORM EOJ-PROCESSING.
        GOBACK.
/
    HOUSEKEEPING SECTION.
        MOVE LOW-VALUES TO LOW-PRIME-KEY
                            HIGH-PRIME-KEY
                            LOW-ALT-KEY
                            HIGH-ALT-KEY.
        MOVE ALL ZEROES TO SORT-PRIME-COUNT-TABLE
                            SORT-ALT-COUNT-TABLE
                            PRIME-BUCKETS.
        MOVE 60 TO LINE-COUNT.
        ACCEPT DATE-IN FROM DATE.
        MOVE MM-IN TO MM-OUT.
        MOVE DD-IN TO DD-OUT.
        MOVE YY-IN TO YY-OUT.
        MOVE DATE-OUT TO TODAYS-DATE.
        OPEN OUTPUT REPORT-FILE.
        IF REPORT-STATUS NOT = 0
            MOVE 04 TO ABEND-PLACE
            CALL 'ILBOABNO' USING ABEND-PLACE.
    HOUSEKEEPING-EXIT.
        EXIT.
/
    SORT-PRIME-IN SECTION.
        OPEN INPUT FILE-IN.
        IF FILE-IN-STATUS NOT = 0
            MOVE 05 TO ABEND-PLACE
            CALL 'ILBOABNO' USING ABEND-PLACE.
*
    READ-FILE-IN.
        READ FILE-IN
            AT END GO TO CLOSE-FILE-IN.
        IF FILE-IN-STATUS NOT = 0
            MOVE 06 TO ABEND-PLACE
            CALL 'ILBOABNO' USING ABEND-PLACE.
*
*       EXTRACT PRIMARY AND ALTERNATE KEYS FROM INPUT FILE
*
        MOVE PRIME-KEY TO SR1-PRIME-KEY.
        MOVE ALT-KEY TO SR1-ALT-KEY.
        RELEASE SR1-PRIME.
        GO TO READ-FILE-IN.
*
    CLOSE-FILE-IN.
        CLOSE FILE-IN.
        IF FILE-IN-STATUS NOT = 0
            MOVE 07 TO ABEND-PLACE
            CALL 'ILBOABNO' USING ABEND-PLACE.
    SORT-PRIME-IN-EXIT.
        EXIT.
/
    SORT-PRIME-OUT SECTION.
        OPEN OUTPUT WORK-FILE-1.
        IF WORK-FILE-1-STATUS NOT = 0
            MOVE 08 TO ABEND-PLACE
            CALL 'ILBOABNO' USING ABEND-PLACE.
*
```

FIGURE F.4 (Continued)

```
        RETURN-PRIME-OUT.
            RETURN SR1
                AT END GO TO RETURN-PRIME-OUT-EXIT.
            ADD 1 TO PRIME-KEY-COUNT.
            IF PRIME-KEY-COUNT = 1
                MOVE SR1-PRIME-KEY TO LOW-PRIME-KEY.
    *
    *        COUNT AND PRINT DUPLICATE PRIMARY KEYS
    *
            IF SR1-PRIME-KEY = HIGH-PRIME-KEY
                ADD 1 TO DUP-PRIME-KEY-COUNT
                PERFORM PRINT-DUP-PRIME-KEY
            ELSE
                ADD 1 TO UNIQUE-PRIME-KEY-COUNT.
            MOVE SPACES TO WORK-RECORD-1.
    *
    *        STORE HIGHEST PRIMARY KEY AND
    *        CREATE WORK RECORD OF ALTERNATE KEY AND PRIMARY KEY
    *
            MOVE SR1-PRIME-KEY TO HIGH-PRIME-KEY
                                  WR1-PRIME-KEY.
            MOVE SR1-ALT-KEY TO WR1-ALT-KEY.
            WRITE WORK-RECORD-1.
            IF WORK-FILE-1-STATUS NOT = 0
                MOVE 09 TO ABEND-PLACE
                CALL 'ILBOABNO' USING ABEND-PLACE.
            GO TO RETURN-PRIME-OUT.
    *
         RETURN-PRIME-OUT-EXIT.
            CLOSE WORK-FILE-1.
            IF WORK-FILE-1-STATUS NOT = 0
                MOVE 10 TO ABEND-PLACE
                CALL 'ILBOABNO' USING ABEND-PLACE.
    *
         SORT-PRIME-OUT-EXIT.
            EXIT.
    /
         SET-PRIME-INCREMENT SECTION.
    *
         FINISH-VANALYZE1.
            IF DUP-PRIME-KEY-COUNT NOT = 0
                GO TO COMPUTE-PRIME-GROUPINGS.
            IF LINE-COUNT GREATER THAN 56
                PERFORM HEADINGS-OVERFLOW.
            MOVE 'NO DUPLICATE PRIMARY KEYS' TO DETAIL-DESC.
            WRITE REPORT-RECORD FROM DETAIL-LINE2 AFTER ADVANCING 1.
    *
    *        DIVIDE PRIMARY KEYS INTO 10 GROUPINGS BY RECORD COUNT
    *        SO THAT THE HIGH AND LOW KEY WITHIN EACH GROUP IS KNOWN
    *
         COMPUTE-PRIME-GROUPINGS.
            COMPUTE PRIME-GROUP-COUNT =
                (PRIME-KEY-COUNT / PRIME-GROUP).
            IF PRIME-GROUP-COUNT = 0
                MOVE 1 TO PRIME-GROUP-COUNT.
            MOVE PRIME-KEY-COUNT TO TEMP-PRIME-GROUP-COUNT.
    *
         INIT-PRIME-TABLE.
            ADD 1 TO SUB.
            MOVE PRIME-GROUP-COUNT TO PRIME-GROUP-TAB-COUNT (SUB).
            SUBTRACT PRIME-GROUP-COUNT FROM TEMP-PRIME-GROUP-COUNT.
            IF TEMP-PRIME-GROUP-COUNT IS NOT GREATER THAN
                    PRIME-GROUP-COUNT
                ADD 1 TO SUB
                MOVE TEMP-PRIME-GROUP-COUNT TO
                        PRIME-GROUP-TAB-COUNT (SUB)
                MOVE 0 TO TEMP-PRIME-GROUP-COUNT
```

FIGURE F.4   (Continued)

```
              MOVE 1 TO SUB
              GO TO SET-PRIME-INCREMENT-EXIT.
          GO TO INIT-PRIME-TABLE.
     SET-PRIME-INCREMENT-EXIT.
          EXIT.
  /
     SORT-ALT-PRIME-IN SECTION.
         OPEN INPUT WORK-FILE-1.
         IF WORK-FILE-1-STATUS NOT = 0
             MOVE 11 TO ABEND-PLACE
             CALL 'ILBOABNO' USING ABEND-PLACE.
  *
  *     PROCESS WORK FILE OF ALTERNATE AND PRIMARY KEYS
  *
     READ-ALT-PRIME-IN.
         READ WORK-FILE-1
             AT END GO TO READ-ALT-PRIME-IN-EXIT.
         IF WORK-FILE-1-STATUS NOT = 0
             MOVE 12 TO ABEND-PLACE
             CALL 'ILBOABNO' USING ABEND-PLACE.
         ADD 1 TO TEMP-PRIME-GROUP-COUNT.
  *
  *     STORE LOW AND HIGH PRIMARY KEY FOR EACH GROUPING
  *
         IF TEMP-PRIME-GROUP-COUNT = 1
             MOVE WR1-PRIME-KEY TO PRIME-GROUP-TAB-LOW (SUB).
         IF TEMP-PRIME-GROUP-COUNT = PRIME-GROUP-TAB-COUNT (SUB)
             MOVE WR1-PRIME-KEY TO PRIME-GROUP-TAB-HIGH (SUB)
             ADD 1 TO SUB
             MOVE 0 TO TEMP-PRIME-GROUP-COUNT.
         MOVE SPACES TO SR2-ALT-PRIME.
         MOVE WR1-ALT-KEY TO SR2-ALT-KEY.
         MOVE WR1-PRIME-KEY TO SR2-PRIME-KEY.
         RELEASE SR2-ALT-PRIME.
         GO TO READ-ALT-PRIME-IN.
  *
     READ-ALT-PRIME-IN-EXIT.
         CLOSE WORK-FILE-1.
         IF WORK-FILE-1-STATUS NOT = 0
             MOVE 13 TO ABEND-PLACE
             CALL 'ILBOABNO' USING ABEND-PLACE.
     SORT-ALT-PRIME-IN-EXIT.
         EXIT.
  /
     SORT-ALT-PRIME-OUT SECTION.
         OPEN OUTPUT WORK-FILE-2.
         IF WORK-FILE-2-STATUS NOT = 0
             MOVE 14 TO ABEND-PLACE
             CALL 'ILBOABNO' USING ABEND-PLACE.
  *
     RETURN-ALT-PRIME-OUT.
         RETURN SR2
             AT END GO TO WRITE-LAST-WR2.
         ADD 1 TO ALT-SORT-OUT-COUNT
  *
  *     STORE LOWEST AND HIGHEST ALTERNATE KEY
  *
         IF ALT-SORT-OUT-COUNT = 1
             MOVE SPACES TO WORK-RECORD-2
             MOVE SR2-ALT-KEY TO LOW-ALT-KEY
                                 HIGH-ALT-KEY
                                 WR2-ALT-KEY
             MOVE 1 TO WR2-COUNT
             GO TO RETURN-ALT-PRIME-OUT.
  *
```

FIGURE F.4   (Continued)

```
*     CREATE WORK RECORD OF ALTERNATE KEY WITHIN
*     COUNT OF PRIMARY KEY POINTERS
*
      IF SR2-ALT-KEY = HIGH-ALT-KEY
          ADD 1 TO WR2-COUNT
      ELSE
          PERFORM WRITE-WORK-RECORD-2
          MOVE SPACES TO WORK-RECORD-2
          MOVE SR2-ALT-KEY TO WR2-ALT-KEY
          MOVE SR2-ALT-KEY TO HIGH-ALT-KEY
          MOVE 1 TO WR2-COUNT.
      GO TO RETURN-ALT-PRIME-OUT.
*
  WRITE-LAST-WR2.
      IF WR2-COUNT = 1
          ADD 1 TO UNIQUE-ALT-KEY-COUNT
      ELSE
          ADD 1 TO DUP-ALT-KEY-COUNT.
      WRITE WORK-RECORD-2.
      ADD 1 TO ALT-KEY-COUNT.
      IF WORK-FILE-2-STATUS NOT = 0
          MOVE 15 TO ABEND-PLACE
          CALL 'ILBOABNO' USING ABEND-PLACE.
      CLOSE WORK-FILE-2.
      IF WORK-FILE-2-STATUS NOT = 0
          MOVE 16 TO ABEND-PLACE
          CALL 'ILBOABNO' USING ABEND-PLACE.
  SORT-ALT-PRIME-OUT-EXIT.
      EXIT.
/
*     DIVIDE ALTERNATE KEYS INTO 10 GROUPINGS BY RECORD COUNT
*     SO THAT THE HIGH AND LOW KEY WITHIN EACH GROUP ARE KNOWN
*
  SET-ALT-INCREMENT SECTION.
      COMPUTE ALT-GROUP-COUNT =
          (ALT-KEY-COUNT / ALT-GROUP).
      IF ALT-GROUP-COUNT = 0
          MOVE 1 TO ALT-GROUP-COUNT.
      MOVE ALT-KEY-COUNT TO TEMP-ALT-GROUP-COUNT
      PERFORM SETUP-VANALYZE2.
*
*     STORE COUNT OF EACH GROUPING IN TABLE
*
  INIT-ALT-TABLE.
      ADD 1 TO SUBA.
      MOVE ALT-GROUP-COUNT TO ALT-GROUP-TAB-COUNT (SUBA).
      SUBTRACT ALT-GROUP-COUNT FROM TEMP-ALT-GROUP-COUNT.
      IF TEMP-ALT-GROUP-COUNT IS NOT GREATER THAN
              ALT-GROUP-COUNT
          ADD 1 TO SUBA
          MOVE TEMP-ALT-GROUP-COUNT TO
                  ALT-GROUP-TAB-COUNT (SUBA)
          MOVE 0 TO TEMP-ALT-GROUP-COUNT
          MOVE 1 TO SUBA
          GO TO STORE-ALT-GROUPINGS.
      GO TO INIT-ALT-TABLE.
*
  STORE-ALT-GROUPINGS.
      OPEN INPUT WORK-FILE-2.
      IF WORK-FILE-2-STATUS NOT = 0
          MOVE 17 TO ABEND-PLACE
          CALL 'ILBOABNO' USING ABEND-PLACE.
*
  READ-WR-2.
      READ WORK-FILE-2
          AT END GO TO CLOSE-WR-2.
      IF WORK-FILE-2-STATUS NOT = 0
```

FIGURE F.4   (Continued)

```
                MOVE 18 TO ABEND-PLACE
                CALL 'ILBOABNO' USING ABEND-PLACE.
            ADD 1 TO TEMP-ALT-GROUP-COUNT.
    *
    *****STORE LOW AND HIGH ALTERNATE KEY FOR EACH GROUPING
    *
            IF TEMP-ALT-GROUP-COUNT = 1
                MOVE WR2-ALT-KEY TO ALT-GROUP-TAB-LOW (SUBA).
            IF TEMP-ALT-GROUP-COUNT = ALT-GROUP-TAB-COUNT (SUBA)
                MOVE WR2-ALT-KEY TO ALT-GROUP-TAB-HIGH (SUBA)
                ADD 1 TO SUBA
                MOVE 0 TO TEMP-ALT-GROUP-COUNT.
            GO TO READ-WR-2.
    *
      CLOSE-WR-2.
            CLOSE WORK-FILE-2.
            IF WORK-FILE-2-STATUS NOT = 0
                MOVE 19 TO ABEND-PLACE
                CALL 'ILBOABNO' USING ABEND-PLACE.
      SET-ALT-INCREMENT-EXIT.
            EXIT.
    /
      SORT-CNT-ALT-OUT SECTION.
            RETURN SR3
                AT END GO TO SORT-CNT-ALT-OUT-EXIT.
            ADD 1 TO TOP-50-CNT-ALT.
    *
    *     PRINT THE 50 ALTERNATE KEYS WITH THE MOST
    *     PRIMARY KEY POINTERS AND THEIR COUNTS
    *
            IF TOP-50-CNT-ALT LESS THAN 51
                PERFORM PRINT-TOP-50-CNT-ALT.
            GO TO SORT-CNT-ALT-OUT.
      SORT-CNT-ALT-OUT-EXIT.
            EXIT.
    /
      MISC-SUBROUTINE SECTION.
      WRITE-WORK-RECORD-2.
            IF WR2-COUNT = 1
                ADD 1 TO UNIQUE-ALT-KEY-COUNT
            ELSE
                ADD 1 TO DUP-ALT-KEY-COUNT.
            WRITE WORK-RECORD-2.
            ADD 1 TO ALT-KEY-COUNT.
            IF WORK-FILE-2-STATUS NOT = 0
                MOVE 20 TO ABEND-PLACE
                CALL 'ILBOABNO' USING ABEND-PLACE.
    *
      HEADINGS-OVERFLOW.
            ADD 1 TO PAGE-NO.
            WRITE REPORT-RECORD FROM RPT-HD1 AFTER ADVANCING T-O-P.
            IF REPORT-STATUS NOT = 0
                MOVE 21 TO ABEND-PLACE
                CALL 'ILBOABNO' USING ABEND-PLACE.
            WRITE REPORT-RECORD FROM RPT-HD2 AFTER ADVANCING 1.
            WRITE REPORT-RECORD FROM RPT-HD3 AFTER ADVANCING 2.
            WRITE REPORT-RECORD FROM  BLANKS AFTER ADVANCING 1.
            MOVE 5 TO LINE-COUNT.
    *
      PRINT-DUP-PRIME-KEY.
            IF LINE-COUNT GREATER THAN 56
                PERFORM HEADINGS-OVERFLOW.
            MOVE SPACES TO DETAIL-LINE2.
            MOVE SR1-PRIME-KEY TO DETAIL-DESC.
            WRITE REPORT-RECORD FROM DETAIL-LINE2 AFTER ADVANCING 1.
            ADD 1 TO LINE-COUNT.
```

FIGURE F.4   (Continued)

```
*
    SETUP-VANALYZE2.
        MOVE 0 TO PAGE-NO.
        MOVE 2 TO RPT-NUMBER.
        MOVE 60 TO LINE-COUNT.
        MOVE 'ALTERNATE KEYS WITH THE MOST POINTERS' TO
                RPT-DESC.
        MOVE '# OF PRIME KEYS               ALTERNATE KEY'
                TO COL-HD.
        MOVE SPACES TO DETAIL-LINE.
*
    PRINT-TOP-50-CNT-ALT.
        IF LINE-COUNT GREATER THAN 56
            PERFORM HEADINGS-OVERFLOW.
        MOVE SR3-COUNT TO DETAIL-COUNT.
        MOVE SR3-ALT-KEY TO DETAIL-KEY.
        WRITE REPORT-RECORD FROM DETAIL-LINE AFTER ADVANCING 1.
        ADD 1 TO LINE-COUNT.
*
    SETUP-VANALYZE3.
        MOVE 0 TO PAGE-NO.
        MOVE 3 TO RPT-NUMBER.
        MOVE 60 TO LINE-COUNT.
        MOVE 'PRIME KEY GROUPINGS' TO RPT-DESC.
        MOVE '# OF RECORDS                 LOW KEY / HIGH KEY'
                TO COL-HD.
        MOVE SPACES TO DETAIL-LINE.
*
    PRINT-PRIME-GROUPINGS.
        IF LINE-COUNT GREATER THAN 56
            PERFORM HEADINGS-OVERFLOW.
        MOVE PRIME-GROUP-TAB-COUNT (SUB) TO DETAIL-COUNT.
        MOVE PRIME-GROUP-TAB-LOW (SUB) TO DETAIL-KEY.
        WRITE REPORT-RECORD FROM DETAIL-LINE AFTER ADVANCING 2.
        MOVE SPACES TO DETAIL-LINE.
        MOVE PRIME-GROUP-TAB-HIGH (SUB) TO DETAIL-KEY.
        WRITE REPORT-RECORD FROM DETAIL-LINE AFTER ADVANCING 1.
        ADD 3 TO LINE-COUNT.
*
    SETUP-VANALYZE4.
        MOVE 0 TO PAGE-NO.
        MOVE 4 TO RPT-NUMBER.
        MOVE 60 TO LINE-COUNT.
        MOVE 'ALTERNATE KEY GROUPINGS' TO RPT-DESC.
        MOVE SPACES TO DETAIL-LINE.
*
    PRINT-ALT-GROUPINGS.
        IF LINE-COUNT GREATER THAN 56
            PERFORM HEADINGS-OVERFLOW.
        MOVE ALT-GROUP-TAB-COUNT (SUBA) TO DETAIL-COUNT.
        MOVE ALT-GROUP-TAB-LOW (SUBA) TO DETAIL-KEY.
        WRITE REPORT-RECORD FROM DETAIL-LINE AFTER ADVANCING 2.
        MOVE SPACES TO DETAIL-LINE.
        MOVE ALT-GROUP-TAB-HIGH (SUBA) TO DETAIL-KEY.
        WRITE REPORT-RECORD FROM DETAIL-LINE AFTER ADVANCING 1.
        ADD 3 TO LINE-COUNT.
*
    SETUP-VANALYZE5.
        MOVE 0 TO PAGE-NO.
        MOVE 5 TO RPT-NUMBER.
        MOVE 60 TO LINE-COUNT.
        MOVE 'RECORD KEY COUNTS' TO RPT-DESC.
        MOVE CONSTANT1 TO RPT-HD3-X2.
        MOVE SPACES TO DETAIL-LINE.
        PERFORM HEADINGS-OVERFLOW.
```

FIGURE F.4   (Continued)

```
*
  PRINT-KEY-COUNTS.
      MOVE '# OF UNIQUE KEYS' TO DETAIL-DESC.
      MOVE UNIQUE-PRIME-KEY-COUNT TO DETAIL-COUNT1.
      MOVE UNIQUE-ALT-KEY-COUNT TO DETAIL-COUNT2.
      WRITE REPORT-RECORD FROM DETAIL-LINE2 AFTER ADVANCING 2.
      MOVE '# OF DUPLICATE KEYS' TO DETAIL-DESC.
      MOVE DUP-PRIME-KEY-COUNT TO DETAIL-COUNT1.
      MOVE DUP-ALT-KEY-COUNT TO DETAIL-COUNT2.
      WRITE REPORT-RECORD FROM DETAIL-LINE2 AFTER ADVANCING 2.
      MOVE 'TOTAL # OF KEYS' TO DETAIL-DESC.
      MOVE PRIME-KEY-COUNT TO DETAIL-COUNT1.
      MOVE ALT-KEY-COUNT TO DETAIL-COUNT2.
      WRITE REPORT-RECORD FROM DETAIL-LINE2 AFTER ADVANCING 2.
      MOVE 'LOW PRIME KEY' TO DETAIL-DESC.
      MOVE SPACES TO DETAIL-LINE2-PART3.
      MOVE LOW-PRIME-KEY TO DETAIL-KEY1.
      WRITE REPORT-RECORD FROM DETAIL-LINE2 AFTER ADVANCING 2.
      MOVE 'HIGH PRIME KEY ' TO DETAIL-DESC.
      MOVE HIGH-PRIME-KEY TO DETAIL-KEY1.
      WRITE REPORT-RECORD FROM DETAIL-LINE2 AFTER ADVANCING 2.
      MOVE 'LOW ALTERNATE KEY' TO DETAIL-DESC.
      MOVE LOW-ALT-KEY TO DETAIL-KEY1.
      WRITE REPORT-RECORD FROM DETAIL-LINE2 AFTER ADVANCING 2.
      MOVE 'HIGH ALTERNATE KEY' TO DETAIL-DESC.
      MOVE HIGH-ALT-KEY TO DETAIL-KEY1.
      WRITE REPORT-RECORD FROM DETAIL-LINE2 AFTER ADVANCING 2.
      MOVE SPACES TO DETAIL-LINE2.
      MOVE 'END OF REPORTS' TO DETAIL-KEY1.
      WRITE REPORT-RECORD FROM DETAIL-LINE2 AFTER ADVANCING 2.
  MISC-SUB-EXIT.
      EXIT.
/
*
*     PRINT THE LAST THREE REPORTS
*
  EOJ-PROCESSING SECTION.
      PERFORM SETUP-VANALYZE3.
      PERFORM PRINT-PRIME-GROUPINGS
          VARYING SUB FROM 1 BY 1
          UNTIL PRIME-GROUP-TAB-COUNT (SUB) = 0.
      PERFORM SETUP-VANALYZE4.
      PERFORM PRINT-ALT-GROUPINGS
          VARYING SUBA FROM 1 BY 1
          UNTIL ALT-GROUP-TAB-COUNT (SUBA) = 0.
      PERFORM SETUP-VANALYZE5.
      PERFORM PRINT-KEY-COUNTS.
      CLOSE REPORT-FILE.
      IF REPORT-STATUS NOT = 0
          MOVE 22 TO ABEND-PLACE
          CALL 'ILBOABN0' USING ABEND-PLACE.
  EOJ-PROCESSING-EXIT.
      EXIT.
*
  END-OF-PROGRAM SECTION.
*     END OF PROGRAM VANALYZE
```

FIGURE F.4   (Continued)

```
//FSBT677A  JOB AK00TEST,'DP4-GUZIK',CLASS=W,MSGCLASS=X,
//  MSGLEVEL=(1,1),NOTIFY=BT05677
//*
//*     COMPILE AND GO JCL FOR VANALYZE
//*     THIS JCL = BT05677.SOURCE.CNTL(JCLFF5)
//*
//COBCMPGO  PROC DEVICE='SYSDA'
//*
//COMPILE  EXEC  PGM=IKFCBL00,
//  PARM='SIZ=262144,BUF=80000,CNT=57,DMA,CLI,SXR,APO,NOADV,LANGLVL(2)'
//SYSLIB    DD   DSN=SYS1.COBLIB,DISP=SHR
//SYSUT1    DD   UNIT=&DEVICE,SPACE=(460,(700,100))
//SYSUT2    DD   UNIT=&DEVICE,SPACE=(460,(700,100))
//SYSUT3    DD   UNIT=&DEVICE,SPACE=(460,(700,100))
//SYSUT4    DD   UNIT=&DEVICE,SPACE=(460,(700,100))
//SYSPRINT  DD   SYSOUT=*
//SYSUDUMP  DD   SYSOUT=*
//SYSLIN    DD   DSN=&LOADSET,
//  UNIT=&DEVICE,SPACE=(3200,(500,100)),
//  DISP=(MOD,PASS)
//*
//LOADGO   EXEC  PGM=LOADER,COND=(5,LT,COMPILE),
//  PARM='MAP,LET,PRINT,CALL,RES,NOTERM,SIZE=307200,NAME=**GO'
//SYSLIB    DD   DSN=SYS1.COBLIB,DISP=SHR
//SYSLIN    DD   DSN=&LOADSET,
//  DISP=(OLD,DELETE)
//SYSLOUT   DD   SYSOUT=*
//SYSPRINT  DD   SYSOUT=*
//SYSUDUMP  DD   SYSOUT=*
//*
//*  VANALYZE PROGRAM DD STATEMENTS
//*
//SYSOUT    DD   SYSOUT=*
//REPORTFL  DD   SYSOUT=*
//TEMPFIL1  DD   UNIT=&DEVICE,
//  DCB=(RECFM=FB,LRECL=250,BLKSIZE=6000),
//  SPACE=(CYL,(10,10),RLSE)
//TEMPFIL2  DD   UNIT=&DEVICE,
//  DCB=(RECFM=FB,LRECL=140,BLKSIZE=6160),
//  SPACE=(CYL,(10,10),RLSE)
//SORTWK01  DD   UNIT=&DEVICE,SPACE=(CYL,(10,10),RLSE)
//SORTWK02  DD   UNIT=&DEVICE,SPACE=(CYL,(10,10),RLSE)
//SORTWK03  DD   UNIT=&DEVICE,SPACE=(CYL,(10,10),RLSE)
//  PEND
//*
//RUNIT    EXEC  COBCMPGO
//COMPILE.SYSIN  DD *

    --- VANALYZE SOURCE CODE GOES HERE ---

//LOADGO.SEQFILIN  DD  DSN=data.set.to.be.evaluated,
//  DISP=SHR
//
```

FIGURE F.5 Typical MVS JCL to compile, linkage edit and load, and run VANALYZE data set key analysis program

mated method to monitor the salient characteristics and performance of all or selected key sequenced data sets in one or more catalogs exists in the form of VMONITOR, a job stream listed in Figure F.6.

Jobstream VMONITOR

VMONITOR (V-monitor) invokes the IDCAMS utility storing printlines for access by other programs. The job stream invokes three programs—VCATSCAN, VEXTRACT, and

```
//FSBT677A   JOB AKOOPROD,'DP4-GUZIK',CLASS=W,MSGCLASS=X,
//  MSGLEVEL=(1,1),NOTIFY=BT05677
//*
//*     VMONITOR KDSD MONITORING JOB STREAM
//*     THIS JCL = BT05677.SOURCE.CNTL(VMONITOR)
//*
//********************************************************************
//*                                                                  *
//*     READ DESIRED CATALOGS                                        *
//*                                                                  *
//********************************************************************
//STEPA     EXEC  PGM=IDCAMS
//SYSUDUMP    DD   SYSOUT=*
//SYSPRINT    DD   DSN=&&LISTC,
//  UNIT=SYSDA,
//  DISP=(NEW,PASS,DELETE),
//  DCB=(RECFM=VBA,LRECL=125,BLKSIZE=629),      '1 BLOCK/FILE
//  SPACE=(629,(300,100),RLSE)                  'APPROX 300 FILES
//SYSIN     DD  *
    LISTCAT CATALOG(SYS1.VSAM.PROJ1CAT)
    LISTCAT CATALOG(SYS1.VSAM.USERCAT)
    LISTCAT CATALOG(SYS1.VSAM.TEST5CAT)
/*
//********************************************************************
//*                                                                  *
//*     CONVERT LISTCAT PRINTLINES FROM VB TO FB                     *
//*                                                                  *
//********************************************************************
//STEPB     EXEC  PGM=IEBGENER
//SYSUT1     DD   DSN=&&LISTC,
//  DISP=(OLD,DELETE)
//SYSUT2     DD   DSN=&&LISTCFB,
//  UNIT=SYSDA,
//  DISP=(NEW,PASS,DELETE),
//  DCB=(RECFM=FB,LRECL=62,BLKSIZE=6200),
//  SPACE=(6200,(15,3),RLSE)
//SYSPRINT   DD   SYSOUT=*
//SYSUDUMP   DD   SYSOUT=*
//SYSIN      DD  *
    GENERATE  MAXFLDS=99
      RECORD  FIELD=(62,1,,1)
/*
//********************************************************************
//*                                                                  *
//*     SELECT VSAM DATA SETS TO MONITOR AND GENERATE                *
//*     A LISTCAT ENTRIES(...) STATEMENT FOR EACH                    *
//*                                                                  *
//********************************************************************
//STEPC     EXEC  PGM=VCATSCAN
//STEPLIB    DD   DSN=SYS1.PRODLIB,DISP=SHR
//VCATSCE1   DD   DSN=&&LISTCFB,
//  DISP=(OLD,DELETE)
//VCATSCU1   DD   DSN=&&LISTENT,
//  UNIT=SYSDA,
//  DISP=(NEW,PASS,DELETE),
//  DCB=(RECFM=FB,LRECL=80,BLKSIZE=6160),
//  SPACE=(6160,(3,1),RLSE)
//SYSOUT     DD   SYSOUT=*
//SYSUDUMP   DD   SYSOUT=*
//********************************************************************
//*                                                                  *
//*     EXECUTE THE GENERATED LISTCAT ENTRIES COMMANDS               *
//*                                                                  *
//********************************************************************
```

FIGURE F.6 MVS JCL for VMONITOR job stream, which invokes three COBOL programs and utilities to produce consolidated performance reports on multiple key sequenced data sets automatically

```
//STEPD     EXEC  PGM=IDCAMS
//SYSUDUMP  DD   SYSOUT=*
//SYSIN     DD   DSN=&&LISTENT,
// DISP=(OLD,DELETE)
//SYSPRINT  DD   DSN=&&RAW,
// UNIT=SYSDA,
// DISP=(NEW,PASS,DELETE),
// DCB=(RECFM=VBA,LRECL=125,BLKSIZE=629),
// SPACE=(629,(18000,3000),RLSE)
//***********************************************************************
//*                                                                    *
//*    CONVERT LISTCAT PRINTLINES FROM VB TO FB                        *
//*                                                                    *
//***********************************************************************
//STEPE     EXEC  PGM=IEBGENER
//SYSUT1    DD   DSN=&&RAW,
// DISP=(OLD,DELETE)
//SYSUT2    DD   DSN=&&RAWFB,
// UNIT=SYSDA,
// DISP=(NEW,PASS,DELETE),
// DCB=(RECFM=FB,LRECL=121,BLKSIZE=6171),
// SPACE=(6171,(30,6),RLSE)
//SYSPRINT  DD   SYSOUT=*
//SYSUDUMP  DD   SYSOUT=*
//SYSIN     DD   *
    GENERATE  MAXFLDS=99
      RECORD  FIELD=(121,1,,1)
/*
//***********************************************************************
//*                                                                    *
//*    EXTRACT VSAM STATS FOR THIS CYCLE AND WRITE TO                  *
//*    NEXT GENERATION OF STATS DATA SET                               *
//*                                                                    *
//***********************************************************************
//STEPF     EXEC  PGM=VEXTRACT
//STEPLIB   DD   DSN=SYS1.PRODLIB,DISP=SHR
//VEXTRAE1  DD   DSN=&&RAWFB,DISP=(OLD,DELETE)    'RAW LISTCAT P/L
//VEXTRAU1  DD   DSN=BT80.A99.VSAMSTAT(+1),       'EXTRACTED STATS
// UNIT=SYSDA,
// DISP=(NEW,CATLG,DELETE),
// DCB=(XX90.A00.DUMMYLBL,RECFM=FB,LRECL=149,BLKSIZE=6109),
// SPACE=(6109,(10,10),RLSE)
//VEXTRAU2  DD   SYSOUT=*
//SYSOUT    DD   SYSOUT=*
//SYSUDUMP  DD   SYSOUT=*
//***********************************************************************
//*                                                                    *
//*    CREATE COMPARISON REPORT FOR THIS CYCLE                         *
//*                                                                    *
//***********************************************************************
//STEPG     EXEC  PGM=VREPORTR
//STEPLIB   DD   DSN=SYS1.PRODLIB,DISP=SHR
//VREPORE1  DD   DSN=BT80.A99.VSAMSTAT(0),
// DISP=SHR
//VREPORE2  DD   DSN=BT80.A99.VSAMSTAT(+1),
// DISP=SHR
//VREPORU1  DD   SYSOUT=(G,,C150)                 '150 COLUMNS WIDE
//VREPORU2  DD   SYSOUT=*
//SYSOUT    DD   SYSOUT=*
//SYSUDUMP  DD   SYSOUT=*
//
```

FIGURE F.6   (*Continued*)

VREPORTR—that produce consolidated, summarized reports listing all of the data sets being monitored. Data sets with CI and CA splits, multiple extents, or a decline in record count from the prior monitoring run are listed on a special report for priority attention. The reports produced can be scanned quickly by a technical support group or designated analyst.

Sample reports output by these programs are illustrated in Chapter 8.

VCATSCAN

COBOL program VCATSCAN (V-catalog-scan), listed in Figure F.7, reads the printlines produced by a LISTCAT of the specified catalogs. For data sets being monitored, the program builds LISTCAT statements for a subsequent invocation of IDCAMS, which will obtain a full LISTCAT of each such data set. The initial IDCAMS LISTCAT and VCAT-SCAN automate the process of composing these additional control statements.

VEXTRACT

The control statements formed by VCATSCAN are processed by an invocation of ID-CAMS, and the printlines from all of the individual KSDS LISTCATS are again saved in machine-readable form. VEXTRACT (V-extract), listed in Figure F.8, examines these printlines and creates several outputs.

A report depicted in Figure F.9 is created containing only the Attributes Group of each LISTCAT, for manual reference purposes. Note that this report presents the printlines

```
IDENTIFCATION DIVISION.
PROGRAM-ID.   VCATSCAN.
AUTHOR.        R. GUZIK.
DATE-WRITTEN. AUGUST 1987.
DATE-COMPILED.
*
*     READ THE PRODUCTION CATALOG AND CREATE A FILE OF LISTC
*     CONTROL CARDS FOR ALL SELECTED VSAM FILES.
*
*     THIS SOURCE CODE IS AVAILABLE IN MACHINE READABLE FORM
*     FOR UPLOAD
*
*
ENVIRONMENT DIVISION.
INPUT-OUTPUT SECTION.
FILE-CONTROL.
    SELECT LISTCIN   ASSIGN UT-S-VCATSCE1.
    SELECT LISTCOUT  ASSIGN UT-S-VCATSCU1.
*
DATA DIVISION.
FILE SECTION.
FD  LISTCIN
    RECORDING F                  LABEL RECORDS STANDARD
    BLOCK 0 RECORDS              RECORD 62 CHARACTERS.
01  LISTC-IN.
    05  FILLER      PIC X(01).
    05  FILE-TYPE   PIC X(04).
    05  FILLER      PIC X(12).
    05  DSN.
        10  DSN-1-10    PIC X(10).
        10  DSN-11-44   PIC X(34).
```

FIGURE F.7 Source code for COBOL program VCATSCAN, which reads print line output of a LISTCAT listing data sets and builds a LISTCAT control statement for each KSDS present

```
       05  FILLER      PIC X(01).
*
 FD  LISTCOUT                      DATA RECORD LISTC-OUT
     RECORDING F                   LABEL RECORDS STANDARD
     BLOCK O RECORDS               RECORD  80 CHARACTERS.
 01  LISTC-OUT.
     05  PREFIX         PIC X(11).
     05  OUT-DSN        PIC X(69).
*
 WORKING-STORAGE SECTION.
 77  VSAM-FILE-COUNT    PIC 9(5)  VALUE O.
 77  ALL-CONSTANT       PIC X(5)  VALUE ') ALL'.
 77  SPACE-CONSTANT     PIC X(5)  VALUE LOW-VALUE.
/
 PROCEDURE DIVISION.
*
 BEGIN.
     OPEN INPUT LISTCIN.
     OPEN OUTPUT LISTCOUT.
*
 READ-EXTRACT.
     READ LISTCIN
        AT END
            GO TO END-OF-JOB.
     IF FILE-TYPE EQUAL 'CLUS' OR 'AIX '
        NEXT SENTENCE
     ELSE
        GO TO READ-EXTRACT.
*
*    MODIFY CODE BELOW TO REFLECT DATA SET EXCLUSION LOGIC
*
     IF DSN-1-10 EQUAL '0000000000' OR 'SYS1.VVDS.'
        GO TO READ-EXTRACT.
     MOVE ' LISTC ENT(' TO PREFIX.
     MOVE SPACES TO OUT-DSN.
     STRING DSN DELIMITED BY SPACE-CONSTANT
         ALL-CONSTANT DELIMITED BY SIZE
             INTO OUT-DSN.
     WRITE LISTC-OUT.
     ADD 1 TO VSAM-FILE-COUNT
     GO TO READ-EXTRACT.
*
 END-OF-JOB.
     DISPLAY 'VCATSCAN'.
     DISPLAY 'VSAM-FILE-COUNT = ' VSAM-FILE-COUNT.
     CLOSE LISTCIN.
     CLOSE LISTCOUT.
     GOBACK.
```

FIGURE F.7   (*Continued*)

```
        IDENTIFICATION DIVISION.
        PROGRAM-ID.    VEXTRACT.
        AUTHOR.        R. GUZIK.
        DATE-WRITTEN.  AUGUST 1987.
        *
        *     CREATE AN EXTRACT FILE OF STATISTICS FOR ALL VSAM
        *     FILES AND REPORT OF FILE CHARACTISTICS.
        *
        *     THIS SOURCE CODE IS AVAILABLE IN MACHINE READABLE FORM
        *     FOR UPLOAD
        *
        *
        ENVIRONMENT DIVISION.
        CONFIGURATION SECTION.
        SPECIAL-NAMES.
            C01 IS T-O-P.
        INPUT-OUTPUT SECTION.
        FILE-CONTROL.
            SELECT LISTCIN    ASSIGN UT-S-VEXTRAE1.
            SELECT FILEOUT    ASSIGN UT-S-VEXTRAU1.
            SELECT RPTOUT     ASSIGN UT-S-VEXTRAU2.
        *
        DATA DIVISION.
        FILE SECTION.
        FD  LISTCIN
            RECORDING F                   LABEL RECORDS STANDARD
            BLOCK 0 RECORDS               RECORD 121 CHARACTERS.
        01  LISTC-IN-TYPE.
            05  FILLER       PIC X(01).
            05  FILE-TYPE-IN   PIC X(03).
                88  RIGHT-TYPE-IN      VALUES 'CLU' 'AIX'.
            05  FILLER       PIC X(13).
            05  DSN-IN       PIC X(44).
            05  FILLER       PIC X(60).
        01  LISTC-IN-DATA.
            03  FRONT-1      PIC X(01).
            03  LISTC-IN-DATA120.
                05  FILLER     PIC X(1).
                05  FRONT-6      PIC X(06).
                    88  NEW-PAGE           VALUE 'DCAMS '.
                    88  STAT-LINE          VALUE '    ST'.
                05  LABEL-1-IN PIC X(04).
                    88  RIGHT-LABEL-1     VALUE 'REC-'.
                    88  RIGHT-STAT-LABEL-1    VALUE 'KEYL'.
                05  FILLER       PIC X(10).
                05  DATA-1-IN  PIC X(10).
                05  FILLER       PIC X(05).
                05  LABEL-2-IN PIC X(14).
                    88  RIGHT-LABEL-2     VALUE 'CREATION------'.
                05  DATA-2-IN   PIC X(10).
                05  DATA-2-IN-R REDEFINES DATA-2-IN.
                    07  FILLER      PIC X(04).
                    07  YY-IN       PIC X(02).
                    07  FILLER      PIC X(01).
                    07  DDD-IN      PIC X(03).
                05  FILLER       PIC X(05).
                05  DATA-3-IN.
                    07  LABEL-3-IN PIC X(20).
                    88  RIGHT-LABEL-3     VALUE 'EXTENTS-------------'.
                05  EXTENT       PIC X(04).
                05  FILLER       PIC X(05).
                05  LABEL-4-IN PIC X(17).
                    88  RIGHT-LABEL-4     VALUE 'CISIZE-----------'.
                05  DATA-4-IN    PIC X(7).
```

FIGURE F.8   Source code for COBOL program VEXTRACT, which reads KSDS LISTCAT printlines and prepares summarized performance monitoring information

```
          05  FILLER        PIC X(2).
*
FD  FILEOUT                         DATA RECORD RECORD-OUT
    RECORDING F                     LABEL RECORDS STANDARD
    BLOCK 0 RECORDS                 RECORD 149 CHARACTERS.
01  DATE-RECORD-OUT.
    05  FILLER               PIC X(01).
    05  DAY-OUT              PIC 9(05).
    05  FILLER               PIC X(01).
    05  TIME-OUT             PIC 9(08).
    05  FILLER               PIC X(134).
01  RECORD-OUT.
    05  DSN-OUT              PIC X(36).
    05  CISIZE-OUT           PIC X(07).
    05  DASH-OUT             PIC X(01).
    05  CREATE-DATE-OUT.
        07  YY-OUT           PIC X(02).
        07  DDD-OUT          PIC X(03).
    05  TOTAL-RECS-OUT       PIC 9(10).
    05  CI-SPLITS-OUT        PIC 9(10).
    05  CA-SPLITS-OUT        PIC 9(10).
    05  RECS-ADDED-OUT       PIC 9(10).
    05  RECS-DELETED-OUT     PIC 9(10).
    05  RECS-READ-OUT        PIC 9(10).
    05  RECS-UPDATED-OUT     PIC 9(10).
    05  EXTENT-OUT           PIC 9(04).
    05  PERCENT-CI-FREE-OUT  PIC 9(08).
    05  PERCENT-CA-FREE-OUT  PIC 9(08).
    05  TOTAL-BYTES-FREE-OUT PIC 9(10).
*
FD  RPTOUT
    RECORDING F                     LABEL RECORDS STANDARD
    BLOCK 0 RECORDS                 RECORD 121 CHARACTERS.
01  REPORT-OUT.
    05  FILLER               PIC X(01).
    05  RPT-BODY             PIC X(120).
*
WORKING-STORAGE SECTION.
01  VSAM-FILE-COUNT          PIC 9(9)  VALUE 0.
01  LINE-COUNT               PIC 9(3)  VALUE 85  COMP-3.
*
01  HEADING-1.
    05  FILLER PIC X(25) VALUE 'VEXTRACT-R1              '.
    05  FILLER PIC X(25) VALUE 'PRACTICAL VSAM PERFORMANC'.
    05  FILLER PIC X(25) VALUE 'E MEASUREMENT STATISTICS '.
    05  FILLER PIC X(25) VALUE '            REPORT DATE '.
    05  RPT-DATE       PIC 9(5).
    05  FILLER PIC X(03) VALUE SPACES.
    05  FILLER PIC X(9)  VALUE '  PAGE '.
    05  RPT-PAGE       PIC 99      VALUE 01.
        05  FILLER PIC X(1)  VALUE SPACES.
*
01  DETAIL-1.
    05  DSN-R                PIC X(36).
    05  FILLER               PIC X(84)  VALUE SPACES.
*
01  DETAIL-2.
    05  FILLER               PIC X(07)  VALUE SPACES.
    05  COL-1-R              PIC X(24)  VALUE SPACES.
    05  FILLER               PIC X(05)  VALUE SPACES.
    05  COL-2-R              PIC X(24)  VALUE SPACES.
    05  COL-2-R-R REDEFINES COL-2-R.
        07  COL-2-FIRST-R    PIC X(2).
            88  COL-2-EMPTY    VALUE LOW-VALUES.
        07  FILLER           PIC X(22).
    05  FILLER               PIC X(05)  VALUE SPACES.
    05  COL-3-R              PIC X(24)  VALUE SPACES.
```

FIGURE F.8   (Continued)

```
            05   COL-3-R-R REDEFINES COL-3-R.
                  07  COL-3-FIRST-R        PIC X(2).
                      88  COL-3-EMPTY      VALUE LOW-VALUES.
                  07  FILLER               PIC X(22).
            05   FILLER                     PIC X(05)   VALUE SPACES.
            05   COL-4-R                    PIC X(24)   VALUE SPACES.
            05   COL-4-R-R REDEFINES COL-4-R.
                  07  COL-4-FIRST-R        PIC X(2).
                      88  COL-4-EMPTY      VALUE LOW-VALUES.
                  07  FILLER               PIC X(22).
            05   TAIL-END-R                 PIC X(02)   VALUE SPACES.
/
 PROCEDURE DIVISION.
*
 BEGIN.
        OPEN INPUT LISTCIN.
        OPEN OUTPUT FILEOUT.
        OPEN OUTPUT RPTOUT.
        ACCEPT RPT-DATE FROM DAY.
        MOVE SPACES TO DATE-RECORD-OUT.
        ACCEPT DAY-OUT FROM DAY.
        ACCEPT TIME-OUT FROM TIME.
        WRITE DATE-RECORD-OUT.
*
 READ-EXTRACT.
        READ LISTCIN
           AT END
              GO TO END-OF-JOB.
*
 IS-IT-AIX-OR-CLUSTER.
        IF RIGHT-TYPE-IN
           NEXT SENTENCE
        ELSE
           GO TO READ-EXTRACT.
        MOVE ALL ZEROES TO RECORD-OUT.
        MOVE DSN-IN TO DSN-OUT DSN-R.
        IF LINE-COUNT > 49
            PERFORM HEADING-OVERFLOW.
        MOVE DETAIL-1 TO RPT-BODY.
        WRITE REPORT-OUT AFTER ADVANCING 2.
        ADD 2 TO LINE-COUNT.
*
 FIND-CREATION-DATE.
        PERFORM READ-EXTRACT.
        IF RIGHT-LABEL-2
           NEXT SENTENCE
        ELSE
           GO TO FIND-CREATION-DATE.
        MOVE YY-IN TO YY-OUT.
        MOVE DDD-IN TO DDD-OUT.
*
 FIND-CISIZE.
        PERFORM READ-EXTRACT.
        IF RIGHT-LABEL-4
           NEXT SENTENCE
        ELSE
           GO TO FIND-CISIZE.
        MOVE DATA-4-IN TO CISIZE-OUT.
        MOVE LISTC-IN-DATA120 TO RPT-BODY.
        WRITE REPORT-OUT AFTER ADVANCING 1.
        ADD 1 TO LINE-COUNT.
*
 FIND-NEXT-STAT-LINE.
        PERFORM READ-EXTRACT.
        IF NEW-PAGE
```

FIGURE F.8   (Continued)

```
            PERFORM READ-EXTRACT.
        IF STAT-LINE
            GO TO FIND-REC-TOTAL.
        MOVE LISTC-IN-DATA120 TO DETAIL-2.
        IF COL-2-EMPTY
            MOVE SPACES TO COL-2-R COL-3-R COL-4-R
            GO TO PRINT-THIS-LINE.
        IF COL-3-EMPTY
            MOVE SPACES TO COL-3-R COL-4-R
            GO TO PRINT-THIS-LINE.
        IF COL-4-EMPTY
            MOVE SPACES TO COL-4-R.
*
    PRINT-THIS-LINE.
        MOVE DETAIL-2 TO RPT-BODY.
        WRITE REPORT-OUT AFTER ADVANCING 1.
        ADD 1 TO LINE-COUNT.
        GO TO FIND-NEXT-STAT-LINE.
*
    FIND-REC-TOTAL.
        PERFORM READ-EXTRACT.
        IF RIGHT-LABEL-1
            NEXT SENTENCE
        ELSE
            GO TO FIND-REC-TOTAL.
        MOVE DATA-1-IN TO TOTAL-RECS-OUT.
        MOVE DATA-2-IN TO CI-SPLITS-OUT.
        PERFORM READ-EXTRACT.
        IF NOT RIGHT-LABEL-1
            PERFORM READ-EXTRACT.
        MOVE DATA-1-IN TO RECS-DELETED-OUT.
        MOVE DATA-2-IN TO CA-SPLITS-OUT.
        MOVE EXTENT TO EXTENT-OUT.
        PERFORM READ-EXTRACT.
        IF NOT RIGHT-LABEL-1
            PERFORM READ-EXTRACT.
        MOVE DATA-1-IN TO RECS-ADDED-OUT.
        MOVE DATA-2-IN TO PERCENT-CI-FREE-OUT.
        PERFORM READ-EXTRACT.
        IF NOT RIGHT-LABEL-1
            PERFORM READ-EXTRACT.
        MOVE DATA-1-IN TO RECS-UPDATED-OUT.
        MOVE DATA-2-IN TO PERCENT-CA-FREE-OUT.
        PERFORM READ-EXTRACT.
        IF NOT RIGHT-LABEL-1
            PERFORM READ-EXTRACT.
        MOVE DATA-1-IN TO RECS-READ-OUT.
        MOVE DATA-2-IN TO TOTAL-BYTES-FREE-OUT.
        MOVE '-' TO DASH-OUT.
        INSPECT DSN-OUT REPLACING ALL LOW-VALUE BY '-'.
        WRITE RECORD-OUT.
        ADD 1 TO VSAM-FILE-COUNT.
        GO TO READ-EXTRACT.
*
    HEADING-OVERFLOW.
        MOVE HEADING-1 TO RPT-BODY.
        WRITE REPORT-OUT AFTER ADVANCING T-O-P.
        MOVE 1 TO LINE-COUNT.
        ADD 1 TO RPT-PAGE.
*
    END-OF-JOB.
        DISPLAY 'VEXTRACT-R2'.
        DISPLAY 'VSAM-FILE-COUNT = ' VSAM-FILE-COUNT.
        CLOSE LISTCIN.
        CLOSE FILEOUT.
        CLOSE RPTOUT.
        GOBACK.
```

FIGURE F.8   (Continued)

```
VEXTRACT-R1              PRACTICAL VSAM PERFORMANCE MEASUREMENT STATISTICS        REPORT DATE 87038        PAGE 31

WCOO.C36.FFSEQCHG
  KEYLEN-------------7      AVGLRECL-------------16      BUFSPACE---------3072      CISIZE-----------1024
  RKP----------------0      MAXLRECL-------------16      EXCPEXIT--------(NULL)      CI/CA-------------15
  SHROPTNS(3,3)  RECOVERY    UNIQUE      NOERASE          INDEXED    NOWRITECHK      NOIMBED    NOREPLICAT
  UNORDERED      NOREUSE     NONSPANNED

WCOO.C36.JCMAINDX
  KEYLEN------------11      AVGLRECL-------------23      BUFSPACE--------16896      CISIZE-----------8192
  RKP----------------5      MAXLRECL-------------23      EXCPEXIT--------(NULL)      CI/CA-------------2
  AXRKP--------------8
  SHROPTNS(3,3)  RECOVERY    UNIQUE      NOERASE          INDEXED    NOWRITECHK      NOIMBED    NOREPLICAT
  UNORDERED      NOREUSE     SPANNED     UNIQUEKEY

WCOO.C36.JCMASTER
  KEYLEN-------------7      AVGLRECL-------------81      BUFSPACE---------6144      CISIZE-----------2048
  RKP----------------1      MAXLRECL-------------81      EXCPEXIT--------(NULL)      CI/CA-------------8
  SHROPTNS(3,3)  RECOVERY    UNIQUE      NOERASE          INDEXED    NOWRITECHK      NOIMBED    NOREPLICAT
  UNORDERED      NOREUSE     NONSPANNED

WMOO.CO5.FVFVSAM
  KEYLEN-------------9      AVGLRECL------------380      BUFSPACE---------9216      CISIZE-----------4096
  RKP----------------0      MAXLRECL------------380      EXCPEXIT--------(NULL)      CI/CA------------116
  SHROPTNS(2,3)  RECOVERY    UNIQUE      NOERASE          INDEXED    NOWRITECHK      IMBED      NOREPLICAT
  UNORDERED      NOREUSE     NONSPANNED

WMOO.CO5.LISCVSAM
  KEYLEN-------------4      AVGLRECL-------------80      BUFSPACE---------6144      CISIZE-----------1024
  RKP----------------0      MAXLRECL-------------80      EXCPEXIT--------(NULL)      CI/CA------------435
  SHROPTNS(2,3)  RECOVERY    UNIQUE      NOERASE          INDEXED    NOWRITECHK      IMBED      NOREPLICAT
  UNORDERED      NOREUSE     NONSPANNED

WMOO.CO5.VIOLVSAM
  KEYLEN------------11      AVGLRECL------------120      BUFSPACE--------12288      CISIZE-----------4096
  RKP----------------0      MAXLRECL------------120      EXCPEXIT--------(NULL)      CI/CA------------116
  SHROPTNS(2,3)  RECOVERY    UNIQUE      NOERASE          INDEXED    NOWRITECHK      IMBED      NOREPLICAT
  UNORDERED      NOREUSE     NONSPANNED

VEXTRACT-R2
VSAM-FILE-COUNT  =  000000258
```

FIGURE F.9 Portion of one report produced by program VEXTRACT, listing in one report the attribute information for all data sets monitored

329

formed by many LISTCATS all in one place. This type of report is not available from any raw LISTCAT function.

VEXTRACT also generates a data set containing critical measurements from each LIST-CAT. The data set is output as the next generation of a two-generation GDG. VREPORTR, executed in the next step, uses both the current and this (+ 1) generation of the data set to do comparison reporting. The data set output by VEXTRACT is used by VREPORTR to create the "problem data set" report and complete performance listing.

A small report is also produced citing the number of VSAM data sets being monitored.

VREPORTR

A reporting program, VREPORTR (V-reporter) is listed in Figure F.10. It creates the consolidated performance monitoring report and a special highly summarized report listing only the key sequenced data sets in need of priority attention.

```
IDENTIFICATION DIVISION.
PROGRAM-ID.     VREPORTR.
AUTHOR.         R. GUZIK.
DATE-WRITTEN.   AUGUST 1987.
DATE-COMPILED.
*
*    PRINT VSAM STATISTICS FOR YESTERDAY AND TODAY AND AN
*    EXCEPTION REPORT LISTING DATA SETS NEEDING ATTENTION.
*
*    NOTE: OUTPUTS 150 BYTE PRINTLINE INTENDED TO BE SENT
*    TO A LASER PRINTER CAPABLE OF HANDLING THIS SIZE LINE
*
*    THIS SOURCE CODE IS AVAILABLE IN MACHINE READABLE FORM
*    FOR UPLOAD -- SEE APPENDIX H FOR INFORMATION ON OBTAINING
*    A NOMINAL COST DISKETTE CARRYING THIS AND OTHER ITEMS
*
ENVIRONMENT DIVISION.
CONFIGURATION SECTION.
SPECIAL-NAMES.
     C01 IS T-O-P.
INPUT-OUTPUT SECTION.
FILE-CONTROL.
     SELECT YESTER     ASSIGN UT-S-VREPORE1.
     SELECT TODAYY     ASSIGN UT-S-VREPORE2.
     SELECT RPTS       ASSIGN UT-S-VREPORU1.
     SELECT RPT2       ASSIGN UT-S-VREPORU2.
*
DATA DIVISION.
FILE SECTION.
*
FD  YESTER                    DATA RECORD YESTER-REC
    RECORDING F               LABEL RECORDS STANDARD
    BLOCK 0 RECORDS           RECORD 149 CHARACTERS.
01  YESTER-DATE-REC.
    05  FILLER                PIC X(01).
    05  DAY-Y                 PIC 9(5).
    05  FILLER                PIC X(01).
    05  TIME-Y                PIC 9(08).
    05  FILLER                PIC X(134).
01  YESTER-REC.
    05  DSN-Y                 PIC X(36).
    05  CISIZE-Y              PIC X(07).
    05  CREATE-DATE-Y.
```

FIGURE F.10 Source code for COBOL program VREPORTR, which compares KSDS summary data from previous and current VMONITOR run and prepares full and "problem data set" monitoring reports

```
              07  FILLER              PIC X(01).
              07  YY-Y                PIC X(02).
              07  DDD-Y               PIC X(03).
         05  TOTAL-RECS-Y             PIC X(10).
         05  CI-SPLITS-Y              PIC X(10).
         05  CA-SPLITS-Y              PIC X(10).
         05  RECS-ADDED-Y             PIC X(10).
         05  RECS-DELETED-Y           PIC X(10).
         05  RECS-READ-Y              PIC X(10).
         05  RECS-UPDATED-Y           PIC X(10).
         05  EXTENT-Y                 PIC X(04).
         05  PERCENT-CI-FREE-Y        PIC X(08).
         05  PERCENT-CA-FREE-Y        PIC X(08).
         05  TOTAL-BYTES-FREE-Y       PIC X(10).
 *
 FD  TODAYY                           DATA RECORD TODAYY-REC
     RECORDING F                      LABEL RECORDS STANDARD
     BLOCK 0 RECORDS                  RECORD 149 CHARACTERS.
 01  TODAYY-DATE-REC.
         05  FILLER                   PIC X(01).
         05  DAY-T                    PIC 9(5).
         05  FILLER                   PIC X(01).
         05  TIME-T                   PIC 9(08).
         05  FILLER                   PIC X(134).
 01  TODAYY-REC.
         05  DSN-T                    PIC X(36).
         05  CISIZE-T                 PIC X(07).
         05  CREATE-DATE-T.
              07  FILLER              PIC X(01).
              07  YY-T                PIC X(02).
              07  DDD-T               PIC X(03).
         05  TOTAL-RECS-T             PIC X(10).
         05  CI-SPLITS-T              PIC X(10).
         05  CA-SPLITS-T              PIC X(10).
         05  RECS-ADDED-T             PIC X(10).
         05  RECS-DELETED-T           PIC X(10).
         05  RECS-READ-T              PIC X(10).
         05  RECS-UPDATED-T           PIC X(10).
         05  EXTENT-T                 PIC X(04).
         05  PERCENT-CI-FREE-T        PIC X(08).
         05  PERCENT-CA-FREE-T        PIC X(08).
         05  TOTAL-BYTES-FREE-T       PIC X(10).
 *
 FD  RPTS                             DATA RECORD REPORT-OUT
     RECORDING F                      LABEL RECORDS STANDARD
     BLOCK 0 RECORDS                  RECORD 150 CHARACTERS.
 01  REPORT-OUT.
         05  RPT-CC                   PIC X.
         05  RPT-BODY                 PIC X(149).
 *
 FD  RPT2                             DATA RECORD BADGUY-OUT
     RECORDING F                      LABEL RECORDS STANDARD
     BLOCK 0 RECORDS                  RECORD 133 CHARACTERS.
 01  BADGUY-OUT.
         05  BADGUY-CC                PIC X.
         05  BADGUY-BODY              PIC X(132).
 *
 WORKING-STORAGE SECTION.
 01  MATCH-KEY                        PIC X(36).
 01  YESTER-IN-CNT                    PIC 9(7)  VALUE 0   COMP-3.
 01  MATCHED-CNT                      PIC 9(7)  VALUE 0   COMP-3.
 01  MISSING-TODAYY-CNT               PIC 9(7)  VALUE 0   COMP-3.
 01  MISSING-YESTER-CNT               PIC 9(7)  VALUE 0   COMP-3.
 01  TODAYY-IN-CNT                    PIC 9(7)  VALUE 0   COMP-3.
 01  LINE-COUNT                       PIC 9(3)  VALUE 0   COMP-3.
 01  LINE-COUNT2                      PIC 9(3)  VALUE 0   COMP-3.
```

FIGURE F.10   (Continued)

```
01   MATCH-STATUS                  PIC 9      VALUE 2.
     88  YESTER-LO                             VALUE 1.
     88  YESTER-EQ                             VALUE 2.
     88  YESTER-HI                             VALUE 3.
01   TODAYY-EOF                     PIC 9      VALUE 0.
     88  TODAYY-AT-EOF                          VALUE 1.
*
01   HEADING-1.
     05  FILLER PIC X(25) VALUE 'VREPORTR-R1                '.
     05  FILLER PIC X(25) VALUE '                          '.
     05  FILLER PIC X(25) VALUE 'PRACTICAL VSAM PERFORMANC'.
     05  FILLER PIC X(25) VALUE 'E MEASUREMENT STATISTICS '.
     05  FILLER PIC X(25) VALUE '              REPORT DATE '.
     05  RPT-DATE         PIC 9(5).
     05  FILLER PIC X(03) VALUE SPACES.
     05  FILLER PIC X(9)  VALUE '   PAGE '.
     05  RPT-PAGE         PIC 99      VALUE 01.
     05  FILLER PIC X(5)  VALUE SPACES.
*
01   HEADING-2.
     05  FILLER PIC X(25) VALUE '                          '.
     05  FILLER PIC X(25) VALUE 'TOP LINE   PREVIOUS DATE '.
     05  H-DATE-Y PIC X(5).
     05  FILLER    PIC X(8)  VALUE '  TIME '.
     05  H-TIME-Y PIC X(8).
     05  FILLER PIC X(29) VALUE '    BOTTOM LINE CURRENT DATE '.
     05  H-DATE-T PIC X(5).
     05  FILLER    PIC X(8)  VALUE '  TIME '.
     05  H-TIME-T PIC X(8).
     05  FILLER PIC X(28)  VALUE SPACES.
*
01   HEADING-3.
     05  FILLER PIC X(25) VALUE 'DATA-SET-NAME            '.
     05  FILLER PIC X(25) VALUE '             CISIZE CRDAT '.
     05  FILLER PIC X(25) VALUE 'TOTAL-REC CI-SPLITS CA-SP'.
     05  FILLER PIC X(25) VALUE 'LITS   # ADDED   # DELED '.
     05  FILLER PIC X(25) VALUE '  # READ   # UPDED EXT   '.
     05  FILLER PIC X(24) VALUE ' CI%FR   CA%FR  TOT-FREE'.
*
01   DETAIL-1.
     05  DSN-P                     PIC X(36).
     05  CISIZE-P                  PIC X(07).
     05  CREATE-DATE-P             PIC X(07).
     05  TOTAL-RECS-P              PIC X(10).
     05  CI-SPLITS-P               PIC X(10).
     05  CA-SPLITS-P               PIC X(10).
     05  RECS-ADDED-P              PIC X(10).
     05  RECS-DELETED-P            PIC X(10).
     05  RECS-READ-P               PIC X(10).
     05  RECS-UPDATED-P            PIC X(10).
     05  EXTENT-P                  PIC X(04).
     05  PERCENT-CI-FREE-P         PIC X(08).
     05  PERCENT-CA-FREE-P         PIC X(08).
     05  TOTAL-BYTES-FREE-P        PIC X(10).
*
01   HEADING2-1.
     05  FILLER PIC X(25) VALUE 'VREPORTR-R2                '.
     05  FILLER PIC X(25) VALUE '                          '.
     05  FILLER PIC X(25) VALUE 'PRACTICAL VSAM PERFORMANC'.
     05  FILLER PIC X(25) VALUE 'E MEASUREMENT STATISTICS '.
     05  FILLER PIC X(25) VALUE '              REPORT DATE '.
     05  RPT2-DATE        PIC 9(5).
     05  FILLER PIC X(03) VALUE SPACES.
     05  FILLER PIC X(9)  VALUE '   PAGE '.
     05  RPT2-PAGE        PIC 99      VALUE 01.
     05  FILLER PIC X(5)  VALUE SPACES.
*
```

FIGURE F.10   (Continued)

```
01  HEADING2-2.
    05  FILLER PIC X(25) VALUE '                         '.
    05  FILLER PIC X(25) VALUE '                         '.
    05  FILLER PIC X(25) VALUE '        DATA SETS IN NEED OF'.
    05  FILLER PIC X(25) VALUE ' ATTENTION               '.
    05  FILLER PIC X(25) VALUE '                         '.
    05  FILLER PIC X(24) VALUE '                        '.
*
01  HEADING2-3.
    05  FILLER PIC X(25) VALUE 'DATA-SET-NAME            '.
    05  FILLER PIC X(25) VALUE '              TOT-RECS TO'.
    05  FILLER PIC X(25) VALUE 'T-RECS  DIFFER- CI-SPLIT'.
    05  FILLER PIC X(25) VALUE 'S CA-SPLITS EXT          '.
    05  FILLER PIC X(25) VALUE '                         '.
    05  FILLER PIC X(24) VALUE '                        '.
*
01  HEADING2-4.
    05  FILLER PIC X(25) VALUE '                         '.
    05  FILLER PIC X(25) VALUE '              YESTERDAY  T'.
    05  FILLER PIC X(25) VALUE 'ODAY       ENCE          '.
    05  FILLER PIC X(25) VALUE '                         '.
    05  FILLER PIC X(25) VALUE '                         '.
    05  FILLER PIC X(24) VALUE '                        '.
*
01  BAD-GUY-AREA-R.
    05  DSN-R                   PIC X(36).
    05  TOTAL-RECS-Y-R          PIC X(10).
    05  TOTAL-RECS-T-R          PIC X(10).
    05  TOTAL-RECS-DIFF-R       PIC X(10).
    05  CI-SPLITS-R             PIC X(10).
    05  CA-SPLITS-R             PIC X(10).
    05  EXTENT-R                PIC X(04).
*
01  DETAIL2-2.
    05  WORDSS                  PIC X(21).
    05  COUNTS                  PIC 9(07).
    05  FILLER                  PIC X(107)    VALUE SPACES.
*
01  HOLD-AREA.
    05  BAD-GUY-SW    VALUE 'N'    PIC X.
*
    05  TOTAL-RECS-Y-HOLD-X          PIC X(10).
    05  TOTAL-RECS-Y-HOLD-N REDEFINES
        TOTAL-RECS-Y-HOLD-X          PIC 9(10).
*
    05  TOTAL-RECS-T-HOLD-X          PIC X(10).
    05  TOTAL-RECS-T-HOLD-N REDEFINES
        TOTAL-RECS-T-HOLD-X          PIC 9(10).
*
    05  TOTAL-RECS-DIFF-HOLD-X       PIC X(10).
    05  TOTAL-RECS-DIFF-HOLD-N REDEFINES
        TOTAL-RECS-DIFF-HOLD-X       PIC 9(10).
*
    05  EXTENT-T-HOLD-X              PIC X(04).
    05  EXTENT-T-HOLD-N     REDEFINES
        EXTENT-T-HOLD-X              PIC 9(04).
*
    05  CA-SPLITS-T-HOLD-X           PIC X(10).
    05  CA-SPLITS-T-HOLD-N  REDEFINES
        CA-SPLITS-T-HOLD-X           PIC 9(10).
*
    05  CI-SPLITS-T-HOLD-X           PIC X(10).
    05  CI-SPLITS-T-HOLD-N  REDEFINES
        CI-SPLITS-T-HOLD-X           PIC 9(10).
/
```

FIGURE F.10 (Continued)

```
          PROCEDURE DIVISION.
          BEGIN.
              OPEN INPUT YESTER.
              OPEN INPUT TODAYY.
              OPEN OUTPUT RPTS.
              OPEN OUTPUT RPT2.
              READ YESTER      AT END GO TO YESTER-BAD.
              MOVE DAY-Y TO H-DATE-Y.
              MOVE TIME-Y TO H-TIME-Y.
              READ TODAYY       AT END GO TO TODAYY-BAD.
              MOVE DAY-T TO H-DATE-T.
              MOVE TIME-T TO H-TIME-T.
              ACCEPT RPT-DATE FROM DAY.
              ACCEPT RPT2-DATE FROM DAY.
              PERFORM HEADING-OVERFLOW.
              PERFORM HEADING-OVERFLOW2.
      *
          READ-YESTER.
              READ YESTER
                 AT END
                      GO TO FLUSH-TODAYY.
              ADD 1 TO YESTER-IN-CNT.
              MOVE DSN-Y TO MATCH-KEY.
              IF TODAYY-AT-EOF
                 PERFORM PRINT-YESTER-REC-ONLY
                 ADD 1 TO MISSING-TODAYY-CNT
                 GO TO READ-YESTER.
      *
          PROCESS-TODAYY.
              IF YESTER-LO
                 GO TO MATCH-FILES.
      *
          READ-TODAYY.
              READ TODAYY
                 AT END
                      MOVE 1 TO TODAYY-EOF
                      PERFORM PRINT-YESTER-REC-ONLY
                      ADD 1 TO MISSING-TODAYY-CNT
                      GO TO READ-YESTER.
              ADD 1 TO TODAYY-IN-CNT.
      *
          MATCH-FILES.
              IF MATCH-KEY IS GREATER THAN DSN-T
                 MOVE 3 TO MATCH-STATUS
                 PERFORM PRINT-TODAYY-REC-ONLY
                 ADD 1 TO MISSING-YESTER-CNT
                 GO TO READ-TODAYY.
      *
              IF MATCH-KEY IS EQUAL TO  DSN-T
                 MOVE 2 TO MATCH-STATUS
                 PERFORM PRINT-BOTH
                 ADD 1 TO MATCHED-CNT
                 GO TO READ-YESTER.
      *
              MOVE 1 TO MATCH-STATUS.
              PERFORM PRINT-YESTER-REC-ONLY.
              ADD 1 TO MISSING-TODAYY-CNT.
              GO TO READ-YESTER.
      *
          HEADING-OVERFLOW.
              MOVE HEADING-1 TO RPT-BODY.
              WRITE REPORT-OUT AFTER ADVANCING T-O-P.
              MOVE HEADING-2 TO RPT-BODY.
              WRITE REPORT-OUT AFTER ADVANCING 1.
              MOVE HEADING-3 TO RPT-BODY.
              WRITE REPORT-OUT AFTER ADVANCING 1.
              MOVE 3 TO LINE-COUNT.
```

FIGURE F.10   (Continued)

```
            ADD 1 TO RPT-PAGE.
*
   HEADING-OVERFLOW2.
        MOVE HEADING2-1 TO BADGUY-BODY.
        WRITE BADGUY-OUT AFTER ADVANCING T-O-P.
        MOVE HEADING2-2 TO BADGUY-BODY.
        WRITE BADGUY-OUT AFTER ADVANCING 1.
        MOVE HEADING2-3 TO BADGUY-BODY.
        WRITE BADGUY-OUT AFTER ADVANCING 2.
        MOVE HEADING2-4 TO BADGUY-BODY.
        WRITE BADGUY-OUT AFTER ADVANCING 1.
        MOVE 5 TO LINE-COUNT2.
        ADD 1 TO RPT2-PAGE.
*
   PRINT-YESTER-REC-ONLY.
        IF LINE-COUNT > 74
            PERFORM HEADING-OVERFLOW.
        MOVE YESTER-REC TO RPT-BODY.
        WRITE REPORT-OUT AFTER ADVANCING 2.
        MOVE SPACES TO RPT-BODY.
        WRITE REPORT-OUT AFTER ADVANCING 1.
        ADD 3 TO LINE-COUNT.
*
   PRINT-TODAYY-REC-ONLY.
        IF LINE-COUNT > 74
            PERFORM HEADING-OVERFLOW.
        MOVE SPACES TO RPT-BODY.
        WRITE REPORT-OUT AFTER ADVANCING 2.
        MOVE TODAYY-REC TO RPT-BODY.
        WRITE REPORT-OUT AFTER ADVANCING 1.
        ADD 3 TO LINE-COUNT.
*
   PRINT-BOTH.
        IF LINE-COUNT > 74
            PERFORM HEADING-OVERFLOW.
        MOVE YESTER-REC TO RPT-BODY.
        WRITE REPORT-OUT AFTER ADVANCING 2.
        MOVE TODAYY-REC TO DETAIL-1.
        MOVE SPACES TO DSN-P.
        MOVE DETAIL-1 TO RPT-BODY.
        WRITE REPORT-OUT AFTER ADVANCING 1.
        ADD 3 TO LINE-COUNT.
        PERFORM CHECK-FOR-BAD-GUYS.
*
   FLUSH-TODAYY.
        IF YESTER-LO
            PERFORM PRINT-TODAYY-REC-ONLY.
*
   READ-TODAYY-TO-END.
        IF TODAYY-AT-EOF
            GO TO PRINT-TOTALS.
        READ TODAYY
            AT END
                GO TO PRINT-TOTALS.
        ADD 1 TO TODAYY-IN-CNT.
        PERFORM PRINT-TODAYY-REC-ONLY.
        GO TO READ-TODAYY-TO-END.
*
   CHECK-FOR-BAD-GUYS.
        MOVE TOTAL-RECS-Y TO TOTAL-RECS-Y-HOLD-X.
        INSPECT TOTAL-RECS-Y-HOLD-X REPLACING LEADING '-' BY '0'.
        MOVE TOTAL-RECS-T TO TOTAL-RECS-T-HOLD-X.
        INSPECT TOTAL-RECS-T-HOLD-X REPLACING LEADING '-' BY '0'.
        IF TOTAL-RECS-T-HOLD-N IS LESS THAN TOTAL-RECS-Y-HOLD-N
            MOVE 'Y' TO BAD-GUY-SW
            MOVE TOTAL-RECS-Y TO TOTAL-RECS-Y-R
```

FIGURE F.10   (Continued)

```
            MOVE TOTAL-RECS-T TO TOTAL-RECS-T-R
            COMPUTE TOTAL-RECS-DIFF-HOLD-N =
                ( TOTAL-RECS-Y-HOLD-N - TOTAL-RECS-T-HOLD-N )
            INSPECT TOTAL-RECS-DIFF-HOLD-X
                REPLACING LEADING '0' BY '-'
            MOVE TOTAL-RECS-DIFF-HOLD-X TO TOTAL-RECS-DIFF-R.
        MOVE EXTENT-T TO EXTENT-T-HOLD-X.
        INSPECT EXTENT-T-HOLD-X REPLACING LEADING '-' BY '0'.
        IF EXTENT-T-HOLD-N IS GREATER THAN 1
            MOVE 'Y' TO BAD-GUY-SW
            MOVE EXTENT-T TO EXTENT-R.
        MOVE CA-SPLITS-T TO CA-SPLITS-T-HOLD-X.
        INSPECT CA-SPLITS-T-HOLD-X REPLACING LEADING '-' BY '0'.
        IF CA-SPLITS-T-HOLD-N IS GREATER THAN 0
            MOVE 'Y' TO BAD-GUY-SW
            MOVE CA-SPLITS-T TO CA-SPLITS-R.
        MOVE CI-SPLITS-T TO CI-SPLITS-T-HOLD-X.
        INSPECT CI-SPLITS-T-HOLD-X REPLACING LEADING '-' BY '0'.
        IF CI-SPLITS-T-HOLD-N IS GREATER THAN 0
            MOVE 'Y' TO BAD-GUY-SW
            MOVE CI-SPLITS-T TO CI-SPLITS-R.
        IF BAD-GUY-SW = 'Y'
            MOVE DSN-T TO DSN-R
            PERFORM WRITE-BAD-GUY-REPORT.
    *
    WRITE-BAD-GUY-REPORT.
        IF LINE-COUNT2 > 54
            PERFORM HEADING-OVERFLOW2.
        MOVE BAD-GUY-AREA-R TO BADGUY-BODY.
        WRITE BADGUY-OUT AFTER ADVANCING 2.
        ADD 2 TO LINE-COUNT2.
        MOVE SPACES TO BAD-GUY-AREA-R.
        MOVE SPACES TO HOLD-AREA.
        MOVE 'N' TO BAD-GUY-SW.
    *
    YESTER-BAD.
        MOVE 'YESTERDAY IS EMPTY' TO HEADING-3.
        GO TO CLEAN-UP.
    *
    TODAYY-BAD.
        MOVE 'TODAYY IS EMPTY' TO HEADING-3.
    *
    CLEAN-UP.
        PERFORM HEADING-OVERFLOW.
    *
    PRINT-TOTALS.
        PERFORM HEADING-OVERFLOW2.
        MOVE    'YESTER-IN-CNT      = ' TO WORDSS.
        MOVE     YESTER-IN-CNT          TO COUNTS.
        MOVE DETAIL2-2 TO BADGUY-BODY.
        WRITE BADGUY-OUT AFTER ADVANCING 2.
        ADD 2 TO LINE-COUNT2.
    *
        MOVE    'TODAYY-IN-CNT      = ' TO WORDSS.
        MOVE     TODAYY-IN-CNT          TO COUNTS.
        MOVE DETAIL2-2 TO BADGUY-BODY.
        WRITE BADGUY-OUT AFTER ADVANCING 2.
        ADD 2 TO LINE-COUNT2.
    *
        MOVE    'MATCHED-CNT        = ' TO WORDSS.
        MOVE     MATCHED-CNT            TO COUNTS.
        MOVE DETAIL2-2 TO BADGUY-BODY.
        WRITE BADGUY-OUT AFTER ADVANCING 2.
        ADD 2 TO LINE-COUNT2.
    *
        MOVE    'MISSING-TODAYY-CNT = ' TO WORDSS.
        MOVE     MISSING-TODAYY-CNT     TO COUNTS.
```

FIGURE F.10   (Continued)

```
            MOVE DETAIL2-2 TO BADGUY-BODY.
            WRITE BADGUY-OUT AFTER ADVANCING 2.
            ADD 2 TO LINE-COUNT2.
     *
            MOVE     'MISSING-YESTER-CNT = ' TO WORDSS.
            MOVE     MISSING-YESTER-CNT       TO COUNTS.
            MOVE DETAIL2-2 TO BADGUY-BODY.
            WRITE BADGUY-OUT AFTER ADVANCING 2.
            ADD 2 TO LINE-COUNT2.
     *
            CLOSE YESTER.
            CLOSE TODAYY.
            CLOSE RPTS.
            CLOSE RPT2.
            GOBACK.
```

FIGURE F.10   (Continued)

Illustrations of Output

Figure F.11 is a sample of the consolidated report output by program VREPORTR. Figure F.12 depicts the "problem data set" report, the single most important output of the performance monitoring job stream. This report contains one line for each data set for which a decline in record count is noted, or which has CI or CA splits, or which has gone into multiple disk extents. While it is possible that some data sets appearing on this report are not yet candidates for reorganization and/or redesign, all of the data sets cited on this report should be considered for further attention. Compare the utility of this report with the prospect of running and examining several hundred raw LISTCATs in order to monitor production key sequenced data sets.

TOP LINE   PREVIOUS DATE 87024 TIME 14483788 BOTTOM LINE CURRENT DATE 87038 REPORT DATE 87038 TIME 10442883

DATA-SET-NAME	CISIZE-CRDAT	TOTAL-REC	CI-SPLITS	CA-SPLITS	# ADDED	# DELED	# READ	# UPDED	EXT	CI%FR	CA%FR	TOT-FREE
CP00.CO3.ITEMDB	4096-87020	633	0	0	0	0	0	0	1	20	10	471040
	4096-87020	633	0	0	0	0	0	0	1	20	10	471040
CP00.CO3.ITEMXREF	4096-87020	62	0	0	0	0	0	0	1	20	10	565248
	4096-87020	62	0	0	0	0	0	0	1	20	10	565248
CP00.CO3.LEDGER	4096-86128	158	73	0	132	0	816	0	1	5	25	1572864
	4096-86128	172	37	0	146	0	816	0	1	5	25	1556480
CP00.CO3.NULL.REFOPEN	4096-86182	1	0	0	0	0	0	0	1	20	20	36864
	4096-86182	1	0	0	0	0	0	0	1	20	20	36864
CP00.CO3.PAPPOLGL	4096-87020	1	0	0	0	0	0	0	2	20	10	2863104
	4096-87020	0	0	0	0	0	0	0	2	20	10	2863104
CP00.CO3.RCS.CMPRPAGE	4096-86071	297	0	0	0	0	1330	0	15	0	0	0
	4096-87036	129	0	0	0	0	129	0	5	0	0	24576
CP00.CO3.REFERENC	4096-87020	51745	0	0	0	0	47	0	19	20	10	3563520
	4096-87020	51751	0	0	0	6	1039	12	19	20	10	3563520
CP00.CO3.REFOPEN	4096-86321	27995	497	13	57656	54483	1750757	16998	2	15	20	3821568
	4096-86321	27995	497	13	57656	54483	1778976	16998	2	15	20	3821568
CP00.CO3.REPTDISB	8192-87021	20323	3	2	1467	0	17570	0	1	20	10	2260992
	8192-87035	20556	0	0	1	0	35081	0	1	20	10	2260992
CP00.CO3.STEMP	4096-86298	0	0	0	0	0	0	0	1	5	25	5734400
	4096-86298	0	0	0	0	0	0	0	1	5	25	5734400
CP00.CO3.SUSPENSE	4096-87020	4714	0	0	0	0	982	35	2	20	10	3956736
	4096-87020	4732	1	0	18	0	1845	260	2	20	10	3952640

```
CP00.C03.SYSTEM----4096-87021----3697----5----2----384----340----12694----5----2----20----10--1744896
                 --4096-87021----3718----9----5----2331---2271---58717----98---3----20----10--3518464

CP00.C03.TABOPEN---4096-87020----4221----0----0----14----0------73----12---4----20----10--7233536
                 --4096-87020----4227----0----0----14----8----4981----34---4----20----10--7233536

CP00.C03.WTRLED----4096-86268----16----2----0----13----1-----637----6----1----20----20--1708032
                 --4096-86268----16----2----0----13----1-----637----6----1----20----20--1708032

CP00.C03.XCOMMON--16384-86337----0----2----1----1050---6568---6739----0----1----5----25--89915392
                 -16384-87026----30---0----1-----534---1144---1457----0----1----20---10--17809408

CP00.C03.XTEMP-----8192-86298----1----0----0----0----0------1----0----1----5----25--2859008
                 --8192-86298----1----0----0----0----0------1----0----0----5----25--2859008

CP00.C11.UNIONTBL--1024-86337----219----0----0----0----0-----861----1----1----1----1--411648
                 --1024-86337----219----0----0----0----0-----861----1----1----1----1--411648

CP00.C11.UNIONTBL.AIX-1024-86337----50----0----0----0----0------60----0----1----0----0--442368
                 --1024-86337----50----0----0----0----0------60----0----1----0----0--442368

CP00.C56.TESTVSAM--1024-84144----1----0----0----0----0-------0----0----1----0----0--14336
                 --1024-84144----1----0----0----0----0-------0----0----1----0----0--14336

CP00.C58.VSAMSNDX--1024-84216----20----0----0----3----0------20----0----1----0----0--29696
                 --1024-84216----20----0----0----3----0------20----0----1----0----0--29696

CP00.C59.CP59BTCH--2048-85303----3----0----0----0----0------28----4----1----20----5--30720
                 --2048-85303----3----0----0----0----0------28----4----1----20----5--30720

CP00.C59.CP59MAST--2048-85303----101----2----0----54----2----266----54----4----20----5--59392
                 --2048-85303----101----2----0----54----2----266----54----4----20----5--59392

CP00.C59.CP59PYMT--2048-85302----264----2----0----261----1---1209----1----4----20----5--69632
                 --2048-85302----264----2----0----261----2---1254----1----4----20----5--69632

CP00.C70.CP70FXBC--4096-86008----104----0----0----0----0-----100----0----1----11----10--143360
                 --4096-86008----104----0----0----0----0-----159----0----1----11----10--143360
```

FIGURE F.11 Sample of VREPORTR program full KSDS monitoring report, showing previous and current performance monitoring statistics for all key sequenced data sets

339

```
VREPORTR-R2                          PRACTICAL VSAM PERFORMANCE MEASUREMENT STATISTICS           REPORT DATE 87038
                                            DATA SETS IN NEED OF ATTENTION

DATA-SET-NAME                      TOT-RECS  TOT-RECS  DIFFER- CI-SPLITS CA-SPLITS EXT
                                   YESTERDAY TODAY     ENCE

CPOO.CO3.SUSPENSE----------------                      ---------1            ---2
CPOO.CO3.SYSTEM------------------                      ---------9---------5---3
CPOO.CO3.TABOPEN-----------------                                          ---4
CPOO.CO3.WTRLED------------------                      ---------2
CPOO.CO3.XCOMMON-----------------                            ---------1
CPOO.C59.CP59MAST----------------                            ---------2---4
CPOO.C59.CP59PYMT----------------                      ---------2---------2---4
CPOO.C70.CP7OHXBC----------------                      ---------2---------1
CPOO.C70.CP7OHXI2----------------                      ---------1
CSOO.CO4.BEMASTER----------------                                          ---2
CSOO.C23.TTLEORNR----------------                      ---------1
CSOO.C25.PROFILE-----------------                      --------30---------19--21
CSOO.C27.CERTEMPL----------------                                          ---6
CSOO.C27.CSPADEPT----------------                      ---------1
CSOO.C27.CSPCTTLE----------------                      ---------1
CSOO.C27.CSPIFAPL----------------                      ---------3
CSOO.C27.CS14APPL----------------                      ---------9
CSOO.C27.CS14TRAN----------------                      ---------9
CSOO.C27.DPOLEMPL----------------                                          ---7
CTOO.C95.ODE.APPLIBC-------------                      ---------2
DCOO.C1O.VSAMEXT----------------------6852------1596------5256
                                                                          ---5
YESTER-IN-CNT       = 0000265
TODAYY-IN-CNT       = 0000258
MATCHED-CNT         = 0000252
MISSING-TODAYY-CNT  = 0000013
MISSING-YESTER-CNT  = 0000006
```

FIGURE F.12   Sample of VREPORTR program "problem data set" monitoring report, listing data sets in immediate need of attention and tuning, and the characteristics suspect

TEST DATA FOR KSDS EXPERIMENTATION

Figure F.13 lists a small set of test data suitable for use in experimenting with the key sequenced data set defined and loaded in the major examples of Chapters 2 and 5. Although the quantity of test data is small, it was carefully constructed with alternate key values that provide exposure to many distinct unique and nonunique key values. The format of this data is depicted in Figure 2.1 of Chapter 2 and Figure 5.1 of Chapter 5. The records are already in ascending primary key sequence, ready for loading to a KSDS.

This test data can be entered as 80-byte card image records using TSO or another online text editing system, or it can be obtained in machine-readable form on diskette as described in Appendix A and uploaded to a mainframe. Figure F.14 lists the coding for a simple execution of the IEBGENER utility to expand the records to the 250-byte length required for the AK00.C98.CUSTMAST data set used in most examples in this book. Almost all of the data contained in the test data set is for the record key fields. The two letters at the end of each 80-byte test data record comprise the only data content and are present simply to help see the sort order of records at any point as compared to their original order.

```
                1         2         3         4         5         6         7
----+---- |0----+----0----+-- |--0----+- |---0---- |+ |----0----+----0 |----+ |----0 |--
414943675 |FORESTER         |ALVIN    |08716293 |S |DORCHESTER ST    |09710 |      |AA
312872548 |WASIK            |CHARLES  |22168028 |N |KILDARE AVE      |02009 |      |BB
886376533 |KUREK            |BESSIE   |24307091 |W |FULLERTON AVE    |05800 |4-B   |CC
934064961 |HAMPSTER         |HERBERT  |25656631 |S |HALLDALE AV      |08711 |      |DD
206931482 |HAMPSTER         |HENRIETTA|28441269 |S |HALLDALE AV      |08711 |      |EE
968312814 |HAMPSTER         |HARVEY   |28799201 |S |HALLDALE AV      |08711 |      |FF
650038142 |KALKINS          |JANET    |32613729 |N |SHERIDAN RD      |03016 |      |GG
624925399 |HAMPSTER         |HELEN    |32817132 |S |HALLDALE AV      |08711 |      |HH
364787800 |ANCONA           |MINNIE   |33841546 |S |KOLINA PL        |04310 |17    |II
030606384 |EASTON           |JESSIE   |37667140 |W |PRYOR RD         |02059 |      |JJ
008290945 |CHEROSO          |JEROME   |42705117 |N |ELSTON AVE       |00418 |      |KK
463586621 |DEKOVEN          |FRANK    |46712001 |S |LARAMIE DR       |04408 |      |LL
726321341 |SMITH            |JOHN     |48077449 |W |69TH             |01349 |      |MM
468384552 |SMITH            |JOHN     |63735122 |  |KILBOURNE        |00911 |      |NN
385726351 |SMITH            |JOHN     |63817627 |E |135TH ST         |02415 |      |OO
878952284 |FLAGG            |ALLAN    |64070301 |N |KOSTNER AV       |05625 |43    |PP
679912244 |MADISON          |MONROE   |73724695 |W |WRIGHTWOOD LANE  |04849 |      |QQ
036505341 |BILECKI          |PATRICIA |88389992 |S |LEAVITT ST       |00609 |16    |RR

                1         2         3         4         5         6         7
----+---- |0----+----0----+-- |--0----+- |---0---- |+ |----0----+----0 |----+ |----0 |--
```

FIGURE F.13   Test data for programs

```
//FSBT686A   JOB AK00TEST,'DP2-JANOSSY',CLASS=E,MSGCLASS=X,
//   MSGLEVEL=(1,1),NOTIFY=BT05686
//*
//***********************************************************
//*                                                         *
//*      EXPAND 80 BYTE TEST DATA TO 250 BYTE RECORDS        *
//*                                                         *
//***********************************************************
//STEPA     EXEC  PGM=IEFBR14
//DEL1      DD    DSN=AK00.C98.CUSTTEST,
//   UNIT=SYSDA,
//   DISP=(MOD,DELETE),
//   SPACE=(TRK,0)
//*
//STEPB     EXEC  PGM=IEBGENER
//SYSPRINT  DD    SYSOUT=*
//SYSUT1    DD    DSN=BT05686.SOURCE.CNTL(CUSTTEST),
//   DISP=SHR
//SYSUT2    DD    DSN=AK00.C98.CUSTTEST,
//   UNIT=SYSDA,
//   DISP=(NEW,CATLG,DELETE),
//   DCB=(RECFM=FB,LRECL=250,BLKSIZE=6000),
//   SPACE=(6000,(1,1),RLSE)
//SYSIN     DD    *
     GENERATE  MAXFLDS=99,MAXLITS=300
        RECORD  FIELD=(72,1,,1),
                FIELD=(28,'                          ',,73),
                FIELD=(20,'                    ',,101),
                FIELD=(20,'                    ',,121),
                FIELD=(20,'                    ',,141),
                FIELD=(20,'                    ',,161),
                FIELD=(20,'                    ',,181),
                FIELD=(20,'                    ',,201),
                FIELD=(20,'                    ',,221),
                FIELD=(10,'          ',,241)
     /*
     //
```

FIGURE F.14   IEBGENER execution to expand test data from 80 bytes to 250 bytes

VSAM FILE STATUS Values:
Comprehensive Chart for Analysis

The comprehensive table of VSAM verbs and FILE STATUS values that may be returned for each is arranged in the order in which the verbs are most often encountered. FILE STATUS values up to value 30 are somewhat standardized across various IBM access methods; this chart, however, is specific to VSAM.

Although this chart may be used to develop a customized definition of the FILE STATUS field, it is provided primarily as an aid to problem resolution. You will find it helpful to look up a FILE STATUS value here when a program using a VSAM file has been forced to abort.

This chart originally appeared as Appendix G in *Commercial Software Engineering: For Productive Program Design* (James Janossy, John Wiley and Sons, Inc., 1985) ISBN 0-471-81576-4, and is reproduced here with the permission of the publisher.

OPEN

00	File has been successfully opened	Proceed
30	Permanent I/O error due to media or other failure	Terminate run
90	Unusable file; may be OPENing for I/O and file has just been created, is in an "unloaded" condition (has never had any records in it)	Terminate run; load at least one record using OPEN for OUTPUT
91	Password failure (security password either not supplied by program or does not match existing file password)	Terminate run
92	Logic error; the file is already open	Terminate run and correct program logic
93	Resources not available for VSAM; not enough memory for the program, or SHAREOPTIONS prevent use while file is being used by another program	Terminate run; increase region size; check SHARE-OPTIONS
95	Invalid or incomplete file information associated with the program Key length, key position, or record length incorrectly specified in the program file description (FD).	Terminate run; correct program file FD and/or job JCL

OPEN

96	No DD statement in JCL; no file identification	Terminate run; correct JCL
97	File not closed by previous job accessing it; IDCAMS has done a VERIFY to adjust system catalog and make file usable; OPENed OK	Proceed, but installation of prior VERIFY step in job-stream is customary

READ(Not READ . . . NEXT)

00	Read was successful	Proceed
23	Record with specified key not found	Dependent on the program
30	Permanent I/O error due to media or other failure	Terminate run
90	VSAM logic error; no further information available	Terminate run
92	Logic error; file may not be open	Terminate run
93	Resources not available for VSAM; not enough memory for the program	Terminate run; increase region size
95	Invalid file information	Key fields positioned incorrectly in file FD; terminate run and make FD consistent with defined key positions

REWRITE

00	Rewrite was successful	Proceed
02	Record successfully rewritten; an alternate index record has been created with a key that duplicates an existing alternate index key (alternate index specifies duplicates are allowed, and VSAM "UPGRADE" option is defined for the file)	Proceed; extra information from access method may not be of interest
22	Invalid key: an attempt to rewrite a record that would create a duplicate alternate index key, and the alternate index is defined as duplicates not allowed; the VSAM "UPGRADE" option has been defined for the file (Note: This can be a problem to debug because this same value on WRITE may indicate that the primary key is the duplicate. The update that preceded the REWRITE has changed the value of the alternate key field and due to the UPGRADE option, VSAM is updating the alternate index.)	Dependent on program; most often points to a failure in design of alternate index key, or missing alternate key formation MOVEs in program
23	Key of the record to be rewritten not on the file; either key of a record read for update has been changed by mistake, or an unusual update without prior read action is underway and a record thought to be on the file is not there [VSAM permits REWRITE without a prior READ for indexed (KSDS) files when ac-	Dependent on program; most often a logic error

REWRITE

cess is random or dynamic. For ESDS files, a
prior read is necessary before REWRITE.]

30	Permanent I/O error due to media or other failure	Terminate run
90	VSAM logic error; no further information available	Terminate run
92	Logic error; file may not be open or there was no previous READ of the record being rewritten (ESDS only)	Terminate run
93	Resources not available for VSAM; not enough memory for the program	Terminate run; increase region size

WRITE

00	Write was successful	Proceed
02	Record successfully written; an alternate index record has been created with a key that duplicates an existing alternate index key (Alternate index specifies duplicates are allowed, and VSAM "UPGRADE" option is defined for the file.)	Proceed; extra information from access method may not be of interest
21	Sequence error; file is opened for OUTPUT, and access is sequential, as for initial loading; record carried a key value less than or equal to the key of the record previously written	Dependent on program; file loading is usually terminated and load file examined
22	Invalid key: most often an attempt to write a record that carries a primary key value already in the file; can also occur on an attempt to write a record with a unique primary key but an alternate key value already on file, and the alternate index has been defined as "duplicates not allowed"; the VSAM "UPGRADE" option has been defined for the file, meaning that VSAM is updating the alternate index	Dependent on program; may be a defect in the design of the alternate index key, or missing MOVEs in the process of forming the alternate key. Print or display primary key field and all alternate key fields for analysis.
24	"Boundary violation"; an attempt to write more data into a file than the allocated space for the file will allow; occurs on key sequenced (KSDS) or relative record (RRDS) VSAM files only [See 34 for sequential (ESDS) files.]	Terminate run; either purge unneeded records from it (in a batch copy and reload, or with DELETEs) or back it up, do IDCAMS delete, redefine with more space, and reload
30	Permanent I/O error due to media or other failure	Terminate run
34	"Boundary violation"; similar to code 24 but for VSAM entry sequenced datasets (ESDS) only (ESDS datasets are VSAM sequential files, rarely used.)	Terminate run

WRITE

90	VSAM logic error; no other information available	Terminate run
92	Logic error; file may not be open or the file was open for EXTEND, and an attempt was made to write a record to the file that carried a primary key less than or equal to the highest key already in the file	Dependent on program; print or display key of record and continue or terminate run
93	Resources not available for VSAM; not enough memory for the program	Terminate run; increase region size

DELETE

00	Delete was successful	Proceed
23	Record with specified key not found on file	Dependent on specific program
30	Permanent I/O error due to media or other failure	Terminate run
90	VSAM logic error; no further information available	Terminate run
92	Logic error; file may not be open or is opened for SEQUENTIAL access and there was no previous READ to obtain the record to be deleted	Terminate run
93	Resources not available for VSAM; not enough memory for the program	Terminate run; increase region size

START

00	Start was successful	Proceed
23	No record found with a key satisfying the full or partial key requirements specified	Dependent on program
30	Permanent I/O error due to media or other failure	Terminate run
90	VSAM logic error; no further information available	Terminate run
92	Logic error; file is probably not open	Terminate run
93	Resources not available for VSAM; not enough memory for the program	Terminate run; increase region size

READ . . . NEXT(Sequential Read after START)

00	Read . . . Next was successful	Proceed
02	Read . . . Next on an alternate key was successful, and one or more records with the same alternate key exist after this one. (Note: This can only occur when the file was STARTed on and is being read sequentially using an alternate	Proceed; extra information from access method may not be of interest

READ . . . NEXT(Sequential Read after START)

	key, not its primary key, and the alternate key has been defined as "duplicates are allowed.")	
10	End of file has been reached	Program dependent; actions which must be done at "browse" EOF
30	Permanent I/O error due to media or other failure	Terminate run
90	VSAM logic error; no further information available	Terminate run
92	Logic error; file probably not open or previous file status 94 ignored	Terminate run
93	Resources not available for VSAM; not enough memory for the program	Terminate run; increase region size
94	No current record pointer exists to meet sequential read request [Note: This can occur if a START positioned the file after the record with the highest key in the file (i.e., after the last record in the file) or if there was no previous START of the file.]	Terminate run; examine the logic for incorrect file status checking after the prior START or failure to do a START

CLOSE

00	File was successfully closed	Proceed
30	Permanent I/O error due to media or other failure	Terminate run
90	VSAM logic error; no further information available	Terminate run
92	Logic error; file is probably not open	Terminate run
93	Resources not available for VSAM; not enough memory for the program	Terminate run; increase region size

— INDEX —